Student-Managed Investment Funds

Student-Managed Investment Funds

Organization, Policy, and Portfolio Management

Second Edition

Brian Bruce

Hillcrest Asset Management, LLC, Dallas, TX, United States
The Philip M. Dorr Alumni & Friends, Endowed Investment Fund, Baylor University

ELSEVIER

ACADEMIC PRESS
An imprint of Elsevier

Academic Press is an imprint of Elsevier
125 London Wall, London EC2Y 5AS, United Kingdom
525 B Street, Suite 1650, San Diego, CA 92101, United States
50 Hampshire Street, 5th Floor, Cambridge, MA 02139, United States
The Boulevard, Langford Lane, Kidlington, Oxford OX5 1GB, United Kingdom

Notices

Knowledge and best practice in this field are constantly changing. As new research and experience broaden our
understanding, changes in research methods, professional practices, or medical treatment may become
necessary.

Practitioners and researchers must always rely on their own experience and knowledge in evaluating and using
any information, methods, compounds, or experiments described herein. In using such information or methods
they should be mindful of their own safety and the safety of others, including parties for whom they have a
professional responsibility.

To the fullest extent of the law, neither the Publisher nor the authors, contributors, or editors, assume any liability
for any injury and/or damage to persons or property as a matter of products liability, negligence or otherwise, or
from any use or operation of any methods, products, instructions, or ideas contained in the material herein.

Library of Congress Cataloging-in-Publication Data
A catalog record for this book is available from the Library of Congress

British Library Cataloguing-in-Publication Data
A catalogue record for this book is available from the British Library

ISBN 978-0-12-817866-9

For information on all Academic Press publications
visit our website at https://www.elsevier.com/books-and-journals

Publisher: Brian Romer
Editorial Project Manager: Lindsay Lawrence
Production Project Manager: Niranjan Bhaskaran
Cover Designer: Victoria Pearson

Typeset by SPi Global, India

Contents

Introduction to the second edition

We are delighted with the tremendous reception to the first edition of this book and pleased to have been asked by the publisher to produce a second edition. This textbook will continue to be a leading resource for student managed portfolio classes.

For the second edition, the previous chapters have all been updated to reflect suggestions from users of the first edition. The Stock Selection chapter, previously Security Selection, includes additional information regarding fundamental analysis and industry analysis. The chapters on Portfolio Construction and Performance Evaluation have been expanded to include more information on ways for students to manage and evaluate their portfolios. The Presentation chapter, in addition to updated examples of sector and external presentations, now includes a section focused on CFA Research Challenge Presentation Materials. The Tools chapter has been expanded to include how-to-use sections for Morningstar Direct^{SM} and Eikon from Refinitiv.

Finally, this edition includes two new chapters. ETFs, Bonds and Derivatives, has been added as more programs are using these assets in their portfolios. As trading continues to quickly evolve and we have also added the Trading and Operations chapter to cover the latest trading platforms and venues found in s structured investment management organization.

This second edition includes improvements in every chapter which will not only help students in class but also prepare them better for their first job in investments.

Acknowledgments to the second edition

We have included the acknowledgments from the first edition due to the tremendous debt we owe all the contributors and supporters. As we get ready to launch the second edition, the careful reader may notice that Brian's esteemed co-author, Jason Greene, is no longer associated with the book. Since the first edition, Jason has become the Dean of the College of Business at the University of Alabama in Huntsville and was unable to participate in this edition. For the first edition, Brian collected over a 1000 pages of material from student managed portfolios and competitions all over the country. Jason was the driving force that helped form all that material into the first edition. The field owes Jason a great debt for his outstanding contribution in promoting student managed portfolio classes.

Without Jason, we decided to enlist the help of some of the leading professors and investment professionals in the field. Each professor took a chapter and significantly updated it based on suggestions from edition one users or wrote and entirely new chapter. Our contributing authors have well over 100 years of experience teaching students how to invest live portfolios. Combing that experience with Brian's 26 years of teaching and we bring the reader a wealth of knowledge. We have included bios on all the second edition contributors below.

We also thank the following individuals and institutions for graciously providing material for this textbook:

Larry Lockwood, Texas Christian University
Dave Sather, Texas Lutheran/Sather Financial
Quinnipiac University, GAME Forum
ACA Compliance Group
Eikon from Refinitiv
Morningstar Direct[SM]

Finally, we want to thank some people who were instrumental in the second edition. Melinda Estelle has worked to put this material in proper form for the publisher. Melinda works with Brian as a member if the editorial team for The *Journal of Behavioral Finance*, the *Journal of Investing*, the *Journal of Index Investing*, and the *Journal of Impact & ESG Investing*. We also want to thank Scott Bentley for his support of both editions of the book. There would be no book with Scott championing it at Elsevier.

Contributing Authors

Rob Dolan

University of Richmond

Contributor: Chapter 3 Investing with Exchange Traded Funds

Robert Dolan is a Professor of Economics at the Robins School of Business at the University of Richmond. During his tenure at the University of Richmond, he has been named the David Meade White Distinguished Teach Fellow and Faculty Member of the Year by the Richmond College Student Government Association. He is the co-author of multiple articles and books, and he regularly speaks at events around the country.

Jill Foote

Rice University

Contributor: Appendix 2 Forums, Symposiums, Competitions

Jill Foote is Senior Lecturer in Finance, Director of the Rice Business Finance Center, and Director of the M.A. Wright Investment Fund (the MBA student managed portfolio coursework) at Rice University's Jesse H. Jones Graduate School of Business. Her principal teaching responsibilities are in investment management. She is also the faculty advisor of the Rice Finance Club.

Prior to joining the Jones School in 2002, Dr. Foote worked for 13 years at Goldman Sachs in New York, where her later 7 years were spent as a Vice President, managing projects in strategic initiatives, new business ventures, and risk management; and operational, regulatory, and financial audits and risk reviews.

Dr. Foote holds a PhD in Economics from Fordham University, an MA in Economics from New York University, and a BA in Economics and Managerial Studies from Rice University, where she graduated Magna Cum Laude and Phi Beta Kappa. She also has a Chartered Financial Analyst designation and has previously served on the Board of Directors of the CFA Society Houston.

Travis Jones

Florida Gulf Coast University

Contributor: Chapter 1 Investment Philosophy and Process; Chapter 2 Stock Selection

Dr. Travis Jones is a Professor of Finance in the Lutgert College of Business at Florida Gulf Coast University (FGCU). Dr. Jones received his PhD in Finance from the University of Alabama and has been a faculty member at FGCU since 2005. He has been teaching the Student Managed Investment Fund at FGCU since 2007.

Dr. Jones is heavily involved with the CFA Institute and serves on the Board of Directors of the CFA Society Naples (FL). Dr. Jones conducts research in the areas of investments, derivative securities, and finance pedagogy. He has published in *Financial Services Review*, *Journal of Financial Education*, *Journal of Investments*, *Journal of Index Investing*, *Journal of Trading*, and *Quarterly Review of Economics and Finance*, among other finance-related journals.

Prior to his academic career, he worked as a futures and options broker and a swim coach.

Paul Kaplan
Morningstar Canada

Contributor: Chapter 4 Portfolio Construction; Chapter 5 Performance Evaluation

Paul D. Kaplan, PhD, CFA, is a Director of Research for Morningstar Canada and is a senior member of Morningstar's global research team. He led the development of many of the quantitative methodologies behind Morningstar's fund analysis, indices, advisor tools, and other services. He conducts research on asset allocation, retirement income planning, portfolio construction, index methodologies, and other investment topics.

Many of Kaplan's research papers have been published in professional books and publications such as the *Financial Analysts Journal and the Journal of Portfolio Management*. He received the 2008 Graham and Dodd Award and was a Graham and Dodd Award of Excellence winner in 2000. Many of his works appear in his book Frontiers of Modern Asset Allocation published in 2012 by John Wiley & Sons. He is a co-author of the book Popularity: A Bridge between Classical and Behavioral Finance published in 2018 by the CFA Institute Research Foundation.

Prior to that, he served on the Economics Faculty of Northwestern University where he taught international finance and statistics.

Kaplan holds a Bachelor's degree in Mathematics, Economics, and Computer Science from New York University and an Master's degree and Doctorate in Economics from Northwestern University. He has served as a member of the editorial board of the *Financial Analysts Journal* and holds the Chartered Financial Analyst® designation.

Rob Kissell
Kissell Research Group

Contributor: Chapter 6 Trading and Operations

Dr. Robert Kissell is President of Kissell Research Group, a financial and economic consulting specializing in algorithmic trading, quantitative modeling, statistical analysis, risk management, and sports analytics. He has over 20 years of professional experience and advises financial institutions globally on trade execution strategies, portfolio optimization, machine learning, risk management, and best execution. He has developed algorithmic trading models and analytics that are used by brokers, institutions, banks, and hedge funds in the United States, Europe, and Asia.

In addition to his role at Kissell Research Group, Dr. Kissell is a Professor at Molloy College in the School of Business teaching graduate and undergraduate courses in quantitative analysis and finance, and is an Adjunct Professor Instructor at Fordham University teaching courses algorithmic trading and fintech.

Dr. Kissell is an author of the leading industry books "Algorithmic Trading Methods," "The Science of Algorithmic Trading & Portfolio Management," "Multi-Asset Risk Management," "Optimal Sports Math, Statistics, and Fantasy," and "Optimal Trading Strategies."

He has worked with several Investment Banks including UBS Securities where he was the Executive Director of Execution Strategies and Portfolio Analysis, at JP Morgan where he was Executive Director and Head of Quantitative Trading Strategies, at Citigroup/Smith Barney where he was Vice President, Quantitative Research, and at Instinet where he was Director, Trading Research.

Dr. Kissell has a PhD in Economics from Fordham University, a MS in Applied Mathematics from Hofstra University, a MS in Business Management, and a BS in Applied Mathematics & Statistics from Stony Brook University.

K.C. Ma
University of West Florida

Contributor: Chapter 8 Tools

K.C. Ma is the Eminent Scholar and the Mary Ball Washington/Switzer Brothers Endowed Chair of Finance at University of West Florida. Ma is the Director of Argo Investments Institute which enables college students to manage real money stock, bond, and option funds. Ma received his PhD in Finance from University of Illinois. He is also a Chartered Financial Analyst.

Ma has taught at Stetson University, University of Illinois at Urbana-Champaign, University of Toledo, University of Pittsburgh, Loyola University at Chicago, University of Hawaii, and Texas Tech University. He has worked at Investment Research Company, George Weiss Associates, and Ned Davis Research. He is the Principal for KCM Asset Management, KCM Market Neutral Funds, and KCM Analytics.

Lingjie Ma
University of Illinois at Chicago

Contributor: Chapter 4 Portfolio Construction

Lingjie has 15 years of global multiasset investment experience, as both head of research and portfolio manager, with responsibilities for full-spectrum investment process and business management. Lingjie joined UIC in 2016 as a Clinical Associate Professor in Finance and Assistant Dean for partnership programs. Before that, Lingjie worked in PanAgora Asset

Management, Northern Trust Global Investments, Deutsche Bank, and BMO Quantamental Strategies. Lingjie earned a PhD in Economics and a Master in Statistics from the University of Illinois at Urbana-Champaign. In addition to publications in both academic and industrial journals, Lingjie is a frequent public speaker on quantitative strategies and quantamental investments.

Anne Macy

West Texas A&M University

Contributor: Chapter 7 Presentations

Dr. Anne Macy is the Gene Edwards Professor of Finance and Director of the College of Business Student-Managed Investment Fund at West Texas A&M University's Paul and Virginia Engler College of Business. Additionally, Macy has been an Adjunct Professor for the Pacific Coast Banking School since 2007. Since 2012, she has co-advised the WTAMU CFA Research Challenge team. She teaches investments, security analysis, portfolio management, corporate finance, and healthcare financial management. Macy conducts finance and economic education seminars. Macy has been recognized by WTAMU for Teaching Excellence and Outstanding Service. Macy has published over 35 research articles and cases in journals such as *The CASE Journal*, *International Advances in Economic Research*, *SAGE Business Cases*, and the *Southwestern Economic Review*. In 2011, Macy became the Editor of the *Southwestern Economic Review*. Her research interests range from investing to healthcare corporate finance to pedagogy. Macy has a BA in Economics from the University of South Dakota and a MA and PhD in Economics from Texas Tech University.

Jerry L. Stevens

University of Richmond

Vantage Consulting Group

Contributor Chapter 3 Investing with Exchange Traded Funds

Jerry L. Stevens received his MS (1977) and PhD in Economics (1980) from the University of Illinois. He retired in 2020 as a Professor of Finance at the University of Richmond's E.C. Robins School of Business. During his career, he held a number of endowed chairs, won numerous teaching and service awards, and served as an Editor and Associate Editor for several journals. Professor Stevens has a long history of advising and creating student managed funds, to include a fund for economics students based on trading exchange traded funds (ETFs). He has over 50 publications in refereed research journals to include the *American Economic Review*; *Journal of Portfolio Management*; *Financial Management*; *Journal of Accounting, Auditing, and Finance*; *Financial Services Review*; *Journal of Financial Education*; *Journal of Investment Consulting*; and the *Journal of Financial Planning*.

Doctor Stevens is a speaker and educational consultant for the National Alliance where he specializes in the risk analysis portion of the Certified Risk Manager certification body of knowledge. He is currently the Chief Economist and Senior Consultant for the Vantage Consulting Group, a research-based consulting group of academics and practitioners. He has been with Vantage since its founding in 1982 and is the author of the Vantage Quarterly Outlook.

Rusty Yerkes

Samford University

Contributor: Appendix 1 Advisors guide to organization of a SMIF

Rustin T. (Rusty) Yerkes is an Associate Professor of Finance at the Brock School of Business, Samford University, in Birmingham, AL where he teaches Investments, Financial Statement Analysis and Risk Management & Insurance courses in the Masters of Business Administration (MBA), Masters of Accounting (MAcc), and undergraduate finance programs. His research interests are in venture capital, municipal finance and mortgage markets and he has published articles in *The Financial Review, Journal of Investing, The Journal of Biblical Integration in Business, Journal of Private Equity,* and *Journal of Trading.* Rusty has been recognized by Samford with faculty awards for Outstanding Scholarship and Distinguished Service. He received a PhD in Finance from the University of Alabama, MBA in Finance from Auburn University Montgomery and BS in Economics and BS in Operations Research from the US Air Force Academy in Colorado Springs, Colorado. Prior to entering graduate school, he served on active duty as an officer in the US Air Force working as a logistics analyst and Assistant Professor of Economics at the US Air Force Academy. Following active duty he worked as a portfolio manager for AmSouth (now Regions) Asset Management. Rusty holds the Chartered Financial Analyst (CFA, 2003), Certified Financial Planner (CFP, 2005) and Financial Risk Manager (FRM, 2015) designations. In his free time he enjoys running, road and mountain cycling, fiction and non-fiction reading and volunteering with Junior Achievement of Alabama.

Acknowledgments to the first edition

We could not have included as much information about existing practices in student-managed investment funds and the profession without the meaningful contributions of others. We thank the following individuals and their institutions for their generous help in writing this book. This book would not have been possible without their work in their respective programs and their willingness to contribute to this effort.

Leah Bennet, CFA Institute
Stanley Block, Texas Christian University
Jonathan Boersma, CFA Institute
Genna Brown, Georgia State University
Dan Chung, Fred Alger Management, Inc.
Philip Cooley, Trinity University
Sharon Criswell, ALM First
Eric Davis, Tennessee Valley Authority
Steven Dolvin, Butler University
Jill Foote, Rice University
Chinmoy Ghosh, University of Connecticut
Aimee Harmelink, Smith Breeden Associates
Robert Kissell, JP Morgan
Edward Lawrence, University of Missouri St. Louis
Hal Liebes, Fred Alger Management, Inc.
Anna Marie Lopez, Hotchkis & Wiley
David Louton, Bryant University
Terry Maness, Baylor University
John Minnehan, NEPC, LLC
Timothy Nantell, University of Minnesota
David Nawrocki, Villanova University
Max Palmer, FlexTrade
Amanda Quinn, CFA Institute
Steve Ramsey, Austin College
Marc Reinganum, State Street Global Advisors
William Reichenstein, Baylor University

Peter Ricchiuti, Tulane University
Patrick Rice, Baylor University
Adam Schwartz, Washington and Lee University
Carl Schwinn, Bates College
Ronald Singer, University of Houston
Paul Stewart, University of Houston
Brian Stype, CFA Institute
Kristy D. Tarr, FactSet
Todd Williams, Austin College
John Winegender, Creighton University
Faith Yando, Dimensional Fund Advisors LP

We also thank the following institutions and, in the cases of many of these colleges and universities, the participants in their student-managed investment funds, for graciously providing material for this textbook.

Advent Software
Austin College
Bates College
Baylor University
Bentley University
Bloomberg
Bryant University
Butler University
CFA Institute
Connecticut College
Cornell University
Creighton University
FactSet
Fairfield College
FlexTrade
JP Morgan
LSV Asset Management
Northfield Information Services, Inc.
Oberlin College
Rice University
Southern Illinois University Carbondale
Southern Methodist University
State Street Global Advisors
Stetson University
Texas Christian University

Thomson Reuters

Trinity University

Tulane University

UBS

University of California—San Diego

University of Connecticut

University of Minnesota

University of Missouri—St. Louis

University of Toledo

University of Tulsa

Villanova University

Washington and Lee University

We also thank the editors and project managers at Elsevier, especially Scott Bentley and Melissa Murray, for their help and persistence in getting this project off the ground and to completion. Finally, we thank our assistants, Melinda Estelle, Stephen Putbrese, and Bryan Welge for their work in collecting and reviewing material for the book.

About the Author

Brian R. Bruce

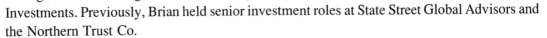

CEO & Chief Investment Officer, Hillcrest Asset Management
Board of Trustee Member, The Philip M. Dorr Alumni and
Friends Endowed Investment Fund, Baylor University

Brian is the CEO & Chief Investment Officer of Hillcrest Asset
Management. He founded Hillcrest in 2007 and is a pioneer in
behavioral portfolio management. Under Brian, Hillcrest has won
numerous awards for outstanding investment performance.
Before founding Hillcrest, Brian was Chief Investment Officer at
PanAgora Asset Management, a subsidiary of Putnam
Investments. Previously, Brian held senior investment roles at State Street Global Advisors and
the Northern Trust Co.

Brian was a Visiting Professor of Investments and taught the student-managed investment class
in the Hankamer School of Business at Baylor University for 18 years and currently serves on
the fund's Board of Trustees. He also taught the student-managed portfolio classes and served
as the Director of the Finance Institute and Founding Director of the Alternative Asset
Management Center at the Cox School of Business at Southern Methodist University.

Brian received his MBA from the University of Chicago, MS from DePaul University, and BS
from Illinois State University. He is a member of the Illinois State University College of
Business Hall of Fame, a recipient of the University of Chicago Graduate School of Business
CEO Award, and won the SMU Cox School of Business Media Expert of the Year Award twice.

Brian has published numerous scholarly articles and books including *Analysts, Lies, and
Statistics* which he co-authored with former Harvard Business School Professor Mark
Bradshaw. He is the Editor of *Journal of Investing*, the *Journal of Index Investing*, the *Journal
of Impact & ESG Investing*, and the *Journal of Behavioral Finance*.

Brian can be found on Linkedin at https://www.linkedin.com/in/brian-bruce-a1b5112/.

CHAPTER 1

Investment philosophy and process

A student-managed investment fund is a pool of real money that is managed by undergraduate or graduate students. Students have the responsibility for deciding how the money is invested. In some cases, this responsibility covers all aspects of the investment process, including asset allocation, security selection, execution and trading, and monitoring and reporting. In other funds, students are responsible for a subset of these activities, perhaps because they are given a mandate to invest in a specific asset class by a board of advisors or the beneficiary of the fund's assets. In all cases, the common element is that students are entrusted with the responsibility and granted the authority to invest real money. As such, a student-managed investment fund is not a game. It is not a simulation. Risks are taken. Profits can be made. Money can be lost.

Given what is at stake, there are some within a university who might question the wisdom in trusting students with real money. After all, students are not professionals. Yet in a student-managed investment fund, students are being trusted with responsibilities that are typically bestowed only on professionals with years of experience. With the help of professional and academic advisors, educational resources—such as this book, and, most importantly, a high level of diligence, students can achieve results on par with those of true professionals. In so doing, students gain valuable experience and insights that apply to business, in general, and investing, specifically—as well as a broad spectrum of other activities.

The real-world experience provides the primary motivation for most colleges and universities to offer a student-managed investment fund. Likewise, this course attracts motivated students who seek a real-world experience and a more practical understanding of business and investments. The student-managed investment fund provides a hands-on learning environment in much the same way as laboratory experiments or exercises would enhance learning physics, chemistry, or biology. As with science labs, in a student-managed investment fund, the theory that is taught in finance textbooks and classroom lectures becomes tangible and its relevance clearer. This book serves as a sort of "lab book" in helping to present traditional classroom material in an applied setting. As such, the emphasis is on the practice of investing. The relevant theories are not developed in as much detail as they might be in some texts. Rather, this book takes the approach of providing more discussion of the issues that arise in the application of such theories and offer a framework for the practice of investing. In doing so, we attempt to

Student-Managed Investment Funds. https://doi.org/10.1016/B978-0-12-817866-9.00001-7

highlight the diversity of approaches to investing in practice by including numerous examples from student-managed investment funds and professional investment firms alike.

The student-managed investment fund as an investment management firm

A student-managed investment fund (SMIF) is an investment organization. In many ways, it will resemble a real investment firm as it often serves nearly the same purpose. For an SMIF that manages a mandate from its university's endowment fund, the SMIF serves the same role as any of the endowment fund's other investment managers. As such, the endowment fund is the SMIF's client, to whom the students in this class must answer. The SMIF has a challenge to conduct its business with the same standards in mind as the other investment firms that the endowment fund has hired. These investment firms are usually considered to be institutional investment managers, in that they cater to the institutional, as opposed to the retail, marketplace. Institutional investors include public pension plans, such as the California Public Employees' Retirement System (aka CalPERS); corporate pension plans, such as the Boeing Company Employee Retirement Plan; Taft-Hartley (i.e., labor union) retirement plans, such as the UMWA Health & Retirement Funds; foundations, such as the Andrew W. Mellon Foundation; endowment funds, such as Harvard's Harvard Management Company; and family offices, such as the family offices of Paul Allen or Michel Dell or group family offices like Rockefeller and Tolleson. These types of investors have many common traits, including a large size (from the hundreds of millions of dollars to tens of billions of dollars), long (often infinite) investment horizons, and professional investment staffs. It is with this clientele in mind that we model this book.

As indicated above, one reason we chose the institutional investment approach is that many SMIFs literally have their universities' endowment funds as clients. More importantly, by catering to the professional investors in the marketplace, institutional investors are often more discerning and reliant on sound principles of finance and investing. As a result, the best practices of investing are often found among those who provide investment services to institutional clients. In addition, many students in student-managed investment fund programs seek careers in the institutional money management industry and our goal is to provide a training and educational resource that will allow student-managed investment fund members to excel as professional investors.

Key steps in meeting the standards of an institutional investor are to provide clear expectations regarding the investment approach, and to have a rational organizational and operational structure that can consistently deliver on those expectations. While this chapter addresses the former and Chapter 2 addresses the latter, it is important to note that these two aspects of a student-managed investment fund and, indeed, any investment firm, are not mutually exclusive. The investment approach must contemplate specific organizational and operational realities. Likewise, the organizational and operational structure must reflect the investment approach.

For example, a quantitative investment approach that relies on a specific economic or financial model and requires little qualitative or subjective input would need significant technology, data, and operations to support such systems. In contrast, a fundamental investment approach that requires research by numerous individual analysts must have the depth of knowledge and headcount to provide adequate coverage of the market.

With this institutional investment framework in mind, we begin by discussing the investment approach. In short, we will be discussing *investing*. As indicated above, we discuss investing from the institutional or professional viewpoint and not necessarily as what is portrayed in the popular media or in commercial advertisements for trading services that are targeted at the retail (i.e., individual) investor. Investing is appropriately a professional pursuit. Like other professions, such as medicine, law, and engineering, investments require a base of knowledge acquired through a coherent program of study, and training on how it is practiced professionally. In short, investing should not be pursued in some *ad hoc* fashion or without an understanding of the field. To do so is irresponsible and unlikely to yield the desired outcomes. Investing that is practiced on behalf of a client or for one's own personal benefit, should be done diligently and in a manner consistent with established knowledge and practices in the field. The thoughtful reader might be tempted to pause to wonder how a group of students, who are, by definition, investing novices and in the process of gaining investing knowledge, might appropriately be expected to build an institutional-quality investment approach. This book takes the view that every investor is a student of investing. Most advanced undergraduates and graduate students have learned the key fundamental material upon which to build an investment approach. Moreover, students are as capable of being diligent and building a thoughtful approach as many professionals. With the help of resources, such as advisors, mentors, and this and other books, students can leverage their own insights to build a compelling and successful fund. Our experience as professors of student-managed investment fund programs has shown us first-hand how even undergraduates can do analysis that rivals that of professional investors.

The key to initiating a program of investing resides in the development of the investment philosophy and process. Together, the investment philosophy and process represent the definition of an individual's or organization's approach to investing. As such, they reflect the purpose and methods that generate the investment results.

Investment philosophy and process

The investment philosophy and process combine to define the investor or the investment organization. The investment philosophy and the investment process provide a framework in which to understand markets and select investments. Without these, the entire endeavor is *ad hoc*. In short, the investment philosophy provides the *why* and the investment process provides the *how*.

To illustrate the importance of philosophy and process for an organization, such as an investment management firm or a student-managed investment fund, consider a sports analogy regarding a game of basketball. Without an investment philosophy and investment process, the investment decisions are like a pickup game in which 10 players meet at the court and are divided into two teams in a random, *ad hoc* manner. Each player in the game follows her own approach to the game, without the benefit of knowing her teammate's approach. Each player on a team is working for the common goal of her team scoring more points, but without a common playbook, a coherent game strategy, or a shared understanding of the opposition. The game evolves without forethought, with offense being improvised and defense being decided on-the-spot. The individual talents of certain players might be revealed. It is more likely, however, that whatever talents each player possesses will not be fully realized in such an *ad hoc* approach to the game.

In contrast, having an investment philosophy and process is like having a coherent team and game plan. A true team approach begins by first defining the goal of the team. It progresses by building a team and understanding the team's strengths and weaknesses. Plays are drawn up, based on this understanding. Each player on the team knows the playbook, which might even be customized for the particular strengths or weaknesses of a particular game's opposition. Each player has a role in the execution of the offense and defense. The plays are practiced until they become second nature. There is a *shared* understanding of purpose and execution for how the game will be played. The same idea applies to investing.

The investment philosophy represents a *shared* sense of purpose for an organization. It explains what the group believes about markets and *why* it believes it can create or add value. The investment process articulates *how* the philosophy is implemented. In takes the philosophy regarding what opportunities are believed to exist and expresses the methods by which those opportunities are realized. Having the investment philosophy and process memorialized for the group defines the organization and assures its continuity and consistency of approach through time. As indicated in Exhibit 1.1, Creighton University's and Florida Gulf Coast University's student-managed investment fund properly begins with a specific exercise to make sure that new students understand the philosophy of the previous students in the fund. In this way, the

---

Exhibit 1.1 Creighton University and Florida Gulf Coast University

Different schools do the transition from class to class, from semester to semester, and from year to year differently. Both the Creighton Student Management equity fund and the Florida Gulf Coast University Eagle Fund are continuous SMIFs. These two funds keep the selected stocks in the portfolio from the previous semester's or year's class. The first requirement of a new class is to understand the philosophy of the past portfolio managers and their management style. This system is similar to students' starting work at a professional mutual fund with their current holdings, their recommended list, and their watch list.

---

continuity and consistency through time are facilitated in an environment in which consistency and continuity are a unique challenge due to the structure of a student-managed investment fund that experiences significant turnover of personnel every semester or every year.

While the philosophy and process are important internally to an investor and investment organization, they are equally important in articulating an investment approach externally to prospective clients. The statement of the philosophy allows prospective clients to judge whether there is a match between their own outlook and philosophy and that of the investment manager. Likewise, an investment process defines the general approach that prospective clients can expect the manager to follow. In this way, there should be a logical link between the philosophy and process that can be judged as reasonable.

Finally, for an aspiring investment professional who is embarking on a career in investment management, the investment philosophy and process shows that the person approaches investing as a professional. Indeed, a common question in institutional RFPs (Request for Proposal) and in employee interviews at investment management firms is to ask the firm or the individual what their investment philosophy or investment process is. The investment philosophy shows thoughtfulness with respect to purpose and an understanding of the problem. The investment process reveals an understanding of a solution through planning, purposeful execution, and diligence in the act of investing.

Investment philosophy

According to Merriam-Webster, the definitions of the word "philosophy" include:

1. "The most basic beliefs, concepts, and attitudes of an individual or group."
2. "A theory underlying or regarding a sphere of activity or thought."

An investment philosophy defines the common set of beliefs for an investment organization. This gives every member of the group a common reference from which to begin doing analysis and contributing ideas to the organization. While individual members need not subscribe to the exact set of beliefs embodied in the group's philosophy, members should use the philosophy as the set of beliefs that define their efforts and activities on behalf of the organization.

Scope of an investment philosophy

When developing an investment organization's investment philosophy, the scope should be limited to the realm of investment-related activities. It should not wander off into irrelevant reflections on the state of the world or the state of the economy. Rather, the philosophy should be focused on what will be most relevant in shaping and guiding the investment approach for the group. Many student-managed investment funds might engage in a number of other educational, career-enhancing, or social activities besides undertaking investment activities.

The investment philosophy should be limited to the investment activities. Likewise, many investment firms include statements about their own client service outlook (e.g., "we put the client first") in their investment philosophies. This might be fine for an overall firm philosophy, but it is unlikely to have any bearing on investment activities. To say that each client's needs are unique begins to suggest that there is no coherent philosophy that the organization has to offer. Any organization should have an overall philosophy or mission statement, but this is not a substitute for a cogent investment philosophy. In short, do not confuse a "business philosophy" or "mission statement" with an investment philosophy. Too many investment companies make this mistake and leave the client wondering what their basic principles are when it comes to investing.

Key elements of an investment philosophy

1. Statement of beliefs about the markets.
2. Statement of beliefs about the opportunities to create value.
3. Statement of beliefs about the group's abilities.
4. Statement of beliefs about the group's abilities to exploit the opportunities to create value.

Statement of beliefs

The investment philosophy should include a statement of beliefs about the state of the market. Ideally, this is one or two sentences that provide a clear and concrete statement of the fund's view of how the world is and perhaps why it is the way it is. This statement should be assailable. By definition, any statement of a belief, as opposed to a fact, is open to agreement or disagreement. Those who agree usually have evidence to support such a position, while the same can be true of those who disagree. Thus, while these are statements of belief, they are not without evidence and therefore are not pure statements of faith. By stating the starting point, potential clients are free to agree or disagree with the statement. The client who hires the manager is implicitly agreeing with the belief or at least admitting the possibility that there is truth in the belief.

For example, consider two funds, E.M. Hutton and Hi-Mark, Ltd., who each pursue very different strategies. E.M. Hutton (or EMH for short), believes that the markets are efficient in the semi-strong form sense. EMH's philosophy might begin with the statement, "We believe the stock prices reflect publicly available information." In contrast, Hi-Mark, Ltd. (or HML for short) might pursue a fundamental equity strategy and begin their philosophy statement with, "We believe that the prices deviate over short horizons from their fundamental values due to investors' overreaction to short-term information." Note that these statements set the foundation for subsequent statements of how each fund will provide valuable services in such a market.

Statement of opportunities

Given the statement of beliefs, the next element of the investment philosophy should articulate the nature and scope of opportunities available in the marketplace to add value. This statement should be closely connected to the statement of beliefs. That is, this statement should follow directly from the statement of beliefs. While the statement of beliefs is quite general, this statement of opportunities should be quite specific and limited to those opportunities that the individual or organization is focused on exploiting.

Continuing with the EMH and HML examples, EMH might continue to say, "We believe that the market rewards risk in well-diversified portfolios over the long-term. Therefore, we believe that since markets are efficient and cannot be outperformed, the best an investor can do is to implement a well-diversified portfolio with low turnover and trading costs." Likewise, HML might continue their philosophy to say, "Opportunities exist to find undervalued firms that have recently released negative information, resulting in depressed market prices relative to intrinsic values." Clearly, these two investment managers should have very different investment approaches. The statements of beliefs and opportunities allow the organizations to convey their starting points and their purpose in offering investment services.

Statement of ability

The statements of belief and opportunity establish the potential for any individual or organization to add value through their investment services. However, the philosophy must also establish the specific abilities of the individual or organization to exploit these opportunities. In other words, an opportunity for added value is necessary, but not sufficient for an investment approach to add value. The beliefs and opportunities say what is available in the market. The statement of ability articulates the capability of the individual or organization to realize those opportunities. In this sense, the statement of ability is a statement of competitive advantage. The statements of beliefs and opportunities are externally focused on the markets. The statement of ability should be internally focused beliefs about the individual or organization.

The statement of ability must also be relevant within the context of the statement of beliefs and opportunities. That is, it must relate to those opportunities. In our EMH-HML example, each manager must state an ability that relates to the opportunities he or she has articulated. In doing so, EMH might point out its own particular expertise in targeting risk and efficient implementation by saying, "EMH has the capability to build well-diversified portfolios with low turnover and low trading costs that are able to realize the risks and returns to passive benchmarks in a real portfolio." In essence, EMH is saying that it can achieve exposure to an index or benchmark and achieve the returns from those passive indexes in practice. Similarly, HML might describe their capabilities in identifying undervalued securities. However, in doing so, HML must be careful to articulate how it does not fall prey to the same overreactions that give rise to the opportunities it seeks to exploit. One way that HML might communicate this ability is to say that, "HML employs a quantitative system that is designed to identify stocks that have experienced negative market sentiment, but that have strong long-term fundamentals."

Note that these statements are specific, yet not too detailed. Statements of philosophy should be only as specific and detailed as necessary, and no more. To provide too much detail would be to put the philosophy at risk of being unnecessarily narrow and rigid. In this sense, there exists a balance. Notice that the HML statement does not describe its quantitative model in detail or provide an itemized list of aspects of a company's fundamentals that classify a company as "strong." Rather, it narrows the scope of analysis to being quantitative and the inputs to the model as being both fundamental (as it relates to intrinsic value) and, perhaps, behavioral (as it relates to market sentiment). This leaves plenty of room for detail to be added in the investment process that describes how such a model works, it makes clear that the philosophy relies on the belief in such a model's capability.

Statement of value

The statement of value may be a separate statement within the philosophy, or it may be incorporated into the statement of ability. Regardless, the philosophy must make clear the expected benefit from pursuing the individual's or organization's investment approach. There must be a positive statement of the value added from the investment approach. This statement might implicitly or explicitly compare its approach to other (competing) approaches. However, it must not be simply a negative statement of the perils from other approaches. Just as in considering one's own life philosophy, the final statement of value should be one of identity and purpose. It should help summarize the intended virtue of adherence to the philosophy.

The EMH philosophy might conclude, "By building a well-diversified portfolio with efficient execution and low turnover, the EMH strategy seeks to realize returns that compensate for risks taken, without losing returns to unnecessary and unrewarded costs." Likewise, HML might conclude, "With a disciplined implementation of its model, the HML strategy has the potential to reap rewards beyond those of passive benchmarks or indexes, without incurring more risk."

With these statements, the individual or organization has defined the scope of its investment approach and its purpose for investing. The individual or organization has bared its soul in hopes of finding a soul mate. That last statement might sound a little over-the-top, but there is more truth in it than there is hype. The key idea behind an investment philosophy is to provide a "soul" that guides the individual or organization in its investment endeavors. The soul keeps the approach on track, especially during times when the environment becomes particularly challenging. It provides something to return to when the path seems unclear. It is something that should be questioned at times (as in "soul searching"), especially in light of evidence or experience to cast doubt on it. But, if the philosophy is founded on solid reasoning, insight, and knowledge, it is very likely to survive challenge and provide an important source of stability and strength to an individual or organization as it invests.

Examples of investment philosophy

Institutional investment management firms provide excellent examples for student-managed investment funds with respect to investment philosophy and process. While not all investment management firms publicly provide clear statements of their investment philosophy and process, those that do are often found on the companies' websites and in their materials provided to current and prospective clients. As discussed in the overview of investment strategy classifications in Appendix A, investment strategies are often classified into "quantitative" or "fundamental" strategies. This distinction is particularly appropriate when considering the investment philosophy and process of an investment manager. Therefore, we provide examples of investment philosophies of quantitative managers in Exhibit 1.2 and fundamental managers in Exhibit 1.3.

Exhibit 1.2 Investment philosophies from investment firms with quantitative strategies

LSV Asset Management
Investment philosophy
The fundamental premise on which our investment philosophy is based is that superior long-term results can be achieved by systematically exploiting the judgmental biases and behavioral weaknesses that influence the decisions of many investors. These include: the tendency to extrapolate the past too far into the future, to wrongly equate a good company with a good investment irrespective of price, to ignore statistical evidence, and to develop a "mindset" about a company.

LSV uses a quantitative investment model to choose out-of-favor (undervalued) stocks in the marketplace at the time of purchase that have potential for near-term appreciation. LSV believes that these out-of-favor securities will produce superior future returns if their future growth exceeds the market's low expectations.

LSV portfolios typically have a deep value orientation relative to the indices. Market timing is not part of the process and portfolios are fully invested (cash levels usually below 2%).

(*Source:* www.lsvasset.com, June 2020.)

Dimensional Fund Advisors
Investment philosophy
Dimensional's investment philosophy is based on the belief that security prices quickly incorporate information and reflect the aggregate forward-looking expectations of market participants. We use the information available in market prices to identify systematic differences

in expected returns among securities, supported by robust theoretical and empirical research. We implement our understanding of reliable drivers of expected returns in broadly diversified, systemic investment solutions that pursue higher expected returns while efficiently managing risks and costs for investors.

(*Source:* Dimensional Fund Advisors, June 2020.)

Exhibit 1.3 Investment philosophies from investment firms with fundamental strategies

Fred Alger Management, Inc.

Investment philosophy

We believe companies undergoing positive dynamic change, offer the best investment opportunities for our clients. Our competitive edge is identifying these companies and capitalizing on the changes before it is recognized in the market.

We embrace change found in "traditional" growth companies as well as in companies experiencing what we call a "growth renaissance".

By positive dynamic change, we mean those companies experiencing:

- High unit volume growth
  - These companies are experiencing rapidly growing demand, have a strong business model, enjoy market dominance. We track the company's growth phases closely, aiming to own its shares during the highest growth period.
  - These "traditional" growth companies have growing revenues, growing unit volume, increasing market share, and are expanding business.
- Positive life cycle change
  - These companies are benefitting from a positive catalyst in their business, allowing them to enter an accelerated growth phase. Positive catalysts for change could include new management, product innovation, acquisition, or new regulations.
  - A catalyst drives the companies to experience a "growth renaissance," resulting in an improving earnings trajectory leading to P/E expansion.

Investment process

Research has been the cornerstone of our investment process for over 50 years and we rely on our talented research professionals to execute our investment process with utmost discipline and precision. Our original, fundamental, bottom-up research process is designed to get the analyst's best ideas into the portfolio. We conduct thorough, original, research, taking into account both quantitative and qualitative data.

What differentiates our research?

Original research to build a differentiated view
- Analysts leverage country/regional and industry/sector expertise to identify potential change beneficiaries.
- Develop a differentiated view of a company's total market and ability to execute its business model.

- Quantify insights in detailed income, balance sheet, and cash flow models specific to a company's key drivers.

Stress test valuation based on key stock drivers
- Fundamentals are explicitly linked to valuation and stock-specific risk factors.
- Assess company fundamentals using detailed, proprietary financial models utilizing a variety of valuation methods.
- Base case price targets are stress tested for both upside surprise and downside risk.

Collaborative dialogue drives decisions
- Portfolio Managers challenge Analysts to test conviction.
- Open door policy.
- Weekly global investment team meetings.
- Regular sector team meetings.
- Shared database for notes on every contact about a company.

Portfolio construction balances reward and risk
- Buy decisions and the position size are based on:
  - Relative investment opportunity.
  - Portfolio constraints.
  - Liquidity.
- Sell decisions are based on:
  - Stock achieving its target price.
  - Company experiencing deteriorating fundamentals with greater reward/risk potential.

(*Source*: www.alger.com, June 2020.)

Hotchkis & Wiley
Philosophy
H&W employs a research-driven, fundamental value investing approach. We invest in companies where, in our opinion, the present value of its future cash flows exceeds the market price. These opportunities often emerge because the market extrapolates current trends into the future, which leads to favoring popular investments and shunning others — regardless of valuation. Empirical evidence suggests that companies generating above average returns on capital attract competition that leads to lower levels of profitability. Conversely, capital leaves depressed areas, often allowing profitability to revert back to normal levels. The difference between a company's price based on an extrapolation of current trends and a more likely reversion to mean creates the value investment opportunity.

To uncover these opportunities, we employ a disciplined, bottom-up investment process emphasizing rigorous, internally generated fundamental research. We believe the consistent application and depth of our independent research can maximize the trade-off between value and risk providing superior returns to a static benchmark over the long term.

(*Source*: www.hwcm.com, May 2020.)

The two companies in Exhibit 1.2, LSV Asset Management (LSV) and Dimensional Fund Advisors (DFA), implement quantitative equity strategies. LSV provides a relatively concise statement encompassing the key elements of an investment philosophy. They indicate that they believe that investors in the market suffer from judgmental biases leading to "out-of-favor" securities that are undervalued in the market. One can infer LSV believes that undervalued securities give rise to an opportunity to outperform the overall market or a passive index. LSV's philosophy statement indicates that its ability resides in its quantitative process to identify these undervalued securities, with their value being the potential for superior long-term returns. LSV supports their investment philosophy with numerous academic research articles, available on the firm's website. Similarly, DFA's investment philosophy is rooted in research and summarized in several pages on the firm's website. A short excerpt from one of those pages is provided in Exhibit 1.2. Readers are encouraged to visit DFA's website for the complete discussion of the firm's investment philosophy.

The investment philosophies of fundamental managers in Exhibit 1.3 range from quite brief to rather lengthy. The common element among these philosophies is that they all emphasize the value of fundamental research in determining the true value of the firms that they hold and the implicit belief that each firm possesses the ability to conduct this research better than others.

Exhibit 1.4 shows the investment philosophy of Baylor University's student-managed investment fund. As indicated in its philosophy, the fund uses a hybrid approach in building its

---

Exhibit 1.4 Baylor University's student investment fund investment philosophy

The fund seeks long-term capital appreciation with returns in excess of the S&P 500 market index. The fund is invested in stocks from the industries within the S&P 500 index, with a nominal amount of cash maintained to facilitate day-to-day operations. To achieve superior returns, the fund relies on superior stock selection.

Portfolio allocation is not a primary strategy of the fund; our target is mirror, as closely as possible, the S&P 500 index sector weights. Analysts give careful consideration and require consensus to be reached before any sector is significantly over- or under-weighted. The primary objective remains the selection of securities that will provide a superior return using qualitative and quantitative fundamental analysis.

As part of the quantitative analysis, the fund follows a multi-factor model involving three components: value, growth, and hybrid measures. The weight allocated to each of these factors within the model is at the analyst's discretion, but the general methodology remains consistent. The overall objective is to achieve a balanced investment approach combining both value and growth factors. Typical metrics utilized by analysts are the following:

Growth	Value	Hybrid
Quarterly earnings surprise	Price/earnings	Price-to-earnings growth (PEG)
Earnings revisions	Price/book	
Return on equity		
5-year consensus growth		

We believe combing multiple measures in these three component areas provide a valuable method of identifying stocks with superior long-term return potential. Additionally, the fund seeks to substantiate quantitative stock analysis with the underlying investment "story." The story of a stock includes the company's strategic vision, core competencies, short- and long-term plans of action; the quality of the management team; an analysis of the industry and competitors; and an understanding of macroeconomic factors affecting the business.

(Source: www.baylor.edu/business.)

portfolio, with a statement that this blend of quantitative and fundamental research reveals the true "story" behind a company and its value.

Investment process

While the investment philosophy establishes the rationale for the opportunity for a particular investment approach, the investment process produces the actual results. As noted in the Cayuga Fund's report of its performance in Exhibit 1.5, the returns from a strategy are the result of the application of an investment process. According to Merriam-Webster, the definitions of the word "process" include:

1. "Something going on"
2. "A series of actions or operations conducing to an end; especially a continuous operation or treatment especially in manufacture."

Exhibit 1.5 The Cayuga Fund at Cornell University's Johnson College of Business

Performance
The fund began as an index-tilt product, with the objective of generating returns above the S&P 500. Since October 2002, the fund has followed a market-neutral strategy. Annual returns since 2003 (the first full year of operation as a market-neutral hedge fund) are shown below. The fund's management believes that its performance over time is the result of a combination of its disciplined investment process, which consists of fundamental analysis layered on the output of a proprietary quantitative model, and careful attention to risk management.

Year	Performance (%)	AUM (m)
2003	19.20	2.8
2004	18.60	6.8
2005	10.40	10.2
2006	14.20	13.5
2007	5.95	14.4
2008	0.42	14.4
2009	−0.39	11.5

We include the first definition because it so eloquently points out the obvious. Any investment approach must have *something going on*! If there is no investment process, a fund risks raising a question as to what, if anything, is going on. As indicated in the second definition, the statement of the investment process explains what is going on by describing the actions. The second definition also alludes to the manufacturing context of the word "process." In manufacturing, the process is what converts raw materials to a final product or output. Indeed, the manufacturing process describes how the raw materials are combined and treated to create the final product. Likewise, in investing, the investment process describes how an investor builds a portfolio from its raw materials. More specifically, the investment process describes the steps that an investor or investment organization follows to arrive at a set of portfolio weights.

A manufacturing process is subject to the laws of physics. For example, a saw blade cannot be made out of cotton, but a comfortable shirt can be. Likewise, a portfolio must be made up of inputs that logically and theoretically contribute to the choice of portfolio weights according to economic and financial theory and principles. An investment process must articulate what the inputs are, how they are used, and what steps are taken to transform the inputs into a useable set of portfolio weights. This process must be motivated by and consistent with the investment philosophy. Like the investment philosophy, the investment process should be informed by the field of knowledge that is relevant. Depending on the investment philosophy and the particular strategy, the field of knowledge might be drawn from the fields of economics, finance, mathematics, and/or psychology, among others.

The philosophy and process are complimentary to one another. In initially conceiving an investment philosophy and process, it is helpful to establish the philosophy first, since the philosophy sets the foundation with a set of beliefs, opportunities, and goals for the process. However, it is often useful to revisit or revise the philosophy after considering the investment process. The creation of the investment process can help clarify both the potential for certain opportunities to be realized and the constraints that make some goals difficult to achieve. Through time, the process is more likely to be adapted to changing market conditions, capabilities, or technology. In making enhancements to the investment process, the investment philosophy provides the framework from which potential changes are conceived. Changes in the process that help more fully realize the opportunities articulated in the philosophy should be sought. In all cases, the investment process and philosophy should be consistent with one another.

An investment process must have a clear beginning, middle, and end. The investment process's beginning or initialization establishes the starting point from which all other decisions and analysis will proceed. The middle of the investment process describes the meat of the process where most of the action takes place through the application of the methods. The end of the investment process implements the strategy and declares the resulting product or output. As the definition above alludes to, the investment process is continuous. As such, there is no specific beginning or end in time. Thus, most investment processes can be thought of as loops, in which the beginning is returned to as soon as one reaches the end. As such, the investment process is typically shown in presentations by institutional investment firms as a flow chart as seen in the example from Baylor University's student-managed investment fund in Exhibit 1.6.

Exhibit 1.6 Baylor University's student investment fund investment process

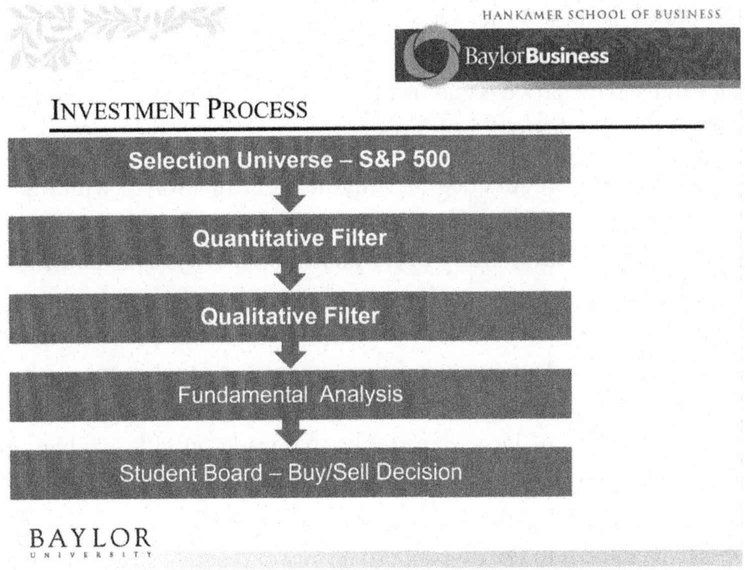

(*Source: www.baylor.edu/business*)

Key elements of an investment process

1. Initialization.
2. Methods.
3. Implementation.

Initialization

The beginning of an investment process can take many different forms. In all forms, the process must be initiated by defining the starting point. Fortunately, the investment philosophy provides the motivation for what form the initialization takes. The form typically depends on whether the investment approach embodied in the philosophy is considered "top-down" or "bottom-up." A top-down approach typically starts with a global or macroeconomic idea that we will identify as a theme. This theme provides the foundation on which the remainder of the process will build. For example, consider an investment philosophy that identifies the forecast of macroeconomic trends as a source of value. This approach's investment process might begin with a measurement or analysis of various economic factors to establish a forecast or a theme. For example, the process might say, "Leading economic indicators are evaluated to forecast which sectors of the economy are expected to experience the most relative growth over the next 12 to 24 months." A more detailed statement might add, "Leading indicators include Corporate Profitability, Inflation, Inventories, Industrial Production, New Manufacturing Orders for Consumer Goods, New Manufacturing Orders for Capital Goods, Building Permits, Housing Starts, Employment, Money Supply, Interest Rates, Consumer Borrowing, and Consumer Confidence." Later steps in the process can further refine this forecast or theme and explain how the ideas are expressed through stock holdings.

For a bottom-up approach, the process begins with the identification of which securities will be the subject of the bottom-up analysis. This step is critical because it often is not feasible for a bottom-up approach to begin with literally every possible security. The identified securities are often referred to as the "eligible universe" or simply the "list of eligible securities." In many cases, the eligible universe is dictated by the specific investment product, mandate, or benchmark. For example, a student-managed investment fund that manages a U.S. large cap core mandate for its university's endowment fund might begin its investment process by saying, "The eligible universe consists of large cap stocks that trade on U.S. exchanges. A stock is considered large cap if it is a constituent of the S&P 500 Index or if its market capitalization is larger than that of the 10th percentile ranking stock in the S&P 500 Index." This example highlights an important contrast to the investment philosophy: the investment process should be quite specific.

Exhibit 1.7 Texas Christian University Educational Investment Fund

Top-down balanced portfolio management approach (TCU)

The TCU-EIF is a well-diversified balanced fund, investing across multiple asset classes. The fund's long-term strategic asset allocation is 70/25/5 percentage allocations to stocks, bonds, and cash, respectively. Exposure to real estate and international assets is also encouraged. Tactical asset deviations from the strategic allocations are exercised within limits. For instance, equity allocations can range between 60% and 80% depending on shorter term capital market forecasts of the fund members. At the beginning of the semester, the Fund's Chief Economist provides a state of the global economy address. Key macroeconomic variables discussed include gross domestic product, industrial production, capacity utilization, inflation, unemployment rates, default risk spreads, maturity risk spreads, intermediate Treasury bond rates, federal debt as a percentage of GDP, U.S. dollar strength relative to key foreign currencies, retail sales, fiscal and monetary policy, housing prices, and foreclosure rates. We use these and other leading indicators to proactively move assets to favorable sectors, evaluate businesses within those sectors using appropriate valuation techniques, and finally, make investment decisions on individual companies.

After the economist's presentation, the class spends one week examining individual sectors. Class members are assigned to examine specific sectors and then to make formal presentations to the class, after which sector allocation targets are established for the semester. Targets are established by majority vote of fund members. Active sector allocations for equities are made relative to the S&P 500 equity industry sector allocations. Allocations can deviate up to 50% relative to the S&P 500 weightings. For instance, if 20% of the S&P 500 is allocated to the information technology sector, the EIF target weight to the sector can be range anywhere from 10% to 30%, depending on the funds expectations for the sector.

Tactical decisions also are made to equities segmented by capital appreciation (dividend yields below the 10-year Treasury yield), income and capital appreciation (dividend yields close to the 10-year Treasury yield) and income (dividend yields higher than the 10-year Treasury yield) stocks. The fixed income portion of the portfolio is invested primarily in fixed income mutual funds, which are monitored by the fund's fixed income analysts. Fixed income deliberations focus on maturity and quality sector weightings. Key factors include interest rate movements, business cycle projections, duration, and convexity.

(*Source: TCU, Larry Lockwood.*)

Exhibit 1.7 shows an example of the Texas Christian University's student-managed investment fund, the Educational Investment Fund (TCU-EIF). After stating the portfolio's overall strategic asset allocation, the entire first paragraph is concerned with the initialization of the TCU-EIF top-down investment process. This stage of the process clearly indicates not only the key inputs of the macroeconomic variables, but notes that these fall under the responsibility of the Chief Economist for the fund.

Methods

The heart of the investment process is the set of methods used to construct the portfolio. This section is where the value that is identified in the investment philosophy is realized. It describes how the initial inputs are refined, analyzed, or treated to come up with investment ideas. An analogy of the investment process is that of a recipe for cake. A cake usually includes: eggs, flour, water, sugar, butter, and seasonings. The recipe starts by discussing the ratios of the ingredients and how they are mixed together. The ratios are important in determining whether you get a cake or a loaf of bread from the same ingredients. The recipe goes on to describe the methods for mixing the ingredients together, such if the dry ingredients, are separated out and mixed before being added to the other ingredients. The mixing is also often important to how the cake turns out. If the batter is mixed too slow or too fast, for too short or too long a time, the batter can have the wrong consistency, affecting the texture of the cake when it is baked. Likewise, the methods used to analyze the inputs to the investment process can affect the quality of the output. Therefore, it is important to memorialize the methods so that they, like a good recipe, can be passed down to future generations.

The specific importance of certain inputs to an investment process is akin to the ratios of the ingredients in a recipe. In the top-down example above, the percentage weight on each economic indicator might be discussed in the methods section of the investment process. Like a recipe's description of how to mix the ingredients, a key element of the investment process is the discussion of methods that are employed. In doing so, it provides the individual or investment organization a clear understanding of the methods so that they can be applied consistently through time. This is especially important for student-managed investment funds that experience significant turnover of personnel. If not for a cogent explanation of the investment methods, the student-managed investment fund might have very different approaches and outcomes from year to year, even starting with the same inputs. In terms of cooking, this would be like trying to bake a cake and sometimes ending up with a cake, sometimes bread, and sometimes a cookie. While the importance for a student-managed investment fund is clear, it would be dangerous to believe that an individual or other investment organization would not realize as much value from an investment process. Indeed, an investment process is just as important to an individual or professional investment firm. The investment process serves the role of providing for a consistent approach over time for an investment firm as employees come and go. For the individual, the process provides a consistent framework and helps to assure that approach has been purposefully and thoughtfully undertaken. These methods define the investment approach or strategy. Thus, a significant change in the methods represents a change in strategy. If the investment process methods vary through time, there is no way to use the investment outcomes to refine the investment approach.

Some of the methods utilized in the investment process can be and usually are proprietary to the individual or organization. Because of this, the full details of the investment process, especially those at the heart of the process, might not be publicly disclosed. However, most steps and methods can be part of a publicly disclosed investment process by simply excluding specific elements that make them proprietary. Returning to the cooking analogy, these items might be considered a baker's secret ingredient, a specific ratio of ingredients, or a specific technique in mixing the ingredients. But, just as ingredients are disclosed on food products, it is possible to disclose quite a bit of an investment process's inputs and methods without risking harm to its proprietary value.

The result of the heart of the investment process is the resulting target portfolio weights. Returning to Exhibit 1.7, the second and third paragraphs discuss the methods of the TCU-EIF in determining the resulting sector and security weights. For some investment approaches, this final result represents the ultimate goal and outcome, while perhaps not technically the end of the investment process. In baking example, the last step might be to bake the cake at 375°F for 23 min. The implication is that the cake is finished at this point. In some sense, it is, but it probably is not in its final form that is to be presented to those who eat it. For the investment process, the target weights define the unadorned end product—perhaps even known as a model portfolio. These weights are ready to be implemented into an actual portfolio.

Implementation

The final step of the investment process is the implementation. This last step might be quite short and of have very little incremental value for some investment approaches or might be a key component of others. The end of the investment process should discuss how the target weights are converted into a real portfolio of security holdings. The implementation stage of the process might also include risk controls that are not integrated into earlier parts of the process. For baking, this might literally be the icing on the cake and describes how the cake is to be presented to those who actually eat it. This part of the investment process typically gives consideration to the direct and indirect costs of transactions and the trading methods used to affect such costs. For example, the final step might be to adapt the target weights to hold each stock in round lots of 100 shares each. An example of this is shown in the portfolio construction panel from Baylor's student-managed investment fund in Exhibit 1.8.

Finally, the end of the investment process discusses how the portfolio will be rebalanced or adjusted through time. In some cases, this part of the process might describe a specific rebalancing approach using the same target weights. In nearly all cases, rebalancing occurs as the result of a new iteration of the complete investment process. In this way, the end of the investment process directs us back to the beginning of the process, just as would occur in continuous loop.

Exhibit 1.8 Baylor University's student investment fund portfolio construction

HANKAMER SCHOOL OF BUSINESS

BaylorBusiness

RISK MANAGEMENT

- Portfolio Construction
  - Minimize risk by not making sector bets
  - Aware of industry exposure
  - Avoid short-term, speculative investments
- Continuous monitoring of portfolio positions
- Strong sell discipline - we sell when:
  - Fundamentals deteriorate
  - Story changes
  - Our expectation of future earnings growth changes
  - Valuation is no longer attractive
  - Better opportunities exist

BAYLOR
UNIVERSITY

(*Source: www.baylor.edu/business.*)

Examples of investment process

Exhibit 1.9 shows examples of the investment process from the same investment firms whose philosophies are shown in Exhibit 1.2. Recall that these firms' philosophies motivate the quantitative approaches that these firms pursue. For example, LSV's philosophy discussed the opportunities that are created by human biases. It would be surprising, therefore, if human judgment, subject to the same biases, were an integral part of the investment process. LSV's investment process outlines the key *quantitative* steps of the process that govern the selection of securities and their weights in the resulting portfolio. Similarly, DFA's investment process focuses on the steps to building diversified portfolios with targeted risk characteristics, as is consistent with the firm's investment philosophy.

Unlike quantitative firms' emphasis on quantitative methods and quantifiable variables, firms pursuing fundamental strategies must have processes that describe how economic conditions or company attributes are used to determine buy or sell decisions in the portfolio. Exhibit 1.10 shows the investment processes from the same firms whose philosophies are shown in Exhibit 1.3. As with quantitative firms, these firms' processes are consistent with their philosophies, which emphasize the particular opportunities these firms seek to realize.

Exhibit 1.9 Investment processes from investment firms with quantitative strategies

LSV Asset Management

Investment process

LSV uses quantitative techniques to select individual securities in what would be considered a bottom-up approach. The investment process is similar for each of our investment strategies but is segmented into different capitalization ranges or regions.

A proprietary investment model is used to rank a universe of stocks based on a variety of factors we believe to be predictive of future stock returns. The process is continuously refined and enhanced by our investment team although the basic philosophy has never changed—a combination of value and momentum factors. We then overlay strict risk controls that limit the over- or under-exposure of the portfolio to industry and sector concentrations. We also limit exposures in individual securities to ensure the portfolios are broadly diversified, further controlling risk.

The competitive strength of this strategy is that it avoids introducing the process to any judgmental biases and behavioral weaknesses that often influence investment decisions.

Portfolio turnover is approximately 30% for each strategy.

LSV has a strict policy against using soft dollars. Socially Responsible Investing (SRI) screens are available.

(*Source: www.lsvasset.com, June 2020.*)

Dimensional Fund Advisors

Investment process

Dimensional's core investment principle is that security prices contain reliable information about systematic differences in expected returns among securities. We use the information available in prices to increase expected returns and manage risks within each phase of our investment process—research, portfolio design, portfolio management, and trading.

Research

  Our research is focused on conducting rigorous empirical analysis to understand the drivers of expected returns. Through our relationships with leading financial economists and our internal research team, we continually work to improve our understanding of what drives differences in expected returns among securities and how we can extract information about those differences to improve outcomes for our investors.

Portfolio design

  Dimensional designs portfolios to pursue a balance between increasing expected returns, managing risks, and reducing costs. Our strategies are designed to target multiple drivers of expected return in an efficient, broadly diversified investment framework that considers daily information from markets.

Portfolio management

  Through a daily order generation process, our portfolio managers use current information to generate buy and sell candidates that each meaningfully improve expected returns for the portfolio, balancing tradeoffs between expected returns, risks, and costs. Once a security is held in our portfolios, portfolio managers seek to maximize the value of that holding while managing risk each day.

Trading

Dimensional's trading approach is designed to continually rebalance our portfolios through time to maintain focus on higher expected returns while retaining flexibility each day to limit the costs of executing trades. Our process allows our traders to participate in the available liquidity in the marketplace rather than demand immediacy and incur higher potential trading costs from crossing spreads and market impact.

(*Source: Dimensional Fund Advisors, June 2020.*)

Exhibit 1.10 Investment processes from investment firms with fundamental strategies

Fred Alger Management, Inc.
Investment process

NEW IDEAS	Analysts identify companies experiencing positive dynamic change in their sectors and regions to generate potential investment ideas
ANALYSIS	Analysts perform in-depth company analysis to develop a differentiated view supported by detailed financial models and stress-tested for a range of potential outcomes
DIALOGUE	Analysts present their ideas to portfolio managers and have their investment thesis and assumptions challenged
CONSTRUCTION	Portfolio managers construct portfolios of the highest conviction ides while managing risk
MONITORING	Risks are collaboratively managed by analysts, portfolio managers, the Director of Quantitative and Risk Management, and compliance

(*Source: www.alger.com, June 2020.*)

Hotchkis & Wiley
Process

H&W subscribes to a team-oriented, four-stage process. The goal is to employ a consistent, repeatable approach and create a diversified portfolio that exhibits attractive risk/return characteristics.

Stage	Purpose	Responsibility
1. Idea generation	Identify investment candidates and prepare initial review	Entire team
2. In-depth evaluation	Prepare detailed assessment of investment opportunity	Analysts
3. Recommendation	Review analysis, assess risk/return profile	Analysts/portfolio Managers
4. Portfolio construction	Buy, sell, and monitor	Portfolio managers

1. **Idea generation**

   We source investment ideas from screens of financial databases and from our investment team.

   Financial database screens

   We use dynamic and flexible quantitative screens designed to filter a large universe of securities to identify those that appear to have attractive risk/reward characteristics. These screens evaluate similar risk and valuation criteria but can be tailored for specific sectors/industries to emphasize the most relevant factors.

   Investment team

   We augment our quantitative screens with ideas sourced from our Analysts and Portfolio Managers. Based on their industry knowledge, contacts, and experience, our investment team identifies opportunities that automated screens can miss due to data issues or other limitations inherent with screens.

   Once investment ideas are generated, an initial review is conducted to highlight the key investment merits and risks, verify the validity of the characteristics that attracted us to the security in the first place, identify any obvious issues/warning signs that need to be addressed, and provide a rough estimate of the risk/return profile.

2. **In-depth evaluation**

   The in-depth evaluation stage of the process is by far the most vigorous and time-consuming. This stage involves detailed research at the industry, company, and security level.

   Industry

   Analysts conduct industry research concentrated on determining long-run margins and returns on capital. We seek to understand the factors that influence changes in supply and demand in order to determine normal industry profitability. Competitive analysis, akin to a Porter's Five Forces approach, is also evaluated to obtain a better understanding of industry risks. Our analysts accumulate a body of knowledge over years that enable them to respond to dynamic markets quickly.

   Company

   Using the industry research as a backdrop, the Analyst conducts detailed fundamental research at the company level. We focus on the company's long-run normal earnings power, which is the sustainable cash earnings of a company under equilibrium economic and competitive market conditions. Company analysis focuses on full cycle profitability, capital intensity, free cash flow, and financial leverage. Analysts meet with company management to better understand the company's business model by its various divisions, capital allocation policy, return potential of current capital programs, shareholder orientation, and overall competence.

   Next, we do a risk assessment, which entails a variety of both financial and non-financial factors. We assess the company's ability to survive temporary, short-term distress without impairing the long-term value of its franchise. This includes a review of its financial leverage, historical cash flow volatility, available liquidity, access to capital, exposure to extreme events, and unusual profit concentrations. To augment the risk evaluation process we have developed a red flags analysis, which is a list of questions that helps identify subtle but potentially meaningful risks. The ultimate goal is to identify attractively valued companies with acceptable risk profiles.

Security

To quantify return potential, we employ an internally developed, three-stage dividend discount model ("DDM"), using market-derived discount rates. The first stage uses explicit earnings projections for years one through five, which are derived from the Analyst's financial model.

We assume that a company achieves normal earnings in year five. The second stage of the DDM reverts the company's returns to market averages over the next 15 years. The third stage determines the terminal value of the stock. We determine the present value (price target) by discounting these values back at the cost of equity. Next the analyst provides a risk assessment highlighting critical issues that could affect the company and its stock price. Finally, the analyst summarizes the recommendation with an investment thesis and recommended weight.

3. **Recommendation**
   Each step of the in-depth evaluation is subject to peer review by the Portfolio Managers. In addition to reviewing financial models and ensuring integrity/consistency, the reviewers play a devil's advocate role to challenge the thesis and modeling assumptions. The primary objective is to solidify our belief in valuation and security risk. Once ideas are thoroughly vetted, the Analyst and Portfolio Managers jointly decide on a target weight.

4. **Portfolio construction**
   We employ a bottom-up, risk-controlled portfolio construction process with the primary goal of generating attractive risk-adjusted returns. Portfolio Managers assess recommendations within the context of the overall portfolio. They consider the relative attractiveness of opportunities and assess the complementary nature of new ideas with the existing portfolio. Portfolio Managers have responsibility for creating and maintaining a target portfolio for the investment strategy, generating trades, and assuring compliance with client guidelines— buy, sell, and monitor.

(*Source: www.hwcm.com, May 2020.*)

The Hotchkis & Wiley process is particularly thorough in discussing all aspects of the investment process, including a description of the personnel in whom certain responsibilities reside. Note how Alger's investment process is articulated with a chart, emphasizing the continuous nature of the process.

Internal and external uses of the investment philosophy and process

The discussions of investment philosophy and process focus primarily on the internal value to an individual or organization in having a documented philosophy and process. For student-managed investment funds and investment firms, the internal benefits help promote the consistent application of an investment approach in an environment of personnel turnover. Most student-managed investment funds experience nearly 100% turnover every semester or at least every academic year. While the turnover in investment firms is lower than this, turnover does occur in any organization. The existence of the philosophy and process helps to assure a firm's clients that the strategy that is followed when the investment firm is hired is likely to be the same strategy that is followed in the future, regardless of turnover in firm personnel. Likewise, if a student-managed investment fund manages a portion of its university's endowment fund, the existence of the investment philosophy and process provides the endowment fund's board of trustees with some confidence that students will employ the same approach 5 years from now, even though none of those students will be involved in the fund.

The external benefits of a clearly articulated investment philosophy and process are critically important in establishing a mutual understanding between an investment organization and its client. The disclosure of the investment philosophy to the organization's clients and prospective clients allows the clients to judge whether there is a shared outlook of the market and available opportunities. Moreover, it allows the client to determine its own confidence in the individual's or investment organization's capabilities. Very simply, if there is a mismatch between the prospective client's and the investment firm's philosophies, then the client should not employ the investment firm to manage investments on its behalf. Similarly, confidence in the investment organization's stated capabilities are required for a client to retain the services of the investment organization. (Additional discussion of this issue is found in "The Role of Investment Philosophy in Evaluating Investment Managers: A Consultant's Perspective on Distinguishing Alpha from Noise," by John Minahan, formerly of New England Pension Consultants (NEPC), available in Appendix B online).

The investment process helps in a different but no less important way to help manage the relationship between a client and an investment organization. The documented investment process provides the client with an understanding of the methods used in constructing the client's portfolio as well as the expected characteristics and range of outcomes from the resulting portfolio. The ultimate outcome that is the goal in hiring a portfolio manager is its performance (i.e., return on investment). However, return on investment over a given time period is a noisy indicator of whether an investment manager has diligently employed its own investment process. Indeed, the signal-to-noise ratio of most investment processes is very low. Therefore, investment returns should not be the only evidence that a client considers when evaluating whether a manager has done what it was hired to do. Rather, the client should consider whether the manager continues to employ the methods as set out in the investment process and whether those methods have resulted in the expected characteristics and range outcomes. Likewise, the manager must provide transparent communication to the client that establishes whether the methods are being followed and whether characteristics and the range of outcomes are consistent with the investment process. Thus, the investment process provides an important part of the transparency that is critical for the effective monitoring of investment managers.

To help understand the importance of the role of the investment process in the manager-client relationship, consider the following example of two investment managers who were hired by an endowment fund. Prior to being hired by the endowment fund, both managers had recorded very good performance compared to the S&P 500 index. Manager A provides very little detail in its investment process, and just discloses that it has a team of analysts who pick the stocks that they consider to be the best. Manager B, on the other hand, has a detailed, step-by-step description of its investment process that makes clear that it seeks to hold firms with high dividend yields, low P/E ratios, and solid growth prospects, as forecasted by a team of analysts. The process provides further details of how the analysts are trained in a specific type of fundamental analysis that was developed by the firm's founder. The founder is known to have long ago retired, but her approach remains a hallmark of the firm. The final fact is that each firm has lost about one quarter of its investment personnel, including those that make up their analyst teams.

A few years after hiring these two firms, the endowment fund's board of trustees feels pressure to make a decision on whether to retain or fire these firms, since each firm's investment returns have been below the benchmark return and far less than expected. Can the endowment justify retaining either firm? If so, on what basis? Both managers are likely to correctly point out that no investment process can yield outperformance every year, or even every 3-year period. However, the board of trustees must have confidence in each manager's ability in order to make a decision to retain the firm. In the case of Manager A, the board of trustees has little to go on except the faith and hope that the "good" analysts who were responsible for the good performance long ago have not left the firm—or at least that they have been replaced by equally good analysts. In other words, the board must hope that the bad performance is not because the firm no longer has the talent that it once had. However, the board has little information to verify that the same investment process that had been followed before (during a period of good performance) is still being followed now (during this period of bad performance). In other words, it must try to distinguish if the underperformance is just noise. In contrast, Manager B can point to specific elements of its investment process that have led to specific characteristics of the portfolio. Manager B can point to how clear its investment process is in providing for the training of any new analysts to replace the analysts it lost. This training would still emphasize the same investment principles and approach that the firm has used throughout its history. Finally, Manager B can establish whether the return outcomes are consistent with its approach in the current market environment and the expected range of outcomes from such an approach. That is, there may be evidence to support the claim that the underperformance really is just a result of "noise." In summary, it is likely that the board of trustees has more reason to remain confident in the capability of Manager B to deliver good performance in the future, assuming that the board had this confidence to begin with. Therefore, the board is less likely to fire Manager B than it is to fire Manager A.

This example highlights the importance of an investment process in the decision to retain or fire an investment manager. However, it is easy to see that the investment process is equally important in hiring an investment manager. Indeed, the board of trustees in the example possibly should not have hired Manager A in the first place, because Manager A either lacks a proper investment philosophy and process or cannot articulate the investment philosophy and process in a way that gives a prospective client a clear understanding of how it invests.

For a student-managed investment fund, this example serves as a cautionary tale. No one seems to pay attention to a fund or its investment process when returns are good (even though they should!). When returns are "bad" (negative or below that of a benchmark), interested parties such as boards of trustees, alumni, and administrators, pay very close attention—and attention during times of underperformance is usually stressful and unpleasant. Consistent adherence to, implementation of, and good communication of a specific investment philosophy and process are crucial in maintaining a positive ongoing experience and represent best practices. In short, the student-managed investment fund should strive to meet the same standards as an institutional investment firm.

Finally, while this example also takes the perspective of the client, it could have easily taken the perspective of the investment firm. If the investment firm has a clearly thought-out investment philosophy and process, such as Manager B, then it is more likely to maintain its approach, even during periods in which the approach is not yielding the desired results. Investing at a professional level requires a consistent and disciplined application of a process that is built on the foundation of a sound investment philosophy.

Summary of key points

- Diligent investing is not *ad hoc*.
- The investment philosophy describes the beliefs about the market environment, the opportunities that the firm seeks to exploit in their investment process, and the capabilities of the individual or organization that help to realize those opportunities.
- The investment philosophy facilitates a shared understanding of purpose, opportunity, and direction.
- The investment process describes the key inputs into investment decisions, the methods employed to refine those inputs to create portfolio weights, and the implementation procedures.
- The investment process helps to assure that a plan is in place to provide for a continuous and consistent investment approach through time, even in the presence of personnel turnover.

Exercises

1. Navigate the following links to investment philosophy and investment process. These are some examples of real investment firms' philosophy and process statements. Not all of them are very good in that they do not necessarily fit the requirements of stating

a philosophy or clearly articulating the process. However, they are informative as to the approach of well-established investment managers.

   a. Alger: www.alger.com

   b. Dimensional Fund Advisors: www.dimensional.com

   c. INTECH: www.intechinvestments.com

   d. Invesco: www.invesco.com

   e. Janus: www.en-us.janushenderson.com

   f. LSV: www.lsvasset.com

   g. Perkins: www.perkinsinvestmentmanagement.com/perkins

   h. Waddell & Reed: www.waddell.com.

2. Develop separate investment philosophy statements for each of the following starting points:

   a. A market that is semi-strong-form efficient

   b. A market that is weak-form efficient

   c. A market that is not efficient

   d. A market in which there is overreaction

   e. A market in which there is underreaction

3. Develop separate investment processes for of the following strategies:

   a. A U.S. small cap index fund

   b. A Eurozone large cap index fund

   c. A global all cap index fund

   d. An active U.S. mid cap value fund

   e. An active growth fund

4. Obtain a list of active managers employed by your university's endowment fund. Critique the investment philosophy statements of several managers. In cases in which you find the statements deficient, try to glean the information from other information about the manager and rewrite a statement to meet the standards of a good investment philosophy.

5. Obtain a list of active managers employed by your university's endowment fund. Critique the investment process statements of several managers. In doing so, identify the parts of the process that you believe are proprietary.

6. Critique your own university's student-managed investment fund investment philosophy and process.

Appendix A: Common investment strategy classifications

Most investment strategies fit into commonly used classifications. While these classifications are useful for a quick, broad understanding of an investment approach, they are only "headlines" that help provide a hint at the details of the story that are revealed in the investment process.

The most basic level of classifications is that of its asset class, such as *equity*, *fixed income*, or *real assets* (such as real estate). Further refinement of the asset class might also be appropriate for some funds. Most of these refinements are along the lines of the specific characteristics of the assets. In the equity asset class, securities are typically categorized by size and style. The size refers to the market capitalization of the target securities. A *small cap* strategy would typically target the smaller stocks in the market, such as those found in the Russell 2000 Index. Some strategies that target the smallest stocks in the market are often referred to as *micro cap* strategies. Likewise, *large cap* strategies would hold the largest stocks in a specific market, while *mid cap* strategies would hold stocks in the middle capitalization range. We have purposefully not defined the capitalization ranges using dollar values because the dollar cutoffs of these ranges are ever-changing. More specifically, the ranges are all relative to the current market of securities. The style of a stock typically refers to whether the stock is considered a *growth* stock or a *value* stock. Unfortunately, these two styles lack precise definitions, but are commonly understood to break down as follows. Value stocks provide relatively high dividends and low price-to-earnings ratios and/or price-to-book ratios, among other measures. Growth stocks are those that do not have these features, but instead whose prices are relatively high compared to their earnings or book values presumably due to their growth prospects. As with size, the style classifications are relative to the current universe of stocks, not absolute.

In the fixed income class, refinements are typically made along the lines of default risk, issuer, and/or duration or term. For example, bond funds might fall into the categories of (federal) *government* or *government agency*, *municipal*, *corporate*, and/or *high yield corporate*. These fund classifications might also have a term or duration modifier, such as *short-term* corporate debt or *long-term* government debt. In short, many classifications reveal the category off securities held.

Geographic focus provides additional classification for an investment strategy. Unless otherwise noted, most strategies are assumed to be *domestic* in scope (e.g., *U.S.* for a U.S.-based investment organization). However, it is best to be specific in referring to the geographical scope of a strategy. For example, a fixed income portfolio that seeks to purchase debt of countries worldwide would be classified as *global* fixed income fund. Likewise, the geographic scope should be classified as narrowly as appropriate. It is common to see U.S. state-classified municipal bond funds, such as a New York municipal bond fund.

Finally, one of the most important classifications of a strategy is the breakdown between *active* or *passive*. A passive investment strategy seeks to have exposure to a specific asset class or perhaps even a narrower segment of the market. However, a passive approach only seeks to track but not outperform that segment of the market as a whole. Passive strategies are typically broadly diversified within the segment and individual security weights are typically based on market capitalization. For example, an S&P 500 Index fund is a passive strategy that tracks the S&P 500, capitalization-weighted index. An *active* strategy seeks to outperform passive benchmarks and accordingly hold securities in weights that are different from those found in the strategy's benchmark. The expected source of the outperformance from an active strategy should be discussed in the strategy's investment philosophy and the methods for choosing the active weights should be covered in the investment process. Actives strategies also are typically classified by their broad investment approach. Two commonly used broad classifications are *fundamental* or *quantitative*. Methods that include research by analysts who make growth forecasts or valuation decisions based on their own judgment and interpretation of the facts are a common part of a fundamental approach. When a specific computer model is employed to make those forecasts without human judgments (other than those that created the model or computer program!), the approach is usually considered quantitative. Quantitative models also make heavy use of factor-based models. Of course, some approaches can employ a mix of these two approaches and would not be classified as either purely quantitative or fundamental.

Appendix B

(Provided online) "The Role of Investment Philosophy in Evaluating Investment Managers: A Consultant's Perspective on Distinguishing Alpha from Noise", published in *The Journal of Investing*, Summer 2006, Vol. 15, No. 2, pp. 6–11. Reprinted with permission.

CHAPTER 2

Stock selection

The resulting product of a student-managed investment fund—indeed, of any investment manager—is a portfolio. A portfolio is a collection of securities, held at specific proportions or weights. As such, portfolio management can be considered as a combination of two activities: security selection and portfolio construction. This chapter focuses on the selection of the securities within the portfolio. The following chapter focuses on how those securities are combined to construct the portfolio. In most student-managed portfolios, the emphasis, the importance, and the majority of the time spent are on security selection. The amount of time spent on security selection versus portfolio construction should depend on the investment strategy as defined by the investment philosophy and investment process. In other words, the approach to security selection and portfolio construction should be governed by the investment philosophy and process. In some investment processes, security selection and portfolio construction might be mutually exclusive activities, while in others, there may be no discernible separation of the two. These chapters will treat security selection and portfolio construction separately, but attempt to point out areas in which dependencies and overlap exist between the two activities.

Security selection is made up of two separate activities: security analysis and quantitative modeling or screening. A good security selection process will feature both. For the majority of investment firms, the quantitative analysis comes at the beginning of the process. Below are the typical steps in building an equity portfolio.

1. Eligible Universe:
   a. Determine the appropriate benchmark.
   b. Pick a universe of stocks based on that benchmark.
2. Sector or Factor Allocation and Security Selection:
   a. Decide how to deal with macroeconomic or sector weightings.
   b. If actively weighting sectors, choose factors to research.
   c. Determine how to rank stocks within the portfolio or sector.
   d. Quantitative: Build a quantitative model:
   e. Determine factors that cause stocks to outperform.
   f. Backtest those factors.
   g. Use those factors to screen or rank stocks.
   h. Qualitative: Write a research report:

Student-Managed Investment Funds. https://doi.org/10.1016/B978-0-12-817866-9.00002-9

   i.   Determine which factors cause stocks to outperform.
   j.   Do research into those areas/factors and determine criteria to compare them.
3.   Portfolio Construction:
   a.   Build the portfolio based on understanding the risks involved.
   b.   Establish risk controls.
   c.   Use an optimizer or a set of portfolio construction rules and guidelines.

Exhibit 2.1 shows a graphical representation of the steps of this type of process from the Tulane student-managed portfolio.

Like most solutions to complex problems, the above steps break a big problem into smaller pieces. It starts by narrowing down the scope of research and analysis from all possible securities to a specific universe of securities, usually based on the benchmark against which the portfolio is compared. It is important to note that the absence of a benchmark and some very broad benchmarks result in a very large eligible universe. The absence of a benchmark also creates issues for the fund in determining acceptable performance, as discussed in Chapter 5. Quantitative processes are especially adept at dealing with large numbers of securities, while fundamental processes that rely on a limited number of human analysts to conduct research must whittle the number of securities down to a manageable number. As such, fundamental approaches typically rely on at least some quantitative process to screen stocks in order to find a smaller set of candidates for further in-depth research in the security selection steps. In some processes, security selection might begin by carving the universe into separate pieces by sector or economic factor exposure, while other processes might consider all stocks together, regardless of sector or economic factor exposure. This chapter begins by looking at the first step

Exhibit 2.1 Tulane student-managed investment fund security selection process

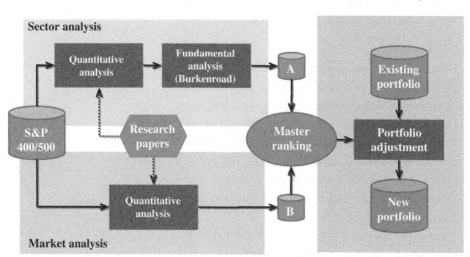

of screening and modeling and then focuses on the analysis of securities in the second step, with the result being a long (hold or buy) or short (do not hold, sell, or short sell) decision. The final step of portfolio construction is discussed in detail in the following chapter.

Quantitative analysis

The goal of quantitative analysis in a student-managed portfolio setting is to narrow down the universe of stocks for further in-depth research. Quantitative analysis is the activity of researching securities using characteristics, factors, or variables using quantitative models. As such, quantitative analysis relies on aspects of a security that are quantified or quantifiable, such as financial statement information, market price and trading activity, and historical stock return and risk characteristics. Some institutional investment processes are strictly quantitative. For example, of the investment philosophy and process examples in Chapter 1, LSV represents an investment manager that uses quantitative analysis exclusively. Recall that LSV's investment philosophy indicates that it believes opportunities exist because of traders' judgment biases. Its quantitative investment process specifically addresses these biases in human judgment by, among other things, not allowing human judgments to enter into its process.

Traditional fundamental processes often have quantitative components. In some cases, these quantitative components are blended with traditional fundamental analysis so that the investment process is a fully integrated mixture of the two approaches. In other investment processes, the role of quantitative analysis is to screen securities to be used in a primarily fundamental approach. Stock screens typically serve the purpose to reduce a set of stocks from a large number to a smaller number, resulting in a subset of securities for further fundamental analysis. In this way, quantitative analysis can help improve the efficiency of an investment process by focusing human research and analysis on securities with the most potential for added value within the portfolio. Exhibit 2.2 shows examples of security screening processes from two student investment funds. The first example in Panel A shows a screen used by a student in Southern Methodist University's SMIF to identify stocks within the Consumer Staples sector. The screen narrows the sector's 42 stocks to five that the student would then use in further research and analysis. Panel B shows parameters used in the screening process in the University of Houston's student-managed investment fund. Appendix A discusses the use of Z-scores and ranking models, which are often used in quantitative analysis to help select stocks to include in a portfolio.

Security analysis

Security analysis, also referred to as fundamental analysis, is the key element resulting in security selection for many active investment strategies. Typically, its ultimate purpose is to identify mispriced securities by comparing the intrinsic value of the stock to its market price.

Exhibit 2.2 Examples of stock screens

Panel A: Southern Methodist University Student's Screening Process

1. To begin the screening process, I first compiled Market Cap, Beta, industry, LT and ST growth rates, PE, dividend yield, and analyst recommendations on all S&P 500 Consumer Staples firms. Companies Remaining: 42
2. From Consumer Staples sector averages, I eliminated companies with a PE above the sector average of 14.66. Companies Remaining: 22
3. Then I eliminated companies with dividend yields below the sector average of 2.81. Companies Remaining: 11
4. Finally, I eliminated companies with an analyst recommendation absolute minimum below "4." Companies Remaining: 5

Panel B: University of Houston Screening Parameters

Screening parameters include:
- Market capitalization
- Sector
- Risk metrics
- Discounted Cash Flow model

As such, security analysis is only relevant in the context of an investment philosophy that articulates a belief that securities are not fairly priced at all times. In other words, security analysis is only relevant within the context of a strategy that seeks to exploit an inefficient market. As a practical matter, the belief that securities can be mispriced is only a necessary condition that motivates the use of security analysis. There must also be a mechanism by which mispricings lead to profits. A sufficient condition that provides for the realization of profits from security analysis is when market prices adjust toward intrinsic values (i.e., the market moves toward efficiency). Therefore, security analysis is often the central value-generating activity of a fundamental active strategy.

Security analysis is part science and part art. Many finance courses spend a substantial amount of time on the science aspect that includes ratio analysis, time value of money calculations, and estimation of the cost of capital and its components. While this chapter reviews some of the relevant science, we devote a substantial amount of time to discussing the role of the art in security analysis, as the art of security analysis is often the distinguishing factor between good and bad security selection. We note, however, that art by its nature is not subject to formulaic approaches or clearly identifiable steps that, when followed, will always lead to masterpieces. Rather, the art in security analysis resides in the creative choices, assumptions, or estimates that must be made to apply the science. The art arises because the science requires quantities from the future, such as future earnings, as inputs. As such, the art involves making calculated estimates about unknown quantities and often requires the analyst to quantify something that represents a subjective judgment.

Security analysis is a necessarily broad term and admits many specific methods. As such, we can consider security analysis to be a toolbox that holds many different tools. We cover below various tools or approaches and note how each is typically used. As with other chapters, we provide the basic theoretical motivation for the tools, but emphasize the practical application of these tools within the context of a student-managed investment fund. We provide an extended example from Texas Christian University's Educational Investment Fund at the end of the chapter to further illustrate the application of many of the tools discussed herein. In addition, Appendix B of this chapter contains excerpts from *Analysts, Lies and Statistics* that discuss the role analysts play and information about some of the key financial information on which analysts make estimates. Appendix B is intended to provide valuable context to student-managed investment fund analysts who struggle with the same issues as Wall Street analysts.

Company analysis

Before proceeding to the quantitative aspects of security analysis, it is important to recognize that a substantial part of security analysis is of a more qualitative nature, which we refer to as company analysis. Company analysis provides the context for the financial information and analysis that makes up the bulk of this chapter. Without this context, it is impossible to have a meaningful understanding of the business that generates the financial information. Revenues, costs, and capital expenditures, which will play key roles in the following valuation discussion, differ in character from industry to industry and business to business. It is the security analyst's job to know not only the numbers but also the story behind the numbers. In short, the analyst must know the company.

Company analysis involves researching any and all aspects of a company that affect its success, from its products and services to its leadership team. A key part of this research focuses on identifying sources of sustainable competitive advantages or value. That is, the company analysis aims to determine the key aspects of the firm's business that are likely to generate value.

The approach to analyzing the company depends on the investment philosophy and process. For example, in a top-down process that begins by identifying themes in the overall economy that represent investment opportunities, the role of company analysis is to first identify companies that are likely candidates to contribute to those economic themes. If there is a view that the market for new houses is about to boom, the analyst might make a list of all firms that are directly affected by such a boom and then a list of all firms that are indirectly but significantly affected by such a boom. In a bottom-up investment process, the analysts might seek an understanding of each company and its opportunities or risks.

Company analysis should also follow a process in terms of systematically developing an understanding of a firm's business. One approach might be to research a company from the standpoint of its financial statements. This approach is not necessarily concerned with specific numbers on the financial statements, but is concerned with the sources of those numbers. From the income statement, the analyst might start with the top line to determine the sources of the firm's revenues, answering questions such as, "Who are the firm's customers?," "What are the firm's major business/product segments?," "Where (in the world or in the country) are sales made?," "When (both in time and in economic conditions) are sales made?" In short, this aspect of company analysis concerns itself with the firm's marketing, sales, and distribution strategy. This might involve research on the firm's target market or current customer base. As will be seen later in this chapter, of particular concern here will be the opportunity for revenue growth. Therefore, the analyst would want to understand such opportunities and how the company is positioned to realize them. This often involves an analysis of the firm's position relative to competitors and an understanding of those competitors' businesses.

Moving down the income statement, the analyst would ask similar questions about the firm's costs and expenses throughout the production chain, including those about suppliers, opportunities to achieve cost efficiencies, or risks of increasing costs. Finally, the analyst might turn to the balance sheet and determine the strategy the firm uses to manage its assets and liabilities. Of particular importance is the firm's investment in assets and technology to help it increase its profits. Outside of the financial statements, analysts typically try to understand who the executives of the firm are and what strategy they have for the future of the firm. After all, the assets of the firm belong to the shareholders and the executive team is entrusted with managing those assets. Potential shareholders should understand who they are "hiring" to manage their assets when they purchase stock.

In some sense, company analysis is the qualitative side of security analysis. As such, it is the least technical aspect of security analysis. Student-managed investment funds can utilize student analysts who have had less exposure to accounting and finance courses to undertake basic company research and analysis and contribute such an understanding of the firm to a team in which others focus on the more technical or quantitative aspects.

A good company versus a good investment

A good company is not the same thing as a good investment. Some people think that successful investing or stock picking is all about finding good companies. However, this seemingly commonsense approach ignores a simple fact: To earn a profit, an investor must not overpay for a stock. In other words, *price* and *value* are not necessarily the same things. The discussion that follows focuses on determining the value of a company and its stock.

There may be times when market participants "fall in love" with a company, its products, or its characteristics and bid its stock price up. While the market might be "right" that the company, its products, or its characteristics are very good, those who buy into the stock at a price above its true or intrinsic value are less likely to realize the expected benefits or profits from such a purchase. Conversely, there may be companies that fall out of favor in the market—a company whose stock price is beat down beyond what is justified. For example, this might happen to companies that suffer a scandal, a product liability claim, or simply bad press. Even if such a company might not be considered a "good company" by some measure, its market price might represent such a discount to its intrinsic value that it is a good stock.

We raise the point about a good company versus a good investment (or good stock) because there appear to be some who do not understand or appreciate this truth. Successful business-people understand it. Good investments are those that are worth more than the price paid for them. Whether or not a stock is a good investment depends on whether the value of the stock is greater than its current price within the context of the investment philosophy and process. The following discussion reviews the underlying financial theory regarding the intrinsic value of a firm and provides tips for developing practical valuation models.

In focusing on the intrinsic value of the future cash flows of the stock or the firm as criteria for security selection, the discussion implicitly assumes that a stock's price and its intrinsic value can be different. That is, we implicitly assume that the market might not be efficient in that the price may not reflect the information used in the analysis. This assumption may not be consistent with every investment managers' investment philosophy. However, this implicit assumption is common among active managers who engage in security selection.

Valuation

Our discussion of valuation reviews the theory and application of several important valuation models. The common element among all valuation models is that they begin with the same first principle: The value of any asset is the present value of its future cash flows. That is, the scientific aspect of determining the intrinsic value of a stock is as simple as discounting the future cash flows from the stock. If its future cash flows and the appropriate discount rate are known, then the value of the stock is determined by the application of a time value of money principles. We start with this simple abstraction even though it relies on the naive notion that future cash flows are known.

We first review the Dividend Discount Model, which uses dividends paid to the company's shareholders as the key cash flow paid by a stock. Beyond its usefulness in its own right, the Dividend Discount Model offers an important conceptual framework upon which we will base the other models. We next discuss the DCF approach using the firm's cash flows that are available to equity-holders. This model considers the cash flows to the entire firm and, therefore, models the value of the entire firm. The company's stock represents the residual value available to equity shareholders after all senior claims, such as those of bondholders, are paid. Finally, we discuss the use of earnings or earnings per share as a measure of cash flow. While not technically a cash flow, the use of earnings in firm valuations has its virtues, primarily from a practical standpoint. We conclude this chapter with a discussion of commonly cited valuation metrics. Specifically, we emphasize the link between these metrics and the valuation models.

Dividend Discount Model

If an investor buys a stock and holds it indefinitely, the investors derives value from the stock's stream of dividends. The Dividend Discount Model (DDM), also known as the Gordon Growth Model, formalizes the valuation of a stock as follows.

Suppose a stock will pay dividend of D_1 a year from now. Subsequent dividends will grow at a rate of g_D and investors demand a required return of k_E. Today's price of the stock, V_0^{DDM}, is equal to the present value of this constant growth in perpetuity, given as

$$V_0^{DDM} = \frac{D_1}{k_E - g_D} \tag{2.1}$$

The assumptions underlying this valuation model seem to be quite restrictive. For starters, the model implicitly assumes that a stock currently pays dividends. Therefore, its use seems limited to only those stocks that currently pay dividends. Furthermore, the explicit assumption that dividends will grow at a constant rate in perpetuity seems almost certain to be violated for nearly every stock. Fortunately, the model's usefulness is not as restrictive as it might seem.

A more general form of the Dividend Discount Model allows for any pattern of dividends throughout time. In this case, the value of a stock today is just the infinite sum of all future dividends, as given by:

$$V_0^{DDM} = \sum_{t=1}^{\infty} \frac{D_t}{(1+k_E)^1} \tag{2.2}$$

or

$$V_0^{DDM} = \frac{D_1}{(1+k_E)} + \frac{D_2}{(1+k_E)^2} + \frac{D_3}{(1+k_E)^3} + \cdots + \frac{D_t}{(1+k_E)^t} + \frac{D_{t+1}}{(1+k_E)^{t+1}} + \cdots \tag{2.3}$$

Note that, by specifying, D_1, D_2, D_3, etc., we are implicitly assuming these dividends must be individually forecast. Eqs. (2.1–2.3) are equally "correct" from a theoretical perspective. However, applying this theory of valuation to practice requires either an assumption of constant growth rate for all future dividends (for Eq. 2.1), or a year-by-year forecast of all future dividends (for Eq. 2.2 or 2.3). Good security analysis balances the need for tractability and simplicity with the desire to capture critical details and complexities. Fortunately, the DDM's flexibility allows the analyst to balance such interests.

Before proceeding, we consider that the constant growth formula from Eq. (2.1) is relevant at any point in time after which dividends grow at a constant rate. In other words, if dividends grow at a constant rate g_D starting at time t, then the price at time t can be calculated using the constant growth of a perpetuity formula, given by:

$$V_t^{DDM} = \frac{D_{t+1}}{k_E - g_D} = \frac{D_t(1 + g_D)}{k_E - g_D} \tag{2.4}$$

Note that D_{t+1} appears in both Eqs. (2.3) and (2.4). Indeed, if all dividends grow at a constant rate subsequent to time t, we can rewrite Eq. (2.3) as:

$$V_0^{DDM} = \frac{D_1}{(1 + k_E)} + \frac{D_2}{(1 + k_E)^2} + \cdots + \frac{D_{t-1}}{(1 + k_E)^{t-1}} + \frac{D_t + V_t^{DDM}}{(1 + k_E)^t} \tag{2.5}$$

In this way, we now need only make forecasts of individual dividends between now and time t and then assume a constant growth rate of dividends beyond time t. Indeed, this version of the DDM, often referred to as the multistage Dividend Discount Model, allows for any pattern of dividends over the short term (even admitting the case of no dividends, where $D_1 = D_2 = 0$) and allows a simplifying assumption to be made about the level and growth rate of longer term dividends. That is, dividends, $D_1, D_2, D_3, \ldots$ in the near-term future periods, such as the next several years, can be individually forecast. Beyond those first few years, dividends can be assumed to grow at a constant rate, often referred to as the terminal growth rate. Those dividends get summarized into a single value or price according to Eq. (2.3), which we refer to as the terminal value. Together, the dividends and terminal value get discounted to the present according to Eq. (2.4).

Finally, we note that we have used the precise and seemingly restrictive language of referring to g as the constant growth rate of dividends. This need not be the only interpretation of g within this dividend discount model of valuation. In practice, we can consider g as the future *average* growth rate of dividends and still be precisely accurate and consistent with the theory.

In summary, the security analyst can value stocks using the DDM by applying the following steps:

Steps to using the multistage Dividend Discount Model

1. Forecast each year's dividend over the near term (e.g., the next 5 years).
2. Estimate an average terminal growth rate of dividends beyond the near future (e.g., beyond the next 5 years).
3. Estimate the appropriate discount rate for the stock.

4. Discount the dividends in step 2 to find the terminal value of the stock at the beginning of the terminal growth stage.
5. Discount the terminal value and the dividends during the abnormal growth stage to find the intrinsic value of the stock.

These steps are easily implemented or modeled using an Excel spreadsheet, as shown in the example in Exhibit 2.3. The exhibit distinguishes between cells that are inputs and those

Exhibit 2.3 Example of Dividend Discount Model in Excel

Assumptions, estimates, and forecasts
1. Stock will pay a dividend of $0.60 next year.
2. The dividends per share over the following 4 years will be: $0.80 in 2 years; $0.96 in 3 years; $1.08 in 4 years; and $1.16 in 5 years.
3. The terminal growth rate will be 4% per year, starting after 5 years.
4. The discount rate will be calculated using the Capital Asset Pricing Model.
5. The risk-free rate is 3.5% per year.
6. The market risk premium is 5.50% per year.
7. The stock's beta, calculated from the last 5 years of monthly returns, is 0.92.

	A	B	C	D
1	Dividend Discount Model			
2	Risk Free Rate	3.50%		
3	Market Risk Premium	5.50%		
4	Equity Beta	0.92		
5	Required Return on Equity	8.56%		=B2+B4*B3
6				
7	Terminal Growth Rate	4.00%		
8				
9	Year	Dividend per Share ($)	Terminal Value ($)	
10	1	0.60		
11	2	0.80		
12	3	0.96		
13	4	1.08		
14	5	1.16	26.46	=B14*(1+B7)/(B5-B7)
15				
16	Year	Present Value ($)		
17	1	0.55		=(B10+C10)/(1+$B$5)^A17
18	2	0.68		=(B11+C11)/(1+$B$5)^A18
19	3	0.75		=(B12+C12)/(1+$B$5)^A19
20	4	0.78		=(B13+C13)/(1+$B$5)^A20
21	5	18.32		=(B14+C14)/(1+$B$5)^A21
22				
23	Intrinsic Value per Share ($)	21.07		=SUM(B17:B21)
24				
25	Inputs	Calculated		
26				

that are calculated. It is common practice to estimate the required return to equity (i.e., the firm's cost of equity capital) using a model of the fair expected return, such as the Capital Asset Pricing Model (CAPM). Of course, the CAPM requires inputs of the risk-free rate, the market risk premium, and the stock's beta. The inputs should match the horizon of the model. Because the DDM values an infinite stream of future dividends, the risk-free rate and market risk premium are based on a long-term historical average of these values. There are numerous methods for estimating the beta of the firm's equity. If using historical data for the estimate, the analyst must decide on the horizon (e.g., 3, 5, 10, etc. years) for the data, frequency of the data (e.g., daily, weekly, monthly, etc.), and the market proxy (e.g., S&P 500, all U.S. stocks, all world) stocks. We note that a student-managed investment fund, and indeed any investment organization, should agree on these issues, as the required return model and its parameters should be the consistent across the analysis of every firm, since these are not firm-specific measures. That is, the risk-free rate and market risk premium assumption for one stock should be the same as those of every other stock, regardless of the analyst using the model. Otherwise, the results of the analysis are not comparable or compatible across analysts.

A correctly programmed spreadsheet model will perform these calculations flawlessly. However, the old adage applies: Garbage in, garbage out. In other words, the model's output is only as good as its inputs or assumptions. The inputs of the model shown in the exhibit must be estimated or forecasted by the analyst. Herein is the "part science, part art" aspect of security analysis. The science of the model requires forecasts of variables that are inherently unknown with any certainty. Therefore, analysts must develop their skills in the art of making forecasts and estimates of these inputs.

The DDM is deceptively simple when it comes to making estimates or forecasts of its inputs. Indeed, for a stock that currently pays a dividend, it appears that the dividend is effectively known with certainty. While it may be the case that a company's current dividend is known, a key issue is whether this known dividend currently reflects a large portion of the source of value from holding the stock. This issue is best understood by considering the source of a firm's dividends. In general, the source of a company's dividends is the company's earnings or profits. When the firm earns a profit, it has two choices as to what to do with those earnings: (1) it can pay the earnings out to shareholders as a return on the shareholders' capital; or (2) it can retain those earnings, effectively reinvesting them in the company. For a stock to be valuable, capital must eventually be returned to shareholders. Indeed, the stock of a company that never returns cash to its shareholders is worth nothing. Therefore, retained earnings must be paid back to shareholders eventually. In this sense, retained earnings can be thought of as capital that is reinvested on behalf of shareholders for the purpose of delivering a higher rate of return—or a higher rate of growth—when the capital is eventually returned. This highlights the importance of considering the dividend payout ratio when performing security analysis using the DDM.

The dividend payout ratio is calculated as the ratio of the per-share dividend paid to the per-share earnings of the company. The ratio indicates what proportion of the firm's capital is paid out to shareholders, with the remainder being what proportion is retained. In some cases, a low payout ratio might be considered good or desirable, as it might reflect the fact that a firm has valuable growth opportunities for which it needs to reinvest its earnings. Indeed, as is covered in many corporate finance courses, earnings could represent a relatively low-cost source of capital for the firm. A growing firm might benefit its shareholders by reinvesting earnings in high-return activities in order to pay out larger dividends in the future.

For companies in some industries or sectors, such as utilities or REITs, the payout ratio is typically a high proportion of earnings. For others, the ratio might be quite low. For those firms in which the dividend payout ratio is high, the dividends might be expected to grow at the same rate as the firm's earnings. Therefore, the security analyst might forecast the long-term average growth rate of the firm's earnings and assume that the dividends will grow at the same rate, implicitly assuming that the payout ratio will remain the same. For companies with low payout ratios, there is capacity for the stock's dividend to grow substantially, even if the earnings of the company do not grow. This implies that the growth rate can play a relatively larger role in the DDM for a stock with a low payout ratio than for a stock with a higher payout ratio, holding all other things constant. For these stocks, the security analyst must forecast the growth rate of earnings *and* the change (and its timing) in the payout ratio in order to forecast the growth in future dividends. In this way, there may be more uncertainty surrounding the DDM valuation for stocks that have low payout ratios. In the extreme circumstance of a company that does not currently pay a dividend, the DDM provides a particular challenge because of the added uncertainty surrounding the forecast of the timing and amount of the initial dividend. While we just described this as an "extreme circumstance," we note that it is hardly uncommon, as only 50.7% of the stocks in the Russell 3000 Index and only 22.6% of all U.S. actively traded stocks paid dividends in 2012, according to Bloomberg.

Discounted Cash Flow model

The Dividend Discount Model considers the cash flows that accrue directly to the shareholder of a firm's stock in the form of dividends. An alternative method of valuing the stock of a company is to value the entire firm and then determine the amount of that value on which equity shareholders have a claim. We refer to this model as the Discounted Cash Flow (DCF) model or the Free Cash Flow model, because it discounts the firm's future free cash flows to determine the intrinsic value of the firm available to equity holders. The time-value-of-money calculations in the DCF model are nearly identical to those in the DDM. However, we replace the forecast of dividends with a forecast of the firm's total free cash flows. Another subtle difference is that the resulting present value reflects the value available to all of the firm's claimholders. Recognizing that equity holders represent residual claimants, we must first subtract the value of the firm's debt in order to determine the value of the firm's stock, accounting for the number of shares outstanding.

We derive the DCF model in a similar manner as we developed the calculations of the DDM. We begin by considering the stream of future cash flows available to an infinitely lived firm. The cash flow in year t is forecast to be FCF_t. Because we are valuing the entire firm and not just considering the value of the firm's equity, the weighted average cost of capital, denoted by k_{WACC}, represents the appropriate discount rate for the time-value-of-money calculations. The total value of the firm is just the present value of the infinite stream of cash flows, as given by:

$$V_0^{DCF} = \frac{FCF_1}{(1+k_{WACC})} + \frac{FCF_2}{(1+k_{WACC})^2} + \cdots + \frac{FCF_t}{(1+k_{WACC})^t} + \cdots \tag{2.6}$$

Notice the similarities between Eqs. (2.6) and (2.3). As with the Dividend Discount Model, some simplifying assumptions are necessary to make this model tractable, since it would otherwise require the security analyst to forecast an infinite number of inputs. If we assume that free cash flows grow at terminal growth rate g_{FCF} beyond time t, then we can utilize the valuation formula for a constantly growing perpetuity. We reflect the value of all dividends beyond time t in a terminal value at time t as:

$$V_t^{DCF} = \frac{FCF_t(1+g_{FCF})}{k_{WACC} - g_{FCF}} \tag{2.7}$$

Eq. (2.6) can be restated to create a multistage version of the DCF model, given by:

$$V_0^{DCF} = \frac{FCF_1}{(1+k_{WACC})} + \frac{FCF_2}{(1+k_{WACC})^2} + \cdots + \frac{FCF_{t-1}}{(1+k_{WACC})^{t-1}} + \frac{FCF_t + V_t^{DCF}}{(1+k_{WACC})^t} \tag{2.8}$$

Just as with the Dividend Discount Model, the multistage DCF model allows the analyst to forecast near-term year-by-year cash flows and then summarize the long-term cash flows through an assumed constant average terminal growth rate, resulting in a terminal value. An analyst can easily implement such calculations in an Excel spreadsheet, as shown in the example in Exhibit 2.5. Note that Eq. (2.8) results in a calculation of the intrinsic value of the overall firm. This valuation should be useful for both bond and stock analysts. Bond analysts could determine whether the company's value exceeds the value of the firm's debt. Equity analysts could use this model to determine the residual value of the firm, after debt holders are paid. To do so, the market value of the firm's debt can be subtracted from the firm value V_0^{DCF} to get the total value of the firm available to equity holders, V_0^{DCF}. Finally, the intrinsic per-share value of the firm can be determined by dividing V_0^{DCF} by the number of shares outstanding.

Steps to using the multistage discounted cash flow model

1. Forecast each year's cash flow over the near-term (e.g., the next 5 years).
2. Estimate an average terminal growth rate of cash flows beyond the near-term (e.g., beyond the next 5 years).
3. Estimate the firm's weighted average cost of capital to be used as the discount rate.
4. Discount the cash flows in step 2 to find the terminal value of the firm at the beginning of the terminal growth stage.
5. Discount the terminal value and the cash flows during the abnormal growth stage to find the intrinsic value of the firm.
6. Estimate the market value of the firm's debt.
7. Subtract the market value of the firm's debt from the intrinsic value of the firm to get the intrinsic value of the firm's equity.
8. Divide the intrinsic value of the firm's equity by the shares outstanding to find the intrinsic per-share value of the firm's stock.

We illustrate these steps in Exhibit 2.4. Note that the DCF model requires more inputs and more steps than the DDM model in Exhibit 2.3. In particular, the calculation of the discount rate, the weighted average cost of capital (WACC), to be applied to the firm's cash flows requires both the cost of equity and cost of debt. The cost of equity follows the same approach of relying on the Capital Asset Pricing Model beta for the stock and the assumptions of the risk-free rate and market risk premium. In addition, the weighted average cost of capital utilizes the required return on the firm's debt. To get the required return on the firm's debt, there are at least two approaches. The first approach is to simply find the average yield to maturity on the firm's existing long-term debt. Alternatively, the yield spread on the firm's debt can be used and added to the risk-free rate. The latter approach has the benefit of utilizing a long-term measure of the cost of debt rather than one that is possibly influenced by abnormally high or low current interest rates. The final ingredient to calculating the WACC is the firm's mix of equity and debt. The example has an implicit assumption that the firm is currently at its optimal or long-term average capital structure. As such, it uses the current market value of the firm's equity and debt in the WACC calculation. An alternative approach would be to forecast and specify the firm's long-term target capital structure directly for this calculation. The Excel formulas that calculate the terminal value and the present values are identical to the DDM, given the inputs.

The security analyst must do a bit more research in order to implement the DCF model, as it requires the use of the firm's financial statements to calculate cash flows. In theory, cash flow is a straightforward measure of the change in a firm's cash over a period of time, accounting for all of the sources and uses of that cash. In practice, cash flow can have several different, but related, definitions. Each measure has its usefulness in specific applications. Because the DCF model is valuing the entire firm, it is useful to consider the

Exhibit 2.4 Example of Free Cash Flow to Equity model in Excel

Assumptions, estimates, and forecasts

1. Stock will pay a dividend of $0.60 next year.
2. The dividends per share over the following 4 years will be: $0.80 in 2 years; $0.96 in 3 years; $1.08 in 4 years; and $1.16 in 5 years.
3. The terminal growth rate will be 4% per year, starting after 5 years.
4. The discount rate will be calculated using the Capital Asset Pricing Model.
5. The risk-free rate is 3.5% per year.
6. The market risk premium is 5.50% per year.
7. The stock's beta, calculated from the last 5 years of monthly returns is 0.92.

	A	B	C	D
1	Free Cash Flow to Equity Model			
2	Risk Free Rate	3.50%		
3	Market Risk Premium	5.50%		
4	Equity Beta	0.92		
5	Cost of Equity	8.56%		=B2+B4*B3
6				
7	Yield Spread on Firm Debt	1.20%		
8	Pre-Tax Cost of Debt	4.70%		=B2+B7
9	Effective Tax Rate	30%		
10	After-Tax Cost of Debt	3.29%		=B8*(1-B9)
11				
12	Market Value of Debt ($)	500,000,000		
13	Market Value of Equity ($)	4,306,000,000		
14				
15	Wtd Avg Cost of Capital	8.01%		=(B13/(B12+B13))*B5+(B12/(B12+B13))*B10
16				
17	Terminal Growth Rate	3.00%		
18				
19	Year	Free Cash Flow ($)	Terminal Value ($)	
20	1	240,000,000		
21	2	260,000,000		
22	3	280,000,000		
23	4	300,000,000		
24	5	320,000,000	5,928,057,554	=B24*(1+B17)/(B5-B17)
25				
26	Year	Present Value ($)		
27	1	221,075,903		=(B20+C20)/(1+$B$5)^A27
28	2	220,614,310		=(B21+C21)/(1+$B$5)^A28
29	3	218,850,996		=(B22+C22)/(1+$B$5)^A29
30	4	215,994,114		=(B23+C23)/(1+$B$5)^A30
31	5	4,143,771,968		=(B24+C24)/(1+$B$5)^A31
32				
33	Intrinsic Firm Value ($)	5,020,307,290		=SUM(B27:B31)
34	Intrinsic Value of Equity ($)	4,799,231,387		=SUM(B28:B32)
35	Shares Outstanding	190,000,000		
36				
37	**Intrinsic Value per Share ($)**	**25.26**		=B34/B35
38				
39	Inputs	Calculated		

cash flows independent of the firm's source of capital or its capital structure decisions, which could affect the overall cash flow. For this model, the common method of measuring a cash flow to the firm is the after-tax value of earnings before interest and taxes (EBIT), plus depreciation, minus capital expenditures and changes to working capital. This method of calculating cash flow reflects the operating cash flows to the firm because it begins with EBIT rather than using net income. While it might seem that this valuation gives no tax credit for an interest expense, we note that the tax benefit of debt is already reflected in the after-tax cost of debt component of the weighted average cost of capital. We add back the non-cash component of EBIT, depreciation, but subtract capital expenditures and changes to working capital. In doing so, free cash flow to the firm reflects that amount of cash the firm earns during a period, net of the cash it spends to assure the company's ongoing ability to conduct business.

Sidebar: Free Cash Flow to the firm calculation

$$FCF = EBIT \times (1 - t) + Depr - CapEx - \Delta WC$$

FCF	Free cash flow to the firm
EBIT	Earnings before interest and taxes
t	Marginal tax rate
Depr	Depreciation
CapEx	Capital expenditures
ΔWC	Changes or investments in working capital

The approach that the security analyst takes to making forecasts of the free cash flow to the firm can vary from analyst to analyst. At one extreme of sophistication (or, at least, complexity), the analyst might make forecasts of the components of every aspect of DCF, starting with the top-line revenue forecast, proceeding to the costs and its driving factors, and finishing with the ongoing capital investment needs of the firm. Each item might be subject to different influences. For example, the firm's revenues might depend on its product development plans and its competitive position in the product markets. The costs for one firm might be highly variable depending on quantities sold and/or on commodity prices, while another firm might have a high degree of operating leverage. The firm's capital investment plan might influence both costs and revenues. These forecasts might be made at the geographical, market segment, and/or product level. Clearly, a detailed model of a conglomerate has the potential to be quite elaborate. At the other extreme, an analyst might consider recent years' free cash flows to form the baseline to which future year's cash flow growth is applied. Analysis anywhere between the elaborate, complex model and the baseline model exists.

Two analysts (or analysts from two firms or student-managed investment funds) can both conduct valuation using a DCF model, yet apply the model in substantially different methods. Indeed, the differences are likely to depend on the differences in the investment philosophy and represent differences in the investment process. Whether the elaborate, the baseline, or some approach in between is the best depends many factors. The superiority of one over the other is impossible to establish. The usefulness is likely to depend on the type and structure of the firm's business, the quality of information available about the firm, and the analyst's ability. We caution that a higher level of complexity does not always lead to a higher level of accuracy. Making forecasts of the components of EBIT, for example, requires many different forecasts to be made. If each forecast is made with error, then the errors could compound each other in a way that is not readily apparent. On the other hand, if the forecast errors are independent of one another, then they might average out.

Free Cash Flow to Equity model

A variant on the Discounted Cash Flow model is the Free Cash Flow to Equity (FCFE) model. As its name suggests, the FCFE model discounts future cash flows to equity holders, taking into account receipt of cash from or payment of cash to debt holders. Specifically, the free cash flow to equity starts with net income, which is the earnings available to shareholders after interest and taxes have been paid. Just as in the total free cash flow calculation, depreciation and amortization are added back because they are non-cash charges that decreased the net income. Likewise, investments in working capital (additions to current assets and decreases to liabilities) are subtracted out as uses of cash. Finally, new issues of debt less debt repaid is added to the cash available to equity holders. The sidebar shows the calculation of the free cash flow to equity, which can be compared with free cash flow to the firm calculation in the earlier sidebar.

We note that the free cash flows to equity account for the portion of cash flows that are to be paid to debt holders (via the interest expense) and are discounted by the required return on equity. As such, the FCFE mode results in the intrinsic value of the firm that is claimed by equity holders. Given consistent measurement of the inputs to the DCF and the FCFE models, they should result in the same valuations for the firm. Therefore, one or the other model is commonly chosen by a security analyst. We note, however, that the DCF model may be more appropriate in the analysis of the firm's debt and equity, as it provides for the overall firm value available to all security holders.

Sidebar: Free cash flow to equity calculation

$$FCFE = NI + Depr - CapEx - \Delta WC + \Delta Debt$$

FCFE	Free cash flow to equity
NI	Net income
Depr	Depreciation
CapEx	Capital expenditures
ΔWC	Changes or investments in working capital
$\Delta Debt$	Net new borrowing

Steps to using the Free Cash Flow to Equity model

1. Forecast each year's free cash flow to equity over the near term (e.g., the next 5 years).
2. Estimate an average terminal growth rate of free cash flows beyond the near term (e.g., beyond the next 5 years).
3. Estimate the firm's required return on equity.
4. Discount the cash flows in step 2 to find the terminal value of the firm at the beginning of the terminal growth stage.
5. Discount the terminal value and the cash flows during the abnormal growth stage to find the intrinsic value of the firm's equity.
6. Divide the intrinsic value of the firm's equity by the shares outstanding to find the intrinsic per-share value of the firm's stock.

Valuation using earnings

An earnings-based valuation model can be considered middle ground between the Dividend Discount Model and a Discounted Cash Flow model, such as the Free Cash Flow to Equity model. The earnings approach, which we will call the Earnings Model, focuses on the value of the firm's equity (or price per share), just as the DDM does. Like the FCFE model, the Earnings Model considers the intrinsic value deriving from the firm's ongoing business, not just from the cash flows paid out to shareholders. Indeed, under certain assumptions the Earnings Model is equivalent to the FCFE model. We consider the Earnings Model in its basic form for both simplicity and to show how common practical valuation metrics are derived from valuation principles.

The Earnings Model considers the relevant cash flow in a discounted cash flow model to the earnings (or earnings per share) of the firm, discounted to the present using the required return on the firm's equity. As such, the growth rates used in the model refer to the growth rate in the firm's earnings. The steps to calculate the intrinsic value of the firm's equity follow the derivations for both the DDM and DCF as shown in the above equations. The resulting Earnings Model value of the firm's stock, given earnings per share each period, a terminal growth rate of earnings g_E, and the required return on the firm's equity is given by:

$$V_0^E = \frac{E_1}{(1+k_E)} + \frac{E_2}{(1+k_E)^2} + \cdots + \frac{E_{t-1}}{(1+k_E)^{t-1}} + \frac{E_1 + V_t^E}{(1+k_E)^t}, \text{where} \tag{2.9}$$

$$V_t^E = \frac{E_t(1+g_E)}{k_E - g_E} \tag{2.10}$$

Just as in the DDM and DCF models, the Earnings Model requires the analyst to make forecasts of the key variables used in the analysis. Specifically, the analyst must forecast the amount and timing of earnings, their growth over time, and the discount rate appropriate to the firm's equity. For completeness, we list the steps of for using the Earnings Model of stock valuation below.

Steps to using the Earnings Model

1. Forecast each year's earnings over the near term (e.g., the next 5 years).
2. Estimate an average terminal growth rate of earnings beyond the near term (e.g., beyond the next 5 years).
3. Estimate the firm's cost of equity capital to be used as the discount rate.
4. Discount the earnings in step 2 to find the terminal value of the stock at the beginning of the terminal growth stage.
5. Discount the terminal value and the earnings during the abnormal growth stage to find the intrinsic value of the firm's stock.

As with the Discounted Cash Flow and Free Cash Flow to Equity models, the forecast of the earnings can apply short- and long-term growth forecasts to baseline earnings based on the current year's earnings or an average of recent past years' earnings and apply short- and long-term growth forecasts. Alternatively, the Earnings Model's application can be more complex and detailed by building earnings forecasts from estimates of the various components of earnings. Of course, earnings forecasts rely on similar research and analysis that goes into the Discounted Cash Flow model and vice versa. As such, these models should result in consistent intrinsic values, assuming that the inputs and forecasts are consistent with one another. Indeed, the Earnings Model and the Discounted Cash Flow model will yield the same result if the market value of debt is calculated accurately and the after-tax value of the firm's depreciation is equal to value of the firm's capital expenditures over time. The interested reader can prove this algebraically by solving for the conditions that set the intrinsic value of equity in the Earnings Model equal to the intrinsic value of equity in the Discounted Cash Flow model.

Market valuation measures

Rather than modeling the value of the firm using the Discounted Cash Flow to Equity, Dividend Discount Model, or Earnings Model, some analysts utilize market valuation measures to judge a stock's valuation relative to other stocks. Indeed, the above discussion focuses on absolute measures of valuation and ignores the pragmatic view that portfolio management is often an exercise in relative judgments: one stock's valuation relative to another stock's valuation. Market valuation ratios, such as Price-to-Earnings (P/E), Price-to-Cash Flow (P/CF), and Price-to-Book (P/B) serve as valuable tools in judging such relative values. These measures are motivated by the valuation models discussed above. As such, market valuation ratios provide yet another tool for use in security analysis.

Price-to-earnings

The most popular market valuation measure is the price-to-earnings ratio, often just referred to as the P/E. The P/E is best interpreted within the context of the Earnings Model. To facilitate the interpretation, we consider the simplification of the EM in which we have a forecast of next year's earnings, E, which are expected to subsequently grow at a constant rate g. Therefore, we can rewrite Eq. (2.9) simply as:

$$V_0^E = \frac{E_0(1+g_E)}{k_E - g_E}$$ (2.11)

Before proceeding, we adapt our notation to emphasize that the remainder of the analysis will be used to infer the market's forecast of the inputs into the EM. Consider variables with "hats" to be the market's forecast of the variable, so that $\hat{k}$ is the market-determined discount rate, $\hat{g}$ is the market's forecasted long-term growth rate, and P_0 is the market price for the stock. We rewrite Eq. (2.10) as:

$$P_0 = \frac{E_0(1+\hat{g})}{\hat{k} - \hat{g}}$$ (2.12)

To obtain the P/E ratio, we simply divide both sides of Eq. (2.12) by the earnings per share, to get:

$$\frac{P_0}{E_0} = \frac{(1+\hat{g})}{\hat{k} - \hat{g}}$$ (2.13)

Eq. (2.13) shows that the P/E ratio reflects the market's forecast of the growth rate of earnings and the required return on the firm's equity. In other words, the market is willing to pay more per dollar of earnings when it forecasts a higher growth rate of earnings and/or when it has a lowered required return on the firm's stock. The higher the expected growth, the higher the P/E ratio is, holding the required return on equity constant.

Eq. (2.13) illustrates that the P/E ratio can also be thought of as a time-value-of-money multiplier that is applied to a year's earnings to determine the present value of a growing stream of earnings. Simply put, the required rate of return and growth rate combine to determine the P/E. Any terminal value that is calculated in Eq. (2.10) of an Earnings Model could be considered as the last year's earnings multiplied by some future P/E ratio that represents the appropriate combination of required return and long-term growth rate in earnings. As such, analysts can check their long-term growth forecasts and required return assumptions against the average market P/E for similar stocks. An analyst should question any forecast of a terminal growth rate relative to the required return that results in too high of a P/E compared to what is typical in the market.

Eq. (2.13) is also useful when comparing the valuation of two stocks with similar characteristics. For example, stocks from the same industry or subsector might be assumed to have the same cost of equity capital. Assuming the same $\hat{k}$, the stock with the higher P/E ratio is the stock that has higher long-term growth prospects according to the market's expectation. The security analyst who evaluates these two companies might have a different view of which company has the better growth prospects, making one company appear undervalued relative to the other. In the case in which the security analysts shares the consensus of the market as to which stock has the higher growth prospects, then the issue of which stock represents the better relative value is less clear.

The security analyst who has a good forecast of the required return on equity can rearrange Eq. (2.13) to determine the market's implied long-term growth forecast of a stock, as given by:

$$\hat{g} = \frac{\dfrac{P_0}{E_0}\hat{k} - 1}{1 + \dfrac{P_0}{E_0}} \tag{2.14}$$

By comparing the growth estimate from Eq. (2.14) with her own long-term growth estimate, the analyst can judge whether the market is too optimistic or pessimistic about a firm's future long-term growth. That is, rather than arriving at a price estimate for the firm, the analyst need only forecast the growth rate for the firm's earnings and compare it to the implied growth rate from the market price. Any stock for which the market's implied growth rate is too low is undervalued, while stocks with too high an implied growth rate are overvalued by the market. Together, Eqs. (2.13) and (2.14) illustrate that security analysis and valuation depend critically on future long-term growth prospects. This is akin to calculating an implied volatility from an option premium and using that implied volatility rather than a calculated premium.

Price-to-sales

The same approach as used in the analysis of the P/E ratio can be used in examining a firm's price-to-sales (P/S) ratio. P/S can be especially useful in comparing the valuations among companies that have comparable profit margins. Consider using the company's sales, S_0, and its net profit margin, π, to define earnings as $E_0 = \pi S_0$. We can rewrite Eq. (2.12) to express the firm's stock price in terms of the firm's sales per share, as given by:

$$P_0 = \frac{\pi S_0(1+\hat{g})}{\hat{k}-\hat{g}} \tag{2.15}$$

In this case, we might assume that the profit margin remains constant over the long term and any growth in earnings comes from a growth in sales. Therefore, the price-to-sales ratio can be expressed in terms of the firm's growth rate of sales, profit margin, and required return on equity, as given by:

$$\frac{P_0}{S_0} = \frac{\pi(1+\hat{g})}{\hat{k}-\hat{g}} \tag{2.16}$$

Applying the same analysis as was applied to the P/E ratio, the growth rate becomes the key differentiator between the value of two companies that have similar profit margins and required rates of return. As discussed in the Appendix, the profit margins for some types of companies are found to be quite stable over time. This implies that growth in earnings, and perhaps even cash flows, are driven primarily by growth in sales. Therefore, some analysts view sales-driven valuation approaches, such as that reflected in the price-to-sales ratio, to have the virtue of reducing the valuation problem to its fundamental elements.

Price-to-cash flow

The price-to-cash flow (P/CF) ratio can be evaluated in the context of the Free Cash Flow to Equity model. As with the Earnings Model, we can simplify Eq. (2.7) by assuming a constant growth rate for the firm's cash flows. Since Eq. (2.7) relies on cash flows to the firm, we also simply the model by expressing cash flows on a per share basis. Using the latest cash flow, the firm's cost of capital, and the long-term growth rate, the value of the firm is given by:

$$V_0 = \frac{CF_0(1+g_{CF})}{k_{WACC}-g_{CF}} \tag{2.17}$$

Again, we adapt the notation to emphasize that the remainder of the analysis will be used to infer the market's forecast of the firm's valuation. The variables with "hats" refer to the market's forecast of the variable, so that $\hat{k}$ is the market-determined cost of capital, ghat is the market's forecasted long-term growth rate, and P is the market price for the stock. We rewrite Eq. (2.17) as:

$$P_0 = \frac{CF_0(1+\hat{g}_{CF})}{\hat{k}_{WACC}-\hat{g}_{CF}} \tag{2.18}$$

Dividing both sides of Eq. (2.18) by the per share cash flow results in the P/CF ratio, given by:

$$\frac{P_0}{CF_0} = \frac{(1+\hat{g}_{CF})}{\hat{k}_{WACC}-\hat{g}_{CF}} \tag{2.19}$$

Notice the similarities between Eqs. (2.18) and (2.13). While there are technical differences in the parameters on the right-hand side between the two equations, the interpretations of the parameters are essentially the same. While the weighted average cost of capital might be lower than the cost of equity (i.e., the required return on the firm's equity), the growth rate in cash flows might be expected to be equivalent to the growth rate in earnings. For the growth rates in earnings and cash flows to be different, there must be some long-term change in capital expenditures or non-cash items in proportion to the firm's earnings. As discussed earlier, these growth rates might also be considered equal to the long-term growth rate in the firm's cash flows, assuming a constant net profit margin. While these subtleties and technicalities are sometimes important, they can be minor when using these ratios to make relative valuation judgments across securities in related subsectors or industries.

Security analysis application

We illustrate the application of the security valuation models by discussing the equity valuation approach used in Texas Christian University's Educational Investment Fund (TCU-EIF). Chapters 2 and 4 also utilize the TCU-EIF example in demonstrating the role of security analysis in the construction of the overall portfolio and the importance of the written investment idea. presentation, respectively. We thank Stanley Block, Larry Lockwood, and Ben Wyatt of the TCU-EIF for their significant contributions to this material.

Example: Texas Christian University's Educational Investment Fund

By Stanley Block and Larry Lockwood

Valuation

While the EIF employs various methods to value assets, we rely heavily on the Free Cash Flow to Equity (FCFE) and Dividend Discount Models (DDM). We believe that these models, especially the FCFE model, force the analyst to carefully consider all the factors that can affect firm value, including profitability, risk, working capital, debt, and capital expenditures.

Our analysis begins with the income statement in which we forecast revenues, expenses, and net income. While we follow a standard framework of analysis, we leave no stone unturned when deriving our pro forma forecasts and valuation estimates. While company guidance can be helpful, we tend to consider them with a healthy dose of skepticism. We do not simply look at the bottom line numbers; instead we constantly stress the importance of the quality of earnings and attempt to identify any potential latent problems that may surface for the company in the future.

Much consideration is given to our projections as these figures are the main drivers of the DDM and FCFE values. To confirm our forecasts are reasonable, we report the annualized growth in forecasted earnings per share (EPS) and compare the growth rates to the past 3 years' EPS growth rate. After forecasting the income statement, the balance sheet and cash flow statements are projected.

After generating the pro forma statements for the next three fiscal years, we then forecast dividends and free cash flow to equity. To estimate the terminal stock price (for year 3), we use the P/E multiple method: We derive a forecast for the year 3 P/E and multiply it times the predicted year 3 earnings per share. To forecast the year 3 P/E, we consider determinants such as the company's historical P/E, industry average P/E, earnings growth, systematic risk, and key macroeconomic factors. For the DDM, we discount the projected dividends through year 3, along with the forecast year 3 stock price. For the FCFE model, we discount the projected FCFE through year 3, along with the forecast of the year 3 stock price.

For both the DDM and the FCFE, we discount the pertinent cash flows using the appropriate risk-adjusted discount rate based on the Capital Asset Pricing Model (CAPM). In our CAPM, we use the currently quoted 30-year U.S. Treasury bond yield as the risk free rate and the historical geometric average market risk premium (i.e., the historical geometric average market return less the 30-year Treasury bond return, which is equal to 5.7%). Geometric averages are a preferred metric for long-term asset comparisons. Individual stock betas are gathered from various sources, such as Bloomberg and Value Line, but are also compared against historical betas using regression analysis over the past 60 months. Fund members have the flexibility to choose a beta believed to best represent the company's systematic risk over the coming years. We also compare our CAPM projections against other models such as the bond build-up approach. In all our calculations, we emphasize reliance on intuitive understanding of models and their output, and not strict adherence to mathematical rules at the expense of good logic and common sense.

After forecasting the key cash flows and determining the appropriate risk-adjusted discount rate, we run sensitivity analyses based on different earnings per share and P/E forecasts. Through the sensitivity analysis, the members can see forecasts and valuations scenarios ranging from worst to best case. From here, the members can also obtain some understanding of the potential undervaluation or overvaluation of the evaluated stock. Comparisons between the valuations derived from the DDM and the FCFE models are made and considered when making buy (undervalued) and sell (overvalued) decisions.

Checks and balances

We run our predictions through various checks and balances. For instance, we use stock price multiple comparisons such as price to earnings, price to book value, price to sales, price to cash flow, and price-to-EBITDA across similar competitors within the industry. Fund members use these comparisons to either support or refute the recommendation made by the (student) analyst. We also derive the present value of growth opportunities (PVGO) for each stock, equal to the current stock price minus the stock's zero growth value (current year forecast earnings divided by the discount rate). The PVGO calculation separates the existing earnings of the firm from investors' perception of future incremental earnings generated from the firm's growth opportunities. A high PVGO relative to current stock price is indicative of a growth stock. To justify the purchase of a high PVGO stock, fund members must be convinced of the high growth potential of the company's earnings.

DDM and FCFE models: An illustration

In this section, we provide a simplified example for both the DDM and FCFE models used by the TCU Educational Investment Fund. Our analytical framework relies heavily on the valuation principles established in the Chartered Financial Analysts program.

We present a condensed pro-forma income statement in Exhibit 2.5, in which we forecast key variables for the next 3 years, after which we estimate a horizon value for the stock. The analysis begins with revenue forecasts, which are derived after a thorough examination of main

Exhibit 2.5 Pro forma income statement

	2009	2010	2011	2012
Revenues	7000.00	7350.00	7864.50	8572.31
EBITDA	1400.00	1617.00	1808.84	2057.35
Depreciation and Amortization	200.00	218.00	239.80	268.58
Interest	70.00	73.50	80.85	92.98
Pretax Profit (EBT)	1130.00	1325.50	1488.19	1695.80
Tax	169.50	265.10	312.52	373.08
Net Income	960.50	1060.40	1175.67	1322.72
Shares Outstanding	500	500	500	500
Earnings/Share	$1.92	$2.12	$2.35	$2.65
Dividend/Share Assumptions	$0.77	$0.85	$0.94	$1.06
Revenue Growth		5%	7%	9%
EBITDA Margins	20%	22%	23%	24%
Depreciation and Amortization Growth		9%	10%	12%
Interest Expense Growth		5%	10%	15%
Effective Tax Rate	15%	20%	21%	22%
Capital Expenditure Growth		10%	10%	10%

revenue drivers of the company. For our example, revenues are predicted to grow at 5%, 7%, and 9%. All dollar figures reported in the exhibit are in millions, except per share variables. Other assumptions are listed at the bottom of the exhibit.

To forecast earnings, we often rely on margin forecasts such as an operating profit (EBITDA) margin, and then proceed to the forecasts of interest, taxes, depreciation, and amortization. Key inputs when forecasting EBITDA include labor costs, operating leverage, inflation, and stage of the business cycle. For our example, predicted EBITDA margins equal 22%, 23%, and 24%, over the next 3 years, respectively.

We forecast depreciation and amortization, interest, and taxes separately, and subtract them from EBITDA to derive net income. Because depreciation generally rises and falls as a percentage of property, plant, and equipment, we generally predict depreciation after formulating our PP&E forecasts. In our example, depreciation is expected to grow 9%, 10%, and 12% for the next 3 years.

We forecast interest expense as a percentage (interest rate) of debt outstanding (e.g., increasing 5%, 10%, and 15%, over the next 3 years, respectively, in our example). Taxes are deducted, based on tax rates determined by current and anticipated tax legislation. Finally, after calculating net income, shares outstanding are forecast (often based on company guidance, or recent trends). For simplicity, in our example, we assume no changes in shares outstanding.

To predict dividends, we often apply a dividend payout rate (e.g., based on historical data or company guidance) against our net income forecasts. In our example, we use a 40% dividend payout.

After applying the growth and margin assumptions, predicted dividends equal $0.85, $0.94, and $1.06, for 2010, 2011, and 2012, respectively. To determine the intrinsic value for the stock using the dividend discount model, we discount the predicted dividends along with the predicted year 3 stock price. As explained earlier, we derive our year 3 stock price forecast by using the combined P/E and earnings model: 2012 stock price estimate equals predicted 2012 P/E ratio times predicted 2012 earnings per share.

Exhibit 2.6 presents our CAPM and P/E assumptions, and Exhibit 2.7 presents the DDM valuation. Assume that the fiscal year ends December 31, and that the current date is March 14, 2010 (80% of the year remains).

As explained earlier, we also rely heavily on the free cash flow to equity (FCFE) model, especially in cases for which dividends are either not paid by the company or show a weak relationship with the firm's profitability. To derive the FCFE, we begin with net income and subtract changes in net working capital, capital expenditures, and add non-cash expenses and net new borrowing.

Exhibit 2.6 Capital asset pricing model and P/E assumptions

Risk Free Rate	4.50%
Risk Premium	5.70%
Beta	1.25
CAPM	11.625%
2012 Predicted EPS	$2.65
2012 Predicted P/E	12.0
2012 Predicted Stock Price	$31.80

Exhibit 2.7 Valuation using the dividend discount model

Year	Dividends	Period	Present value
2010	$0.85	0.80	$0.78
2011	$0.94	1.80	$0.77
2012	$1.06	2.80	$0.78
	PV of Dividends	$2.33	
	PV of 2012 Stock Price	$23.34	
	Intrinsic Value		$25.67

Changes in net working capital (excluding cash) are derived after a thorough examination of accounts receivable, inventory, and accounts payable. An increase in accounts receivable and inventory result in a decrease in cash flow, while an increase in accounts payable results in an increase in cash flow.

Next, capital expenditures are predicted (often as a percentage of sales), and must be consistent with the student's growth forecasts for the company. For instance, if the company is in an expansionary phase, capital expenditures should exceed depreciation. Conversely, if the company is in a declining phase, capital expenditures should be less than depreciation. While the analyst usually focuses on the purchase of assets when discussing capital expenditures, also included in the figure would be any cash received from the sale of a fixed asset such as equipment.

Finally, net new borrowing is determined, often predicted by using the company's target capital structure (e.g., target debt ratio times capital expenditures net of depreciation). By including additional debt that would be needed to finance new capital expenditures, the analyst debt forecasts remain close to the company's target capital structure. Also included in net new borrowings would be any principal debt payments due within the year.

The FCFE intrinsic value of the stock equals the present value of the FCFE for the next 3 years, plus the horizon value. An illustration of the FCFE model is provided in Exhibit 2.8. We begin with our pro-forma net income (see Appendix—Exhibit A2.1) Once again, we assume the current date is March 14, 2010 (80% of the year remains).

Therefore, our analysis leads us to an intrinsic value of $27.26 using the FCFE model and to $25.67 using the DDM. We can rely on just one model or use a weighted average of the two depending on our relative levels of confidence in the two models.

Exhibit 2.8 Free Cash Flow to Equity

	2010	2011	2012
Net Income	1060.40	1175.67	1322.72
Non-cash Charges	218.00	239.80	268.58
Total	1278.40	1415.47	1591.30
Changes in Working Capital			
Accounts Receivable	(100.00)	(125.00)	(150.00)
Inventory	(50.00)	(100.00)	(150.00)
Accounts Payable	125.00	175.00	200.00
Total Changes in Working Capital	(25.00)	(50.00)	(100.00)
Operating Cash Flow	1253.40	1365.47	1491.30
Capital Expenditures	(735.00)	(786.45)	(857.23)
Free Cash Flow to the Firm	518.40	579.02	634.07
Net New Borrowings	206.80	218.66	235.46
FCFE	725.20	797.68	869.53
Shares Outstanding	500	500	500
FCFE per Share	1.45	1.60	1.74
PV of FCFE per Share	1.33	1.31	1.28
Sum of PV of FCFE			$3.92
PV of 2012 Price			$23.34
Intrinsic Equity Value			$27.26

Potential variations

Clearly, there are many variations to our methods that we can consider. First, we could forecast individual year dividends or free cash flows for more than 3 years, presumably forecasting until the firm's competitive advantage ends, after which we would apply the industry average P/E to derive the horizon value. In our experience, however, it is exceedingly difficult attempting to forecast the period in which a competitive advantage will end. Consequently, we prefer to forecast dividends and free cash flows for 3 years and to then apply either a discount or premium P/E to reflect the firm's strength or weakness within the industry at year 3.

Second, we could forecast the horizon value using a constant growth assumption, rather than using the combined P/E and earnings method. Clearly, we could solve for the constant growth that would equalize the two methods. But we prefer the combined method because it forces the analyst to draw price-multiple comparisons, which many investors deem essential in their buy and sell decisions.

Third, we could use the free cash flow to the firm (FCF) rather than free cash flow to equity. In the FCF model, the weighted average cost of capital is used to discount the predicted FCF, equal to net income minus change in net working capital and capital expenditure, plus non-cash expenses and after-tax interest expense. In the FCF model, equity value equals the discounted value of the FCF minus the market value of the firm's outstanding debt. The FCF and FCFE procedures will give the same intrinsic value, and we feel the FCFE method is a more direct method for stock valuation purposes.

Summary of valuation models

- Security analysis is the driving force in security selection.
- The role of security analysis in an investment process should be consistent with the strategy's investment philosophy and process.
- Quantitative models can be used to screen securities for further research and analysis or to rank securities as part of a quantitative security selection model.
- Company analysis is a part of, but not equivalent to, security analysis. A good company is not necessarily a good investment.
- The goal of security valuation is to determine the intrinsic value of a firm or its securities.
- The value of any security is the present value of that security's future cash flows.
- The Dividend Discount Model uses a stock's dividends as the future cash flows that are relevant to the security's intrinsic value.
- The Discounted Cash Flow model and its variants use the future cash flows to the firm in calculating the intrinsic value.
- Market valuation measures, such as P/E, P/S, and P/CF are motivated by and related to theoretical valuation models.

Financial statement analysis

Analysis of a company's financial statements is crucially important to determine whether to invest in its stock or bonds. A company's financial statements provide a picture into the overall financial health of a firm. It can (and should) be noted that financial statements can be subject to "manipulation," even in accordance with Generally Accepted Accounting Principles (GAAP), which allow some wiggle-room for reporting various items or outright accounting fraud by managers (such as was the case with Enron in 2001). Nonetheless, the financial statements of most firms provide valuable information for the analysts and when properly examined provide key insights into whether a firm might be a "good" or "bad" company, as discussed above.

The income statement

The income statement is the primary source of information of a firm's profitability and shows the revenues and expenses of the firm over time. The fact that the income statement gives information over time is important to note. The income statement draws a picture of what the firm has earned and spent (revenues and expenses) over the period of the statement. This allows the analyst to see what has happened in the firm over time and compare this to prior years. One of the most common pieces of information pulled quickly from the income statement is Net Income or Earnings of the firm. This is often referred to as "the Bottom Line" because it is at the bottom of the income statement. The Net Income of the firm should not be the only piece of information pulled from the income statement, but it is a quick read into the firm's health after it has paid all of its expenses. We discuss financial ratios using information from the income statement below.

The balance sheet

The balance sheet of a company is a second source of valuable financial information. The balance sheet presents a snapshot of what the firm owns, owes, and what is left over for the stockholders; in the assets, liabilities, and stockholder's equity, respectively. The balance sheet shows the balance of accounts at a given time. This is important to note, since a lot may have changed within a firm over a year, quarter, or any other period. Thus, it is important not to rely too much on a single time period balance sheet. However, the balance sheet is a good source to glean a quick snapshot of where the firm stands financially, what assets it owns, how much in liabilities it owes, and the book value of its equity. It is also important to realize that the balance sheet reports historical numbers, or book values. The market values of the assets, liabilities, and stockholder's equity may (and are usually) greatly different from the reported book values. As such, while it is important to begin to paint a picture of a firm's financial health from its balance sheet, an analyst should not think of this as a complete picture.

Statement of cash flows

The statement of cash flows is often a less used financial statement when analyzing securities. However, it is not less important. The statement of cash flows reconciles the cash balance from the balance sheet(s) from the beginning of one period to the end of a period. It provides a breakdown of a firm's Cash From Operations, Cash From Investments, and Cash From Financing. The end result of the statement of cash flows is the increase (or decrease) in cash for the period. Thus, the statement of cash flows is like the income statement in that it presents a change in accounts over a period and not a snapshot of accounts at a point in time. It is important to note that the statement of cash flow does not present Free Cash Flow (either Free Cash Flow to the Firm or Free Cash Flow to Equity) as discussed in the stock valuation models above. Both of these cash flow calculations are performed using figures gathered from the financial statements.

Ratio analysis

An analyst can use a number of financial statement ratios to assess a company's financial health. We will discuss a few of these ratios below, but keep in mind that there are other ratios that may also be useful when assessing the stock of a firm. The ratios of a single-year from a single firm cannot be analyzed in isolation. The analyst must compare each ratio to some baseline to determine if the ratio is high or low, good or bad. This baseline can be the same ratio of the same firm from prior years or it can be the same ratio of a competitor firm or, better yet, the average of the ratio for the industry that the firm being analyzed is in.

Liquidity ratios

The first category of financial ratios are liquidity ratios. These ratios measure how well a firm is using their current assets and cash along with the overall short-term financial health of a company. It is important to know whether a firm is liquid, in the short-term, so that one can assess the possibility of problems in the future. The primary liquidity ratio is the Current Ratio, which is the firm's current assets divided by its current liabilities. In general, the current ratio tell how well a firm can cover (or pay) its current liabilities with its current assets. The quick ratio is similar to the current ratio but is the current assets minus inventory divided by current liabilities. The quick ratio is primarily used to analyze a firm that relies heavily on selling of inventory to pay current liabilities.

Activity ratios

Activity ratios, also called Asset Management ratios, are helpful in determining how well a firm is using it assets. The primary ratio in this category if the Total Asset Turnover ratio. The total assets turnover is calculated as sales divided by total assets and gives a picture of how well a firm is using its assets to generate sales. This ratio is part of the DuPont analysis, discussed below. The other ratios include in the spreadsheet with this chapter include Inventory Turnover, Average Collection Period and Average Payment Period. These ratios show how well a firm is managing its inventory, accounts receivable, and accounts payable, respectively.

Leverage ratios

Leverage ratios, or debt ratios, give a sense of clarity of the leverage (or level of debt) that a firm currently holds. The Debt Ratio is calculated as the firm's long-term debt divided by its total assets and shows what percentage of assets are finance with long-term debt. The debt ratio is often influenced by the industry that a firm is in. so it is best to compare debt ratios of firms within the same industry.

This is a good place to point out that different analysts may calculate a given ratio in different ways. For example, the debt ratio is often times calculated as total liabilities divided by total assets. Here, we are using only long-term debt in the numerator. Thus, for financial statement analysis, it is crucial to either calculate each ratio yourself, know how your source calculates a ratio, or use ratios from the same source.

The Times Interest Earned (TIE) is a second leverage ratio. This ratio examines the income statement and looks at how well a firm can cover its interest payments. It is calculated as a firm's earnings before interest and taxes (EBIT—the earnings that a firm can pay interest from) divided by the firms interest payment. The TIE ratio illustrates how many times over a firm can make its interest payments with its current earnings. This give more of a picture of the servicing of a firm's debt, rather than the level of the debt that the debt ratio gives.

Profitability ratios

The fourth category of financial ratios is the profitability ratio. These ratios are often the most exciting (but not necessarily the most important) when analyzing a stock, because they mostly involve income statement numbers. The Gross Profit Margin ratio shows how much of its revenue a firm is keeping after paying costs of goods sold. This ratio is a very "top line" sort of ratio in that it involves nothing but gross profit (revenue minus cost of goods sold) divided by revenue. Moving down the income statement, one can calculate the Operating Profit Margin ratio. This ratio is calculated as the firm's operating profit or earnings before interest and taxes (EBIT) divided by revenue and is a picture of how much a firm keeps from revenue after paying all expenses expect interest and taxes. The final three profitability ratios that we highlight in this section are calculated using Net Income. These are Net Profit Margin, Return on Assets (ROA), and Return on Equity (ROE). Since each of these use net income in the numerator, the denominator is what separates the interpretation of each of these ratios. The Net Profit Margin equals net income divided by revenue and measure the percentage of revenue that flows to the bottom line (how much of the revenue goes to stockholders or what the firm keeps after paying all expenses). The firm's Return on Assets

(ROA) equals net income divided by total assets and shows how well the firm is using its assets to generate net income. The Return on Equity (ROE) give a picture of how well the firm is using equity (book value) to generate net income and is equal to the net income divided by stockholder's equity.

Market-based ratios

Market-based (or just market) ratios combine a financial statement metric with a market-based statistic. For example, one of the most widely used market-based numbers (though it is not a ratio, per se) is Earnings per share (EPS). EPS takes the net income of a firm and divides it by the number of shares outstanding of that firm's stock. In addition, dividends per share takes the total dividends of the firm and divides this by the number of shares. In the valuation discussion above, we used price-to-earnings (P/E) and price-to-sales (P/S). Both of these are market-based ratios. P/E is often widely quoted along with EPS, since P/E is just the market price of the firm divided by the EPS (EPS used in the P/E ratio can either be trailing/historical EPS or forward/forecasted EPS). Similarly, P/S is simply the firm's market price divided by the sales per share. Both of these ratios show how much the market is paying for a dollar of earnings or a dollar of sales, respectively. A third ratio in this category is Market-to-Book (or price-to-book), which is the price of the firm divided by the stockholder equity per share (or book value per share). Market-to-book tells how much investors are paying for a dollar of the firm's book value. This ratio is often expressed as the reciprocal, book-to-market, so be aware of which version of this ratio is reported in a given source.

DuPont analysis

The last two ratios mentioned (ROA and ROE) are often segmented using a technique called DuPont analysis. DuPont breaks apart ROA and ROE into other ratios to provide a better picture of what is actually going on in the firm and shows why ROA and ROE are changing. DuPont for ROA equals a firm's Net Profit Margin multiplied by the Total Asset Turnover. Since ROA equal net income divided by total assets, net profit margin (net income/revenue) times total asset turnover (revenue/total assets) lead to ROA. DuPont is not used to calculate ROA, but is used to show why ROA changes. For example, in the spreadsheet example, ROA in 2019 is 84.30% and in 2018 is 60.71%. This increase from 2018 to 2019 is due to the fact that the example firm's total asset turnover increased from 4.35 (in 2018) to 6.11 (in 2019), and net profit margin actually declined. For ROE, the DuPont analysis is ROA multiplied by Total Assets divided by Stockholder's Equity (this ratio, Assets/Equity, is the Equity Multiplier). Thus, for the example firm in the spreadsheet, the ROE increased from 46.38% (in 2018) to 58.32% (in 2019). Like with ROA, this change was primarily due to the increase in total asset turnover (since neither net profit margin nor the equity multiplier changed from 2018 to 2019). So, with the DuPont analysis, you can separate ROA and ROE and better analyze the source of the change.

Industry analysis

Industry analysis is an important component of stock analysis. Here we take a step back and look at the sector or industry that the firm under analysis is competing in. As we step back in our analysis and begin to look at a bigger picture, it is good to examine two general approaches to analysis. The bottoms-up approach begins with the analysis of individual companies and moves "up" in scope. Much of the discussion in this chapter so far has been from a bottoms-up perspective, screening for and analyzing individual securities. The bottoms-up approach moves from individual security analysis to industry analysis, then to the broader sector analysis, and so forth. The other approach to analysis is called top-down. In the top-down approach, the analysis begins with examination of the macro (global) economy, then moves to sector and industry analysis, then to individual security analysis. We will stick with the bottoms-up approach for discussion in this chapter, but just remember that the order can be reversed.

At first glance, it might seem easy to determine the industry of a given company, and for many companies, this is easy. However, for some companies, the industry in which it competes may be difficult to determine, or the company may technically compete in several industries. Take Amazon, for example, are they a retail/consumer discretionary company, or are they a technology company? Most might say they are (or can be considered) both. One (more ad hoc) way to conduct industry analysis is to compare the firm in question to its competitors, but seeking out sources that specify the firm's industry is often a better way to go. For example, the analyst could look up the NAICS (North American Industry Classification System) or SIC (Standard Industrial Classification) code(s) for the firm under analysis. Both of these codes (and others) group individual firms into industry clusters based on their operations. The first digits of each industry code number classifies the broader grouping and third, fourth, and later digits begin to further narrow the specific industry.

A large component to industry analysis concerns an industry's sensitivity to the economic or business cycle. Different industries respond differently at difference points in the economic cycle. For a portfolio manager, it may be prudent to engage in sector/industry rotation as a results of industry analysis. One strategy involving sector rotation might be to increase portfolio weights in stocks that compete in industries that are expected to do well over the forecasted economic cycle and decrease the weight of stocks in industries that are expected to do not as well. For example, if the economy is going into a period of expansion, the analyst and portfolio manager might want to increase weight in stocks in the information technology, consumer discretionary and communication services sectors and industries within these sectors. If the economy if moving into a period of contraction, the analyst migsht recommend increasing weights in stock in the healthcare, consumer staples, and utilities sectors and industries within these sectors.

Exercises

1. What key beliefs must be embedded in an investment philosophy for security analysis to be a valuable part of the investment process? That is, what conditions are necessary to believe that security analysis is a valuable activity?
2. What is the difference between a good company and a good stock?
3. Explain the difference between a firm's earnings and its cash flows.
4. Discuss the meaning of *relative value*.
5. This chapter focuses on stock valuation models. Using the valuation concepts in this chapter, explain how you would value a firm's bond and how you would value the firm's debt.
6. List all the assumed or forecasted inputs to the Dividend Discount model. For each input, explain how the resulting calculated intrinsic value of the stock changes when the value of the input is increased.
7. List all the assumed or forecasted inputs to the Dividend Discount model. Identify each input as either universal or firm-specific. Universal inputs take on the same value for all firms. Firm-specific inputs take on different values for different firms.
8. List all the assumed or forecasted inputs to the Discounted Cash Flow model. For each input, explain how the resulting calculated intrinsic value of the stock changes when the value of the input is increased.
9. List all the assumed or forecasted inputs to the Discounted Cash Flow model. Identify each input as either universal or firm-specific. Universal inputs take on the same value for all firms. Firm-specific inputs take on different values for different firms.
10. What conditions must be met (or assumptions made) for the calculated intrinsic value using the Discounted Cash Flow model to be equal to the intrinsic value using the Earnings Model for the same firm? Discuss your answer in words and show your answer algebraically.
11. Discuss the advantages and disadvantages of each valuation model.
12. Some security analysts utilize price-per-*unit* valuation heuristics, where examples of *units* are customer, subscriber, store, mile, acre, square foot, or hit (referring to the Internet, not organized crime).
    a. Relate these heuristics to the fundamental valuation models discussed in this chapter. Specifically, discuss how each heuristic could be considered equivalent to one of the valuation models.
    b. Discuss the implicit or explicit assumptions the make these heuristics useful.
    c. Are these heuristics more or less useful relative valuations? Why?
13. Suppose a firm has a negative long-term growth rate of earnings and/or cash flows. Does this firm have a positive intrinsic value? Why or why not?
14. Some are tempted to claim that the Dividend Discount Model is useless for stocks that do not currently pay dividends. Explain why this claim is not true.

Appendix A: Ranking stocks and Z-score

Investment processes that are more heavily tilted to the quantitative side typically seek to rank stocks. The development of ranking models can be complex and time-consuming, requiring significant design and backtesting or historical analysis. For this reason, ranking models may not be as common among student-managed investment funds. Still, ranking models can be a useful tool by themselves, or in combination with traditional fundamental analysis.

The objective in a quantitative ranking model is to sort stocks from "best" to "worst." Ranking along one dimension appears quite simple: rank stocks according to the characteristic of interest. For example, suppose an investor believes in holding the most profitable stocks. The investor would find a source, such as Morningstar or Bloomberg, to determine the profit margin of each company. This list could then be sorted from highest to lowest. Of course, the quantitative analyst must take care to assure that the characteristic is measured consistently among the stocks that are being ranked. Furthermore, since the average measure of a characteristic such as profitability might vary significantly across industries or sectors, perhaps depending on how the measure is defined, ranking might be done only within a suitable set of peers (e.g., industry or sector). Alternatively, the analyst might want to adjust profitability by sector or industry. A popular method to standardize ranking measures is known as a "Z-score."

Z-score

Suppose peer group (or sector) s has N_s securities as members of that peer group. The Z-score for characteristics c for each security i in the peer group can be calculated as

$$Z_{s,i} = \frac{C_{s,i} - \overline{C}_s}{\sigma_{c_s}}$$

$C_{s,i}$ Characteristic or factor of security i within peer groups s.

$\overline{C}_s$ The average of characteristic c in peer groups s, where $\overline{C}_s = \frac{1}{N_s} \sum_{i=1}^{N_s} C_{s,i}$.

σ_{C_s} The standard deviation of characteristics C in peer groups S, where

$$\sigma_{C_s} = \sqrt{\frac{1}{N_s - 1} \sum_{i=1}^{N_s} \left(C_{s,i} - \overline{C}_s\right)^2}$$

As shown in the sidebar, the Z-score adjusts for both the mean (i.e., average) and standard deviation (i.e., variation) of a variable. More precisely, the Z-score provides a measure of the number of standard deviations above (positive) or below (negative) the mean for a particular observation. In the case of ranking along a single characteristic, the Z-score adjusts for differences in that characteristic across different subsets, such as industries or sectors. For example, in the case of profit margin, the quantitative analyst might use the Z-score to adjust for the average and standard deviation of the profit margin within each GIC sector. A Z-score of zero would indicate that a company is at the average profit margin for its sector. A Z-score of 1.00 would indicate that the company's profit margin is one standard deviation above its peer-group average and Z-score of −2.50 would indicate that a company's profit margin is

2.50 standard deviations below its peer group average. By standardizing by dividing by the standard deviation, two observations with the same Z-score are equally "extreme" within their peer group.

In general, ranking models attempt to combine multiple factors, characteristics, or dimensions to arrive at an overall ranking of stocks rather than just ranking along one dimension. The Z-score becomes especially important when trying to combine different measures into a single ranking. A common ranking process is to combine different factors by calculating a weighted average of the factors' Z-scores. The use of Z-scores assures that rankings are not disproportionately influenced by the variation (or lack thereof) within a single factor. The weights chosen by the quantitative analyst determine the importance of that factor in the ranking scheme. Exhibit A2.1 shows several examples of security ranking models. Panel A illustrates various weighting schemes and Panel B shows an example of a ranking model's results.

Exhibit A2.1 Examples of quantitative ranking models

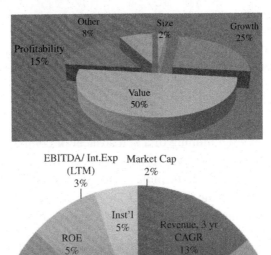

Factor	% Weight
ROE	6.00
ROA	6.00
PM	8.00
Dividend yield	10.00
Best Est. LTG	6.00
3 Yr Sales Average Growth	13.00
P/E	11.00
P/B	11.00
P/S	11.00
Market Cap	18.00

Revised Financial Industry Ranking Model Comparables	Value				Growth		Momentum	Efficiency		Size	Score	Rank
	Trailing E/P Z	Forward E/P Z	S/P Z	Book / Price Z	Est. 2-Yr EPS	1m Upward EPS Analyst	12m Mom. Z	NI Margin Z	ROE Z	BV Z		
Hartford Financial Services Group Inc.	1.04	2.35	2.55	1.63	0.20	2.68	(0.22)	(0.12)	0.18	(0.10)	0.90	1
Capital One Financial Corp.	2.25	1.43	(0.04)	0.70	(1.10)	3.22	0.95	0.49	0.47	0.05	0.86	2
Prudential Financial, Inc.	1.16	1.49	1.53	0.71	(0.23)	3.22	0.18	(0.09)	0.39	0.22	0.82	3
Ameriprise Financial Inc.	0.50	1.05	0.15	(0.30)	0.24	2.68	1.79	0.03	0.54	(0.30)	0.79	4
Torchmark Corp.	1.50	1.75	(0.79)	0.09	(0.30)	1.05	0.55	2.34	0.71	(0.46)	0.73	5
Lincoln National Corp.	0.83	2.05	1.09	1.10	0.06	2.13	(0.16)	(0.05)	0.06	(0.27)	0.62	6
Principal Financial Group Inc.	0.43	1.23	0.50	0.36	(0.05)	2.13	0.82	(0.08)	0.07	(0.33)	0.56	6
Citigroup, Inc.	0.64	1.10	(0.20)	0.77	0.45	(0.04)	1.15	0.28	(0.04)	3.24	0.59	7
MetLife, Inc.	0.42	1.77	1.50	0.40	0.02	1.05	0.25	(0.22)	(0.05)	0.56	0.47	10
T. Rowe Price Group, Inc.	(0.38)	(0.09)	(0.82)	(1.43)	0.44	2.13	0.52	0.74	1.60	(0.49)	0.46	11
Wells Fargo & Company	0.46	1.00	(0.29)	(0.33)	0.68	(0.58)	(0.20)	0.30	0.36	2.37	0.25	24
The Goldman Sachs Group, Inc.	0.85	1.54	(0.21)	(0.01)	0.29	(0.58)	(1.05)	0.45	0.45	1.19	0.14	31

The results of a quantitative ranking model are entirely dependent on the formulaic analysis of data. Small errors in the programming of a spreadsheet or computer model can cause the output of the model to be totally unrelated to what was intended. As such, care must be taken in checking (and double-checking) the formulas that comprise the model. In addition, the results are critically dependent on the input data. Care must be taken to maintain the quality and integrity of the data. Some common challenges and potential solutions are as follows:

- **Choice of factors.** There are many sources for factors. If an investment process does not have a stated bias toward growth, value, large, small, etc., then a balance of factors would be reasonable.
- **Missing data.** There must be a consistent procedure for handling missing data. When data are missing, many utilize an average for that factor for the security, peer group, or universe, depending on the data item. Be careful when doing this as missing data may be missing for a reason that could be negative and informational. Using the average is most appropriate when the reason for the missing data is unrelated to the actual conditions of the security and due to errors in the data sources.
- **Outliers.** The must be a strategy for dealing with outliers or extreme data points, which may or may not represent errors or inconsistencies in the data. It is sometimes desirable, though not always appropriate, to reduce the influence of outliers or extreme values. A good

method for doing so is Winsorization, which sets values beyond the 5th (or 1st) percentile to the 5th (or 1st) percentile value.

- **Data integrity and consistency.** When buy and sell decisions are being made based on data about a stock, it is critical to ensure the data are as accurate as possible. Always double-check your data. Even with large, popular stocks listed in the United States, it is surprising how different data can be from one source to another. Try to find the best source of data and double-check the data when possible. Resolve any inconsistencies within or among sources with as many other sources as possible.
- **Standardization.** Z-scores are a way to deal with variables that are of various scales or magnitudes (see example above).
- **Consistent positives and negatives.** Make sure to score each factor so that the positives and negatives are in the right direction. For example, if high profitability and a low debt ratio are positives, then a highly profitable firm should rank high and a firm with low debt should rank high.
- **Timing of data.** Be sure to measure the data so that they are aligned in time. Since fiscal years are different for each firm, it is often necessary to assemble quarterly financial statements into yearly numbers rather than use fiscal year reports.
- **Weighting.** Decide on a weighting scheme for your factors. If there are no strong prior reasons for differential weighting, decision theory suggests that you should equal weight.
- **Refine the data.** There are too many data available. The key is to choose wisely the data used for the quantitative model.

Appendix B: Cutting through the hype

This material is excerpted from *Analysts, Lies, and Statistics: Cutting through the Hype in Corporate Earnings Announcements* by Brian Bruce and Mark T. Bradshaw with permission from the authors.

The role of analysts

A reasonable investor might ask, "What role do analysts serve? Why can't we get rid of them? At the very least, let's replace them with independent research firms and not rely on analysts tied to brokerage firms." In this Appendix we will show the critical function that analysts play in the flow of information from companies to investors.

Buy and sell recommendations

Recently, analyst recommendations have been subject to much scrutiny. The best place to start looking at those recommendations is at the overall recommendation from analysts. Each analyst issues a strong buy, buy, hold, sell or strong sell recommendation for each stock that they follow. What did each of three leading compilers of earnings estimate data show with their data recently?

Thompson Financial/First Call aggregated these recommendations in July of 2001 and found that almost 50% of all recommendations are buy while less than 1% were sell. A similar study done by Zacks Investment Research of over 8000 recommendations of stocks in the S&P 500 showed that only 29 were sells or less than one-half of 1%. This compared to 214 strong buy recommendations.

The third firm I/B/E/S had their data analyzed in a study by Li (2002) over time. It showed startling consistency across 7 years and nearly a quarter million recommendations.

IBES rating	Strong buy	2	3	4	Sell	Total recommendations
1994	25%	33%	37%	2%	3%	29,521
1995	27	32	36	2	3	30,854
1996	30	33	32	2	2	29,734
1997	31	37	29	1	2	30,350
1998	29	39	30	1	1	35,445
1999	30	40	28	2	1	37,318
2000	31	40	27	1	1	32,663
Average	29%	36%	32%	2%	2%	

(Source: Li, X., 2002. Career Concerns of Analysts: Compensation, Termination and Performance. Vanderbilt University Working Paper.)

This pattern cannot appear by chance. Consistently averaging 2% of all recommendations as sells is not because only 2% of all companies followed are worthy of that recommendation. What causes analysts to have such a significant bias in their recommendations?

The analyst cycle and the critical role of analysts

To understand analyst recommendations, you first must understand the analyst cycle. This cycle is a description of all the forces that act on analysts in their making a recommendation. The first part is the source of much information to an analyst: company management. Company management provides financial projections about future earnings and allows the analyst to discuss the firm's prospects. In this part of the relationship, the analyst is a non-paying client of the company.

There is a second part to the relationship between company and analyst. Many analysts work for firms that are investment banks. Investment banks market to companies to do the companies' investment banking business like issuing bonds or a new class of stock for the company. The relationship now may be that the company is the client to the analyst and his firm. Since the analyst works for the firm, he must not get in the way of the investment banking marketing effort and, in fact, may be asked to help in that effort.

The next relationship is that of the analyst to the investor. The analyst provides the investor with critical information about a security that may be difficult to obtain by the investor. In return, the analyst needs the investor to trade with the analyst's firm in order for his/her firm to "get paid." Many times in a portfolio manager's career does he or she get a call from an analyst asking if the portfolio manager values the information that the analyst sends. If the portfolio manager answers yes, the analyst will generally ask for a certain level of trading commissions to flow to his/her firm. Many analysts are judged based on the amount of trading flow they bring into a firm.

Finally is the link back to the company. The investor will act on the information provided by the analyst (along with other information). This will affect the price, which is of great concern to company management. As stock options became more prevalent in the 1990s, the concern of senior management turned from earning a large cash bonus to getting lots of stock options and maximizing their value. This causes senior management of a company to be very concerned about what investors think about the company.

The changing nature of analyst estimates

Over the years, it has been the job of CFOs of major corporations to tweak the books in order to make earnings appear more stable than they really are. They did this because they believed that investors would reward them for predictability. Then came the internet mania and CFOs stretched the envelope even further in trying to show good results to investors. So how do companies smooth out their earnings? Firms that issue credit can report higher earnings by adjusting their default rates on loans to levels that are too low, which pushes up earnings. Once the company is doing better, the default rate can be pushed up to bring earnings down. These actions in combination create a smoothed earnings pattern. Likewise, a company can push product out to dealers and distributors and book the revenue, even if the merchandise can be returned at a later date, bringing profits up. Later, when revenues have improved, the returns can be booked.

All of the above manipulations can occur within Generally Accepted Accounting Principles (GAAP). These are the numbers created by a firm's auditors and reported to the Securities & Exchange Commission. However, the 1990s popularized a new set of earnings numbers, the pro-forma earnings. These numbers are not regulated like GAAP earnings and allow firms to exclude such basic costs as marketing and interest. One famous pro-forma story is a firm who repainted their fleet of vehicles on a regular schedule. After deciding to paint the vehicles before their schedule date, the firm excluded the cost of painting, claiming that since it wasn't scheduled it was an extraordinary item and should not be included as an expense in their pro-forma earnings numbers.

Pro-forma has become such a fixture in the press that it was the subject of a column by Rob Walker on cnbc.com. An excerpt is illuminating:

PRO FORMA literally means "for the sake of form," but the Wall Street Journal sheds light on what the phrase means to corporations in America when it explains that "a growing number present their earnings on a 'pro forma' basis, 'as if' certain expenses didn't exist." This is not a scandalous idea; it's a delightful one.

On a pro forma basis, I'm having an outstanding year. In calendar year 2002 I've gone to the gym on a regular basis and expect this trend to continue and to have a material impact on my health going forward. Year-to-date, my health has improved by a solid 15% on an annualized basis.

BETWEEN THE LINES

These results do not reflect certain items. Loss of good health and potential mortality stemming from 62 consecutive quarters of above-plan intake of assorted spirits, tobacco, and other substances reliant on mouth-to-lung delivery systems, and miscellaneous off-book chemical and pharmaceutical substances, are addressed in a one-time write-down. Results also include the application of "good will" regarding those days, and in some cases weeks, when actual gym attendance was negatively impacted or curtailed by visits to the racetrack, where I ate oysters and drank Budweiser.

Finally, a recent post-workout lunch of a 22-oz, bone-in rib steak at Smith & Wollensky and three shots of bourbon is treated here as a non-recurring expense. I'll never do that again! I encourage you to focus on these pro forma results as a truer portrait of the state of my health than "traditional measures," which suggest that I have been dead for at least a year.

The problems with pro-forma earnings have led the SEC to issue a warning to companies to stop using pro-forma earnings. Pro-forma earnings "can make it hard for investors to compare an issuer's financial information with other reporting periods and with other companies," the SEC wrote. The SEC warned investors to be especially careful looking at reports that contain alternative calculations of financial results, leave out non-recurring transactions, and vary widely from GAAP results.

Effect of pro-forma versus GAAP earnings on the investor

The current gap between pro-forma and GAAP earnings are the widest in history. In, fact Standard & Poor's and First Call, both using pro-forma earnings, still estimated that earnings fell by 32% versus 17% in 2001 based mainly on how special items were treated. This caused a valuation difference that is significant. In looking at the price/earnings ratio of the S&P 500, it was approximately 36 using GAAP earnings, 24 using S&P earnings and 22 using First Call earnings. Looking at the chart below you can see how clearly the gap has widened between GAAP and pro-forma earnings for the S&P 500.

An exhaustive report on the subject by Keon (2001) looked at the differences. First, he found that a key difference was whether the ratio was calculated based on trailing or estimated earnings. Another difference was the way pro-forma earnings were calculated. Reported earnings "could be whatever the company could convince analysts were correct" according to Keon, a former executive at I/B/E/S. He speculates that when the gaps began they were driven by two changes in corporate practices: the merger and acquisition boom and the re-structuring movement. Due to a need to show the results from an acquisition or to deal with poor performance discontinued, many companies sold or cut back on marginal operations, thereby taking a one-time charge against earnings. By the 1990s companies like General Motors were taking charges due to how pension liabilities were accounted for. Since there was no change in the actual liability, companies excluded these charges from earnings. By the late 1990s internet firms had taken this practice to extremes, excluding marketing costs, shipping costs, and other normal expenses associated with doing business.

This has caused investors to push analysts to take a deeper look at pro forma earnings. In early 2002, Merrill Lynch told its analysts to use a variety of methods to judge financial performance rather than relying on pro forma earnings when reporting on a company. In an internal memo, Merrill is adopting in its research "the use of broad measures beyond pro-forma earnings to evaluate a company's quality of earnings with the objective of establishing an enhanced standard of accountability and transparency for our clients." The goal is to use the tougher GAAP standards more rigorously in evaluating firms.

Earnings surprise

This section will focus on the topic of earnings surprise. What is earnings surprise? It is an earnings report that differs from what analysts were expecting. Earnings surprise often causes a substantial movement in the stock's price. Parts of the above description came from a web-based investment site. It shows how common the ideas of earnings surprise have become. In the 1960s, the concept of earnings surprise was limited to a few academics doing research on an effect that wasn't known to many sophisticated investors.

History

The relationship between corporate earnings information and stock prices has been an active area of financial research since the 1960s. The origins of this research can be traced to the notion of stock market efficiency, which implies that all publicly available information should rapidly get reflected in stock prices in an unbiased manner. Because of this security prices should quickly react to earnings numbers when they are released. The magnitude and direction of the market reaction should be related to the degree to which the information contained in earnings disclosures is new (unexpected). In an early study on this effect, Ball and Brown were able to document a significant pre-earnings announcement drift in the stock prices of the companies in their sample. Fig. 2.1 shows that for two measures of unexpected earnings (variable 1: net income and variable 2: EPS), this drift was positive for companies that reported higher earnings than expected (an excess return of about 7% over the 12 months preceding the announcement), and negative for companies whose earnings came in below expectations (an approximate −9.5% excess return over the same period). Furthermore,

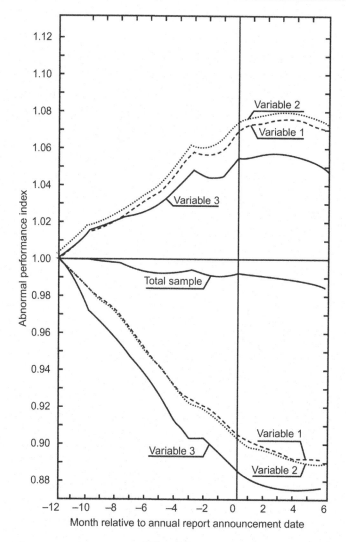

Fig. 2.1

Abnormal performance indexes for various portfolios. *Reproduced with permission from the Journal of Accounting Research.*

companies that had the largest earnings deviations from the prior year (i.e., the biggest surprises) experienced the greatest reaction.

Two features of Fig. 2.1 deserve further comment. First, consistent with the thesis of informational efficiency of the stock market, Ball and Brown found that about 85–90% of the market reaction to earnings announcements occurred in the months preceding the announcement and only 10–15% during the announcement month itself. This is consistent with the existence of analysts whose forecasts and forecast revisions cause prices to continuously move up (down) during the year, in accord with favorable (unfavorable) news. Subsequent studies obtained even stronger results. Brown, Griffin, Hagerman and Zmijewski (1987) attributed this improvement to the fact that analysts' forecasts are better predictors of actual earnings than mechanical forecasts of the type used by Ball and Brown because they are likely to incorporate the more timely and broader sources of information typically available to market participants. Their work led to the widespread use of analysts' forecasts as proxies for market expectations. The availability of large historical databases of analysts' forecasts in electronic form and readily accessible online updates to such data served to further popularize the use of analysts' forecasts in investment research and practice.

The second noteworthy aspect of Fig. 2.1 is that the market reaction to positive and negative earnings surprises is not symmetric. Firms whose reported earnings fall below expectations appear to experience a larger negative reaction before, during and after the month of the earnings announcement than those that surprise on the upside.

Finally, as Fig. 2.1 indicates, excess returns associated with extreme earnings surprises seemed to persist for several months after the earnings report. This implies that abnormal returns could be earned by forming portfolios based on the sign and magnitude of earnings surprises. This observation led to the use of standardized unexpected earnings (SUE) scores in stock valuation. We discuss SUE scores in the next section in context of our discussion of earnings surprise measurement.

Measurement issues

As mentioned above, one key component in measuring the earnings surprise for a company is the analyst's forecast of earnings for the company. Unless the company is very small, it is likely to be covered by more than one analyst, and earnings forecasts issued by different analysts for the same company and fiscal period may differ. A conventional approach to incorporating the divergent views of multiple analysts is to construct a consensus forecast, such as a mean (or median) of all currently available forecasts. If one believes that each individual analysts' forecast of earnings measures the company's actual earnings with some error, but that these errors are idiosyncratic across analysts, this approach has the merit of reducing the error (noise) inherent in the individual forecasts.

Stock returns from an earnings surprise strategy depend on variation in the magnitude and direction of the surprises. The magnitude of the surprise cannot be measured in purely monetary terms, since the impact of an actual earnings report of 10 cents a share by a company for which the mean analyst expectation was five cents (a 100% surprise) is likely to be much greater than the case where the analysts' forecast was one dollar and the company reported actual earnings of $1.05 per share (a 5% surprise). Note that in both cases, the actual reported earnings beat expectations by the same amount (5 cents per share). The example illustrates the need to account for differences in scale when studying the relation between earnings surprises and stock prices.

The earnings surprise number can be normalized by a variety of deflators, such as the actual or forecast earnings, as indicated in the above example. One problem with these approaches is that they tend to break down when the actual (or forecast) earnings are negative. An alternative is to use the absolute value of the actual or forecast earnings instead. Even so, difficulties can arise in cases where the earnings number used for scaling is very small. Deflators close to zero magnify the actual surprise, leading to large cross-sectional variations that are unrelated to significant differences between expectations and the actual outcomes. In such cases, the stock price at the time of the forecast is often used as a deflator.

The above discussion has focused on operational factors that can affect the robustness of earnings surprise measures. However, when constructing such measures, it is equally important to consider the reliability of the consensus earnings forecasts. The market reacts to a company's earnings announcement because it triggers a revision of beliefs about the company's future (e.g., its ability to grow or pay a certain stream of dividends). The extent of this revision depends on the strength (consistency) of investors' preannouncement views about a particular earnings outcome. If the market is fairly certain about what the earnings for a company are likely to be, an earnings announcement that deviates from that expectation constitutes unambiguously good (or bad) news, and the resulting price reaction is likely to be sharp and swift. On the other hand, if there is considerable uncertainty about the earnings outcome, the announcement of earnings primarily serves to dispel uncertainty about future outcomes. A widely accepted measure of earnings surprise that incorporates this notion is the standardized unexpected earnings or SUE score proposed by Latane and Jones (1977). The SUE score is the difference between the actual earnings and expected earnings deflated by a measure of uncertainty in the earnings forecast. To calculate a stock's SUE, three items of data are needed: the company's latest reported earnings, the last consensus earnings estimate before the release of the actual earnings, and the standard deviation of the individual analysts' forecasts that make up the consensus. The SUE can then be calculated as:

$$SUE = \frac{\text{Actual earnings} - \text{Consensus earnings forecast}}{\text{Standard deviation of analysts' forecasts}}$$

The more extreme the value of the resulting number, the more likely it is that the company's earnings announcement will have a significant effect on its share price. The intuition underlying the SUE score follows from our earlier observation that the market reaction to the surprise associated with an earnings announcement depends not only on the magnitude of the surprise (captured in the numerator of the calculation), but also on the uncertainty inherent in the forecast of expected earnings. The denominator of the SUE score captures this uncertainty by directly gauging the extent to which analysts disagree about the earnings outcome for a company. However, as with other earnings surprise measures, caution needs to be exercised in the computation of SUE scores in cases where sufficient data is not available for computation. For small companies, the number of analysts following the company may be small (often one or two), making it difficult or impossible to compute the standard deviation of forecasts.

Clearly, the benefits of using any particular deflator are debatable, and much depends on one's view of what drives the stock price reaction to earnings surprises and the nature of the data available. If the time series process underlying earnings is considered stable, focusing on large percentage changes will capture the stock market effects of unusual earnings events. On the other hand, price deflation is appealing since it directly associates earnings changes with the valuation impact of those changes. SUE scores are intuitively pleasing because they allow us to incorporate not only the effect of extraordinary earnings reports, but also the characteristics of the forecasts themselves into the surprise metric in a logical fashion. This reason and the fact that SUE was the first published indicator of surprise have made the SUE scores the most commonly used measure of earnings surprise.

Earning abnormal returns from earnings surprises

In our discussion of the Ball and Brown (1968) study, we alluded briefly to the nature of the market reaction to earnings surprises around the time of the earnings announcement. In a pattern confirmed by several independent academic studies, Fig. 2.1 (above) indicated that stocks with the largest positive (negative) surprises move higher (lower) before the earnings announcement, jump (drop) dramatically during the report week and then continue to drift up (down) during subsequent weeks. The pattern of market reaction to earnings surprises during and before the announcement month confirms our intuition that as the uncertainty about future earnings is gradually resolved during the year, the good or bad news should manifest itself in stock prices via continual revisions of forecasts by analysts, interim corporate disclosures, and leakage of information into the market through the information search activities of other market participants. However, the post-announcement reaction is counter-intuitive in that after earnings have been publicly announced, the information in the earnings release should be rapidly incorporated into market prices in an unbiased fashion, rather than continuing to drift up or down over a prolonged period. In the early 1970s some researchers examined this post-announcement drift in greater detail, noting that it was contrary to the notion of market efficiency. The post announcement drift persisted well into the 1990s and was subjected to rigorous academic research because it contradicted the notion of market efficiency. The anomaly could not be explained even after controlling for risk, size and a variety of other factors that could affect stock returns, and with investors eyeing potential short-term gains from trading on earnings surprises, SUE scores soon became a standard component of stock valuation models. SUE scores performed well from 1987 to 1998, displaying correlations of as much as 30% with 1-month ahead stock returns and predicting the direction of subsequent stock price movements correctly over 83% of the time. Results for longer holding periods (2 or 3 months) were similar and enabled investors to earn excess returns of 4–5%. However, of late the ability of SUE scores to forecast 1 month ahead returns has begun to diminish. For example, in 1999, the correlation between the two was negative for six out of 12 months. To a large extent, this should have been expected, for discovery of information inevitably leads to its reflection in market prices. Indeed, what was surprising was the fact that the effect persisted for so long after its discovery and exploitation. However, two additional factors have contributed to the decline in the effectiveness of SUE scores: (1) the corruption of consensus estimates as a measure of market expectations over this period; and (2) the manipulation of reported earnings by corporate management, subjects to which we shall return at the end of this chapter.

Factors affecting the strength of the earnings surprise-stock return relationship

The relationship between SUE scores and stock returns at and after the earnings announcement depends not only on the magnitude and direction of the reported surprise but also on the characteristics of the reporting companies. Companies with low P/E multiples (value stocks) tend to show greater reaction on the upside when the earnings surprise is positive, while those with high P/E ratios (growth stocks) experience greater negative fallout from an earnings report that disappoints. This is consistent with Stickel (1998) who finds that stocks with higher analyst ratings tend to have higher P/E ratios. The reasons for this phenomenon may be traced back to the earnings expectations life cycle discussed earlier. Recall that in the late part of the cycle, as the estimate revisions for positive surprise stocks turn positive, momentum investors pile into these stocks, causing their P/E ratios to go up. When expectations rise to unrealistic levels, subsequent negative surprises "torpedo" these very same growth stocks, causing them to "sink" rapidly at the time of the earnings announcement. Dreman suggests that the above relationship between P/E ratios and market reaction to earnings surprises can be used to earn abnormal returns, as depicted in the chart below:

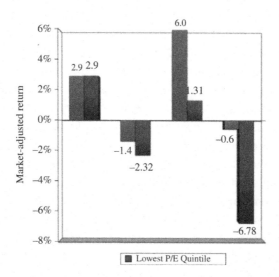

Another factor that affects this relationship is firm size. Bhushan (1989), has shown that smaller firms tend to have fewer analysts following their stock. If analysts are viewed as information intermediaries whose forecasting activities serve to incorporate value-relevant information into market prices, one would expect smaller firm size (lower analyst following) to be associated with larger earnings surprises. This is because in the case of smaller companies, less information is likely to have been impounded into its stock price prior to its earnings announcement. The quantity and quality of predisclosure information increase, earnings surprises, and the market's reaction to them, is smaller. They also report that the speed of stock prices adjustment following earnings surprises is greater when the quality and quantity of analysts' forecasts is high. There is an inverse relationship between the degree of prominence of a firm (as measured by the amount of coverage it receives in the financial press) and the market reaction to its earnings announcements. However, firm size can proxy for a variety of factors, such as risk, therefore any conclusions should be drawn with caution. For example, the level of institutional shareholding in a firm has been shown to vary directly with firm size.

Observed earnings distributions

Overall, the search for evidence of earnings management around specific corporate events and within specific accounts has resulted in somewhat mixed or weak evidence that managers manipulate earnings, with much of the evidence limited to a particular industry (e.g., banks) or corporate event (e.g., acquisition). Thus, one possible reason why evidence is somewhat mixed is that most of the studies focus on a small number of firms, which results in earnings management tests that have low power. In response to this, researchers have begun to look not at specific accounts or corporate events, but at overall distributions of earnings across large numbers of firms. By considering large numbers of firms, researchers are able to appeal to the "law of large numbers" that suggests that many distributions tend to be normal (i.e., the bell-curve).

In these studies of earnings distributions, it is hypothesized that managers dislike reporting negative earnings, and will avoid reporting negative earnings if they have the opportunity to exercise discretion and bump earnings up to positive earnings. Also, it is hypothesized that managers would prefer to exercise discretion to manipulate earnings upwards to avoid a decrease in reported earnings from an earlier fiscal quarter or year.

As an example of the results in these studies, we constructed the graph below. It plots the distribution of earnings before extraordinary items scaled by market value for all firms from 1976 to 2000. The figure presents the frequencies of reported earnings numbers (scaled by market value) for intervals of width 0.005 across the range −0.25 to +10.35. The overall shape of the distribution of earnings reflects the bell-curve that characterizes normal distributions. However, around earnings of zero, there is an unexplained kink in the distribution. There are fewer than expected frequencies of earnings just below zero, and more than expected frequencies of earnings just above zero. It appears that, barring some inexplicable property of earnings, managers who would have reported just slightly negative earnings intervened in the accounting process to produce earnings figures that were just above zero.

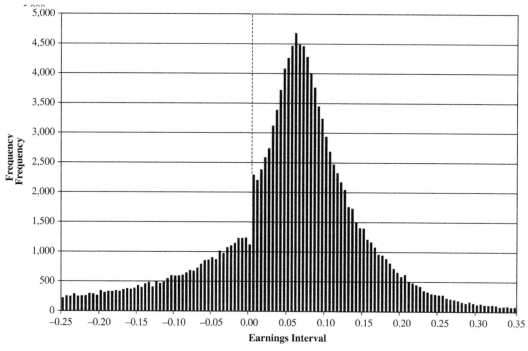

(Source: Compustat.)

Summary

It is a widely held belief that managers manipulate accounting earnings. These beliefs underlie a large number of academic studies where researchers attempt to uncover evidence of earnings management. While there are a number of studies that provide evidence that is consistent with earnings management, those results are sometimes sensitive to the way earnings management is measured. Although many studies interpret their analysis as evidence of earnings management, a fair number lack evidence of earnings management. The closest evidence we have to a "smoking gun" that earnings are managed is the analysis of overall distributions of earnings, which provide compelling evidence that managers avoid reporting slightly negative earnings or slightly decreasing earnings. This area remains interesting because of the unyielding beliefs that managers freely manipulate earnings.

Accruals versus cash flows

How well does accrual accounting accomplish the objective of providing a better summary measure of performance than cash flows? Dechow (1994) studied the relative performance of cash flows and earnings at explaining stock returns. She first showed that as you lengthen the measurement interval, say several years, earnings and cash flows become more similar in their ability to measure a company's performance, i.e., explain stock returns. This makes sense, because over the life of a firm, the total earnings will equal the total cash flows. The key to her findings, however, is the analysis of earnings over shorter intervals, such as quarterly and annual earnings. For the shorter intervals, she shows that earnings dominate cash flows in their ability to explain stock returns. She concludes:

> *"[The results] demonstrate that cash flows are not a poor measure of firm performance per se. In steady-state firms, where the magnitude of accruals is small and cash flows and earnings are most similar, cash flows are a relatively useful measure of firm performance. However, when the magnitude of accruals increases, indicating that the firm has large changes in its operating, investment, and financing activities, cash flows suffer more severely from timing and matching problems. Therefore, as accruals increase in magnitude net cash flows' association with stock returns declines. Overall, the results are consistent with the hypothesis that accountants accrue revenues and match expenditures to revenues so as to produce a performance measure (earnings) that better reflects firm performance than realized cash flows."*

The evidence is compelling in favor of accrual accounting, and it is consistent with what we observe when we see analysts predominantly forecasting earnings rather than cash flows.

Accounting numbers as a measure of performance

Even though accrual accounting leads to financial reports that provide better summary information than would a cash-flow based report, accruals can be too much of a good thing. That is, rather than accruals providing enhanced earnings figures, they do the opposite.

At the Harvard Business School, the core accounting class emphasizes that the best accounting can do is provide a picture of a company's true economics, but that discretion available in accounting rules makes accounting numbers fuzzy. As a heuristic for communicating this idea in class, the following representative formula is used.

$$\text{Accounting numbers} = \text{Economic substance} + \text{Measurement error} + \text{Bias}$$

The formula is suggestive rather than an attempt to partition accounting numbers into separate quantities. Accounting numbers constitute any of the numbers from any of the financial statements, but the most common number is earnings. Economic Substance is what accountants are trying to measure. For example, did a company generate value for its investors? Clearly, accountants would prefer that all Accounting Numbers reflect Economic Substance.

However, because accrual accounting requires that estimates be made (e.g., the estimated life of a machine, its expected salvage value, etc.), the resulting accounting numbers will often be wrong, reflecting misestimates. This "noise" in the Accounting Numbers is labeled Measurement Error. Some measurement is expected and tolerable, but the hope is that overestimates from one period will be offset by small underestimates from another period, leading to just a small amount of Measurement Error.

Unfortunately, because managers are aware that accountants and financial statement users understand and tolerate some measurement error, they turn this to their advantage. Rather than provide estimates that increase the correspondence between Accounting Numbers and Economic Substance, dubious managers with incentives to overstate Accounting Numbers can infuse Bias into those numbers. For example, managers can intentionally overestimate the useful lives of machinery, resulting in lower periodic depreciation charges.

This bias cannot go on forever, because of the disciplined nature of double-entry accrual accounting. If a manager intentionally overstated the useful life of a machine, then the lower depreciation expense would result in an asset that is likely overstated. When the firm sells or disposes of the asset, it will likely record a loss on the sale or disposal. Such a loss is the "catch-up" for the under-depreciation that resulted from the manager's intentional bias.

Another source of bias is actually built into accounting by accountants themselves. Despite the fact that the FASB does not actively seek conservative accounting methods, most of the rules that it issues are inherently biased toward being conservative (e.g., recognizing unrealized losses but not unrealized gains). Thus, the conservative nature of accounting rules serves as an additional source of bias. If we generally believe that managers have incentives to bias accounting numbers upwards, then the conservative nature of accounting rules provides some offset.

Accruals are sometimes not so good

The subjective nature of accruals recorded by managers makes them a dangerous thing. If managers are upstanding and transparent, then accruals enhance the financial statements' ability to convey the economic condition and performance of the firm. If, however, managers have less than noble objectives, then accruals are an easy to use tool to artificially modify the financial reports in some desired direction (usually up). We will see a detailed discussion of this in the next chapter.

By way of introduction, in this chapter we want to simply visit accounting accruals from the perspective of their time-series behavior. It is useful to consider a simple example to appreciate further how accruals work.

Consider a simple sale of $100,000 to be booked by a company. A customer places an order for products, and the company ships them to the customer. The customer receives them, and agrees to pay for the products within 30 days. Even though the accountant sees no cash coming in the door, the financial statements are nevertheless adjusted to reflect this transaction. In other words, accrual accounting is employed to better reflect the economic substance of the sale of products to a customer.

The accountant would record an account receivable asset for the amount that the customer owes the company, and would also go ahead and recognize the sales revenue for the sale of the products. The increase in the accounts receivable asset goes on the balance sheet and will stay there until the customer pays off their account.

Suppose further that nothing else happened during this year. The increase in accounts receivable represents an "income increasing" accrual. Nothing is wrong with income-increasing accruals per se. However, a small dose of healthy skepticism will trigger a concern that unscrupulous managers might abuse their discretion. In a real company, there is not just one sales transaction per year, but often thousands. With all the transactions, what is to keep a manager from bumping up the amount recorded as sales by some artificial amount? Auditors come in at the end of the year and spot check transactions recorded by managers, but they cannot view all transactions. As it turns out, most of the Accounting Enforcement Actions issued by the Securities and Exchange Commission, in which companies are admonished for fraudulent accounting, reveal that fictitious or overstatement of sales is usually the violation.

Note that we are not arguing that all managers "bump up" the amount of revenues beyond that which is justified. Instead, we wish to provide a simple exposition of how accruals impose discipline on managers through the reversing process. To that end, we are introducing the possibility that accruals might be recorded at the wrong amounts initially, but that this will work its way back out of the accounting system eventually.

To provide a contrasting example to the account receivable accrual, suppose also that the company discussed above rewards its sales staff with paid vacations in the year following a big sale, and that the sales agent who made the $100,000 sale gets vacation time during which the company will pay her $1000. The company would record the cost of this paid vacation in the current period during which the sale was recorded. This would require the company to record an expense and a corresponding accrued vacation liability. This is an example of an "income decreasing" accrual.

Neither the income increasing nor the income decreasing accruals can continue indefinitely. They eventually reverse when the company either collects the account receivable or pays the employee her vacation time. However, over short periods of time, it should be clear that managers could adjust too much for income increasing accruals and too little for income decreasing accruals.

Now back to the sales example. Suppose that the manager decided to record the sale at $120,000 rather than $100,000. Eventually, the customer will pay but will only pay what was invoiced to them—$100,000. This leaves an uncollectible $20,000 account receivable on the books. Sooner or later, the manager will have to clean out that receivable. To make things simple, suppose that when the manager writes off the bogus account receivable they have to record some kind of "loss." The loss decreases earnings in the period recorded. And, the amount of the loss is exactly equal to the amount by which sales were initially "overbooked." It is important to again restate that we do not believe or mean to imply that the overbooking of revenues or the underbooking of expenses is routine.

Thus, if a manager overbooked revenue in the first year leading to an overstatement of income in that year, the undoing of that overbooked revenue would come in the second year when the useless account receivable had to be written off. This provides a stylized example of a basic fact: All else equal, income increasing accruals in one period are generally followed by reversals in later periods. Similarly, income decreasing accruals in one period are generally followed by reversals in later periods.

Where to look

How is an investor to keep track of accruals made by managers? Fortunately, the statement of cash flows provides an investor with such information summarized nicely. For example, contrast the two excerpts from the operating section of the cash flow statements of Ebay and E-Trade:

Ebay

	2001	2000	1999
Net income	$90,448,000	$48,294,000	$10,828,000
Depreciation	$89,732,000	$45,191,000	$25,331,000
Adjustments to net income	$113,023,000	$54,245,000	$6,522,000
Changes in accounts receivables	($50,221,000)	($48,862,000)	($28,884,000)
Changes in liabilities	$2,310,000	$42,055,000	$68,103,000
Changes in other operating activities	$6,820,000	($40,775,000)	($15,336,000)
Cash flows from operating activities	$252,112,000	$100,148,000	$66,564,000

E-Trade

	2001	2000	1999
Net income	($241,532,000)	$1,353,000	$19,152,000
Depreciation	$188,268,000	N/A	$97,638,000
Adjustments to net income	($241,495,000)	N/A	($140,719,000)
Changes in accounts receivables	N/A	N/A	($3,586,689,000)
Changes in liabilities	$20,738,000	N/A	$3,306,275,000
Changes in other operating activities	$19,327,000	N/A	$165,651,000
Cash flows from operating activities	($254,694,000)	$40,911,000	($138,692,000)

The operating section of the cash flow statement reconciles net income to cash flows from operating activities. The reconciling items reflect accruals recorded under GAAP. For Ebay, the reconciling items indicate a predominance of income-decreasing activities, because the net of the adjustments is positive. In contrast, for 1999 and 2001, the net adjustments for E-trade are negative, indicating that accounting accruals during those years were, on average, income increasing. These two companies are symbolic of an average phenomenon that characterizes the behavior of future earnings conditional on accruals, which is discussed next.

Accruals and earnings behavior

Sloan (1996) investigated the time-series properties of earnings unconditionally, and conditional on the level of accruals embedded in earnings in the base year. He found that extreme earnings that contain a large amount of income increasing accruals tend to revert toward lower levels in the future years at a much quicker rate than extreme earnings unconditionally revert. However, extreme earnings levels that contain a disproportionately low level of income increasing accruals (which is another way of saying the earnings reflect a high level of cash flows), persist for longer periods before reverting.

The following graph was constructed based on net income scaled by total assets (ROA). We ranked firms into deciles according to ROA, then tracked ROA in the years prior to and after the ranking period.

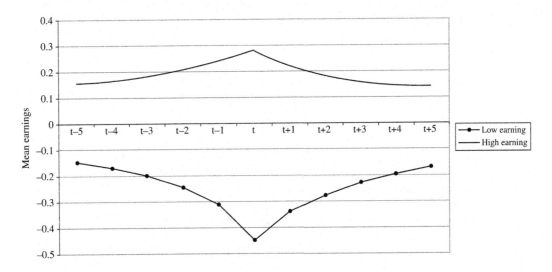

The figure demonstrates the well-known mean reversion in earnings levels. The next figure was similarly constructed and tracks the level of ROA as well. However, in period $t = 0$, the ranking variable was accruals scaled by total assets, not net income scaled by total assets.

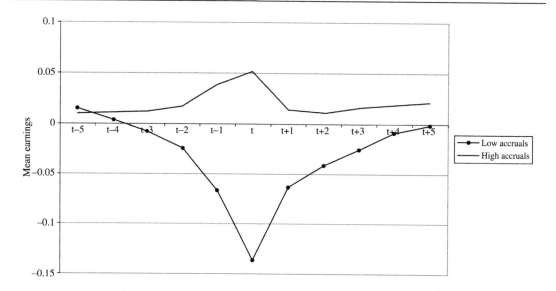

Clearly, the rate of mean reversion in earnings for extreme levels of accruals is much greater. This is a manifestation of the reversing nature of accounting accruals discussed in the stylized examples earlier.

Another way to construct the figure is to initially rank on the level of cash flows scaled by assets and track the mean reversion in levels of earnings.

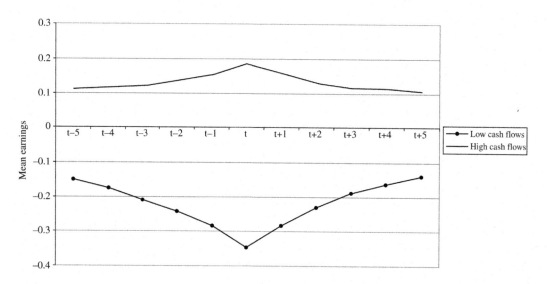

This figure provides complementary evidence to the second figure. However, when extreme levels of earnings are largely supported by underlying cash flows, the earnings levels, although reverting on average, tend to revert at a much slower rate than earnings that largely reflect accounting accruals.

Sloan (1996) documented that the stock market apparently does not appreciate these patterns in earnings. The following data covers the period 1988–1998 and reflects annual raw returns, value-weighted market adjusted returns, and size-decile adjusted returns for the 3 years subsequent to a portfolio formation year, across deciles formed on the basis of the level of accruals (e.g., as in the second figure above).

Rank	Raw returns			Market-Adj. returns			Size-Adj. returns		
	$t+1$	$t+2$	$t+3$	$t+1$	$t+2$	$t+3$	$t+1$	$t+2$	$t+3$
Low	0.203	0.249	0.217	0.037	0.076	0.038	0.048	0.073	0.025
2	0.211	0.229	0.235	0.049	0.060	0.060	0.064	0.065	0.048
3	0.183	0.185	0.227	0.022	0.018	0.056	0.038	0.021	0.049
4	0.161	0.165	0.187	−0.002	0.000	0.019	0.010	0.006	0.017
5	0.141	0.158	0.176	−0.019	−0.009	0.007	−0.002	−0.001	0.004
6	0.154	0.173	0.153	−0.006	0.006	−0.018	0.013	0.017	−0.025
7	0.152	0.175	0.213	−0.009	0.008	0.038	0.011	0.016	0.036
8	0.146	0.192	0.185	−0.017	0.024	0.012	0.000	0.033	0.010
9	0.117	0.149	0.219	−0.047	−0.017	0.041	−0.031	−0.012	0.033
High	0.080	0.147	0.210	−0.082	−0.023	0.034	−0.063	−0.018	0.025
Nc	35,956	28,608	22,429	35,956	28,608	22,429	35,107	27,951	21,932

The figure replicates the original findings of Sloan. Companies reporting high levels of accruals in a base year realize substantially lower returns in the following 2 years. On the other hand, companies with the lowest levels of accruals realize substantially higher levels of accruals in the subsequent 2 years. Together, these observed patterns in stock returns suggest a market that is either pleasantly or unpleasantly surprised when subsequent earnings either increase (after low and typically income decreasing accruals) or decrease (after high and typically income increasing accruals).

References

Bhushan, R., 1989. Firm characteristics and analyst following. J. Account. Econ. 11 (2–3), 255–274.

Dechow, P.M., 1994. Accounting earnings and cash flows as measures of firm performance: the role of accounting accruals. J. Account. Econ. 18 (1), 3–42.

Keon, 2001. What's the P/E ratio of the S&P 500? Prudential Equity Res.

Li, X., 2002. Career Concerns of Analysts: Compensation, Termination and Performance. Vanderbilt University Working Paper.

Sloan, R.G., 1996. Do stock prices fully reflect information in accruals and cash flows about future earnings? Account. Rev. 71 (3), 289–315. July.

Accruals versus cash flows:

Dechow, P.M., 1994. Accounting earnings and cash flows as measures of firm performance: the role of accounting accruals. J. Account. Econ. 18 (1), 3–42.

Accruals:

Bhushan, R., 1989. Firm characteristics and analyst following. J. Account. Econ. 11 (2–3), 255–274.

Bradshaw, M.T., Richardson, S.A., Sloan, R.G., 2001. Do analysts and auditors use information in accruals? J. Account. Res., 39 (1), 45–74 June.

Sloan, R.G., 1996. Do stock prices fully reflect information in accruals and cash flows about future earnings? Account. Rev. 71 (3), 289–315, July.

The classic paper on this topic was written by Lang Wheeler and included in Brian's earlier book "The Handbook of Corporate Earnings Analysis."

Wheeler, L., 1994. Changes in consensus earnings estimates and their impact on stock returns. Handb. Corp. Earnings Anal.

Morgan Stanley's earnings revisions study is:

Whither Analysts Revisions? December 2001. Global Equity and Derivative Markets Quantitative Strategies.

Other useful papers include:

Angwin, J., Peers, M., November 1, 2001. Cold calls: AOL may be snubbing merrill. Wall Street J.

Bagnoli, M., Beneish, D., Watts, S., 1999. Whisper forecasts of quarterly earnings per share. J. Account. Econ.

Bernstein, R., January 16, 2001. Five-year growth rates haven't budged. Merrill Lynch Quant. Strategy Update.

DeBondt, W., Forbes, W., 1999. Herding in analyst earnings forecasts: evidence from the United Kingdom. Eur. Financ. Manage. 5(2).

DeBondt, W., Thaler, R., May 1990. Do security analysts overreact? Am. Econ. Rev. 80, 52–57. AEA Papers and Proceedings.

Dechow, P., Skinner, D., 2000. Earnings management: reconciling the views of accounting academics, practitioners, and regulators. Account. Horiz. 15(2).

Dreman, D., 1998. Contrarian Investment Strategies: The Next Generation. Simon and Schuster.

Edmonston, P., 2001. Focus on Whisper numbers fades as pundits sidestep the informal targets. Wall Street J. 26, July.

Healy, P.M., Wahlen, J.M., 1999. A review of the earnings management literature and its implications for standard setting. Account. Horiz. 13(4).

Jha, V., Mozes, H., April 2001. Forecasting Changes in Consensus Earnings Estimates, Working Paper.

Keon, 2001. What's the P/E ratio of the S&P 500? Prudential Equity Res.

Li, X., 2002. Career Concerns of Analysts: Compensation, Termination and Performance. Vanderbilt University Working Paper.

Lauricella, T., September 4, 2001. Analyst reports pressures of employer's trading. Wall Street J.

Schipper, K., 1989. Commentary on earnings management. Account. Horiz. 3(4).

Williams, N., February 21, 2002. The Quality and Quantity of Earnings: Both are Cyclical. Goldman Sachs Global Portfolio Strategy.

In this Appendix, we limited our definition of earnings management to what we termed "classical" earnings management. We omitted discussion of several related areas such as fraud, accounting choices, and operating decisions. The following papers and their included references address fraud through an analysis of Accounting and Auditing Enforcement Releases by the SEC.

Beneish, M.D., 1999. Incentives and penalties related to earnings overstatements that violate GAAP. Account. Rev. 74 (4), 425–457.

Bonner, S.E., Palmrose, Z.V., Young, S.M., 1998. Fraud type and auditor litigation: an analysis of SEC accounting and auditing enforcement releases. Account. Rev. 73 (4), 503–532.

Dechow, P., Sloan, R.G., Sweeney, A.P., Causes and consequences of earnings manipulation: an analysis of firms subject to enforcement actions by the SEC Contemp. Account. Res., 13 (1), 1–36.

Feroz, E.H., Park, K., Pastena, V.S., 1991. The financial and market effects of the SEC's accounting and auditing enforcement releases. J. Account. Res. 29 (Suppl), 107–142.

Additionally, the following summary papers discuss the evidence regarding management accounting method choices, and to a lesser extent, operating decisions that impact reported income.

Fields, T.D., Lys, T.Z., Vincent, L., 2001. Empirical research on accounting choice. J. Account. Econ. 31 (1–3), 255–307.

Holthausen, R.W., Leftwich, R.W., 1983. The economic consequences of accounting choice—implications for costly contracting and monitoring. J. Account. Econ. 5 (2), 77–117.

For an analytical model supporting the notion that current shareholders demand earnings management, see:

Dye, R., 1988. Earnings management in an overlapping generations model. J. Account. Res. 26, 195–235.

The Jones model and several of its subsequent modifications may be found in the following papers

Dechow, P.M., Sloan, R.G., Sweeney, A.P., Detecting earnings management Account. Rev., 71 (2), 193–227, April

Jones, J., 1991. Earnings management during import relief investigations. J. Account. Res. 29 (2), 193–228.

The following references are a very limited sampling of studies investigating specific accruals.

Ayers, B.C., Deferred Tax Accounting Under SFAS No. 109: An empirical investigation of its incremental value-relevance relative to APB No. 11. Account. Rev., 73 (2), 195–212.

Beatty, A., Chamberlain, S., Magliolo, J., 1995. Managing financial reports of commercial banks: the influence of taxes, regulatory capital and earnings. J. Account. Res. 33 (2), 231–261. Autumn.

Beaver, W.H., Engel, E.E., 1996. Discretionary behavior with respect to allowances for loan losses and the behavior of security prices. J. Account. Econ. 22 (1–3), 177–206. August–December.

Elliott, J.A., Hanna, J.D., 1996. Repeated accounting write-offs and the information content of earnings. J. Account. Res. 34, 135–155.

Francis, J., Hanna, J.D., Vincent, L., 1996. Causes and effects of discretionary asset write-offs. J. Account. Res. 34, 117–134.

Miller, G.S., and D.J. Skinner, Determinants of the valuation allowances for deferred tax assets under SFAS No. 109. Account. Rev., 73 (2), 213–233.

Petroni, K.R., 1992. Optimistic reporting in the property casualty insurance industry. J. Account. Econ. 15, 485–508.

Petroni, K.R., Ryan, S.G., Wahlen, J.M., 2000. Discretionary and non-discretionary revisions of loss reserves by property-casualty insurers: differential implications for future profitability, risk and market value. Rev. Account. Stud. 5, 95–125.

These studies examine the manipulation of earnings in order to affect compensation:

Gaver, J., Gaver, K., Austin, J., 1995. Additional evidence on bonus plans and income management. J. Account. Econ. 18, 3–28.

Guidry, F., Leone, A., Rock, S., 1999. Earnings-based bonus plans and earnings management by business unit managers. J. Account. Econ. 26, 113–142.

Healy, P., 1985. The effect of bonus schemes on accounting decisions. J. Account. Econ. 7, 85–107.

See the following studies for examinations of earnings management to avoid debt covenant violations:

DeFond, M.L., Jiambalvo, J., 1994. Debt covenant effects and the manipulation of accruals. J. Account. Econ. 17, 145–176.

Healy, P., Palepu, K.G., 1990. Effectiveness of accounting-based dividend covenants. J. Account. Econ. 12 (1–3), 97–124.

Incentives and results surrounding management buyouts are found in these papers:

DeAngelo, L. Accounting numbers as market valuation substitutes: a study of management buyouts of public stockholders. Account. Rev., 41, 400–420.

Perry, S.E., Williams, T.H., 1994. Earnings management preceding management buyout offers. J. Account. Econ. 18 (2), 157–180.

Stock-for-stock acquisitions and the existence of earnings management are addressed in the following papers:

Erickson, M., Wang S., Earnings management by acquiring firms in stock for stock mergers. J. Account. Econ., 27 (2), 149–176.

To read more about the anomalous distributions of earnings and earnings changes, see the following papers:

Burgstahler, D., Dichev I., Earnings management to avoid earnings decreases and losses. J. Account. Econ., 24 (1), 99–126.

Degeorge, F., Patel, J., Zeckhauser, R., 1999. Earnings management to exceed thresholds. J. Business 72 (1), 1–33.

CHAPTER 3

Investing with exchange traded funds

Student managed investment funds (SMIFs) are experiential learning programs typically located in finance departments of many colleges and universities. Most of these student funds follow a "bottom up" approach to portfolio construction. The bottom-up model focuses on stock selection based on fundamental analysis of a security's intrinsic value relative to the security's market value. Bottom-up student funds are consistent with the emphasis on cash flow projections, financial statement analysis, and valuation models learned in finance courses. This chapter describes an experiential student managed fund that is unique in three respects. First, the portfolio construction follows a true "top-down" analysis. The top-down approach requires students to develop investment strategies based on global macroeconomic and sector themes. These themes direct investment decisions for asset allocations, global region exposure, country exposure, sector exposure, and final ETF selections. Second, exchange traded funds (ETFs) are the only investment vehicles in the portfolio. The ETF is generally regarded as the most significant new financial security of the last three decades. Third, the ETF fund presented in this chapter naturally builds interdisciplinary participation, providing experiential learning beyond the traditional cohort of finance students. The opening sections of this chapter provide background on ETFs and highlight the merits of using ETFs as the investment vehicle in a student managed fund. While this chapter focusses on the use of ETFs within the pedagogical medium of student managed funds, the broader benefits from learning about ETFs will also serve students well. The last portion of the chapter provides examples and details for implementing an ETF fund. In this way we describe the "what" the "why" and the "how" of ETF investing for student funds.

What is so special about ETFs?

Exchange traded funds (ETFs) are a relatively recent addition to the menu of securities available to investors. An ETF share represents a prorated ownership claim on a portfolio of securities, just like a mutual fund, but the ETF trades like a share of stock. An ETF may track a generic index such as the S&P 500 or it can contain a wide variety of underlying investments to include stocks, commodities, bonds, futures, or a mixture of investments. ETF holdings may be domestic, international, or a blend of both. An ETF may hold thousands of securities across different industries or it may be indexed to a specific industry, investment style, or sector. An investor does not need a large amount of funding to achieve diversification with ETFs, since

Student-Managed Investment Funds. https://doi.org/10.1016/B978-0-12-817866-9.00003-0

each holding is already a portfolio. ETFs accommodate investment exposures and access to a wide range of assets that were once only available to large investors.

ETFs evolved from the concept of passive indexing based on the efficient market view that it is better to buy the market than try to beat the market by actively trading. The oldest continuous ETF is the Standard and Poor's Depositary Receipt (S&P 500 SPDR) designed to track the S&P 500 index, which is still a dominant ETF in the market today. Since the creation of the SPDR in the early 1990s, the menu of available ETFs has exploded. In 2017, the research firm ETFGI (https://etfgi.com/) reported that there were 5,024 ETFs trading worldwide. David Nadig, an early and leading proponent of ETFs, predicted that the value of assets in ETFs will reach $12 trillion by 2024, a sum likely to surpass the total assets in mutual funds.[a]

ETFs versus mutual funds

The growth of ETFs is commonly attributed to five characteristics: (1) diversification; (2) low cost; (3) tradability; (4) transparency; and (5) tax efficiency.[b] Although an ETF has similarities to a mutual fund, the mutual fund is more of an investment mule while the ETF is more like an investment thoroughbred. Like the mutual fund, the ETF offers exposure to almost any part of the financial markets and to almost any investment style. Both mutual funds and ETFs can be either passively or actively managed producing expense ratios that vary widely. Since ETFs trade like a share of stock through a broker, there are a number of advantages for ETF investors. An ETF share can be margined, loaned, shorted, or applied to other strategies used by stock investors. Unlike a mutual fund, ETFs trade throughout the day. This provides continuous pricing data upon which to trade and also offers better liquidity. In contrast, mutual funds require intra trading-day orders that transact at after-close prices producing delayed settlement and thus lower liquidity. ETFs also offer transparency in the sense that the holdings of an ETF are easily identified. Daily transparency and ease of arbitrage between an ETF and the underlying holdings means an ETF will trade very close to the net asset value of the securities in the ETF portfolio. Knowing the content of specific ETFs is particularly important when constructing a portfolio of ETFs because redundancy in holdings across ETFs can lower the risk-return efficiency of the portfolio. ETFs are also more tax efficient because they allow investors to manage tax liabilities. With mutual funds, the timing and magnitude of capital-gain distributions is institutionally driven (i.e., market movements in conjunction with regulatory requirements regarding distributions). With an ETF, the timing and magnitude of capital-gain income is completely at the discretion of the investor because, as with a share of stock, the capital gain (loss) on an ETF is only taxable (deductible) when the ETF is sold. Although tax efficiency is an important advantage of ETFs, taxation does not apply in the specific instance of SMIFs since they operate exclusively in a non-profit environment.

---

[a] "Why ETFs?" This is a video narrated by David Nadig under the website tab "ETF University." This video is part of an educational series titled "ETF University" offering more than 50 videos that cover introductory through advanced topics on ETFs. (https://www.etf.com/etf-education-center/etf-university-video-why-etfs).

[b] Extensive discussion of the history and evolution of ETFs is well beyond the purpose of this chapter. For more complete coverage of the topic, see Hill et al. (2015). The monograph is available from the CFA (www.cfapubs.org).

"Smart beta" ETFs use rules as a basis for selecting the underlying investments. For example, an investment style, such as a high dividend yield, defines the rules for selecting the stocks in a high dividend smart beta ETF. Other investment styles, such as small cap growth or momentum, may also be implemented in an ETF. Owning shares in a smart beta ETF allows investors to follow an investment strategy without building the portfolio themselves. The smart beta approach generates performance that is highly correlated with the predetermined set of screening rules that define the investment style, allowing investors to participate in a style of investment without the actual research and transactions associated with individual stock selection. An investment strategy such as style rotation, based on the view that the market rewards different styles at different times, may be implemented at very low costs by simply moving from one smart beta ETF to another that is most in favor at the time.

ETF asset classes and expenses

Exhibit 3.1 presents a hypothetical ETF portfolio that includes all ETF asset classes. The information provided in the exhibit is easily obtained using any of several websites that provide ETF screeners. This portfolio is an example designed to present a few descriptive details about ETFs; it is not the product of the analysis described later in the chapter. Exhibit 3.1 illustrates that the ETF universe covers the full range of asset classes that one could include in a portfolio, although the number of ETFs within a particular asset class varies considerably. For example, investors looking for U.S. equity can choose from almost 900 ETFs. The menu for U.S. fixed-income exposure contains more than 300 ETFs. In contrast, there are roughly 60 ETFs that offer exposure to alternatives assets or asset allocation strategies. The order in which the asset classes appear in Exhibit 3.1 generally reflects how the number of ETFs declines by asset class.

Exhibit 3.1 also reports the expense ratios for specific ETFs. The low-cost appeal of ETFs is clearly evidenced by the fee for the Vanguard S&P 500 (VOO) of just three basis points. For example, consider a portfolio that equally weights U.S. and international equity and fixed income. These asset classes are represented by the first four ETFs listed in Exhibit 3.1. Equal stakes in the four ETFs would incur a total portfolio expense of less than 15 basis points. However, the low-cost virtue of the ETF wanes considerably for asset classes beyond equity and fixed-income. This trend is not surprising since these assets classes move increasingly from passive to active management and tend to be more volatile, thus losing some of the operational efficiency achieved in a pure index fund. Also note how the asset size of these ETFs varies enormously and is roughly correlated with asset class. The largest ETF in Exhibit 3.1, Vanguard's U.S. equity funds, has $116.1 billion in assets under management compared to ProShares' leveraged fund with just $38 million in assets. In fact, the distribution of assets in the ETF market is highly concentrated. Marketwatch.com

Exhibit 3.1 An ETF portfolio spanning all asset classes

Ticker	Description	Asset class	Expense ratio	Assets under management
VOO	Vanguard S&P 500 ETF	U.S. Equity	0.03%	$116.1 B
ACWX	iShares MSCI ACWI excluding U.S. ETF	Intl. Equity	0.31%	$3.7 B
LQD	iShares iBoxx USD Corporate Bond ETF	U.S. Fixed Income	0.15%	$36.2B
BNDX	Vanguard Total International Bond ETF	Intl. Fixed Income	0.09%	$18.0 B
GSG	iShares S&P GSCI Commodity Indexed Trust	Commodities	0.80%	$970.9 M
FXE	Invesco Currency Shares Euro Trust	Currency	0.40%	$225.8 M
MDIV	Multi-Asset Diversified Income Index Fund	Asset Allocation	0.71%	$679.6 M
JPHF	JPMorgan Diversified Alternatives ETF	Alternatives	0.85%	$149.5 M
HDGE	Advisor Shares Ranger Equity Bear ETF	Inverse Equity	2.72%	$138.7 M
XPP	ProShares Ultra FTSE China 50	Leveraged	0.95%	$38.4 M

reported that just 20 ETFs, or less that 1 percent, accounted for half of the new capital inflows to the ETF market in 2017.[c]

ETF risks

Investment portfolios should be well diversified to eliminate unsystematic risk. Beyond that, risk averse investors seek higher returns to compensate for taking more risk. Investors generally view risk as the degree of uncertainty and/or potential loss inherent in an investment decision. Investors who trade individual securities normally make trading decisions frequently, making risk measures over relatively short holding periods relevant. Commonly used measures of risk for short term investors include the standard deviation (volatility) and market risk exposure (beta). In contrast, ETFs tend to be part of a longer-term investment approach where trading ETFs occurs infrequently. The investment thesis is based on a long-term return objective and trades do not occur based on daily, weekly, or monthly movements in the investment or market return. Rather than try to know when to get out of an investment and get back in again, longer

---

[c] https://www.marketwatch.com/story/less-than-1-of-etfs-getting-half-of-all-inflows-in-2017-2017-07-19.

term investors hold on to an investment during market volatility if the long-range investment thesis remains viable. ETF risk analysis tends to be less attuned to short run volatility and more concerned with long run time-series deviations from a benchmark, commonly called tracking errors. Trading ETFs occurs when there are changes in the investment thesis or corrections in implementing the thesis.

There are also a number of unique risks in ETFs that the investor must consider. Probably the biggest risk starts with not understanding how the particular ETF operates. Many of the ETF asset classes are very complex and involve valuations of derivative products. For example, commodity ETFs do not track the spot rate of the commodity, rather they are based on rolling positions in futures. Movements in the prices of futures and derivatives break the link between the NAV and ETF price. These valuation issues are normally beyond the scope of the individual or student investor. Student funds may want to focus on only the equity and fixed income ETF categories. The risk of not implementing the investment thesis gets higher when students probe less familiar investment securities and global regions.

Liquidity risk, which is the degree to which an investor can get money back from an investment, also varies widely with ETFs. While ETFs have continuous trading through brokers, the bid-ask spreads are very different for different classes of ETFs. Differences in size and trading volume create differences in the liquidity of the ETF. In general, using ETFs with high daily volume of trading provides liquidity. Liquidity risk is especially important if trading is frequent.

The ETF student fund and the "top-down" investment approach

Since ETF securities are portfolios, the investment perspective for constructing a portfolio of ETFs is inherently different from a bottom-up approach focused on selecting individual securities. ETFs offer a wide choice of exposures to global regions, countries, styles, and sectors that require investment decisions on relative weights to these exposures compared to the weights in a passive global index benchmark. Student managers must formalize the investment philosophy and strategy for making the exposure decisions that ultimately lead to their ETF portfolio. Like all investment organizations, students gain focus and a better understanding of the direction of the fund by writing an investment policy statement that clearly defines how they approach the markets. A detailed discussion of the value and content of an IPS appears in a previous chapter. Exhibit 3.2 presents the investment policy statement for a top-down ETF SMIF that is currently in operation.

Stages of analysis in a top-down fund

A process for a top-down ETF fund unfolds in five stages. The conceptual elements of each stage are outlined in Exhibit 3.3. The first four stages in Exhibit 3.3 lead to the construction of the ETF portfolio while stage V involves analysis and monitoring of the portfolio.

Stage I requires students to research global macroeconomic and political conditions (e.g., growth, inflation, monetary policy, political instability). The focus at this level is on the U.S., major countries (e.g., Germany, India, China) and global regions (North America,

Exhibit 3.2 Investor policy statement

Portfolio:	University of Richmond Endowment (Richmond, Virginia)
Tax ID:	Tax Exempt
Initial Asset Value:	$25,000
Holdings:	ETFs with U.S. Equity, International Equity, U. S. Fixed Income, and / or International Fixed Income exposure. Temporary cash balance during rebalancing and portfolio transitions
Restrictions:	No holdings with leverage, inverse structure, or derivative exposure
Return Goal:	Outperform a Benchmark defined as 70% (MSCI's Global Equity Fund, Ticker: ACWI) + 30% (Vanguard's Total Bond Fund, Ticker: BND)

Portfolio selection guidelines: The ETF Fund performance depends on selected asset class performance, portfolio sector weights, and specific ETFs within asset and sector classifications. The student group tilts the equity, fixed income, and cash asset mix around the 70/30/0 long run target. Global exposures follow from macroeconomic themes likely to unfold over the 2-year investment horizon. Sector weights deviate from the weights in the passive index funds to reflect expected opportunities, given the macroeconomic thesis and corresponding sector and industry implications. Specific ETFs selected for the portfolio survive a rigorous screening process to find the best ETF within a desired global region, country, and sector/industry exposure.

Historically, equities offer higher rates of return along with greater volatility than fixed income or cash assets. The ETF fund portfolio uses diversification to moderate risk and seeks the maximum return per unit of risk expected in the markets. The ETF Fund uses geographic diversification combined with efficient portfolio algorithms to construct the portfolio. Investments in exchange traded funds (ETFs) provides added diversification without holding large numbers of securities.

Investment objectives:
- Enhanced return consistent with an intermediate time horizon of 2–3 years.
- Risk profile: Moderate with a tilt toward above market risk when warranted
- Short term liquidity needs: None
- Annual Rate of Return Expectation: 8% (based upon global equity and bond return expectations and pension fund actuarial assumption)
- ETF selections with minimal transaction costs.

Duties and responsibilities include:
- Annual reporting requirements with periodic updates for the Advisory Board. Ongoing weekly updates and consultations with faculty advisors.
- Selection of assets to achieve efficient diversification of risk and returns.
- Control trading costs with low turnover and screening to find lowest operating cost funds.
- Monitor all investments using prudent buy and sell discipline to minimize turnover consistent with a 2-year investment horizon.
- Trades executed through TD Ameritrade/Scottrade at the lowest available online commission.
- Annual and mid-year reports on holdings, trading activity, and change in value.
- Strictly adhere to investment restrictions.

Exhibit 3.3 Stages in NXG's active ETF portfolio construction

Stage I	Stage II	Stage III
Global macro analysis by region and country	**Investment thesis (desired factor exposures)**	**ETF screener (consistent with thesis)**
GDP/Growth Prospects	Key Drivers / Catalysts	Screen based on Stage II
Interest Rates	Asset Class Mix	Seek best in Category
Inflation Rates	Country/Region Mix	Eliminate Restricted Funds[a]
Currency Strength	Sector/Industry	Eliminate Low Volume Funds
Balance of Payments		
Spreads (credits, maturity, etc.)		
Commodity Prices		
Political Risk		

Stage IV	Stage V
Identify optimal ETF Mix	**Performance review and analysis**
Benchmark Weights	Attribution Analysis[b]
Target Risk Tolerance	Value at Risk[b]
Set "Intuitive" Sector Weights	
Construct Efficient Frontier[b]	
Identify ETF Combinations[b]	

[a]The nature of a student fund may justify restrictions on certain types of asset classes such as leveraged, alternatives, and inverse equity funds.
[b]These areas require student analysts with strong quantitative skills.

Europe/Middle East, Latin America, and Asia-Pacific). This research is the basis for developing an investment theme at Stage II. This theme then guides decisions regarding asset class allocations, regions, countries, and sectors. For example, expectation of a robust U.S. economy relative to Europe and Emerging Markets would tilt the portfolio toward U.S. equities, probably with a further tilt toward sectors such as consumer discretionary goods, industrials, and financial services. The nature of economic conditions may alter the portfolio's orientation with respect to large versus mid- or small-cap ETFs, or value versus growth ETFs. Any investment theme would also integrate secular trends. The aging population worldwide favors the healthcare sector. The pace of technological progress assures a place for the tech sector in the portfolio as well as sectors where new technologies have particular traction (e.g., telecom, social media, healthcare). Within fixed income, the investment theme will shape the duration and quality of credit in the portfolio. Specific commodities are highly sensitive to the business cycle (e.g., metals, energy) or supply shocks that might emerge due to political currents (e.g., energy, agriculture). Exhibit 3.4 schematic shows how business cycle phases can be linked to specific sectors.

In Stage III, students select specific ETFs to achieve the portfolio composition as prescribed by the investment theme. The tasks at this stage demonstrate very clearly why ETFs are ideally suited to operating a top-down SMIF in three respects. First, unlike the traditional bottom up SMIF, implementing the investment theme does not involve valuation of fundamentals of any financial asset. Second, the costs associated with an ETF portfolio are low. For example, Schwab charges $4.95 per trade with a zero fee for Schwab ETFs and there are no account

Exhibit 3.4 Sector weighting linked to phases of the macroeconomic cycle

Cycle phase	Macroeconomic conditions	Links to sectors	Overweight sectors	Underweight sectors
Early Expansion	Sharp recovery, positive growth, rate of growth picks up, credit eases, margins expand, profit growth, low inventories, sales growth picks up	*GDP*: Growth rebounding *Inflation*: Low *Interest Rates*: Low *Unemployment*: High *Wages*: Low *Sentiment*: Low but rising	Consumer Discretionary Industrials Technology Credit Cyclical Capital Goods Cons. Cyclical	Utilities Financials Telecomm. Health Care Cons. Staples
Mid Expansion	Longest phase of the cycle, moderate but sustained growth, momentum in activity, credit more available, easy monetary policy moves to neutral, inventory and sales grow, inventory/sales ratio about equal to long run average	*GDP*: Growth Sustained *Inflation*: Rising *Interest Rates*: Rising *Unemployment*: Falling *Wages*: Low growth *Sentiment*: Rising	Technology Industrials Capital Goods Credit Cyclical Industrials	Materials Utilities
Late Expansion	Overheated economy, inflation picks up above trend, growth rate slows, monetary policy becomes restrictive, credit becomes tight, profit margins narrow, inventories build, and sales fall	*GDP*: Peak flattening *Inflation*: High *Interest Rates*: Low *Unemployment*: Low *Wages*: Improving *Sentiment*: Peaked	Materials Capital Goods Health Care Energy Utilities Cons. Staples	Cons. Discr. Cons. growth Technology

| Recession | Contraction with negative growth rates, profits decline and credit is tight at all levels, monetary policy becomes accommodative, sales fall with lagging inventory reductions | *GDP*: Falling (negative) *Inflation*: Falling *Interest Rates*: Falling *Unemployment*: Rising *Wages*: Falling from peak *Sentiment*: Falling | Consumer Staples, Utilities, Health Care, Telecomm. | Cap. Goods Cons. growth Cons. Cycl. Basic Ind. Technology Materials Financials |

minimums. A single ETF provides diversification via the basket of stocks defined by the orientation of the index, thus diversification in a region, country, or sector is achieved at the transactions cost of a single trade. Third, the phenomenal growth of ETFs has been accompanied by many websites that provide free-access to a wide range of ETF information that is easily managed by user-friendly "screeners". These screeners allow students to identify cohorts of ETFs that are consistent with the criteria of the portfolio's composition (e.g., asset class, regions, sectors).

A free ETF "screener" is available at ETF.com (https://www.etf.com/etfanalytics/etf-finder). The screener is easy to navigate and provides a remarkable amount of free information. The "asset" tab provides a dropdown menu with six asset classes. Clicking on "equity" in this menu reveals another dropdown menu that allows one to apply filters for regions, countries, sectors, capitalization size, and investment style (i.e., value, growth, or blend). The table content reloads as additional filters are selected. The default content in the table presents the elements listed under the "Overview" tab (e.g., total assets, trading volume, yield-to-date) but selecting other tabs (e.g., "returns," "expenses," "dividends") prompts the table to reload accordingly. Clicking on a specific ETF in the table displays a new page that provides extensive detail.

At the completion of Stage III students have a list of ETFs that match the investment thesis, pass the filtering criteria for portfolio composition, and meet the restrictions imposed on the student fund. Likely restrictions on a student fund would include prohibition of certain ETF asset classes (e.g., leveraged, inverse, alternatives). Stage IV involves a range of a tasks necessary to finalize the portfolio. After deciding on the asset classes, students set the long-run target weight for each asset class. These long-run weights reflect the fund's policy statement that is prepared for the target investor.

Analyzing the tentative ETF portfolio holdings

Student managers must identify an appropriate benchmark for performance comparison. The benchmark not only reflects the fund's investment philosophy but is investable and measurable. For example, the MSCI ACWI ETF provides a diversified passive benchmark portfolio with wide exposure over different equity subclasses and countries. ACWI tracks large and mid-cap equities in developed and emerging markets covering 64 countries and representing 85% of the global investable equities. A sector breakdown of the ACWI fund also allows benchmarking for active rotation of sector weights in accordance with the investment thesis. The Vanguard Total Bond market ETF (BND) represents a viable passive index for fixed income based on high liquidity and a broad mix of long and intermediate bonds.

Stage IV involves quantitative analysis of the tentative portfolio before making the final trades, conducting an analysis of performance for current holdings, and providing suggestions for rebalancing the portfolio. Identifying the correlation between specific holdings is particularly important in the case of ETFs. Since an ETF is a basket of securities, there are instances where different filters will produce very similar holdings. For example, filters that identify large-cap equity ETFs will produce a cohort similar to the holdings from of an ETF for the technology sector (e.g., Microsoft, Apple, Facebook, Alphabet). Fortunately identifying these overlaps is easy because the structure of the ETF is "transparent". The ETFdb screener permits an examination of the complete underlying holdings of 2280 ETFs. Applications of Markowitz efficient portfolio algorithms also play a role in this process. Although the analysis is *ex post*, students compare their tentative portfolio performance with alternative portfolios using different weights.

Additional quantitative analysis occurs in Stage V. Portfolio performance is monitored by using an attribution model and analyzing tracking errors relative to the benchmark. The attribution analysis fosters learning by breaking down returns relative to a benchmark to identify where active decisions were good or bad. If the attribution analysis shows poor performance, the challenge is to decide if more time would allow the thesis to develop more fully or if the thesis is wrong. Analysis of *ex post* tracking errors provides a longer-term perspective from which students can see where the portfolio has under or overperformed.

Constraints and student issues with ETF funds

Although one of the purposes of a SMIF is to give responsibility and discretion to student managers, advisors need to place some restrictions on the full range of ETFs available for investing. As the ETF market has become more sophisticated, the complexity of many ETFs has increased. Student managers may not work well with the risk and return characteristics of the more exotic ETFs such as levered, inverse, and derivative ETFs. Investing in only U.S. equity and U.S. fixed income accommodates a basic but complete top down analysis with ETFs. Expanding to include international equity and international fixed income opens the analysis to global considerations. Expanding the universe much beyond this opens up more sophisticated analysis of the risks and returns involved. The primary goals of a student managed fund are easily met with plain vanilla ETF structures.

The costs of trading ETFs include the operating cost, the bid-ask spread, and trading costs. In general, ETFs have low operating costs with expense ratios averaging roughly 45 basis points, but the costs are much lower for equity and fixed income ETFs than leverage, derivatives, or commodity exposures. The ultimate cost of trading depends on the number of ETFs traded, frequency of trading, total amount invested, and return on the investment. Although ETFs do not require large investments, students are typically tempted to hold a large number of ETFs or to turn the portfolio over frequently. Either impulse will place substantial drain on the performance of a fund with a small amount of capital. The drag of transaction costs on performance can be reduced by applying four criteria: (1) screen out ETFs with higher operating expenses; (2) select ETFs with high trading volume; (3) minimize the number of holdings consistent with a fully diversified portfolio; and (4) adopt a longer-term investment horizon consistent with an endowment or a client with a long term lock up period.

Implementing a student managed ETF fund—A detailed example

Several aspects of organizing and implementing a student managed fund are common for all investment strategies and portfolio holdings. Exhibit 3.5 lists many of these questions. For ETF student funds, the process starts with a top-down analysis culminating in the selection of specific ETFs that offer a portfolio with desired exposures in global regions, countries, and sectors. The investment horizon and holding period are long term since the scenarios that determine the investment thesis typically do not change rapidly. A course limited to one semester does not work well with the top down structure and broader global, macroeconomic, and required industry analysis. An ETF fund may require a longer calendar time commitment to complete a broad global analysis. Once constructed, students must also consider rebalancing and performance reporting at later dates. A continuous portfolio with ongoing analysis and rebalancing serves the long run performance goals best.

The top-down investment framework described in this chapter requires a broader skill set that expands beyond a single discipline. Much of the added breadth is economic analysis. Knowledge of macroeconomic measurement and trends is essential. Macroeconomics is increasingly becoming international macro due to the regional and country-specific interdependences of trade. The content of the more technical deliverables that students submitted were conducted with the most current programming skills (e.g., R and Python). Although not included in this chapter, one economics and computer science major student used extensive macro data in a value at risk (VaR) forecast of inflation and GDP growth for several

---

Exhibit 3.5 Questions about setting up a student managed fund

- Should the fund be administered as a scheduled class each semester or should it be a student activity allowing participation over multiple semesters?
- What are the appropriate course prerequisites and background experiences for fund managers?
- How are student fund managers determined?
- What is an appropriate incentive structure for an academic advisor's work on the fund?
- What is the source of funding?
- Is the fund's investment horizon a semester or longer? How does this affect the investment strategy?
- How is risk tolerance determined? How is risk measured?
- How much discretion do student managers have in making investment decisions?
- What are the appropriate investment constraints for a student fund?
- What data sources are needed to implement the investment fund?
- What procedures and work products should be required to support investment decisions?
- How should sell discipline be structured to avoid behavioral biases to hold losers too long?
- How is the buy decision justified? How can small sample size, recency effects, and "follow the crowd" issues be addressed in the buy recommendations?
- What is an appropriate process for performance analysis and fund monitoring?
- How should student managers codify the investment process, procedures, and constraints of the fund to allow an easy transition from one management team to another.

---

major countries. This chapter focuses on describing the deliverables associated with a top down model, but does not reference the construction of a website on which most of the deliverables currently appear (URetf.com). This cite was designed by a computed science major in collaboration with an English major. To be sure, the team has included finance students and their contribution should not be understated; but this contribution has been a part of a team in an interdisciplinary setting. Specific responsibilities for subsets of the students come together to form a collective organizational investment process. For these reasons, an ETF fund serves a wider set of students than funds focused on selecting stocks.

ETF fund structure

The University of Richmond began an ETF SMIF in 2016. The fund operates as a one-half unit course that can be repeated twice (two semesters) for credit and may be extended for no academic credit if participation is acceptable to advisors. Since one advisor is in charge of the Honors Program in economics, some students have extended participation in the ETF fund to an honors thesis around some aspect of the fund experience. A second academic advisor from the

Finance Department completes the advising team and helps integrate the economics and finance components of the ETF analysis. A weekly seminar with advisors is supplemented by a weekly meeting of student managers. The current faculty advisors created the fund without academic teaching credit—their participation is valued as part of their university service. Oversight of the program is structured and time consuming although the level of preparation required for the weekly seminar is low compared to a normal class. Other universities may need to develop another form of academic advising to be sustainable, but once involved, advisors will almost surely find this activity to be rewarding. The reputation of the ETF SMIF has grown quickly and attracts a very strong applicant pool. Many former team members now hold research positions at major banks and investment firms.

The Richmond ETF SMIF started with $25,000 of university funds. To start, the ETF fund defines its "customer" to be an endowment with a very long run investment horizon, which is likely to be most appropriate for an ETF fund. Student managers apply and are recruited based on courses in intermediate macroeconomics, econometrics, advanced macroeconomics, investments, portfolio theory, and/or math economics courses. About half of the management team is new each academic year and about half are continuing from the prior year without academic credit.

The investment policy statement (IPS) for the Richmond ETF fund appeared early in the chapter as Exhibit 3.2. The fund is constrained to investment in only the U.S. equity, International equity, U. S. fixed income, and International fixed income ETF asset classes. More complex ETFs are not followed, allowing a focus on global, country, and sector economic analysis. A target benchmark of 70% equity and 30% fixed income represents a long run target, but managers may deviate within 30% on each side of the target. The IPS also outlines specific objectives and duties of managers for the University of Richmond fund. A concise summary of the top-down investment process for the ETF fund appears as Exhibit 3.6. This statement introduces new managers to the top-down stages of analysis for the fund. New managers are required to review this document and study examples of work products provided by managers in the prior year.

Detailed examples of deliverable student work products

The remainder of this chapter contains detailed examples of documents, work products, and performance analysis from the ETF Student Fund at the University of Richmond. The order of exhibits corresponds to the stages of portfolio construction and evaluation presented in Exhibit 3.3.

The first phase of the ETF portfolio construction begins with a global regional analysis. Management teams are assigned to four regions: North America, Latin America, Europe and the Middle-East, and Asia-Pacific. Analysts cover the region and the countries within the

Exhibit 3.6 ETF investment fund process

Given our focus on top-down analysis we first look at the benchmark weights for asset classes and sectors. To outperform the benchmark, we conduct in-depth analysis of global, country, sector, and industry conditions with the goal of creating more favorable portfolio exposures than the benchmark exposures. To simplify the global analysis, we organize research assignments around four main global regions (North America, Asia-Pacific, Europe/Middle East, and Latin America/Africa), with two or three managers assigned to each region. For each region, we focus on key economic factors and catalysts driving growth prospects, interest rates, labor markets, inflation rates, demographic shifts, trade policy, currency strength, balance of payments, spreads, commodity risks, political risk and more. Each regional research group prepares written reports on each country in the region and presents the analysis to the overall management group and fund advisors in one of the weekly seminars. In a subsequent meeting each region and countries within the region receive a grade ranging from A to D with respect to prospects for equity growth and relative debt performance. After presenting, debating, and reconciling views on each country, the management team decides on the most attractive weights for each country of the world.

After deciding on the countries and regions offering the most promising investment opportunities, the management team organizes an analysis of sectors and industries. At this point, the menu of available ETFs presents a constraint, since some country ETFs only provide exposure to the overall economy rather than exposure to specific sectors or industries. In some cases, available ETFs allow a focus on specific sectors within an entire region, rather than a country. The managers review key drivers, catalysts, and risks for each sector, as well as asset class mix, and interconnections among industries. Research group assignments for five prominent sectors in each region result in written summaries and presentations to the entire management group and advisors. The emphasis is on linking expected sector and industry performance to the projected macroeconomic outlooks. Ultimately, fund managers present more specific suggestions on desirable weights and combinations of country and sector combinations.

In the final ETF selection phase, managers screen for ETFs in line with the investment thesis. Screens also eliminate ETFs with average trading volume under 20,000 and with high bid/ask spreads in order to manage liquidity risk and transaction costs. Managers within each global region pitch their ETFs to the management group and construct a tentative portfolio of selected ETFs. Analysis of this portfolio occurs with back tests of risks and returns for different weights. A correlation matrix reveals whether certain ETFs are redundant and if a collection of fewer ETFs might offer equal or better performance. Finally, managers conduct an analysis of portfolio exposures to make sure the portfolio is in line with the outlooks and sector/industry research. At this point managers present the tentative portfolio to the advisors for a complete discussion and presentation of the analysis behind the recommendation. Final trades follow if there are no areas of concerns raised in this meeting.

region. Exhibit 3.7 is an example of a student's deliverable work product covering North America. These regional analyses open with summary economic performance measures, survey the economic implications of a range of political and policy developments, and conclude with commentary on specific sectors. Work products for each region are delivered to the academic advisors and presented for discussion to the full management team. After several rounds of discussions, the management team adopts the weight for each global region. This weighting is shown in Exhibit 3.8 along with a brief discussion.

Exhibit 3.7 Global regional analysis (deliverable work product example)

Region: North America
Region Rating: B
Date: 09/19/2018

Summary of recent economic performance (recent quarter)

Country	GDP growth rate	Inflation	Interest rate	Unemployment rate
United States	4.20%	2.00%	3.05%	3.90%
Canada	1.90%	3.00%	2.41%	5.87%
Mexico	2.04%	4.90%	4.43%	3.34%

Key summary points

- U.S. fiscal stimulus provided solid short-term boost to domestic firms. However, perceptions of increased wealth and political risk may neutralize the stimulus's longer-term effect.
- The United States is renegotiating NAFTA with hard ball being played on both sides. A breakdown of this deal will likely affect Canada more than the United States, especially if Trump executes his threat of a tariff on Canadian automobiles.
- The trade dispute between the U.S. and China has caught headline attention and caused market volatility. While combined tariffs have totaled $260B in the past week of this report, fears have eased for a full-blown trade war.
- The U.S. Federal Reserve is on track to normalizing interest rates. It is doing so at a faster rate than other developing economies who also had historically low rates after the financial crisis. Increasing interest rate differentials, paired with solid growth and future increased deficits, are likely to cause an appreciation of the U.S. dollar up until mid-to-late 2019.
- Energy reform and a shift away from carbon-based sources in Mexico is a noble pursuit, however, corruption and a new executive is likely to hinder its execution.

Key trends and issues

U.S. Tax Stimulus, "Tax Cuts and Jobs Act"

U.S. President Donald Trump signed the "Tax Cuts and Jobs Act" into law on December 22, 2017, the largest tax overhaul since 1986. The tax rate is effectively a stimulus to U.S. corporations, as it establishes a single corporate tax rate of 21%, down from the previous top corporate tax rate of 35%. With this tax cut, the statutory rate for the United States, including state and local taxes, is 26.5%. This figure is significant because the weighted average tax rate for European Union countries is 26.9%, likely reducing the incentive for U.S. firms to transfer their tax regimes abroad. In addition, the tax law requires the repatriation of overseas profit for U.S. companies at a rate of 15.5% for cash and 8.0% for reinvested profits. This is speculated to increase the strength of the U.S. dollar relative to other currencies. However, according to the Brookings Institution, about 95% of foreign profits are held in USD currency, which do not need to be exchanged in the forex market, translating to this effect likely being minimal.

The positive effects of the tax law are likely to be short-term albeit real. S&P 500 companies had positive earnings growth after the Tax Cuts and Jobs Act but this growth will likely diminish going forward. Tax cuts also offered a boost to consumers. According to the Tax Policy Center, a middle- income household on average should save $980 in taxes, making individuals feel richer. In addition, Congressional auditors say that 30 million people in the U.S. had their income tax liabilities under-withheld. This will result in those 30 million individuals having to pay a larger tax bill in spring 2019, which could partially offset the boost in consumer spending gained in 2018. In addition, the U.S. midterm elections pose a risk to the fiscal stimulus delivered by the tax law.

Currently, the Democratic party is forecasted to take seats in the House of Representatives, which given that 0 Democrats in both the House and the Senate voted for the passing of the Tax Cuts and Job Act, a swing in the House could be detrimental to the future of the law.

North American trade woes, NAFTA stalemate

The North America Free Trade Agreement is in its 13th month of negotiations. Currently, negotiations are at an apex between Canada and the United States, with Mexico and the U.S. already having agreed on a preliminary deal. Currently, negotiations are ongoing, but concern of the deal being scrapped has diminished slightly. The U.S. has backed down from its Buy American demand for lucrative procurement projects. This would have prevented Canada and Mexico from bidding on American government infrastructure projects. An externality of these negotiations may be a renewed interest in U.S. infrastructure investment. The Buy American demand is cited to be a cause of dispute between the Canada and the U.S. Donald Trump has threatened the Canadian automobile industry with tariffs if Canada does not meet its demands in renegotiation. Other core issues are dairy and panel disputes. Despite these issues, Canada is the number one buyer of U.S. exports, and some form of a renegotiated deal is likely. Also, the U.S. Congress has permitted a trilateral deal—it is not certain that a Mexico-only deal will be allowed.

Tic-for-Tac trade war

The trade war between the United States and China has dominated headlines and ensued market volatility. On September 19, the United States imposed a 10% tariff on $200B of Chinese goods. This action has a step-up feature—January 1, 2019, the tariffs will increase to 25%. In retaliation, as has been the mantra from Beijing, China imposed a 10% tariff on $60B of U.S. goods. This is relatively optimistic because China's choice of weighing levies on $60B of U.S. goods versus $200B and its choice of a 10% tariff as opposed to a 25% tariff is seen as an easement of a full out trade war. In sum, the trade dispute between the United States and China is over the United States' disapproval of China's practices regarding U.S. intellectual property, the devaluation of their currency to make their exports more competitive, and government subsidies to dump goods in the U.S. Premier Li Keqiang said China won't devalue its currency, even after the latest exchange of tariffs, providing some optimism for future compromise.

Monetary policy and interest rate differentials

The United States Federal Reserve is on a path to normalize domestic interest rates. Currently, the Fed has increased rates twice this year, and the market is currently expecting two more rate hikes in 2018 and three hikes in 2019 of likely 25 bps. While this is the largest hike in over a decade, rates are still historically low, and the Federal Open Markets Committee forecasts real GDP growth to be 2.8% in 2018 and slightly lower in 2019 at 2.4%. Currently, the Fed is targeting a Federal Funds Rate in the bounds of 1.75–2.0%. The latest Fed dot plot suggests a targeted Fed Funds Rate of 3.125% and 3.375% for 2019 and 2020, respectively. Given the strong labor market, and inflation approaching the 2% Fed mandate, the central bank is likely to execute hiking rates in 2018–19. In addition to the United States strong economic growth in 2018 (GDP for 2Q18 was 4.2%) and future expected budget deficits, interest rate differentials are helping lead the appreciation of the U.S. dollar. U.S. sovereign debt is seen as a haven among investors, and the U.S. is a leader among developed economies regarding normalizing its interest rate to prerecession levels. In comparison, the European Central Bank's key interest rates are 0.00%, 0.25% and −0.40%, and the Bank of Japan has set rates near zero percent. Currently, investors want to allocate to the United States, and it's showing in the value of the dollar.

Mexico energy reform

Mexico is hoping to improve its energy sector. Mexico has ended its 75 year-long state-controlled oil and gas industry. If executed correctly, it will attract private capital and skilled labor to the industry. Mexico has significant oil and gas resources that are currently not exploited. According to Petroleos Mexicanos, a state-controlled energy company, there is an estimated total of 89B barrels of oil available for extraction. Despite this, Mexico's oil production has declined as well as oil exports from the weak commodity prices in 2014 and 2015. Reuters reported, "Oil Service and Mapping firms in Mexico are recovering from an industry recession and received $800 million in data sales to energy firms considering bidding for Mexican oil and gas blocks." These blocks are in the Gulf of Mexico and have received $61B in investment pledges. Energy reform may lead Mexican oil and gas industries out of a trough if successful. Per-capita energy use in Mexico is less than 40% of the OECD average, resulting in opportunity for growth. Mexico launched PRODESEN, a 15-year development program for the national electric system. From the years 2017 to 2031, PRODESEN estimates $110B in power related infrastructure projects. In addition, the plan's goal is to expand clean energy's share of power generation to 35% from 25% by 2024. While this plan looks promising, investors must continue with caution. Mexico's energy grid is weak and inefficient, a significant portion of the energy generated in Mexico is lost due to inefficiency and illegal usage. In addition, newly elected President Andres Manuel Lopez Obrador, has ambitious goals but the current state of the nation's finances could limit what his government can accomplish. However, he also stated no campaign promises would be broken. Mexico's debt currently stands at 54% of its GDP, this is almost twice the long-run average from 1990–2017 of 27.94% of GDP.

North American sectors/industries of interest

- **Technology**—The S&P 500 technology index has increased around 30% from a year ago. Cloud computing and artificial intelligence are attractive ideas that will certainly be prevalent in the future both in North America and globally. However, the growth potential comes at a cost. P/E ratios for the investable universe of S&P 500 technology companies have increased on a forward basis for the past 4 years. Current risk factors leave this sector vulnerable to a correction and will have to be taken into consideration going forward.
- **Infrastructure**—The American Society of Civil Engineers' most recent infrastructure report card grades U.S. infrastructure as a D+. Water pipelines are in serious need of repair. Water pipelines have a useful life between 75–125 years. Given the current replacement rate of about 0.5%, it will take about 200 years to turn over the current pipeline infrastructure. While this area is attractive given the critical nature and need for an infrastructure overhaul, the current political gridlock in the United States and the reluctance to direct serious capital to non-viewable improvements results in any expected timeframe for growth from an investment perspective to be elusive.
- **Insurance**—Insurance companies tend to fare well in rising interest rate environments and will benefit from the Fed normalizing rates. In addition, the 10-year treasury has very recently broken out, surpassing the 3% mark. Peter Tchir of Academy Securities Inc said investors have gotten complacent regarding the Fed keeping rates low and the yield curve staying flat. The yield curve has been relatively flat and long-term rates could breakout further on the possibility of successful trade deal negotiations and continued solid economic growth. In addition to growth, diminishing pension fund demand for long-term Treasuries could help steepen the curve. Greater convexity in the yield curve would be beneficial for insurance companies. Also, the tax law has increased health insurance premiums, which may also help bolster insurance companies' earnings.

Exhibit 3.8 Global region exposure composite—Student manager's example (4/18/2019)

Our analysis suggests that the region with the most opportunistic macroeconomic environment is North America. We want our portfolio to be very conservative in risk this year given our outlook on the global economy. We allocated the most to North America because there is a greater variety of ETFs available, the outlook is generally clearer, and much of the growth in the rest of the world depends on North American growth. We were easily able to invest in desired sectors to include non-cyclicals, healthcare, insurance, and medical devices in North America with less opportunities in these sectors elsewhere. Emerging Markets appear to very distressed with the strong dollar and high debt loads and the distress will mount if global growth slows. Overall, we expanded our exposure in North America and allocated 36.4% to the region.

Asia-Pacific and Europe/Middle East received nearly equal weights in our portfolio. Both regions have strong fundamental characteristics but political uncertainty and upcoming elections raise concerns about the course of these economies in the near term. We see comparable risks in each region, leading us to allocate nearly equal weights to each region. We chose the lowest exposure to Latin America because of increased political uncertainty and slowing growth in the region. Latin American countries recently recovered from a recession but GDP in many countries are missing estimates. Within the region, we believe there is potential for renewed stability and growth in Brazil and Chile, resulting in an overall allocation of 13.9% to the region. The pie chart below summarizes the target weights from our global allocation view.

Global exposures

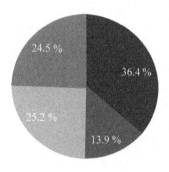

North America	36%
Latin America	13.9%
Europe and Middle East	24%
Asia-Pacific	25%

The second phase of the ETF portfolio construction examines countries and sectors within each global region. These regional and country allocations are the result of extensive discussion among the fund managers and advisors. Exhibit 3.9 shows the weights for each country that evolved in the student analysis following discussions of the global region reports.

Exhibit 3.10 provides an example of a sector analysis report describing conditions in agriculture, metals and oil, renewable energy, infrastructure, and technology in Latin America. Students discuss all the various sectors and region reports to narrow the focus to the desired exposures. Exhibit 3.11 shows the composite target for sector weights that managers believed to be appropriate after discussing and combining the various sector reports.

The final phase of the ETF portfolio construction requires analysis of the individual ETFs that fit the global region, country, and sector objectives. The specific ETF analysis uses the free screener available at ETFdb.com. Exhibits 3.12 and 3.13 provide examples of deliverable work products for two specific ETFs. The discussions of each ETF take place with a priority on consistency with the global, country, and sector perspectives developed throughout the top-down process.

Before a tentative ETF portfolio recommendation occurs, managers examine the correlations between ETFs to see if there are redundant ETF selections. An example of the correlation analysis appears as Exhibit 3.14. Highly correlated ETFs are identified and managers reduce the number of holdings going into the next stage of analysis. At this point the managers break open the ETFs and look at the combined underlying holdings with respect to the weights on global regions, countries, and sectors implied by the collection of ETFs. The weights on each ETF are varied in a simulation to identify the ETFs and weights that give the desired target exposures in global regions, countries, and sectors.

As a final consideration of how the tentative portfolio might fit the investment objectives, managers construct a Markowitz efficient frontier for the ETFs in the tentative portfolio. Exhibit 3.15 shows the frontier along with a discussion of how it was constructed. The tentative portfolio also appears in Exhibit 3.15 (shown as the dot just inside the frontier) to illustrate how it compares to a hypothetical *ex post* efficient frontier. In this particular case, the portfolio exhibits slightly higher risk for the corresponding rate of return.

A listing of the ETF holdings along with the weights and returns over the spring semester appear as Exhibit 3.16. This is a short run snapshot of the portfolio after a rebalancing on 1/7/2019. The fund's investment objectives are long term, so the data in Exhibit 3.16 are really just a part of the monitoring process rather than an investment horizon analysis. For example, the India Infrastructure fund (INXX) had not performed well prior to the rebalance. Long discussions revolved around whether the thesis supporting INXX was wrong, in which case the fund would be sold at the next rebalance point, or if the holding period had not been long enough to see the anticipated return results. In this case, INXX never recovered; in fact, this ETF was liquidated in

Exhibit 3.9 Country exposure composite—Student manager's example (4/18/2019)

Our country exposures reflect present our views on the best countries within the global regions. Our highest concentration overall is in the United States with 40.3% of our exposure. The concentration is high since many ETFs, even those not centered on North America, include companies that are in the United States. Our second, third, and fourth largest holdings are Japan, Germany and Chile, with 9.8%, 9.8%, and 8.2%, respectively. We chose these exposures because we believe these countries offer the best potential for appreciation over the 2-year horizon for the fund. We hold a 6.5% stake in the Netherlands largely because we believe it is one of the best performing European countries. We have smaller positions in the emerging markets of China, Brazil, and India with 6.2%, 5.6% and 4.3%, respectively. While we know emerging market countries are prone to a higher downturn in a slowing economic environment, these countries possess characteristics that we believe will withstand any negative global market weakness.

Top 10 country exposures

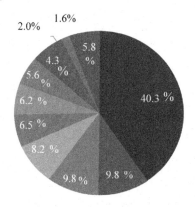

United States	40.3%
Japan	9.8%
Germany	9.8%
Chile	8.2%
Netherlands	6.5%
China	6.2%
Brazil	5.6%
India	4.3%
South Korea	2.0%
Switzerland	1.6%
Other	5.8%

Exhibit 3.10 Sector analysis by global region (deliverable work product example)

Sectors: Agriculture, Metals & Oil, Renewable Energy, and Infrastructure
Region: Latin America
Sector Ratings: Buy Agriculture, Renewable Energy, Technology, and
Date: 10/23/2018

Sector	Countries affected	Recommendation
Agriculture	All Latin American Countries	Buy
Metals & Oil	Chile, Brazil	Hold
Renewable Energy	Uruguay, Brazil, Peru	Buy
Infrastructure	Brazil, Argentina, Chile, and Colombia	Hold
Technology	Argentina, Brazil, Chile, Peru	Buy

Agriculture—Buy

The agricultural sector has seen an immense sell-off in the Latin American region ever since it experienced its worst drought of the century. This caused Latin American countries to miss output goals and trade partners disappointed. However, prices are beginning to pick up and given the trade uncertainty, Latin American countries are expected to prosper. China is already signing on contracts to export soybean from Brazil and other agricultural products. Soybean used to be a commodity that China purchased from the US, but that is no longer the case. More importantly, weather forecasts are positive and global demand is strong, so with improved output, Latin American countries will be able to experience synergies for their economy. Therefore, this sector is rated as a "Buy" given that tariffs are not going to impact this region and is expected to primarily experience benefits from any trade uncertainty.

Renewable energy—Buy

Foreign Direct Investment for renewable energy has increased exponentially in the last 5 years. Before, approximately 6% of total FDI was sent toward renewable energy, but now it is up to 18%. Uruguay leads in having effective renewable energy systems placed within the country. 95% of it runs on multiple forms of renewable energy including solar and wind. Brazil is conducting research and looks to start creating renewable energy in cars, in order to be more competitive in the market. Since FDI as a whole is going down for non-renewable energy, it is spiking up for alternative forms of energy that are renewable. Chile is also a front-runner in the renewable energy frontier. They are heavily investing in this technology and after their elections, they are expected to come out of their stagnating economic cycle back into a booming one according to World Finance. Renewable energy is contributing to the increase in employment in Latin America. Approximately 2 million jobs in the region are associated with renewables and the rate is expected to grow. Renewable energy is also associated with infrastructure building. Governments in Brazil and Uruguay are working to make the power grid as green as possible, leading to increased jobs and overall growth. An important aspect to keep in mind about renewable energy is that it may not be prevalent in our time horizon, however, as more technological innovation in the space occurs, there is great potential.

Infrastructure—Buy

There is increased investment in infrastructure expected to occur in Latin America as economies begin to kick-start after being in a recession. Brazil is expected to ramp up infrastructure investment in the telecommunications space, in order to advance the country's technological scope. Uruguay is building windmills and dams in order to make their country "greener." Colombia has a $70 billion plan that will extend to 2035 in which thousands of roads, railroads, and airports will be built. This is so the country becomes more interconnected with major cities. Peru also has a $1 billion plan to have potable sewage systems for the entire country. Finally, Chile's new president, Sebastian Pinera, has made it his agenda to improve infrastructure within the nation. This includes building new roads, bridges, telecommunication towers, and schools. The country has already seen a subtle decrease in the unemployment rate and more is expected under the Pinera administration.

Money also continues to pour into Latin America from China and private equity firms. China hopes to increase its influence on the region as trade relationships fall apart with the US. China has increased its infrastructure investment by 20% in the region and is credited for financing high profile projects such as the Nicaragua Canal. Along with China, private equity firms are seeing an influx of investors coming to them with money to put into infrastructure. Equities are no longer enough to get yields and private equity investors are looking for creative ways to find returns. Infrastructure funds are launching every month with KKR being one of the latest with a $3 billion fund launched in early September 2018.

This sector is given a "Buy" rating because as the region begins to emerge from a recession, infrastructure is top-of-mind for Latin American countries. This will lead to improved employment rates, technological innovation, and overall well-being for the region due to competitive edges emerging.

Technology—Buy
Argentina lifted a tariff on technology, which made the country the most expensive place to buy an iPhone. FDI for technology has been steadily increasing along with renewable energy. FDI coming into the region focusses on telecommunication enhancements. Brazil is expected to increase investment into telecom infrastructure in 2018. Brazil is actively integrating technology into its manufacturing and automobile services. Trade prospects are opening up for the region with NAFTA falling apart, deals with Europe in place, and the Pacific Alliance gaining dependence on each other. With heavy investment expected in technology, Latin America is rated a "Buy" region.

July of 2019. Often, students learn more from their mistakes than from their successes. INXX will now forever be an example of a bad decision from holding a loser too long. Going forward, new managers will be given an initial task of reviewing the INXX example and supporting materials to discuss what went wrong. Overall, the tracking errors around the benchmark are provided for the short-run holding period (semester) in Exhibit 3.17 and for the fund since inception in December of 2016 in Exhibit 3.18. An analysis of these tracking errors is a large part of the educational process. The tracking analysis prompts the discussion of whether poor performance resulted from a bad thesis or because there has not been enough time for the thesis to develop. This perspective provides a good test of the long-term investment patience of managers and their commitment to the longer-term ETF investment philosophy.

Exhibit 3.11 Sector/industry composite exposure—Student manager's example (4/18/2019)

Our industry analysis suggested that the technology sector offers the most promising growth over the 2-year horizon. Specifically, we felt that global robotics and artificial intelligence, and global financial technology presented excellent investment avenues. Furthermore, Technology in Asia also presented an excellent opportunity as the industry is still growing at high rates, has significant governmental support, and large populations that have not yet accessed the internet's full capabilities. Since we are being conservative in our portfolio construction, we made sure our weight in technology did not significantly overpower other industries. Our exposure to technology does not consist of FAANG stocks and is more specialized toward less volatile technology firms. The next largest sectors were industrials, financial services, and consumer defensive. We also have exposure to other defensive industries including utilities and healthcare. While we sought diversification from basic materials, communication services, energy, and real estate but we wanted lower exposures than the benchmark in these sectors.

Sector exposures

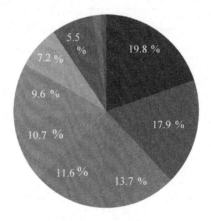

Technology	19.8%
Industrials	17.9%
Financial Services	13.7%
Consumer Defensive	11.6%
Utilities	10.7%
Healthcare	9.6%
Consumer Cyclicals	7.2%
Basic Materials	5.5%
Communication Services	1.5%
Energy	1.5%
Real Estate	1%

The nature of ETFs makes it difficult to limit specific exposures in some regions. This results in positions in ETFs that are very diversified with holdings across sectors that we do not think are great opportunities. This could cause our region, country, and industry exposure to be slightly different from what the fund managers prefer to hold. As the ETF market grows and more selections are available, we hope to select more specific ETFs with exposures that directly correlate with our views.

Exhibit 3.12 ETF analysis and recommendation (deliverable work product example)

ETF: Global X Robotics and AI—BOTZ

Recommendation: Buy
Current Price: $19.35
Date: 11/27/2018

Ticker	BOTZ
52 Week 2Price Range	$18–$27
MSCI Index YTD Return	4.03%
YTD Return	−18.35%
1 Year Return	−23.97%
3 Month Return	−15.35%
Beta	1.10
Expense Ratio	0.68%
Bid-Ask Spread %	2.70%
Average Volume	970K
50 Day Moving Average	$20.79
200 Day Moving Average	$22.61
NAV	$19.18

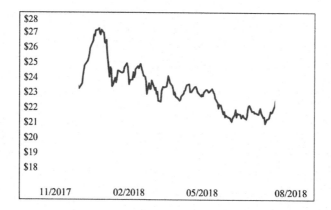

The Global X Robotics and Artificial Intelligence ETF (BOTZ) seeks to invest in companies that potentially stand to benefit from increased adoption and utilization of robotics and artificial intelligence (AI), including those involved with industrial robotics and automation, non-industrial robots, and autonomous vehicles.

Country breakdown		Sector breakdown
Japan—43.66%	Israel—1.88%	Technology—45.18%
United States—32.95%	Canada—1.7%	Industrials—38.72%
Switzerland—10.49%	Germany—1.17%	Healthcare—14.59%
United Kingdom—3.47%	South Korea—1.04%	Energy—1.51%
Finland—3.07%		

Region and sector outlook

Artificial intelligence was valued as a 2.42B market in 2017, and it is forecasted to grow exponentially in the coming years. As many technology companies face decreased differentiation and increased competition, they turned to artificial intelligence to propel them into the future, keeping their brands relevant. Artificial intelligence and robotics have an incredible amount of applications, and as the technology is perfected and advanced, these will only increase. From defense applications to commercial trucking and manufacturing applications to everyday consumer uses, this industry and its applications will only grow.

Upside catalysts

- **Revenues from licensing**: The majority of revenues in this industry come from licensing. Once these companies are able to perfect their projects, other industries will want to implement their technologies to differentiate themselves from their competition. This can be a very lucrative business given the high barriers to entry due to R&D in the industry.
- **Room for growth**: Because of the unlimited potential of these technologies, this market should offer good growth from here. The industry is expected to achieve a cumulative average growth rate of 28.73% between 2018 and 2023. Getting into this market now will lead to incredible returns, should these forecasts come to fruition. Robotics & AI are a disruptive force that's not limited to industrial manufacturing. The holdings of this ETF are some of the biggest players in the AI industry who will likely see proportional growth.
- **Movement to task-specific robots**: The concept of a single robot that can do anything is compelling to both robot manufacturers and to robot purchasers. Yet limitations in engineering, artificial intelligence, and costs, have led to the rise of task-specific robots. It is much easier and cheaper to develop a robot that can do one thing really well. By leveraging proven technologies, these robots are designed to be low cost, reliable, and easily integrated into existing business processes. In doing so, they lower the barriers to adopting robotics and expand the range of industries that can utilize robots in their everyday functions.
- **Increasing labor costs**: Labor costs are expensive and rising, which is a particularly challenging prospect for competitive industries like manufacturing. While many businesses turned to offshoring such jobs, many companies are finding robots to be even more cost efficient. One analysis found that offshoring jobs could save a firm approximately 65% on labor costs while replacing workers with robots can achieve an estimated 90 % in savings.

Downside risk

- **Regulation**: Because these technologies are so new, regulation is lagging behind. Uber's recent incident in Arizona where one of its self-driving cars hit a pedestrian brought up some of these potential issues. How do you handle ethical issues or place blame on a machine? Will the company be punished? Because everything in this industry is so new, we are not able to understand what regulation could look like down the line.
- **Dependence on pace of R&D**: The performance of these holdings will depend on the success and pace of research and development. Therefore, this may be a better fund to hold in the long term. This is an up and coming market with a lot of runway, but it may take a period of time to become profitable. However, the ETF has been performing very well, and I do not believe this should be something to turn us away.
- **China**: As wages in China continue to rise, firms are increasingly looking elsewhere for new sources of low-cost labor. In response, China has made massive investments into robotics to maintain its pole position in global manufacturing. In 2017, the country was the largest market for industrial robotics and saw its purchases of robots increase 58% year-over-year.

Ultimately, China will likely be both a major purchaser of robotics as well as an emerging competitor to existing firms, making it a true x-factor for the industry.

Investment thesis

We rank BOTZ as a "Buy" rating. The ETF presents an opportunity to invest in robotics and AI companies in Japan and the US. BOTZ offers long run potential and could reach an accelerated growth stage in our time horizon. With economic growth conditions finally improving in Japan in 2019, this ETF can allow us to capture superior returns.

Exhibit 3.13 ETF Analysis and recommendation (deliverable work product example)

ETF: iShares MSCI Netherlands—EWN

Recommendation: Buy
Current Price: $28.26
Date: 11/26/2018

Ticker	EWN
52 Week Price Range	$27–$34
MSCI Index YTD Return	4.03%
YTD Return	−10.32%
1 Year Return	−8.89%
3 Month Return	−9.06%
Beta	0.95
Expense Ratio	0.49%
Bid-Ask Spread %	0.04%
Average Volume	230K
50 Day Moving Average	28.93
200 Day Moving Average	30.95
NAV	$28.06

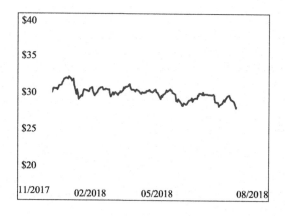

EWN is an ETF that seeks to track the results of an index composed of Dutch equities

Country breakdown	Sector breakdown	
Netherland—91%	Consumer Non-Cyclical—29%	Healthcare—6%
United States—9%	Technology—20%	Communications—2%
	Financials—18%	Energy—2%
	Industrials—11%	Real Estate—1%
	Basic Materials—9%	Consumer Cyclical—1%

Region and sector outlook

After seeing the economy rising to positive-zone growth in the past 2 years, Europe is expected to continue delivering growth in the next year. However, finding a suitable investment option for the region is challenging, due to country-specific risks that a lot of the major economies face. Specifically, France faces multiple labor strikes and sluggish domestic demand; Spain deals with one of the highest unemployment rates in the EU, a structural unemployment that would require a long-term solution; Italy became the second-most indebted country in the region, and sends negative sentiment to investors as its current government is seen as fiscally irresponsible. Between these options, the Netherlands rises as one of the more stable economies within the developed countries in Europe. The Dutch economy faced uncertainty from the global trade tension in the past year, and yet still delivered a strong economic performance in 2018.

Notable sectors in the region are aerospace & defense and technology. The aerospace & defense sector is poised to increase as European countries attempt to reach their target NATO defense contribution while technology development in various aspects has become a race around the world.

Upside catalysts

- **Strong economic fundamentals**: Household expenditure picked up pace and resilient growth in goods exports contributed positively to economic growth, despite accelerating import growth and lingering global trade tensions. Looking at the final quarter, consumer confidence edged down in October but remained elevated. This, coupled with low unemployment levels, bodes well for the continuation of healthy household expenditure growth.
- **Strong domestic demand**: The Dutch economy is likely to continue growing at a robust pace for the rest of 2018 and into the next year, driven by solid domestic demand. Private consumption is strong and residential investment remains very dynamic. Favorable financial conditions have supported both consumption and business investment growth. However, the contribution of net exports is expected to moderate on higher oil prices and slower world trade.

Downside risk

- **Eurozone downturn**: Exports play an important role in the economic growth of the Netherlands. Therefore, any macro trend that hurts the global economy would be a considerable headwind for the Dutch economy. Currently, uncertainty regarding the future trade relationship between the EU and the United Kingdom from Brexit remains a downside risk as is a possible increase in tensions between the EU and the United States.

Investment thesis

We rank EWN as a "Buy" rating. The ETF presents an opportunity to invest in larger-cap companies within the Netherlands. Europe is an economically developed region with a lot of attractive investment options, but currently, most countries are facing specific challenges of their own, those that would make them risky investment options. The Netherlands is one of the more developed economies in the region without any notable issues, both economic and political, that could hinder economic growth. This ETF will give us exposure to the European region and allow us to capture returns without facing riskier investment options from other countries in the region.

Exhibit 3.14 Correlation matrix of the tentative ETF portfolio

Below is the portfolio's correlation matrix:

Color legend: 0.99 / 0.75 / 0.25 / -0.25 / -0.75 / -0.99

	ACWI	EWZ	ECH	BOTZ	EMQQ	HEWJ	INXX	EWN	HEWG	ICLN	ITA	FINX	XLP	KIE	VPU	IHI	UUP
ACWI	1.00																
EWZ	0.42	1.00															
ECH	0.52	0.63	1.00														
BOTZ	0.89	0.16	0.43	1.00													
EMQQ	0.76	0.42	0.45	0.80	1.00												
HEWJ	0.65	-0.04	0.21	0.67	0.48	1.00											
INXX	0.41	0.32	0.37	0.33	0.42	0.20	1.00										
EWN	0.85	0.33	0.50	0.79	0.74	0.60	0.41	1.00									
HEWG	0.70	0.12	0.27	0.66	0.51	0.66	0.36	0.73	1.00								
ICLN	0.70	0.48	0.61	0.54	0.69	0.38	0.47	0.64	0.50	1.00							
ITA	0.78	0.21	0.37	0.76	0.57	0.56	0.13	0.60	0.57	0.48	1.00						
FINX	0.81	-0.12	0.19	0.83	0.68	0.52	0.10	0.66	0.49	0.43	0.72	1.00					
XLP	0.55	0.30	0.24	0.41	0.34	0.27	0.26	0.52	0.37	0.35	0.39	0.35	1.00				
KIE	0.74	0.19	0.21	0.63	0.44	0.65	0.24	0.65	0.54	0.44	0.75	0.55	0.47	1.00			
VPU	0.20	0.16	0.11	0.23	0.03	-0.02	0.29	0.21	0.10	0.24	0.08	0.23	0.55	0.23	1.00		
IHI	0.76	0.14	0.20	0.76	0.56	0.48	0.35	0.62	0.58	0.50	0.65	0.79	0.48	0.58	0.26	1.00	
UUP	-0.32	-0.51	-0.40	-0.43	-0.39	0.20	-0.20	-0.31	-0.28	-0.28	-0.07	-0.29	-0.13	-0.07	-0.05	-0.18	1.00

Note: ETF ticker symbols represent the rows and columns. The bar at the right represents a color code for correlations. The correlation matrix was constructed using daily returns beginning with February 28, 2014 and ending with February 28, 2019. The correlation matrix identifies which ETFs are highly correlated with our other ETF holdings. If correlations are stable, it would be redundant to hold two ETFs with high correlations. The correlation matrix shows that ACWI (our benchmark) has the most consistently high correlations with the rest of the ETFs in the portfolio. This is not bad since we want to track the benchmark and we believe we selected sectors and ETFs that can outperform the benchmark going forward.

Exhibit 3.15 *Ex post* **Markowitz efficient frontier**

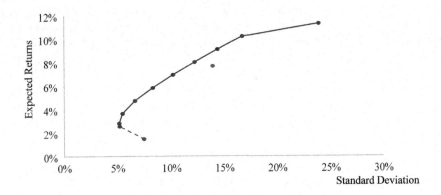

The model uses standard deviations and average returns calculated from monthly returns for 16 ETFs with available data from February 28, 2014 to February 28, 2019. The solver tool in Excel provided the basic model for construction of the frontier. With solver we find the weights in a hypothetical portfolio that minimizes the standard deviation to achieve a set amount of expected return. There are vital limitations to the model. As noted above, this is a back-testing method that goes 3 years in the past to construct the frontier. The past does not always predict the present, but there are good insights that can be made from looking at how the efficient portfolios could be constructed.

Exhibit 3.19 presents a breakdown of return performance to be used in an attribution model. By sorting the semester performance by asset class, sector, and ETF performance the managers identified which active decisions, relative to the benchmark, added or subtracted from performance. Exhibit 3.20 provides this summary showing good asset allocation, poor global region distributions, and good ETF selection in this case. This pattern is not unusual since student managers often take more risk with asset allocation and do a better job of analyzing ETFs than fully predicting global economic conditions. Over time, a fund could focus on pure ETF selection by matching the benchmark in asset allocation and global region allocation. This would shorten the calendar time needed to run the fund but would limit the educational experience of a broader global perspective.

As part of an ongoing effort to add more risk analysis, a student manager conducted a Value at Risk (VaR) analysis of the ETF fund. The VaR model estimates the expected maximum loss with a given confidence level based on different assumptions about the return-loss distribution of portfolio returns. The monthly VaR of the portfolio relative to each ETF's contribution to the overall measure appears in Exhibit 3.21. The VaR model assumed a normal distribution, which is an assumption to be explored more fully in the future. The table in Exhibit 3.21 shows the additional risk provided by each item in the portfolio in absolute terms as well as the percentage

Exhibit 3.16 Performance overview

As of April 18, 2019, the fund's assets under management (AUM) were $30,161.19, up 13.10% from the portfolio rebalance on January 7, 2019. We have 16 holdings. Our 70/30 equity/fixed income benchmark was up 9.75% over the same period. On a total return basis, we beat the 70/30 benchmark by 3.35%. Since our asset allocation decision resulted in a 100% equity allocation, we also compared our returns to an equity only benchmark. The 100% equity benchmark was up 13.24% over the rebalance period, with 0.14% underperformance on an all equity basis. This is not surprising since our view led us to a very conservative equity portfolio focused on sectors that could weather a financial slowdown. The rebalance period was a short-term snapshot of portfolio performance while we maintained a 2-year window for our ultimate projections. As a result, we did not immediately react to poor performing funds but we reviewed the analysis that led to the fund selections to make sure the longer-term justification for holding each ETFs remained valid. Our portfolio holdings and return performance for the rebalance period appear in the table below.

ETF holdings and return performance 1/7/2019 to 4/18/2019

Ticker	ETF sector	% Exposure	Weight	Total rate of return
FINX	Global FinTech	$1704.95	5.65%	27.05%
ITA	US Aerospace and Defense	$1645.28	5.45%	13.13%
KIE	Insurance	$1484.42	4.92%	12.60%
ICLN	Global Clean Energy	$1710.28	5.67%	10.12%
XLP	Consumer Staples	$2047.32	6.79%	9.55%
HEWJ	Japanese Equities	$1449.92	4.81%	9.07%
VPU	Vanguard Utilities	$1147.86	3.81%	8.63%
IHI	U.S. Medical Devices	$1505.00	4.99%	7.64%
BOTZ	Robotics and AI Tech	$3374.35	11.19%	5.73%
EWN	Netherlands Equities	$2504.00	8.30%	4.72%
HEWG	Currency Hedged German Equities	$2650.56	8.79%	4.15%
UUP	USD Index Bullish	$1332.63	4.42%	2.47%
EWZ	Brazilian Equities	$1254.26	4.16%	2.09%
ECH	Chilean Equities	$2444.20	8.10%	<0.55%>
EMQQ	Asia Internet and E-Commerce	$2296.09	7.61%	<10.96%>
INXX	India Infrastructure	$1326.45	4.44%	<23.59%>

contribution of each ETF to the overall portfolio VaR. ETFs that contributed a greater percentage of risk to the overall portfolio than their corresponding weight were flagged for further analysis. A student manager developed general code that allows changes in dates of the results, additions and removal of ETFs, changes in the weights in the portfolio, and automatic creation of the VaR measures and tables. In future work student managers will continue this work and explore ideal percentage allocations to each ETF from a risk management perspective.

Exhibit 3.17 Short run portfolio tracking errors over the period 1/7/2019 to 4/18/2019

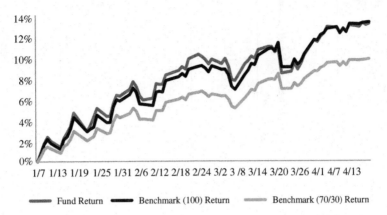

Since inception on 1/12/2016, the ETF fund achieved a 20.62% cumulative total rate of return compared to benchmark performance of 19.08% over the same period. Performance above the benchmark was 1.54%.

Exhibit 3.18 Long run portfolio tracking errors since inception on 1/12/2016

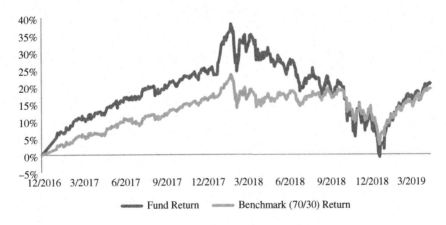

Student managers provide one last deliverable work product demonstrating how they are monitoring the fund with an eye toward moving to the next rebalance. Exhibit 3.22 illustrates what this basic report entails. The key is to generate thoughtful review of the intended outcomes relative to the short run outcome with an identification of what changes might be in order. This final product represents the starting point for the next semester's managers along with a complete review of all deliverable work products generated by the managers in the prior semester.

Exhibit 3.19 Attribution analysis data

Benchmark and ETF portfolio weights and return performance

A. Benchmark Returns = 13.76% Equity and 1.66% Fixed Income; 70% Equity/30% Fixed Income

Benchmark regions

	North America	Latin America	Europe	Asia-Pacific
Region Weight	57.73	1.47	20.96	19.84
[Region Return]	[14.12]	[0.26]	[11.44]	[9.83]

Benchmark sectors

	Basic materials	Consumer cyclicals	Financial services	Real estate	Communication services	Energy	Industrials	Tech.	Consumer defensive	Healthcare	Utilities
Sector weight	4.80	11.13	18.57	2.93	3.91	6.55	10.07	17.89	8.91	12.05	3.19
[Sector Return]	[11.91]	[15.02]	[11.05]	[3.84]	[11.94]	[11.12]	[15.61]	[24.34]	[10.17]	[0.61]	[6.26]

B. ETF Portfolio Returns = 13.35% Equity and 0% Fixed Income; 100% Equity Weight

ETF portfolio—Regions

	North America	Latin America	Europe	Asia-Pacific
Region Weight	36.57	13.80	25.18	24.45
[Region Return]	[15.58]	[2.44]	[15.07]	[15.18]

ETF portfolio—Sectors

	Basic materials	Consumer cyclicals	Financial services	Real estate	Communication services	Energy	Industrials	Tech.	Consumer defensive	Healthcare	Utilities
Sector weight	5.42	7.24	13.71	1.02	1.76	1.34	18.22	20.34	11.43	9.20	10.34
[Sector Return]	[5.66]	[11.83]	[11.105]	[8.40]	[6.98]	[7.23]	[16.88]	[21.87]	[11.06]	[14.24]	[0.54]

Exhibit 3.20 Attribution analysis of active ETF decisions relative to the benchmark

Passive Return for 70/30 Index Mix	9.75%
Active ETF Portfolio Return	13.26%
Overall Excess Return	**3.51%**
Passive Return for 70/30 Index mix	9.75%
Active Asset Allocation 100% Equities, Passive Sector Weights	13.24%
Excess Return due to Active Asset Allocation	**3.50%**
Active Asset Allocation 100% Equities, Passive Sector Weights	13.24%
Active Asset Allocation, Active Region Allocation, Passive Sector Weights	10.46%
Excess Return due to Active Region Allocation	**−2.78%**
Active Asset Allocation, Active Region Allocation, Passive Sector Weights	10.46%
Active Asset Allocation, Active Region Allocation, Active Sector/ETF	13.26%
Excess Return due to Sector/ETF Selection	**2.79%**

Exhibit 3.21 Value at risk analysis

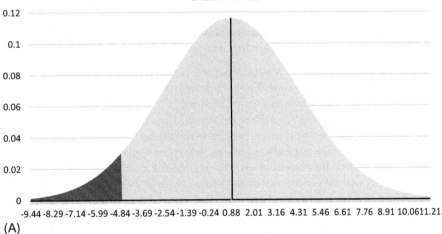

Monthly Profit-Loss Distribution Assuming Normal Distribution

(A)

Note: Estimates were obtained by fitting a distribution (through Maximum Likelihood Estimations) to the observed profit-loss returns of the portfolio based on historical data with a 95% confidence level. The graph above illustrates a 5% chance that a monthly return could fall below −4.84%.

5% Value-at-Risk			
Ticker	**Component Contribution**	**Percent Contribution**	**Portfolio Weight**
BOTZ	1.01%	20.13%	10.54%
EMQQ	0.57%	11.28%	6.95%
ECH	0.53%	10.58%	8.67%
EWN	0.47%	9.36%	8.15%
HEWG	0.39%	7.76%	8.48%
ICLN	0.31%	6.21%	5.62%
ITA	0.30%	6.07%	5.77%
FINX	0.30%	6.05%	5.55%
HEWJ	0.26%	5.24%	4.86%
IHI	0.25%	4.99%	5.43%
XLP	0.22%	4.36%	6.78%
INXX	0.21%	4.26%	4.01%
KIE	0.19%	3.86%	5.01%
VPU	0.05%	1.00%	3.87%
EWZ	0.00%	−0.08%	4.77%
UUP	−0.05%	−1.07%	4.56%
Portfolio VaR		5.01%	
Worst Monthly Loss (out of $25,000)		$1,252.50	

(B)

Exhibit 3.22 Monitoring and rebalancing issues (deliverable work product)

While the fund's second semester is typically focused on analyzing the portfolio and reviewing previous decisions, we also updated our macroeconomic research to account for any new events that we felt could impact our portfolio moving forward.

Since the initial analysis and the fund's first rebalance in January, several important events have occurred around the globe. The most prominent issue for our portfolio is the change in monetary policy expectations, specifically in the United States. When our regional expectations were formed in October, the U.S. Federal Reserve was expected to continue its monetary tightening path. The Fed was expected to raise the Federal Funds Rate three times in 2019, and two times in 2020 in increments of likely 25 basis points. The Fed "Dot Plot" suggested a Federal Funds Rate of 3.125% in 2020, and 3.375% in 2021. However, persistently low inflation and slowing global growth has motivated the Fed to take a more dovish stance. Currently, the Fed is not planning on raising interest rates in 2019, potentially making a cut in the latter half of the year.

Our investment thesis for the U.S. insurance sector was partly dependent on higher interest rates that would improve profitability, as well as Insurtech, technological innovations designed to improve the current insurance industry model. While we still believe Insurtech will drive value in the industry, our financial technology (fintech) ETF gives us the exposure we want to technological innovations that will drive future efficiency and productivity in the U.S. The capital gained from the sale of the U.S. insurance ETF will be equally split in other current holdings, Vanguard Utilities ETF (VPU) and iShares Dow Jones U.S. Medical Devices ETF (IHI). Given a more recent review, we believe the following rebalancing decisions are in order.

- Sell our entire stake in U.S. Insurance (KIE)
- Increase our US Utilities ETF (VPU) position by 2.88–6.35%
- Increase our US Medical Devices ETF (IHI) position by 2.54–7.93%

Summary

Colleges and universities now have easy access to the technology, data, and guidance by investment professionals required to provide practical investment experience for students. Student funds may adopt one of the many investment strategies used in practice, to include active use of ETFs. Exhibit 3.23 provides a list of sources and ETF data available for student managers. The ETF fund presented in this chapter continues to evolve by building on broader global analysis of financial markets and use of quantitative tools. This approach is a fertile area for both practice and learning in higher education where some of the dominant themes are globalization and integration of disciplines. The ETF approach for student managers expands the experiential learning format beyond what has traditionally been an exercise for finance students.

Many facets of the ETF approach for student funds remain a work in progress. Students must build on the "intuitive" ETF selection process to develop stronger quantitative analysis skills that work well with ETFs. The examples presented in this chapter illustrate both the starting points as well as the introduction of more advanced applications of efficient portfolio concepts, VaR, and attribution analysis. Additional work on applications of factor analysis and use of smart beta portfolios will follow. Unlike real world investment practice, student fund management moves slowly as students learn from mistakes of their predecessors and work on corrections. Although the use of ETFs by student funds is in the formative stages, added insight and guidance from professional ETF investors will ultimately allow more creative use of ETFs as vehicles for experiential learning.

Exhibit 3.23 Sources of information and data

In the ETF Fund, we largely use sources that are free and readily available to the entire campus. The key exception is the Bloomberg data feed in our finance "lab" that is also used by managers in our other student managed funds. The Bloomberg data are expensive but not necessary for management of an ETF fund.

Finance/economy focused websites

Market Realist—http://marketrealist.com/

The Economist—http://www.economist.com/

Wall Street Journal—https://www.wsj.com/

Investopedia—http://www.investopedia.com/

Daily Shot—http://blogs.wsj.com/dailyshot/

Economy.com—https://www.economy.com/

Bloomberg Businessweek—https://www.bloomberg.com/businessweek

Bloomberg—https://www.bloomberg.com/

Forbes—https://www.forbes.com/

Market Watch—http://www.marketwatch.com/

Yahoo Finance—https://finance.yahoo.com/

Google Finance—https://www.google.com/finance

Barron's—http://www.barrons.com/

Planet Money—http://www.npr.org/sections/money/

Business Insider—http://www.businessinsider.com/

Blackrock Blog—https://www.blackrockblog.com/

Economist View—http://economistsview.typepad.com/economistsview/

Bloomberg TV—https://www.bloomberg.com/live

ETF focused websites

ETF.com—http://etf.com/

ETFDatabase—http://etfdb.com/screener/

DATA

IMF—http://www.imf.org/external/datamapper/

Bloomberg Terminals

Exercises

1. **Principles of investment funds**. Professional investment funds require a clear sense of "who they are." This means identifying the fund's client base, general guidelines, and investment objectives. As student managers, clearly and concisely address each of the following:
   - Who is the client?
   - What are the investment objectives?
   - What is the risk tolerance?
   - What time horizon (years) is appropriate given the factors noted above?
   - How often will you rebalance your ETF portfolio?
   - What is the appropriate benchmark to be used in evaluating your fund.
   - Write a brief investment policy statement.
   - Reflect upon all of your responses above. Broadly, is there a clear and consistent message?

2. **Developing an investment thesis**. The first dimension of portfolio construction is to determine asset class allocations (i.e., stocks, bonds, cash, commodities, real estate, etc.). This decision should follow from an investment thesis based on global, regional, and national macroeconomic conditions as well as government policy actions throughout the world. For example, the 2010–20 decade was characterized by slow but sustained economic growth, historic monetary accommodation both in terms of duration and degree, and significant regional political developments (e.g., Brexit, deterioration in international trade agreements, political regime changes). These events define the investment environment as we enter a new decade.
   - Discuss the implications of the environment for a portfolio's asset allocations.
   - Assign weights to each asset class and explain the basis for each weight.
   - Is this asset allocation consistent with the first four items you considered in Question 1?
   - Examine two specific countries and two regions (e.g., Latin America, emerging markets, Europe). Assign weights to these geographic areas and explain the basis for each weight (do not rule out the likelihood of assigning a zero weight but still explain).
   - Based on your global investment thesis, identify the sectors/industries that offer the best opportunities over the next two-year investment horizon. Assign target weights for the specific industry and sector groups. Concisely explain.

3. **The ETF selection process**. Implementation of the portfolio requires identifying specific ETFs that capture the asset class, region, and sector elements of the investment thesis. The exercises below use the free ETF "screener" available at ETF. com (https://www.etf.com/etfanalytics/etf-finder). Follow this link and scroll down to the "ETF Results" table. This table has several levels of functionality. The specific ETFs listed in the table reload as successive filter criteria are applied. The resulting number of ETFs is reported in the "ETF Results" title. In the website's *de novo* table, this entry is 2,342, which is the total number of ETFs covered by ETF.com since no screens are applied. Seven column headings appear immediately below the "ETF Results" title (e.g., Fund Basics and Performance). The "Custom" feature requires a subscription. Each of these categories offer more specific content that can be selected for display in the body of the table. The default display is "Fund Basics" (e.g., ticker symbol, name, segment description, expense ratio). Click the other headings to examine how the ETF-specific information changes. Clicking on a specific column heading *within* the table will sort the selected item in ascending or descending value (e.g., from lowest to highest expense ratio). Clicking on a specific ETF ticker symbol in the table loads a separate web page containing extensive information on the ETF. The steps below are an example of using the screener on the equity asset class.
   - Scroll to the bold heading "ETF Filters" and click the hypertext "Classification." This action presents a menu of six asset classes. Check the "Equity" box. When this criterion is selected, the specific ETFs listed in the table change immediately.
   - Below the "Asset Class" list, scroll down and click the "Location" hypertext. This action prompts a menu of 10 global regions. Alternatively, explore "Geography." This option produces a list of many countries and some more narrowly defined regions. Select a region or country and note that the number of qualifying ETFs can decline dramatically. Examine this phenomenon by comparing a screen of the U.S. versus individual European countries, then consider Latin American countries.
   - The two steps above filter by asset class and region, two of the main aspects of an investment thesis. "Sector" selection is another important element. Click the "Reset All" text

above the table. Return to the "Asset Class" options under "Classification," again select "Equity," and then click the "Focus" hypertext. This menu supports searches filtered by 11 sectors. The "Niche" hypertext adds 17 sectors that are more narrowly defined. Experiment with different sector searches.

- In the context of any search, it is useful to examine the range of ETF-specific information that is available by changing the categorical content of the table (i.e., rotate through the seven column options at the top of the table).

- The precise composition of any ETF is available by clicking on the ticker symbol in "ETF Results" Table. Why is this information important? Consider an investment thesis that includes equity as an asset class, the U.S. as a region, and technology as a sector. Use the screen path, "equity/location/geography/US" to identify U.S. equity ETFs; *iShares' Core S&P 500 (IVV)* appears among the top two ETFs. Click on the *IVV* ticker symbol, scroll down slightly, and click on "Fit." This provides a listing and weights for all the stocks in *IVV*. Note the largest components of this index. Next use the screen path: "equity/focus/technology." Examine the composition of *iShares' Global Tech (IXN)*. What do you notice about the two indexes? What does this observation imply about maintaining a desired level of diversification while implementing an investment thesis? This specific exercise recommends a broader analysis be performed after the proposed portfolio is finalized. Download a time-series for each of the ETFs and construct the co-variance matrix. Does this procedure reveal any surprising degree of correlation between specific ETFs? If so, examine the ETFs' compositions.

4. **Performance evaluation**. Performance evaluation is an important final phase for a student fund. A subsequent chapter offers a complete discussion of performance evaluation for a portfolio. While we do not go into detail here, the following questions should be addressed by student managers.
   - How would you compare the risk and returns of your ETF portfolio performance to the benchmark?
   - How would you use the Sharpe ratio to measure performance?
   - How would you calculate a Jensen alpha for your portfolio?
   - Use the Markowitz efficient portfolio concept to generate the frontier for the ETFs you chose. Look back over the past five years and construct the efficient set for the various weights and combinations of the ETFs you chose for your portfolio. How does your portfolio compare to the portfolios on the efficient frontier?

Reference

Hill, J.M., Nadig, D., Hougan, M., 2015. A Comprehensive Guide to Exchange Graded Funds (ETFs). CFA Research Foundation.

CHAPTER 4

Portfolio construction

Constructing a multi-asset class portfolio is a complex process that can involves up to three levels of decisions: asset allocation, manager selection and weighting, and security selection and weighting. At each decision level, asset classes, mangers, or securities are combined to obtain the combination of risk and expected return that best fits with the goals for the portfolio or a specific part of the portfolio. In this chapter, we discuss each of these levels in turn.

Asset allocation

Asset allocation is the selection of asset classes and their weights for the overall portfolio.[a] The combination of a set of asset classes and their corresponding is often called an *asset mix*. The asset allocation process does not select any specific investments, but rather sets the stage for the later stages of the portfolio construction process. In some governance structures, the top-level investment committee approves the asset mix and delegates its implementation to one or more portfolio managers or portfolio management teams, each of which could internal or external.

Asset class selection

There is no standard way to define asset classes. They can be very broad, for example, U.S. Stocks, or more narrowly defined, such as U.S. Large-Cap Value Stocks. At a minimum, they should include equities, fixed income, and cash.

A few general principles for selecting asset classes are:

(1) They should be based on the investment philosophy and approach of the portfolio.
(2) There should be an index for each.
(3) They should not overlap with each other.
(4) Their returns should be fairly uncorrelated with each other.

Exhibit 4.1 shows a set of asset classes and indexes that are often used to represent them. Note that many of these overlap so it is important that when choosing from a list this, to pick only

---

[a] Sometimes, a distinction in made between strategic and tactical asset allocation. Strategic asset allocation sets the long-term asset class weights to set the portfolio benchmark. In tactical asset allocation, the weights are actively adjusted over short periods in an attempt to outperform the strategic asset allocation benchmark. In this chapter, only discuss strategic asset allocation.

Student-Managed Investment Funds. https://doi.org/10.1016/B978-0-12-817866-9.00004-2

Exhibit 4.1 Asset classes and corresponding indexes that can serve as benchmarks

Asset class	Index for benchmarking
U.S. All-Cap Stocks	Russell 3000 Morningstar U.S. Market
U.S. Large-Cap Stocks	Russell 1000 S&P 500 Morningstar U.S. Target Market Exposure
U.S. Large-Cap Growth Stocks	Russell 1000 Growth S&P 500 Growth Morningstar U.S. Large-Mid Growth
U.S. Large-Cap Value Stocks	Russell 1000 Value S&P 500 Value Morningstar U.S. Large-Mid Value
U.S. Mid-Cap Stocks	Russell Midcap S&P 400 Morningstar U.S. Mid Cap
U.S. Mid-Cap Growth Stocks	Russell Midcap Growth S&P 400 Growth Morningstar U.S. Mid Growth
U.S. Mid-Cap Value Stocks	Russell Midcap Value S&P 400 Value Morningstar U.S. Mid Value
U.S. Small-Cap Stocks	Russell 2000 S&P 600 Morningstar U.S. Small Cap
U.S. Small-Cap Growth Stocks	Russell 2000 Growth S&P 600 Growth Morningstar U.S. Small Growth
U.S. Small-Cap Value Stocks	Russell 2000 Value S&P 600 Value Morningstar U.S. Small Value
Global All-Cap Stocks	FTSE Global All Cap MSCI ACWI S&P Global Broad Market (BMI) Morningstar Global Markets
Global Large-Cap Stocks	S&P Global 1200 Russell Global Large Cap
Global Large/Mid-Cap Stocks	FTSE All World Morningstar Global Markets Large-Mid Cap
Global Small-Cap Stocks	Russell Global Small Cap
Global Shariah-compliant Large/Mid-Cap Stocks	FTSE Shariah Global
Developed Market All-Cap Stocks	MSCI World Morningstar Developed Markets

Non-U.S. All-Cap Stocks	FTSE Global All Cap ex-U.S. Morningstar Global Markets ex-U.S.
Non-U.S. Large/Mid-Cap Stocks	FTSE All World ex-U.S. Morningstar Global Markets ex-U.S. Large-Mid Cap
Europe, Asia and Far East Developed Large-Cap Stocks	MSCI EAFE Morningstar Developed Markets ex-North America
Europe Large/Mid-Cap Stocks	Russell Europe
Emerging Market Stocks	FTSE Emerging MSCI EM S&P/IFCI Composite Morningstar Emerging Markets
U.S. Bonds	Bloomberg Barclays U.S. Govt/Credit
USD-denominated Inv. Grade Bonds	Bloomberg Barclays U.S. Aggregate Morningstar U.S. Core Bond
U.S. Treasury Bonds	Bloomberg Barclays U.S. Treasury Morningstar U.S. Treasury Bond
U.S. State and Local Bonds	Bloomberg Barclays U.S. Municipal
USD-denominated Inv. Grade Corporate Bonds	Bloomberg Barclays U.S. Corporate Morningstar U.S. Corporate Bond
USD-denominated Corp. High Yield Bonds	Bloomberg Barclays U.S. Corporate High Yield
Global Bonds	Bloomberg Barclay Global Aggregate
Global Inv. Grade Corporate Bonds	Bloomberg Barclays Global Corporate Morningstar Global Corporate Bond
Global Inv. Grade Government Bonds	Bloomberg Barclays Global Treasury Morningstar Global Treasury Bond
Global Government and Corp. High Yield Bonds	Bloomberg Barclay Global High Yield
Non-U.S. Govt. Bonds	FTSE WGBI Non-USD
EUR-denominated Inv. Grade Bonds	Bloomberg Barclays Euro Aggregate Morningstar Eurozone Core Bond GR EUR
GBP-denominated Inv. Grade Bonds	Bloomberg Barclay Sterling Aggregate Morningstar UK Core Bond
Asian-Pacific Investment Grade Bonds	Bloomberg Barclays Asian-Pacific Aggregate
U.S. Treasury Inflation Protected Bonds	Bloomberg Barclays U.S. TIPS Morningstar U.S. Treasury Inflation-Protected Securities
Commodities	Dow Jones-UBS S&P GSCI Morningstar Long-Only Commodity
Cash	FTSE Treasury Bill 3 Mon

nonoverlapping asset classes and indexes. For example, if you select U.S. Large Cap Stocks as an asset class, you should not select U.S. Large Cap Growth and U.S. Cap Value Stocks. Conversely, if you select U.S. Large Cap Growth and U.S. Cap Value Stocks as asset classes, you should not select U.S. Large Cap Stocks.

As we discuss in this chapter, the indexes allow us to estimate the statistical properties of the asset classes that we need at all levels of portfolio construction. In the next chapter, we discuss how they are used to evaluate performance.

Asset allocation with mean-variance optimization

While there are several approaches to asset allocation, *mean-variance optimization* (MVO) is probably the best known. Based on the work of Nobel laureate Harry Markowitz in the 1950s, MVO, also known as Modern Portfolio Theory (MPT), is based on the idea that investors prefer higher expected return to lower and lower risk to higher. Therefore, for a given level of expected return, the best asset mix would be the one with the lowest level of risk. By varying the level of expected return, we can trace out a curve called the *efficient frontier*. Exhibit 4.2 shows two efficient frontiers formed from the seven asset classes indicated. (We explain the two efficient frontiers later.) Each efficient frontier shows that there is a trade-off between risk and expected return.[b] In theory, we should select an asset mix along an efficient frontier.

Inputs to MVO

In order to generate an efficient frontier, we need to run a special piece of software called a mean-variance optimizer, or simply, an *optimizer*. An optimizer requires three sets of parameters:

(1)   Arithmetic expected returns—one for each asset class[c]
(2)   Standard deviations—one for each asset class
(3)   Correlations—one for each *pair* of asset classes

These parameters govern the statistical properties of the asset class returns and therefore any asset mix. Together, they are sometimes called *capital market assumptions*.

The arithmetic expected returns are the centers of the distributions of each asset classes. The expected return of an asset mix is the center of the distribution of the asset mix. It is the weighted average of the arithmetic expected returns of the asset classes. Let.

m = the number of asset classes.
M_i = the arithmetic expected return of asset class i.

---

[b]   Note that the trade-off is only between efficient asset mixes. In general, if one asset is riskier than another, it does not follow that it has a higher expected return.

[c]   We explicitly say that the expected returns are arithmetic because below we introduce geometric expected returns. In the context of MVO, expected returns are usually understood to be arithmetic.

Exhibit 4.2 Mean-variance efficient frontiers

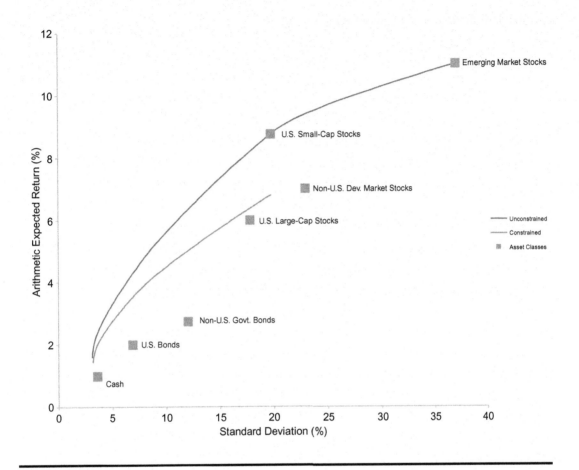

x_i = the asset class's weight on asset class i (Note that $\sum_{i=1}^{m} x_i = 1$).
M_p = the arithmetic expected return on the asset mix.

We have:

$$\sum_{i=1}^{m} x_i M_i = M_p \tag{4.1}$$

In MVO, risk is measured by standard deviation of return. The standard deviation of an asset mix's return depends on both the standard deviation of the returns on the asset classes and on all of the pairwise correlations. Let

S_i = the standard deviation of return on asset class i.

ρ_{ij} = the correlation of the returns on asset classes i and j.
S_p = the standard deviation of return of the asset mix.

The standard deviation of the asset mix is given by:

$$S_p = \sqrt{\sum_{i=1}^{m}\sum_{j=1}^{m} x_i x_j S_i S_j \rho_{ij}} \tag{4.2}$$

In standard MVO, the asset class weights are subject to two constraints:

(1) No short positions: For each asset class i, $0 \leq x_i \leq 1$.

(2) Budget constraint: Weights must sum to 1, $\sum_{i=1}^{mx_i=1}$.

As we discuss below, additional constraints can be added.

The endpoints of the efficient frontier are:

(1) The asset mix that minimizes standard deviation. This is the *minimum variance portfolio* (MVP).
(2) The asset mix that maximizes arithmetic expected return (regardless of risk).

The optimizer find the MVP by finding the set of weights $(x_1, x_2, ..., x_m)$ that minimizes S_p in Eq. (4.2), subject to the constraints. Let M_{mvp} denote the expected return of the MVP. The optimizer also finds the asset mix that maximizes expected return, subject to the constraints. Let M_{max} denote the expected return of this asset mix. For values of the expected return between M_{mvp} and M_{max}, M_T, the optimizer finds the asset mix that minimizes S_p, subject to the constraints placed on all asset mixes plus the constraint that $M_p = M_T$. The efficient frontier chart is a plot of (S_p, M_p) points for the mixes calculated in this way.

Estimation of parameters

Typically, the standard deviations and correlations are estimated from the historical returns on the indexes that represent the asset classes using standard statistical formulas.

Estimating the expected returns on the asset classes is a more nuanced problem. While it common to use average historical returns, it is no advisable. If we run MVO on purely historical data, we will find what asset mixes were best in the past. But asset mixes should reflect our forecasts of the future, especially expected returns. There are several techniques for formulating expected returns on asset classes which are covered in the exercises for this chapter.

Example of optimization

Exhibit 4.3 shows a set of capital market assumptions for the seven-asset class model. The standard deviations were estimated from the historical returns of the indexes shown, while the

Exhibit 4.3 Capital market assumptions

Asset class	Index	Expected return (%)		Standard deviation (%)	Correlation with						
		Arithmetic	Geometric		U.S. Large-Cap Stocks	U.S. Small-Cap Stocks	Non-U.S. Dev. Market Stocks	Emerging Market Stocks	U.S. Bonds	Non-U.S. Govt. Bonds	Cash
U.S. Large-Cap Stocks	S&P 500	6.00	4.54	17.75	1.00	0.89	0.84	0.67	-0.19	-0.01	0.07
U.S. Small-Cap Stocks	Russell 2000	8.75	7.00	19.73	0.89	1.00	0.77	0.73	-0.28	-0.13	-0.03
Non-U.S. Dev. Market Stocks	MSCI EAFE	7.00	4.64	22.87	0.84	0.77	1.00	0.72	-0.19	0.19	-0.04
Emerging Market Stocks	S&P/IFCI Composite	11.00	5.33	36.90	0.67	0.73	0.72	1.00	-0.31	-0.10	-0.12
U.S. Bonds	Bloomberg Barclays U.S. Govt/Credit	2.00	1.77	6.84	-0.19	-0.28	-0.19	-0.31	1.00	0.58	0.11
Non-U.S. Govt. Bonds	FTSE WGBI Non-USD	2.75	2.06	11.97	-0.01	-0.13	0.19	-0.10	0.58	1.00	-0.03
Cash	FTSE Treasury Bill 3 Mon	1.00	0.94	3.58	0.07	-0.03	-0.04	-0.12	0.11	-0.03	1.00

Exhibit 4.4 Asset mixes along constrained efficient frontier

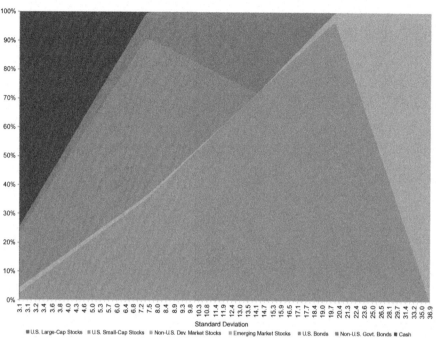

arithmetic expected returns were estimated using other techniques.[d] The efficient frontiers in Exhibit 4.2 were generated by running MVO using the capital market assumptions in Exhibit 4.3. The frontier labeled Unconstrained was generated with only the minimum constraints of no short selling and the budget constraint Exhibit 4.4 shows the asset mixes along this frontier.

A striking feature of the unconstrained frontier is the absence of U.S. Large-Cap Stocks and Non-U.S. Developed Market Stocks from any asset mix, and the dominance of U.S. Small-Cap Stocks until near the right end of the frontier where Emerging Market Stocks dominate. In an unconstrained optimization, the asset mix with the highest expected return is 100% in the asset class with the highest expected return. In this case, this is Emerging Market Stocks. It is unlikely that an investment committee in the U.S. would accept the asset mixes along the unconstrained frontier. They would expect small-cap stocks and emerging market stocks to make up a small part of the asset mix and they would expect U.S. assets to make up a large part of it.

---

[d] The geometric expected returns, which are derived from the arithmetic expected returns and standard deviations, are not part of the capital market assumptions. We have included them in Exhibit 4.1 because we discuss them below.

There are two main ways of getting an optimizer to produce more balanced and acceptable asset mix:

(1) Calibrate the capital market assumptions, especially the expected returns, to make the asset classes that would otherwise be omitted from the efficient frontier more desirable, and those that would otherwise dominate the efficient frontier less desirable.
(2) Impose additional constraints.

In the example presented here, we did some of each. We imposed additional constraints to force all asset classes to be represented in the efficient frontier and then calibrated the expected returns to achieve balanced asset mixes. (The expected returns in Exhibit 4.3 are the calibrated values.) The additional constraints that we imposed are:

(1) The minimum allocation to cash is 2%.
(2) U.S. Small-Cap Stocks and Emerging Markets Stocks together cannot make up more that 10% of equities.
(3) Non-U.S. stocks must be less than U.S. stocks.
(4) Non-U.S. bonds must be less than U.S. bonds.

The efficient frontier labeled "Constrained" is the result of running MVO using the capital market assumptions in Exhibit 4.3 with the standard constraints plus these four. Note how this frontier is entirely below the unconstrained frontier and it is much shorter. Instead of the asset class that maximizes expected return being 100% in a single asset class, as Exhibit 4.5 shows, it is much more balanced consisting of:

(1) 49.0% in U.S. Large-Cap Stocks
(2) 39.2% in Non-U.S. Developed Market Stocks
(3) 9.8% in Emerging Market Stocks
(4) 2.0% in Cash

This asset mix has a lower expected return and much less risk than Emerging Market Stocks. Hence it lower and to the left of the endpoint of the unconstrained frontier.

Exhibit 4.5 shows that over a large stretch of the constrained frontier, all seven asset classes are represented and in proportions that a U.S.-based investment committee could find acceptable (perhaps with some adjustments). The need to balance the mathematical precision of MVO with the need to form asset mixes that investors will find acceptable shows why asset allocation is a blend of art and science.

Beyond mean-variance optimization

While MVO is a powerful asset allocation framework, it does have some drawbacks and limitations:

Exhibit 4.5 Asset mixes along unconstrained efficient frontier

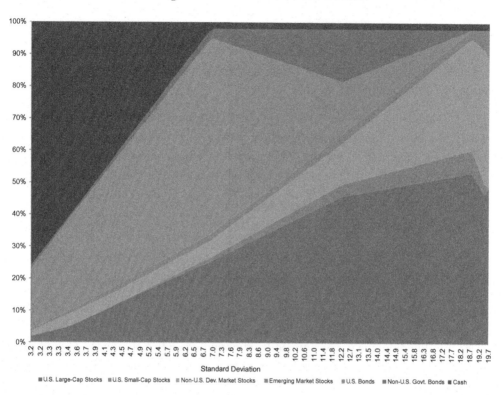

(1) Return distributions are described by only two parameters: mean and variance (the square of standard deviation.) While this does not mean that we are assuming that returns are normally distributed (as it is often mistakenly alleged), it does mean that the possibilities of extremes that markets occasionally exhibit, *fat tails*, are not being modeled.

(2) The statistical relationships between returns on different asset classes are limited to be linear. In MVO, the statistical relationship between the returns on any two asset classes is given solely by the correlation coefficient between them. This means that if we were to plot the returns of one against the other, we would be modeling their relationship with a linear regression line. But a linear regression line may not be an adequate model. A nonlinear relationship might be a more suitable model.

(3) The benefit from holding an asset mix is measure by its arithmetic expected return. This implies that the investor is only looking one period ahead when evaluating the distribution of future returns.

(4) Risk is measured by standard deviation of return which measures uncertainty about returns but makes no distinction between good returns and bad returns. However, to investors, risk is not just uncertainty. Rather, it is uncertainly about possible losses.

Markowitz himself has addressed these issues and has developed various alternatives to MVO. Paul Kaplan and Sam Savage, building on the work of Markowitz and others, developed a general framework for asset allocation optimization that they call *Markowitz 2.0*, which includes MVO as a special case (Kaplan and Savage, 2012).

Markowitz 2.0 address the limitations of MVO as follows:

Scenario approach

Rather than using a set of parameters to describe the joint distribution of asset class returns, in Markowitz 2.0, the model builder creates a list of all possible scenarios and the return on each asset class under each scenario. This allows for the possibility of fat tails. Also, it places no restrictions on the relationships between asset class returns, so nonlinear relationships are possible. The scenarios can be based on historical data (adjusted for forward-looking expected returns) or Monte Carlo simulation based on statistical models of returns that can include fat tails.

Geometric expected return

As we have already discussed, in MVO, expected return is the arithmetic mean of possible future returns, one period out. In the scenario approach, assuming that all scenarios are equally likely, we can write the expected arithmetic expected return of an asset class or asset mix as:

$$M = \frac{1}{n}(r_1 + r_2 + \cdots + r_n) \tag{4.3}$$

where

> n = the number of scenarios.
> M = the expected arithmetic mean expected return of the asset class or asset mix.
> r_i = the return on the asset class or asset mix under scenario i.

Over the long run, an investor would not be interest so much in a single-period return of an investment, but rather in the *time-weighted return*. As we discuss in Chapter 5, the time-weighted return measures an asset manager's performance. If the scenario model is correct, over the long-run, the time-weighted return should approach the geometric expected return (G) implied by the scenario model. This is given by:

$$G = \sqrt[n]{(1+r_1)(1+r_2)\cdots(1+r_n)} - 1 \tag{4.4}$$

There are several formulas for approximating geometric expected return from arithmetic expected return using several formulas. If returns follow a lognormal distribution, we have:

$$G = \frac{(1+M)^2}{\sqrt{(1+M)^2 + S^2}} - 1 \tag{4.5}$$

In the Markowitz 2.0 framework, either M or G can take be the expected return to be maximized; i.e., the property of the asset mix that the investor wants to maximize for a given level of risk.

Risk measures

Since to investors, risk is a matter of possible losses, it has been argued that any meaningful risk measure should only take into account only possible losses. Such a risk measure is called a *downside risk measure*.

Several downside risk measures have been proposed. Some require the selection of a target return to define what is meant by a loss. Letting τ denote the target return, the *below-target qth lower partial moment* is:

$$LPM_q(\tau) = \frac{1}{n} \sum_{i=1}^{n} \max(\tau - r_i, 0)^q \tag{4.6}$$

Alternatively, the arithmetic mean can be the target, in which case we have *below-mean qth lower partial moment*:

$$LPM_q^* = \frac{1}{n} \sum_{i=1}^{n} \max(\tau - r_A, 0)^q \tag{4.7}$$

A second lower partial moment is called a *semivariance*. Just as the square root of variance is called standard deviation, the square root of a second lower partial moment is called a *semideviation* or a *downside deviation*. The formulas for below-target downside deviation and below-mean downside deviation are as follows:

$$DD(\tau) = \sqrt{LPM_2(\tau)} \tag{4.8}$$

$$DD^* = LPM_2^* \tag{4.9}$$

Some proponents of using below-target semideviation instead if standard deviation have called their approach *postmodern portfolio theory*, although their approach is merely a special case of portfolio theory broadly defined as we discuss here (see Kaplan, 2017).

Another approach to measuring downside risk is *value-at-risk* (VaR). VaR is defined with respect to a given percentile which we denote as p. VaR(p) of a return distribution is the number such that there a p probability losing VaR(p) or more. In the notation of probability theory:

$$Prob\left[\tilde{r} \leq -VaR(p)\right] = p \tag{4.10}$$

The most common value for p is 5%.

VaR is not very useful itself because it only tells the location of the left tail of the distribution. It does not measure the severity of the losses of the left tail returns. This is measured by *conditional value-at-risk* (CVaR), also called *expected shortfall*. CVaR(p) is minus the average of returns less than $-$VaR(p). In the notation of probability theory:

$$CVaR(p) = -E\left[\tilde{r}\mid \tilde{r} \leq -VaR(p)\right] \tag{4.11}$$

CVaR is related to the 1st lower partial moment as follows:

$$CVaR(p) = VaR(p) + \frac{1}{p}LPM_1(-VaR(p)) \tag{4.12}$$

Markowitz 2.0 optimization

In summary, there are two forms of expected return (arithmetic and geometric) and six risk measures that can be used in optimization:

(1) Standard deviation
(2) Below-target 1st lower partial moment
(3) Below-mean 1st lower partial moment
(4) Below-target semideviation
(5) Below-mean semi-deviation
(6) Conditional value-at-risk

Hence, there are least 12 different Markowitz 2.0 optimization models. Note that MVO and so-called postmodern portfolio theory (expected arithmetic mean and below-target semideviation) are each just one of these models.

Example: Geometric expected return-CVaR optimization

To illustrate Markowitz 2.0, we generated 1000 scenarios of annual returns on the seven asset classes that we used in the MVO example using a Monte Carlo technique. We optimized on expected geometric return and 5% CVaR. Exhibit 4.6 shows the expected geometric return and CVaR of each asset classes based on the simulated returns as well as two efficient frontiers. Note that under in this model, Emerging Market Stocks has a lower expected geometric mean and a higher CVaR than U.S. Small-Cap Stocks. This reflects the high volatility of Emerging Market Stocks. Recall from Eq. (4.5) that for a given value of the arithmetic expected return, the higher the standard deviation of return, the lower the geometric expected return. Also, for a given level of arithmetic expected return, the higher the standard deviation, in general, the higher the CVaR.

We generated the efficient frontier labeled Unconstrained with only the minimum constraints of no short selling and the budget constraint. Exhibit 4.7 shows the asset mixes along this frontier. As in the MVO example, the asset mixes tend to be concentrated in certain asset classes, with U.S. Small-Cap Stocks being the dominate asset class at higher levels of risk. Asset classes that are usually considered core to a U.S. multi-asset class portfolio, U.S. Large-Cap Stocks and Non-U.S. Developed Market Stocks, are missing entirely.

Exhibit 4.6 Expected geometric return/CVaR Markowitz 2.0 efficient frontiers

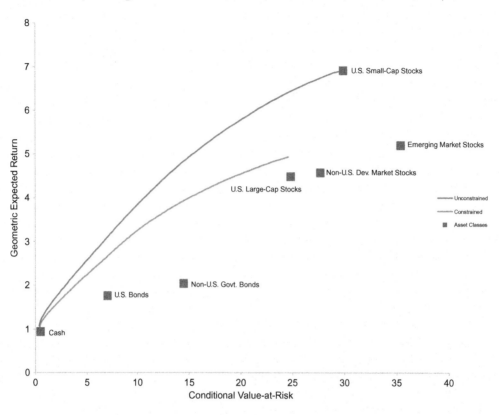

As in MVO, in Markowitz 2.0, we can address some of the issues of asset classes being over or underrepresented by imposing additional constraints. We impose the same additional constraints that we did in the MVO example. The result of this is the Constrained efficient frontier in Exhibit 4.6. Exhibit 4.8 shows the asset mixes along this frontier. While these asset mixes generally contain more asset classes that those of the unconstrained frontier, Emerging Markets Stocks are completely omitted. This asset class would have to be forced into the efficient frontier with a constraint that sets a minimum on its allocation.

So, while Markowitz 2.0 provides a more general and flexible framework for asset allocation, it still requires the same sort of calibration as MVO to produce acceptable asset mixes.

Manager allocation

Once the asset mix for a multi-asset class portfolio is selected, it needs to be implemented with investments. These investments can include:

Exhibit 4.7 Caption: asset mixes along unconstrained Markowitz 2.0 efficient frontier

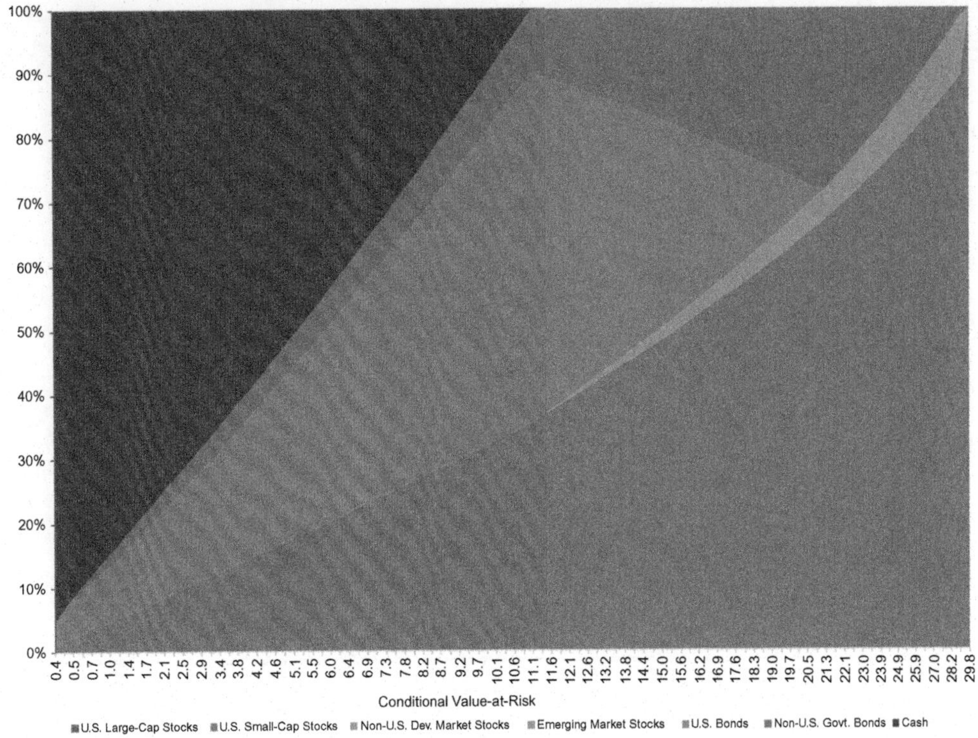
100%
90%
80%
70%
60%
50%
40%
30%
20%
10%
0%
0.4 0.5 0.7 1.0 1.4 1.7 2.1 2.5 2.9 3.4 3.8 4.2 4.6 5.1 5.5 6.0 6.4 6.9 7.3 7.8 8.2 8.7 9.2 9.7 10.1 10.6 11.1 11.6 12.1 12.6 13.2 13.8 14.4 15.0 15.6 16.2 16.9 17.6 18.3 19.0 19.7 20.5 21.3 22.1 23.0 23.9 24.9 25.9 27.0 28.2 29.8
Conditional Value-at-Risk
U.S. Large-Cap Stocks
U.S. Small-Cap Stocks
Non-U.S. Dev. Market Stocks
Emerging Market Stocks
U.S. Bonds
Non-U.S. Govt. Bonds
Cash

(1) Passively managed (internally or externally) portfolios to directly implement asset class exposures through portfolios that replicate asset class indexes.
(2) Actively managed (internally or externally) portfolios of individual securities, selected and weighted over time by portfolio managers or management teams who are trying to outperform benchmarks.

To relate actively managed portfolios to asset classes, we use multi-factor models of the form[e]:

$$R_j = \alpha_j + \sum_{k=1}^{M} \beta_{j,k} R_{Ik} + e_j \tag{4.13}$$

where

M = the number of risky asset classes.
R_j = the return (in excess of the risk-free rate) on managed portfolio j.

[e] We discuss multi-factor models in more detail in Chapter 5.

Exhibit 4.8 Asset mixes along constrained Markowitz 2.0 efficient frontier

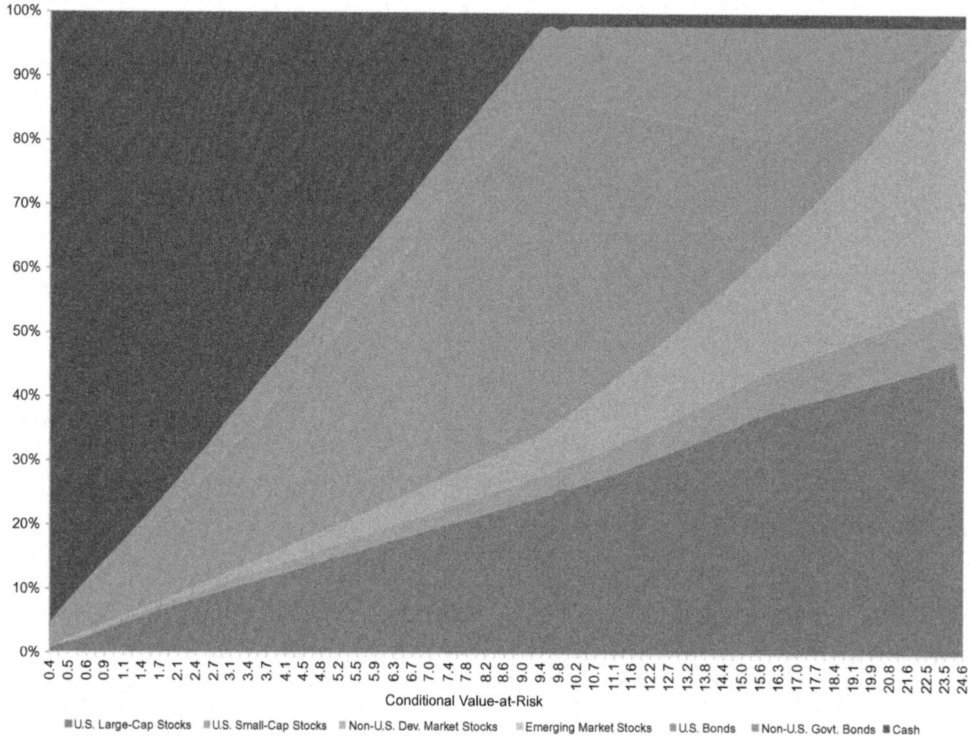

R_{Ik} = the return (in excess of the risk-free rate) on managed asset class index k.

α_j = the expected active return (alpha) on managed portfolio j.

$\beta_{j,k}$ = actively managed portfolio j's exposure to asset class k.

e_j = the unsystematic component of managed portfolio j's return.

Actively managed portfolio j's exposure to cash is:

$$\beta_{j,0} = 1 - \sum_{k=1}^{M} \beta_{j,k} \qquad (4.14)$$

The alphas should not be taken from the intercepts of regressions on historical returns. Rather, they should be estimated as forecasts of future active returns. There are several ways to do this. An article by Waring and Ramkumar (2008).

By definition, the unsystematic component of return, e_j, has the following properties:

(1) Has a mean of zero
(2) Is independent of the asset class index returns
(3) Is independent of the unsystematic components of other managed portfolios

We denote the standard deviation of e_j as σ_{ej}. This is the *unsystematic risk* (or *idiosyncratic risk*) of managed portfolio j.

Let

$\omega_j =$ the allocation to actively managed portfolio j in the overall portfolio.
$y_k =$ the allocation to the index fund for asset class k.

The exposure of the overall portfolio is:

$$\hat{x}_k = \sum_{j=1}^{N} \omega_{j,k} \beta_{j,k} + y_k \tag{4.15}$$

where N is the number of actively managed portfolios.

Let $\bar{x}_k$ denote the target allocation to asset class k for the portfolio as a whole. In manager allocation, we take this as given. Ideally, $\hat{x}_k = \bar{x}_k$ for each asset class. This could be achieved by investing in asset class index funds. However, in order to benefit from active management, it may be necessary to allow the overall portfolio's asset allocation to differ from the target. This creates *misfit risk* for the overall portfolio. Misfit risk is given by:

$$S_{MR} = \sqrt{\sum_{i=1}^{M} \sum_{k=1}^{M} (\hat{x}_i - \bar{x}_i)(\hat{x}_k - \bar{x}_k) S_i S_k \rho_{ik}} \tag{4.16}$$

where, as in the section on MVO, S_i denotes the standard deviation of return on asset class i and ρ_{ik} denotes the correlation between the returns on asset classes i and k.

Active management also introduces unsystematic risk into the overall portfolio. This is given by:

$$\sigma_{UR} = \sqrt{\sum_{j=1}^{N} \omega_j^2 \sigma_{ej}^2} \tag{4.17}$$

Taken together, misfit and unsystematic risk constitute *active risk*[f]

$$\sigma_{AR} = \sqrt{S_{MR}^2 + S_{UR}^2} \tag{4.18}$$

---

[f] Also called *tracking error*.

Of course, there is a positive side to active management; namely, the addition of alpha to the overall portfolio. The alpha for the overall portfolio is just the weighted average of the alphas of the managed portfolios:

$$\alpha_P = \sum_{j=1}^{N} \omega_j \alpha_j \qquad (4.19)$$

Manager structure optimization

The purpose of manager allocation is to strike a balance between alpha and the two forms of active risk, misfit and unsystematic. We do this using a special form of optimization, which is sometimes called *manager structure optimization* (MSO).[g] In MSO, the goal is to maximize the following objective function:

$$Q = \alpha_P - \frac{\lambda_{MR}}{2} S_{MR}^2 - \frac{\lambda_{UR}}{2} \sigma_{UR}^2 \qquad (4.20)$$

where λ_{MR} and λ_{UR} are *risk aversion* parameters for misfit and unsystematic risk respectively. The higher their values, the less risk will be taken in the solution.

The maximization of Q is subject to certain constraints:

(1)   Actively managed portfolios cannot be held short. Hence, $\omega_j \geq 0$ for $j = 1, 2, \ldots, N$.
(2)   The budget constraint:

$$\sum_{j=1}^{N} \omega_j + \sum_{k=0}^{M} y_k = 1 \qquad (4.21)$$

Note that in Eq. (4.21), y_0 denotes the allocation to cash.

If constraints (1) and (2) above were the only constraints, it would mean that cash and all of the asset class index funds (or exposure to the asset through some other means such as derivatives can be shorted. If that is the case, we have *portable alpha*. This means that we can select actively managed portfolios solely for their alphas, with their unsystematic risks as the only risks. We can use the asset class index funds (or equivalents) to make up the differences between the asset class exposures and the target asset allocation. With portable alpha, the allocation to each actively managed portfolio j is given by[h]:

$$\omega_j = \frac{\max(\alpha_j, 0)}{\lambda_{UR} \sigma_{ej}^2} \qquad (4.22)$$

---

[g] This term comes from Waring et al. (2000).

[h] Since it is possible for alpha to be negative (a forecast that the manager will detract value), and since actively managed portfolios cannot be shorted, we must take the greater of alpha and zero.

The allocation to each asset class index funds k, and cash ($k = 0$) is:

$$y_k = \bar{x}_k - \sum_{j=1}^{N} \omega_{j,k} \beta_{j,k} \qquad (4.23)$$

This eliminates misfit risk.

If cash and the asset class index funds cannot be shorted, so that $y_k \geq 0$ for $k = 0, 1, ..., M$, there will usually be some misfit risk. An exception is when we impose (4.23) as a constraint together with the constraint against shorting cash the asset class index funds. This can lead to considerable limits on allocations to actively managed portfolios as we demonstrate in the example below.

Example of manager structure optimization[i]

MSO requires the following inputs:

(1) The target asset class weights
(2) Standard deviations and correlations for the asset class returns
(3) For each actively managed portfolio:
    a. Alpha
    b. Exposure to each asset class
    c. Unsystematic risk
(4) Risk aversion coefficients for misfit and unsystematic risk

Exhibit 4.9[j] shows the target asset weights, standard deviation of returns, and correlations of returns for an eight-asset class model. Exhibit 4.10 shows the alphas, asset class exposures, and unsystematic risk for 20 actively managed portfolios. Note that some of the alphas are negative, meaning that these managers are forecast to detract value. Also note that some of the asset class exposures are negative. This is indicative that the asset class exposures where estimated from an unconstrained multifactor model.

---

[i] This example is taken from Kaplan (2016).

[j] © [2020] Morningstar, Inc. All Rights Reserved. The information contained herein: (1) is proprietary to Morningstar and /or its content providers; (2) may not be copied or distributed; (3) does not constitute investment advice offered by Morningstar; and (4) is not warranted to be accurate, complete, or timely. Neither Morningstar nor its content providers are responsible for any damages or losses arising from any use of this information. Past performance is no guarantee of future results. Use of information from Morningstar does not necessarily constitute agreement by Morningstar, Inc. of any investment philosophy or strategy presented in this publication.

Exhibit 4.9 Target asset mix and asset class parameters for manager structure optimization

Asset class	Benchmark weight (%)	Std. dev. (%)	Correlation with						
			U.S. Large-Cap Stocks	U.S. Small-Cap Stocks	Non-U.S. Developed Markets Stocks	Emerging Markets Stocks	U.S. Investment Grade Bonds	U.S. High Yield Bonds	Non-U.S. Bonds
U.S. Large-Cap Stocks	34	15.54	1.000						
U.S. Small-Cap Stocks	14	19.99	0.808	1.000					
Non-U.S. Developed Markets Stocks	8	15.00	0.825	0.790	1.000				
Emerging Markets Stocks	4	21.80	0.760	0.787	0.798	1.000			
U.S. Investment Grade Bonds	20	3.78	−0.223	−0.185	−0.146	−0.191	1.000		
U.S. High Yield Bonds	6	8.07	0.463	0.558	0.470	0.582	0.094	1.000	
Non-U.S. Bonds	4	8.52	−0.035	−0.027	0.247	0.011	0.520	0.094	1.000
Cash	10	—	—	—	—	—	—	—	—
Benchmark	100	9.66	0.957	0.914	0.897	0.848	−0.110	0.587	0.085

Exhibit 4.10 Parameters of managed portfolios for manager structure optimization

Asset class exposures (%) (betas)

Fund	Alpha	Unsystematic risk	U.S. Large-Cap Stocks	U.S. Small-Cap Stocks	Non-U.S. Developed Markets Stocks	Emerging Markets Stocks	U.S. Investment Grade Bonds	U.S. High Yield Bonds	Non-U.S. Bonds	Cash
U.S. Large-Cap Stock Fund 1	0.48	4.65	64.6	14.0	4.3	7.4	-13.3	-3.4	2.2	24.3
U.S. Large-Cap Stock Fund 2	0.19	4.10	79.1	2.3	11.5	2.0	26.7	-4.9	-9.5	-7.2
U.S. Large-Cap Stock Fund 3	0.12	3.62	87.1	-2.7	3.0	-0.9	-0.9	4.1	1.4	9.0
U.S. Large-Cap Stock Fund 4	0.04	2.98	93.6	-6.0	-0.4	-4.1	-3.5	5.7	4.6	10.1
U.S. Large-Cap Stock Fund 5	0.03	1.37	74.9	15.7	5.6	0.0	10.4	1.5	-4.9	-3.3
U.S. Large-Cap Stock Fund 6	0.02	1.31	92.0	-1.2	8.6	-0.8	2.5	3.6	-6.1	1.3
U.S. Small-Cap Stock Fund 1	0.12	8.84	-5.8	59.3	9.5	-1.0	-16.5	18.1	16.4	20.0
U.S. Small-Cap Stock Fund 2	0.03	4.59	-8.4	95.6	-6.8	3.1	16.0	-13.7	7.9	6.3
Non-U.S. Developed Markets Stock Fund 1	0.32	3.76	-4.2	-0.5	78.5	16.5	14.7	-3.7	-14.7	13.4
Non-U.S. Developed Markets Stock Fund 2	0.03	2.57	-1.3	-0.2	90.8	7.0	5.1	-3.4	3.3	-1.3

Fund										
Non-U.S. Developed Markets Stock Fund 3	-0.01	4.80	7.3	8.4	103.1	-11.9	-8.8	1.8	0.2	-0.1
Non-U.S. Developed Markets Stock Fund 4	-0.10	3.72	-1.2	2.8	101.5	-2.4	4.6	-3.0	-6.2	4.1
Emerging Markets Stock Fund	0.54	4.65	-8.6	11.0	24.8	84.2	32.3	-18.0	-9.7	-15.9
U.S. Investment Grade Bond Fund 1	0.12	1.12	-0.3	-0.3	1.3	0.4	74.3	-1.6	-3.0	29.1
U.S. Investment Grade Bond Fund 2	0.04	0.86	-0.7	-1.1	3.4	-0.4	103.2	3.5	-1.9	-6.0
U.S. Investment Grade Bond Fund 3	0.03	0.85	1.7	-2.0	0.1	-0.7	48.0	1.1	-0.8	52.6
U.S. Investment Grade Bond Fund 4	-0.01	0.76	-2.6	1.2	2.0	-0.4	95.5	3.9	-1.7	2.2
U.S. Investment Grade Bond Fund 5	-0.03	0.61	2.0	-1.5	-1.5	0.3	86.0	-1.7	2.6	13.8
U.S. High Yield Bond Fund	0.03	2.04	0.6	-0.1	11.4	-4.8	29.2	74.0	-7.4	-2.9
Non-U.S. Bond Fund	0.08	3.82	7.5	-0.1	-7.3	1.2	37.1	2.0	42.8	16.7

Exhibit 4.11 shows three efficient frontiers in alpha/active risk space. They all use the assumptions in Exhibits 4.9 and 4.10, but differ in their constraints:

(1) *Portable Alpha.* No constraints on cash and asset class indexes
(2) *With Misfit Risk.* No shorting cash and asset classes
(3) *No Misfit Risk Allowed.* No shorting cash and asset classes and no misfit

All three efficient frontiers start at the origin with an alpha of zero and active risk of zero. This portfolio consists of the index funds allocated according to the target asset mix. Portfolio A is a portable alpha portfolio and is therefore on all three efficient frontiers. This is because it takes only long positions in the index funds and cash so that the long-only constraints are not binding. This portfolio is 34.7% allocated to active fund and 65.3% allocated to index funds and cash.

Note that the Portable Alpha frontier is a straight line. This is because when we have portable alpha, all optimal portfolios have the same *information ratio*:

$$IR = \frac{\alpha_P}{\sigma_{UR}} \tag{4.24}$$

Exhibit 4.11 Efficient frontiers in alpha/active return space

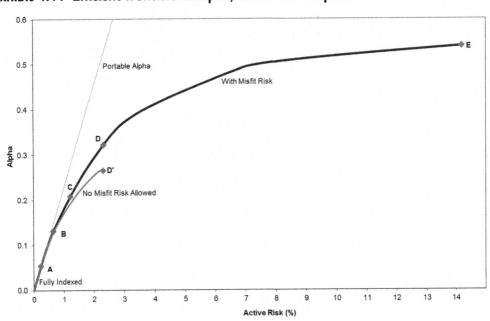

(Data Source: © [2020] Morningstar, Inc. All Rights Reserved, Reproduced with Permission.)

This information ratio is the highest possible for portfolios of actively managed portfolios that have positive alphas.

Portfolios B, C, D, and E are only on the "With Misfit Risk" efficient frontier. The allocation to active funds increases along this efficient frontier as we move up and to the right, taking an increasing amount of active risk. By Portfolio D, we are using only active funds. Misfit risk increases with the increase in allocation to active funds.

Portfolio E is the most extreme point on the "With Misfit Risk" efficient frontier. It is 100% allocated to the fund with the highest alpha, the Emerging Markets Stock Fund. While it has a high alpha, it has an extremely high level of active risk, most of which is due to misfit risk, so it would be of interest only to the most risk tolerant of investors.

Portfolio D′ is the most extreme point on the "No Misfit Allowed" efficient frontier. In order to fit the benchmark asset allocation exactly, this portfolio allocates 11.3% to index funds and cash. Portfolio D on the "With Misfit Risk" frontier has the same active risk as Portfolio D′. As can be seen graphically in Exhibit 4.11 and numerically in Exhibit 4.12, Portfolio D has a higher alpha than Portfolio D′. This difference in alpha is the cost of not allowing misfit risk.

Risk budgeting

The process of taking selected risks to obtain returns higher that the risk-free rate is sometimes *called risk budgeting*. Setting the target asset mix is the first step in risk budgeting. In this step, whoever has responsibility for the overall portfolio is taking on the *systematic risks* of the asset classes because each asset class has an associated *premium*, that is, expected return in excess of the risk-free rate. This step is complicated by the fact that there are no agreed upon values for these premiums, so judgment is involved.

The next step is the manager allocation step. In this step, whoever is responsible for the overall portfolio needs to select managers to implement the target asset mix. The easiest thing to do at this stage is to just use an index fund for each asset class. However, if there is a strong belief that active managers (internal or external) can generate alpha, it may be worth taking on additional risk in the forms of misfit risk and unsystematic risk. The manager structure optimization approach provides a what to carry out this stage of risk budgeting.

We now turn to process by which each manager constructs a portfolio of individual securities to fulfill the manager's specific mandate.

Portfolio construction at the security level

A security's portfolio weight is the proportion of the portfolio's value that is allocated to that security. Securities' portfolio weights define the portfolio and determine the portfolio outcomes and performance. Portfolio construction is the process through which these weights are set and

Exhibit 4.12 Details on selected portfolios from manager structure optimization

		Portfolio					
	Origin	A	B	C	D	D'	E
Active funds (%)	–	**34.7**	**67.0**	**88.3**	**100.0**	**88.7**	**100.0**
U.S. Large-Cap Stock Fund 1	–	2.4	8.9	19.7	40.4	49.5	–
U.S. Large-Cap Stock Fund 2	–	1.2	4.1	8.4	6.9	2.6	–
U.S. Large-Cap Stock Fund 3	–	1.0	3.9	7.8	–	–	–
U.S. Large-Cap Stock Fund 4	–	0.5	2.4	4.3	–	–	–
U.S. Large-Cap Stock Fund 5	–	1.5	4.3	2.4	–	–	–
U.S. Large-Cap Stock Fund 6	–	1.2	3.7	–	–	–	–
U.S. Small-Cap Stock Fund 1	–	0.2	0.6	1.3	2.7	–	–
U.S. Small-Cap Stock Fund 2	–	0.1	0.2	0.3	0.2	–	–
Non-U.S. Developed Markets Stock Fund 1	–	2.4	6.1	7.3	8.8	–	–
Non-U.S. Developed Markets Stock Fund 2	–	0.4	–	–	–	–	–
Non-U.S. Developed Markets Stock Fund 3	–	–	–	–	–	3.2	–
Non-U.S. Developed Markets Stock Fund 4	–	–	–	–	–	–	–
Emerging Markets Stock Fund	–	2.6	4.2	5.4	8.5	1.5	100.0
U.S. Investment Grade Bond Fund 1	–	9.7	23.7	24.0	29.7	–	–
U.S. Investment Grade Bond Fund 2	–	6.0	–	–	–	22.2	–
U.S. Investment Grade Bond Fund 3	–	4.2	–	–	–	–	–
U.S. Investment Grade Bond Fund 4	–	–	–	–	–	–	–
U.S. Investment Grade Bond Fund 5	–	–	–	–	–	–	–
U.S. High Yield Bond Fund	–	0.8	3.2	4.7	1.0	9.8	–
Non-U.S. Bond Fund	–	0.6	1.6	2.7	1.8	–	–
Index Funds and Cash	**100.0**	**65.3**	**33.0**	**11.7**	**–**	**11.3**	**–**
U.S. Large-Cap Stocks	14.0	28.4	12.8	–	–	–	–
U.S. Small-Cap Stocks	8.0	13.2	11.0	8.2	–	6.9	–
Non-U.S. Developed Markets Stocks	4.0	4.2	–	–	–	–	–

Emerging Markets Stocks	20.0	1.2	—	—	—	—	—
U.S. Investment Grade Bonds	6.0	2.7	—	—	—	—	—
U.S. High Yield Bonds	4.0	5.8	3.9	1.0	—	—	—
Non-U.S. Bonds		5.0	5.4	2.6	—	4.5	—
Cash		4.7	—	—	—	—	—
Aversion to Misfit Risk	∞	0.94	0.24	0.10	0.04	∞	0.00
Aversion to Specific Risk	∞	0.94	0.24	0.10	0.04	0.00	0.00
Alpha	—	0.054	0.131	0.208	0.322	0.265	0.540
Active Risk	—	0.239	0.652	1.230	2.329	2.328	14.211
Misfit Risk	—	—	0.141	0.463	1.173	—	13.429
Specific Risk	—	0.239	0.636	1.140	2.012	2.328	4.651

(Data Source: © [2020] Morningstar, Inc. All Rights Reserved. Reproduced with Permission.)

maintained. As such, portfolio construction is typically viewed as dealing primarily with a portfolio's risk, while security analysis and selection deal primarily with the portfolio's return.

Once a security is selected, its weight must be determined. As discussed in the previous chapter, these activities often are not mutually exclusive. Indeed, the selection of a security for inclusion in the portfolio results in the stock having a non-zero weight. However, there can be a meaningfully different outcome from holding a specific security at a weight of 1% compared to a weight of 5%, though both are non-zero weights. While the previous chapter discussed how security analysis results in the selection of securities in the portfolio, this section of this chapter focuses on the how to determine security weights of those selected securities and how to rebalance a portfolio to maintain security weights.

As with security analysis and selection, portfolio construction should be a clearly articulated component of the investment process. As such, portfolio construction should be motivated by and consistent with the investment philosophy and contribute to the overall objectives of the investment process. In some investment processes, security selection and portfolio construction might be fully integrated and inseparable components, while they might be mutually exclusive activities in others. Moreover, the emphasis within the investment process might be heavily skewed toward one activity or evenly split. That is, security selection and portfolio construction both contribute to value in an investment process. Therefore, the methods that yield the resulting portfolio weights should be clear in any investment process.

This section of this chapter covers numerous aspects of portfolio construction and the contribution of portfolio weights to portfolio performance. We use the term "performance" broadly to mean portfolio performance outcomes. As such, performance will at times refer to the expected or realized average returns, while at other times it will refer to the risk or distribution of returns.

We begin with a review of basic portfolio mathematics. While the review might be unnecessary for many readers, we also use introduce here the notation that we will use for the remainder of the book.

Portfolio weights and returns

Consider a portfolio worth a total of $V_{p,t}$ dollars at time t. Suppose for each stock i, the portfolio holds $S_{i,t}$ shares at a price per share of $P_{i,t}$ at time t. The weight of the stock in the portfolio is given by:

$$w_{i,t}^p = \frac{S_{i,t} \times P_{i,t}}{V_{p,t}} \tag{4.25}$$

The superscript on the weights identifies the weights as belonging to portfolio p. The weights of the N securities in the portfolio must sum to one at every point in time:

$$\sum_{i=1}^{N} w_{i,t}^p = 1 \tag{4.26}$$

Note that we have explicitly included time subscripts for the number of shares, stock price, weight, and portfolio value. Holding the number of shares constant, a stock's portfolio weight will change over time if the price of the stock changes and/or the value of the portfolio changes.

In the latter case, the weight of the stock might change when other securities' prices change, even if there is no change in the number of shares held in the portfolio. For convenience, we will often drop the time subscript from our notation if the time over which these are measured is unambiguous. However, we retain the time subscript for now and note that a time subscript on the number of shares is required if the number of shares changes over the time periods of interest.

The return for a stock over time t is defined as its percentage change in value from the end of the previous period to the end of the current period:

$$r_{i,t} = \frac{P_{i,t} - P_{i,t-1}}{P_{i,t-1}} \tag{4.27}$$

A portfolio's return is similarly defined:

$$r_{p,t} = \frac{V_{p,t} - V_{p,t-1}}{V_{p,t-1}} \tag{4.28}$$

Combining Eqs. (4.25), (4.27), and (4.28), a portfolio's return is the weighted average of the returns of the securities in the portfolio, as given by:

$$r_{p,t} = \sum_{i=1}^{N} w_{i,t-1}^p \times r_{i,t} \tag{4.29}$$

These equations make clear that two portfolios that hold the same securities at different weights are different portfolios and have different realized returns. For example, a value-weighted portfolio of 500 stocks will perform differently from an equally weighted portfolio of the same 500 stocks. Likewise, two portfolios that have different rebalancing schemes will have weights that evolve differently over time as number of shares changes. Therefore, an equally weighted portfolio that is rebalanced on a quarterly basis will perform differently from an equally weighted portfolio that is rebalanced on a daily basis, even ignoring transaction costs. In either case, portfolio construction has direct impacts on portfolio performance.

Active returns and active weights

An investment strategy that aims to beat a specific benchmark's return is often referred to as an active return strategy. This reflects the fact that the portfolio's absolute return is less important than its return relative to or against the benchmark. For example, an investment manager who is hired by his or her client to manage a large cap core mandate with the S&P 500 Index as the benchmark is likely to be evaluated exclusively against that benchmark. The absolute performance of the portfolio is of little concern. If the portfolio has a 15% return in a given year, the firm's clients may view this as a terrible year if the S&P 500 experiences a 25% return. Likewise, if the portfolio loses 5% in a year, the client may celebrate this if the S&P 500 loses 12% that year.

The selection of securities and their weights distinguish one benchmark from another. The most popular benchmarks used in institutional portfolios in the United States are the S&P (e.g., S&P 500, S&P 400, and S&P 600) and Russell (e.g., Russell 1000, Russell 2000, and Russell 3000) equity indexes and the Barclays (e.g., Barclay's Aggregate and Barclay's U.S. Treasury). The FTSE (e.g., FTSE All World) and MSCI indexes (e.g., MSCI EAFE and MSCI EM) are among the most popular non-U.S. and global indexes. (Recall Exhibit 4.1 which lists asset classes and indexes that can serve as their benchmarks.) In general, good benchmarks are those that clearly define the set of securities and weights so that a passive investment in the benchmark is feasible. The benchmark should be consistent with the portfolio's target asset class mix and style.

Finally, the benchmark for any active strategy should be declared in advance so that outcomes can be measured against it.

We can express a portfolio's active return in terms of a weighted average of the underlying security's active returns. Defining $rr_{i,t} = r_{i,t} - r_{b,t}$ to be the active return on security i, relative to the portfolio's benchmark, the portfolio's active return is given by:

$$rr_{p,t} = r_{p,t} - r_{b,t} = \sum_{i=1}^{N} w_{i,t-1}^{p} \times rr_{i,t} \tag{4.30}$$

Thus, the higher the weight on securities with higher active returns, the higher the active return of the portfolio. This is just one way to express the active return of the portfolio. It is also useful to consider alternative forms of calculating the portfolio's active return. Specifically, we can use the fact that the benchmark is simply a portfolio that has a specific weight on each constituent security, and zero weights on non-constituent securities. Therefore, the benchmark's return can be written as:

$$r_{b,t} = \sum_{i=1}^{N} w_{i,t-1}^{b} \times r_{i,t} \tag{4.31}$$

Using the securities' benchmark weights and portfolio weights, the portfolio's active return can be written in terms of the securities' portfolio and benchmark weights and the securities' returns, as given by:

$$
\begin{aligned}
r_{p,t} - r_{b,t} &= \sum_{i=1}^{N} w_{i,t-1}^{p} \times r_{i,t} - \sum_{i=1}^{N} w_{i,t-1}^{b} \times r_{i,t} \\
&= \sum_{i=1}^{N} \left(w_{i,t-1}^{p} - w_{i,t-1}^{b} \right) \times r_{i,t}
\end{aligned} \tag{4.32}
$$

In this calculation, the number of securities, N, refers to the number of securities in the benchmark plus any non-benchmark securities in the portfolio. More generally, N could represent all securities in the market, with the portfolio and the benchmark having significant numbers of securities with zero weights.

The difference between the security's weight in a portfolio and the benchmark is known as a security's active weight. We define $\delta_{i,t-1}^{p} = w_{i,t-1}^{p} - w_{i,t-1}^{b}$ as the *active weight* in portfolio p.

on security i at time t-1. Therefore, the active return on an actively managed portfolio is the sum of the product of all portfolio and benchmark securities' active weights and returns:

$$r_{p,t} - r_{b,t} = \sum_{i=1}^{N} \delta_{i,t-1}^{p} \times r_{i,t} \tag{4.33}$$

where

$$\sum_{i=1}^{N} \delta_{i,t-1}^{p} = 0 \tag{4.34}$$

Notice that the portfolios' active weights sum to zero. Clearly, a passive portfolio that mimics the benchmark exactly would have an active weight of zero for every benchmark security. Any other portfolio has at least some non-zero active weights, while still having the property that the active weights sum to zero. Securities with active weights that are positive are known as overweighted securities, or just overweights. Likewise, those securities with negative active weights are known as underweighted securities, or just underweights. Another interpretation of overweights and underweights is to think of them as *long* positions and *short* positions, respectively, relative to the benchmark. Indeed, any benchmark security that is not held in the portfolio is short relative to the benchmark. Furthermore, the amount by which the non-held security is short is its benchmark weight. Any other security for which the portfolio weight is less than the benchmark weight is also short relative to the benchmark by the difference between the benchmark weight and the portfolio weight.

The framework of an active return strategy as given above is useful in both security analysis and portfolio construction. This framework reveals that value can be added in a active return strategy by overweighting good securities and/or underweighting bad securities. That is, both picking winners and avoiding losers within the target benchmark contribute to the outperformance of a portfolio relative to its benchmark. Thus, a strategy need not actually short sell securities on an absolute basis to benefit from the ability to identify underperforming securities. Rather, such a strategy benefits relative to its benchmark by underweighting securities that underperform.

Furthermore, the above framework is flexible in its application to securities or groups of securities. Heretofore, we have focused the discussion on security weights and returns. However, this framework can be applied to weights and returns of groups of securities, such as groupings based on asset class, sector, characteristic, or factor. For example, the S&P 500 Index can be split among GICS sectors. Exhibit 4.13 provides the definitions for the GICS sectors. For a portfolio that has N_s securities from group s, the portfolio's weight in group s is the sum of the weights of the securities in group s:

$$w_{s,t}^{p} = \sum_{i=1}^{N_s} w_{i,t}^{p} \tag{4.35}$$

where each i is a member of group s. Note that Eq. (4.35) can also be written in active weight terms along the lines of Eqs. (4.33) and (4.34). As such, group weights and active weights

Exhibit 4.13

(A) Introducing Communication Services Sector in 2018

The last several years have seen rapid evolution in the way people communicate, access entertainment content and other information. This evolution is a result of the integration between telecommunications, media, and internet companies. Companies have moved further in this direction by consolidating through mergers and acquisitions and many now offer bundled services such as cable, internet services, and telephone services. Some of these companies also create interactive entertainment content and aggregate information that is delivered through multiple platforms such as cable and internet, as well as accessed on cellular phones.

Summary of changes

Telecommunication Services Sector renamed to Communication Services Sector

The Telecommunication Services Sector is renamed to Communication Services to include companies that facilitate communication and offer related content through various media. It includes: Media companies moved from Consumer Discretionary to Communication Services. Internet services companies moved from Information Technology to Communication Services.

Information Technology Sector

The Internet Software & Services Industry and Sub-Industry is discontinued.

A new Sub-Industry is created under the IT Services Industry called Internet Services & Infrastructure. The Application Software Sub-Industry is updated to include cloud-based software companies.

Consumer Discretionary Sector

The Media Industry Group is moved out of Consumer Discretionary and into the Communication Services Sector, and renamed Media & Entertainment.

E-commerce companies are moved from Information Technology to Consumer Discretionary.

These changes were implemented after the close of business (ET) on Friday, September 28, 2018 in GICS Direct and in the MSCI Equity Indexes in one step as part of the November 2018 Semi-Annual Index Review (source: https://www.msci.com/gics).

(B) Global Industry Classification Standard (GICS) Sector Definitions

Now, GICS has 11 sectors which are described below.

Energy Sector: The GICS Energy Sector comprises companies whose businesses are dominated by either of the following activities: The construction or provision of oil rigs, drilling equipment, and other energy-related service and equipment, including seismic data collection. Companies engaged in the exploration, production, marketing, refining, and/or transportation of oil and gas products.

Materials Sector: The GICS Materials Sector encompasses a wide range of commodity-related manufacturing industries. Included in this sector are companies that manufacture chemicals, construction materials, glass, paper, forest products and related packaging products, and metals, minerals, and mining companies, including producers of steel.

Industrials Sector: The GICS Industrials Sector includes companies whose businesses are dominated by one of the following activities: the manufacture and distribution of capital goods, including aerospace and defense, construction, engineering and building products, electrical equipment, and industrial machinery. The provision of commercial services and supplies, including printing, data processing, employment, environmental, and office services. The provision of transportation services, including airlines, couriers, marine, road and rail, and transportation infrastructure.

Consumer Discretionary Sector: The GICS Consumer Discretionary Sector encompasses those industries that tend to be the most sensitive to economic cycles. Its manufacturing segment includes automotive, household durable goods, textiles and apparel, and leisure equipment. The services segment includes hotels, restaurants and other leisure facilities, media production and services, and consumer retailing.

Consumer Staples Sector: The GICS Consumer Staples Sector comprises companies whose businesses are less sensitive to economic cycles. It includes manufacturers and distributors of food, beverages, and tobacco and producers of nondurable household goods and personal products. It also includes food and drug retailing companies.

Health Care Sector: The GICS Health Care Sector encompasses two main industry groups. The first includes companies who manufacture health care equipment and supplies or provide health-care-related services, including distributors of health care products, providers of basic health care services, and owners and operators of health care facilities and organizations. The second regroups companies primarily involved in the research, development, production, and marketing of pharmaceuticals and biotechnology products.

Financials Sector: The GICS Financial Sector contains companies involved in activities such as banking, consumer finance, investment banking and brokerage, asset management, insurance and investment, and real estate, including REITs.

Information Technology Sector: The GICS Information Technology Sector covers the following general areas: first, Technology Software and Services, including companies that primarily develop software in various fields such as the Internet, applications, systems, and/or databases management, and companies that provide information technology consulting and services; second, Technology Hardware and Equipment, including manufacturers and distributors of communications equipment, computers and peripherals, electronic equipment and related instruments, and semiconductor equipment and products.

Communication Services Sector: The GICS Communication Services Sector contains companies that provide communications services primarily through a fixed-line, cellular, wireless, high bandwidth, and/or fiber optic cable network.

Utilities Sector: The GICS Utilities Sector encompasses those companies considered electric, gas, or water utilities or companies that operate as independent producers and/or distributors of power. This sector includes both nuclear and non-nuclear facilities.

Real Estate Sector: Real Estate is being moved out from under the Financials Sector and being promoted to its own Sector under the code 60. The Real Estate Investment Trusts Industry is being renamed to Equity Real Estate Investment Trusts (REITs), and excludes Mortgage REITs. Mortgage REITs remain in the Financials Sector under a newly created Industry and Sub-Industry called Mortgage REITs.

---

combine with group returns to generate portfolio returns and active returns. Specifically, a portfolio might generate relative performance from overweighting and underweighting specific sectors, smaller stocks, or growth-oriented stocks. For a fixed income portfolio, such active performance might originate from active weights to a particular duration or credit risk.

An example of group weightings appears in the TCU EIF investment process. Recall that the TCU EIF investment process was discussed in Chapter 2 regarding its approach to security selection and analysis. Of importance here is how the TCU EIF constructs its portfolio with specific allocation to asset classes and sectors within the equity class as described in Exhibit 4.14. Notice that the TCU EIF portfolio construction specifically contemplates the benchmark weights in setting sector weights. In this way, the group makes an explicit consideration of active sector weights in constructing the fund.

Exhibit 4.14 Texas Christian University Educational Investment Fund top-down balanced portfolio construction approach

The TCU-EIF is a well-diversified balanced fund, investing across multiple asset classes. The fund's long-term strategic asset allocation is 70/25/5 percentage allocations to stocks, bonds, and cash, respectively. Exposure to real estate and international assets is also encouraged. Tactical asset deviations from the strategic allocations are exercised within limits. For instance, equity allocations can range between 60% and 80% depending on shorter term capital market forecasts of the fund members.

At the beginning of the semester, the Fund's Chief Economist provides a state of the global economy address. Key macroeconomic variables discussed include gross domestic product, industrial production, capacity utilization, inflation, unemployment rates, default risk spreads, maturity risk spreads, intermediate Treasury bond rates, federal debt as a percentage of GDP, U.S. dollar strength relative to key foreign currencies, retail sales, fiscal and monetary policy, housing prices, and foreclosure rates. We use these and other leading indicators to proactively move assets to favorable sectors, evaluate businesses within those sectors using appropriate valuation techniques, and finally, to make investment decisions on individual companies.

After the economist's presentation, the class spends 1 week examining individual sectors. Class members are assigned to examine specific sectors and then to make formal presentations to the class, after which sector allocation targets are established for the semester. Targets are established by majority vote of fund members. Active sector allocations for equities are made relative to the S&P 500 equity industry sector allocations. Allocations can deviate up to 25% relative to the S&P 500 weightings. For instance, if 20% of the S&P 500 is allocated to the information technology sector, the EIF target weight to the sector can range anywhere from 15% to 25%, depending on the funds expectations for the sector.

Tactical decisions also are made to equities segmented by capital appreciation (dividend yields less than 2%), income and capital appreciation (dividend yields between 2% and 4%) and income (dividend yields over 4%) stocks. The fixed income portion of the portfolio is invested primarily in fixed income mutual funds, which are monitored by the fund's fixed income analysts. Fixed income deliberations focus on maturity and quality sector weightings. Key factors include interest rate movements, business cycle projections, duration, and convexity.

Equities are valued based on dividend discount (DDM) and discounted cash flow (DCF) models. DCF models include both the free cash flow to the firm (FCFF) and free cash flow to equity methods (FCFE). The discount rate used for the DDM and FCFE is determined using the Capital Asset Pricing Model (CAPM). In the CAPM, we use the currently quoted yield on 30-year U.S. Treasury bonds to proxy for the risk-free rate and we use the long-term (since 1926) geometric average difference in returns between large cap U.S. stocks and long-term government bonds to proxy for the market equity risk premium. As a check, we also use a bond build-up method to determine each stock's cost of equity. The bond build-up return equals the currently quoted yield on the firm's longest dated bond plus a 300 to 400 basis point equity premium. For all models, we forecast out 3–5 years. Terminal values are determined using two methods (1) applying a perpetual growth to dividends or free cash flows and (2) applying a multiple (P/E or EV/EBIDTA) on earnings or EBITDA. To reduce group-think biases, decisions to buy or sell are based on a super-majority 70% vote from class members.

Expected returns

The expected return of a portfolio is the weighted average of the expected returns of the portfolio's securities. In short, if the investment manager selects securities with high expected returns, the portfolio should have a high expected return. As such, the expected return is largely determined by security selection and analysis that is covered in Chapter 2. However, the resulting portfolio expected return is also impacted by the choice of portfolio weights. We show this by taking the statistical expectation of Eq. (4.29) to get the portfolio's expected return. Assuming that portfolio weights are constant, the expected return of the portfolio is given by:

$$E[r_p] = \sum_{i=1}^{N} w_i^p \times E[r_i] \qquad (4.36)$$

where $E[r_i]$ is the expected return of asset i.

Similarly, we can determine the average portfolio return using the average of the portfolio securities' returns by taking the average of Eq. (4.29). Assuming constant portfolio weights, the arithmetic average portfolio return is given by:

$$\bar{r}_p = \sum_{i=1}^{N} w_i^p \times \bar{r}_i \qquad (4.37)$$

where $\bar{r}_i$ is the expected return of asset i.

Earlier in this chapter we discussed the geometric expected return calculated over a set of scenarios. When the calculation is performed over a period of time, it is called the *geometric mean* of returns. Hence, the geometric mean of returns is the multiplication of one plus return for each period for T periods and then powered by $1/T$. The geometric mean of returns makes fundamental sense in investments simply because wealth is cumulative. For example, with 100 dollars invested in a security that had return of 50% for yesterday and −50% for today, then the wealth is 75 dollars by end of today, that is the return for those 2 days are −25%. While by the algebraic mean, we would have the return of 0% for those 2 days.

The assumption that weights are constant is unlikely to be true. Indeed, other than extreme coincidence, weights are constant only if the portfolio is rebalanced to the same weights at least as often as, or more often than, the data are observed. For example, to use Eq. (4.37) to calculate the average return of an equally weighted portfolio using monthly returns, the portfolio must be rebalanced at least monthly to maintain the equal weights. If the portfolio is not rebalanced monthly, the security weights drift away from their starting values due to price changes. Consequently, the average return of a rebalanced portfolio can differ from the average return of a portfolio that is not rebalanced, even if both portfolios start with the same security weights. For the constant weight formula in Eq. (4.36) to work exactly, the frequency of rebalancing must match the frequency with which returns are measured.

The constant weight formulas also apply to the calculation of relative returns (realized or expected). The expected relative return of a portfolio is the expected portfolio return minus the expected benchmark return,

$$E\left[r_p\right] - E[r_b] = E\left[r_p - r_b\right] = \sum_{i=1}^{N} w_i^p \times E[r_i - r_b] = \sum_{i=1}^{N} w_i^p \times E[rr_i] \tag{4.38}$$

Likewise, the average relative return of the portfolio is given by:

$$\overline{rr}_p = \overline{r}_p - \overline{r}_b = \sum_{i=1}^{N} w_i^p \times (\overline{r}_i - \overline{r}_b) = \sum_{i=1}^{N} w_i^p \times (\overline{r}_i - \overline{r}_b) \tag{4.39}$$

These equations illustrate that the portfolio's expected or average relative return depends on securities' portfolio weights and their relative returns. The higher the weight on securities with higher active returns, the higher the portfolio's average relative return.

We can also express a portfolio's average relative return in terms of each security's average relative return:

$$\overline{r}_p - \overline{r}_b = \sum_{i=1}^{N} w_i^p \times (\overline{r}_i - \overline{r}_b) = \sum_{i=1}^{N} w_i^p \times (\overline{r}_i - \overline{r}_b) \tag{4.40}$$

Total risk of a portfolio

A common measure of total risk in a portfolio is the portfolio's variance of returns. It is also common to use standard deviation, which is the square root of the variance. The return variance of a constant weight portfolio depends on the variances and covariances of the portfolio's underlying securities. Denote the covariance between security i and security j as $\sigma_{i,j}^2 = Cov(r_i, r_j)$ and the variance of security i as $\sigma_i^2 = Var(r_i) = Cov(r_i, r_i) = \sigma_{i,i}^2$. For a portfolio of N securities, the $N \times N$ covariance matrix has off-diagonal (i.e., when $i \neq j$) elements of $\sigma_{i,j}^2$

and diagonal (i.e., when $i = j$) elements of the covariance matrix are σ_i^2. The portfolio variance is given by[k]:

$$Var(r_p) = \sigma_p^2 = \sum_{i=1}^{N}\sum_{j=1}^{N} w_i^p w_j^p \sigma_{i,j}^2 \tag{4.41}$$

However, when the number of securities is large, the elements of the covariance should not be estimated directly. Rather, a factor model should be used. In a factor model, the covariation of returns between securities is due to exposure to a set of common factors. A security-level factor model for security i can be written as follows:

$$r_i = E[r_i] + \sum_{k=1}^{K} \beta_{i,k} f_k + e_i \tag{4.42}$$

where

K = the number of factors.
$\beta_{i,k}$ = the *factor loading* for the security on factor k. Also called *beta*, it is the security's exposure to the factor.
f_k = the kth factor. Each factor has an expected value of 0.
e_i = the residual. It has an expected value of 0 and is uncorrelated with all the factors, and uncorrelated with residuals of other securities.

The factors can be derived from index returns. But they also be derived from any variable that has a pervasive effect on security returns, such as macroeconomic variables (GDP growth, interest rates, inflation, etc.).

Using a factor model, we can calculate the variance of any security i:

$$Var(r_i) = \sum_{k=1}^{K}\sum_{q=1}^{K} \beta_{i,k}\beta_{i,q} S_{k,q}^2 + \sigma_{ei}^2 \tag{4.43}$$

where

$S_{k,q}^2$ = the covariance of factors k and q
σ_{ei}^2 = the variance of the residual of the security

The first term on the right-hand side of Eq. (4.43) captures the security's systematic risk. The second term is unsystematic risk.

---

[k] Using matrix notation, we can define the N-dimensional vector of security weights as w and the covariance matrix as V, so that portfolio variance is $w'Vw$.

The covariance between the returns on securities i and j is:

$$Cov(r_i, r_j) = \sum_{k=1}^{K} \sum_{q=1}^{K} \beta_{i,k} \beta_{j,q} S_{k,q}^2 \qquad (4.44)$$

To calculate the variance of a portfolio, we first calculate the betas of the portfolio. For each factor k, the portfolio beta is:

$$\beta_k^p = \sum_{i=1}^{N} w_i^p \beta_{i,k} \qquad (4.45)$$

The variance of the return on the portfolio is:

$$Var(r_p) = \sum_{k=1}^{K} \sum_{q=1}^{K} \beta_k^p \beta_q^p S_{k,q}^2 + \sum_{i=1}^{N} (w_i^p)^2 \sigma_{ei}^2 \qquad (4.46)$$

The standard deviation of the portfolio is, of course, given by:

$$\sigma_p = \sqrt{\sigma_p^2} \qquad (4.47)$$

The formula for portfolio variance illustrates that portfolio risk increases when more weight is placed on securities with (1) higher factor exposures and (2) higher unsystematic risk. Total risk is often important when the portfolio is considered as an investor's only portfolio or investment.

Factor models are important in modeling the risk of portfolios of individual securities for at least three reasons:

(1) *Parsimony.* If 100 stocks are being considered for the portfolio, the covariance matrix will have 5050 distinct values. Estimating and processing this many parameters is unworkable.

(2) *Mathematical soundness.* If the covariance matrix is estimated with fewer observations than there are securities, it would make it possible to form riskless portfolio of risky securities, which is of course impossible. By keeping systematic risk to a few factors and the systemic risk of each security uncorrelated with all else, factor models allow us to model the covariance of security returns in a mathematically sound way in which these is no limit on the number of securities.

(3) *Factor-based optimization.* Optimization software for creating portfolios at the security level is almost always based on factor models. Factor models allow the optimization software to find solutions quickly for large numbers of securities.

The simplest factor model is the single-factor model. In this model, the factor is usually based on a broad market index, such as the S&P 500. Hence, it is sometimes called the *market model*.[1] Therefore, we can write the single-factor model as follows:

$$r_i = E[r_i] + \beta_i(r_{Mkt} - E[r_{Mkt}]) + e_i \tag{4.48}$$

where r_{Mkt} denotes the return in the market index.

In the single factor model, the variance of return on security i is:

$$Var(r_i) = \beta_i^2 S_{Mkt}^2 + \sigma_{ei}^2 \tag{4.49}$$

where S_{Mkt}^2 is the variance of the return on the market index.

The covariance of the returns on securities i and j is:

$$Cov(r_i, r_j) = \beta_i \beta_j S_{Mkt}^2 \tag{4.50}$$

The variance of a portfolio is:

$$Var(r_p) = (\beta^p)^2 S_{Mkt}^2 + \sum_{i=1}^{N} (w_i^p)^2 \sigma_{ei}^2 \tag{4.51}$$

where β^p is the portfolio beta, calculated using Eq. (4.45).

Exhibit 4.15 shows estimates of beta and unsystematic risk for 10 stocks. The estimation was carried out by regressing the monthly excess returns on the stocks on the S&P 500 over a 60-month period. The exhibit also shows the R-squareds of the regressions, some of which are quite low, showing that a lot of the volatility of returns is not due to general movements in the market, but rather to stock-specific risk or factors not included in the model. For the purposes of illustration, we use the single-factor model for the remainder of this chapter, even though it has this limitation. Exhibit 4.15 also shows three portfolios of the 10 stocks and the portfolio risk for each of them.

To show how to calculate risk using the single-factor model, we created Exhibit 4.15 is the image of a spreadsheet. Exhibit 4.16 presents the formulas for the calculated cells in Exhibit 4.15.

Tracking error and relative risk

Tracking error is the risk of a portfolio's returns relative to its benchmark. This measure of relative risk is often important when the mandate for the investment manager is to outperform a specific benchmark, but to also have a similar exposure to that benchmark's asset class. For example, a client might grant an active U.S. small cap core mandate to an investment manager with either the Russell 2000 Index or the S&P Small Cap 600 Index as a benchmark. The client

---

[1] The market model is sometimes mistakenly called the Capital Asset Pricing Model (CAPM). While both focus on market return, they differ in the CAPM is a model of expected returns, while the market model is a model of realized returns.

Exhibit 4.15 Calculating portfolio risk using the single-factor model in Excel

| Workbook Views | | | Show | | Zoom | | | | Window | | | |

H18 fx =SQRT(H16^2*F13^2+H17^2)

	A	B	C	D	E	F	G	H	I	J	K
1									Portfolios		
					Monthly Unsystematic	Factor Model		Equal	Basic Constraints	Upper & Lower	
2	Stock	Ticker	Beta	R-Squared	Risk (%)	Total Risk (%)		Weights	Only	Bounds	
3	Microsoft Corp	MSFT	1.22	45.93%	4.61	6.25		10.00%	0.04%	5.00%	
4	Canon Inc	CAJFF	0.54	16.64%	4.16	4.55		10.00%	24.79%	20.00%	
5	Apple Inc	AAPL	1.25	31.18%	6.43	7.73		10.00%	0.00%	5.00%	
6	Oracle Corp	ORCL	1.16	53.91%	3.71	5.45		10.00%	3.07%	7.71%	
7	International Business Machines Corp	IBM	1.34	50.60%	4.60	6.52		10.00%	0.00%	5.00%	
8	Coca-Cola Co	KO	0.45	18.09%	3.35	3.70		10.00%	42.81%	20.00%	
9	Wells Fargo & Co	WFC	1.11	41.79%	4.55	5.94		10.00%	3.49%	7.29%	
10	Dillard's Inc Class A	DDS	1.14	11.21%	11.15	11.82		10.00%	0.42%	5.00%	
11	Rockwell Automation Inc	ROK	1.41	55.36%	4.41	6.56		10.00%	0.00%	5.00%	
12	CenterPoint Energy Inc	CNP	0.47	12.55%	4.31	4.60		10.00%	25.37%	20.00%	
13	S&P 500		1.00	100.00%	0.00	3.44					
14											
15						Total Weights		100.00%	100.00%	100.00%	
16						Beta		1.01	0.53	0.78	
17						Unsystematic Risk (%)		1.76	2.09	1.63	
18						Total Risk (%)		3.89	2.76	3.14	

Exhibit 4.16 Excel formulas for calculating risk using the single-factor model

Variable	Cells	Algebraic formula	Example Excel formula
Security Total Risk	F3:F12	$\sqrt{\beta_i^2 S_{Mkt}^2 + \sigma_{ei}^2}$	=SQRT($C3^2*$F$13^2 + $E3^2)
Portfolio Total Weights	H15:J15	$\sum_{i=1}^{N} w_i^p$	=SUM(H$3:H$12)
Portfolio Beta	H16:J16	$\sum_{i=1}^{N} w_i^p \beta_i$	=SUMPRODUCT($C$3:$C$12,H$3:H$12)
Portfolio Unsystematic Risk	H17:J17	$S_{UR}^p = \sqrt{\sum_{i=1}^{N} \left(w_i^p\right)^2 \sigma_{ei}^2}$	=SQRT(SUMPRODUCT(H$3:H$12, H$3:H$12,$E$3:$E$12,$E$3:$E$12))
Portfolio Total Risk	H18:J18	$\sqrt{\left(\beta^p\right)^2 S_{Mkt}^2 + \left(S_{UR}^p\right)^2}$	=SQRT(H16^2*F$13^2 + H$17^2)

might expect the investment manager's portfolio to outperform the Russell 2000 Index over time, but to generally track the index's ups and downs. Tracking error is a measure of how poorly the portfolio tracks the benchmark. More precisely, tracking error is the standard deviation of the portfolio's relative returns versus the benchmark index. As such, the average active return of a portfolio does not count as tracking error. Rather, the variation around the average active return counts as tracking error.

Mathematically, the tracking error of a portfolio p relative to benchmark b (i.e., the relative return variance of the portfolio is defined to be $\tau_p = \sqrt{\tau_p^2}$, where $\tau_p^2 = Var(r_p - r_b)$). Again, the tracking error is simply the standard deviation of relative returns.

We can use active weights with a factor model to calculate portfolio tracking error. To do this with a factor model, we first need to calculate the betas using active weights ($\delta_i^p = w_i^p - w_i^b$):

$$\hat{\beta}_k^p = \sum_{i=1}^{N} \delta_i^p \beta_{i,k} \tag{4.52}$$

The portfolio's relative return variance is given by:

$$\tau_p^2 = \sum_{k=1}^{K} \sum_{q=1}^{K} \hat{\beta}_k^p \hat{\beta}_q^p S_{k,q}^2 + \sum_{i=1}^{N} \left(\delta_i^p\right)^2 \sigma_{ei}^2 \tag{4.53}$$

In some cases, the benchmark is entirely made up of factor exposures. Letting β_k^b denote the benchmark's exposure to factor k, we define security i's relative beta on factor k to be:

$$\hat{\beta}_{i,k} = \beta_{i,k} - \beta_k^b \tag{4.54}$$

Hence, the portfolio's relative beta on factor k is:

$$\hat{\beta}_k^p = \sum_{i=1}^{N} w_i^p \hat{\beta}_{i,k} \tag{4.55}$$

The since there is no unsystematic risk in the benchmark, the portfolio's relative return variance is given by:

$$\tau_p^2 = \sum_{k=1}^{K} \sum_{q=1}^{K} \hat{\beta}_k^p \hat{\beta}_q^p S_{k,q}^2 + \sum_{i=1}^{N} \left(w_i^p\right)^2 \sigma_{ei}^2 \tag{4.56}$$

In the case of the market model, if the market index is also the benchmark, the relative beta of each security i is:

$$\hat{\beta}_i = \beta_i - 1 \tag{4.57}$$

The portfolio's relative beta is:

$$\hat{\beta}^p = \sum_{i=1}^{N} w_i^p \hat{\beta}_i \tag{4.58}$$

The portfolio's relative return variance is:

$$\tau_p^2 = \left(\hat{\beta}^p\right)^2 S_{Mkt}^2 + \sum_{i=1}^{N} \left(w_i^p\right)^2 \sigma_{ei}^2 \tag{4.59}$$

Note that the number of securities in Eqs. (4.52)–(4.59) is greater than or equal to the number of securities in Eqs. (4.45) and (4.46). Eqs. (4.45) and (4.46) need only consider the securities held in the portfolio at a non-zero weight, while Eqs. (4.52)–(4.59) must consider all securities that appear in both the portfolio and the benchmark.

Exhibit 4.17 shows the calculation of portfolio tracking error in Excel using the single-factor model applied to portfolios of the same 10 stocks in Exhibit 4.15. estimates of beta and unsystematic risk for 10 stocks. We created Exhibit 4.17 from Exhibit 4.15 by replacing the betas with the relative betas. The calculations shown in Exhibit 4.16 also apply to Exhibit 4.17, but with each β replaced by its corresponding $\hat{\beta}$. Exhibit 4.17 shows three portfolios of the 10 stocks and the tracking for each of them.

Exhibit 4.17 Calculating portfolio tracking error using the single-factor model in Excel

H18		f_x	=SQRT(H16^2*F13^2+H17^2)									
	A	B	C	D	E	F	G	H	I	J	K
1									Portfolios		
			Relative			Monthly Unsystematic	Factor Model		Equal	Basic Constraints	Upper & Lower	
2	Stock	Ticker	Beta	R-Squared	Risk (%)	Total Risk (%)		Weights	Only	Bounds	
3	Microsoft Corp	MSFT	0.22	45.93%	4.61	4.67		10.00%	9.97%	9.59%	
4	Canon Inc	CAJFF	-0.46	16.64%	4.16	4.46		10.00%	10.61%	10.32%	
5	Apple Inc	AAPL	0.25	31.18%	6.43	6.48		10.00%	5.15%	5.00%	
6	Oracle Corp	ORCL	0.16	53.91%	3.71	3.75		10.00%	15.16%	14.59%	
7	International Business Machines Corp	IBM	0.34	50.60%	4.60	4.75		10.00%	10.23%	9.82%	
8	Coca-Cola Co	KO	-0.55	18.09%	3.35	3.84		10.00%	16.08%	15.66%	
9	Wells Fargo & Co	WFC	0.11	41.79%	4.55	4.56		10.00%	10.03%	9.66%	
10	Dillard's Inc Class A	DDS	0.14	11.21%	11.15	11.16		10.00%	1.68%	5.00%	
11	Rockwell Automation Inc	ROK	0.41	55.36%	4.41	4.63		10.00%	11.32%	10.85%	
12	CenterPoint Energy Inc	CNP	-0.53	12.55%	4.31	4.68		10.00%	9.77%	9.51%	
13	S&P 500		0.00	100.00%	0.00	3.44					
14											
15						Total Weights		100.00%	100.00%	100.00%	
16						Relative Beta		0.01	-0.03	-0.03	
17						Unsystematic Tracking Error (%)		1.76	1.42	1.47	
18						Tracking Error (%)		1.76	1.42	1.47	

Tracking error derives from the general scale of the active weights of a portfolio. Consider a reference portfolio with an active weight of δ_i^r on security i. As discussed earlier, each active weight represents a view or a "bet" on security i. A negative active weight is a negative or bearish view and a positive active weight is a positive or bullish view on the security. Now consider a portfolio that has the same view on each security, only differing in the magnitude of this view. That is, scale the active weight in the reference portfolio to arrive at the portfolio's active weight. Therefore, the portfolio's active weight on security I is given by $\delta_i^p = a_s \delta_i^r$, where a_s is the scale factor for the active weights. Letting τ_r denote the tracking error of the reference portfolio, it follows that $\tau_p = a_s \tau_r$. (To see this, substitute $a_s \delta_i^r$ for δ_i^p in Eqs. (4.52) and (4.52), pull out a_s^2, and take the square root.) That is, the tracking error of a portfolio scales with its active weights. An alternative way to think about this result is to consider an overall portfolio that invests in two assets: the reference portfolio and the benchmark portfolio. In this case, a_s represents the proportion of the overall portfolio that is invested in the reference portfolio and $1 - a_s$ is the proportion invested in the benchmark portfolio. Clearly, if $a_s = 0$, there is no tracking error. If $a_s = 2$, the tracking error is doubled. In general, the larger (in magnitude) the active weights, the higher the tracking error.

The variance and covariance structure of the market can be quite complex, though some general relationships tend to hold in theory and in practice. Securities within the same category (e.g., country, asset class, size group, sector, or factor) tend to be more highly correlated with each other than with securities in different categories due to their similar exposures to common factors. An active portfolio that seeks to be neutral to categories but to achieve abnormal performance through security selection can diversify within categories and achieve relatively low tracking error. In contrast, a strategy that diversifies within a category but is concentrated along limited dimensions might still have a high tracking error. Cremers and Petajisto, 2009) distinguish between these two sources of active management by developing a measure of a how active a portfolio is. They call this measure the portfolio's *active share* (see Cremers and Petajisto, 2009). Active share is measured as:

$$ActiveShare = \frac{1}{2} \sum_{i=1}^{N} |\delta_i^p| \tag{4.60}$$

Intuitively, active share is another measure of the "distance" of a portfolio from the benchmark. The farther away from the benchmark, the larger the active weights. This means a portfolio is more active or less passive. As discussed above, tracking error will increase with an increase in active share unless the portfolio is constructed such that larger active weights are placed on securities that have lower relative return covariances. Similarly, a portfolio can have a lower active share with higher tracking error if the active weights are focused on companies that share similar factor exposures and, therefore, covary more with one another.

Portfolio optimization

In its strictest sense, portfolio optimization is a solution, in the form of portfolio weights, to a specific formal mathematically stated portfolio problem or objective. As we discussed in the context of asset allocation, and as we discuss in several examples below, even this seemingly scientific exercise is subject to considerable "art" in its implementation. Of course, portfolios are optimized according to the objectives reflected in the individual or organization's investment process. Formalized optimizations are typically characterized by either maximizing or minimizing a portfolio measure. However, portfolio optimization can be considered less formally and more generally to be the setting of portfolio weights according to overall goals or rules, without a formal mathematical solution. In this sense, portfolio optimization involves setting portfolio weights to achieve a general orientation in the portfolio. Some portfolio goals may not have unique solutions that lend themselves to mathematical solutions. In either case, portfolio mathematics governs the resulting portfolio performance and provides the framework for portfolio optimization. As such, portfolio optimization can be the central step in portfolio construction, resulting in a set of portfolio weights.

Minimize total risk

One example of a formal objective for setting portfolio weights is the minimization of the portfolio's total risk. This objective seeks a set of weights that achieve the lowest possible portfolio volatility. Many readers will recognize the resemblance of this objective to the minimum variance portfolio that is discussed in many introductions to portfolio theory. It is important to note that this portfolio is similar to the minimum variance portfolio in its solution method, but is likely to differ in a very meaningful way. Specifically, the portfolio optimization for an investment process is generally done in combination with other security selection methods, while the minimum variance portfolio represents the portfolio of all market securities that achieves the least possible variance. In other words, the resulting portfolio here seeks to find the lowest risk portfolio among a set of securities which represent a subset of the overall universe of securities.

Our focus is on the practical implementation of such an objective. We begin with the simplest form of the optimization by stating our objective in terms of total portfolio risk, understood to be the function of portfolio weights defined by Eqs. (4.45) and (4.46). The mathematical problem is:

$$\underset{w_i^p}{\text{Min }} Var(r_p) \; s.t. \sum_{i=1}^{N} w_i^p = 1, w_i^p \geq 0 \; i = 1, 2, \cdots, N \tag{4.61}$$

In words, this expression reflects that we are minimizing the portfolio variance function by choosing the portfolio weights, subject to the constraint that the weights sum to one and that each weight be nonnegative (so that there is no short selling). The minimization of the portfolio's total variance (or standard deviation) is the objective function. As noted above, we have constrained this problem to the N securities that make it to this step of the investment process—to the point of having the weights optimized. If there were prior steps that screened securities or otherwise narrowed the universe of securities, then this problem has effectively constrained the excluded securities to have zero weight.

This problem is usually solved numerically with optimization software. Since security level optimizers are based on factor models, optimization and factor model estimation are often both capabilities of the same software package. However, for illustrative purposes, when we are dealing with small number of securities, Microsoft Excel has a useful optimization tool, known as the "Solver" and we will demonstrate its use in several examples below.

We return to the 10-stock examples shown in Exhibit 4.15. The first portfolio (cells H3:H12) is the equally weighted portfolio of 10% in each stock. The second portfolio (cells I3:I12) is the minimum variance portfolio, subject to constraints in Eq. (4.61).

To find the minimum variance portfolio, we use the Excel Solver. You can open the Solver from the "Data" menu ribbon. "Solver" should appear on the right end of the menu ribbon. (If it does not appear, go to the "Developer" menu ribbon, click on "Excel Add-ins," and check "Solver Add-in.") To use the Solver to find the minimum variance portfolio, set up the Solver's dialog box as shown in Exhibit 4.18. Then press the "Solve" button.

Before proceeding further in discussing the use of optimizers, we caution that optimizers are inherently "dumb" in that they do not have an innate knowledge of a specific problem, its context, or the data being used. As such, an optimizer does not know whether a solution is reasonable or unreasonable. The optimizer simply arrives at a solution according to the problem, parameters, and input data that are provided by the user. It is up to the optimizer's user to understand the problem, parameters, and input data and judge the reasonableness of the optimizer's solution. For this reason and others discussed below, optimizers must be used carefully and constrained responsibly. Otherwise, they can produce portfolios that are highly concentrated in a few securities, as is the case in Exhibit 4.15, where the portfolio is concentrated in three stocks.

One particular problem is that the optimizer treats the inputs as the Truth about the distributions of future returns, when in fact, we only have estimates which are largely based on the past. This is the case with optimization at all levels: asset allocation, manager allocation, and security allocation. At the asset allocation level, we discussed this issue regarding asset class expected returns and with manager allocation, we mentioned it with respected to alphas. But it is an issue with all inputs at all levels of portfolio construction.

In the example of minimizing the portfolio standard deviation, the Solver acts as if all of the estimated parameters are known with certainty. In practice, however, we do not have the luxury of knowing the true values for the parameters, since we typically estimate the parameters from

Exhibit 4.18 Excel Solver dialog box to find the minimum variance portfolio

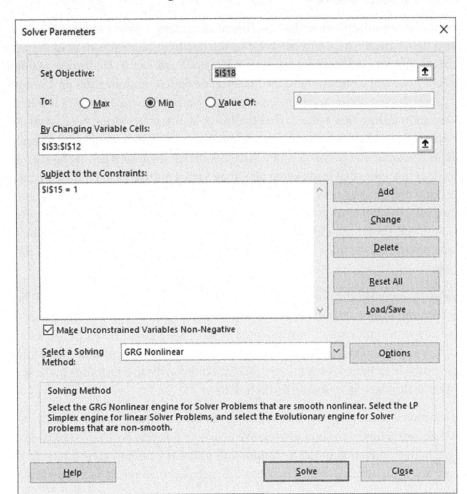

past data. The Solver in the example above found a solution for what portfolio *should have been held* in order to minimize portfolio risk. Of course, an investment manager would want to know what portfolio to hold going forward, not what portfolio she should have held. The Solver cannot solve the real problem unless it is provided with data from the future. Since this is clearly not possible, we must rely on historical data, forecasts, or estimates that might (or might not!) be informative about the future. Note that forecasts or estimates using historical data will only represent the true data with error. Being "dumb," the optimizer treats these errors as facts. Therefore, an investment manager must operate the optimizer in a way that takes into account the fact that the optimizer cannot find the best solution because it is not being provided with the true parameters or data. As with the asset allocation optimization, one way to address this problem is the use of constraints.

Constraints to the optimization use the investment managers' a priori knowledge about the problem and the characteristics and behavior of the portfolio securities to help the optimizer find a practical solution. In theory, constraints cause optimizations to find worse solutions, not better. Indeed, if we add a constraint to the standard deviation minimization problem above, it would defy logic for the optimizer to arrive at a better solution in the form of a lower portfolio standard deviation *during that period*. Had the lower standard deviation been available, the optimizer would have been free to choose that solution in the absence of the constraint. It is impossible to constrain an optimizer and arrive at a better solution when using true data or parameters. It is this logic that leads some people to view constraints in an investment process negatively. However, it is critical to understand that these seemingly ill effects of constraints apply to theoretical situations in which the true data and known parameters are being used in the optimization. In practice, well-chosen constraints can, and generally do, result in better portfolio outcomes since the true (future) data and parameters are never known at the time of the optimization.

We have already included the constraint that weights to be non-negative. This is a basic feasibility constraint since institutional investment funds typically do not engage in short selling. We now constrain each of the 10 stocks to have a weight of between 5% and 20%. In Exhibit 4.15, the portfolio that minimizes variance subject to these constraints in addition to the constraints shown in Exhibit 4.18 is in cells J3:J12. To set up these constraints in the solver, we set the Solver dialog box as shown in Exhibit 4.19.

While the additional constraints result in a more diversified portfolio, we note that weights on 8 of the 10 stocks are at one of the boundaries. We also note that that portfolio standard deviation significantly higher compared to the portfolio with only the minimal constraints. In the next example, we show minimizing risk relative to a benchmark can result in a more diversified portfolio.

Minimize tracking error

Many investors, especially institutional investors such as pension and endowment plans, are more concerned with the tracking error of a particular investment strategy or mandate than they are with its total risk This type of client might be concerned with the total risk of its overall portfolio, portfolio but hires a specific investment manager in an asset class or sub-class, such as long-term corporate debt or U.S. small cap equity. The client would expect the investment manager to be exposed to the same risks as the underlying passive benchmark.

If a portfolio is mandated to track a particular underlying benchmark or index, the tracking error of the portfolio might be more important than the total risk of the portfolio. The tracking error of

Exhibit 4.19 Excel Solver dialog box to find the minimum variance portfolio with bounds on the weights

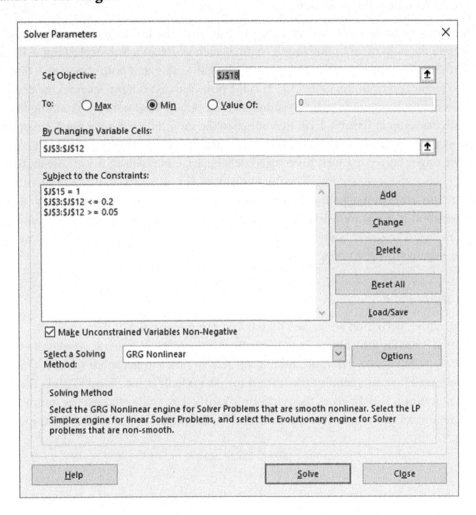

a portfolio can be optimized in a similar manner as the portfolio standard deviation. In this case, the objective function becomes the tracking error as the function of portfolio weights defined by Eqs. (4.52) and (4.53). The mathematical problem is:

$$\underset{w_i^p}{\text{Min}} \ \tau_p^2 \ s.t. \ \sum_{i=1}^{N} w_i^p = 1, w_i^p \geq 0 \ i = 1, 2, ..., N \qquad (4.62)$$

This minimization problem is similar to the minimization of portfolio variance. If the benchmark can is entirely made of factor exposures, the only difference is that relative betas replace betas (compare Eq. 4.53–4.46).

As with minimization of portfolio variance, we can solve the tracking error minimization problem with the help of an optimization routine, such as Excel's Solver. Exhibit 4.17 shows three portfolios. The first (in cells H3:H12) is the equally weighted portfolio with 10% in each stock. The second portfolio (in cells I3:I12) is the portfolio that minimizes tracking error, with the weights only subject to the basic constraints in Eq. (4.62). We found it by running the Excel Solver with the setup in Exhibit 4.18. In contrast to the minimum variance portfolio in Exhibit 4.15, this portfolio is fairly well diversified among the 10 stocks. This is a small illustration on how optimizing relative to a well diversified benchmark can result in a well-diversified portfolio, even without constraints. The third portfolios (in cells J3:J12) is the result of running the Solver with lower and upper bounds on the weights of 5% and 20% respectively. Since the optimal portfolio is fairly well-diversified without these bounds, imposing the bounds has minimal impact. The lower bound of 5% only impacts one stock in a significant way and no stocks are impacted by the upper bound.

Maximize Sharpe Ratio

Our optimization discussion so far has focused on minimizing risk. Of course, risk minimization is not the only objective in portfolio management. In general, investors attempt to maximize some reward-to-risk ratio, trading off risk in order to get more reward. One of the most widely sued measurement for the reward-to-risk tradeoff is the Sharpe Ratio. The Sharpe Ratio for a portfolio is defined as the portfolio's (arithmetic) expected excess return (i.e., its expected return net of the risk-free rate) divided by the portfolio's standard deviation:

$$SR_p = \frac{E[r_p] - r_f}{\sigma_p} \tag{4.63}$$

Note that the Sharpe ratio is a measurement for the risk-adjusted expected return for a portfolio, not active return again a benchmark. Thus, in the finance industry, Shape ratio is usually applied to total return strategies such as hedge funds.

To construct a portfolio using the Sharpe Ratio, the investor would optimize the set of weights by maximizing the objective function. Because portfolio expected return enters into the objective function, the maximization must utilize an estimate of securities' expected returns, in addition to estimates of a factor model for the securities' covariances. The expected return estimates may be generated as part of security analysis and security selection, discussed in the prior chapter. The optimization would favor stocks with relatively high expected returns and low covariances with other securities. We caution that expected returns are especially difficult to forecast. As discussed above regarding all of the optimization problems discussed in this chapter, the inputs to risk minimization, the optimizer treats errors as the Truth. If a security in a Sharpe Ratio optimization has a very large expected return compared to other securities, the optimizer is susceptible to "falling in love" with the security and placing a very large weight on it. Constraints become even more important in such situations.

An alternative form of constraints that can be useful in optimizations such as those involving the Sharpe Ratio is to constrain the estimated inputs rather than the optimized weights. For example, consider an investment manager engaged in a fundamental stock selection process that wishes to maximize the Sharpe Ratio. After screening the universe of securities, the investment managers' analysts arrive at a "short list" of securities that are deemed to be future outperformers. However, the analysts do not have precise enough expected return estimates for the short-listed securities to allow them to confidently rank these securities. In essence, the analysts view these chosen securities like parents would view their children: they love them all and cannot say which one they love more than another. If this investment manager wants to maximize the Sharpe Ratio, then a reasonable assumption would be to set all of the chosen securities' expected returns to be the same. This way, the numerator of the Sharpe Ratio is the same, regardless of the set of weights chosen. Assuming these expected returns are positive, the maximization of the Sharpe Ratio is equivalent to a minimization of the portfolio standard deviation. That is, minimizing the denominator of a fraction (the Sharpe Ratio, in this case) maximizes the fraction when the numerator is held constant.

The maximization of the Sharpe Ratio through risk minimization can also be viewed as a constraint on the optimization. This might work well when there is relatively high confidence in the covariance estimates of the securities, but relatively low confidence in the expected return estimates. This avoids the problem of the optimizer "falling in love" with securities whose estimated expected returns are high. If these estimated expected returns are known to have large errors, then this effectively constrains the optimizer from treating these errors as Truth. Other constraints discussed above can also help. However, we caution that when there are a few securities with very large expected returns, the optimizer is likely to want to put a very large weight on those securities, usually placing the constrained maximum weight on them.

Maximize Information Ratio

Another important metrics to measure portfolio performance is Information Ratio. Different from the Sharpe Ratio, the information ratio measures active performance against a benchmark. The Information Ratio is defined as the portfolio's expected relative return, $E[r_p]$-$E[r_b]$, divided by the tracking error, $\tau_p{}^{m}$:

---

[m] Note that this definition of the Information Ratio differs from that in Eq. (4.24) which we presented in the context of manager allocation. There the numerator is alpha, which is expected return in excess of the premiums due to factor exposures, i.e., the portion of excess return due that arises from misfit risk. Here, the numerator is excess return from all sources, be they due to systematic misfit risk or unsystematic risk.

$$\frac{E[r_p] - E[r_b]}{\tau_p} \qquad (4.64)$$

As with the Sharpe Ratio, the Information Ratio can be maximized by minimizing the tracking error if the expected relative return of each portfolio security is the same. The Southern Illinois University Saluki Student Investment Fund, as discussed above, is an example of such an optimization. The SSIF recognizes that their estimates of expected returns are very noisy. While they have confidence in their chosen securities, they have very little confidence in ranking the expected returns of securities relative to one another. One factor that contributes to the difficulty in ranking or differentiating securities' expected returns is the organizational structure of the SSIF, in which analysts are assigned to sector teams for in-depth research. Therefore, the uncertainty surrounding intra-sector rankings gets compounded with the uncertainty of inter-sector ranking, resulting in very low confidence in forecasting one chosen security to have a higher expected relative return than another chosen security. By using the objective function of tracking error minimization, the SSIF is effectively maximizing the portfolio's Information Ratio.

Practical considerations

There is a popular story that tells of the U.S. Space Program's discovery in the early days of space flight that a ballpoint pen would not write in the zero-gravity environment of space. After years of research and analysis costing millions of dollars, a ballpoint pen was developed that could write in zero gravity. Meanwhile, the Soviets sent their cosmonauts to space with pencils. While the veracity of this parable is questionable, the lesson is no less valuable. Sometimes, common sense is far more valuable than complex analysis. This chapter has covered many of the technical aspects of portfolio construction and described methods for completing quantitative optimizations—much of it for the sake of risk management. At times, we have discussed the possible hazards in relying too much on quantitative methods. We take this opportunity to emphasize the virtues of common sense and practical considerations.

As discussed above, quantitative methods work very well in theory. However, real portfolio management occurs in the real world, not in the theoretical world. The mathematics of portfolio theory are known ... and known to work when all of the parameters are known. Two key issues that arise in the real world that are not problems in the theoretical world are (1) parameter uncertainty and (2) human error. We discuss above how constraints can help limit the problem of parameter uncertainty. In some cases, however, there is so much parameter uncertainty that it is not advisable to use such parameters at all, even in conjunction with constraints. In such circumstances, proportional weighting (e.g., equal weighting) within a sector or factor group might result in as good of a realized outcome as an optimized approach.

Exhibit 4.20 Examples of portfolio policies

Security, Sector, and Factor Weight Constraints	Minimum and/or maximum weights or active weights for individual securities, sectors, and factors
Factor or Characteristic Exposure Targets	Target or target ranges for exposures, such as average betas or characteristic ratios
Security, Sector, and Factor Weight Tolerances	Tolerances for deviations of portfolio weights from targets to determine when a rebalancing transaction is necessary
Minimum Trade Sizes	Minimum number of shares or dollar value for a rebalancing transaction
Number of Holdings	Minimum and/or maximum number of portfolio holdings
Diversification Requirements	Minimum and/or maximum number of holdings, weights, factors, or characteristics
Prototyping	Applying a method or model to a small model portfolio prior to deploying on a live portfolio
Redundancy and Error Checks	Have multiple people use independent sources, methods, and/or platforms for analysis. Build automated error-checks where possible
Reasonableness Checks	Check that outputs match expected results and reconcile any discrepancies
Documentation	Document methods, protocols, and procedures so that any work can be replicated without additional instruction

We summarize practical portfolio policies in Exhibit 4.20 that may be appropriate depending on the portfolio objectives, investment philosophy, and investment process. As many of these items are discussed above, we do not repeat their discussion here. However, this list also includes policies aimed at reducing the likelihood and impact of human error. Our failure to emphasize these considerations until now should not be taken to mean that they are of little importance. To the contrary, these considerations are essential in any investment process, especially those that make use of a quantitative optimization. We begin with prototyping to assure that a process works well on a small scale prior to deploying it on a larger scale. For example, it is helpful to do calculations by hand using only two or three securities while also programming an optimizer to do the same calculations. Doing these calculations at least once by hand checks that an optimizer, such as Excel's Solver, is set up to solve the desired problem correctly. In many cases, optimizations can become quite complex. Simplicity is often the friend of a robust outcome. Therefore, extra caution is required when building complex, elaborate, and unwieldy models. In some cases, a simpler model can achieve most of the benefit at a far lower fraction of the cost or risk of error. When possible, build a model multiple times, by multiple people, and/or on multiple platforms. This redundancy again helps assure that the solution is consistent and accurate.

The seemingly redundancy is costly but reaps large benefits. Any data being added to a model or optimizer should be checked by at least two people. Again, the redundancy of having different people utilize different sources of data can also help reduce the likelihood that errors affect the outcomes. Check every solution for reasonableness. Are constraints met? Is the process placing the most weight on securities that were expected to get the most weight, given the objectives? If not, these issues should be resolved and reasoned to make sure that the result is accurate. Finally, document every step of the process, including revisions to the process and requirements for maintenance, updates, and input data. As turnover in a student-managed investment fund is a particular challenge, documentation becomes even more important to successfully maintaining the investment process.

Summary of key points

- Constructing a multi-asset class portfolio is a complex process that can involves up to three levels of decisions: asset allocation, manager selection and weighting, and security selection and weighting.
- At each decision level, asset classes, mangers, or securities are combined to obtain the combination of risk and expected return that best fits with the goals for the portfolio.
- Modern Portfolio Theory (MPT) is a framework for forming asset allocations Based upon risk, expected return, and risk preferences. It is also called Mean-Variance Optimization (MVO).
- MVO finds the asset mix with the highest expected return for each level of standard deviation.
- The inputs to MVO should be forward-looking, especially expected returns.
- MVO can result in asset mixes that concentrated a few asset classes.
- To obtain more diversified asset mixes, we can (1) impose constraints on the asset class weights, and (2) calibrated the expected returns.
- Markowitz 2.0 is a generalization of MPT of which MVO is a special case.
- In MVO, the joint distribution of asset class returns is fully described by a set of parameters (arithmetic expected returns and standard deviation of returns for asset class, and the correlations of returns). In Markowitz 2.0, the joint distribution of returns of all asset classes is described by a set of scenarios.
- Scenarios of asset class returns can be based on historical returns or Monte Carlo simulation.
- In MVO, expected is arithmetic. In Markowitz 2.0, expected return can be either arithmetic or geometric.
- In MVO, risk is measured by standard deviation. In Markowitz 2.0, risk can not only measure by standard deviation, but also a variety of downside risk measures, including Conditional Value at Risk (CvaR).
- As in MVO, Markowitz 2.0 optimization may require some calibration of the inputs (scenarios) and imposing some constraints.
- Manager Structure Optimization (MSO) is a framework for implanting an asset mix with a set of actively and passively managed portfolios (which can include portfolios managed inhouse.)

- The inputs to MSO include the target asset mix and the standard deviations and correlations of return for the asset classes.
- For each actively managed portfolio, MSO requires a factor model consisting of a forward-looking alpha and active risk, as well as the exposure to each asset class.
- MSO is usually run with the constraint that the sum of all allocations (actively managed portfolios, index funds, and cash) is 100% and that all allocations are non-negative (so no shorting.)
- MSO generates an efficient frontier of active risk versus alpha. Active risk consists of misfit risk (due to deviations from the target asset mix) and unsystematic risk from the actively managed portfolios.
- If the non-negativity constraint is not binding on cash or the index funds, we have portable alpha, meaning that the information ratio (as defined in the context of MSO) is maximized and allocations cash and the index funds eliminate all misfit risk.
- MSO is a method of risk budgeting, i.e., taking on systematic risk through asset allocation and unsystematic through actively managed portfolios to obtain an expected return greater than risk-free rate. Systematic risk provides the premiums of the asset classes and unsystematic risk provides the alphas of the actively managed portfolios.
- Factor models of security returns allow us to create parsimonious, mathematical sound models of the variances and covariances of returns and covariance across all securities that can be used in security-level optimization.
- In a factor model, each security has a set factor loadings (betas) and a level of unsystematic risk.
- Market model is a single-factor model in which the factor is based on a broad market index.
- Special cases of security-level optimization include minimizing portfolio variance and maximizing the Sharpe Ratio. However, optimization based on absolute return can result in concentrated portfolios.
- An alternative approach is to optimize relative to a benchmark. This includes minimizing tracking error and maximizing the Information Ratio. Optimization relative to a benchmark can result in diversified portfolios.
- When a benchmark can be expressed purely as factor exposure, we only need to replace betas with relative betas to optimize.
- It is important to not overly rely on quantitative methods such as portfolio optimization. This is because of parameter uncertainty and the possibility of human error. Every solution should be checked for reasonableness.

Exercises

1. Select a group of asset classes from Exhibit 4.1 that you think should be represented in a university endowment and a corresponding index for each.
2. In Morningstar® Direct^SM, go to the Learning Center on the left-hand side, and select Online Training. From there, go to "H. Determining Optimal Asset Allocation

Strategies." Select "Getting Started with Asset Allocation." Read through this document and use it to familiarize yourself with the asset allocation software. (This is to help you complete the following exercises.)

3. Using the asset classes and indexes that you selected in Exercise 1, create a set of capital market assumptions (for annual returns) from historical data and generate an MVO efficient frontier. What do you notice about the optimal asset mixes?

4. Try one or more of the other methods for estimating the expected returns on the asset classes. Reoptimize. What changes to you see in the optimal asset mixes?

5. If you notice that the optimal asset mixes tend to be concentrated, try imposing constraints and reoptimize. Do the optimal asset mixes change as you expect them to?

6. Redo Exercises 3–5 using the alternative measures of expected return and risk. This means using geometric rather than arithmetic expected return (mean in the software) and a downside risk measure. (You can do this on the Optimization Settings dialog box that appears when you press the Optimization button.)

7. Select a set of mutual funds from Morningstar® Direct^{SM} and download their historical monthly returns over the same period that you used to estimate the capital market assumptions in Exercise 3. (Use the Morningstar Category field to be sure that each all asset classes that you selected in Exercise 1 are represented by the funds.) Also, download a time series of monthly returns on cash to subtract from each fund's monthly returns and the monthly returns on each asset class index. Use this data to estimate the betas of each fund in Eq. (4.13) and the cash betas using Eq. (4.14).

8. Estimate the unsystematic risk of each fund. To do this, for each fund, calculate the monthly residuals $(e_{jt} = R_{jt} - \alpha_j - \sum_{k=1}^{M} \beta_{j,k} R_{lk})$, and then $\sigma_{ej} = \sqrt{\frac{12}{T-(M+1)} \sum_{t=1}^{T} e_{jt}^2}$, where T is the number of months in the regression. (The multiplication by 12 is to annualize unsystematic risk to match annualized systematic risk estimated in Exercise 3.)

9. Read the article by Waring and Ramkamar on estimating forward-looking alpha. Create a spreadsheet that can take the inputs and calculate an alpha for any number of funds. Apply the spreadsheet to the portfolio that your class is managing and to other actively managed portfolios within your school's endowment. Apply it to the funds that you selected in Exercise 7. If you are not familiar enough with the portfolios and funds that you are applying the model to, make some assumptions that you think that you would make sense.

10. Select a target asset mix. Combine it with the standard deviations and correlation of returns from the capital market assumptions in Exercise 3 in a spreadsheet file. In the same file (possibly in a different tab), combine the alphas from Exercise 9 with and the unsystematic risk and betas of each fund that you selected in Exercise 7 in a fashion similar to Exhibit 4.10. (You can use Eq. (4.14) to get the cash allocations.)

Add a column for weights on actively managed funds and a row below the fund asset class exposures for weights on index funds and cash. (As a placeholder for values for these weights, you can set them all to $1/(N + M + 1)$.) Add a cell for the sum of all these weights based on Eq. (4.21) so that you can impose the budget constraint. Based on Eqs. (4.15)–(4.19), add cells with formulas for portfolio alpha, misfit risk, and unsystematic risk. Add two cells for values of the two risk aversion parameters and add a cell for the objective function given in Eq. (4.20).

11. Experiment with different values of the risk aversion parameters in the spreadsheet you created in Exercise 10. At what point do the results switch from portable alpha solutions to solutions with misfit risk?

12. Select 10 stocks from Morningstar® Direct^{SM} and download their historical monthly returns over a 60-month period. Download monthly returns on a broad market index and on a cash to subtract from the stock returns and the index returns to form excess monthly returns. Estimate the market model for each stock in this form:
$R_{it} = \alpha_i + \beta_i R_{Mkt,\, t} + e_{it}$. Calculate the residuals for each stock ($e_{it} = R_{it} - \alpha_i - \beta_i R_{Mkt,\, t}$)

and then estimate unsystematic risk: $\sigma_{ei} = \sqrt{\frac{1}{T-2}\sum_{t=1}^{T} e_{it}^2}$, where T is the number of months in the regression. Also, calculate the standard deviation of excess returns on the market index. (Note that in this exercise, all standard deviations are monthly.)

13. Use the results from Exercise 12 to set up a spreadsheet like Exhibit 4.15. Place an equally weighted portfolio in columns H, I, and J. Using the formulas in Exhibit 4.16, complete the spreadsheet.

14. Minimize the total risk of the portfolio in cells I3:I12 by running the Excel Solver with the setup shown in Exhibit 4.18. What do you observe about this portfolio?

15. Minimize the total risk of the portfolio in cells J3:J12 by running the Excel Solver with the setup shown in Exhibit 4.19. (You can also try optimizing with a different set of constraints.) What do you observe about this portfolio?

16. Make a copy of the spreadsheet that you created in Exercise 13, but change the betas to relative betas. Minimize the tracking error of the portfolio in cells I3:I12 by running the Excel Solver with the setup shown in Exhibit 4.18. What do you observe about this portfolio?

17. Minimize the tracking error of the portfolio in cells J3:J12 by running the Excel Solver with the setup shown in Exhibit 4.19. (You can also try optimizing with a different set of constraints.) What do you observe about this portfolio?

Appendix: Tracking error and relative risk explained[n]

Tracking error is the risk of a portfolio's returns relative to its benchmark. This measure of relative risk is often important when the mandate for the investment manager is to outperform a specific benchmark, but to also have a similar exposure to that benchmark's asset class. For example, a client might grant an active U.S. small cap core mandate to an investment manager with either the Russell 2000 Index or the S&P Small Cap 600 Index as a benchmark. The client might expect the investment manager's portfolio to outperform the Russell 2000 Index over time, but to generally track the index's ups and downs. Tracking error is a measure of how poorly the portfolio tracks the benchmark. More precisely, tracking error is the standard deviation of the portfolio's relative returns versus the benchmark index. As such, the average active return of a portfolio does not count as tracking error. Rather, the variation around the average active return counts as tracking error.

Before proceeding to the mathematical analysis, we illustrate tracking error using two actively managed portfolios, Portfolio A and Portfolio B, benchmarked to the S&P 500 index. The cumulative returns for these two portfolios, along with the benchmark S&P 500, are shown in Exhibit A4.1 for a three-year period ending in December 2012. These portfolios take active risk by holding securities at weights different from the capitalization weighted S&P 500, but generally track the large cap benchmark in it moves up and down. That is, the two portfolios generally track the S&P 500 as it rises from around August 2010 through April 2011, and then track its decline over the subsequent 5 months. Portfolio A appears to deviate a bit more from the track of the S&P 500, while Portfolio B mimics the movements of the index quite closely. The two portfolios and the S&P 500 generally have the same direction and similar magnitude of monthly returns as shown in the second graph. However, there is some deviation from the S&P 500 from month to month, as more clearly shown in the graph of monthly relative returns. Recall that relative return each month is simply the return of the portfolio minus the return of the benchmark (the S&P 500, in this case). The relative returns of Portfolio A are more volatile than those of Portfolio B, showing that Portfolio A has more tracking error—it deviates more from the S&P 500 in each month.

Finally, the distribution of monthly returns and relative returns for the 10-year period ending December 2012 for these two portfolios is shown in the set of histograms in Exhibit A4.2. The distribution of the S&P 500 and the two portfolios' returns appear to have a similar spread or width, as confirmed by their having similar overall standard deviations. Specifically, the

---

[n] This material provides an alternate method for evaluating tracking error and calculating relative risk. This material was reproduced from the previous version, Trading and Money Management in a Student-Managed Portfolio. The factor model presented in the main text of the chapter is recommended when dealing with a large number of stocks.

Exhibit A4.1 Portfolio returns and tracking error against a benchmark

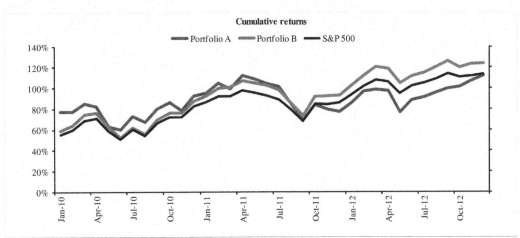

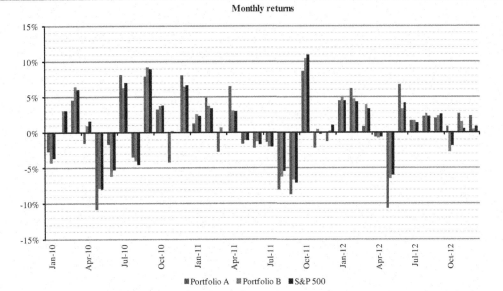

Exhibit A4.2 Distribution of returns, standard deviation, and tracking error

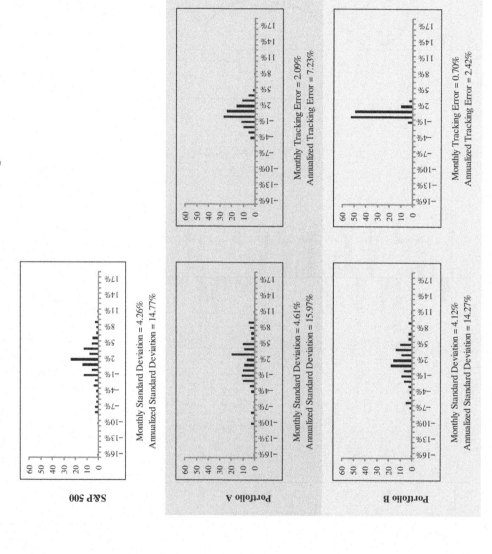

standard deviation of monthly returns for the S&P 500 is 4.26%, while the standard deviation for portfolios A and B is 4.61% and 4.12%, respectively. Because it is common to use annualized numbers, we also report the annualized standard deviation as calculated from the monthly returns.[°] The widths of the relative return distributions are very different, with Portfolio B's monthly relative returns being distributed more closely around the mean compared to Portfolio A's monthly active returns. Indeed, the tracking error (i.e., the standard deviation of relative returns) of Portfolio A is approximately three times as large as the tracking error of Portfolio B.

Mathematically, the tracking error of asset i relative to benchmark b (i.e., the relative return variance of security i) is defined to be $\tau_i = \sqrt{\tau_i^2}$, where $\tau_i^2 = Var(r_i - r_b)$. Again, the tracking error is simply the standard deviation of relative returns. Similarly, we define the covariance of relative returns between securities i and j to be $\tau_{i,j}^2 = Cov(r_i - r_b, r_j - r_b)$. Note that the covariance of relative returns between two securities is a function of the covariance of the securities' returns, their covariances with the benchmark, and the benchmark's variances, as given by:

$$Cov(r_i - r_b, r_j - r_b) = Cov(r_i, r_j) - Cov(r_i, r_b) - Cov(r_j, r_b) + Var(r_b) \tag{A4.1}$$

or:

$$\tau_{i,j}^2 = \sigma_{i,j}^2 - \sigma_{i,b}^2 - \sigma_{j,b}^2 + \sigma_b^2 \tag{A4.2}$$

Note that this means that a security's relative return variance can also be written as a function of the security's own variance, the benchmark's variance, and the security's covariance of returns with the benchmark returns.

With these preliminaries in mind, we can write the tracking error of a portfolio in several different ways. First, the variance of the portfolio's relative return can be expressed as a function of the portfolio securities' weights and variances and covariances of relative returns, as given by:

$$Var(r_p - r_b) = \tau_p^2 = \sum_{i=1}^{N} \sum_{j=1}^{N} w_i^p w_j^p \tau_{i,j}^2 \tag{A4.3}$$

This formula should look familiar, as it is nearly identical to the portfolio variance formula in Eq. (4.41). Indeed, the relative return variance formula (Eq. A4.3 replaces the plain covariance matrix in the portfolio variance formula (Eq. 4.41 with the relative return covariance. With

---

[°] We employ the common practice of using the "square root of time" rule when annualizing standard deviations by multiplying the monthly return standard deviation by the square root of 12. The "square root of time" rule has an implicit assumption that the sub-period (e.g., monthly) returns are uncorrelated through time, which may not be accurate. However, this common practice provides a nice approximation for our purposes here. The same approach is used in annualizing tracking error.

portfolio variance, we are confident that most securities have positive covariance with one another. As such, portfolio variance cannot be diversified away or reduced to zero because of securities' average positive covariance. With relative return variance or tracking error, the intuition changes a bit. Because we are now dealing with relative or residual risk, we should expect some securities' relative returns to be negatively correlated (i.e., to covary in a negative way), with the average covariance of relative returns being approximately zero. Eq. (A4.3) illustrates that tracking error in a portfolio can be reduced in two ways: (1) placing more weight on securities that lower tracking error; (2) placing more weight on securities whose relative returns have a negative covariance with one another. That is, there is a possibility of achieving a relatively low tracking error with a subset of the benchmark securities.

We extend our previous example of 10 stocks to consider tracking error relative to the S&P 500 Index. Exhibit A4.3 shows the relative return correlation and covariance matrices. The

Exhibit A4.3 Relative return covariance matrix and correlation matrix

Correlation of Monthly Relative Returns (2003 – 2007)

	MSFT	DELL	AAPL	ORCL	IBM	KO	WFC	DDS	ROK	CNP	
MSFT		0.24	0.10	−0.05	0.07	0.06	−0.25	0.03	−0.21	−0.06	
DELL	0.24		0.15	0.06	0.11	−0.06	−0.27	0.26	0.22	−0.13	
AAPL	0.10	0.15		0.22	0.06	−0.04	−0.17	0.07	0.36	−0.06	
ORCL	−0.05	0.06	0.22		0.16	−0.13	−0.12	0.05	0.18	−0.30	
IBM	0.07	0.11	0.06	0.16		−0.13	−0.04	−0.19	−0.01	−0.01	
KO	0.06	−0.06	−0.04	−0.13	−0.13		−0.08	−0.35	−0.18	0.07	
WFC	−0.25	−0.27	−0.17	−0.12	−0.04	−0.08		0.00	−0.02	−0.09	
DDS	0.03	0.26	0.07	0.05	−0.19	−0.35	0.00		0.27	−0.02	
ROK	−0.21	0.22	0.36	0.18	−0.01	−0.18	−0.02	0.27		−0.23	Overall
CNP	−0.06	−0.13	−0.06	−0.30	−0.01	0.07	−0.09	−0.02	−0.23		Average
Average	−0.01	0.07	0.08	0.01	0.00	−0.09	−0.11	0.01	0.04	−0.09	−0.01

Covariance of Monthly Relative Returns (2008 – 2012)

	MSFT	DELL	AAPL	ORCL	IBM	KO	WFC	DDS	ROK	CNP	
MSFT		0.19	0.16	0.25	−0.15	0.03	0.10	0.10	−0.21	−0.03	
DELL	0.19		0.14	0.29	0.04	−0.31	−0.05	−0.10	0.22	−0.02	
AAPL	0.16	0.14		0.04	0.07	−0.19	−0.31	0.24	0.03	−0.03	
ORCL	0.25	0.29	0.04		0.07	−0.31	−0.13	−0.04	0.00	−0.07	
IBM	−0.15	0.04	0.07	0.07		0.16	−0.28	−0.22	−0.28	0.18	
KO	0.03	−0.31	−0.19	−0.31	0.16		−0.05	−0.17	−0.34	0.37	
WFC	0.10	−0.05	−0.31	−0.13	−0.28	−0.05		0.17	0.11	−0.33	
DDS	0.10	−0.10	0.24	−0.04	−0.22	−0.17	0.17		0.08	−0.22	
ROK	−0.21	0.22	0.03	0.00	−0.28	−0.34	0.11	0.08		−0.05	Overall
CNP	−0.03	−0.02	−0.03	−0.07	0.18	0.37	−0.33	−0.22	−0.05		Average
Average	0.05	0.04	0.02	0.01	−0.05	−0.09	−0.08	−0.02	−0.05	−0.02	−0.02

Exhibit A4.4 Return covariance matrix and correlation matrix

Correlation of Monthly Returns (2003 – 2007)

	MSFT	DELL	AAPL	ORCL	IBM	KO	WFC	DDS	ROK	CNP	
MSFT		0.37	0.24	0.15	0.27	0.22	−0.08	0.14	−0.05	0.06	
DELL	0.37		0.29	0.27	0.34	0.19	0.00	0.36	0.34	0.02	
AAPL	0.24	0.29		0.35	0.25	0.16	0.05	0.17	0.44	0.05	
ORCL	0.15	0.27	0.35		0.38	0.15	0.16	0.18	0.32	−0.12	
IBM	0.27	0.34	0.25	0.38		0.17	0.23	0.02	0.19	0.15	
KO	0.22	0.19	0.16	0.15	0.17		0.11	−0.15	0.02	0.20	
WFC	−0.08	0.00	0.05	0.16	0.23	0.11		0.14	0.14	0.06	
DDS	0.14	0.36	0.17	0.18	0.02	−0.15	0.14		0.35	0.06	
ROK	−0.05	0.34	0.44	0.32	0.19	0.02	0.14	0.35		−0.10	**Overall**
CNP	0.06	0.02	0.05	−0.12	0.15	0.20	0.06	0.06	−0.10		**Average**
Average	0.15	0.24	0.22	0.20	0.22	0.12	0.09	0.14	0.18	0.04	0.16

Correlation of Monthly Returns (2008 – 2012)

	MSFT	DELL	AAPL	ORCL	IBM	KO	WFC	DDS	ROK	CNP	
MSFT		0.59	0.55	0.66	0.38	0.41	0.49	0.58	0.45	0.35	
DELL	0.59		0.48	0.63	0.52	0.22	0.33	0.33	0.56	0.38	
AAPL	0.55	0.48		0.48	0.49	0.26	0.15	0.55	0.45	0.34	
ORCL	0.66	0.63	0.48		0.54	0.23	0.35	0.47	0.53	0.35	
IBM	0.38	0.52	0.49	0.54		0.31	0.23	0.45	0.42	0.36	
KO	0.41	0.22	0.26	0.23	0.31		0.35	0.46	0.32	0.44	
WFC	0.49	0.33	0.15	0.35	0.23	0.35		0.47	0.46	0.09	
DDS	0.58	0.33	0.55	0.47	0.45	0.46	0.47		0.45	0.33	
ROK	0.45	0.56	0.45	0.53	0.42	0.32	0.46	0.45		0.44	**Overall**
CNP	0.35	0.38	0.34	0.35	0.36	0.44	0.09	0.33	0.44		**Average**
Average	0.49	0.45	0.42	0.47	0.41	0.33	0.32	0.45	0.45	0.34	0.42

summary matrices show the average covariances and correlations for two groups of stocks: Information Technology stocks and the five stocks that are not in the Information Technology sector. In Exhibit A4.4, notice that 10 (or 10%) of the return covariances are negative in 2003 through 2007 and none are negative in 2008 through 2012. In Exhibit A4.3, 52% of the relative return covariances are negative in 2003 through 2007 and 46% are negative in 2008 through 2012. Furthermore, the relative return covariances are generally lower, having an average relative return covariance of near 0.0005 in both periods, compared to an average return covariance of 0.0012 in 2003 through 2007 and 0.0041 in 2008 through 2012. The same relationships hold for the relative return correlations compared to the return correlations.

Overall, the heat map of the relative return covariance matrix is very similar to the heat map for the return covariance matrix in 2003 through 2007. However, the relative return covariance matrix heat map looks quite different from the return covariance matrix heat map during 2008 through 2012, indicating that there can be meaningful differences in the patterns of covariances when using relative returns compared to plain returns. This indicates that portfolios constructed to have low total risk or standard deviation might not have low tracking error. In other words, the portfolio must be constructed in consideration of the specific type of risk that is targeted.

Exhibit A4.5 shows the tracking error for the same portfolios that appear in Exhibit A4.6. Not surprisingly, the resulting portfolio relative return variances and tracking errors shown in Exhibit A4.5 are smaller compared to the return variances and standard deviations in Exhibit A4.6. Also, given the similarity in the ranking of stocks' return covariances and relative return covariances in 2003 through 2007, the pattern of resulting tracking errors is similar to the pattern of standard deviations across different sets of portfolio weights during that period. Specifically, the equally weighted portfolio, P1, has a tracking error that is larger than when more weight is placed on KO and WFC, which have the lowest average relative return covariances among these 10 stocks. However, the tracking error results in 2008 through 2012 show a different pattern across portfolios than the standard deviation results. Specifically, both P1 and P2 have higher tracking errors than the equally weighted portfolio. This illustrates the usefulness of the relative return covariance matrix to an investment manager who wishes to construct a portfolio with tracking error risk management as one of the portfolio goals.

Exhibit A4.5 Portfolio weights and tracking error

	Portfolio weights										Tracking error	
Portfolio	MSFT	DELL	AAPL	ORCL	IBM	KO	WFC	DDS	ROK	CNP	2003–2007	2008–2012
P1	10%	10%	10%	10%	10%	10%	10%	10%	10%	10%	**2.23%**	**2.54%**
P2	5%	5%	5%	5%	5%	25%	25%	5%	5%	15%	**1.79%**	**2.80%**
P3	5%	5%	5%	5%	5%	5%	5%	25%	25%	15%	**3.43%**	**4.69%**

Exhibit A4.6 Portfolio weights and standard deviations

	Portfolio weights										Standard deviation	
Portfolio	MSFT	DELL	AAPL	ORCL	IBM	KO	WFC	DDS	ROK	CNP	2003–2007	2008–2012
P1	10%	10%	10%	10%	10%	10%	10%	10%	10%	10%	**3.52%**	**6.95%**
P2	5%	5%	5%	5%	5%	5%	25%	25%	5%	5%	15%	**2.97%**	**6.28%**
P3	5%	5%	5%	5%	5%	5%	5%	5%	25%	25%	15%	**4.39%**	**9.04%**

References

Cremers, K.J.M., Petajisto, A., 2009. How active is your fund manager? A new measure that predicts performance. Rev. Financ. Stud. 22 (9), 3329–3365.

Kaplan, P.D., 2016. Combining alpha with beta. It takes both art and science to make a practical portfolio-construction tool. Morningstar, (December/January), 48–54.

Kaplan, P.D., Savage, S., 2012. Markowitz 2.0. In: Kaplan, P.D. (Ed.), Frontiers of Modern Asset Allocation. John Wiley & Sons, Hoboken, NJ.

Kaplan, P.D., 2017. From Markowitz 1.0 to Markowitz 2.0 with a detour to postmodern portfolio theory and back. J. Invest, 26 (1), 122–130.

Waring, M.B., Ramkumar, S.R., 2008. Forecasting fund manager alphas: the impossible just takes longer. Financ. Anal. J. 64 (2), 65–80.

Waring, M.B., Whitney, D., Pirone, J., Castille, C., 2000. Optimizing manager structure and budgeting manager risk. A user's guide for active management. J. Portf. Manag. 26 (2), 90–94.

CHAPTER 5

Performance evaluation

Every investment manager must report his or her portfolio's performance. However, the obligation of an investment manager goes beyond simply reporting performance—the investment manager must understand performance and provide an explanation of it that is consistent with the manager's investment process. This understanding and explanation help both internally and externally. Internally, the investment manager can use the understanding of past performance to monitor performance and assure that the investment process is working as expected. Performance evaluation can help identify opportunities to enhance the investment process, increase returns, or mitigate risks. Externally, the investment manager can use performance evaluation to help explain how the investment process works to capitalize on the opportunities identified in the investment philosophy.

We distinguish between *performance reporting*, which usually emphasizes the percentage return on an investment, and *performance analysis*, which aims to provide an understanding of the performance. Performance reporting is an *accounting* exercise. Performance analysis is an *economic* exercise. In both cases, such reports help provide transparency both internally and externally as to the returns and risks of the investment strategy, as well as their sources.

This chapter begins by discussing the importance and methods of performance reporting standards. In a basic performance report, an investment manager should report annualized returns over specific time periods for the portfolio and, if applicable, the portfolio's benchmark. Beyond the basic report, the chapter discusses how performance evaluation reveals the story behind the annualized returns. We provide discussions of two general classes of performance evaluations: performance attribution and returns-based performance analysis. These methods complement each other in providing insights into the sources of returns and relative returns, as well as the risk exposures in the portfolio. We show numerous equations in order to provide the technical background of these methods before applying them in several examples. Finally, we discuss transaction cost analysis as an important element in understanding the overall performance of a portfolio.

Student-Managed Investment Funds. https://doi.org/10.1016/B978-0-12-817866-9.00005-4

Performance calculation

There are two overarching goals in reporting performance: accuracy and consistency. Accuracy comes from using the right information and carefully applying the appropriate calculation methods. An investment manager achieves consistency in the performance report by developing a process and implementing it the same way through time. Performance reporting standards, such as GIPS™ (Global Investment Performance Standards) maintained by the CFA Institute, assist the investment manager in achieving both goals. We reprint the GIPS standards in Exhibit 5.1. Exhibit 5.2 contains a discussion by ACA Compliance Group on implementing GIPS-compliant performance measurement standards.

Performance calculations for a portfolio can be done from two perspectives: (1) the perspective of the portfolio managers, and (2) the perspective of the investors. Cashflows in and out of the portfolio are irrelevant from the managers' perspective since they are outside of the managers' prevue. However, cashflows are relevant to the investors' since it is the investors who generally decide when and how much to add or remove money from the portfolio.

For these two perspectives there are two types of returns that serve as performance measures: time-weighted returns and dollar-weighted returns. Time weighted returns are standard in performance reporting as are often called total returns are simply returns. Dollar-weighted returns (also called money-weighted returns or internal rates of return) are less prevalent but can be useful to highlight how the cashflow decisions of investors' impacted how successfully they deployed the portfolio.

Time-weighted returns

The calculation of portfolio performance, as measured by time-weighted returns, seems to be quite straightforward. For a portfolio that has no cash flows and that holds securities for which market values are readily available, the calculation of the portfolio return over period t, r_t, is simply the percentage change from the beginning portfolio value, MV_{t-k}, to the ending portfolio value, MV_t, as given by:

$$r_{t-k,t} = \frac{MV_t - MV_{t-k}}{MV_{t-k}} \tag{5.1}$$

A challenge in performance calculations arises when the market values are not readily available. For U.S. publicly traded equity securities, market values are usually readily available in the form of the daily closing price. Likewise, any other security or commodity that is actively traded has its market value readily available in the form of its market-determined price. Since market prices are unavailable for illiquid securities, such as equity or debt securities, that are not regularly traded on a daily basis, the fair market value of those securities must be

Exhibit 5.1 Global Investment Performance Standards

Global Investment Performance Standards

GUIDANCE STATEMENT ON CALCULATION METHODOLOGY

Adoption Date: 9/28/10

Effective Date: 1/1/2011

Retroactive Application: Not Required

CFA Institute

www.gipsstandards.org
© 2014 CFA Institute

GIPS GUIDANCE STATEMENT ON CALCULATION METHODOLOGY

Introduction

Achieving comparability among firms' compliant presentations requires as much uniformity as possible in the methodology used to calculate portfolio and composite returns. The uniformity of the return calculation methodology is dependent on accurate and consistent input data, a critical component to compliance with the GIPS® standards. Although the GIPS standards allow flexibility in return calculation, the return must be calculated using a methodology that incorporates the time-weighted rate of return concept for all portfolios except for private equity. For information on calculating performance for private equity, see the private equity provisions and guidance.

The GIPS standards require a time-weighted rate of return because it removes the effects of external cash flows, which are generally client-driven. Therefore, a time-weighted rate of return best reflects the firm's ability to manage the portfolios according to a specified mandate, objective, or strategy, and is the basis for the comparability of composite returns among firms on a global basis.

In this Guidance Statement, the term "return" is used, rather than the more common term "performance," to emphasize the distinction between return and risk and to encourage the view of performance as a combination of risk and return. Risk measures are valuable tools for assessing the abilities of asset managers; however, this Guidance Statement focuses only on the return calculation.

Money- or dollar-weighted returns may add further value in understanding the impact to the client of the timing of external cash flows, but are less useful for return comparisons and are therefore not covered by this Guidance Statement.

Guiding Principles

Valuation Principles
The following are guiding principles that firms must use when determining portfolio values as the basis for return calculations:
- For periods beginning on or after 1 January 2011, portfolios must be valued in accordance with the definition of fair value and the GIPS Valuation Principles in Chapter II of the GIPS standards.
- For periods prior to 1 January 2011, portfolio valuations must be based on market values (not cost basis or book values).
- Firms must value portfolios in accordance with the composite-specific valuation policy.
    - For periods prior to 1 January 2001, portfolios must be valued at least quarterly.

Guidance Statement on Calculation Methodology

o For periods beginning on or after 1 January 2001, portfolios must be valued at least monthly.

o For periods beginning on or after 1 January 2010, firms must value portfolios on the date of all large cash flows. Firms must define large cash flow for each composite to determine when portfolios in that composite must be valued.

o Portfolios must not be valued more frequently than required by the composite-specific valuation policy.

- For periods beginning on or after 1 January 2010, firms must value portfolios as of the calendar month end or the last business day of the month.

- Firms must use trade date accounting for periods beginning on or after 1 January 2005. [Note: for purposes of the GIPS standards, trade date accounting recognizes the asset or liability on the date of the purchase or sale, not on the settlement date. Recognizing the asset or liability within three days of the date the transaction is entered into (trade date, $T + 1$, $T + 2$, or $T + 3$) satisfies the trade date accounting requirement for purposes of the GIPS standards.]

- Accrual accounting must be used for fixed-income securities and all other investments that earn interest income. The value of fixed-income securities must include accrued income.

- Accrual accounting should be used for dividends (as of the ex-dividend date).

Calculation Principles for Portfolios

The following are guiding principles that firms must use when calculating *portfolio* returns:

- All returns must be calculated after the deduction of the actual trading expenses incurred during the period. Firms must not use estimated trading expenses.

- Total returns must be used. Total return is defined as the rate of the return that includes the realized and unrealized gains and losses plus income for the measurement period.

- The calculation method chosen must represent returns fairly, must not be misleading, and must be applied consistently.

- Firms must calculate time-weighted rates of return that adjust for external cash flows. External cash flow is defined as capital (cash or investments) that enters or exits a portfolio and is generally client driven. Income earned on a portfolio's investments is not considered an external cash flow unless it is paid out of the portfolio.

- For periods beginning on or after 1 January 2005, firms must calculate portfolio returns that adjust for daily-weighted external cash flows. An example of this methodology is the Modified Dietz method.

- For periods beginning on or after 1 January 2010, at the latest, firms must calculate performance for interim sub-periods between all large cash flows and geometrically link performance to calculate periodic returns. (Note: For periods beginning on or after 1 January 2010, firms must define prospectively, on a composite-specific basis, what constitutes a large cash flow.) For information on calculating a "true" time-weighted return, see the "Time-Weighted Rate of Return" section below.

- External cash flows must be treated in a manner consistent with the firm's documented composite-specific policy.
- For periods beginning on or after 1 January 2001, firms must calculate portfolio returns at least monthly. For periods prior to 2001, portfolio returns must be calculated at least quarterly.
- Periodic and sub-period returns must be geometrically linked.

Calculation Principles for Composites

The following are guiding principles that firms must use when calculating *composite* returns:

- Composite returns must be calculated by asset-weighting the individual portfolio returns using beginning-of-period values or a method that reflects both beginning-of-period values and external cash flows.
- The aggregate return method, which combines all the composite assets and cash flows to calculate composite performance as if the composite were one portfolio, is acceptable as an asset-weighted approach.
- For periods beginning on or after 1 January 2006 and prior to 1 January 2010, firms must calculate composite returns by asset-weighting the individual portfolio returns at least quarterly. For periods beginning on or after 1 January 2010, composite returns must be calculated by asset-weighting the individual portfolio returns at least monthly.
- Periodic and sub-period returns must be geometrically linked.

Cash Flow Principles

The following are guiding principles that firms must consider when defining their composite-specific cash flow policies:

- An *external cash flow* is a flow of capital (cash or investments) that enters or exits a portfolio, which is generally client driven. When calculating approximated rates of return, where the calculation methodology requires an adjustment for the daily-weighting of cash flows, the formula reflects a weight for each external cash flow. The cash flow weight is determined by the amount of time the cash flow is held in the portfolio.
- When calculating a more accurate time-weighted return, a *large cash flow* must be defined by each firm for each composite to determine when the portfolios in that composite are to be valued for performance calculations. It is the level at which the firm determines that an external cash flow may distort performance if the portfolio is not valued. Firms must define the amount in terms of the value of the cash/asset flow or in terms of a percentage of the portfolio assets or the composite assets. The large cash flow determines when a portfolio is to be valued for performance calculations.
- A large cash flow is differentiated from a *significant cash flow*, which occurs in situations where the firm determines that a client-directed external cash flow may temporarily prevent the firm from implementing the composite strategy and the portfolio is temporarily removed from the composite or the external cash flow is placed in a temporary new account. Please see the Guidance Statement on the Treatment of Significant Cash Flows, which details the procedures and criteria

Guidance Statement on Calculation Methodology

that firms must adhere to and offers additional options for dealing with the impact of significant cash flows on portfolios.

Time-Weighted Rate of Return

Valuing the portfolio and calculating interim returns each time there is an external cash flow results in the most accurate method to calculate the time-weighted rates of return.

The formula for calculating the time-weighted portfolio return when there are no external cash flows is:

$$r_i = \frac{V_i^E - V_i^B}{V_i^B},$$

where

r_i = the return for period i in which there are no external cash flows
V_i^E = the ending value of the portfolio for period i
V_i^B = the beginning value of the portfolio for period i

When a portfolio experiences external cash flows during a period, the most accurate return is calculated by valuing the portfolio at the time of the external cash flow, calculating the time-weighted return for each sub-period (defined as the period between external cash flows), and then geometrically linking the sub-period returns using the following formula:

$$r_t^{TWR} = \left[(1 + r_1) \times (1 + r_2) \times \cdots (1 + r_I)\right] - 1,$$

where r_t^{TWR} is the time-weighted return for period t and period t consists of I sub-periods.

Approximation of Time-Weighted Rate of Return

As mentioned in the introduction, the GIPS standards require firms to calculate a time-weighted rate of return, except for private equity. The GIPS standards allow flexibility in choosing the calculation methodology, which means that firms may use alternative formulas, provided the calculation method chosen represents returns fairly, is not misleading, and is applied consistently.

Calculating a time-weighted rate of return is not an easy task and may be cost intensive. For these reasons, firms may use an approximation method to calculate the total return of the individual portfolios for the periods and sub-periods. The most common approximation methods combine specific rate of return methodologies (such as the original Dietz method, the Modified Dietz method, the original IRR (internal rate of return) method, and the Modified BAI (Bank Administration Institute) method) for sub-periods, and then geometrically links the sub-period returns.

Just as the GIPS standards transition to more frequent valuations, the GIPS standards also transition to more precise calculation methodologies. Therefore, the GIPS standards require firms to calculate approximated time-weighted rates of return that adjust for daily-weighted external cash flows (e.g., Modified Dietz method) for periods beginning on or after 1 January 2005. For periods beginning on or after 1 January 2010, firms are required to calculate a more accurate time-weighted rate of return and are required to value portfolios at the time of each large cash flow, as well as at calendar month-end or on the last business day of the month.

According to the *Modified Dietz* method the portfolio return can be calculated using the formula:

$$r_t^{MD} = \frac{V_t^E - V_t^B - \sum_{i=1}^{I} CF_{i,t}}{V_t^B + \sum_{i=1}^{I} \left(CF_{i,t} \times w_{i,t}\right)},$$

where

r_t^{MD} = the Modified Dietz return for the portfolio for period t

V_t^E = the ending value of the portfolio for period t

V_t^B = the beginning value of the portfolio for period t

i = the number of external cash flows (1, 2, 3…I) in period t

$CF_{i,t}$ = the value of cash flow i in period t

$w_{i,t}$ = the weight of cash flow i in period t (assuming the cash flow occurred at the end of the day), as calculated according to the following formula:

$$w_{i,t} = \frac{D_t - D_{i,t}}{D_t},$$

where

$w_{i,t}$ = the weight of cash flow i in period t, assuming the cash flow occurred at the end of the day

D_t = the total number of calendar days in period t

$D_{i,t}$ = the number of calendar days from the beginning of period t to cash flow i

While this Guidance Statement only contains details about the Modified Dietz method, other formulas for calculating approximate time-weighted rates of return are also permitted.

Composite Return Calculation

The GIPS standards require that composite returns must be calculated by asset weighting the individual portfolio returns using beginning-of-period values or a method that reflects both beginning-of-period values and external cash flows.

Guidance Statement on Calculation Methodology

The intention is to show a composite return that reflects the overall return of the set of the portfolios included in the composite.

To calculate composite returns, firms may use alternative formulas so long as the calculation method chosen represents returns fairly, is not misleading, and is applied consistently.

According to the *Beginning Assets Weighting* method the composite return, R_t, can be calculated using the formula:

$$R_t = \frac{\sum_{k=1}^{K} \left(V_{k,t}^{B} \times r_{k,t} \right)}{\sum_{k=1}^{K} V_{k,t}^{B}},$$

where

R_t = the beginning assets weighted return for the composite for period t

k = number of portfolios (1, 2, 3,..., K) in the composite at the beginning of period t

$V_{k,t}^{B}$ = the beginning value of portfolio k for period t

$r_{k,t}$ = the return of portfolio k for period t

The *Beginning Assets Weighting* method can also be expressed as:

$$R_t = \sum_{k=1}^{K} \left(\frac{V_{k,t}^{B}}{\sum_{k=1}^{K} V_{k,t}^{B}} \times r_{k,t} \right) = \sum_{k=1}^{K} w_{k,t}^{B} r_{k,t}$$

where $w_{k,t}^{B}$ is the weight of the value of portfolio k as a fraction of total composite asset value based on beginning asset values for period t, and can be calculated according to the following formula:

$$w_{k,t}^{B} = \frac{V_{k,t}^{B}}{\sum_{k=1}^{K} V_{k,t}^{B}}$$

The *Beginning Assets Plus Weighted Cash Flow* method represents a refinement to the beginning assets weighting method. Consider the case in which one of two portfolios in a composite doubles in value as the result of a contribution on the third day of a performance period. Under the beginning assets weighting method, this portfolio will be weighted in the composite based solely on its beginning value (i.e., not including the contribution). The beginning assets plus weighted cash flow method resolves this problem by including the effect of external cash flows in the weighting calculation.

Assuming that external cash flows occur at the end of the day, the weighting factor for each cash flow is calculated as:

$$w_{i,k,t} = \frac{D_t - D_{i,k,t}}{D_t},$$

where

$w_{i,k,t}$ = the weight of cash flow i in portfolio k in period t, assuming the cash flow occurred at the end of the day
D_t = the total number of calendar days in period t
$D_{i,k,t}$ = the number of calendar days from the beginning of period t to cash flow i in portfolio k

The *Beginning Assets Plus Weighted Cash Flow* composite return can be calculated as follows:

$$R_t = \frac{\sum_{k=1}^{K} \left\{ \left[V_{k,t}^B + \sum_{i=1}^{I_k} \left(CF_{i,k,t} \times w_{i,k,t} \right) \right] \times r_{k,t} \right\}}{\sum_{k=1}^{K} \left[V_{k,t}^B + \sum_{i=1}^{I_k} \left(CF_{i,k,t} \times w_{i,k,t} \right) \right]},$$

where

R_t = the beginning assets plus weighted cash flow composite return for period t

$V_{k,t}^B$ = the beginning value of portfolio k for period t

I_k = the number of cash flows (i = 1, 2, 3,..., I_k) in portfolio k
$CF_{i,k,t}$ = the ith cash flow in portfolio k for period t
$w_{i,k,t}$ = the weight of cash flow i in portfolio k for period t
$r_{k,t}$ = the return for portfolio k for period t

The *Beginning Assets Plus Weighted Cash Flow* composite return method can also be expressed by the following formula:

$$R_t = \sum_{k=1}^{K} \left(\frac{V_{k,t}}{\sum_{k=1}^{K} V_{k,t}} \times r_{k,t} \right),$$

where

R_t = the beginning asset plus weighted cash flow composite return for period t

Guidance Statement on Calculation Methodology

$r_{k,t}$ = the return for portfolio k for period t

$V_{k,t}$ = the beginning value plus weighted cash flows of portfolio k for period t as calculated according to the following formula:

$$V_{k,t} = V_{k,t}^B + \sum_{i=1}^{I_k} \left(CF_{i,k,t} \times w_{i,k,t} \right),$$

where

$V_{k,t}$ = the value of portfolio k's beginning assets plus weighted cash flows for period t

$V_{k,t}^B$ = the beginning value of portfolio k for period t

I_k = the number of cash flows ($i = 1, 2, 3,..., I_k$) in portfolio k

$CF_{i,k,t}$ = the ith cash flow in portfolio k for period t

$w_{i,k,t}$ = the weight of cash flow i in portfolio k for period t

The *Aggregate Return* method combines all the composite assets and external cash flows before any calculations occur to calculate returns as if the composite were one portfolio. The method is also acceptable as an asset-weighted approach.

Geometric Linking of the Periodic Composite Returns

To calculate the composite return over more than one period or sub-period, the composite return over the total period is calculated by geometrically link the individual composite periodic returns using the following formula:

$$R_t^{TWR} = \left[(1 + r_1) \times (1 + r_2) \times \cdots (1 + r_I) \right] - 1,$$

where R_t^{TWR} is the time weighted composite return for period t and period t consists of I sub-periods.

Additional Considerations

Changes to the Methodology
Where appropriate, in the interest of fair representation and full disclosure, firms should disclose material changes to their calculation and valuation policies and/or methodologies.

Third-Party Performance Measurement
Firms may use portfolio returns calculated by a third-party performance measurer as long as the methodology adheres to the requirements of the GIPS standards.

Different Valuation and/or Calculation Method
Firms are permitted to include portfolios with different valuation and/or calculation methodologies within the same composite as long as the methodologies adhere to the requirements of the GIPS standards. Firms must be consistent in the methodology used for a portfolio (e.g., firms cannot change the methodology for a portfolio from month to

Guidance Statement on Calculation Methodology

month).

Month End Valuations

Firms must be consistent in defining the (monthly) valuation period. The valuation period must end on the same day as the reporting period. In other words, firms must value the portfolio/composite on the last day of the reporting period or the nearest business day. Including portfolios with different ending valuation dates in the same composite is not permitted for periods beginning on or after 1 January 2006. For periods beginning on or after 1 January 2010, firms must value portfolios as of the calendar month end or the last business day of the month.

Trading Expenses

Returns must be calculated after the deduction of the actual trading expenses. Trading expenses are the actual costs of buying or selling investments. These costs typically take the form of brokerage commissions, exchange fees, taxes, bid-offer spreads from either internal or external brokers, and any other regulatory fee, duty, etc. associated with an individual transaction. Custodial fees charged per transaction should be considered custody fees and not trading expenses.

Trade Date Accounting

Firms must use trade date accounting for periods beginning on or after 1 January 2005. Trade-date accounting recognizes an asset or liability on the date of the purchase or sale, not on the settlement date. Recognizing the asset or liability within three days of the date the transaction is entered into satisfies the trade-date accounting requirement.

Taxes

Firms must disclose relevant details of the treatment of withholding taxes on dividends, interest income, and capital gains, if material. Returns should be calculated net of non-reclaimable withholding taxes on dividends, interest, and capital gains. Reclaimable withholding taxes should be accrued.

Grossing Up or Netting Down of Investment Management Fees

Firms are allowed to include portfolios with different grossing-up methodologies within the same composite. Firms must be consistent in the methodology used for a portfolio (e.g., firms cannot change the methodology for a portfolio from month to month). Please see the Guidance Statement on Fees.

Large Cash Flows

The firm must have an established composite-specific policy on defining and valuing for large cash flows and apply this policy consistently. Actual valuation at the time of any large cash flow is required for periods beginning on or after 1 January 2010.

Disclosures

Firms must disclose that policies for valuing portfolios, calculating performance, and preparing compliant presentations are available upon request.

Effective Date

Guidance Statement on Calculation Methodology

The effective date for this Guidance Statement is 1 January 2011. When bringing past performance into compliance, firms may comply with this version of the Guidance Statement or with prior versions in effect at the time. Prior versions of this Guidance Statement are available on the GIPS standards website (www.gipsstandards.org).

Exhibit 5.2 Global Investment Performance Standards:
A practical guide to implementing the GIPS

WHITE PAPER
Table of Contents

WHITE PAPER

An Introduction to the GIPS Standards

According to eVestment[1] about 67 percent of firms are now GIPS® compliant. Compliance with the GIPS standards is recognized as an industry best practice and has become a de facto requirement, especially in the institutional money management space, in order to stay competitive. A firm's claim of GIPS compliance facilitates "apples-to-apples" comparisons between investment managers for prospective clients and fosters invaluable client trust. This white paper should help both firms considering GIPS compliance, and also those looking to improve a current framework, by providing an overview of the building blocks necessary to manage a successful claim of GIPS compliance and to have confidence in the ultimate manifestation of the claim of GIPS compliance in the compliant presentation.

CFA Institute administers the Global Investment Performance Standards, or GIPS standards, based on the underlying principles of "full disclosure and fair representation." There is no formal enforcement mechanism, though in the United States, the SEC and savvy institutional investors act as de facto policing agents for the GIPS standards. The GIPS standards are exactly as the name implies—a global set of standards for measuring, calculating, and presenting investment performance. Though the GIPS standards are adopted voluntarily, institutional investors often require investment managers to be in compliance. As a result, investment managers and prospective clients alike can benefit. Investment firms benefit from strengthened internal controls and smoother processes while prospective clients can have greater confidence when evaluating performance among different managers.

While CFA Institute initiated the GIPS standards and funded its development, an executive committee made up of CFA Institute officials, investment practitioners, and investors from around the world is responsible for governance. As of the end of 2017, 41 countries have adopted the GIPS standards or have had their local performance reporting standards endorsed by the GIPS Executive Committee.

---

[1] eVestment. Analytics for Institutional Managers, Investors & Consultants, www.evestment.com. Accessed 4 June 2018.

Drafting Policies and Procedures

To effectively become, and remain, compliant with the GIPS standards firms first need comprehensive, well-thought-out policies and procedures. These policies and procedures, often published in a manual, provide the blueprint for a firm's compliance efforts. The manuals are firm specific and vary in form and length, though between 12 and 25 pages appears to be the norm. These manuals are often the first document requested and reviewed by third parties such as verifiers and/or regulators. A manual that vaguely documents policies and omits procedures will quickly raise a red flag and ensure an in-depth review.

An effective manual, on the other hand, details how the firm complies with every applicable provision of the GIPS standards. It also has a procedure for each policy that describes who will implement the policy, when the implementation will occur, and how the implementation will take place.

As part of the development process, the individual(s) charged with creating this document should solicit feedback and buy-in from all departments affected by any policies and procedures. This is necessary because views on particular topics can vary widely across an organization's groups. For example, regarding materiality thresholds for an error correction policy, the marketing and legal/compliance groups may have disparate opinions on what an investor considers a material error. By having collaborative discussions while drafting the manual, firms can avoid creating policies that may not make sense for them down the road.

Best practice often dictates that firms create a GIPS oversight committee whereby each group impacted by the requirements of the GIPS standards is represented. Among other duties, this committee should create the policies and procedures document and then review and update it periodically. During its meetings, the committee should also discuss any external or internal changes that affect the firm and its claim of GIPS compliance. GIPS oversight committees typically include members from groups such as compliance, legal, marketing, operations, and portfolio management. The manual should not be left static after its creation, but rather should be maintained as a "live" document and should reflect current practices, while also preserving historic ones. It is expected that changes to policies and procedures will be relatively minimal, though material strategic or organizational changes, as well as product introductions or discontinuations, will almost always require a revision.

Action Items for Policies and Procedures:

☐ **Review or draft the GIPS compliance manual.**
- Is it up to date and accurate? Is it comprehensive and complete?
- For each policy, is there an associated procedure to ensure proper execution?
- Do the policies make sense for the firm?
- Have changes occurred in areas such as systems, policies, procedures, organizational structure, or personnel that need to be addressed in the manual?
- Are the documented procedures being implemented in practice?

☐ **Consider creating a GIPS oversight committee that meets periodically to review GIPS-specific issues and that has ultimate responsibility for policies and procedures.**

Defining the Firm

One of the first steps involved in becoming compliant is defining the firm for GIPS compliance purposes. A common misconception is that firms can claim compliance on only one investment product or strategy. This is not the case and the provisions of the GIPS standards must be applied on a firm-wide basis.

It is utterly important that firms are defined fairly and appropriately. If a firm is not defined properly, issues can arise when determining firm assets under management, constructing composites, and marketing the firm as GIPS compliant.

One of the key determinants when defining the firm is how the firm is held out to the public. The GIPS standards require a firm to be defined as "an investment firm, subsidiary, or division held out to clients or prospective clients as a distinct business entity."[2]

A "distinct business entity" is one that:

(1) is organizationally and functionally segregated from other units, divisions, departments, or offices;

(2) retains discretion over the assets it manages; and

(3) has autonomy over the investment decision-making process."[3]

Additionally, there are other factors that may also need to be considered, including whether the entity has a distinct market or client type or whether it has a separate, distinct investment process compared to other entities within the broader organization.

---

[2] GIPS Handbook, p. 340.
[3] Ibid.

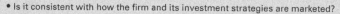

Action Items for Firm Definition:

❑ **Establish or review the firm definition.**
- Is it consistent with how the firm and its investment strategies are marketed?
- Has the firm been defined too narrowly or too broadly?

❑ **Evaluate any changes in the firm definition.**
- Has the firm undergone a restructuring or will it in the near future?
- Has the firm consolidated or separated any business lines?
- Are there any new business lines that should be included or excluded from the firm definition (e.g., a hedge fund launch or entry into wrap programs)?
- Have any mergers or lift outs occurred that could affect the firm definition?

The GIPS standards suggest that firms adopt the broadest, most meaningful firm definition. In some cases, such as when a firm includes all assets within the legal entity, defining the firm can be simple. In other circumstances, defining the firm is more complex. The latter is common in cases where a parent organization has multiple entities and business lines operating under one brand. If the underlying entities hold themselves out to the public as distinct business entities, it may be appropriate to define the GIPS-compliant firm to only include one of the underlying entities rather than the entire firm at the parent level. The illustration below shows different options and can differ depending on how a firm is structured.

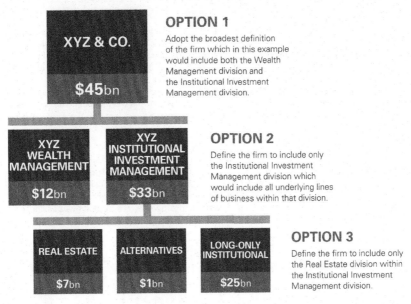

OPTION 1

Adopt the broadest definition of the firm which in this example would include both the Wealth Management division and the Institutional Investment Management division.

OPTION 2

Define the firm to include only the Institutional Investment Management division which would include all underlying lines of business within that division.

OPTION 3

Define the firm to include only the Real Estate division within the Institutional Investment Management division.

XYZ & CO. $45bn

XYZ WEALTH MANAGEMENT $12bn

XYZ INSTITUTIONAL INVESTMENT MANAGEMENT $33bn

REAL ESTATE $7bn

ALTERNATIVES $1bn

LONG-ONLY INSTITUTIONAL $25bn

Figure 1. Illustration of Firm Definition Options

Practically speaking, the definition of the firm is the foundation for firm-wide compliance and creates defined boundaries that determine the value of total firm assets under management that must be presented. It is important for firms to periodically review the firm definition and these reviews should determine whether any material changes within the organization have altered how the firm is held out to the public. Such changes are typically associated with corporate restructuring or mergers and acquisitions.

 Defining Discretion

Discretion, according to the GIPS standards, is the ability of the firm to implement its intended investment strategy. This can often be different from the firm's legal discretionary authority. A firm may have legal discretion and yet be able to classify a portfolio as non-discretionary under the GIPS standards. A well-thought-out and consistently applied definition of discretion is critical to coming into and maintaining GIPS compliance as a firm's definition of discretion is fundamental to satisfying one of the main requirements of the GIPS standards; specifically, all actual, fee-paying, discretionary accounts must be included in at least one composite.

If documented client-imposed restrictions significantly hinder the firm from fully implementing its intended strategy, the firm may determine the portfolio is non-discretionary. Non-discretionary portfolios must not be included in any of a firm's composites. There are degrees of discretion and not all client-imposed restrictions will necessarily cause a portfolio to be non-discretionary. Client-imposed constraints can include restricting asset allocation decisions, restricting the purchase or sale of certain securities, imposing specific cash flow requirements, and applying tax considerations. The firm must determine if the restrictions will, or could, interfere with the implementation of the intended strategy to the extent that the portfolio is no longer representative of the strategy. Both discretionary and non-discretionary portfolios will be included in the total assets of the GIPS-compliant firm.

Each firm must document its definition of discretion and must apply the definition consistently. Only client-imposed restrictions can cause an account to be classified as non-discretionary. Deviations caused by tactical decisions made by the investment manager would not justify a loss of discretion. Ideally, discretion is defined at the firm level, but may be defined at the composite level, or by asset class. Firms must maintain records to support why a portfolio was assigned to a specific composite or was excluded from all composites.

Action Items for Definition of Discretion:

☐ **Establish or review the firm's definition of discretion.**
  • Have the circumstances that may cause a portfolio to be deemed non-discretionary been clearly and completely documented?
  • Has the policy been applied consistently over time and for all portfolios?

☐ **Institute and monitor a process to ensure the appropriate employees understand the firm's process for determining the discretionary status of portfolios.**

☐ **Periodically review portfolios not in composites to ensure they are appropriately excluded.**

☐ **Institute and monitor a process to ensure the supporting documentation for non-discretionary accounts is retained.**

☐ **Institute and monitor a process to notify appropriate personnel when changes to a portfolio may affect its discretionary status.**

Instituting Sound Recordkeeping Practices

Good recordkeeping is fundamental to any sound compliance program. The same is true for GIPS compliance. The GIPS standards require firms to capture and maintain the data and information needed to support all items included in their compliant presentations. GIPS-compliant presentations often come in single-page format, and it would be easy to assume that this would be a simple undertaking. However, the data behind the statistics can become voluminous and this requirement can be quite a task.

For account and composite-level performance, firms must maintain records sufficient to recalculate portfolio and composite-level returns. For account returns, this information might include portfolio market value reports, transaction summaries showing external cash flow days and amounts, accrued income reports, and the calculation methodologies used for different time periods. Non-performance-related information, such as investment management agreements and investment objective questionnaires may also be necessary to prove that a portfolio is included in its proper composite. For composites, depending on the calculation methodology used, a firm might have to maintain all historical monthly account returns, monthly account market values, transaction and external cash flow reports at the composite level, and documentation for portfolios included or excluded for the month being replicated.

Other recordkeeping concerns to be mindful of are instances when performance is calculated outside of a system, such as in spreadsheets, and any time performance track records have been brought over from a different firm. Firms should also institute an added review level when they use spreadsheets to reduce the risk of human error. Another area where recordkeeping is important is ported performance. To be specific, firms must maintain all records needed to support performance presented for periods when managers were at another firm. Regulators often pay very close attention to how firms present ported performance, so the recordkeeping for this area should be thoroughly and regularly reviewed.

Action Items for Recordkeeping:

❏ Select a random set of statistics from the compliant presentation(s) and check to see how easily the supporting records for these statistics can be obtained.

❏ Replicate a sample of account and composite-level returns to ensure the necessary underlying records are available.

❏ Scrutinize any ported performance presented to be sure the records on hand support that performance.

Composite Construction

Once a firm has created an appropriate firm definition and identified discretionary accounts using its definition of discretion, the next crucial step towards GIPS compliance is composite construction. The GIPS standards define a composite as "the aggregation of one or more portfolios managed to a similar investment mandate, objective, or strategy and...the primary vehicle for presenting performance to prospective clients."[4]

Composites form a material component of a firm's marketing efforts and, consequently, need to be constructed accurately and fairly. While the GIPS standards offer some flexibility regarding composites, firms should make sure defined composites are reasonable and consistent with any marketing efforts and with the products and strategies that are offered.

Well-constructed composites provide prospective investors with a true representation of a manager's ability to implement a particular strategy. In contrast, allowing composites to be defined too broadly or narrowly can pose unnecessary risk to a firm. For example, if a firm constructs a composite for a strategy that combines accounts that can use leverage with accounts that prohibit leverage, then the composite returns would be of little use to a prospective investor that disallows leverage. In this situation, constructing separate composites for these accounts would likely be the most appropriate resolution.

---

[4] GIPS Handbook, p. 331.

Action Items for Composite Construction:

☐ **Ensure proper placement of portfolios.**
- Organize a list of accounts that includes not only currently managed portfolios, but also closed accounts that were previously under the firm's management – this will eliminate any potential survivorship bias.
- Apply the firm's definition of discretion, flagging accounts that should be classified as non-discretionary.
- Any fee-paying account that is not classified as non-discretionary must be in a composite. Non-fee-paying accounts may be included in composites as well, but this is not required.

☐ **Review the firm's existing composite structure.**
- Are the composites consistent with the strategies that are offered?
- Are there too few composites (i.e., too broadly defined) or too many composites (i.e., too narrowly defined)?
- Would composite performance provide a prospective investor with an accurate and fair depiction of how their account would be managed?

☐ **Test composites for proper construction.**
- Conduct a dispersion analysis of composite accounts for a given year. If the returns are wildly different, this suggests the composite may be defined too broadly or that errors exist in its construction.
- Select a sample of composite accounts and compare the account holdings to ensure they all have similar securities and the holdings are in line with the composite definition.
- Compare the allocation of accounts within a composite at a high level to ensure they are in line with one another. This comparison could involve allocations to different asset classes if the composite is multi-strategy or it could require a sector allocation review.

WHITE PAPER A Practical Guide to Implementing the GIPS Standards 7

As noted above, the GIPS standards require that composites include all accounts managed according to the same investment mandate, objective, or strategy. They also require portfolios to be added to and removed from composites on a timely, consistent basis. In addition, portfolios must not be switched from one composite to another unless the firm can show documented changes to the portfolios' mandates, objectives, or strategies or that it has redefined the composite in a way that makes the switch appropriate. Having these requirements in place ensures the consistency of account additions and removals and prevents a firm from cherry picking best-performing accounts for a composite at any given time. Adherence to these rules is particularly important because, from a compliance perspective, such cherry picking could be viewed as misleading.

Composite creation is not a singular event. Portfolio holdings constantly fluctuate, accounts are opened and/or closed, discretionary status changes (through a GIPS-compliant lens), and sometimes client mandates change. For this reason, composites must be monitored and managed continuously.

 ## Creating Compliant Presentations and Marketing Material

Perhaps the biggest risk a firm faces when it claims GIPS compliance is in how it presents performance in compliant presentations and marketing materials. Seemingly in most cases where the SEC has cited a firm for a GIPS compliance-related deficiency, the issue pertains to marketing materials that provide inadequate disclosures or statistics, or omit them entirely. A firm's compliant presentation must include all statistics and disclosures required by the GIPS standards. As with any performance-related information disseminated to prospects or the public, compliance departments should review compliant presentations to ensure all required statistics and disclosures are present.

Action Items for Compliant Presentations and Marketing Materials:

☐ Implement and monitor a process to ensure the firm is complying with provision 0.A.9.

☐ Train compliance staff to review any information intended for dissemination to ensure adherence to GIPS standards requirements.

☐ Review compliant presentations, and cross reference sections 4 and 5 of the GIPS standards, to ensure all required disclosures and statistics are included and are accurate.

☐ Implement tracking to document who receives a presentation, which presentation they receive, and when they receive it.

☐ If the firm markets its claim of compliance using the GIPS advertising guidelines, establish and monitor a review process to ensure all disclosure and presentation requirements are met.

See Appendix B for an example of what a compliant presentation often looks like.

Provision 0.A.9 of the GIPS standards requires firms to make every reasonable effort to provide their compliant presentations to all prospective clients. That is, they cannot distribute these presentations selectively. Compliant presentations are often delivered to prospects during an initial meeting as part of a pitch book.

When providing compliant presentations, firms should have a system in place to track who receives a presentation, which presentation they receive, and when they received it. Maintaining this log gives firms an efficient, easily accessible means to demonstrate their adherence to provision 0.A.9. These logs also facilitate any republishing of materials to appropriate prospects and clients should the firm uncover errors that require a restatement of performance information. Such tracking can typically be done as part of a firm's existing process to evidence approval and distribution of marketing materials and advertisements.

 ## Verification

The GIPS Executive Committee strongly recommends (but does not require) that firms claiming GIPS compliance undergo a verification. Verification provides firms, existing clients, and prospective clients with additional confidence that the firm has complied with all the composite construction requirements of the GIPS standards on a firm-wide basis and has designed its policies and procedures to calculate and present performance in compliance with the GIPS standards.

If the firm plans to undergo third-party verification, then a specialist firm should be engaged early on, because the costs of pre-compliance services are usually nominal if such services are provided in conjunction with a verification, experienced verifiers serve as informed GIPS compliance consultants. Specialized GIPS compliance consultants bring to the process the experience of working with other firms facing similar challenges and solutions.

While maintaining independence is critical, verification firms and other specialists can often provide suggestions on how to implement a GIPS-compliant framework, yet also conduct the verification of a firm's claim of GIPS compliance. They can assess books and records and data integrity challenges and also prevent ineffective decision making around fundamental composite construction issues.

For firms further along in the process, GIPS compliance consultants can suggest any necessary adjustments to ensure that GIPS-compliant performance measurement and reporting practices are sound. Additionally, they can assist firms with staying current on any changes to the GIPS standards requirements and interpretations - something many firms simply do not have time for on their own. Working with experts can help keep overhead and training costs down, while providing greater assurance that the right guidance is followed when establishing and maintaining GIPS compliance.

Dedicated Resources

Implementing and maintaining GIPS compliance requires time, resources, and expertise. The prevailing question is often: how much dedicated GIPS standards expertise can the firm afford to have on staff? It may make sense for the largest firms to hire or train several specialists in GIPS compliance. It's a bigger challenge for smaller firms, where portfolio managers, traders, and operations staff already serve various roles, and chief compliance officers have their hands full with everyday regulatory compliance. The price of compliance, however, is far outweighed by the potential costs of noncompliance, including fewer growth opportunities, damage to the firm's reputation by not keeping up with industry best practices, and ultimately, lost business.

When claiming GIPS compliance, firms must satisfy all applicable requirements, including those disseminated in updates, guidance statements, interpretations, Q&As, and clarifications. These resources are available on the GIPS standards website and in the handbook. Historically, CFA Institute reviewed and updated the GIPS standards every five years. While it is expected that new guidance and other information will come out intermittently, the latest version of the GIPS standards is in the works (2020 edition of the GIPS Standards) and is expected to be effective 1/1/2020. To stay current with changes published by CFA Institute and the GIPS Executive Committee, firms should periodically review the website (www.gipsstandards.org) as well as referencing the most recent version of the handbook.

Appendix A: Common Terms

Composite – an aggregation of one or more portfolios managed according to a similar investment mandate, objective, or strategy. Composites are the primary vehicle for presenting performance to prospective clients. The firm must include all actual, fee-paying, discretionary portfolios in at least one composite.

Discretion – the ability of the firm to implement its intended investment strategy. If documented client-imposed restrictions significantly hinder the firm from fully implementing its intended investment strategy, the firm may determine the portfolio is non-discretionary. Non-discretionary portfolios must not be include in a firm's composites.

Compliant Presentation – a presentation for a composite that contains all the information required by the GIPS standards and may also include additional information or supplemental information.

Prospective Client – any person or entity that has expressed interest in one of the firm's composite strategies and qualifies to invest in the composite. Firms can also refine the definition of a prospective client further if they choose. Existing clients may also qualify as prospective clients for any strategy that is different from their current strategy.

Verification – the review of an investment management firm's performance measurement processes and procedures by an independent third-party. Verification also tests whether the firm's policies and procedures are designed to calculate and present performance in compliance with the GIPS standards.

Performance Examination – detailed testing of any of the firm's composites and their associated compliant presentations by an independent verifier. A performance examination may only be performed concurrently with the verification or upon completion of the verification.

Appendix B: Compliant Presentation Example

Year	Gross-of-Fees Return (%)	Net-of-Fees Return (%)	Benchmark Return (%)	Composite 3-Yr St Dev (%)	Benchmark 3-Yr St Dev (%)	Number of Portfolios	Internal Dispersion (%)	Total Composite Assets (USD mil)	Composite Percentage of Firm Assets (%)	Total Firm Assets
2008	10.01%	9.36%	8.52%	N/A	N/A	5	N/A	171.9	18.0%	955.0
2009	47.65%	46.58%	41.45%	N/A	N/A	5	N/A	265.6	19.4%	1,369.1
2010	21.28%	20.39%	11.15%	N/A	N/A	5	N/A	378.4	22.6%	1,674.3
2011	-8.83%	-9.95%	-9.71%	21.89%	22.72%	7	0.03%	317.4	19.6%	1,619.4
2012	20.92%	20.03%	16.83%	18.68%	19.26%	5	N/A	318.5	15.1%	2,109.3
2013	19.28%	18.41%	15.29%	15.44%	16.23%	6	1.09%	474.5	16.7%	2,841.3
2014	-0.74%	-1.48%	-3.87%	12.22%	12.81%	8	0.08%	424.5	14.6%	2,907.5
2015	-4.56%	-5.24%	-5.66%	11.31%	12.13%	4	N/A	354.3	15.8%	2,242.4
2016	6.12%	5.34%	4.50%	12.01%	12.51%	5	N/A	375.2	16.1%	2,330.4
2017	33.12%	32.14%	27.19%	11.82%	11.87%	7	2.35%	454.8	17.1%	2,659.6

XYZ Investment Management claims compliance with the Global Investment Performance Standards (GIPS®) and has prepared and presented this report in compliance with the GIPS standards. XYZ has been independently verified for the periods 1/01/08 – 12/31/17. The verification report is available upon request. Verification assesses whether (1) the firm has complied with all the composite construction requirements of the GIPS standards on a firm-wide basis and (2) the firm's policies and procedures are designed to calculate and present performance in compliance with the GIPS standards. Verification does not ensure the accuracy of any specific composite presentation.

Firm and Composite Information

XYZ Investment Management is an independent investment management firm that manages equity, balanced, and fixed income portfolios. The firm invests primarily in U.S. stocks and bonds.

The ABC Composite invests in small, mid, and large capitalization common stocks. The minimum account size for inclusion into the ABC Composite is $500,000.

The ABC Composite was created in January 2008. A complete list and description of firm composites is available upon request.

Benchmark

The benchmark is the S&P 500 Index, which is a market-capitalization weighted index containing the 500 most widely held companies (400 industrial, 20 transportation, 40 utility and 40 financial companies) chosen with respect to market size, liquidity, and industry. The volatility of the S&P 500 Index may be materially different from that of the strategy depicted, and the holdings in the strategy may differ significantly from the securities that comprise the S&P 500 Index. The S&P 500 Index is calculated on a total return basis with dividends reinvested and is not assessed a management fee.

Performance Calculations

Valuations and returns are computed and stated in U.S. Dollars. Results reflect the reinvestment of dividends and other earnings.

Gross-of-fees returns are presented before management and custodial fees, but after all trading expenses and withholding taxes. Net-of-fees returns are calculated using actual management fees that were paid and are presented before custodial fees but after management fees, all trading expenses, and withholding taxes.

The standard management fee for the ABC strategy is 1.25% per annum on the first $1 million USD and 1.00% per annum on additional assets. Additional information regarding ABC's fees is included in its Part II of Form ADV.

Internal dispersion is calculated using the asset-weighted standard deviation of all accounts included in the composite for the entire year; it is not presented for periods less than one year or when there were five or fewer portfolios in the composite for the entire year.

The three-year annualized standard deviation measures the variability of the composite and the benchmark returns over the preceding 36-month period. The standard deviation is not presented for 2008 through 2010 as it is not required for periods prior to 2011.

Policies for valuing portfolios, calculating performance, and preparing compliant presentations are available upon request.

Past performance does not guarantee future results.

About ACA Performance Services

ACA Performance Services, a division of ACA Compliance Group, offers GIPS compliance verification and consulting services to investment managers around the globe. ACA Performance Services is the largest team of professionals solely dedicated to GIPS compliance verification and investment performance services worldwide.

ACA Compliance Group
1370 Broadway, 12th Floor
New York, NY 10018 USA
Phone: +1 (212) 951-1030
www.acacompliancegroup.com

www.acacompliancegroup.com/performance

For more information regarding ACA Performance Services, please contact your verification team or **Christie Dillard** at 1.866.279.0750 or cdillard@acacompliancegroup.com.

Source: © *2018 ACA Compliance Group. Used with permission from ACA Compliance Group.*

determined using a "fair value" method. Fair value methods generally utilize the observed market value of related securities to impute the values of illiquid securities. For example, the current fair value of a plot of land is generally not its last sale price, since real estate trades very infrequently and the sale price might have been the result of a transaction that occurred years or decades ago. The value of land can be imputed by observing the recent sale prices of land with similar characteristics and in a similar location, adjusting for acreage. Likewise, the imputed fair value of illiquid securities relies on the observed market prices of related securities. Investment firms who hold such securities typically utilize third party vendors who specialize in fair value analysis. Having a third party calculate the fair value also helps avoid the moral hazard problem of having the investment manager determine the value of something that affects the manager's reported performance.

Another complexity in portfolio return calculations arises when there are cash flows in the form of cash withdrawals from the account or cash deposits to the account. The return calculation must account for the cash flow by splitting the return calculation into two periods and linking those periods' returns. Specifically, consider a month in which there is a significant cash flow of CF_{t-k} in the middle of the month. Let time t denote the last day of the month and assume that the cash flow arrives k days before the end of the month, where $k < 21$. Finally, we consider a month that has 21 days, since the average number of trading days in a month is 21. In this way, there are three relevant dates: $t-21$, $t-k$, and t.

As in Eq. (5.1), the beginning market value for our calculation is MV_{t-21}. The market value of those same assets at time $t-k$ is reflected in the pre-flow market value or MV_{t-k}^{pre}. Note that the pre-flow market value at time $t-k$ ignores the cash flow that comes in during that same day. Using the pre-flow market value and the value at the beginning of the month, we calculate the return over the first period within the month as:

$$r_{t-21,t-k} = \frac{MV_{t-k}^{pre} - MV_{t-21}}{MV_{t-21}} \tag{5.2}$$

We now calculate the post-flow value of the assets by adding the cash flow at time $t-k$. The post-flow market value of the portfolio at time $t-k$ is:

$$MV_{t-k}^{post} = MV_{t-k}^{pre} + CF_{t-k} \tag{5.3}$$

The post-flow assets are a part of the portfolio from this point on, so the performance for the second period within the month utilizes this post-flow market value as its beginning value. The portfolio return from time $t-k$ to time t is calculated as:

$$r_{t-k,t} = \frac{MV_t - MV_{t-k}^{post}}{MV_{t-k}^{post}} \tag{5.4}$$

Note that we omit the superscript (pre or post) for periods in which there is no flow, since the market values are unambiguous in these periods. The final step is to link the two periods' returns to calculate the entire month's returns, as given by:

$$r_{t-21,t} = (1 + r_{t-21,t-k})(1 + r_{t-k,t}) - 1 \qquad (5.5)$$

In summary, the first period's return is calculated using the pre-flow value of the portfolio as the ending market value. The second period's return then uses the post-flow market value of the assets as the beginning market value. The full month's return is calculated by compounding the two periods' returns.

A further complication in the calculation of performance arises from cash flows relating to the initiation of the performance calculation. This issue becomes especially important for strategies that are benchmarked to a particular non-cash index. Any cash into a fund must be invested in the underlying portfolio securities. This process, known as a transition, results in direct transaction costs and indirect performance gains or losses as the cash is being traded for the portfolio's underlying securities. For example, suppose a portfolio is benchmarked to the S&P 500 Index and holds a large number of S&P 500 stocks. On the day the cash flow arrives, the cash effectively earns 0% until it is "equitized" (i.e., converted to stock). The portfolio manager must trade the cash for the portfolio stocks, which results in transaction costs. As a result, the portfolio performance will look relatively low compared to the S&P 500 on this day, since the cash earns nothing until converted to stock and the transaction costs lower the account value. Note that this negative relative performance has nothing to do with the portfolio manager's strategy or ability. Rather, the relative performance is due to the cash flow. Therefore, most investment managers and clients set a performance date that is subsequent to the cash flow date.

To illustrate how the performance calculation can be done in the presence of a large cash flow, consider the example shown in Exhibit 5.3. In this example, a portfolio is benchmarked to the S&P 500 Index. It has a market value of approximately $700,000 when a cash inflow of $300,000 occurs at the beginning of the day on November 7, 2012. The portfolio manager has agreed with the client that performance begins as of the same-day market close if the cash flow arrives before 3 PM New York time or as of the next-day market close if the cash flow arrives after 3 PM New York time. The 3 PM cutoff is to allow the investment manager time to determine and submit an order to convert the cash to the strategy's weights prior to the close of the market that day. Furthermore, the agreement sets forth that the manager will attempt to equitize the cash with "market on close" orders.

The exhibit shows the market value of the portfolio's holdings on the four dates in 2012: October 31, November 6, November 7, and November 30. Notice that November 7, 2012, is shown with both pre-flow and post-flow values. Furthermore, the post-flow values reflect the portfolio after the cash has been equitized. In this case, the commissions on the trades to

Exhibit 5.3 Example of a monthly performance calculation when a large cash flow occurs during the month.

A cash flow of $300,000 arrives at the beginning of the day on November 7, 2012. Performance begins as of Market Close on November 7, 2012. The cash flow is equitized (i.e., converted to equity securities through transactions) using "Market on Close" on November 7, 2012. No other cash flows during the month of November. The calculation requires that the market values be calculated at the end of the previous month (October 31, 2012), on the day of the cash flow, and at the end of the current month (November 30, 2012). Note that the market value of the portfolio on the day of the cash flow is calculated both Pre-Flow and Post-Flow. The Pre-Flow market value reflects only the value of the securities and cash that were held prior to the cash flow. The Post-Flow market value reflects the value of all securities, including those that were purchased as a result of the cash flow.

Security	October 31, 2012			November 6, 2012			November 7, 2012 (Pre-flow)		
	Shares Held	Price at Close	Market value at Close	Shares Held	Price at Close	Market value at Close	Shares Held	Price at Close	Market value at Close
A	800	35.99	28,792.00	800	38.28	30,624.00	800	37.58	30,064.00
AEE	1200	32.88	39,456.00	1200	32.10	38,520.00	1200	31.39	37,668.00
APC	600	68.81	41,286.00	600	73.07	43,842.00	600	70.41	42,246.00
BF/B	500	64.06	32,030.00	500	64.60	32,300.00	500	64.40	32,200.00
BMS	800	33.05	26,440.00	800	33.79	27,032.00	800	33.55	26,840.00
FLR	600	55.85	33,510.00	600	54.49	32,694.00	600	53.23	31,938.00
FOSL	400	87.10	34,840.00	400	84.24	33,696.00	400	83.93	33,572.08
FSLR	1400	24.30	34,020.00	1400	24.79	34,707.82	1400	23.67	33,142.48
GWW	200	201.41	40,282.00	200	203.08	40,616.00	200	198.44	39,688.00
JBL	2000	17.34	34,680.00	2000	18.48	36,960.00	2000	17.85	35,700.00
L	800	42.28	33,824.00	800	42.33	33,864.00	800	41.20	32,960.00
MAC	700	57.00	39,900.00	700	57.36	40,152.00	700	56.69	39,683.00
MCK	400	93.31	37,324.00	400	93.48	37,392.00	400	94.69	37,876.00
MDLZ	1500	26.55	39,825.00	1500	26.49	39,735.00	1500	26.25	39,375.00
MMC	1000	34.03	34,030.00	1000	34.92	34,920.00	1,000	34.50	34,500.00
NTAP	600	26.91	16,146.00	600	28.14	16,884.00	600	27.73	16,638.00
NVDA	3100	11.98	37,122.50	3100	13.01	40,331.00	3100	12.61	39,090.38
OXY	500	78.96	39,480.00	500	79.58	39,790.00	500	77.45	38,725.00
PETM	500	66.39	33,195.00	500	67.25	33,625.00	500	66.64	33,320.00
T	500	34.59	17,295.00	500	34.80	17,400.00	500	33.64	16,819.10
WYNN	200	121.06	24,212.00	200	112.21	22,442.00	200	111.03	22,206.00
Cash			5823.43			6043.62			6,043.84
Portfolio Market Value			$703,512.93			$713,570.44			$700,294.88

Security	November 7, 2012 (Post-flow)	November 30, 2012	Trades on November 7, 2012

	Shares Held	Price at Close	Market value at Close	Shares Held	Price at Close	Market value at Close	Shares Held	Trade Price	Market value at Close	Comm.
A	1100	37.58	41,338.00	1100	38.29	42,119.00	300	37.58	11,274.00	8.95
AEE	1700	31.39	53,363.00	1700	29.97	50,949.00	500	31.39	15,695.00	8.95
APC	900	70.41	63,369.00	900	73.19	65,871.00	300	70.41	21,123.00	8.95
BF/B	700	64.4	45,080.00	700	70.18	49,126.00	200	64.40	12,880.00	8.95
BMS	1100	33.55	36,905.00	1100	33.60	36,960.00	300	33.55	10,065.00	8.95
FLR	800	53.23	42,584.00	800	53.08	42,464.00	200	53.23	10,646.00	8.95
FOSL	600	83.9302	50,358.12	600	86.44	51,864.00	200	83.93	16,786.00	8.95
FSLR	2000	23.6732	47,346.40	2000	26.99	53,980.00	600	23.67	14,202.00	8.95
GWW	300	198.44	59,532.00	300	194.02	58,206.00	100	198.44	19,844.00	8.95
JBL	2900	17.85	51,765.00	2900	19.00	55,100.00	900	17.85	16,065.00	8.95
L	1100	41.2	45,320.00	1100	40.88	44,968.00	300	41.20	12,360.00	8.95
MAC	1000	56.69	56,690.00	1000	56.50	56,500.00	300	56.69	17,007.00	8.95
MCK	600	94.69	56,814.00	600	94.47	56,682.00	200	94.69	18,938.00	8.95
MDLZ	2100	26.25	55,125.00	2100	25.89	54,369.00	600	26.25	15,750.00	8.95
MMC	1400	34.5	48,300.00	1400	35.22	49,308.00	400	34.50	13,800.00	8.95
NTAP	900	27.73	24,957.00	900	31.71	28,539.00	300	27.73	8,319.00	8.95
NVDA	4400	12.6098	55,483.12	4400	11.97	52,668.00	1,300	12.61	16,393.00	8.95
OXY	700	77.45	54,215.00	700	75.21	52,647.00	200	77.45	15,490.00	8.95
PETM	700	66.64	46,648.00	700	70.66	49,462.00	200	66.64	13,328.00	8.95
T	700	33.6382	23,546.74	700	34.13	23,891.00	200	33.64	6,728.00	8.95
WYNN	300	111.03	33,309.00	300	112.40	33,720.00	100	111.03	11,103.00	8.95
Cash			8,059.89			9,974.00				
Portfolio Market Value			**$1,000,108.27**			**$1,019,367.00**			**$297,796.00**	**$187.95**

Cash at Close on 11/7/2012 = Cash at Close on 11/6/2012 + Interest on 11/7/2012 + Cash Inflow − Cost of Security Purchases − Cost of Commissions

$5,011.67 = $6,043.62 + $0.12 + $300,000.00 − $297,796.00 − $187.95

Return from October 31, 2012 to November 7, 2012 (Pre-Flow):

$$r_1 = \frac{700,294.88 - 703,512.93}{703,512.93} = -0.4574\%$$

Return from November 7, 2012 (Post-Flow) to November 30, 2012:

$$r_2 = \frac{\$1,019,367.00 - \$1,000,108.27}{\$1,000,108.27} = +1.9257\%$$

?

Return for month of November 2012: $r_{November} = (1 - 0.004574) \times (1 + .019257) - 1 = 1.46\%$

convert the cash to portfolio holdings are not counted against the investment manager, since the post-flow market values are determined after the equitizing transactions have taken place. Had the cash flow remained as cash until after the performance date, any transaction costs would be counted in the manager's performance. Following Eq. (5.2), we calculate the performance between October 31 and November 7 (using the pre-flow market values) to be −0.46%. Similarly, the post-flow market values are used according to Eqs. (5.3) and (5.4) to calculate the performance from November 7 through November 30 to be 1.93%. These returns are compounded according to Eq. (5.5) to determine the strategy's performance 1.46% for the entire month of November.

We include as an end-of-chapter exercise the calculation of the portfolio's performance in this example if there had not been a cash flow during the month. In this case, the difference in the return is less than 10 basis points and is due to the fact that the trades are executed in round lots, which causes the security weightings to differ slightly after the cash flow occurs.

As illustrated in the example, the determination of the performance date can be particularly important for investment managers and student-managed investment funds at the start-up stage, since the calculated performance, and especially the relative performance of the fund against a specific benchmark, can be greatly affected. No single performance date is considered correct, though the market close date described above is quite common. It is critical that the investment manager and the client or portfolio beneficiary understand and agree on the performance date and the portfolio transition prior to the funding of the account. Having the transition plan and performance date that are clearly articulated in the investment management agreement helps assure that the parties share a mutual understanding of an issue that could have a significant impact on the portfolio's reported performance.

Dollar-weighted returns

The value of portfolio evolves over time due to the total returns on investments and cash flows. Letting MV_t denote the market value of a portfolio at time t, r_t denote the periodic total return over the period time t-1 to time t, and CF_t denote the net cashflow over the period time t-1 to time t, the value of the portfolio evolves according to Eq. (5.6):

$$MV_t = (1 + r_t)MV_{t-1} + CF_t \tag{5.6}$$

Exhibit 5.4 illustrates how to implement Eq. (5.6) in an Excel spreadsheet. It shows the monthly returns for a portfolio in cells B3:B14 and monthly cashflows C3:C14 over the period January 31, 2019 through December 31, 2019. It also shows the market value of the portfolio on December 31, 2018, in cell D2 and the month-end market values from January 31, 2019 through in cells D2:D14, calculated using Eq. (5.6).

Exhibit 5.4 Example of calculation of dollar-weighted return

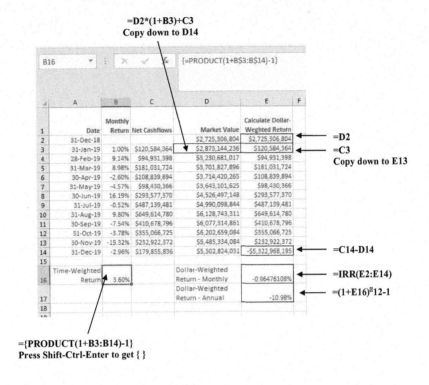

The dollar-weighted return is the constant rate of return which result in the portfolio evolving in value from its initial value (MV_0) to the final value (MV_T). In other words, if we replace r_t in Eq. (5.6) with a constant r, the value of the portfolio would still evolve from MV_0 to MV_T, but along a different path as illustrated in Exhibit 5.5.

The dollar-weighted return is the value of r that solves Eq. (5.7):

$$MV_0 + \sum_{t=1}^{T} \frac{CF_t}{(1+r)^t} - \frac{MV_T}{(1+r)^T} = 0 \qquad (5.7)$$

The Excel function *IRR* (internal rate of return) solves Eq. 5.7. Exhibit 5.4 shows how to do this. First, we need to set up the data for the calculation. To do this, first enter = D2 in cell E2. Then enter =D2*(1+B3)+C3 in cell D3 and copy down to D14. Then, in cell E3, enter = C3 and copy down this cell though cell E13. Finally, enter = C14-D14 in cell E14. Enter = IRR (E2:E14) in cell E16. The result is −0.96%. Since the data in this example are monthly, this is the monthly dollar-weighted return. To annualize it, enter = (1 + E16) ^12–1 in cell E17. The result is −10.98%.

Exhibit 5.5 Evolution of portfolio value with actual returns and dollar-weighted return.

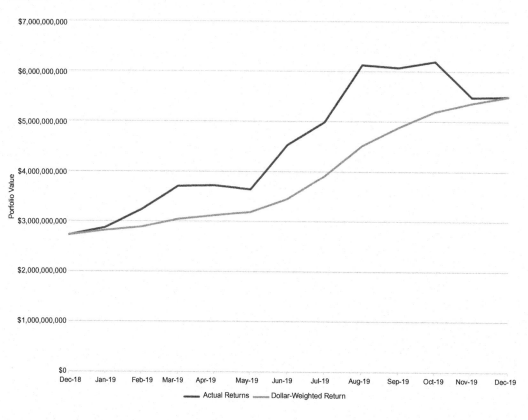

With monthly total return data, the annual time-weighted return is given by:

$$TWR = \sqrt[\frac{T}{12}]{(1+r_1)(1+r_2)\cdots(1+r_T)} \tag{5.8}$$

Using Eq. (5.8), we find that the annual time-weighted return on the portfolio is 3.60% (see cell B16 in Exhibit 5.4). Hence, in this case, the dollar-weighted return is far below the time-weighted return. This is because the large cashflow into the portfolio in August was followed by highly negative returns in subsequent months and large cashflows and large cashflows continues during those months.

An example of performance reporting

Whether the ultimate goal is to preserve capital or to earn a high growth rate, the (time-weighted) percentage return on a portfolio is the ultimate goal of investment management and the portfolio performance report is the ultimate scorecard. Performance reports allow an investor to monitor the portfolio's progress. As such, performance reports should be made on a regular basis. It is common for investment managers to issue formal performance reports on a quarterly basis, though monthly reports or updates are also common.

Exhibit 5.6 shows a quarterly performance summary from Southern Illinois University's student-managed investment fund. This summary contains several items that are standard in most investment management firms' reports to clients. First, note that there are multiple periods reported. Each period ends on the "as of" date of the report, which is June 30, 2013, in this case.

It is common practice to report the most recent quarter, year-to-date (YTD), and one-year periods as the actual percentage return on the portfolio over those horizons. For reports that are made on months that are not quarter-ends (e.g., January, February, April, etc.), the one-month and/or quarter-to-date returns are also commonly reported. The returns over 3-month and 6-month periods are reported by some managers. We caution against reporting too many short-term periods, as this might suggest that the investment manager puts too much emphasis on short-term returns. Beyond 1 year, it is most common to report 3-, 5-, and 10-year returns.

Exhibit 5.6 Quarterly performance summary from Southern Illinois University's Saluki Student Investment Fund

Saluki Student Investment Fund
SIU Foundation Portfolio
Performance Summary
As of June 30, 2013

	Quarter	Calendar YTD	1-Year	3-Year	5-Year	7-Year	10-Year	Since Inception
SSIF	**1.24%**	**15.15%**	**25.31%**	**22.34%**	**10.01%**	**9.67%**	**11.81%**	**6.97%**
S&P 400 Benchmark[a]	1.00%	14.59%	25.18%	19.45%	8.91%	7.72%	10.74%	8.48%
Difference	*0.24%*	*0.56%*	*0.12%*	*2.89%*	*1.10%*	*1.95%*	*1.06%*	*−1.51%*
Tracking Error[b]			1.75%	2.42%	4.36%	4.37%	4.86%	5.74%
Information Ratio[c]			0.07	1.20	0.25	0.45	0.22	−0.26
Months > Benchmark			42%	56%	55%	52%	52%	49%

[a]Performance of the benchmark is reported for the S&P Midcap 400 Total Return Index (Source: Bloomberg SPTRMDCP Index).
[b]Tracking error is annualized and based on monthly return differences relative to the benchmark.
[c]Information ratio is the ratio of the annualized relative return divided by the tracking error. SIU Foundation portfolio value as of June 30, 2013: $1,203,239.08.
Periods greater than one year are annualized. Inception date is June 1, 2000.

Beyond 10 years, multiples of 5 years are also common. The seven-year horizon is also often used, especially for a strategy that has existed for more than 7 years, but less than 10 years. Finally, the "Since Inception" (also sometimes referred to as inception-to-date, or ITD) period reflects the performance of the portfolio or strategy since it began its most recent continuous run.

In words, the performance summary in Exhibit 5.6 shows that the SSIF portfolio has a return of 1.24% for the 3-month period ending June 30, 2013, compared to the benchmark's return of 1.00% over the same period. That is, the portfolio outperformed the benchmark by 0.24% in the second quarter of 2013. Likewise, the portfolio outperformed the benchmark by 56 basis points for the first 6 months of 2013. The average annualized return on the portfolio over the 3 years ending June 30, 2013, is 22.34%, which is 2.89% higher than the benchmark S&P Midcap 400 Index's 19.45% average annualized return over the same period.

The SSIF's performance summary notes that "periods greater than one year are annualized." Reporting annualized time-weighted average returns is standard practice. It is also best practice to use geometric (i.e., compounded) average (time-weighted) returns, which are typically calculated from monthly time-weighted returns. Eq. (5.8) above presents the formula for calculating a compound time-weighted annual return from monthly time-weighted returns. The annualized average puts the average return on a "per year" basis, making each period easy to compare the others. It is not good practice to annualize returns for periods less than 1 year. That is, monthly or quarterly returns should be reported without an adjustment.

The performance summary in Exhibit 5.6 reports the benchmark returns over the same periods as the portfolio or strategy. The benchmark returns are particularly important for strategies that have an explicit benchmark. For those that do not have a formal benchmark, the performance of one or more indexes of similar asset classes may be reported for informal benchmarking purposes. The benchmark returns are calculated using the same method as is used to calculate the portfolio returns. With compound (i.e., geometric average) returns, the order of operation matters. Note that the compound returns are first calculated for the portfolio and the benchmark in Exhibit 5.6. The average arithmetic relative return is reported as the "Difference" in the row below the SSIF and S&P 400 Benchmark returns. It is incorrect to calculate an average arithmetic annualized relative return by using compounding monthly arithmetic relative returns.[a] We illustrate this in two exercises at the end of this chapter. In short, the relative return calculation should be the last calculation, and it is simply the difference between the portfolio return and the benchmark return over that horizon.

The last three rows of data in the performance summary in Exhibit 5.6 report the tracking error, information ratio, and months greater than the benchmark. Recall from Chapter 4 that the

---

[a] It is however correct to calculate an average *geometric* annualized relative return by compounding monthly geometric relative returns. As we discuss later, this is the motivation for geometric performance attribution.

information ratio is the average relative return divided by the tracking error. In some sense, the information ratio is redundant in this report, since it can be calculated from the numbers already present in the report. However, it is convenient to have important performance measures calculated in the report. The "months greater than the benchmark" is commonly referred to as the batting average of a strategy. The baseball-inspired statistic counts a month in which the portfolio beats the benchmark as a "hit." While the batting average does not provide information about the magnitude of the relative return (just as a "hit" does not indicate how many bases the batter achieves), it does provide an indication of how consistently the strategy beats the benchmark. A batting average less than 0.500 might still result in a positive average relative return if the amount by which the strategy beats the benchmark in "hit" months exceeds the amount by which it lags the benchmark in other months.[b]

The statistics in the last three rows of Exhibit 5.6 are not compulsory items in all performance summaries, though they may be relevant for both the investment manager and its client. Tracking error may be of concern for strategy that has a specific benchmark, especially if tracking error is an integral part of the strategy. Indeed, the tracking error might be as important as the average relative return for a strategy that is mandated to track a specific benchmark. For example, an index fund that claims to track the S&P 500 might have an average relative return close to zero but would only be deemed a good substitute for the index if its tracking error is low. Additionally, if tracking error minimization or information ratio maximization are objectives of the investment process, as they are for the SSIF, they are relevant statistics for any performance summary.

As with the presentations discussed in the previous chapter, it is important that performance reports and summaries be presented in a clear and consistent manner. Frequent changes to the format of information that is presented can be confusing, especially to those who only see the performance once each quarter. Think of the layout of the report in terms of the layout of a grocery store. Customers of a grocery store appreciate consistency in the layout so that they can readily find the items they need. When the customer only needs a gallon of milk and loaf of bread, the consistent layout allows the customer to quickly and efficiently find those items. The customers are happy to shop at the grocery store, knowing that they can get in and out of the store quickly with the items they need. Likewise, such consistency in an investment manager's performance summary allows clients to become familiar with the location of information that is important to them. In return, such familiarity and ease of access help build confidence in the quality of the information and perhaps even in the manager. This is especially important in a student-managed investment fund, since the turnover in personnel

---

[b] Baseball fans might think of the average relative return as akin to the slugging percentage. In baseball, the batting average and slugging percentage are different, but related to one another. Similarly, in investment management, the batting average and average relative return are related, but the average relative return is almost always the more relevant statistic.

means that the same people will not be present to answer to the client year after year. Furthermore, graduates of the program would be able to view a performance report years later and be familiar with the content of the report.

Supplemental performance reports can also provide useful information to an investment manager's internal and external constituents. A common supplemental report is a history of period-by-period (such as monthly or annual) returns for a strategy. Such reports might be used internally or externally to conduct performance analysis as describe later in this chapter. Additionally, these reports provide information about the historical distribution of returns from an investment strategy. For example, Exhibit 5.7 shows the annual returns for the student-managed investment fund from Exhibit 5.6. In this case, the report shows both calendar-year returns and fiscal-year returns for the SSIF's client, the SIU Foundation. It is easy to verify that the geometric average of the calendar-year returns is equal to the annualized since inception returns in Exhibit 5.6 using a total of 157 months from the inception to the "as of" date of the report. So, it might seem that this supplemental report adds little information. However, this report shows that the strategy generally rises and falls with the benchmark index. Indeed, the portfolio and the benchmark had their best years in 2003, 2009, and 2010 and had their worst years in 2002 and 2008. Furthermore, the variability of the relative returns is shown, with the portfolio having returns 1230 basis points below the benchmark in its first partial year and 594 basis points above the benchmark in 2010. Moreover, the story of how the SSIF lagged the benchmark by an average of 151 basis points per year since inception (from Exhibit 5.6) is clearer, showing that most of the negative relative performance occurred in its first few years, while the portfolio underperformed the benchmark in only three of the last 10 calendar years. Such supplemental reports can help provide context to the performance summary information.

In conclusion, performance reports should be consistent. The report should provide information that is consistent with the strategy or mandate. As such, the report should include not only the average annualized returns of the portfolio, but also the returns of relevant benchmarks and statistics, such as standard deviation or tracking error, that are meaningful to the investment process. The report should also be consistent through time, allowing the consumer of such reports to become familiar with the layout and content so that information is readily accessible.

Portfolio and performance analysis

Performance analysis is an attempt to provide an understanding of the sources of risk and returns to an investment strategy. In short, the goal of performance analysis is to explain a strategy's performance. Such an explanation can be beneficial both internally to an investment organization and externally to the organization's current and prospective clients because it has the potential to provide insight into the investment philosophy and process of the organization. To do so, the performance analysis should be constructed in a way that is consistent with the investment philosophy and process. In other words, performance analysis

Exhibit 5.7 Supplemental year-by-year historical performance report from Southern Illinois University's Saluki Student Investment Fund

As of June 30, 2013

Fiscal years	2001	2002	2003	2004	2005	2006	2007	2008	2009	2010	2011	2012	2013
SSIF	-2.62%	-13.03%	-4.01%	18.75%	19.31%	12.95%	24.99%	-5.28%	-29.40%	24.67%	48.10%	-1.34%	25.31%
S&P 400 Benchmark[a]	8.87%	-4.72%	-0.71%	27.99%	14.03%	12.98%	18.51%	-7.34%	-28.02%	24.93%	39.38%	-2.33%	25.18%
Difference	*-11.50%*	*-8.31%*	*-3.29%*	*-9.23%*	*5.29%*	*-0.03%*	*6.49%*	*2.05%*	*-1.38%*	*-0.26%*	*8.72%*	*0.99%*	*0.12%*

Calendar year	2000[b]	2001	2002	2003	2004	2005	2006	2007	2008	2009	2010	2011	2012	2013[c]
SSIF	-2.88%	-10.12%	-19.13%	34.14%	13.69%	13.97%	13.64%	9.93%	-34.43%	30.84%	32.59%	3.40%	16.25%	15.15%
S&P 400 Benchmark[a]	9.41%	-0.60%	-14.51%	35.62%	16.48%	12.56%	10.32%	7.98%	-36.23%	37.38%	26.64%	-1.73%	17.88%	14.59%
Difference	*-12.30%*	*-9.52%*	*-4.62%*	*-1.48%*	*-2.79%*	*1.42%*	*3.32%*	*1.95%*	*1.80%*	*-6.54%*	*5.94%*	*5.13%*	*-1.63%*	*0.56%*

[a]Performance of the benchmark is reported for the S&P Midcap 400 Total Return Index (Source: Bloomberg SPTRMDCP Index).
[b]Partial year. Performance begins June 1, 2000.
[c]Partial year. Fiscal Year ends on June 30 of the given year.
[c]Partial year.

should be constructed to measure the contributions from the opportunities identified in the investment philosophy and the objectives defined in the investment process.

We discuss the two primary forms of performance analysis: holdings-based performance attribution and returns-based performance analysis. Performance attribution breaks performance into components based on security-specific characteristics, such as sector or size. Attribution analysis relies on portfolio weights and the underlying security returns over a specific period. Returns-based analysis utilizes portfolio-level returns to estimate their statistical relationship to economic or market factors. Each form has its strengths and each type of analysis can complement the other.

Performance attribution

The goal of performance attribution is to identify the sources of a portfolio's relative returns compared to a benchmark. We build on the analysis in Chapter 4 discussing the sources of portfolio returns and utilize similar terminology and notation relating to portfolio weights and returns, benchmark weights and returns, active weights, and relative returns. We focus on performance attribution methods of performance that are attributed (pun intended) to Brinson and are commonly referred to as "Brinson Attribution" (Brinson, and Fachler, 1985; Brinson et al., 1986, 1991). The general attribution method is widely accepted, but its implementation can differ in subtle ways. We attempt to point out where there are commonly seen variations in practice.

Performance attribution analysis should mirror the portfolio construction process. Recall from Chapter 4 that a multi-asset class portfolio can be managed at three levels: asset allocation, manager allocation, and security allocation. If the overall portfolio is managed this three-step top-down fashion, performance attribution should be performed at these same three levels. Exhibit 5.8 shows this. The top-level decisions are the asset allocation decisions. The strategic asset allocation decision sets the benchmark for the overall portfolio. The top-level active decision is the tactical asset allocation decision which consists of deviations from the strategic asset mix. The next level is the manager allocation decision which is the decision to allocate the portfolio to a set of active managers, strategic beta portfolio, and asset class index portfolios. The third level consists of the decisions each manager makes regarding allocation to the various sectors (such consumer goods, energy, etc.) of a market and finally, the allocation to securities within each sector.

At each level of attribution, there is a benchmark portfolio and an actual portfolio. For each of these portfolios, there is a set of weights on asset classes, managers, or sectors, depending on the level of the analysis. For each weight, there is a corresponding return on the portfolio of the constituents of the given asset class, managed portfolio, or sector. Thus, there are two sets of weights and two sets of returns so that there are four possible portfolios that we can

Exhibit 5.8 Levels of attribution analysis

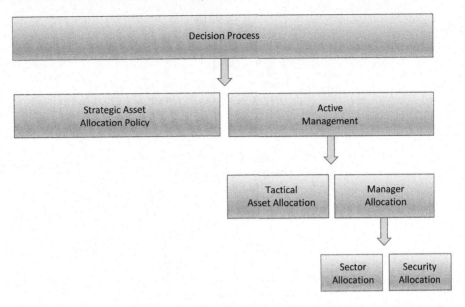

(Source: Based on a chart in Tsai, Cindy Sin-Yi, "Identifying a sponsor's impact on total returns," Morningstar Institutional Perspective, July 2010.)

create from these weights and returns. Brinson et al. present a four-quadrant diagram to show this, which we duplicate as Exhibit 5.9. They number these four portfolios as follows:

The Brinson quadrants	
Quadrant	Return
I	$r_I = \sum_{s=1}^{S} w_s^b r_s^b$
II	$r_{II} = \sum_{s=1}^{S} w_s^p r_s^b$
III	$r_{II} = \sum_{s=1}^{S} w_s^b r_s^p$
IV	$r_{IV} = \sum_{s=1}^{S} w_s^p r_s^p$

where:

w_s^b = the weight on sector s in the benchmark

r_s^b = the return on the portfolio of securities in the benchmark in sector s

w_s^p = the weight on sector s in the portfolio being analyzed

r_s^b = the return on the portfolio of securities in the portfolio being analyzed in sector s

Exhibit 5.9 Formation of the quadrant portfolios in the Brinson framework

Selection

	Actual	Passive
Actual (Timing)	(IV) Actual Portfolio Return	(II) Policy and Timing Return
Passive (Timing)	(III) Policy and Security Selection Return	(I) Policy Return (Passive Portfolio Benchmark)

Source: Brinson, G.P., Hood, L.R., Beebower, G.I., 1986. Determinants of portfolio performance. Financial Anal. J. 42 (4), 39–44. Reprinted by permission of publisher Taylor & Francis, Ltd. http://www.tandfonline.com.

Using these four quadrant-returns, Brinson et al. decompose the difference between the return on the portfolio and the benchmark as follows:

Brinson attribution Effect	Symbol	Calculation
Allocation	AE_I^A	$r_{II} - r_I = \sum_{s=1}^{S}(w_s^p - w_s^b)r_s^b$
Selection	SE_I^A	$r_{III} - r_I = \sum_{s=1}^{S}w_s^b(r_s^p - r_s^b)$
Interaction	IE^A	$r_{IV} - r_{III} - r_{II} + r_I = \sum_{s=1}^{S}(w_s^p - w_s^b)(r_s^p - r_s^b)$
Total Value Added	TE^A	$r_{IV} - r_I = \sum_{s=1}^{S}w_s^p r_s^p - w_s^b r_s^b$

Arithmetic attribution

We introduce the symbols for the effects in the above table to facilitate the discussion below. In our notation, the superscript A means that the calculation of the effect is *arithmetic*, meaning that it is calculated from the quadrant returns using subtraction or addition and subtraction. (We discuss the alternative, geometric attribution below). The subscript I means that there is an interaction term so that:

$$TE^A = AE_I^A + SE_I^A + IE_I^A \tag{5.9}$$

Generally, we can think of a portfolio construction process as being either top-down or bottom-up. In a top-down process, the portfolio manager first allocates capital to each sector, and then members of the management team pick and weight securities within each sector. In a bottom-up approach, the portfolio manager picks securities without regard to sector. Hence, the sector weights are merely the consequences of the security allocations. The presence of the interaction term in the Brinson attribution framework is an attempt to avoid the question as to whether the portfolio construction process is top-down or bottom-up. But if we can answer this question, we can choice a more appropriate approach to attribution and eliminate the need for an explicit interaction term.

For arithmetic top-down attribution, we make the following calculations:

Arithmetic top-down attribution

Effect	Symbol	Calculation
Allocation	AE_T^A	$r_{II} - r_I = \sum_{s=1}^{S}(w_s^p - w_s^b)r_s^b$
Selection	SE_T^A	$r_{IV} - r_{II} = \sum_{s=1}^{S}w_s^p(r_s^p - r_s^b)$
Total Value Added	TE^A	$r_{IV} - r_I = \sum_{s=1}^{S}w_s^p r_s^p - w_s^b r_s^b$

The subscript T denotes top-down attribution.

In arithmetic top-down attribution, Total Value Added is the sum of the Allocation Effect and the Selection Effect:

$$TE^A = AE_T^A + SE_T^A \qquad (5.10)$$

The interaction term of the Brinson framework is subsumed in the Selection Effect so that:

$$AE_T^A = AE_I^A \qquad (5.11a)$$

$$SE_T^A = SE_I^A + IE^A \qquad (5.11b)$$

For arithmetic bottom-up attribution, we make the following calculations:

Arithmetic bottom-up attribution

Effect	Symbol	Calculation
Selection	SE_B^A	$r_{III} - r_I = \sum_{s=1}^{S}w_s^b(r_s^p - r_s^b)$
Allocation	AE_B^A	$r_{IV} - r_{III} = \sum_{s=1}^{S}(w_s^p - w_s^b)r_s^p$
Total Value Added	TE^A	$r_{IV} - r_I = \sum_{s=1}^{S}w_s^p r_s^p - w_s^b r_s^b$

The subscript B denotes bottom-up attribution.

In arithmetic bottom-up attribution, Total Value Added is the sum of the Selection Effect and the Allocation Effect:

$$TE^A = SE_B^A + AE_B^A \qquad (5.12)$$

The interaction term of the Brinson framework is subsumed in the Allocation Effect so that:

$$SE_B^A = SE_I^A \qquad (5.13a)$$

$$AE_B^A = AE_I^A + IE^A \qquad (5.13b)$$

Geometric attribution

In geometric attribution, effects are measured by the geometric differences of the returns of the quadrant portfolios. As we discuss below, this allows effects to be linked together over time so that we can perform attribution over any period.

In general, the geometric difference between the returns on portfolio A (r_A) and portfolio B (r_B) is:

$$\frac{1 + r_A}{1 + r_B} - 1 \qquad (5.14)$$

So, for geometric top-down attribution, we make the following calculations:

Geometric top-down attribution		
Effect	Symbol	Calculation
Allocation	AE_T^G	$\frac{1+r_{II}}{1+r_I} - 1$
Selection	SE_T^G	$\frac{1+r_{IV}}{1+r_{II}} - 1$
Total Value Added	TE^G	$\frac{1+r_{IV}}{1+r_I} - 1$

Total Value Added is related to the Allocation Effect and the Selection Effect multiplicatively:

$$TE^G = \left(1 + AE_T^G\right)\left(1 + SE_T^G\right) - 1 \qquad (5.15)$$

Geometric bottom-up attribution can be defined in a similar fashion.

Details of attribution calculations

In the previous section, we presented the attribution calculations at the level of the Brinson quadrant portfolios. In this section, we take a more detailed look at the calculations by focusing on the *contributions* of each portfolio level calculation. For example, looking at the formula for the single-period return, quadrant I portfolio, we see that it the sum of $w_s^b r_s^b$ over all sectors s. We refer to $w_s^b r_s^b$ as a return contribution.

It is important to understand the difference between a contribution and the return or effect of which it is a part. Based on a contribution, we might conclude overweighting a given sector relative to the benchmark added some amount to the relative return on the portfolio. However, it is not possible to overweight one sector without underweighting one or more other sectors. The effect that we are measuring is due to the impact of all of the sector weights taken together. No contribution can serve as the explanation of relative performance.

Before getting into the contribution-level attribution calculations, let us look at the arithmetic return relative in terms of the individual securities. Recall from Chapter 4 that a portfolio's arithmetic relative return is calculated by subtracting the benchmark return. We restate

Eq. (4.32), but drop the time subscript for ease of exposition here, so that the portfolio's arithmetic relative return on a security-by-security basis is:

$$TE^A = \sum_{i=1}^{N} w_i^p r_i - \sum_{i=1}^{N} w_i^b r_i = \left(w_i^p - w_i^b\right) r_i \tag{5.16}$$

where w_i^p is the weight in the portfolio on security i, w_i^b is the weight in the benchmark on security i, and r_i is the return on security i. Our goal is to determine and identify the sources of the relative returns. As we have discussed, to do so, we group securities by characteristics into sectors. Depending on the level of the portfolio and the investment process, a sector might be a proper sector (e.g., financials, industrials, etc.), an asset class (e.g., stocks, bonds, etc.), or a characteristic (firm size, duration or term, etc.).

Eq. (4.35) show how weights on individual securities roll up into sector weights. We restate this equation here, but without the time subscript for ease of exposition. Let Ω_s denote the set of of securities in sector s in the market. The portfolio's overall exposure to this sector is the sum of all portfolio weights for securities that belong to sector s, as given by:

$$w_s^p = \sum_{i \in \Omega_s} w_i^p \tag{5.17}$$

Note that Ω_s refers to the set of securities in sector s in the entire market, not just the securities in the portfolio. Any sector securities that exist in the market but not in the portfolio have a portfolio weight of zero. Recall that we denote the number of sectors in the market as S. Of course, the weight in all sectors must sum to one, as given by:

$$1 = \sum_{i=s}^{S} w_s^p \tag{5.18}$$

Portfolio p experiences a return to sector s over a given time period of:

$$r_s^p = \frac{1}{w_s^p} \sum_{i \in \Omega_s} w_i^p r_i \tag{5.19}$$

Note that we divide the weighted sum of the returns by the total portfolio weight in sector s in order to get a proper weighted average of all sector s securities' returns within the portfolio. In essence, we are treating each sector as its own sub-portfolio.

Since the benchmark is simply another portfolio, we can express the same quantities from Eqs. (5.17) and (5.19) for the benchmark. Specifically, the benchmark's weight in sector s is:

$$w_s^b = \sum_{i \in \Omega_s} w_i^b \tag{5.20}$$

and the benchmark's return in sector s is:

$$r_s^b = \frac{1}{w_s^b} \sum_{i \in \Omega_s} w_i^b r_i \tag{5.21}$$

The differences between the sector weights of the portfolio and of the benchmark lead to the allocation effect, since the weights represent allocations to sectors. Specifically, when performing arithmetic attribution, the contribution to the portfolio's relative return that is due to an allocation to sector s is given by:

$$CAE_{I,s}^A = \left(w_s^p - w_s^b\right) r_s^b \tag{5.22}$$

Note that we use the return to the sector for the benchmark (not the portfolio) in this calculation, since the purpose is to isolate the impact of the portfolio active sector weight, not its security selection within the sector. In essence, this calculation would explain all of the portfolio's relative return if the investment manager simply invests proportionally in all of the benchmark's stocks, but alters the weights allocated to each sector.

An alternative calculation of the contributions to the arithmetic sector allocation effect is to use the sector's relative return compared to the overall benchmark, as given by:

$$CAE_{I,s}^{A(rel)} = \left(w_s^p - w_s^b\right) \left(r_s^b - r^b\right) \tag{5.23}$$

To determine the sector allocation effect arising from all sectors, we sum across all sector contributions to the Allocation Effect. This gives us the arithmetic Allocation Effect that we discussed earlier:

$$AE_I^A = \sum_{s=1}^{S} CAE_{I,s}^A = \sum_{s=1}^{S} CAE_{I,s}^{A(rel)} \tag{5.24}$$

Note that the total portfolio sector allocation contribution is the same regardless of whether the specification in Eqs. (5.22) or (5.23) is used. As we discuss in the example below, the decision of whether to use sector contributions as in Eq. (5.22) or sector relative contributions as in Eq. (5.23) usually depends on the objective of the portfolio and the desired meaning of the performance attribution.

When performing geometric attribution, the contribution to the portfolio's relative return that is due to an allocation to sector s is given by:

$$CAE_{I,s}^G = \frac{\left(w_s^p - w_s^b\right) r_s^b}{1 + r^b} \tag{5.25}$$

Use the sector's relative return compared to the overall benchmark, as the geometric contribution to the allocation effect is given by:

$$CAE_{I,s}^{G(rel)} = \frac{\left(w_s^p - w_s^b\right) \left(r_s^b - r^b\right)}{1 + r^b} \tag{5.26}$$

Summing across all sector contributions to the geometric Allocation Effect gives us the geometric Allocation Effect:

$$AE_I^G = \sum_{s=1}^{S} CAE_{I,s}^G = \sum_{s=1}^{S} CAE_{I,s}^{G(rel)} \tag{5.27}$$

The attribution of portfolio returns to stock selection derives from the returns to the portfolio's sector securities compared to returns of the benchmark's sector securities. As with sector allocation, the goal is to isolate the security selection skill from the asset allocation skill. Using the same approach as above, we first consider the situation in which there is no active weight to the sector and only consider the return of the portfolio's sector securities relative to the return of the benchmark's sector securities. As such, sector s's contribution this arithmetic "pure security selection effect" for sector s is given by:

$$CSE_{I,s}^A = w_s^b \left(r_s^p - r_s^b \right) \tag{5.28}$$

Earlier, we called the pure security effect the arithmetic Selection Effect. It is sum of the sector contributions to the pure security selection effect:

$$SE_I^A = \sum_{s=1}^{S} CSE_{I,s}^A \tag{5.29}$$

If the attribution analysis is not clearly specified as being top-down or bottom-up, there is a third effect that arises that is not so easily classified. In general, an investment manager can have both an active weight to the sector and a sector portfolio return that differs from the sector benchmark return. For example, an investment manager might overweight a sector that generally does poorly, but for which the manager's security selection is so good that the portfolio's sector does well. This is the *interaction effect* that we discussed earlier, so called because the sector allocation effect from relative sector weights and the security selection effect from relative sector returns interact with one another. The sector s contribution to the interaction effect is given by:

$$CIE_s^A = \left(w_s^p - w_s^b \right) \left(r_s^p - r_s^b \right) \tag{5.30}$$

The arithmetic Interaction Effect is the sum of the sector contributions:

$$IE^A = \sum_{s=1}^{S} CIE_s^A \tag{5.31}$$

It is common to "count" the interaction effect as part of security selection. As we discussed above, this is appropriate if the investment process is top-down and leads to top-down attribution However, as we also discussed earlier, if the investment process is bottom-up, it is appropriate to count it with the sector allocation so that the attribution analysis is bottom-up. For the remainder of our discussion on attribution, we take the top-down approach. Hence, we add the contribution of sector s to the pure selection effect in Eq. (5.25) with the sector's contribution to the interaction effect in Eq. (5.27) to obtain contribution to the total security selection effect, which we will hereafter refer to as the contribution to the security selection effect. Note that the contribution to the security selection effect reduces to simply using the portfolio's sector weight multiplied by the difference between the portfolio's and benchmark's sector return, as given by:

$$CSE_{T,s}^A = w_s^p \left(r_s^p - r_s^b \right) \tag{5.32}$$

The arithmetic Selection Effect, is the sum of the sector contributions to security selection:

$$SE_T^A = \sum_{s=1}^{S} CSE_{T,s}^A \tag{5.33}$$

From here on, we will use Eqs. (5.32) and (5.33) when referring to arithmetic security selection and, as is quite common in practice, making the interaction effect as a separate part of performance attribution unnecessary.

Adding sector s's contribution to the arithmetic sector allocation effect in Eqs. (5.22) or (5.23) to the sector's contribution to the security selection effect in Eq. (5.32), we have the sector's contribution to the portfolio's total relative return, as given by:

$$CTE_s^A = CAE_{T,s}^A + CSE_{T,s}^A \tag{5.34}$$

Together, the relative return of a portfolio is the sum of the allocation and the security selection contributions:

$$TE^A = \sum_{s=1}^{S} CTE_s^A \tag{5.35}$$

This is arithmetic Total Valued Added as we have shown earlier in Eq. (5.10).

Performance attribution examples

Consider Example A in Exhibit 5.10. The table shows all of the inputs and resulting calculations for arithmetic top-down performance attribution for a single period. The beginning-of-period weight in each sector appears in columns (A) and (B) for the portfolio and the benchmark, respectively. The benchmark and the portfolio have positions in Treasury bonds, corporate bonds, and stocks. The portfolio's 20% weight in Treasury bonds results in an underweight of 5% compared to the benchmark's 25% weight in that sector. The portfolio has 10% underweight in stocks and a 5% overweight in corporate bonds. Finally, the portfolio has a 10% weight in cash, a "sector" in which the benchmark has no position, resulting in a 10% overweight to cash. These overweights and underweights are shown in column (C).

The sector returns for the portfolio and benchmark are shown in columns (D) and (E), respectively. Column (F) shows the out- or underperformance of the portfolio's sector

Exhibit 5.10 Examples of attribution calculations using alternative methodologies.

Example A

	Sector weights			Returns			Quadrant portfolios				Arithmetic return contributions		
	(A) Port.	(B) Bench.	(C) +/−	(D) Port.	(E) Bench.	(F) +/−	(I)	(II)	(III)	(IV)	Sector allocation	Security allocation	Total
Cash	10.00%	0.00%	10.00%	0.00%	0.00%	0.00%	0.00%	0.00%	0.00%	0.00%	0.00%	0.00%	0.00%
Treasury Bonds	20.00%	25.00%	−5.00%	4.00%	4.00%	0.00%	1.00%	0.80%	0.80%	0.80%	−0.20%	0.00%	−0.20%
Corporate Bonds	30.00%	25.00%	5.00%	16.00%	12.00%	4.00%	3.00%	3.60%	3.60%	4.80%	0.60%	1.20%	1.80%
Stocks	40.00%	50.00%	−10.00%	26.00%	30.00%	−4.00%	15.00%	12.00%	12.00%	10.40%	−3.00%	−1.60%	−4.60%
Total	100.00%	100.00%	0.00%	16.00%	19.00%	−3.00%	19.00%	16.40%	16.40%	16.00%	−2.60%	−0.40%	−3.00%

Allocation Effect −2.60%

Selection Effect −0.40%

Total Effect −3.00%

Example B

	Sector weights			Returns				Quadrant portfolios				Arithmetic return contributions		
	(A) Port.	(B) Bench.	(C) +/−	(D) Port.	(E) Bench.	(E') Arith. Bench. Rel.	(F) +/−	(I)	(II)	(III)	(IV)	Relative sector allocation	Security allocation	Total
Cash	10.00%	0.00%	10.00%	0.00%	0.00%	−19.00%	0.00%	0.00%	0.00%	0.00%	0.00%	−1.90%	0.00%	−1.90%
Treasury Bonds	20.00%	25.00%	−5.00%	4.00%	4.00%	−15.00%	0.00%	1.00%	0.80%	0.80%	0.80%	0.75%	0.00%	0.75%
Corporate Bonds	30.00%	25.00%	5.00%	16.00%	12.00%	−7.00%	4.00%	3.00%	3.60%	3.60%	4.80%	−0.35%	1.20%	0.85%
Stocks	40.00%	50.00%	−10.00%	26.00%	30.00%	11.00%	−4.00%	15.00%	12.00%	12.00%	10.40%	−1.10%	−1.60%	−2.70%
Total	100.00%	100.00%	0.00%	16.00%	19.00%	0.00%	−3.00%	19.00%	16.40%	16.40%	16.00%	−2.60%	−0.40%	−3.00%

Allocation Effect −2.60%

Selection Effect −0.40%

Total Effect −3.00%

Example C

| | Sector weights | | | Returns | | | Quadrant portfolios | | | Geometric relative |
| | (A) | (B) | (C) | (D) | (E) | (E") | (I) | (II) | (IV) | sector allocation |
	Port.	Bench.	+/−	Port.	Bench.	Geo. Bench. Rel.				
Cash	10.00%	0.00%	10.00%	0.00%	0.00%	−15.97%	0.00%	0.00%	0.00%	−1.60%
Treasury bonds	20.00%	25.00%	−5.00%	4.00%	4.00%	−12.61%	1.00%	0.80%	0.80%	0.63%
Corporate bonds	30.00%	25.00%	5.00%	16.00%	12.00%	−5.88%	3.00%	3.60%	4.80%	−0.29%
Stocks	40.00%	50.00%	−10.00%	26.00%	30.00%	9.24%	15.00%	12.00%	10.40%	−0.92%
Total	100.00%	100.00%	0.00%	16.00%	19.00%	0.00%	19.00%	16.40%	16.00%	−2.18%

Allocation Effect	−2.18%
Selection Effect	−0.34%
Total Effect	−2.52%

securities relative to the benchmark's sector securities. For example, the portfolio's positions in corporate bonds average a return of 16% this period, compared to only 12% for the benchmark in the corporate bond sector–an outperformance of 4%. The portfolio's positions in stocks underperformed the benchmark's position in stocks by 4% over this period. The total row at the bottom of the table shows portfolio and benchmark returns, as well as the total relative return of the portfolio compared to the benchmark. During this period, the portfolio's return of 16.00% lags the benchmark return of 19.00% by 3.00%. In other words, the portfolio's relative return is negative 3.00%.

The columns labeled (I), (II), and (IV) show the calculation of Brinson quadrant portfolios indicated by the column headings. As we have discussed, these are the portfolio returns that we need for top-down attribution. The right-most three columns of the table the sector allocation and stock selection components within each sector and in total.

The sector allocation contributions result from the combination of the investment manager's sector over $-$/underweight choices and the market's sector performance. The product of these two components, as in Eq. (5.22), is shown in the Sector Allocation Return Contribution column. The portfolio's 10% overweight to cash contributes nothing to the portfolio's return, since cash has a zero return during this period. The 5% underweight to Treasury bonds contributes -20 basis points to the portfolio's return, since Treasury bonds have a 4% return. Likewise, the 10% underweight and 30% benchmark return in stocks results in a -300 basis point contribution.

The portfolio's exposure of 30% to its corporate bond outperformance of 4% compared with the benchmark's corporate bond performance results in a 120 basis point security selection contribution to the portfolio's total relative return. Conversely, the portfolio's 40% weight in stocks combines with the 4% underperformance of its stocks compared to the benchmark's stocks, resulting in a security selection contribution of -160 basis points for that sector. For the stocks sector, the sector allocation and security selection contributions combine to decrease the portfolio's relative return by 460 basis points. The contribution from the Treasury bonds sector reduces the portfolio's relative return by another 20 basis points, while the corporate bond's total contribution adds 180 basis points to the portfolio's relative return. Note that the sector total relative returns sum up to the portfolio's total relative return of -300 basis points. In summary, we have used performance attribution to explain the sources of the portfolio's 300 basis points of underperformance relative to the benchmark. Most of the negative relative performance originates in the stocks sector, with both an underweight (or underallocation) to stocks during that sector's high return and an underperformance of the portfolio's securities within that sector. According to this attribution model, corporate bonds contributed positively from both allocation and security selection impacts, while cash contributed nothing.

The careful reader might notice that we attributed a zero contribution to the cash sector in Example A, even though a 10% overweight on cash exists when cash earns zero and all other sectors earn a positive return. The model in Example A attributes a positive allocation contribution of 60 basis points to corporate bonds, even though corporate bonds have a 12% sector return while the benchmark's return overall is 19%. Likewise, Example A attributes a negative impact to sector allocation in Treasury bonds, even though the investment manager underweighted this sector at a time when its return is below that of the benchmark. While the attribution model in Example A provides an accurate measure of the total relative return, it treats asset allocation in terms of absolute returns, as if the benchmark for a sector return is zero. For this reason, we have labeled this method "Return Attribution." If the investment manager's mandate is to beat this specific benchmark, then it we might prefer an attribution method that is focuses more on relative returns when assessing asset allocation skill, such as the method in Eq. (5.23).

Example B in Exhibit 5.10 illustrates arithmetic Relative Return Attribution for a single period utilizing the same portfolio and benchmark as in Example A. The difference appears in the use of sector relative returns for the benchmark, which are shown in columns (E'). The relative return in each sector is calculated by subtracting the benchmark's total return from the sector's return.

The relative return sector allocation in Example B identifies positive contributions when sectors that outperform the benchmark are overweighted or sectors that underperform the benchmark are underweighted. Specifically, underweight to the Treasury bonds sector results in a positive sector allocation contribution because Treasury bonds underperform the benchmark by 15%. The interpretation is that the decision by the investment manager to underweight Treasury bonds was accretive to (i.e., benefitted) the portfolio, since the other sectors, on average, had higher returns. The negative sector allocation contribution of 190 basis points for the cash sector reflects the fact that the investment manager held a position in a sector that substantially underperformed the benchmark. Likewise, the overweight in the corporate bonds sector reduces the portfolio's overall relative return by 35 basis points because the corporate bonds sector underperforms the benchmark. Finally, the stocks sector allocation contribution is −110 basis points. Any decision to underweight one sector is necessarily a decision to overweight another sector. The relative return attribution method assigns the sector allocation to both decisions, reflecting the impact of an over- or underweight in the context of that sector's return compared to the overall benchmark return.

Example C illustrated geometric relative top-down attribution for a single period using the same data as in Examples A and B. Here, we have added column (E") which contains the relative return in each sector calculated by taking the geometric difference the sector's benchmark return benchmark and benchmark's total return:

$$\frac{1 + r_s^b}{1 + r^b} - 1$$

The last column shows the calculation of the geometric relative Sector Allocation Effect, each row but the last being product of the different in weights in column (C) and geometric benchmark relative returns. The results below the table are calculated using the formulas for top-down geometric attribution we discussed earlier.

All three methods shown in the three examples in Exhibit 5.10 are common in practice. Student-managed investment funds should choose the method that best fits the objective of the investment strategy or investment process. To the extent that the portfolio is benchmarked to a specific index, the relative return contributions might be more meaningful.

Performance attribution commentary and interpretation

Performance analysis utilizes performance attribution to provide insights into the performance and behavior of the investment process. This means that performance attribution should not be simply a quantitative exercise of calculating the contributions of sector allocation and security selection. Rather, performance attribution requires thoughtful consideration in designing the performance attribution and care in interpreting the results. As with all other aspects of investment management, the investment philosophy and process should be employed in conducting performance attribution. Specifically, the performance attribution should be designed to identify the sources of performance that the investment philosophy indicates exists and the objectives that the investment process seeks to achieve.

Sectors should be defined in a way that matches the investment process objectives or methods. Sectors can be defined along any dimension by which assets can be classified. For equity strategies, sectors might be defined in terms of capitalization range (e.g., micro-cap, small-cap, mid-cap, etc.), industry groups (e.g., computer and office equipment, household appliances, aircraft, life insurance, etc.), sectors (e.g., Materials, Utilities, Information Technology, etc.), geographic regions (e.g., Asia, Europe, North America, etc., or Midwest, Northeast, Southeast, etc.), style (growth, value, distressed, etc.), economic status (frontier, emerging, developed, etc.), or any other relevant scheme. For fixed income strategies, sectors might be defined in terms of term or duration (e.g., ultra-short, short, medium, long), credit quality (e.g., AAA, BAA, BBB, etc.), issuer characteristic (municipal, Treasury, corporate, etc.), geography (e.g., Asia, Europe, North America, etc., or Midwest, Northeast, Southeast, etc.), or, again, any other relevant scheme. While some classification schemes are more common than others, the key consideration should be whether the classification scheme is relevant to the investment strategy. For example, if an investment philosophy identifies opportunities in predicting which broad asset classes (e.g., stocks, bonds, etc.) will be "in favor" over a given time period, then the performance attribution should define sectors accordingly, perhaps similar to the broad asset classes definitions in Exhibit 5.10. The success of the associated investment process could be measured by the total contribution from sector allocation, since successfully picking the outperforming asset class should result in positive sector allocation contributions. Furthermore, we might expect the security selection component to be small in magnitude, unless security selection is also an integral part of the investment philosophy and process.

Southern Illinois University's Saluki student investment fund utilizes a fundamental, bottom-up investment process and is benchmarked by mandate to the S&P Midcap 400 Index. A key element of the SSIF's investment philosophy is that student members' focused company research and application of fundamental valuation techniques help them identify stocks that have the potential to outperform the market. Furthermore, the SSIF's investment process is executed by members who are organized into teams according to GICS sectors. Each sector team is responsible for using fundamental analysis to pick the best stocks (i.e., those with the most potential to outperform) from within their sector. To this end, the SSIF has a "sector neutral" policy in which it maintains it sector weights within a narrow range of the benchmark's sector weights. This background motivates the SSIF's use of performance attribution in which it defines sectors according to the GICS sector classifications. Furthermore, the SSIF's success in implementing its investment process can be judged along several dimensions. First, if the sector neutral policy is successful, not only should the total sector allocation relative return contribution be zero, each sector's allocation contribution should be zero. Second, if the SSIF members successfully pick stocks that outperform, the portfolio should have a positive relative return that is due to a positive total security selection contribution. In sum, the contribution from security selection should explain all of the portfolio's relative return in a given period and over time. Furthermore, the security selection within each sector can be used to determine which sector teams have been the most successful.

The SSIF's quarterly performance attribution report appears in Exhibit 5.11 in graphical form. Consistent with the investment philosophy and process described above, the relative return contribution from sector allocation in each quarter is nearly zero, both in total and within sectors. This indicates that the SSIF's sector neutral policy appears to be implemented consistently through time. In contrast, the security selection contributions are relatively large in magnitude, indicating that the SSIF is making active security selection decisions. In some cases, the outcomes of these security selection decisions have not added to the relative return of the portfolio. For example, the SSIF's chosen stocks in the Consumer Discretionary sector underperformed the benchmark significantly in the second and third quarters of the year. On the other hand, the security selection contribution from the Financials sector is consistently positive in all four quarters of the fiscal year. Most other sectors have mixed results throughout the year, while the Information Technology sector has positive security selection contributions in three of the four quarters that appear to outweigh the negative contribution in the fourth quarter.

Exhibit 5.12 shows the detailed calculations behind the graphs in Exhibit 5.11. We provide these details to illustrate several issues that arise when doing performance attribution. As we emphasized in the discussion of Exhibit 5.10, the sector allocation contributions can be calculated using either returns or relative returns. Columns (D) and (E) in Exhibit 5.12 report the portfolio and benchmark returns that are used to calculate the return contributions. Columns (E') and (E") report the relative returns that are used for the relative return contributions in arithmetic and geometric attribution, respectively. As in the example in Exhibit 5.10, the sector

Exhibit 5.11 Performance attribution report from SIU's Saluki Student Investment Fund for one fiscal year

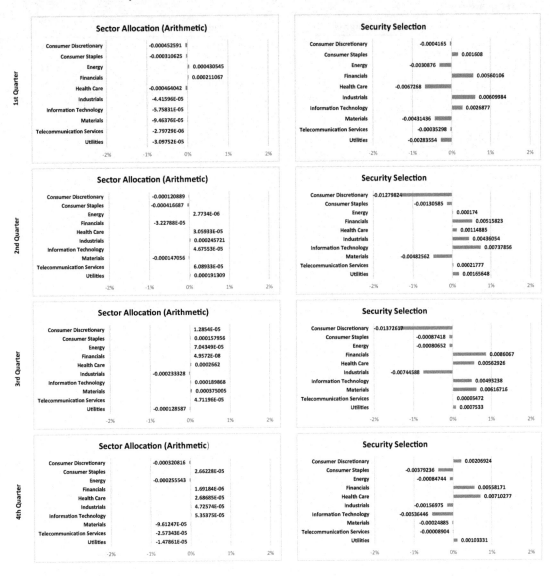

Exhibit 5.12 Example of quarterly performance attribution calculations

First quarter

	Sector weights			Returns			
	(A)	(B)	(C)	(D)	(E)	(E')	(E")
						Arith.	Geo.
	Port.	Bench.	+/−	Port.	Bench.	BM Rel.	BM Rel.
Cash	1.19%	0.00%	1.19%	0.00%	0.00%	−5.46%	−5.18%
Consumer Discretionary	11.90%	13.41%	−1.51%	8.11%	8.46%	3.00%	2.84%
Consumer Staples	4.00%	3.54%	0.46%	2.73%	−1.29%	−6.75%	−6.40%
Energy	6.20%	5.37%	0.83%	5.67%	10.65%	5.19%	4.92%
Financials	21.46%	22.30%	−0.84%	5.56%	2.95%	−2.51%	−2.38%
Health Care	10.04%	11.03%	−0.99%	3.45%	10.15%	4.69%	4.44%
Industrials	17.28%	16.21%	1.07%	8.58%	5.05%	−0.41%	−0.39%
Information Technology	15.81%	15.54%	0.27%	5.03%	3.33%	−2.13%	−2.02%
Materials	6.28%	6.88%	−0.60%	0.17%	7.04%	1.58%	1.50%
Telecommunication Services	0.53%	0.54%	−0.01%	1.60%	8.26%	2.80%	2.65%
Utilities	5.31%	5.18%	0.13%	−2.26%	3.08%	−2.38%	−2.26%
Total	100.00%	100.00%	0.00%	5.14%	5.46%	0.00%	0.00%
Actual Returns				5.02%	5.44%		

Second quarter

	Sector weights			Returns			
	(A)	(B)	(C)	(D)	(E)	(E')	(E")
						Arith.	Geo.
	Port.	Bench.	+/−	Port.	Bench.	Bench. Rel.	Bench. Rel.
Cash	0.58%	0.00%	0.58%	0.00%	0.00%	−3.58%	−3.46%
Consumer Discretionary	14.56%	13.92%	0.64%	−7.10%	1.69%	−1.89%	−1.82%
Consumer Staples	2.87%	3.29%	−0.42%	8.95%	13.50%	9.92%	9.58%
Energy	6.00%	5.88%	0.12%	4.10%	3.81%	0.23%	0.22%
Financials	22.33%	22.14%	0.19%	4.19%	1.88%	−1.70%	−1.64%

(F)	Quadrant portfolios			Return contributions			
				Relative sector allocation			
						Security	Arith.
+/−	(I)	(II)	(IV)	Geometric	Arithmetic	selection	total
0.00%	0.00%	0.00%	0.00%	−0.06%	−0.07%	0.00%	−0.07%
−0.35%	1.13%	1.01%	0.97%	−0.04%	−0.05%	−0.04%	−0.09%
4.02%	−0.05%	−0.05%	0.11%	−0.03%	−0.03%	0.16%	0.13%
−4.98%	0.57%	0.66%	0.35%	0.04%	0.04%	−0.31%	−0.27%
2.61%	0.66%	0.63%	1.19%	0.02%	0.02%	0.56%	0.58%
−6.70%	1.12%	1.02%	0.35%	−0.04%	−0.05%	−0.67%	−0.72%
3.53%	0.82%	0.87%	1.48%	0.00%	0.00%	0.61%	0.61%
1.70%	0.52%	0.53%	0.80%	−0.01%	−0.01%	0.27%	0.26%
−6.87%	0.48%	0.44%	0.01%	−0.01%	−0.01%	−0.43%	−0.44%
−6.66%	0.04%	0.04%	0.01%	0.00%	0.00%	−0.04%	−0.04%
−5.34%	0.16%	0.16%	−0.12%	0.00%	0.00%	−0.28%	−0.29%
−0.32%	5.46%	5.32%	5.14%	−0.14%	−0.15%	−0.17%	−0.32%
−0.42%							−0.10%
				Arith.	Geo.		
		Allocation Effect		−0.15%	−0.14%		
		Selection Effect		−0.17%	−0.16%		
		Total Effect		−0.32%	−0.30%		

(F)	Quadrant portfolios			Return contributions			
				Relative sector allocation			
						Security	Arith.
+/−	(I)	(II)	(IV)	Geometric	Arithmetic	selection	total
0.00%	0.00%	0.00%	0.00%	−0.02%	−0.02%	0.00%	−0.02%
−8.79%	0.24%	0.25%	−1.03%	−0.01%	−0.01%	−1.28%	−1.29%
−4.55%	0.44%	0.39%	0.26%	−0.04%	−0.04%	−0.13%	−0.17%
0.29%	0.22%	0.23%	0.25%	0.00%	0.00%	0.02%	0.02%
2.31%	0.42%	0.42%	0.94%	0.00%	0.00%	0.52%	0.51%

Health Care	10.35%	10.41%	−0.06%	−0.41%	−1.52%	−5.10%	−4.92%
Industrials	16.58%	16.21%	0.37%	12.85%	10.22%	6.64%	6.41%
Information Technology	15.12%	15.52%	−0.40%	7.29%	2.41%	−1.17%	−1.13%
Materials	6.46%	6.96%	−0.50%	−0.95%	6.52%	2.94%	2.84%
Telecommunication Services	0.51%	0.57%	−0.06%	−2.30%	−6.57%	−10.15%	−9.80%
Utilities	4.64%	5.10%	−0.46%	2.99%	−0.58%	−4.16%	−4.02%
Total	100.00%	100.00%	0.00%	3.66%	3.58%	0.00%	0.00%
Actual Returns				3.62%	3.61%		

Third Quarter

	Sector weights			Returns			
	(A)	(B)	(C)	(D)	(E)	(E')	(E")
						Arith.	Geo.
	Port.	Bench.	+/−	Port.	Bench.	Bench. Rel.	Bench. Rel.
Cash	1.26%	0.00%	1.26%	0.00%	0.00%	−13.47%	−11.87%
Consumer Discretionary	13.11%	13.30%	−0.19%	2.32%	12.79%	−0.68%	−0.60%
Consumer Staples	4.01%	3.82%	0.19%	19.60%	21.78%	8.31%	7.33%
Energy	5.72%	6.08%	−0.36%	10.10%	11.51%	−1.96%	−1.72%
Financials	21.90%	21.93%	−0.03%	17.38%	13.45%	−0.02%	−0.01%
Health Care	10.31%	9.39%	0.92%	21.82%	16.36%	2.89%	2.55%
Industrials	16.77%	17.34%	−0.57%	13.12%	17.56%	4.09%	3.61%
Information Technology	15.13%	15.51%	−0.38%	11.73%	8.47%	−5.00%	−4.40%
Materials	6.66%	7.22%	−0.56%	16.03%	6.77%	−6.70%	−5.90%
Telecommunication Services	0.48%	0.51%	−0.03%	−1.10%	−2.24%	−15.71%	−13.84%
Utilities	4.65%	4.90%	−0.25%	20.23%	18.61%	5.14%	4.53%
Total	100.00%	100.00%	0.00%	13.70%	13.47%	0.00%	0.00%
Actual Returns				13.74%	13.45%		

1.11%	−0.16%	−0.16%	−0.04%	0.00%	0.00%	0.11%	0.12%
2.63%	1.66%	1.69%	2.13%	0.02%	0.02%	0.44%	0.46%
4.88%	0.37%	0.36%	1.10%	0.00%	0.00%	0.74%	0.74%
−7.47%	0.45%	0.42%	−0.06%	−0.01%	−0.01%	−0.48%	−0.50%
4.27%	−0.04%	−0.03%	−0.01%	0.01%	0.01%	0.02%	0.03%
3.57%	−0.03%	−0.03%	0.14%	0.02%	0.02%	0.17%	0.18%
0.08%	3.58%	3.54%	3.66%	−0.03%	−0.03%	0.12%	0.08%
0.01%							−0.07%

	Arith.	Geo.
Allocation Effect	−0.03%	−0.03%
Selection Effect	0.12%	0.11%
Total effect	0.08%	0.08%

(F)	Quadrant portfolios			Return contributions Relative sector allocation		Security selection	Arith. total
+/−	(I)	(II)	(IV)	Geometric	Arithmetic		
0.00%	0.00%	0.00%	0.00%	−0.15%	−0.17%	0.00%	−0.17%
−10.47%	1.70%	1.68%	0.30%	0.00%	0.00%	−1.37%	−1.37%
−2.18%	0.83%	0.87%	0.79%	0.01%	0.02%	−0.09%	−0.07%
−1.41%	0.70%	0.66%	0.58%	0.01%	0.01%	−0.08%	−0.07%
3.93%	2.95%	2.95%	3.81%	0.00%	0.00%	0.86%	0.86%
5.46%	1.54%	1.69%	2.25%	0.02%	0.03%	0.56%	0.59%
−4.44%	3.04%	2.94%	2.20%	−0.02%	−0.02%	−0.74%	−0.77%
3.26%	1.31%	1.28%	1.77%	0.02%	0.02%	0.49%	0.51%
9.26%	0.49%	0.45%	1.07%	0.03%	0.04%	0.62%	0.65%
1.14%	−0.01%	−0.01%	−0.01%	0.00%	0.00%	0.01%	0.01%
1.62%	0.91%	0.87%	0.94%	−0.01%	−0.01%	0.08%	0.06%
0.24%	13.47%	13.37%	13.70%	−0.08%	−0.09%	0.33%	0.24%
0.29%							0.05%

Fifth Quarter

	Sector weights			Returns			
	(A)	(B)	(C)	(D)	(E)	(E')	(E")
						Arith.	Geo.
	Port.	Bench.	+/−	Port.	Bench.	Bench. Rel.	Bench. Rel.
Cash	0.57%	0.00%	0.57%	0.00%	0.00%	−0.96%	−0.95%
Consumer Discretionary	11.56%	12.48%	−0.92%	6.24%	4.45%	3.49%	3.45%
Consumer Staples	3.74%	3.68%	0.06%	−4.74%	5.40%	4.44%	4.39%
Energy	6.42%	5.99%	0.43%	−6.30%	−4.98%	−5.94%	−5.89%
Financials	22.97%	23.29%	−0.32%	3.34%	0.91%	−0.05%	−0.05%
Health Care	9.69%	9.65%	0.04%	15.01%	7.68%	6.72%	6.65%
Industrials	17.25%	17.45%	−0.20%	−2.31%	−1.40%	−2.36%	−2.34%
Information Technology	14.86%	15.13%	−0.27%	−4.63%	−1.02%	−1.98%	−1.96%
Materials	7.11%	6.78%	0.33%	−2.30%	−1.95%	−2.91%	−2.89%
Telecommunication Services	0.42%	0.44%	−0.02%	11.71%	13.83%	12.87%	12.74%
Utilities	5.41%	5.11%	0.30%	2.38%	0.47%	−0.49%	−0.49%
Total	100.00%	100.00%	0.00%	1.29%	0.96%	0.00%	0.00%
Actual Returns				1.24%	1.00%		

				Arith.	Geo.
	Allocation Effect			−0.09%	−0.08%
	Selection Effect			0.33%	0.29%
	Total Effect			0.24%	0.21%

(F)	Quadrant portfolios			Return contributions Relative sector allocation		Security selection	Arith. total
+/−	(I)	(II)	(IV)	Geometric	Arithmetic		
0.00%	0.00%	0.00%	0.00%	−0.01%	−0.01%	0.00%	−0.01%
1.79%	0.56%	0.51%	0.72%	−0.03%	−0.03%	0.21%	0.17%
−10.14%	0.20%	0.20%	−0.18%	0.00%	0.00%	−0.38%	−0.38%
−1.32%	−0.30%	−0.32%	−0.40%	−0.03%	−0.03%	−0.08%	−0.11%
2.43%	0.21%	0.21%	0.77%	0.00%	0.00%	0.56%	0.56%
7.33%	0.74%	0.74%	1.45%	0.00%	0.00%	0.71%	0.71%
−0.91%	−0.24%	−0.24%	−0.40%	0.00%	0.00%	−0.16%	−0.15%
−3.61%	−0.15%	−0.15%	−0.69%	0.01%	0.01%	−0.54%	−0.53%
−0.35%	−0.13%	−0.14%	−0.16%	−0.01%	−0.01%	−0.02%	−0.03%
−2.12%	0.06%	0.06%	0.05%	0.00%	0.00%	−0.01%	−0.01%
1.91%	0.02%	0.03%	0.13%	0.00%	0.00%	0.10%	0.10%
0.33%	0.96%	0.90%	1.29%	−0.06%	−0.06%	0.39%	0.33%
0.24%							−0.09%

				Arith.	Geo.
	Allocation Effect			−0.06%	−0.06%
	Selection Effect			0.39%	0.38%
	Total Effect			0.33%	0.32%

allocations are different, depending on whether returns or relative returns are used, while security selection contributions are the same, regardless. The SSIF uses the relative return contributions, since its mandates is performance relative to the S&P Midcap 400 Index. By using relative returns, the impact of maintaining a cash balance becomes clearer, since the benchmark holds no cash. The impact from cash is especially large in Q3, when the benchmark returns more than 13%. The cash position of 1.26% has a measurable negative impact on the relative returns of the portfolio, contributing 17 basis points of underperformance in that quarter. In contrast, an overweight of close to 1% to the Health Care sector contributes only three basis points to the relative return, since the Healthcare sector's return is only a few percentage points higher than the benchmark in Q3.

Had the SSIF used returns (rather than relative returns) in its attribution method, the impact of allocations to cash would have appeared to have been zero and the contribution from a slight overweight to Health Care would have appeared to have been a significant contributor. In short, for the SSIF's investment process, the attribution method employing relative returns is more meaningful. While we present the use of returns or relative returns as a choice, we note that this choice should be made *ex ante* as a matter of policy, not *ex post* as a way to choose numbers that "look better."

In summary, performance attribution reports can be used externally to give clients or constituents insight into how the investment process works. Oftentimes, performance attribution is the integral part of performance "commentary," which tells the story of the investment manager's performance over a specific time horizon, such as a quarter or year. Such transparency is essential in helping clients to have confidence in their hired managers' ability. Furthermore, performance analysis allows clients to understand the sources of performance for each manager so that they can make informed decisions about how they allocate their assets among their hired managers to maximize their portfolio's objectives. Internally, the performance attribution can be used to extract lessons about "what worked" and "what didn't work" as the investment manager implemented the investment process. For a student-managed investment fund, such analysis can meaningfully enhance the educational value of the experience by identifying sources of out- and underperformance and comparing those sources to expected outcomes. In an investment firm, the information in the performance attribution might be used to assign bonuses, allocated resources to remedy "problem" areas, or identify aspects of the investment process that need to be enhanced. For these reasons, performance attribution is a standard tool in performance analysis for nearly every investment manager.

Performance attribution complexities

There are several complexities that arise when calculating performance attribution. The impact of these complexities can be quite small in most cases or surprisingly large in others. We address them here and emphasize that the purpose in our presentation of performance attribution is to provide an estimate of the sources of relative performance instead of a perfect accounting of them.

Eqs. (5.9) through (5.35) are mathematical relationships that hold exactly when there is no rebalancing of the portfolio during the period of measurement. That is, traditional performance attribution assumes no rebalancing during the period over which the attribution is calculated. If there is rebalancing, then the beginning-of-period weights generally will not reflect the exposure to a given sector throughout the entire period. Therefore, the calculation of sector allocation and selection contributions will not add up to the actual portfolio's relative return. Indeed, if there is rebalancing within the portfolio during the period of measurement, the total portfolio return in the attribution model will generally not equal the actual portfolio return for the period, since the portfolio performance will not simply be the sum of the product of the portfolio's beginning sector weights and sector returns. This issue is illustrated in Exhibit 5.12, which shows the full calculations behind Exhibit 5.11's quarterly performance attribution for the SSIF. The SSIF portfolio's actual return for Q4 is 1.24%, which is 0.24% above the benchmark's 1.00% return for the quarter. However, the total portfolio returns in column (D) are 1.29% while the benchmark's total return is 0.96%. That is, the actual portfolio return does not equal the product of the beginning-of-period sector weights and sector returns. The same inconsistency exists between the benchmark's total and actual returns.

While it seems especially odd that a passive benchmark would experience rebalancing, we note that there are usually numerous additions and deletions to most indexes throughout a year. Importantly, when a name is deleted from an index, such as the S&P Midcap 400 Index, it is not necessarily replaced with a company from the same sector. For example, in April 2013, a stock in the Health Care sector was replaced in the S&P 400 with a stock in the Materials sector.[c] An actively managed portfolio is even more likely to experience trading or rebalancing, causing the total return calculation to be different from the actual portfolio return. Indeed, the difference between the portfolio's calculated total return and actual return for each quarter is larger than the difference for the benchmark in Exhibit 5.12. However, we note that the difference is relatively small compared to the actual return and can be either positive or negative. For example, the SSIF portfolio's calculated total return is four basis points lower than the actual portfolio return of 13.74% in Q3, while the calculated total return is four basis points higher than the actual return of 3.62% in Q2.

A solution to this issue is to calculate attribution during periods between portfolio (and benchmark) trades and rebalancing. These periods could then be linked together for the period of interest. Depending on the significance of such trades, this might not result in significantly more precise attribution calculations, as discussed in the next section. Alternatively, some widely available commercial attribution methods utilize average weights rather than beginning-of-period weights.

---

[c] In the first half of 2013, there were 12 days in which a stock was added and a stock was deleted from the S&P 400, and the stocks generally were not from the same sector.

Attribution over multiple periods

It is often desirable to perform performance attribution over longer time horizons, such as a year. This is usually done by linking to the results of series of single period attribution results.

With geometric attribution, linking results across periods is straightforward and unambiguous. Let $AE^G_{T,\,t}$, $SE^G_{T,\,t}$, and TE^G_t denote the Allocation Effect, Selection Effect, and Total Value Added respectively from geometric top-down attribution for period t. The effects from the periods 1, 2, ..., τ can be linked together by multiplication:

$$AE^G_{T,1:\tau} = \prod_{t=1}^{\tau} \left(1 + AE^G_{T,t}\right) - 1 \tag{5.36a}$$

$$SE^G_{T,1:\tau} = \prod_{t=1}^{\tau} \left(1 + SE^G_{T,t}\right) - 1 \tag{5.36b}$$

$$TE^G_{1:\tau} = \prod_{t=1}^{\tau} \left(1 + TE^G_t\right) - 1 \tag{5.36c}$$

Exhibit 5.13 shows the results of linking the four quarters of results of geometric attribution presented in Exhibit 5.12. Note that with geometric attribution, we can only link the overall effects, and not the sector level contributions.

In multiperiod arithmetic attribution, the Total Value Added over periods 1, 2, ..., τ combined is the arithmetic difference between the compound return of the portfolio and on the benchmark Let

$$r_{IV,1:\tau} = \prod_{t=1}^{\tau} \left(1 + r_{IV,t}\right) - 1 \tag{5.37a}$$

Exhibit 5.13 Example of geometric linking of attribution results

Period	Sector allocation	Security selection	Total effect
First Quarter	−0.14%	−0.16%	−0.30%
Second Quarter	−0.03%	0.11%	0.08%
Third Quarter	−0.08%	0.29%	0.21%
Fourth Quarter	−0.06%	0.38%	0.32%
Year	−0.32%	0.62%	0.30%

$$r_{I,1:\tau} = \prod_{t=1}^{\tau} (1 + r_{I,t}) - 1 \qquad (5.37b)$$

We have:

$$TE^A_{1:\tau} = r_{IV,1:\tau} - r_{I,1:\tau} \qquad (5.38)$$

where $r_{IV,t}$ and $r_{I,t}$ are the period t returns on the portfolio and the benchmark, respectively.

Because of compounding, Total Value Added over periods 1, 2, ..., τ combined is <u>not</u> the sum of Total Value Added over the periods:

$$TE^A_{1:\tau} \neq \sum_{t=1}^{\tau} TE^A_t$$

Hence, the results of arithmetic attribution over multiple periods cannot be linked through summation. To work around this, various linking methods have been proposed. Some of these methods using linking coefficients for each period, $\beta_1, \beta_2, ..., \beta_\tau$, so that:

$$TE^A_{1:\tau} = \sum_{t=1}^{\tau} \beta_t TE^A_t \qquad (5.39)$$

The linking coefficients are applied to each effect to form modified versions that can be summed. The following equations, each variable with a hat () denotes its modified version and time subscripts have been added:

$$\widehat{AE}^A_{T,t} = \beta_t AE^A_t \qquad (5.40a)$$

$$\widehat{SE}^A_{T,t} = \beta_t SE^A_t \qquad (5.40b)$$

$$\widehat{TE}^A_{T,t} = \beta_t TE^A_t \qquad (5.40a)$$

Similarly, contributions can be modified in the same way:

$$\widehat{CAE}^{A(rel)}_{T,s,t} = \beta_t CAE^{A(rel)}_{T,s,t} \qquad (5.41a)$$

$$\widehat{CSE}^A_{T,s,t} = \beta_t CSE^A_{T,s,t} \qquad (5.41b)$$

$$\widehat{CTE}^A_{s,t} = \beta_t CTE^A_{s,t} \qquad (5.41c)$$

With the modified variables, linking can be done by summation:

$$\widehat{AE}^A_{T,1:\tau} = \sum_{t=1}^{\tau} \widehat{AE}^A_{T,t} \qquad (5.42a)$$

$$\widehat{SE}^A_{T,1:\tau} = \sum_{t=1}^{\tau} \widehat{SE}^A_{T,t} \tag{5.42b}$$

$$\widehat{TE}^A_{T,1:\tau} = \sum_{t=1}^{\tau} \widehat{TE}^A_{T,t} \tag{5.42c}$$

$$\widehat{CAE}^A_{T,s,1:\tau} = \sum_{t=1}^{\tau} \widehat{CAE}^A_{T,s,t} \tag{5.43a}$$

$$\widehat{CSE}^A_{T,s,1:\tau} = \sum_{t=1}^{\tau} \widehat{CSE}^A_{T,s,t} \tag{5.43b}$$

$$\widehat{CTE}^A_{T,s,1:\tau} = \sum_{t=1}^{\tau} \widehat{CTE}^A_{Ts,t} \tag{5.43c}$$

There are several methods for coming up with the linking coefficients, one of which is the Menchero method which we present here (Menchero, 2000, 2004).

Menchero argues that the most accurate way to link arithmetic attribution effects over multiple periods is to minimize the deviation around some value A that corresponds to a natural scaling from the single-period to the multiperiod active return space. He finds the value of A to be:

$$A = \frac{TE^A_{1:\tau}/\tau}{(1+r_{IV,1:\tau})^{1/\tau} - (1+r_{I,1:\tau})^{1/\tau}} \tag{5.44}$$

He then finds the linking coefficients that minimize the square deviations from A subject to the constraint that Eq. (5.39) holds. The solution to this problem is given by:

$$\beta_t = A + C \cdot TE^A_t \tag{5.45}$$

where:

$$C = \frac{TE^A_{1:\tau} - A \sum_{t=1}^{\tau} TE^A_t}{\sum_{t=1}^{\tau} \left(TE^A_t\right)^2} \tag{5.46}$$

Exhibit 5.14 show how to apply the Menchero linking method to the SSIF portfolio using the data presented in Exhibit 5.12. In Panel A, we bring together the quarterly total returns on the portfolio and benchmark portfolios for the four quarters and show their compound rates of return for the year. We also show the arithmetic differences of the portfolio and benchmark returns for each quarter and for the year. These are the Total Value Added for each of these periods. From these data we calculate A and C using Eqs (5.44) and (5.46), respectively. We then calculate the linking coefficients using Eq. (5.45), with the results as shown in the last column of Panel A.

Exhibit 5.14 Example of linking arithmetic attribution results using the Menchero method

Panel A

	Returns		Total value added	Linking coefficients
	Port.	Bench.		
Q1	5.14%	5.46%	−0.32%	1.19
Q2	3.66%	3.58%	0.08%	1.18
Q3	13.70%	13.47%	0.24%	1.18
Q4	1.29%	0.96%	0.33%	1.18
Year	25.52%	25.14%	0.38%	
A	1.18			
C	−22.81%			

Panel B

	Modified relative sector allocation					Modified security selection				
	Q1	Q2	Q3	Q4	Sum	Q1	Q2	Q3	Q4	Sum
Cash	−0.08%	−0.02%	−0.20%	−0.01%	−0.31%	0.00%	0.00%	0.00%	0.00%	0.00%
Consumer Discretionary	−0.05%	−0.01%	0.00%	−0.04%	−0.10%	−0.05%	−1.52%	−1.63%	0.24%	−2.95%
Consumer Staples	−0.04%	−0.05%	0.02%	0.00%	−0.06%	0.19%	−0.15%	−0.10%	−0.45%	−0.52%
Energy	0.05%	0.00%	0.01%	−0.03%	0.03%	−0.37%	0.02%	−0.10%	−0.10%	−0.54%
Financials	0.03%	0.00%	0.00%	0.00%	0.02%	0.66%	0.61%	1.02%	0.66%	2.95%
Health Care	−0.06%	0.00%	0.03%	0.00%	−0.02%	−0.80%	0.14%	0.67%	0.84%	0.85%
Industrials	−0.01%	0.03%	−0.03%	0.01%	0.00%	0.72%	0.52%	−0.88%	−0.19%	0.17%
Information Technology	−0.01%	0.01%	0.02%	0.01%	0.03%	0.32%	0.87%	0.58%	−0.64%	1.14%
Materials	−0.01%	−0.02%	0.04%	−0.01%	0.00%	−0.51%	−0.57%	0.73%	−0.03%	−0.38%
Telecommunication Services	0.00%	0.01%	0.01%	0.00%	0.01%	−0.04%	0.03%	0.01%	−0.01%	−0.02%
Utilities	0.00%	0.02%	−0.02%	0.00%	0.00%	−0.34%	0.20%	0.09%	0.12%	0.07%
Total	−0.17%	−0.04%	−0.11%	−0.07%	−0.40%	−0.21%	0.14%	0.39%	0.46%	0.78%

Exhibit 5.15 Example of linked arithmetic attribution results using the Menchero method

In Panel B, we apply the linking coefficients to the contributions to Relative Sector Allocation and Security Selection in each quarter, multiplied by each quarter's linking coefficient. Summing across the quarters gives use the contributions to each effect for the year. In Exhibit 5.15, we show the contributions to the effects for the year graphically.

Holdings-based style analysis

Research has shown that equity portfolio performance can largely be explained by various factors which are associated with stocks that have particular characteristics. The two main characteristics that are associated with equity factors are:

1)   Size as measured by market capitalization—the size factor
2)   Value/growth orientation—the value factor

Value/growth orientation is a point on a spectrum with value on one side and growth on the other. A value stock is one in which has a relatively low price per unit of earnings, sales, and other cashflows. A growth stock typically has high growth potential for cashflows and a high price relative to value stocks.

These two characteristics are often used as the two dimensions of a chart called a *style box*. Morningstar.[d] popularized the style box by applying it to equity mutual funds. In its initial version, the Morningstar Equity Style Box™ was a 3 × 3 grid with the vertical axis

---

[d]   © [2020] Morningstar, Inc. All Rights Reserved. The information contained herein: (1) is proprietary to Morningstar and/or its content providers; (2) may not be copied or distributed; (3) does not constitute investment advice offered by Morningstar; and (4) is not warranted to be accurate, complete or timely. Neither Morningstar nor its content providers are responsible for any damages or losses arising from any use of this information. Past performance is no guarantee of future results. Use of information from Morningstar does not necessarily constitute agreement by Morningstar, Inc. of any investment philosophy or strategy presented in this publication.

representing size and the horizonal axis representing value/growth orientation. From top to bottom, the vertical axis is divided into three ranges: Large, Mid, and Small. From left to right, the horizonal axis is divided into three ranges: Value, Core (or Blend), Growth. Later the style box was expanded into a 5 × 5 grid with the vertical axis divided into five ranges: Giant, Large, Mid, Small, and Micro, and the horizontal axis divided into Deep-Value, Core-Value, Core, Core-Growth, and High Growth. Exhibit 5.16 shows the 5 × 5 Morningstar Equity Style Box™ grid.

To perform holdings-based style analysis, first, each stock in the equity universe has to be assigned a pair of numerical scores representing its position on the style box grid. The pair of scores of a portfolio are the asset-weighted averages of the pairs of scores of the stocks that constitute the portfolio. As Exhibit 5.16 shows, Morningstar plots the portfolio's pair of scores on the style box grid, calling the plot point the *centroid* of the portfolio. The location of centroid determines the investment style assigned to the portfolio.

Exhibit 5.16 Morningstar Equity Style Box™ Grid with Ownership Zone[SM]

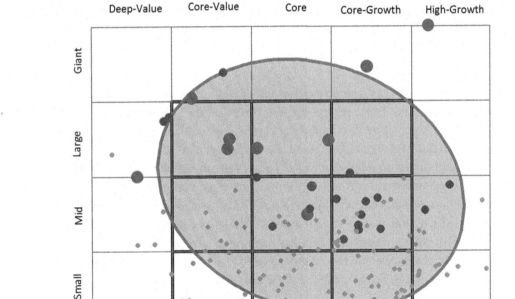

This exhibit is not an exact copy of the chart that appears in Morningstar Direct. Rather it is a rendition.
Source: © [2020] Morningstar, Inc. All Rights Reserved. Reproduced with permission.

Since the centroid is only average, it cannot fully describe how a portfolio is invested. To give a more complete picture of how a portfolio is invested, As Exhibit 5.16 shows, Morningstar plots each stock in the portfolio on the style box grid. To show which stocks have more weight in the portfolio and which less, the plot points vary in size, based on their portfolio weights. Finally, to show focused the portfolio is, as Exhibit 5.16 shows, Morningstar plots the *ownership zone* around the centroid. The ownership zone is the smallest tilted ellipse around the centroid that contains 75% of the portfolio by asset weight. As Exhibit 5.16 shows, although the portfolio's centroid is in the Mid Core square, it contains stocks from several of the other squares that fall within its ownership zone.

Returns-based performance analysis

Returns-based analysis is a popular method to accomplish the goal of identifying the sources of a portfolio's risk and explaining the portfolio's performance. Unlike performance attribution and holdings-based style analysis, returns-based analysis does not require detailed knowledge of the portfolio's holdings and weights. Rather, returns-based analysis only uses the observed returns of a portfolio combined with the returns of other market factors, such as market returns, returns to characteristic-based portfolios, or changes in economic variables. By employing factor models to estimate the sensitivity of a portfolio's returns or relative returns to the factor returns, the analysis provides an understanding of the determinants of a portfolio's performance.

The underlying premise of returns-based analysis is that factor exposures are under the control of the investment manager, but factor returns are not. For example, a portfolio manager might hold a portfolio of large cap, growth-oriented stocks. It is reasonable to expect the value of such a portfolio to rise and fall with the market, but to also do better than the market when large stocks and growth-oriented stocks do relatively well. The question of interest would be whether the portfolio's returns are attributable to these factors or whether the portfolio's performance exceeds those factor returns as a result of security selection skill. Thinking of the performance attribution analysis from the discussion above, we aim to allocate relative returns to large and growth-oriented "sectors" in order to discern the security selection component of the portfolio's returns. Unlike performance attribution, we rely on portfolio returns to infer or estimate exposures to factors rather than assigning factor exposures based on portfolio weights.

Multifactor performance analysis has two objectives: (1) explain the variance of portfolio returns or relative returns, and (2) explain the average portfolio returns or relative returns. The first objective is motivated by the observation that portfolio returns are sensitive to certain factors in the market or the economy. These factors have been found to be associated with period-to-period asset returns, but may or may not be associated with long-term average returns. Such factors include the level of or changes in an economic variable (e.g., inflation, interest rates, unemployment, GDP, etc.) or an index or portfolio (e.g., a portfolio formed on the basis of size, style, price-momentum, etc.). The second objective is motivated by the observation that some factors, usually labeled as "risk factors," have historically had risk premia associated with them. That is, some factors appear to explain assets' long-term average returns. The most popular such factors for equity portfolios are market returns, size, and growth/value style, which were popularized in research by Fama and French in the 1990s (Fama, and French, 1993, 1996).

Single factor model

We begin with a discussion of a single factor model in order to establish some intuition that carries over to multifactor models. Consider a single factor, F, that influences a portfolio's return. This factor has a return (in excess of the risk-free rate) of $R_{F,t}$ in period t.[e] The portfolio's return in period t can be written as a function of the factor's return during the same period, as given by:

$$R_{p,t} = \alpha + \beta_F R_{F,t} + e_t \tag{5.47}$$

The sensitivity of the portfolio returns to the factor returns is reflected in the "beta" parameter. The beta reflects the covariance (and correlation) between the portfolio returns and the factor returns. Specifically:

$$\beta_F = \frac{Cov(R_{p,t}, R_{F,t})}{\sigma_F^2} = \rho_{p,F} \frac{\sigma_p}{\sigma_F} \tag{5.48}$$

where σ_F is the standard deviation of the returns to factor F and $\rho_{p,F}$ is the correlation between returns to factor F and the portfolio returns. Since we generally do not believe that the factor is fully responsible for the exact return of the portfolio in each period, Eq. (5.47) allows for the portfolio to have a constant (or average) return component, α, that applies over all periods. Likewise, an "error" term, e_t, accounts for any portfolio returns in a given period t that are not related to the factor or reflected in the constant α. Eq. (5.47) is also considered to be a regression equation in which the dependent variable is the series of portfolio returns and the single independent variable is the series of factor returns. A regression is used to estimate the parameters α and β_F, since they are not directly observable.

Exhibit 5.17 illustrates how to estimate a single factor model from monthly excess returns on a portfolio and its benchmark over a 36-month period.[f] In this example, α is estimated to be -0.57% and β_F to be 1.01. Exhibit 5.17 also shows the R^2 statistic which measures what percentage of the variance of the return on the portfolio can be explained by the factor. In this

---

[e] Since portfolio returns analysis typically employs excess returns (i.e., returns net of the risk-free rate), in this section, we adopt the convention of capitalizing the returns variable to emphasize that it is an excess return; however, we will refer to excess returns throughout this section simply as "returns."

[f] Regressions to estimate factor are often run on a 36- or 50-month period.

Exhibit 5.17 Example of a single factor model

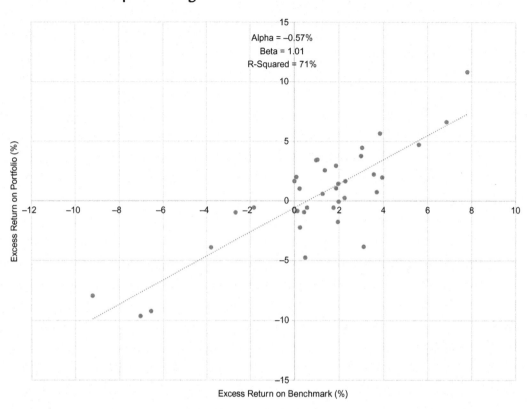

example, R^2 is 71%, indicating that the returns on the portfolio are strongly related to the returns on the benchmark.

Average returns in the single factor model

The single factor model allows us to derive the relationship between the average portfolio return and average factor return by taking the mathematical average of each side of Eq. (5.47). Since the average of a sum is the sum of the averages, we have:

$$\overline{R}_{p,t} = \alpha + \beta_F \overline{R}_{F,t} + \overline{e}_t \tag{5.49}$$

where a bar over a variable indicates the average over the estimation period. Since in regression mode, the average of the error term is zero, we have:

$$\overline{R}_{p,t} = \alpha + \beta_F \overline{R}_{F,t} \tag{5.50}$$

Eq. (5.50) provides the primary method by which returns-based analysis is used to assess performance or to attribute performance to a factor. Specifically, we employ a univariate (i.e., single factor) linear regression model using the portfolio returns as the dependent (left-hand side) variable and the factor returns as the independent variable model to estimate the slope (β_F) and intercept (α). Rather than using portfolio and factor returns, it is common to use excess returns (i.e., returns net of the risk-free rate) for both the portfolio and the factor, when estimating the regression model. The association between the portfolio and factor returns, as estimated by β_F, control for the contribution of the factor to the portfolio's average returns. The average return that is not attributed to the factor appears in the estimated parameter α.

When the "market portfolio" or a proxy index is used as the factor in this model, it is common to interpret the alpha as an "abnormal return."[g] More specifically, a positive abnormal return is interpreted to mean that the portfolio outperformed the "fair" return for its given level of exposure to the non-diversifiable risk associated with the proxy index. It is inferred, therefore, that an investment manager with a significantly positive alpha possesses skill and that the application of the investment process creates value over and above what is available on average in the market. We note that this interpretation applies to the time period over which the portfolio and market returns are measured. As such, any such observations or statements about skill or value are inherently *ex post* in nature. To the extent that an investor believes that skill or value in an investment process persists through time, the investor may believe such analysis to be a valuable ex ante tool.

Analysis of portfolio risk in the single factor model

We can also utilize the single index model to reveal insights about the risk exposures in the portfolio. To do so, we decompose the variance of the portfolio's returns by taking the variance of both sides of Eq. (5.47), so that:

$$Var\left[R_{p,t}\right] = Var[\alpha] + Var[\beta_F R_{F,t}] + Var[e_t] \tag{5.51}$$

We have omitted the covariance term between the factor returns and the error term, since in a regression model, the error term and factor returns are uncorrelated. Since α is a constant, its variance is zero. If we define the variance of the factor returns as σ_F^2 and the variance of the error term as σ_e^2, then the portfolio variance, σ_p^2, is given by:

$$\sigma_p^2 = \beta_F^2 \sigma_F^2 + \sigma_e^2 \tag{5.52}$$

---

[g] This interpretation is rooted in the Capital asset pricing Model of Sharpe, Black, and Mossin (c.f., Lintner, 1965; Mossin, 1966; Sharpe, 1964). The CAPM's "normal" return is based on an asset's equilibrium risk premium that is a function of only the beta of the asset with the market portfolio and the market risk premium.

The portfolio's risk is comprised of two sources: (1) a source due to the risk of the factor and (2) a source due to the error term. If the factor is the market portfolio or its proxy index, we interpret the first term on the right-hand side of Eq. (5.52) to be the systematic risk of the portfolio that is due to the variance of the index. The second term represents the diversifiable (i.e., unsystematic or idiosyncratic) risk of the portfolio. The variance of the error term is known as the residual variance in the context of a regression. When evaluating performance using the portfolio's benchmark as the single factor, an alternative definition of the tracking error is the square root of the residual variance from the regression model.

Dividing both sides of Eq. (5.52) by the portfolio variance, we see that:

$$\frac{\beta_F^2 \sigma_F^2}{\sigma_p^2} + \frac{\sigma_e^2}{\sigma_p^2} = 1 \tag{5.53}$$

Eq. (5.53) states the sources of portfolio risk as proportions that sum to 100%. The first term on the left-hand side of Eq. (5.53) is the regression R^2. When the market portfolio or proxy index is used as the model's single factor, then the R^2 indicates what proportion of the portfolio's risk is explained by market risk. In general, if the factor is the excess return on a broad market index, a more diversified portfolio has a higher R^2, while a less diversified portfolio has a lower R^2.

We have been quite abstract heretofore in our discussion of the single factor model in usually referring to the factor only generically. In practice, the portfolio's benchmark is commonly used as the single factor in such a model. As indicated above, the parameters of the single factor model have a convenient interpretation when the portfolio's benchmark is used. The portfolio's beta measures the sensitivity or risk exposure of the portfolio to the benchmark, while the alpha measures the average return of the portfolio over and above (or below if negative) what a passive investor would earn by holding the same exposure to the benchmark. In this way, the single factor model provides a concise measure of the ability of the investment manager to beat the benchmark. From the viewpoint of the investor, the alpha represents the reward for taking "active risk," rather than remaining with a passive exposure to the benchmark. Indeed, the active risk is even measured in the model's residual variance or its square root, σ_e. As discussed below, these measures are used to calculate a portfolio's information ratio.

Multifactor models

Multifactor models are a generalization of single factor models. The difference is that in a multifactor model, there is more than one factor in the regression equation. In short, the interpretation that is applied to the results remains similar to what we applied to the single factor model, except that we can attribute average returns and risk to more sources. As with the single factor, we begin with a generic definition of the model in which we have N factors, $F1$, $F2$, ..., FN, with factor returns $R_{F1,t}$, $R_{F2,t}$, ..., $R_{FN,t}$ at time t. We estimate the parameters of the regression model:

$$R_{p,t} = \alpha + \beta_1 R_{F1,t} + \beta_2 R_{F2,t} + \cdots + \beta_N R_{FN,t} + e_t \qquad (5.54)$$

The factor betas reflect the sensitivity or exposure of the portfolio returns to the factor. If portfolio returns are positively correlated with a factor's returns, the beta for that factor will be positive. If the portfolio returns have a negative covariance with a factor's returns, the beta for that factor will be negative. Note that the alpha and the error term are different in Eq. (5.54) compared the same terms in Eq. (5.47), but the meaning of these terms remains the same. Alpha is the average return in excess of the average return that is explained by the model's factors. The error term has a zero average but captures any period-to-period variation in returns that are not accounted for by the factor return variation. As such, the decomposition of the portfolio's average return and variance of returns is analogous to the decompositions using the single factor. Specifically, the average return of the portfolio is given by:

$$\overline{R}_p = \alpha + \beta_1 \overline{R}_{F1} + \beta_2 \overline{R}_{F2} + \cdots + \beta_N \overline{R}_{FN} \qquad (5.55)$$

Because factor returns can be correlated to one another, the variance of portfolio returns is not quite as straightforward as it is for the single factor model. Rather, instead of attributing the variance of portfolio returns to each factor individually (which is possible, but beyond the scope of this discussion), we separate the portfolio variance again into the variance explained by the model and the unexplained or idiosyncratic variance, as given by:

$$\sigma_p^2 = Var[\beta_1 R_{F1,t} + \beta_2 R_{F2,t} + \cdots + \beta_N R_{FN,t}] + \sigma_e^2 \qquad (5.56)$$

In this case, the multivariate regression's R^2 reports the proportion of the portfolio's return variance that is explained by the multiple factors.

Fama-French 3-factor model

The Fama-French 3-factor model is one of the most popular multifactor models for analysis of equity portfolio returns. As its name suggests, the model utilizes three factors: a market factor, a size factor, and a style (growth vs. value) factor. These three have been shown in research to not only explain the variation in asset returns, but to also be associated with stocks' long-term returns. The equity market factor is the excess return on the market index. Which is usually a capitalization-weighted broad-market index. Exposure to this market factor reflects a portfolio's systematic risk. In other words, this factor captures the impact of market-wide movements on the portfolio's returns.

To capture the size and style factors, Fama and French create "characteristic" portfolios based on size and style and calculate the returns to the factors based on the difference in the return on one portfolio compared to another. Specifically, the size factor is calculated as the return to a portfolio of small stocks minus the return to a portfolio of big stocks. This "Small Minus Big" return is labeled as the SMB factor. Likewise, Fama and French create the style factor based on the book-to-market ratio, which is used to identify stocks as "growth" or "value" stocks. Stocks with low book values relative to their market values (i.e., low book-to-market) are considered growth-oriented firms. Recall from our valuation discussion in Chapter 3 that a high growth rate raises the market value of the firm, and hence would cause the book value of the firm's assets to be low compared to its market value. Conversely, "value stocks" have relatively high book-to-market ratios. The style factor is calculated as the return to a portfolio of high book-to-market (i.e., value) stocks minus low book-to-market (i.e., growth) stocks. This "High Minus Low" factor is labeled as the HML factor.

The Fama-French 3-factor regression model is specified as:

$$R_{p,t} = \alpha + \beta_M R_{M,t} + \beta_{SMB} SMB_t + \beta_{HML} HML_t + e_t \tag{5.57}$$

The Fama-French model's parameters provide important insights into a portfolio's risk exposures. Since the market factor is positive when the overall stock market rises, a positive beta on the market factor would be expected for most long-oriented equity portfolios. Portfolios that hold stocks with high systematic risk exposure would be expected to have higher betas. The SMB factor returns are positive when small stocks outperform large stocks. Portfolios that place heavier weight on the smaller capitalization stocks in the market would likely have a positive exposure to the SMB factor (i.e., $\beta_{SMB} > 0$), while portfolios that have a tilt toward large cap stocks would be expected to have a negative SMB beta. The HML factor is generally positive when value stocks outperform growth stocks and negative when growth stocks outperform value stocks. In this way, a positive HML beta reflects an exposure to value stocks. Portfolios that hold more weight on growth-oriented stocks than value-oriented stocks would likely have a negative exposure to the HML factor (i.e., $\beta_{HML} < 0$). Portfolios that have no tilt toward growth or value are sometimes referred to as style-neutral or core.

Example of returns-based attribution using the Fama-French 3-factor model

Exhibit 5.18 illustrates the regression analysis of portfolio returns using various mutual funds. Specifically, the exhibit summarizes the regression results for both a single factor model and the Fama-French 3-factor model applied to monthly returns over a five-year period. The exhibit also reports the average returns to the factors and the funds. Consider first the Fama-French 3-factor model (FF 3-factor) for the Technology fund. The Technology fund's market beta is 1.09, indicating that the portfolio has a bit more market risk than a market index fund. Indeed, when the market goes up by 10%, this portfolio goes up by 10.9%, on average. The Technology fund has an SMB beta of 0.01. This small positive exposure to the SMB factor indicates is statistically insignificant, indicating that the Technology fund has no bias relative to the market portfolio with respected to the market capitalization of the stocks it holds.

Exhibit 5.18 Regression estimates using the single factor and Fama-French 3-factor model

Morningstar category	Model	Coefficient estimates					P-values			
		Alpha	Market	SMB	HML	R²	Alpha	Market	SMB	HML
Technology	Single factor	0.30	1.12			0.81	26%	0%		
	FF 3-factor	0.07	1.09	0.01	−0.58	0.90	73%	0%	94%	0%
Large Value	Single factor	−0.38	1.08			0.93	1%	0%		
	FF 3-factor	−0.25	1.10	−0.01	0.34	0.97	2%	0%	86%	0%
Large Growth	Single factor	0.15	1.07			0.81	55%	0%		
	FF 3-factor	−0.07	1.07	−0.10	−0.49	0.89	71%	0%	19%	0%
Small Value	Single factor	−0.41	1.08			0.76	17%	0%		
	FF 3-factor	−0.07	0.97	0.68	0.42	0.97	57%	0%	0%	0%
Small Growth	Single factor	−0.29	1.15			0.78	34%	0%		
	FF 3-factor	−0.15	0.98	0.83	−0.21	0.96	25%	0%	0%	0%
Large Blend (S&P 500 Index)	Single factor	0.02	0.95			0.99	63%	0%	0%	
	FF 3-factor	−0.02	0.97	−0.11	−0.03	1.00	46%	0%	0%	1%

Factor	Average
Market	0.88
SMB	−0.10
HML	−0.43

Fund category	Average excess return
Technology	1.29
Large Value	0.58
Large Growth	1.10
Small Value	0.54
Small Growth	0.73
Large Blend (S&P 500 Index)	0.87

The negative HML beta indicates that the fund holds growth-oriented stocks. It is not surprising that a technology fund would hold riskier, smaller, and more growth-oriented stocks relative to the overall market.

If a portfolio has a significant (positive or negative) beta on one of the factors, then that factor helps explain the variation in the portfolio's returns.[h] Furthermore, the average return of the portfolio can be attributed to that factor. Over a given time period, the average return of the portfolio that is attributed to the factor is the product of the portfolio's factor beta and the average return on the factor. For example, the Technology fund has an HML beta of -0.58 in the Fama-French 3-factor model during a period in which the average monthly return on the HML factor was -0.43%. That is, the average monthly return on the portfolio of value stocks fell behind that of the growth stocks by 0.43% over this period. Therefore, an exposure of -0.58 to the HML factor increases the Technology fund's average monthly return by 25 basis points ($0.25\% = (-0.58) \times (-0.43\%)$) over this period. Likewise, the market and SMB factors contribute 96 basis points and 0 basis points, respectively. Together, the Technology fund's factor exposures contribute 122 basis points ($1.22\% = 0.96\% + 0\% + 0.25\% + 0.01\%$ (correction for rounding error)). In other words, an investor who has a passive exposure to the same risk factors averages a 122 basis points return per month over this period, while the actively managed portfolio with the same factor exposures averages a 129 basis point return in excess of the risk-free rate, resulting in an alpha of +7 basis points.

We note that the alpha of seven basis points for the Technology fund is not statistically significant, since its P-value is 73%. The P-value indicates that the chance of observing an alpha as high as 0.0007 or higher by random chance is 73% if the true alpha is zero. Since 73% is quite a bit higher than the typical cutoff level of 5% (or the more lenient 10%), the alpha for the Technology fund would be labeled as statistically insignificantly different from zero and the conclusion would be that its alpha is indistinguishable from zero, in a statistical sense. The only fund with a statistically significant alpha in Exhibit 5.18 is the Large Value fund. This fund has a statistically significant negative estimated alpha. Interpreting the positive alpha as skill, it appears that we cannot be statistically confident that any of the funds in the exhibit have skill and it appears that the Value fund's monthly average underperformance of 25 basis points is statistically significant at the 5% level.

As discussed above, the R-squared indicates how much variation in the portfolio returns is explained by the variation of the model's factor returns. Not surprisingly, the S&P 500 Index fund has the highest R-squared of the group, with nearly all of the variation in their returns being explained by the variation in factor returns. The S&P 500 Index fund, which is intended to

---

[h] Statistical significance is indicated by the parameter's "P-value." Recall that a p-value (i.e., a probability of observing a parameter at least as extreme by random chance, if the true parameter is zero) of 0.05 (or sometimes 0.10) or less is commonly considered statistically significant. Parameters with -values of 0.05 (or sometimes 0.10) or more are usually considered to be statistically indistinguishable from zero.

mimic the S&P 500 index, has a significant negative exposure to the SMB factor due to its tilt toward large cap stocks. Likewise, the three-factor model adds significant explanatory power beyond the single factor model for the Small Value and Small Growth funds. The significantly positive estimated regression coefficients on the SMB and HML factors for the Small Value fund allow us to infer that this fund holds small-cap, value-oriented stocks. Similarly, the significantly positive coefficient on the SMB factor together with the significantly negative coefficient on the HML factor for the Small Growth fund indicate that this fund holds small-cap, growth-oriented stocks.

Consider again the case of the Technology fund. Recall that 122 basis points of the fund's return are attributed to the Market, SMB, and HML factors. In one sense, the 122 basis points return represents a sort of benchmark return based on the risk factors to which the fund is exposed. The alpha of 0.0007 indicates that the fund outperforms this "benchmark" by seven basis points over this period. However, it is important to recognize that the factor exposure "benchmark" is an imputed benchmark, not necessarily one that was mandated by the manager. The portfolio may have an explicit benchmark against which its performance is measured. In such a case, it might be inappropriate to measure out- or underperformance of the portfolio with the multifactor model's alpha. However, this does not mean that the multifactor model is of no use. Rather, it might be more appropriate in such a case to use the portfolio's relative returns as the regression's left-hand side variable. That is, we can employ the multifactor model to analyze the portfolio's relative returns.

Beyond the Fama-French 3-factor model

While the Fama-French model is a popular performance analysis tool, there are many variations on the theme. In some cases, other specifications of the size and growth/value-style factors are employed. For example, rather than using the Fama-French SMB factor, a size factor can be created by subtracting the return of a large cap index (e.g., the S&P 500 or S&P 100) from the return of a small cap index (e.g., the S&P 600 or Russell 2000). Likewise, growth and value index returns can be used to create a growth/value-style factor akin to HML. Some methods utilize other factors. Among them, a popular equity factor, known as Momentum, is calculated by subtracting the return to a portfolio of recent "losers" (i.e., underperforming stocks) from the return of recent "winners" (i.e., outperforming stocks) (Carhart, 1996).

More generally, securities have various characteristics that investors like or dislike. These investor preferences cause some securities to be popular and others to be unpopularity. Roger Ibbotson, Thomas Idzorek, Paul Kaplan, and James Xiong have developed a framework as to how such preferences impact returns on securities call popularity (Ibbotson, et al., 2018). Some of the characteristics that they identified include the brand value, reputation, and competitive advantage of stock issuer. For each of these characteristics, they form portfolios from the least popular to most popular and find that over the long run, portfolios of the stocks of the least popular companies outperform portfolios of the stocks of the most popular companies. Factors formed from such portfolios could serve to measure how much portfolios are exposed to popular and unpopular characteristics.

Our use of equity portfolios as examples should not be taken as a suggestion that multifactor analysis is restricted to such portfolios. Indeed, multifactor models are common in the analysis of fixed income portfolios, typically including factors relating to the level of interest rates, the credit spread, and the term spread. The latter two factors are typically calculated in the utilizing an approach similar to that of the Fama-French factors in which the return to a portfolio of low-risk bonds (e.g., Treasury bonds) is subtracted from the return to a portfolio of high-risk bonds (e.g., corporate or high yield bonds) and a return on a short portfolio of is subtracted from the return on a long duration portfolio. Inflation and other economic measures, such as GDP, energy prices, and unemployment round out the list of other commonly used factors.

Returns-based style analysis

Another special case of multifactor models is *returns-based style analysis*, often abbreviated RBSA. In RBSA, the factor returns are the returns on a set of indices, each representing an asset class are or pure investment style, chosen to capture a wide range of possible asset allocations or blends of investment styles. In RBSA, the coefficients on the indices are interpreted as weights on a portfolio of indices. Hence, they are constrained to sum to 100%.

There are two forms of RBSA: unconstrained and constrained. In unconstrained RBSA, the coefficients can be negative, representing short positions. In constrained RBSA, the coefficients are constrained to be nonnegative, so that RBSA portfolio of indices is a long-only portfolio. In general, the term RBSA usually refers to constrained RBSA, which was the original form of RBSA introduced by Sharpe (1988, 1992).

An unconstrained RBSA model can be estimated using Eq. (5.54). The coefficients on the indices are interpreted as the portfolio weights. The weight on cash is given by:

$$\beta_0 = 1 - \sum_{i=1}^{N} \beta_i \tag{5.58}$$

A constrained RBSA model cannot be estimated using conventional regression. Instead, we need to use a form of constrained quadratic programming to estimate the coefficients. To do this, we first need to rewrite the regression equation using total returns rather than excess returns so that the return on cash ($r_{F0,t}$) is an explicit factor:

$$r_{p,t} = \alpha + \beta_0 r_{F0,t} + \beta_1 r_{F1,t} + \beta_2 r_{F2,t} + \cdots + \beta_N r_{FN,t} + e_t \tag{5.59}$$

Using a quadratic programming routine, we select the values of β_0, β_1, ..., β_N subject to the constraints:

$$\sum_{i=0}^{N} \beta_i = 1 \text{ and } \beta_i \geq 0 \tag{5.60}$$

Example of returns-based style analysis

To illustrate RBSA, we apply it to the six U.S. equity funds that we used to illustrate the Fama-French 3-factor model in Exhibit 5.18. These are U.S. equity funds, so we only include indices that represent the U.S. equity market.[i]

We want to model the investment styles of these funds along the dimensions of size and value/growth orientation. To do this, we select U.S. equity indices that capture these dimensions as follows:

Investment style	Abbr.	Index	Plot point
Large-cap Value	LV	Russell 1000 Value	$(-1,+1)$
Large-cap Growth	LG	Russell 1000 Growth	$(+1,+1)$
Small-cap Value	SV	Russell 2000 Value	$(-1,-1)$
Small-cap Growth	SG	Russell 2000 Growth	$(+1,-1)$

So that the RBSA regression equation is[j]:

$$r_{p,t} = \alpha + \beta_0 r_{F0,t} + \beta_{LV} r_{LV,t} + \beta_{LG} r_{LG,t} + \beta_{SV} r_{SV,t} + \beta_{SG} r_{SG,t} + e_t \tag{5.61}$$

Exhibit 5.19 reports the results of both unconstrained and constrained RBSA. For the Technology fund, the weights on LV and SV stocks are negative while the weight on LG stocks is just above 100%. The weight on SG is positive and large. These weights are consistent with results of the Fama-French 3-factor model presented in Exhibit 5.18 shows that this fund a large large-cap growth orientation. Imposing the long-only constraints of standard RBSA analysis leads to 91% in LG and 9% in SG and 0% in LV and LG. In contrast, the results of the unconstrained and constrained model are the same for the Small Value fund since in the constrained model, the constraints that the weights be nonnegative do not come into effect.

Exhibit 5.19 presents a third model labeled FF-Based. This model recasts the results of the Fama-French 3-factor in the RBSA framework. One motivation for this model is that the SMB and HML coefficients may not be easy to interpret for many users of the model. By recasting the three Fama-French coefficients as the portfolio weights in RBSA, the results should be more intuitive for many users of the model. Also, since the Fama-French model has three parameters for equities whereas the RBSA model has four, the Fama-French model could be more restrictive in what styles in could model.

To estimate the FF-Based RBSA model, first estimate the Fama-French 3-factor model and calculate the fitted values:

---

[i] An RBSA on multi-asset class portfolios should include indices that represent all of the asset classes that the portfolios could be included in portfolios.

[j] A version of this model, applied in a similar way, was used in Kaplan (2012).

Exhibit 5.19 Returns-based style analysis results

Morningstar category	Model	Weight estimates						R²	P-values				
		Alpha	LV	LG	SV	SG	Cash		Alpha	LV	LG	SV	SG
Technology	Unconstrained	0.02	−10%	101%	−37%	48%	−2%	0.92	90%	53%	0%	1%	0%
	Constrained	0.19	0%	91%	0%	9%	0%	0.90					
	FF-Based	0.11	24%	77%	−44%	49%	−5%	0.92					
Large Value	Unconstrained	−0.19	98%	10%	10%	−3%	−14%	0.96	12%	0%	29%	30%	72%
	Constrained	−0.08	85%	2%	5%	8%	0%	0.96					
	FF-Based	−0.25	68%	36%	33%	−22%	−14%	0.95					
Large Growth	Unconstrained	−0.10	6%	93%	−36%	37%	−1%	0.91	60%	71%	0%	2%	2%
	Constrained	−0.01	0%	97%	0%	3%	0%	0.89					
	FF-Based	−0.04	34%	77%	−42%	36%	−4%	0.90					
Small Value	Unconstrained	−0.08	10%	4%	77%	9%	1%	0.97	47%	36%	70%	0%	33%
	Constrained	−0.08	10%	4%	77%	9%	1%	0.97					
	FF-Based	−0.07	19%	−1%	70%	12%	0%	0.97					
Small Growth	Unconstrained	−0.08	−8%	1%	−4%	101%	10%	0.97	45%	44%	94%	68%	0%
	Constrained	−0.08	0%	0%	0%	93%	7%	0.97					
	FF-Based	−0.12	−20%	22%	24%	68%	6%	0.97					
Large Blend	Unconstrained	−0.01	53%	53%	0%	−5%	0%	1.00	55%	0%	0%	69%	0%
	Constrained	0.00	48%	50%	0%	0%	2%	1.00					
	FF-Based	−0.01	52%	51%	−4%	0%	1%	1.00					

$$\hat{R}_{p,t} = \hat{\alpha} + \hat{\beta}_M R_{M,t} + \hat{\beta}_{SMB} SMB_t + \hat{\beta}_{HML} HML_t \qquad (5.62)$$

Where a hat () over a parameter indicates its estimated value and over $R_{p,t}$ indicates a fitted value. The second step is to run unconstrained RBSA using $\hat{R}_{p,t}$ instead of $R_{p,t}$.[k,l]

RBSA provides a way of presenting investment style on a two-dimensional grid that is similar to a style box. To this, we first calculate the total exposure to equity implied by the weights. Let

$$\hat{\beta}_{EQ} = \hat{\beta}_{LV} + \hat{\beta}_{LG} + \hat{\beta}_{SV} + \hat{\beta}_{SG} \qquad (5.63)$$

The weights on the four style indices on equity only are:

$$\theta_{LV} = \frac{\hat{\beta}_{LV}}{\hat{\beta}_{EQ}} \qquad (5.64a)$$

$$\theta_{LG} = \frac{\hat{\beta}_{LG}}{\hat{\beta}_{EQ}} \qquad (5.64b)$$

$$\theta_{SV} = \frac{\hat{\beta}_{SV}}{\hat{\beta}_{EQ}} \qquad (5.64c)$$

$$\theta_{SG} = \frac{\hat{\beta}_{SG}}{\hat{\beta}_{EQ}} \qquad (5.64d)$$

Hence,

$$x = \theta_{LV} + \theta_{LG} + \theta_{SV} + \theta_{SG} \qquad (5.65)$$

The x- and y-coordinates for the portfolio being analyzed are given by:

$$x = -\theta_{LV} + \theta_{LG} - \theta_{SV} + \theta_{SG} \qquad (5.66a)$$

$$y = \theta_{LV} + \theta_{LG} - \theta_{SV} - \theta_{SG} \qquad (5.66b)$$

A 100% allocation to one of the style indices with a 0% allocation to the other three results in plot point which is a corner of the square shown in Exhibit 5.20.

---

[k] The R^2s reported for the FF-Based model are not those of the unconstrained regressions that we run to estimate the parameters because those would measure the relationship between the fitted fund excess returns rather than the actual excess fund returns. So instead, we measured the correlation of the actual fund excess returns and the fitted excess returns of the unconstrained model and reported the square of this correlation.

[l] In Exhibit 5.19, we only report *P*-values for the unconstrained model. This is because *P*-values for the constrained and FF-Based models cannot calculated using standard regression tools.

Exhibit 5.20 Style Map of Funds based on returns-based style analysis

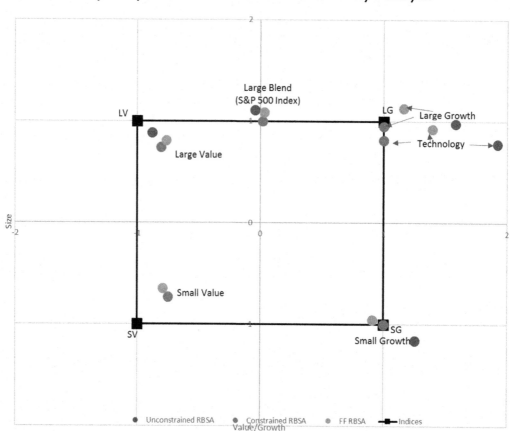

On Exhibit 5.20, we have plotted the (x,y) points for all six of the funds shown in Exhibits 5.18 and 5.19. Note how the points representing the Large Value, Large Growth, Small Value, and Small Growth funds all end up near where we would expect then to be based on their strategies as indicated by their Morningstar categories.[m] Also, the S&P 500 Index fund ends up where we would expect it since it is a Large Blend fund. However, note that while the

---

[m] For the Small Value fund, the point representing the unconstrained model is covered up by the point that represents the constrained model since these two models have identical results for this fund.

Technology and Large Growth funds end up in the large growth area of the chart, the unconstrained and FF-based models place them quite a bit to the right of the square. Constrained RBSA pulls them onto the edge of the square, but in doing so, it loses what could be important information on the extend to with they are growth oriented.

Risk-adjusted return and reward-to-risk measures

Alpha is the most common risk-adjusted measure of portfolio performance. Indeed, the word alpha is often used in conversations about investment strategies to mean "outperformance," as if there is only one way to measure it. In practice, alpha can be defined as (1) the average portfolio return minus the average return on the benchmark; (2) the intercept in the single factor model; and (3) the intercept in a multifactor model; among other less common definitions of alpha. Since we have used all three different definitions of "alpha" in this book, we have tried to make clear which specification of alpha is meant by the context in which it is used. Fortunately, all of these definitions of alpha are qualitatively similar, though not mathematically the same. In all cases, alpha uses the return to a portfolio with similar risk exposures to adjust the return of the portfolio, though "Jensen's Alpha" specifically means using the single factor model (using the market index) (Jensen, 1969). A student-managed investment fund should adopt the definition of alpha that best fits its portfolio mandate and is consistent with its investment philosophy and process.

Chapter 4 discussed other risk-adjusted measures of portfolio performance. Specifically, another popular measure of a portfolio's overall performance is the Sharpe Ratio, which measures the excess return per unit of total portfolio risk. The Sharpe Ratio is less often applied to portfolios that have a specific mandate in a particular asset class, since return per unit of total risk is not necessarily the objective of such portfolios. In such circumstances, the Information Ratio may be more appropriate.

As discussed in Chapter 4, the Information Ratio is typically defined as the average relative return of the portfolio divided by the tracking error of the portfolio. The interpretation of the ratio is akin to that of the Sharpe Ratio, except that it measures the average relative return (i.e., alpha!) per unit of benchmark-relative risk. If we consider that single factor and multifactor models create implicit benchmarks via the factors and factor exposures, then the Information Ratio can also be calculated using these models' measures of alpha and residual risk (i.e., σ_e in Eqs. 5.52 and 5.56). Regardless of the exact specification used, the Information Ratio measures the reward to active management per unit of active risk. It is useful to consider this as the signal-to-noise ratio of active management. The higher the signal or the lower the noise, the more clearly the investment manager's signal becomes. This signal-to-noise ratio helps distinguish skill from luck. For example, if an investment manager holds a relatively concentrated portfolio in which only one or two holdings have significant outperformance, then the alpha might be positive, but the tracking error and residual risk are likely to be high. Indeed, the noise here raises the question as to whether the manager is just lucky with the one or two "hits" in the portfolio. Conversely, if a manager has the same alpha, but a low tracking error or residual risk, then it is likely that the abnormal return is due to multiple "hits" and less likely that the manager is a "one hit wonder." The higher the Information Ratio, the more confident we can be about the alpha truly being "signal" rather than "noise."

Finally, the casting of the Information Ratio as a signal-to-noise ratio is beyond just an intuitive notion. The Information Ratio is mathematically related to the statistical significance of the alpha, which is determined by the alpha's t-statistic. The t-statistic for a regression alpha is calculated by dividing the alpha by its standard error. The standard error of the alpha from a linear regression is approximately equal to the standard deviation of the residual divided by the square root of the number of observations. Therefore, the t-statistic is approximately equal to the Information Ratio multiplied by the standard deviation of time. A higher t-statistic implies a lower P-value and a higher degree of statistical confidence. Therefore, a higher degree of statistical confidence comes with a higher information ratio and/or a longer time with the same information ratio. That is, a higher positive signal-to-noise ratio or a longer time with the same (positive) signal-to-noise ratio allows increased confidence in the signal. In sum, it is difficult to distinguish skill from luck if the Information Ratio is low.

Limitations of performance analysis

Kaplan and Kowara published an article with the provocative title "Are Relative Performance Measures Useless?" (Kaplan and Kowara, 2019). Using both historical returns on funds and simulated returns, they found that a fund that outperforms its benchmark over a 15-year period could have underperformed over long subperiod of perhaps 8–10 years. Similarly, a fund that ultimately underperforms over a 15-year period could outperform over an 8–10-year subperiod. Since these subperiods can be longer that the standard performs of performance measurement, making investment decisions based on past performance over fixed periods can lead to poor investment decisions. The authors conclude that the results of relative performance analysis can be "nothing more than random noise."

The noisy nature of relative performance analysis needs to be kept in mind when using the techniques described in this chapter. While performance analytics are an important part of evaluating investment managers and strategies, they should not be the sole criteria for making investment decisions. Qualitative factors and judgments should also be part of the process.

Summary of key points

- Performance reporting is about how well a portfolio did over some past period. Performance analysis seeks to explain why the portfolio performed as it did.
- There are two main measures of performance: time-weighted return and dollar-weighted return.

- Performance attribution analysis should mirror the portfolio construction process.
- Attribution analysis separates a portfolio's performance in excess of a benchmark using the sector weights and returns of the portfolio and the sector weights and returns of the benchmark.
- There are various forms of attribution analysis. The calculations can be arithmetic or geometric and the analysis can be top-down or bottom up.
- Attribution analysis can be performed over a series of short periods and the results can be linked together to obtain results for longer periods.
- Research has shown that equity portfolio performance can largely be explained by various factors, especially size and value. Expose to these factors can be presented graphically with a style box chart.
- Returns-based analysis usually takes the form of a time-series linear regression model with the returns on the portfolio (in excess of the risk-free) as the dependent variable and one or more factors as the independent variable or variables.
- The single-factor model is often used for measuring systematic risk (beta) and risk-adjusted performance (alpha).
- The Fama-French 3-factor model is a popular multifactor model. The three factors are (1) excess return on a market index, (2) a factor designed to capture exposure to the size factor, and (3) a factor designed to capture exposure to the value factor.
- The 3-factor model has been extended by including other factors such a factor to capture the momentum effect. Other extensions are possible by developing factors based on security characteristics that go beyond risk, but rather are based on characteristics that are popular or unpopular with investors for other reasons.
- Returns-based style analysis (RBSA) is a multifactor model in which the factor returns are the returns on a set of asset class or style indices. In RBSA, the coefficients are interpreted as allocation weights, so they are constrained to sum to 100% and are often constrained to be nonnegative.
- There are several definitions of alpha. A student-managed investment fund should adopt the definition of alpha that best fits its portfolio mandate and is consistent with its investment philosophy and process.
- Performance analysis should not be the sole criteria for making investment decisions.

Exercises

1. Taking the monthly returns, net cashflows, and initial market value as given, replicate the calculation of time-weighted and dollar-weighted return in Exhibit 5.4 in an Excel spreadsheet. Reorder the net cashflows and recalculate. What impact does the order of the cashflows have on the time-weighted and dollar-weighted returns?

2. Taking the portfolio and benchmark sector (asset class) weights and returns as given, replicate the calculations in Exhibit 5.10. What is different between Example A and Example B? How do the results of geometric attribution (Example C) compare to those of arithmetic attribution?

3. Taking the quarterly allocation and selection effects as given in Exhibit 5.13, replicate the calculation of the total effect for each quarter, the allocation and selection effects for each year, and the total effect for the year.

4. Taking the data and results in Exhibit 5.11, replicate the calculation of the linking coefficients in Exhibit 5.14. Then apply them to the quarterly total arithmetic allocation and security effects in Exhibit 5.11 to replicate the modified total quarterly and annual effects in Exhibit 5.14.

5. In Morningstar Direct, select U.S. funds from the Large Value, Large Blend, Large Growth, Mid-Cap Value, Mid-Cap Growth, Small Value, Small Blend, and Small Growth categories. Plot their centroids using the HB Style Map action. See how well their categories align with their positions on the style box grid. Pick a few of them to go in depth by plotting all of their holdings and their ownership zones.

6. From Professor Ken French's website, download 60 monthly values for the risk-free return, the excess return on the market, and the SMB and HML factors. Using Excel, estimate the single-factor model and the Fama-French 3-factor model for the funds that you selected in Exercise (5). How do the alphas from the single-factor and 3-factor compare? Are the coefficients on the SMB and HML factors consistent with the locations of the fund centroids in Exercise (5)?

7. Download the monthly returns on the four indices used in the text for RBSA. For each fund, run unconstrained using linear regression on the excess returns of the fund vs. the excess returns of the indices. Also, calculate the fitted excess returns from the 3-factor model and use them in an unconstrained RBSA. Then run constrained RBSA using the Excel Solver to minimize the variance of the error term in Eq. (5.61). Then plot the three sets of coefficients on a style map. How do the locations of fund centroids on the holdings-based style box grid compare to corresponding locations on the style map from the three versions of RBSA?

References

Brinson, G.P., Fachler, N., 1985. Measuring non-US equity portfolio performance. J. Portf. Manag. 11 (3), 73–76 (Spring).

Brinson, G.P., Hood, L.R., Beebower, G.L., 1986. Determinants of portfolio performance. Financ. Anal. J. 42 (4), 39–44.

Brinson, G.P., Singer, B.D., Beebower, G.L., 1991. Determinants of portfolio performance II: An update. Financ. Anal. J. 47 (3), 40–48.

Carhart, M.M., 1996. On persistence in mutual fund performance. J. Financ. 52, 57–82.

Fama, E.F., French, K.R., 1993. Common risk factors in stocks and bonds. J. Financ. Econ. 33, 3–53.

Fama, E.F., French, K.R., 1996. Multifactor explanations of asset pricing anomalies. J. Financ. 51, 55–84.

Ibbotson, R.G., Idzorek, T.M., Kaplan, P.D., Xiong, J.X., 2018. Popularity: A Bridge Between Classical and Behavioral Finance. CFA Institute Research Foundation, Charlottesville, VA.

Jensen, M.C., 1969. Risk, the pricing of capital assets, and evaluation of investment portfolios. J. Bus. 42, 167–247.

Kaplan, P.D., 2012. Holdings-based and returns-based style models. In: Kaplan, P.D. (Ed.), Frontiers of Modern Asset Allocation. John Wiley & Sons, Inc., Hoboken, pp. 71–102

Kaplan, P., Kowara, M., 2019. Are relative performance measures useless? J. Invest. 28 (4), 83–93.

Lintner, J., 1965. The valuation of risk assets and the selection of risk investments in stock portfolios and capital budgets. Rev. Econ. Stat. 47, 13–37.

Menchero, J., 2004. Multiperiod arithmetic attribution. Financ. Anal. J. 60 (4), 76–91.

Menchero, J., 2000. An optimized approach to linking attribution effects over time. J. Perform. Meas. 5 (1), 36–42.

Mossin, J., 1966. Equilibrium in a capital asset market. Econometrica 34, 768–783.

Sharpe, W.F., 1964. Capital asset prices: A theory of market equilibrium under conditions of risk. J. Financ. 19, 425–442.

Sharpe, W.F., 1988. Determining a fund's effective asset mix. Invest. Manag. Rev. 2, 59–69.

Sharpe, W.F., 1992. Asset allocation: Management style and performance measurement. J. Portf. Manag. 18, 7–19.

CHAPTER 6

Trading algorithms

This chapter provides an overview of the essential information required for algorithmic trading. The topics covered provide students with the necessary information that will allow them to properly select and specify trading algorithms to execute orders based on different trading needs and investment objectives. The materials and concepts presented will provide students with an understanding of:

- The investment cycle
- Algorithmic and electronic trading
- Different types of trading algorithms
- Algorithmic strategies
- Transaction cost components
- Transact costs analysis (TCA)
- Trading venues (exchanges, ATS, and dark pools)
- Broker dealer trading desk
- Algorithmic decision-making process

Investment cycle

To help understand trading strategies and algorithmic trading it is essential to start with a review of the investment cycle. The investment cycle consists of four distinct phases (Exhibit 6.1). These are: asset allocation, portfolio construction, implementation, and portfolio attribution and are as follows:

Asset allocation

Asset allocation is the process of determining how much of the total investment dollar to allocate to stocks, bonds, cash, and other investment vehicles. This decision is made based on the investment objective of fund or via specified fund mandate.

Portfolio construction

Portfolio construction is the process of selecting the actual individual investment instruments to hold in the portfolio. For example, for an equity portfolio this consist of determining which stocks should be bought and added into the portfolio or which stocks should be sold and removed from the portfolio. Portfolio construction will be based on the investment strategy of the fund and could be based on active or passive management, as well as fundamental, quantitative, or index investing. For a bond portfolio, portfolio construction consists of determining which corporate bonds to purchase and hold in the portfolio. This decision is often based on the bond rating (e.g., investment grade or high yield bond), as well as the current yield to maturity, years to maturity, probability of default, etc.

Implementation

The implementation phase of the investment cycle is the process of executing the portfolio managers' investment decisions. It consists of the actual buying and selling of stocks, bonds, etc. Implementation has historically consisted of selecting the appropriate broker for the execution, but with the advent of algorithmic trading, the implementation decisions are much more involved and require investors to be much more proactive in the trading decisions than ever before. Implementation now consists of selecting the broker, trading algorithm, and specifying the set of algorithmic trading rules and parameters to ensure the execution strategy will be consists with the underlying investment objective of the fund.

Portfolio attribution

Portfolio attribution is the process of evaluating portfolio returns and risk, and comparing these values to expectations at the time of the investment decisions. Money managers are continuously reviewing their decisions to understand if the actual returns are due the investment strategy or due to some unanticipated event such as an economic boom or downturn, or company related news, or other items such as market noise, volatility, and/or luck. Portfolio attribution is a very important step in the investment cycle as it helps fund managers understand how well their strategies are working, and if they should continue with the strategy going forward. Portfolio attribution is a never-ending learning process.

Electronic and algorithmic trading

What is electronic trading?

Electronic trading is the process of entering and transacting order over a computer network. Historically, orders sent to brokers via phone calls and/or via fax and were executed via human traders and manual intervention. Traders were tasked with achieving the best price for their clients and would utilize the services of specialists and market makers. But now, markets are completely electronic and all trading is preformed via computers and the large majority of market trades occur via trading algorithms that are making execution decisions in real time

Exhibit 6.1 **Investment cycle**

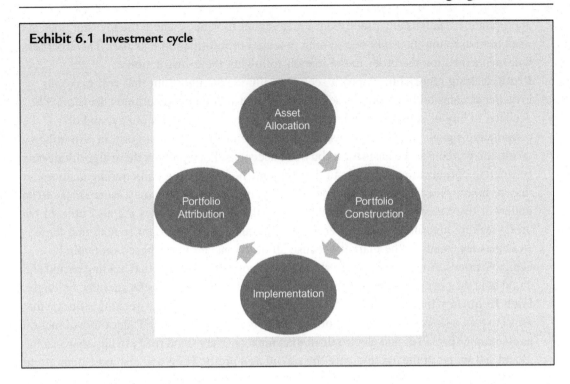

based on actual market conditions and stocks trends. And most importantly, trading algorithms are making decisions without human intervention.

What is algorithmic trading?

Algorithmic trading is the computerized execution of financial instruments following a set of pre-specified trading rules and instructions. These instructions will specify how fast or slow to transact the order in the market, and at what prices, and trading venues. Traditionally, investors would send their order to a broker who would then transact the order in the market using best efforts and their expertise. But with the changing landscape, human traders are no longer best equipped to handle the large quantity of financial data. The process showing how investors specify and determine these algorithmic trading decisions is provided in section "Algorithmic decision-making process."

Trading algorithms can be classified into three categories:

- **Execution algorithm.** An execution algorithm is an algorithm that will transact (trade) a given order following a set of specified rules and guidelines. In these situations, the money manager will determine the order independently of the algorithm and then enters the order characteristics consists of symbol, side, and shares into the algorithm. Investors will also specify other items such as start and end time for the order, price and/or volume limits if appropriate, as well as any preferred trading venues to venues where the investor does not want to transaction (possibly due to high potential of information leakage). The algorithm will then execution the order in the market following these instructions.

- **Profit-seeking algorithm.** A profit seek algorithm is an algorithm that will make the investment decision (e.g., buy or sell decision) and will then execute this decision. The decision to buy or sell shares is based on market prices, investor strategy, and/or quantitative signals. In most of these situations, the profit-seeking algorithm will utilize a quantitative model as the basis for its buy/sell decisions. For example, these algorithms may be running optimizations throughout the day, may be performing pairs trading analysis, or may be monitoring stocks for any type of market mispricing which may cause stocks to be under- or overvalued. Quantitative and statistical arbitrage strategies are also utilized by profit-seeking algorithms to uncover additional value. It is important to note that these strategies are good for the market because all decisions are made based on publicly available prices. Additionally, these strategies do not have any specified holding period and could hold the positions (long and/or short) overnight or for days, weeks, months, or longer.

- **High frequency trading (HFT).** High frequency trading is a profit-seeking strategy that seeks to earn a short-term trading profit in one of two ways. First, HFT algorithms function as electronic specialists and electronic market makers. They stand ready to buy shares at the id and sell shares at the ask and earn the spread as a profit. They will also post liquidity to trading venues to receive a rebate from the venue in additional to earning the spread. Second, other types of HFT algorithms seek to uncover the trading intentions of other market participants by watching trading patterns and the submission of buy and sell order to the market. These algorithms will then use any information that they uncovered to gain an advantage in the market. For example, if a HFT algorithm has uncovered a large buy order in the market they will likely buying shares in conjunction with the investor. Then after prices have increased due to the price impact from the increased buying pressure they will sell the shares they bought at a higher price to earn a profit. It is important to note here that these HFT algorithms are using information that has been publicly disseminated to the market through trade reports and by viewing the order book at different venues. The information is not determined via any type of private information. If the HFT is incorrect with their assessment of an order they will incur a loss. But if the HFT is correct with their assessment they will earn a profit. An HFT strategy will almost always offset their position by the end of the day so that they do not incur any overnight risk (Exhibits 6.2 and 6.3).

Algorithm trading styles

There are many different types of trading algorithms used in the finance, and unfortunately, the naming conventions of these algorithms do not adequately describe what the algorithm is trying to accomplish or how the algorithm will transact in the market. For example, algorithms often have fun and entertaining names such as "Superman," "Tarzan," "Marvelous," as well as

Exhibit 6.2 Electronic and algorithmic trading

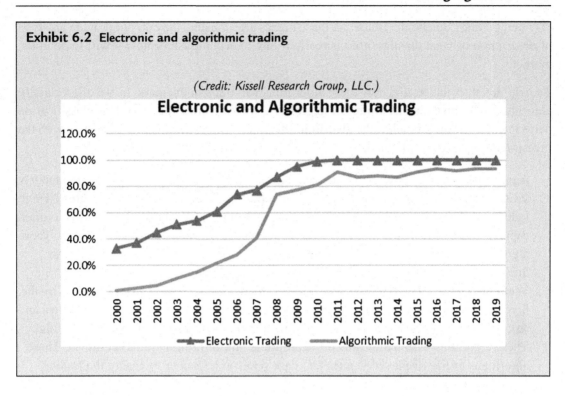

Exhibit 6.3 High turnover trading

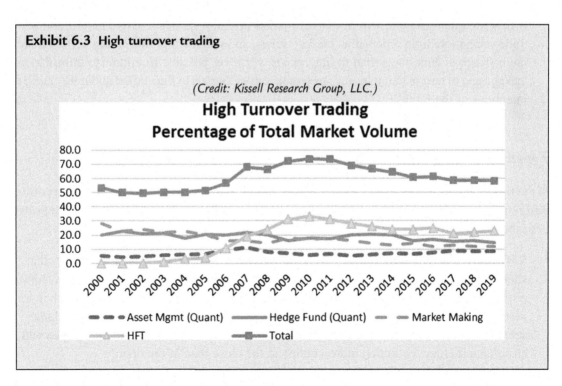

"Dynamic," and "Splendid." But while these names are amusing, they do not provide any type of description of what the algorithm is really trying to accomplish or how it will trade in the market.

To help investors understand how these algorithms will trade in the markets, we often classify algorithms into three distinct groups of aggressive, working order, passive. This classification helps Portfolio Managers select the algorithms that will transact in a manner consistent with the investment objective of the fund.

- **Aggressive.** The algorithm will trade very aggressively in the market and will continuously seek to transact shares at a specified price or better. These algorithms are also referred to in industry as "liquidity seeking" and "liquidity sweeping" algorithms as the goal is to often capture as much available market shares as possible at the specified price or better. These algorithms trade using more market orders than limit orders, and tend to execute in displayed "lite" venues much more often than in dark pools.
- **Working order.** The algorithm will trade in the market following rules specified by the investor. These "working order" algorithms seek to balance the trade-off between cost and risk, and ensure consistence between trading and the investment objective of the fund. These algorithms will trade using an appropriate mix of limit and market orders. These algorithms utilize displayed venues and dark pools in a manner to ensure the trading strategy is most consistent with the investment objective of the fund.
- **Passive.** The algorithm will trade in a passive manner and will seek to transact at prices and with share quantities that will not affect market prices or quotes. Passive algorithms will trade using more limit orders than market orders, and will attempt trade more seek to trade more shares in dark pools than in lite venues whenever possible to minimize information leakage and to ensure that transactions to not convey signals to the market about the trading intentions of the fund.

Types of trading algorithms

In the financial industry there are many types of trading algorithms. And different brokers offer different types and variations of each. The more common types of algorithms used in trading are described below.

- **VWAP.** A VWAP algorithm, e.g., volume weighted average price, is an algorithm that slices the order over the day or over a specified trading period based on the intraday volume profile of the stock. Historically, intraday volume following a U-shaped pattern with more volume at the open and close than during midday. But more recently, intraday volume seems to follow more of a J-shaped pattern where there is more volume at the open and close than midday, but much more volume at the close than at the open.

- **TWAP.** A TWAP algorithms, e.g., time weighted average price, is an algorithm that slices the order over the day or over a specified time period using equal share quantity amounts in each period. In statistics, this type of slicing is often described as a uniform distribution.
- **POV.** A POV algorithm is an algorithm that will trade based on a percentage of market volume. These algorithms are specified in terms of a percentage of volume. For example, POV = 10% indicates that the algorithm is to participate with 10% of the market volume. This means that whenever 1000 shares trades in the market the investor will transact 100 shares.
- **Arrival price.** An arrival price algorithm is an algorithm that will trade aggressive (faster) when market prices are near the arrival price of the order, that is, the market price when the order was entered into the market. As market prices move further away from the arrival price the algorithm will tend to trade at a more passible (slower) manner.
- **Font-load.** A front-load algorithm is an algorithm that trades more aggressive at the beginning of the order and more passible at the end of the order. A front-load algorithm is often used by investors who are trying to capture prices as close to the arrival price as possible and still want to manage the trade-off between trading costs and timing risk.
- **Back-load.** A back-load algorithm is an algorithm is an algorithm that trades more passive at the beginning of the order and more aggressive at the end of the order. A back-load algorithm is often used by investors who are trying to capture prices as close as possible to a future benchmark price, such as the close, and still want to manage the trade-off between trading cost and timing risk.
- **Optimal strategy.** An optimal strategy is an execution strategy that is determined through an optimization process. The more common optimal strategies are (i) minimize the total cost of the trade due to market impact and price appreciation, (ii) balance the trade-off between market impact cost and timing risk, and (iii) maximize the probability of outperforming a specified price.
- **MOC.** A MOC or market on close algorithm is an algorithm that will enter shares into the closing auction of the exchange for execution at the official closing price on the day. Closing auctions require shares to be entered for execution prior to the close. Investors utilizing MOC algorithms are guaranteed to have all shares executed at the closing price but will not know the exact transaction price until after the market closes. Also, once an order is entered into the closing auction of an exchange they are guaranteed to be executed but the order cannot be canceled once entered.
- **Dark pool.** A dark pool algorithm is an algorithm that will only execute shares in the numerous industry dark pools. Investor utilize dark pool algorithms when they wish to remain anonymous and do not want to convey any information to the market regarding their trading intentions. Dark pool algorithms are often used for large orders.
- **Liquidity seeking.** A liquidity seeking algorithm is an algorithm that will utilize all trading venues (displayed and dark venues) to capture liquidity at a specified price or better. The liquidity seeking algorithm will often trade in an aggressive manner to capture as much

liquidity as possible. The liquidity seeking algorithms are often used by investors who are trying to exploit a market mispricing. A liquidity seeking algorithm is also used by investors to execute shares at the tail end of the order. For example, trade aggressively to complete the order. In this situation, investors are not as concerned with information leakage as long as they can complete the order.

- **Dynamic.** A dynamic trading algorithm is an algorithm that adapts to changing market conditions such as prices and volumes based on investor pre-specified trading rules. These rules allow the algorithms to take advantage of market conditions and prices when appropriate. Dynamic algorithmic trading logic is also often integrated into the algorithms mentioned above.
- **Portfolio algorithms.** A portfolio algorithm is a trading algorithm that transacts a basket of stock consisting of one-sided orders such as all buy or all sell orders, or a two-sided order that consists of both buy and sell orders. A portfolio algorithm, also commonly known as Portfolio IS, will make transaction decisions based on the overall cost and risk of the basket. These algorithms will manage the risk of the trade list and take advantage of favorable market conditions whenever possible from the perspective of the trade list. Portfolio algorithms make trading decisions based on the overall trade list and not at the individual stock level.

Exhibit 6.4 shows the usage of different trading algorithms over the 20-year period from 2000 to 2019. Exhibit 6.5 illustrates how different algorithms would slice an order that consists of 10% of the stock's average daily volume.

Algorithmic slicing strategies

Trading algorithms are tasked with managing all transaction costs components over the trading horizon. In most cases, to minimize these costs the algorithms will slice the order and trade over time. There are three main ways that the algorithm will slice the order: time, volume, and price.

These are described below.

- **Time based.** A time based slicing strategy is a strategy that segments the order into trade buckets based on different time periods. The shares in each trade bucket can be based on historical volume profiles (such as a VWAP strategy) or ban be based on equal shares in each buck (such as a TWAP strategy). The number of shares to trade in these groups could also be calculated based on a quantitative model (such as the front-load, back-load, and optimal strategies). The algorithm is then tasked with executing each of these slices during the corresponding time interval.
- **Volume based.** A volume-based slicing strategy is an algorithmic strategy that participates with a specified quantity of volume. For example, a POV algorithm may specific to trade at a rate of POV = 10%. In this case, the algorithm will need to participate with 10% of the

Exhibit 6.4 Trading algorithm usage

(Credit: Kissell Research Group, LLC.)

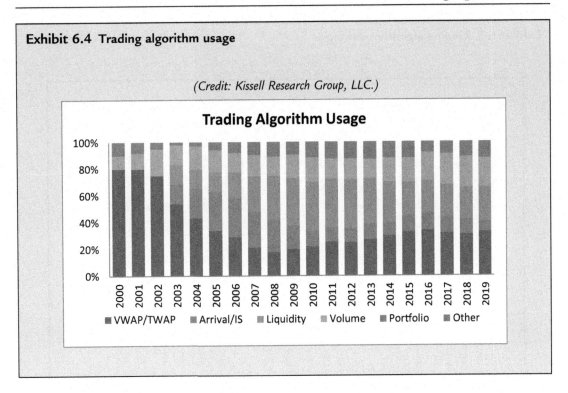

market volume. If 1000 shares trades in the market, the algorithm will need to trade 100 shares. An advantage of a volume based POV algorithm provides the opportunity to participate with increased market volume and complete the order sooner. A disadvantage of a volume based POV algorithm is that if current volume is very low the order many not finish by the end of the day or by the specified end time. In times of illiquidity, investors will need to revise their POV rate to ensure completion of the order.

- **Price based**. A price-based slicing strategy is an algorithmic strategy that will transact different share quantities at different prices. A price-based strategy is used by arrival price algorithms where more shares are transacted when market price is at or near the arrival price than when prices are further away from the arrival price. Some profit seeks and HFT algorithms will also utilize price-based strategies to buy shares only if the price falls below a specified price or to sell shares if the price rises above a specific price.

Some of the more advanced trading algorithms will make use of a combination of the slicing strategies above. This allows investors to customize algorithms for their specific trading and investment needs. For example, we can utilize a combination of a volume-based and price-based slicing strategy so that the algorithm will be able to take advantage of increased volume and also trade at a faster rate when the prices are favorable but trade less urgently when prices are unfavorable.

Exhibit 6.5 Trading algorithm strategies

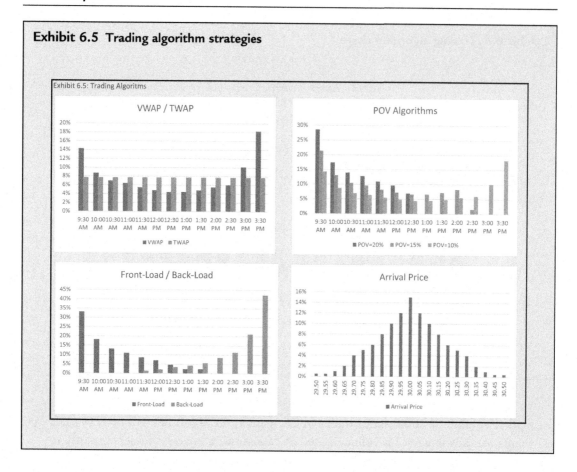

Transaction costs

In economics, transaction costs refer to the fees paid by buyers but not received by sellers and the fees paid by sellers but not received by buyers. In finance, transaction costs refer to the price premium paid above the decision price for buy orders and the discount below the decision price for sell orders.

When investors trade in the market, they encounter transaction costs that could dramatically affect portfolio performance and lead to much lower returns if not properly managers. Trading, unfortunately, is not a frictionless process and is often associated with numerous costs that are both visible (and easy to calculate) and hidden (which can only be observed after trading takes place). In total, there are nine transaction cost components that arise during trading. These are:

Commissions

These are the fees paid to brokers for their service in transacting the order. Commissions are a visible trading cost component.

Fees and rebates

These are the dollars paid to the trading venues (e.g., exchanges, ATS, and dark pools). In some situations, the investor will receive a rebate for the transaction and in other situations investors will pay a fee. Venue fees and rebates are a visible trading cost component.

Spread cost

The difference between the highest bid price and the lowest ask price across all exchanges. In order words, the spread cost is computed from the NBBO (National Best Bid and Offer) prices and is a visible transaction cost component.

Taxes

Consists of SEC tax (on security sales), and income and capital gains taxes. Taxes are a visible transaction cost component.

Delay cost

The cost due to the movement in the stock price from the time of the investment decision to the time that the order is entered into market for execution. For example, if a portfolio manager decides to purchase the stock when it is $30.00/share but by the time the order is entered into the market for execution the price is $30.25/share the manager incurred a cost of $0.25/share. Delay cost is a hidden transaction cost component.

Price appreciation

The price appreciation cost is also referred to as the alpha cost. This is the natural price movement in the stock over the trading period. For example, if the stock price is increasing over the day due price appreciation, the manager will incur a higher transaction price which will make buy orders more expensive and sell orders more profitable since the executions will be made at higher prices. If the stock price is decreasing over the day due to price depreciation, the manager will incur a lower transaction price will make buy orders more favorable and sell orders more costly since the executions will be made at lower prices. Price appreciation is a hidden transaction cost component.

Market impact

Market impact cost, also known as price impact, is defined as the price movement in the stock caused by the investor's trade or order. For example, a buy order causes increased demand i the stock which pushes the stock price up, and a sell order causes increased supply in the stock which pushes the stock price down. This follows the law of supply and demand from economics.

Market impact cost consists of two components: a temporary component and a permanent component. Temporary market impact cost is caused by the liquidity needs of the investor. Here, a buyer of stock may need to offer the market a premium to attract additional sellers into the market to complete the transactions. A seller of stock may need to discount their sale price (ask price) to entice buyers to purchase the shares. This temporary price change due to liquidity needs will be followed by trend reversion after the order is completed where the stock price will return to its fair value equilibrium price (Exhibit 6.6).

Permanent market impact cost is caused by the information content of the trade. At times when trading is perceived as information driven, meaning that we believe that there is some information that is leading the portfolio manager to buy or sell the stock that has not yet been fully disseminated and reflected in to the stock price, the market will reevaluate and adjust the valuation of the stock price which will result in a new fair value. This results in a higher stock price after completion of a buy order and a lower stock price after completion of a sell order.

Market impact cost is one of the more expensive transaction cost components to investors and is caused solely by the order. Portfolio managers try to actively manage and control this cost throughout trading from the first to last trade.

Market impact, unlike other transaction cost components, cannot be completely measured because we are only able to observe stock price movement without the order or stock price movement with the order, but not both. Because of this phenomenon, market impact cost has often been referred to as the Heisenberg Uncertainty Principle of Trading. Market impact cost is a hidden transaction cost component.

Timing risk

Timing risk refers to the price uncertainty over the trading period where prices may increase or decrease due to factors that are not related to the order. Prices may increase or decrease during the trading horizon which makes transaction prices more or less expensive for the investor. Timing Risk is caused by price volatility, volume uncertainty, the buying and selling pressure from other market participants, and market noise. Timing risk is an unavoidable transaction cost component. It is a hidden transaction cost component.

Opportunity cost

Opportunity cost is the cost associated with a missed profiting opportunity by not being able to execute the entire order in the market. For example, a portfolio manager decides to purchase 1,000,000 shares of stock RLK at the opening price of $30.00 and begins to trade at the market open. By the end of the day the price of RLK increases to $30.50, but the manager is only able to purchase 800,000 shares. Thus 200,000 shares of the order were not executed. If the portfolio manager were to execute these 200,000 shares at the market open the fund would have earned an additional $100,000 over the day, e.g., $200,00 * ($30.50 - $30.00) = $100,000$. Opportunity cost is an unavoidable transaction cost component.

One of the primary goals of trading algorithms is to manage and control these transaction costs during implementation of the trade.

Types of implementation and execution

After money managers decide what stocks they want to buy and sell and the corresponding number of shares, they need to decide how they will transact those shares in the market. Investors currently have two ways to execute the shares. These are known as agency execution and capital commitment (principal bid) transaction.

Agency execution

An agency execution is a transaction where the investor pays the broker a commission to facilitate the trade. The broker or really the broker's algorithm then transacts shares in the market using best efforts until the order is completed. In this situation, the investor receives the exact transaction prices achieved by the algorithm. For example, if the investor has a buy order and the market prices increase then the investor will pay a higher price. If the market prices decline for a buy order then the investor will pay a lower price. If the investor has a sell order and the market prices decline the investor will have to sell the shares at a lower price, but if the market prices increase then the investor will be able to sell the shares at a higher price. In an agency execution, the investor does not know the price in advance and incurs all market risk. The investor pays the broker a commission to facilitate the trade.

For example, an investor has a buy order for RLK with a current stock price is $30.00 and the broker agency commission is $0.01. The algorithm completes the order at an average price of $30.10. In this case the investor will incur a total price including commission of $30.11 ($30.10 plus $0.01 commission) and the broker will earn their commission of $0.01.

Exhibit 6.6 Market impact cost

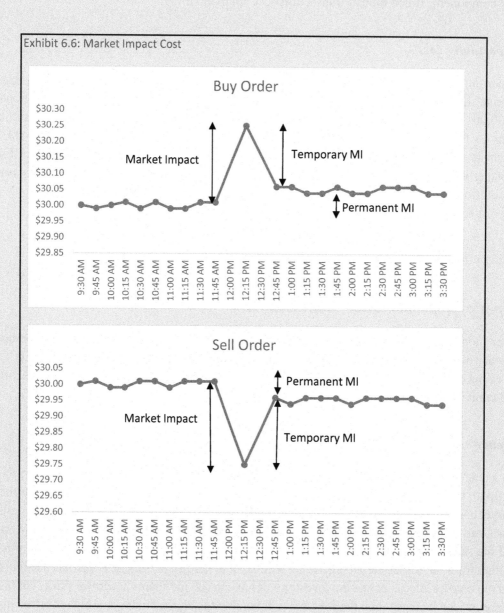

Exhibit 6.6: Market Impact Cost

Capital commitment (principal bid) transaction

A capital commitment trade, also known as a principal bid, risk bid, bid premium., or simply bid, is a transaction where the investor pays the broker a fee to transact the entire order at a specified price. In this case, the investor transacts a known price and transfers all risk to the broker. But the fee (e.g., bid) for this service is much higher than in an agency execution. The broker is then tasked with offsetting the order they just received from the investor in the market. If the broker can transact the order at a cost less than the bid amount received from the investor they will earn a profit. But if the broker incurs a cost higher than the bid received form the investor they will incur a loss.

In a capital commitment trade, the investor is provided with the exact transaction price by the broker and the bid. All risk is then transferred to the broker. The broker charges a higher price for a capital commitment than for an agency execution because they incur all risk of the trade. If the broker can transact in the market at a better price than they charged the investor they will incur a profit, but if they transact at a worse price they will incur a loss.

For example, an investor has a buy order for RLK with a current stock price is $30.00 and the broker bid premium is $0.15. In this case the investor will receive an all-in price (including the bid premium) of $30.15 (current price of $30.00 plus $0.15 bid premium). The broker will then purchase the shares in the market. If the broker purchases shares at a price of $30.15 or lower they will earn a profit. If the broker purchases shares at a price higher than $30.15 they will incur a loss. If the broker purchases shares at a price of exactly $30.15 they will break even. The principal bid premium here will be higher than the agency commission because it is to provide the broker with payment for accepting the risk of the trade.

Trading venues

Historically, stocks were primarily traded on the exchange where they were listed. For example, a blue-chip stock listed on the NYSE exchange traded primarily on the floor of the NYSE and a technology company listed on the NASDAQ OTC exchange would trade primarily via NASDAQ market makers. The blue-chip NYSE listed company would not trade on the OTC exchange and the technology NASDAQ OTC listed company would not trade on the floor of NYSE.

But now, in a new electronic trading area, all stocks now trade in multiple venues consisting of exchanges, alternative trading systems, and dark pools. These are described as follows:

Exchange

An exchange is a venue where companies list their securities to be offered to the market. An exchange will ensure that the listed company has up-to-date financials and is properly adhering to the exchange's listing requirements which may include a minimum price and minimum daily volumes among other items. The exchange will help facilitate trading of the company and provide liquidity in the stocks via electronic market makers that are designated by the exchange. These electronic market maker firms are required to maintain fair and orderly pricings throughout the day, provide competitive bid and offer prices where they stand ready to buy shares and sell shares at their specified prices, and provide on-going market liquidity. A designated market maker firm may be provided with special rebates for their role that might be enticing than what is offered to other investors who are not required to help maintain fair and orderly markets and providing on-going liquidity.

An exchange will maintain an order book for all stocks it trades. The order book includes all buy orders prices and shares, and all sell orders prices and shares. In the case where there may be multiple orders at the same price, the priority for execution will be defined by the exchange. The most common execution priority is given by best price and time (e.g., price-time priority). Some exchanges provide execution priority based on best price and largest share quantity (e.g., price-size priority). If there are multiple orders entered at the same price and share quantity, then the order that has been posted for the time will be executed first (e.g., price-size-time priority).

The exchange is responsible for publicly disseminating its best bid price and the best ask price and corresponding share quantities. The exchange is also required to report all trades executed. Exchanges may also provide order book information to investors which consist of all entered buy orders and sells orders including share quantity). Although investors may be required to pay a fee or an additional fee for access to this service.

Investor will use this information to determine how long it would likely take to execute an order placed at a specified price based on where they are in limit order book and how many orders are ahead of them in the queue.

* An exchange is a displayed market because it disseminates the best bid and best ask prices to the market.

Alternative trading system (ATS)

An alternative trading system (ATS) operates similar to an exchange but does not provide any listing services for companies or provide financial information on the company to investors. An ATS will trade stocks listed on exchanges, and will also disseminate pricing information including its best bid and best ask, as well as order book information. An alternative trading system will most commonly execute orders based on price-time priority.

Investor who seek to transact on an ATS will have access to the prices and order book information. But there may be an additional fee to gain access to the venues full order book. An important note about ATSs is that they have different reporting requirements. This information will allow investor to understand where they are in queue and they can then estimate how long it will likely take to execute their order.

- An alternative trading system is a displayed market because it disseminates the best bid and best ask prices to the market.

Dark pool

A dark pool is a trading venue that does not provide any pricing information to investors. Investors utilizing a dark pool will enter an order and they will receive an execution if there is an offsetting order at the specified price or better. If the dark pool does not have a matching order or does not have an offsetting order at the desired price or better an execution will not occur. Additionally, a dark pool does not report its executed trades directly to public. Instead, trades that occur in a dark pool are publicly disseminated via FINRA's TRF (trade reporting facility) but the only information that is provided is that it was a dark pool trade with giving the exact dark pool where the trade occurred.

An advantage of using a dark pool is that it allows investors to enter large orders for execution without conveying their trading intentions and order size to the public. The order will only execute if there is an offsetting order at the specified price or better. Because neither order information or trade executions for the venue are disseminated publicly, it is often said that dark pools eliminate information leakage. However, investors are always concerned about the possibility of other investors learning information about their trading intentions, especially if they enter a large order, and as a result, will often enter smaller orders into dark pool.

- In most dark pools, orders are matched using the midpoint of the NBBO. Dark pools received their name because they do not provide investors with any pricing information and they do not add to the price discovery process.

Venue pricing models

In the current trading environment, each venue maintains a different pricing model. There are three primary venue pricing models. This is how venues earn their revenue. These are:

- **Commission-fee model.** In a commission-fee model, both the seller and the buyer pay the venue a commission to complete the trade. A commission based pricing model is most common with dark pools. For example, if the commission rate is 10 mills (e.g., $0.0010 per share which is 0.10 cents per share) and a trade occurs both the buyer and the seller pay the venue 10 mills each. Therefore, the venue earns 20 mills on the trade.

- **Maker-taker model.** A maker-taker model is a venue pricing model based on fees and rebates. In this structure, the market participant who posts an order to the exchange (and is disseminated publicly) will receive a rebate from the exchange if a match occurs and the market participant who takes the liquidity will pay a fee. Here, the party who posts an order (e.g., posts liquidity, provides liquidity) is making a market and is rewarded with a rebate for bringing liquidity to the venue when a trade occurs. The party who takes the liquidity is required to pay a fee. For example, in a maker-take pricing structure, the party posting liquidity may receive a rebate of 10 mills and the party taking liquidity may pay a fee of 30 mills for the transaction. In this case, the venue earns a profit of 20 mills per share. A maker-taker venue pricing model is the most common pricing model used with displayed exchanges and venues.

- **Inverted maker-taker model.** An inverted maker-taker model (inverted) behaves in the opposite manner as the maker-taker model. In this case, the party posting liquidity will pay a fee of a match occurs and the party taking liquidity will receive a rebate. For example, an inverted maker-taker model may be one where the liquidity provider pays a fee 30 mills and the liquidity taker receives a rebate of 10 mills. In this case, the venue also earns a profit of 20 mills per share. An inverted maker-taker model is used for displayed exchanges and venues but is much less common than the traditional maker-taker model.

One question that commonly arises with regards to the maker-taker and inverted maker-taker model is why would an investor who is posting liquidity (e.g., entering a limit order) decide to pay a fee on an "inverted" venue when they could receive a rebate on the traditional venue? The answer is simple and comes down to how quick does the investor need to complete the order at their specified price.

For example, suppose an investor wishes to execute an order via a limit order placed at the best market bid but there are many orders at the same price in the queue ahead of the investor. This investor needs to wait until all the order in queue ahead of their order have executed before their order will transact (which may or may not occur). If this investor determines that the time that they will have to wait to have their order executed is too long they have three options that will result in quicker execution. First, they could execute via a market order which results in them paying a fee and a much higher price since they are crossing the entire bid-ask spread. This results in a much higher price and a fee. Second, they could increment the bid price by say a penny. In this case, their order would be the next one in the queue to be transacted because they would have the highest bid price and would be first in-line since they increased the bid. In this case, the investor would receive their rebate but would pay a price that is $0.01 higher. Third, the investor could enter the order on an inverted exchange. In this case, the investor's order would effectively become the next order in the market queue to be executed because a seller would rather receive a rebate for taking liquidity than pay a fee for taking liquidity. In this case, the investor is able to buy shares at their specified price but they pay a fee to the venue rather than collect the rebate. An inverted maker-taker model behaves in the same manner as a fast-pass ticker at amusement parks that allows the customer to cut to the front of the line when the line is too long and the person does not want to wait. The customer receives the fast-pass but paid a premium to receive this luxury. So, the inverted model is the same as a go to the front of the line card for the investor—it comes with an increased cost but this increment cost is still less than the cost corresponding with having to increase the bid price.

Types of orders

There are two main types of orders used in algorithmic trading: market order and limit order. These are:

- **Market order.** A market order is an order that will trade at the best available market price. Here, a buyer would buy shares at the best (lowest) ask price in the market and a seller would sell shares at the best (highest) bid price in the market. There are rules in place that require exchanges and venues to route an order to a different venue if that venue has a better price. Investors who trade via a market order are denoted as liquidity takers since they are taking volume away from the market.
- **Limit order.** A limit order is an order where the investor specifies the highest price (bid) that they are willing to buy shares and the lowest price (ask) that they are willing to sell shares. Investors who trade via limit orders are denoted as liquidity providers since they provide liquidity to the market. Here, the investor would enter their buy or sell order into an exchange or ATS. The order would include the side (buy or sell), price, and share quantity.

Broker dealer trading floor

A full-service broker dealer trading floor will commonly consist of three different trading desks: cash desk, program desk, and electronic desk. Each trading desk is utilized by an investor with a different trading need and serves a different purpose (Exhibit 6.7).

Cash desk

A broker dealer cash trading desk is also known as a single stock trading desk or a block trading desk. Historically, the cash desk was used by investors to transact large block orders, but now, the cash desk is utilized by investors who are trading single orders that are subject to adverse price movement and/or momentum. In these situations, investors will rely on the broker's expertise in understanding stock specific trading patterns and whether or not the stock is likely to experience continued momentum patterns or trend reversal. A cash desk trader will have expertise in both the stock and the stocks sector, and will rely on real time data and market conditions to help structure an appropriate trading strategy for the investor.

The cash desk trader will use the brokers trading algorithms to execute the single stock order. Then as market conditions change, they will likely execute faster or slower so that they can take advantage of the prevailing market conditions.

For example, the investor sends the cash desk a buy order to trade over the day using a POV algorithm. During trading the stock price increases. The broker determines that based on the stock's trading pattern, real time market conditions, and sector movement that the price is likely to exhibit mean reversion. In this case, the broker will likely reduce the algorithm POV rate and trade slower until prices revert to the stocks fair value, and then continue to trade at the initial rate. If the broker determined that they stock was more likely to exhibit continued momentum throughout the day, they would most likely increase the algorithm POV rate and trade faster to avoid the expected higher prices that toward the end of the day. Here the broker would want to complete the order before prices become too high due to the stock's price momentum.

Program desk

A broker dealer program trading desk is also known as the portfolio trading desk. This desk is utilized by investor who are transacting baskets of stocks also known as trade lists, programs, and portfolios. The baskets may be one-sided and consist of buy orders only or sell orders only, or it may be two-sided and consist of buy orders and sell orders.

Investors who utilize a program desk may not necessarily be concerned about short-term price movement for an individual stock, but rather, they are mostly concerned about the overall cost and performance of the entire basket. In these situations, they rely on the expertise of the program trading desk to manage the overall risk of the trade list. The reason that investors are not necessarily concerned about the performance for an individual stock is because the stocks in the basket are likely providing diversification and risk reduction.

For example, consider a basket that consists of buy and sell orders. As the market increases the buy orders become more expensive but the investor receives better prices for the sell orders which helps to offset the higher cost. As the market decreases the sell orders receive less favorable prices but the investor can transact the buys at a better price which helps to offset the less favorable sell prices. Here, the program desk is most concerned about managing the risk of the overall trade basket to protect the investor from market movement. As trading occurs, program traders will fine tune the trade list based on actual market conditions and seek to maintain a minimum risk position throughout trading.

An important consideration for a program trading is with respect to the type of portfolio risk management used during trading. Program algorithms will commonly employ an optimization algorithm that will balance the overall market impact cost across all stocks in the basket and the timing risk of the basket by incorporating price volatility and correlations across all stocks in the basket. The optimizer will be run throughout the day to ensure that trading strategies are consistent with the investment objective of the fund and will adjust to changing market conditions and price movement.

The trade basket can also be executed using "risk minimization" or "cash balancing" constraints which would be incorporated into the optimization process. A risk minimization constraint will ensure that trades occur so that the unexecuted shares will maintain a minimum level of risk given market conditions and prices. A risk minimization constraint is important for investors who are seeking to achieve a desired outcome such as a targeted return, risk level, or factor exposures. It is used for investment optimization and rebalances.

A cash balancing constraint will ensure that the actual executed shares have an equal dollar value across buys and sells. A cash balancing constraint is appropriate for investor who is using the proceeds from sales to finance the buys. It will ensure that the investor will not have to come up with any additional funds at the end of the day in case of unanticipated market movement or trading halts would could results in a higher dollar value bought than sold. In this case, the investor would need to send the broker additional capital to cover the buys.

It is important to note here that the risk minimization and cash balancing constraints behave in an opposite manner and it is essential that investors properly specify these constraints. For example, the risk minimization constraint will manage the "unexecuted shares" to maintain a minimal level of risk. The cash balancing constrain will manage "actual executions" to ensure that the buy value and sell value are the same.

Electronic desk

The electronic trading desk, also known as the algorithmic trading desk, or simply the "Algo" desk, is the used by investors who wish to trade anonymously and want to have full control of their order. These investors will often utilize an electronic desk at times when they are not anticipating any type of short-term adverse price movement, and when they wish to specify exactly how their order is transacted in the market. Investors will use an electronic trading desk for small and large orders, and for both single stock and baskets.

An investor who is using an electronic desk may will use the same tools and algorithms that are used by the broker's cash and program desks. The only difference is that the investor will set and specify all algorithmic parameters. An advantage of using an electronic trading desk to execute an order is that the investor (buy side trader) can to customize an algorithmic trading strategy exactly for their needs and to best achieve their investment objective without having to convey any information about their investment decision to the broker. A disadvantage of using an electronic trading desk is that the investor (buy side trader) will need to understand the intricacies of each algorithm to be able to properly specify trading instructions, which is not easy.

Investors may also select a broker electronic trading desk to utilize the brokers direct market access (DMA) services. DMA allows the investor to use the same algorithmic trading infrastructure as the broker, connect to the same trading venues and dark pools, and receive messages in the same manner as the broker. Here, investors are required to write their own trading algorithms which will often include the logic behind the buy and sell decisions such as via optimization, quant screens, and statistical arbitrage logic.

Using DMA allows investors to customize their own execution algorithms and often in ways that are not available via the broker algorithms. DMA also allows investors to incorporate their own investment instructions and quantitative models as part of the algorithms without conveying any information about their investment decision-making process to the market.

How does the reason behind the trade influence the selection of the trading algorithm?

To help us understand trading algorithms, and more importantly, which algorithms should be selected for with types of situations, it is important to consider the reason behind the trade. Below we discuss some of the more common reasons behind a trade and the most appropriate algorithms for each.

Short-term alpha view

A portfolio manager with a short-term alpha view is expecting the stock price to either increase or decrease in the short-term and often these price movements will occur very fast. In these situations, the portfolio manager will likely trade aggressively to capture as much of the short-term alpha as possible.

- Investors are best served in these situations by utilizing an aggressive trading algorithm.

Long-term alpha view

A portfolio manager with a long-term alpha view believes that the stock will achieve excess returns and long-term growth but the is currently appropriately priced in the market. In these situations, the portfolio manager will often choose to trade in a more passive manner in order to keep their trading intentions hidden and to minimize information leakage that may cause other market participations to draw the same conclusions about the long-term growth opportunity for the stock and thus increase the stock demand and stock prices in short-term.

- Investors are best served in these situations by utilizing a passive trading algorithm.

Exhibit 6.7 Broker dealer trading desks

	Broker-Deal Trading Desks		
Function	Cash Desk	Program Desk	Electronic Desk
Trading:	Single Stock/Blocks	Programs/Baskets Index/ETFs	Single Stocks/Baskets
Trading Concerns:	Price Movement Alpha	Risk Management Cash Balancing	Liquidity Control/Anonymity
Reason:	Company/Relationships Superior Products/Expertise Research Product Capital Commitment	Company/Relationships Superior Products/Expertise Research Product Risk Bids	Company/Relationships Superior Products/Expertise Algorithmic Products
Sales Team:	Equity Sales Corporate Access	PT Sales Quant Sales	Electronic Sales
Research Team:	Equit Research Economic Research Macro Research Sector Analysts	Quant Research Index Research	TCA Research
Research Products:	Price Targets Earnings Ratings	Quant Screens & Research Index & ETF Research Portfolio Analytics Risk Models/Optimizers Price Targets/Returns Pre- & Post-Trade TCA/Market Impact/Cost Curves Risk Bidding Summary	Pre- & Post-Trade Market Microstructure Portfolio Analytics Quant Research TCA/Market Impact Cost Curves Trade Schedule Optimizer

Stock mispricing

At times stocks may be under- or overvalued in the market. While financial theory and the efficient markets hypothesis leads us to believe that securities are properly valued there are times when stocks may be temporary over- or undervalued. In these situations, investors can take advantage of the temporary mispricing and earn a short-term return.

- Investors are best served in these situations by utilizing an aggressive trading algorithm.

Portfolio optimization

A quantitative portfolio manager is launching a new investment strategy to achieve a targeted rate of return. This manager utilizes a portfolio optimizer to determine the best way to achieve the desired portfolio return by minimizing portfolio risk. This results in a list of stock and share quantities that need to be bought for the portfolio. In these situations, investors can utilize a working order algorithm to balance market impact cost and timing risk and ensure consistency between the trading strategy and the investment objective.

- Investors are best served in these situations by utilizing a working order algorithm that balances the trade-off between market impact cost and timing risk. The level of risk aversion for this algorithm will be selected so that it is consistent with the level of total portfolio risk and the expected Sharpe Ratio of the portfolio.

Portfolio rebalance

A quantitative fund manager has determined that the expected return and risk for the portfolio has drifted away from targeted levels due to random market movement and noise. To bring the portfolio back in-line with expectations the manager rebalances the portfolio through a portfolio optimizer. This result in a basket of stock consisting of buys and sells. In these situations, investors can utilize a working order algorithm to balance market impact cost and timing risk and ensure consistency between the trading strategy and the investment objective.

- Investors are best served in these situations by utilizing a working order algorithm that balances the trade-off between market impact cost and timing risk. Because the trade list will consist of buys and sells, the basket of stock achieves risk reduction through diversification and hedging (from buys and sells). This basket can be transacted in the market in a more passive manner than for the portfolio optimization example above because of the increased risk reduction of the list.

Sector fund

A fund manager will often invest in a specified sector. This investment decision may be motivation may be based on a short-term or long-term view. Here, the manager may feel that the sector overall is a great investment opportunity, but has not uncovered any specific stock. Therefore, the manager will likely investor across all stocks in the sector or across a subset of stocks in the sector. It is important to note here that the investment in the sector fund is to capture alpha from the sector. In these situations, the manager will likely trade aggressively if they have a short-term stock view to capture as much alpha as possible, or will trade passively if they have a long-term view and they do not want to alert the market to what they have uncovered.

- If the sector investment strategy is driven based on a short-term alpha view the manager is best served via an aggressive strategy, and using an arrival or POV algorithm.
- If the sector investment strategy is driven is based on a long-term alpha view the manager is best served via a passive strategy, and using a VWAP or a POV algorithm and accessing dark pools as well as lite venues.

Index change

A change has been made to constitutes of the benchmark index for the manager. In this situation, the index manager will need to buy the stocks that are being added to the index and sell the stocks that are being deleted from the index, even if the manager does not have any short-term or long-term expectations for these stocks. An index manager needs to hold the same stocks as the underlying benchmark index and in the same dollar weights. In this situation, the index manager will utilize a back-loaded and or market on close strategy to minimize the market impact cost of the trade and achieve an average execution price as close to the official closing price as possible.

- Investors are best served utilizing a passive strategy and a Back-Loaded and/or a MOC algorithm.

Cash inflow

A portfolio manager received an inflow of cash to invest in the market. In many times the manager will not have expectations for excess alpha in any stocks, because if they did, they would have likely already shifted investment dollars into these stocks. In this situation, managers will often allocate the cash inflow across the stocks already in the portfolio or a subset of these stocks. The manager will likely trade in a passive manner to minimize market impact cost.

- Investors are best served utilizing a passive strategy with a VWAP or POV algorithm.

Cash redemption

Portfolio managers will, at times, receive a cash redemption call from investors. Here the investor is asking to sell stock so that they can receive the cash proceeds. If investors do not specify what stocks to sell, the portfolio manager may sell shares from all positions in the portfolio or from a subset of the positions in the portfolio. In these situations, the portfolio manager will trade in a passive manner to minimize market impact cost and achieve the highest prices for the positions that are sold.

- Investors are best served utilizing a passive strategy with a VWAP or POV algorithm.

Algorithmic decision-making process

Portfolio managers who utilize algorithms to must be very proactive and must specify exactly how the order is to be transacted. Most importantly, portfolio managers need to ensure that the transaction strategy will be consistent with the investment objective of the fund.

The portfolio manager decisions, also known as the algorithm specifications, need to ensure that the order will be transacted in a manner that is consistent with the investment objective of the fund. For example, if the portfolio manager uncovers a stock with a high short-term alpha estimate will need to trade the order in an aggressive manner to capture as much of the alpha as possible. In this case it would not be appropriate to trade the order in a passive manner because doing so may result in the stock increasing in price before the order is completed. Additionally, if a portfolio manager is trying to capture the closing price on the day because that is how the fund is being valued they will need to trade via a back-loaded or MOC strategy. It would not be appropriate for the manager to trade using a front-loaded strategy or high POV rate because this would result in the order being completed before the end of the day and would expose the fund to market risk.

This is accomplished via an algorithmic decision-making process that consists of portfolio manager decisions and order submission rules.

Portfolio manager decisions

The portfolio manager needs to specify two important criteria for every trade. These are the macro strategy and the micro strategy of the trade and are as follows:

- **Macro strategy.** Portfolio managers need to specify their macro trading decision. First, portfolio managers need to select the benchmark price, (e.g., open price, arrival price, VWAP price, closing price). Second, portfolio managers need to specify how to slice the over time (e.g., using a percentage of volume strategy or using a time slicing strategy). Third, portfolio managers need to specify how fast or how slow to trade the order. In many cases, the macro strategy is embedded in the select of the trading algorithm. The macro strategy is the strategy that provides the fund with the highest likelihood of achieving their investment objective based on expected market conditions. At times, the portfolio manager will specify the macro strategy via a quantitative process. For example, (i) minimize the combination of market impact cost and price appreciation, (ii) balance the trade-off between market impact and timing risk at a specified level of risk aversion, and (iii) determine the strategy that provides the highest likelihood of price improvement.
- **Micro strategy.** The micro strategy consists of specifying how the algorithm is to adapt to changing real time market conditions such as price movement, increasing/decreasing volumes, as well as increasing/decreasing volatility. For example, if a manager has a buy

order and price decreases during the day, the manager may decide to trade more aggressively to take advantage of the better market prices, or the manager may elect to trade more passively if she believes the favorable trend will continue throughout the day.

Order submission rules

The next step in the process is that algorithm needs to define and specify the order submission rules to ensure that actual market trades are consistent with the Macro and Micro decisions specified by the investor. These decisions need to be made in real time, and by using real time data across all exchanges, venues, and dark pools. The order submission rules consist of the limit order model (LOM) and the smart order router (SOR) as are as follows:

- **Limit order model (LOM).** The limit order model determines the appropriate mix of limit orders and market orders for each order slice. It is essential that the portfolio manager reviews the limit order logic of the algorithms they employ to ensure these decisions are consistent with and adhere to the macro and micro decisions. Passive strategies will utilize a greater amount of limit orders and aggressive strategies will utilize a larger amount of market orders.
- **Smart order router (SOR).** The smart order router determines where to route a trade. The SOR will determine the destination with the highest probability of executing the limit order and will determine the venue with the best market price known as the national best bid and offer (NBBO) for market orders. The SOR monitors real time data from exchange and venues, and will also assess activity in dark pool. The SOR is also tasked with evaluating trading quality to ensure that the manager's trading intentions are protected, and that valuable trading information is not being conveyed to the market. The SOR is tasked with determining the trading venue that will maximize the likelihood of achieving a fill or trade at the investor's desired price or better. It also provides whether the order should be routed to an exchange, to a displayed venue, or to a dark pool.

Transaction cost analysis (TCA)

Transaction cost analysis (TCA) provides investors, portfolio managers, traders, and brokers with the necessary information to specify a proper algorithmic trading strategy. TCA is comprised of pre-trade, intraday, and post-trade analysis. Each is a very important part of the implementation phase of the investment cycle. These analytical models are provided to investors as either a web-based system or as a standalone system. Many funds have developed their own TCA analytics that are customized for their specific needs.

These are as follows:

Pre-trade analysis

Pre-trade analysis provides investors with the estimated trading costs of an order. This includes the expected market impact, price appreciation, and timing risk. Traders also use pre-trade analysis to evaluate different trading strategies and algorithms based on trading cost and risk. They also allow investors to incorporate their own market views and proprietary alpha forecasts directly into the analyses so that investors can develop a customized analysis for their specified order. Traders use these functions to perform single stock and portfolio multi-period trade schedule optimization.

- The goal of pre-trade TCA is to provide traders with the necessary information to select the most appropriate algorithm and strategy based on the underlying investment objectives of the fund.

Intraday analysis

Intraday analysis provides investors with the necessary real time analytics to monitor transaction costs during trading. These models provide investors with point in time trading costs estimates (for executed shares) and the projected trading costs that will result from completing the order (for those shares that still need to be executed). This is accomplished by incorporating market momentum and actual market conditions (volume, volatility, and aggregated imbalances) directly into the analysis.

- The goal of Intraday analysis is to provide investors with the necessary information to determine when it is advantageous to take advantage of changing market conditions and favorable opportunities.

Post-trade analysis

Post-trade analysis serves as a report card on the trade. It provides investors with the cost of the trade and an evaluation of the trading performance. Post-trade analysis will include a cost comparison to various price benchmarks (e.g., Arrival, Open, VWAP, Close, $T-1$, and $T+1$) as will also compare actual costs to a pre-trade trading cost estimate for the selected strategy.

Post-trade analysis allows funds to determine how well their brokers and algorithms performed given actual market conditions. Investors can rank their brokers and their algorithms to determine which brokers and algorithms are adding value to the fund, and determine which algorithms and which brokers may be underperforming expectations and causing the fund to incur unnecessary higher trading costs. Investors can compute additional statistics related to the trade such as the relative performance measure (RPM) to help determine which brokers are adding value to the trading process and which brokers are causing funds to incur unnecessary trading costs. Customized post-trade reports provide clients with the ability to sort, filter, and evaluate different trading situations right on their own desktop.

- The goal of Post-Trade analysis is to help investors measure trading costs and evaluate trade performance.
- It also helps investors determine which broker and which broker algorithms provide the best results based on order characteristics and market conditions.

Summary of key points

- This chapter provides students with an overview of the electronic and algorithmic trading environment. Ever since the inception of algorithmic trading, investors have been tasked with having to be much more proactive in their trading decision than ever before. Investors can no longer simply route an order to a broker for execution. Investors need to specify exact execution instructions to the algorithm which dictates exactly how and where the order is to be traded in the market. The most important part of these implementation or trading instructions is that they need to specified so that they are consistent with the investment objective of the fund and the motivation behind the trade and investment decision. Students studying today's financial markets will without question encounter a market structure that is much different than in the past, and a market with a new set of nomenclature and decision rules.
- Unfortunately, the academic theory has not kept up with the rapidly changing financial environment. The goal of this chapter was to provide students with an overview of the electronic and algorithmic trading environment, and how they can make the best possible trading decisions and ensure that there is consistency between the trading goal and the investment decision.
- This chapter covered many different algorithmic trading topics, and all of which are extremely important for trading. Students can use this knowledge to make more informed implementation decisions for their fund, and this in turn, will provide improved portfolio performance. In this chapter, students were introduced to different types of trading algorithms, transaction cost components, market impact, displayed markets and dark pools, and different venue pricing structures.
- Most importantly, students were provided with insight into how to best make trading decisions based on the investment objective of the fund.
- Students can utilize and employ the algorithmic decision-making process presented in this chapter to ensure that they are making the best possible trading decisions for fund. And the lessons learned from this chapter can be directly applied into the financial industry in a professional career.

Keyword definition

Algorithmic trading. Algorithmic trading is the computerized execution of financial instruments following a set of pre-specified trading rules and instructions. These instructions will specify how fast or slow to transact the order in the market, and at what prices, and trading venues. There are three different types of trading algorithms in the market: execution, profit-seeking, and high frequency trading (HFT). Execution algorithms are tasked with implementing and trading an order that was determined outside of the algorithms by a portfolio manager. A profit-seeking algorithm is an algorithm that makes both the investment decision (e.g., buy or sell stocks) based on quantitative models and the implementation decision on how to execute and implement the investment decision. An HFT algorithm will commonly be employed to act as an electronic market maker in stocks by providing the market with bid and ask prices throughout the day and helping to maintain a fair an orderly market.

Transaction costs. Transaction costs are the unavoidable cost of doing business that is not incorporated into the price of the product or service. In economic terms, transaction costs are the dollars paid by buyers but not received by sellers, and the dollars paid by sellers but not received by buyers. In finance, transaction costs are the dollars paid above the decision price for buy orders and the dollar discount below the decision price for sell orders. In the trading environment, there are nine transaction cost components incurred by investors that are not incorporated into the stock price at the time of the investment decision. These are: commission, fees and rebates, spreads, taxes, delay cost, price appreciation cost, market impact cost, timing risk and opportunity cost.

Market impact. Market impact is the movement in the price of the stock caused by the trade or order. Market impact consist of two components: temporary impact and permanent impact. Temporary impact is due to the liquidity demands of the investor where a buyer may need to offer the market a premium to attract additional sellers into the market and/or where a seller may need to discount the price of the stock to make the stock more attractive to purchase. Permanent impact is due to the information content of the trade. In this case, the market may perceive that the investor is buying stock because it is currently undervalued in the market or because the stock is expected to achieve excess future returns. Additionally, the market may perceive that the investor is selling stock because the stock price currently overvalued in the market or because the stock is expected to decline in price. Both cases would likely cause the market to reevaluate the fair value of the stock and we would see the price of the buy order increase and the price of the sell order decrease.

Algorithmic decision-making process. The algorithmic decision-making process is used by investors (traders and portfolio manager) to assist with the selection and specification of algorithm and algorithmic trading parameters. Due to the changing financial landscape and shift to electronic markets, investors need to be very proactive in the trading process and need to ensure that the implementation strategy will continuously be consistent with the investment objective of the fund. As part of the algorithmic decision-making process, investors need to make algorithmic trading decisions at the macro and micro level. Macro decisions specify how the algorithm is to trade over the day to ensure consistent with the investment objective of the fund, and micro decisions specify how the algorithm will adapt to real time market conditions.

In additional to the macro and micro rules, investors need to specify appropriate order submission rules including the limit order model (LOM) which determines the appropriate utilization of limit and market orders, and the smart order router (SOR) which determines which exchanges, venues, and dark pools to route the order for execution.

Exercises

1. The investment cycle consists of asset allocation, portfolio construction, implementation, and portfolio attribution. What is the primary role of the trader as part of the investment cycle?

2. In the financial industry, trading algorithms are often given fun and entertaining names. But unfortunately, these names do not often adequately describe what the algorithm is trying to accomplish or how it will trade. Describe the algorithmic classification scheme from this chapter and how it helps traders determine what the algorithms are trying to accomplish.

3. Describe each of the nine transaction cost components from the chapter and provide an example of how they may arise during trading?

4. Describe a VWAP algorithm and a TWAP algorithm. How are they similar? How are they different?

5. What is a POV algorithm? What are the advantages of a POV algorithm compared to a VWAP algorithm? What are the disadvantages of a POV algorithm compared to a VWAP algorithm?

6. An index investor with a large order is trying to execute shares at the closing price on the day. From the list of algorithms in section "Types of trading algorithms," which algorithm would you select and why?

7. An active manager has determined that stock RLK is appropriately priced in the market but has a very strong long-term growth potential. The manager decided to purchase a large block of RLK shares. From the list of algorithms in section "Types of trading algorithms," which algorithm would you select and why?

8. Describe a Displayed "Lite" Venue. Describe a Dark Pool. Why would an investor choose to trade in a displayed market such as an exchange or ATS? Why would an investor choose to trade in a dark pool?

9. Describe each of the three venue pricing models: commission-based, maker-taker, inverted maker-take. Why would an investor choose to use a maker-taker venue? Why would an investor choose to use an inverted maker-taker model? Why would an investor choose to use a commission-based model?

10. Describe each of the following algorithm order slicing strategies (i) time-based, (ii) volume-based, and (iii) price-based.

CHAPTER 7

Presentations

Reports and presentations are a part of any business. Nearly all business units make internal reports and presentations as a way to share information or support a decision. Client-facing business units also make external presentations as part of their efforts to develop new business (i.e., sell products or services) and provide service or support to existing business relationships. At their best, presentations provide information in its most useful form by distilling a thorough understanding of the subject matter into its most relevant points for a particular situation or audience. This chapter provides a discussion of the various types of presentations and reports that are prepared and made by investment organizations in general and student-managed investment funds in particular.

We classify presentations into two general groups: internal presentations and external presentations. Internal presentations are those targeted primarily at constituencies within the organization, such as reports or presentations within a team or by a team for the rest of the organization. Internal presentations, especially within a student-managed investment fund, often serve the purpose of sharing information with the goal of making a key business or investment decision, such as the purchase or sale of a security. External presentations are those targeted at external constituencies, such as clients, prospective clients, oversight boards, or, in the case of student-managed investment funds, interested alumni. As stated above, external presentations often have the purpose of gaining or retaining business or otherwise affecting the organization's external image and future opportunities.

Among the most important internal presentations for a student-managed investment fund are those involving security selection and portfolio construction decisions. As such, this chapter builds on important aspects of the material discussed in Chapters 2 and 4. External presentations can encompass all activities of an investment organization, including its organization structure, but usually have a particular emphasis on the organization's investment philosophy and process, security selection and portfolio construction, and performance. Performance analysis and reporting are important both internally and externally—so important that the material merits the sole attention of Chapter 8.

The practice and experience in making professional presentations in a business setting are among the key benefits to any student participating in a student-managed investment fund. Though this chapter focuses on presentations that support the business of investment

Student-Managed Investment Funds. https://doi.org/10.1016/B978-0-12-817866-9.00007-8

organizations, the presentation skills and experience are applicable to any business, not just investment firms. While the substance of the presentation is derived from the activities involved in managing a portfolio, the lessons from the development and delivery of such reports and presentations are universal.

Internal presentations

For most student-managed investment funds, internal reports and presentations are a key step in making a decision to buy or sell a security. Indeed, some funds require votes under majority rules prior to making a trade. These votes are typically taken at some point after an analyst's report is filed and/or a presentation is made. Given their prominent role, we discuss the elements of such presentations and provide several examples. As discussed earlier in this book, it is important that the content of such presentations be motivated by and consistent with the investment organization's investment philosophy and process. Specifically, most fundamental investment processes should not have reports or presentations that contain quantitative analysis of stock price trends or discussion of elaborate factor models. Rather, reports from such processes would emphasize the fundamental elements that contribute to the investment thesis within the framework of the organization's investment philosophy and process.

We begin by discussing the research report, which is also commonly referred to as an analyst report. Such reports are typical among investment organizations that employ a fundamental investment approach.

Exhibit 7.1 shows an overview of the requirements for security reports as part of the Practicum in Portfolio Management to support Baylor University's student-management investment fund, the Philip M. Dorr Alumni and Friends Endowment Investment Fund. Guidelines such as those in Exhibit 7.1 help assure consistency across securities, fund members, and time within the same organization. Most investment and investment banking firms have such guidelines for reports by their employees. Standards such as these also help share information efficiently, as members of the organization know where certain information will be in the report.

We also note that the guidelines emphasize the importance of being concise. Einstein was known to say, "If I had more time, I would have written a shorter letter." A similar idea applies to all presentations and reports. Even complex ideas can be distilled into their most important elements. Likewise, the investment thesis should be focused on the key elements that lead to the buy, sell, or hold decision. Finally, the report is organized in a clear manner that provides a summary early in the report, along with supporting information throughout the report. By summarizing the investment thesis early on, readers are able to see how the later information helps justify the investment thesis.

Before proceeding to a discussion of specific student-managed investment fund presentations, we discuss considerations in preparing and making such presentations. The list below is

---

Exhibit 7.1 Baylor project guidelines

Remember: A picture says a thousand words. Always be looking for concepts that can be displayed graphically in the form of a table, chart, or graph. Also, follow the page counts listed here. Do not exceed 8 pages plus appendices. Part of a good research report is making your case concisely.

Page 1
Always use the cover page found on the class web page!

Company description
A short description of the company's basic business or businesses. Should be 3–7 lines in length. Should be exclusively factual and should offer no opinions about the company. What do they do?

Bullet points
Look at the cover page example on the web page. Except for Bullet #4, these should be very general and should touch only on the broadest and most important points. Few specific details should be given, as these will appear later on in the report. The goal of Bullet points 1–3 is to tell the most important reasons why a potential investor might want to read the rest of the report or invest in the company. Why is this a good idea?
Bullet point #4 should be similar to every other Bullet #4 in all of our research reports. This gives basic valuations, earnings estimates, the method for valuing the stock, and a price target. See language from example on the web page.

Page 2
Investment opinion
This should be about one page in length, and should expand on the first 3 Bullet points. This section should introduce new ideas about the potential investment merits of the company, as well as giving more specific details about some points already introduced in Bullet points 1–3. In general, this section should be starting to give more specific details about the most important points to the story. However, the focus of this section should continue to be on the main reasons why an investor should invest in the company or industry.

Page 3
Valuation
This section should be 1/3 to 1/2 of a page, and should expand on the fourth bullet point. This should include valuations based on price/book, price/sales, price/earnings, and/or price/cash flow, PEG ratio, equity duration, earnings growth rate estimates, ROE, historical earnings growth, historical trading range, ROA, insider trading, % of insider and institutional holdings, along with earnings revisions and earnings surprise, if possible. These must be compared to the company's industry/SIC code and the appropriate benchmark—i.e., S&P 500 or Russell 2000. Can also compare to other stocks within the industry. This may also include a price target.

Company background
This section should be 1/3 to 1/2 of a page, and should also be very similar to other Company Background sections in our other research reports. This should include details on when the company was formed, the company's IPO, any secondary offerings, private placements or other financings, merger and acquisition activities, and/or spin-offs.

Page 4

Company overview

This section should be one page in length. This section is the heart of the report and includes virtually all details about the company and any operating divisions/subsidiaries. Often included are subsections describing each clearly segmented division. These subsections can include separate pro-formas projecting the financial results for each subsidiary. This section should include discussion of competitive (dis)advantages, barriers to entry, international opportunities, clients, suppliers, distribution system, seasonal or cyclical trends, proprietary technology, the company's long-term growth strategy, etc.

Page 5

Competition

If the company has several publicly traded competitors, this should be a separate section. This section should include a brief 1/3 to 1/2 page description of the competition and a table of their relative valuations. If there are no good comparison companies, a brief description of the competition can be included in the company overview section.

Shareholders

This table should include the holdings of key management and employees. This can be found in the proxy statement. This should also include options or warrants outstanding, as well as major institutional shareholders.

Management

This should include a brief 3–5 line description of the background of the key management members. A one-line description of each member of the Board is also preferred. This information can generally be found in the proxy statement or the annual report.

Page 6

Industry overview

Depending on the company, this section should be one page in length. This should include a fairly detailed description of the trends in the industry, such as consolidation, or other driving factors. This should include the impact of competing or new technology, competition, consumer behavior, etc.

Page 7

Income statement comments

This section should give descriptions of the most recent quarterly period that has been reported, unless it was the fourth quarter, and/or descriptions of the most recent fiscal year end. The focus of this discussion should be to highlight items that are not obvious at first glance. These include reasons for increases (decreases) in sales, one-time gains or losses, reasons for increases/decreases in expenses, etc. This section should also include a discussion of these same concepts that are in the projected results (e.g., if a large one-time gain is expected or a description of the assumptions underlying the earnings estimates). The language should be fairly dry, and should be similar to our other research reports. The information can be obtained from the annual reports, 10-K, or 10-Q.

Balance sheet comments

This section should be very brief, and should only include a discussion of anything that is out of the ordinary. This includes loans to officers, low levels of cash or working capital, high debt, etc. Many times, no discussion about the balance sheet is needed.

Page 8

Key growth drivers

A minimum of 1/2 page should be devoted to an analysis of why you believe the current analyst forecast for earnings growth is accurate or inaccurate. This should be done by examining what drives the growth in the forecast and your assessment of whether that growth can be accomplished.

Risks of investing in this security—What can go wrong?

Much of this information is generic to small cap stocks, such as the risk of the loss of a key management member. Many of these will be the same for all companies, and can be taken directly from our other reports. A discussion of risks that are specific to the company or industry should also be included. A prospectus from a recent IPO or secondary offering is the best place to get ideas of the major risks to a story.

Appendix

Financial statements

In general, the report should contain a quarterly income statement, an annual income statement, and a balance sheet.

The balance sheet should contain only the line items found in the company's 10-K, and should include 2 years of audited year-end information (most recent 10-K) and the most recent unaudited quarterly information (most recent 10-Q). If the last period reported was a year-end, it should contain 3 years of audited year-end information.

The quarterly income statement should include a full year of historical quarterly information, the current year (including estimates), and a future year of quarterly projections. We do not normally project more than 4 quarters in the future, so the periods presented are subject to change depending on where the company is in its fiscal year. The 4Q for historical periods is derived by subtracting the results through the IS 9 months (3Q 10-Q) from the year-end totals (10-K). The annual income statement should contain at least 3 years of historical information and 2–3 years of projections. This should also include an abbreviated cash flow statement (cash flow net income + depreciation/amortization/non-cash expenses) and an abbreviated free cash flow statement (free cash flow = cash flow − capital expenditures).

All of these cash flow figures can be found in the statement of cash flows in the 10-K.

---

purposefully general and primarily stylistic. As such, the suggestions apply to most business presentations. However, these suggestions should not be dismissed or minimized because they focus on style. To the contrary, by following these suggestions, the substance of the presentation should be clearer and more effectively communicated to the audience.

General presentation style and delivery guidelines

1. There should always be (1) an introduction; (2) a body; and (3) a conclusion. The key point of the presentation should be made in each of the three sections. Some describe this rule as, "Tell 'em what you're going to tell 'em. Tell 'em. And then tell 'em what you told 'em."

People remember things that are repeated and this makes clearer to the audience what the presenter thinks his or her key points are. Telling the audience a summary of the key points up front allows the audience to know what to look for in the presentation. By telling them what the key points are (or were) again at the end of the presentation, it leaves them with a reminder.

2. Have clear "takeaways" or "messages" for each presentation. If someone sees and hears the presentation, what are the three or four main points that you want them to realize and remember? Have those points been made clearly in the presentation? Have other points that are not important been made that can be dropped or otherwise minimized? Even if there is a related point that can be made, the decision of whether to include it should be made based on whether the point contributes to the main points of the presentation. This rule can also apply at the section, page, or paragraph level of a report or at the slide level of a presentation. That is, the takeaway or point of each slide should be clear, or the relevance of the slide should be questioned.

3. Slides should …
   a. be clean and not cluttered.
   b. be easy to read from the back of the room. Make sure the font size is large enough, especially on tables and figures that are important.
   c. have bullet points, not long sentences and/or paragraphs.
   d. have a specific purpose or point to make in the presentation.
   e. have a simple and consistent color scheme. More colors are not necessarily better. Also, follow traditional norms with color. Green is usually used to denote a positive value, an upward movement, or something "good." Red usually indicates a negative number, downward movement, etc. Yellow or orange often convey caution. It is best not to report numbers in all red or all green. Color can help add emphasis and should be used accordingly, not for color's sake alone.
   f. have a simple and consistent format. Titles should appear in the same place consistently throughout the presentation. Likewise, the location and formatting of summary or highlight points should be consistent. For example, callout boxes highlighting points might always appear in the right margin. One or two fonts should be chosen that are easy to read. One font can be used for regular text; the other font can be used for emphasis or for special text, such as quotations.
   g. have page numbers. Even when slides are projected and under the control of the presenter, page numbers allow the audience to refer to a specific slide for a question or clarification.

4. Observe the rules of proportionality. Spend time and space on a slide or in the presentation in proportion to the importance of a point or topic. If something is not very important in a 10-min presentation, then do not spend 5 min on it. If something is one of the three key points, then it should have roughly a third of the presentation's time spent on it. By spending too much time on an unimportant point, the audience might infer that the point is

more important than it is. By spending too little time on a point, the audience might infer that the point is of less importance than it is.

5. Be on time. This means many things. Of course, be on time for the presentation. But also be on time in ending the presentation without having to rush at the end (or in the middle, or at the beginning). If the presentation is too long, do not just try to go faster. Instead, whittle the presentation down to its most important aspects or points. Prepare the presentation so that it is concise and to-the-point.

6. Do not read the slides to the audience. This does not mean one or two bullet points or quotes cannot be read verbatim for special emphasis of a point. Keep in mind that the audience can read. It is up to the presenter to fill in the blanks with meaningful discussion, added detail, clarification and emphasis relating to what is on the slide.

7. Give a presentation, not a speech. A presentation involves *sharing* what the presenter understands and what is in his or her head, not what is on a note card or a script. Sharing is an interactive exercise between at least two parties. The audience is important in this exercise and cues should be taken from them. The slides should serve as the presenter's outline, reminding the presenter of the intended talking points. The presenter should know everything else and be able to say what needs to be said from memory, without having memorized specific sentences. Audience feedback, both direct (e.g., questions) and indirect (e.g., body language), can help to steer a presentation. The presenter has the flexibility to alter the delivery of the presentation to best communicate with a particular audience.

8. Keep everyone on the same page. It is common to give a business presentation to an audience that is following the presentation on paper without the benefit of a projected image. In these cases, the audience usually would have a hard copy of the presentation (e.g., in a spiral-bound book or packet). The presenter should, in such cases, explicitly refer to the page number, especially when moving to a new page. For example, the presenter might say, "Turning to page 6, we list the portfolio holdings as of …" or "The graph at the top of page 3 depicts …" or "As indicated in the three bullet points on page 12, …." Be aware if the audience is confused about a slide. Unless later slides help clarify the point, try to resolve the confusion before moving on.

Exhibit 7.2 shows the guidelines for reports in TCU's Educational Investment Fund. The report and its accompanying presentation that are described in this exhibit reflect the investment process discussed in the extended example of security analysis and selection from the TCU-EIF in Chapter 2. Notice that the TCU and Baylor report guidelines both emphasize a discussion of the company and its competitors or competitive environment. The TCU-EIF report also calls for the assumptions used in valuing the security to be explicitly spelled out. As discussed in Chapter 2, the assumptions that go into a valuation model are key in determining the resulting valuation of the security. By having the assumptions clearly stated in the report, readers can judge whether they agree with the valuation in large part based on whether they believe that the inputs and assumptions are reasonable. Both TCU and Baylor

Exhibit 7.2 Texas Christian University's educational investment fund written report and presentation guidelines

By Stanley Block, Larry Lockwood and Jill Foote

The written report

Elements of the written report include the following:

Original purchase rationale: If the stock is an existing holding within the portfolio, the report explains the rationale employed by the student analyst at the time of the purchase. Also, this section is used to see if the factors influencing the original purchase have changed since the original purchase.

Portfolio considerations: The written report describes how the stock fits into the portfolio from a diversification perspective (e.g., lists the current allocation of the fund to the equity sector of the stock, compares current allocation versus the fund's equity sector target).

Industry overview: This section of the student's report discusses recent events within the industry with particular focus on changing trends.

Porter competitive analysis: The competitive forces governing the industry are examined and explained in detail using Porter's Five Forces (power of buyers, sellers, substitutes, potential entrants, and existing competitors). The model allows for the members to see any potential headwinds the company might face going forward. While the "forces" are always changing, an understanding of what the company faces going forward allows for a better feel for future performance. This section provides an overall view of the strength or fragility of the industry and constituent company earnings sustainability.

Company overview: This section begins with a brief discussion of the company's history. Then we examine data related to the company's business segments. We include recent news events, especially those that had significant effects on stock valuation, including recent quarterly performance. This section includes the investment recommendation of the student analyst, along with a discussion of the pros and cons to the recommendation, the latter of which force the analyst to consider factors that move counter to his or her investment recommendation.

Pro forma income statements: This section includes the forecasts of all key income statement variables for the next 3 years, along with a discussion of the assumptions used when deriving the forecasts. The discussion of the assumptions must be specific and quantifiable.

Ratio analysis: These include ratios indicating liquidity (current ratio, quick ratio, accounts receivable), asset utilization (accounts receivable turnover, inventory turnover, total asset turnover), debt utilization (long-term debt to equity, total debt to equity, times interest earned), profitability (gross profit margin, ROE, ROA), valuation ratios (P/E, price-to-book ratio, price-to-cash flow, etc.). We present the ratios for each of the past 3 years for the company under consideration and for the most appropriate competitor and for the industry average in which the subject company operates.

DuPont analysis: We include a separate section reporting the net profit margin, asset turnover, financial leverage, and return on equity. We use averages of all balance sheet numbers in our DuPont Analysis to adjust for companies that might have experienced large changes in assets during the year. The Dupont Analysis allows a nice comparison of the drivers of profitability across time and across competitors.

Valuation assumptions: This section includes a listing of the risk-free rate, market risk premium, beta, and forecasts of earnings per share, dividends, P/E, and free cash flow to equity. Valuation of the stock and sensitivity analyses for the valuation also are presented. Indication of whether the stock is overvalued or undervalued according to the analysis is provided in this section. *Statistical appendix*: An appendix is included for all other valuation considerations including but not limited to historical regression results over the past 60 months, calculation of PEG ratios, alpha, PVGO, earnings growth rates over the past 3 years, and price-to-sales, price-to-cash flow, price-to-book value, and price-to-EBITDA comparisons.

The presentation
After the financial model and the written report are prepared and distributed to fund members (at least 2 days in advance), the student analyst presents his or her findings and recommendation to the class members. The presentation lasts approximately 20 min and is followed by a 20-min question and answer period in which each fund member is expected to participate. After the Q&A, a vote is taken and the recommendation either passes or fails based on a majority rule.

---

utilize an Appendix for more detailed information that might be relevant to some readers or consumers of the report.

Finally, the TCU guidelines provide a discussion of the presentation that supports the research report. The guidelines explicitly contemplate and encourage discussion among the EIF members through questions and answers. The presentation culminates in a vote on the recommendation contained in the report and supported by the presentation. As such, the report and the presentation are the key inputs into the fund's investment decisions. Returning to Baylor's fund, Exhibit 7.3 shows an outline for internal presentations. Again, the existence of a standardized presentation outline assures consistency within the organization. Furthermore, the outline provides a useful checklist that the fund members can use in security analysis and research.

The outline in Exhibit 7.3 is implemented in the presentation shown in Exhibit 7.4. This extended example documents the security selection on stocks from various sub-sectors within the Financials sector in Baylor's fund. There are many noteworthy aspects of this presentation. First, note that presentation generally adheres to many of the applicable stylistic guidelines above. Specifically, the presentation utilizes a consistent style and format. Second, the presentation progresses through the selection of securities in several sub-sectors within the Financials sector. This allows the audience to clearly follow the investment process steps as securities are screened or filtered to arrive at a short list. Once the list has narrowed to two or three securities, specific information is presented about each one.

The presentation in Exhibit 7.4 is also careful to point out recent developments, financial data, and valuation information before presenting a SWOT analysis of the candidate securities. SWOT stands for Strengths, Weaknesses, Opportunities, and Threats. SWOT analysis is a useful framework for summarizing important return and risk considerations when selecting a security. The strengths and weaknesses of a company relate to its ongoing business and existing

---

Exhibit 7.3 Baylor University's general presentation guidelines

The presentations should cover the following material plus any other material information particular to that stock—e.g., lawsuits, etc.

1. Outline of presentation.
2. List current holdings in sector and weight in Dorr Portfolio.
3. List current weight of sector in S&P 500.
4. Filters to reduce stocks in your sector to perhaps eight.
5. Reduce stocks using to one stock (or two if you recommend purchasing two) usually based on fundamental analysis.
6. Company overview.
7. Description of the firm's business model.
8. Discussion of firm's major areas and discussion of prospects and plans.
9. Price chart(s). See BigCharts.com.
10. Ratios including P/E, P/Book, P/CF, P/Sales; long-term projected growth rate; and a PEG ratio. The P/E should be P/forward earnings. These ratios for the firm should be compared to similar ratios for S&P 500, sector or industry, and the firm's major competitors.
11. List of earnings revisions and the up-down ratio probably for the past 30 days.
12. Perhaps the earnings surprise for the most recent quarter.
13. Discuss the CEO or management team.
14. List of growth drivers.
15. List of risks for the stock.
16. Advisor's input.
17. Your recommendation. Hold, sell now, or sell later if we find a better stock.

---

products and/or services. These aspects are typically internally focused and considered to be under the control of the firm itself. The opportunities and threats assess the interactions of the company with the economy, marketplace, or industry that represent potential for gains or losses. After summarizing the rationale and providing input from the faculty advisor, the presentation makes a clear recommendation to buy, hold, pass, or sell the subject securities. By making a clear recommendation, the presentation sets the stage for further discussion and a final vote.

Exhibit 7.5 contains three examples of meeting summaries that were created to memorialize internal presentations, such as the one presented in Exhibit 7.4. Minutes or meeting reports provide important documentation of the discussion surrounding the presentation. While these are not transcripts of the meetings, these reports note significant issues or questions that are raised during the presentation. As indicated elsewhere in this book, saving such reports, presentations, and summaries provides for the "institutional memory" for an organization that would otherwise have little. As discussed in Chapter 8, there are tools available to store and share such documents within an organization. It is important to facilitate access to this documentation for future members of the student-managed investment fund so that they can

Exhibit 7.4 Information technology sector presentation from Baylor University

Information Technology

Spring 2019

Agenda

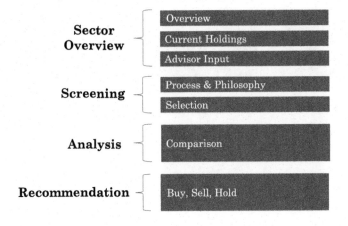

Current Holdings – As of February 4th

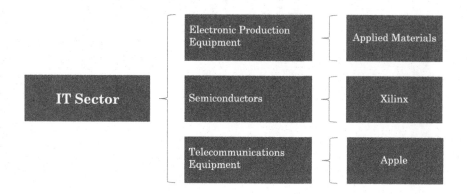

Current Holdings – As of March 14th

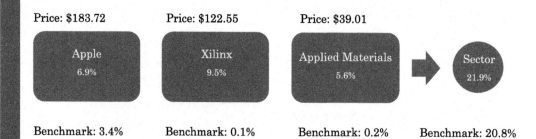

Purchase Rationale

- Apple:
  - Long Term Value Creation
  - Strong Diversified Growth

- Xilinx:
  - Strong innovation at company and product level
  - Strategic position in industry
  - Diversified revenue streams creating strong performance despite volatility

- Applied Materials:
  - Fairly Priced
  - Innovation and Gain Potential

Xilinx

Xilinx: Stock Price (3 Year)

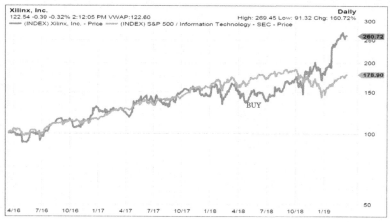

Source: FactSet

Xilinx: Product Segments

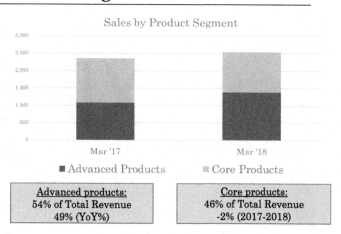

Advanced products:	Core products:
54% of Total Revenue	46% of Total Revenue
49% (YoY%)	-2% (2017-2018)

Applied Materials

Applied Materials: Stock Price (3 Year)

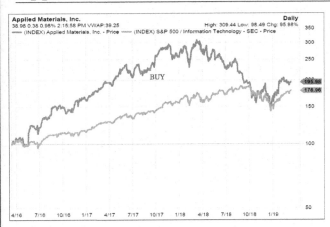

Source: FactSet

Applied Materials: Opportunity

- "Much as PCs and smartphones drove earlier stages of demand for semiconductors, we expect IoT, AR/VR, Big Data, and AI to drive demand for semiconductor manufacturing solutions for years to come."

- "The company's increasingly efficient operations and growing volume leverage are leading to expanded margins and accelerating profit growth."

- Display Equipment segment has grown at a 25% CAGR over past 6 years.

Source: Argus Report

Apple

Apple: Stock Price (3 Year)

Source: FactSet

Apple: Opportunity

Revenue outside of iPhone business grew by almost 19% year-over-year.

- Wearables grew by almost 50%.
- Services generated over $10.8 billion in revenue in Q4'18: a new quarterly record in every geographic segment.

Source: 10-K and Open Letter to Investors

Apple: Current News

- Price movement: $166.52 => $183.72
- Now offering interest-free loans for Chinese customers who are deterred by high prices.
- Expected to announce new TV streaming service and News Subscription service on March 25
- Laserlike acquisition (machine learning startup)
- Negative sentiment beginning to reverse
  - March 11: Merrill Lynch increases target price from $180 to $210 and gives buy rating
  - March 14: Cowen raises target price to $220

Source: SeekingAlpha

Analyst Input

- Sector-wide screen may not be effective due to vast differences in growth indicators across industries
  - Revenue Growth in the Software space
  - Strong Cash flows in the Hardware space
- Good companies should demonstrate consistent growth trends over past 5-10 years
- Good companies should have lower standard deviation of sales growth over time
- Good companies should have high Gross margin, ROE, and ROC

Screening Methodology

- Back-test the cumulative returns of each IT industry against the cumulative returns of the IT sector.
    - Philosophy: we want exposure to the best performing industries in the IT sector.
    - Method: create an equal-weighted portfolio composed of each firm in a specified industry, rebalance monthly, and compare cumulative returns of the portfolio to those of the IT Sector.
- Results of Back-test: the Semiconductor Devices industry (14 firms, on average) and Software industry (14 firms, on average) have outperformed the S&P 500 Info Tech index over the past 3 years.

Semiconductor Devices (3 Years)

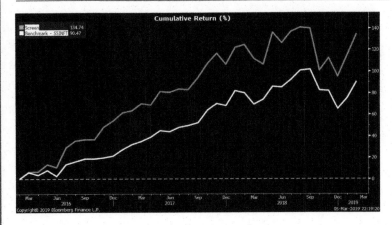

Source: Bloomberg

Software (3 Years)

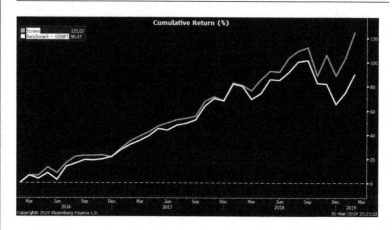

Source: Bloomberg

Semiconductor Devices Rank

Ticker	Short Name	Rank(LF ROE)	Rank(Current FCF Yld)	Rank(Latest Quarterly GM)	ROE LF	FCF Yld	GM:Q
TXN US	TEXAS INSTRUMENT	1	6	3	57.31%	5.87%	64.76%
MU US	MICRON TECH	2	1	6	52.29%	20.38%	58.32%
AVGO US	BROADCOM INC	3	3	10	52.23%	7.23%	53.91%
NVDA US	NVIDIA CORP	4	10	9	49.27%	3.38%	54.74%
MXIM US	MAXIM INTEGRATED	5	9	4	38.34%	4.95%	64.66%
AMD US	ADV MICRO DEVICE	6	14	14	36.20%	-0.60%	37.84%
XLNX US	XILINX INC	7	11	1	32.42%	3.13%	69.01%
INTC US	INTEL CORP	8	7	5	29.07%	5.83%	60.18%
SWKS US	SKYWORKS SOLUTIO	9	5	12	28.54%	6.34%	49.91%
IPGP US	IPG PHOTONICS	10	12	11	19.11%	2.84%	50.52%
QCOM US	QUALCOMM INC	11	13	8	15.66%	2.20%	54.81%
ADI US	ANALOG DEVICES	12	8	2	14.43%	5.40%	67.46%
MCHP US	MICROCHIP TECH	13	4	7	7.86%	6.76%	56.71%
QRVO US	QORVO INC	14	2	13	1.26%	7.54%	40.65%

Source: Bloomberg

Software Rank

Ticker	Short Name	Rank(Latest Quarterly Rev - 1 Yr Gr)	Rank(LF GM - 5 Yr Geo Gr)	Rank(Latest Quarterly ROE - 5 Yr Geo Gr)	Rev - 1 Yr Gr:Q	GM - 5 Yr Geo Gr LF	ROE - 5 Yr Geo Gr:Q
ANSS US	ANSYS INC	1	1	8	37.41%	1.55%	7.32%
ADSK US	AUTODESK INC	2	6	N.A	33.13%	0.41%	N.A
CRM US	SALESFORCE.COM	3	11	N.A	26.36%	-0.63%	N.A
ADBE US	ADOBE INC	4	8	2	22.83%	-0.10%	46.34%
FTNT US	FORTINET INC	5	2	3	21.68%	1.41%	38.76%
CDNS US	CADENCE DESIGN	6	5	5	13.58%	0.54%	13.87%
RHT US	RED HAT INC	7	7	7	13.21%	0.14%	10.58%
MSFT US	MICROSOFT CORP	8	14	9	12.29%	-1.39%	6.33%
INTU US	INTUIT INC	9	3	4	12.17%	0.78%	19.82%
AKAM US	AKAMAI TECHNOLOG	10	12	10	8.34%	-1.02%	-5.05%
SNPS US	SYNOPSYS INC	11	10	6	6.63%	-0.37%	13.51%
CTXS US	CITRIX SYSTEMS	12	4	1	3.09%	0.70%	47.89%
ORCL US	ORACLE CORP	14	9	11	-0.28%	-0.36%	-18.45%

Source: Bloomberg

Screening Elimination

Company	
Texas Instruments	Weak growth drivers; Dividend payout ratio is at 50% over 5 years.
Micron Technology	Pricing volatility; over-exposure to memory industry; trade war issues
Broadcom Inc.	**Selected**
Ansys Inc.	**Selected**
Adobe Inc.	Currently initiating competition with MSFT and AAPL; not an industry leader; most of growth from acquisitions
Fortinet Inc.	Trades at a premium to peers; high P/B; growth drivers are weak

Final Selections

Broadcom, Inc.

Broadcom: Company Profile

- Founded in 1961, Broadcom Inc. is a leading provider of semiconductor and infrastructure solutions.
- Broadcom Inc. business segments include:
  - Wired Infrastructure
  - Wireless Communications
  - Enterprise Storage
  - Industrial & Other
- In April, 2018, relocated from Singapore to San Jose, CA.

Source: Argus Report, FactSet

Broadcom: Management

Hock E. Tan, President, Chief Executive Officer & Director of Broadcom

Thomas Harry Krause Jr, Chief Financial Officer of Broadcom

Boon Chye Ooi, Senior Vice President of Global Operations at Broadcom

Source: FactSet

Broadcom: Investment Thesis

BUY
- Moving from saturated mobile device industry toward enterprise and cloud data center industries in order to continue growth.
- Recent acquisitions and partnerships reflect growth in enterprise storage space.
- Positive margin outlook going forward.
- Above-average growth with discounted valuation multiples.

Broadcom: Revenue Streams

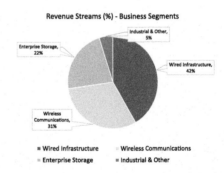

Source: FactSet

Broadcom: Revenue Streams

Total Revenue (%) - Geographic

United States, 13%

Other, 38%

China, 49%

▪ United States   ▪ China   ▫ Other

Source: FactSet

Broadcom: Opportunity

- November 5, 2018: Acquisition of CA Technologies
- Everything-as-a-service (XaaS) offerings through PLAs (Portfolio License Agreement)
  - Ex: Barclays
- Expansion into the cloud data center industry and away from mobile devices

Source: FactSet, Globe News Wire

Broadcom: Risk

- The CA deal adds $18 Billion in new debt, increasing LT Debt to $36-37 Billion.
- Market skepticism toward CA deal initially created a downward pull on stock price, indicating concern for Balance Sheet debt position.
  - Stock Price recovered within 3 months and is currently at a high.
  - Residual skepticism persists.
- Concentrated Customer base
- Shifting focus toward Infrastructure Technology from Semiconductor Solutions

Source: FactSet

Broadcom: Balance Sheet Analysis

Balance Sheet Analysis	OCT '18	OCT '17	OCT '16	OCT '15	OCT '14
Current Ratio	3.90	6.26	2.31	3.37	3.77
Quick Ratio	3.41	5.68	1.86	2.91	3.26
Cash Ratio	1.84	4.43	1.01	1.65	1.60
Cash & ST Inv/Current Assets (%)	47.13	70.81	43.47	48.82	42.45
CFO/Current Liabilities (%)	379.81	259.04	110.82	207.15	115.65

Source: FactSet

Broadcom: Earnings Analysis

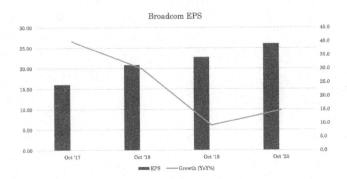

Source: FactSet

Broadcom: Earnings Analysis

Source: FactSet

Broadcom: Earnings Analysis

Broadcom Earnings Revisions

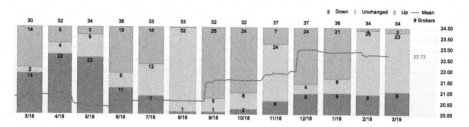

Source: FactSet

Broadcom: Competition

Broadcom: Valuation

Valuation	OCT '18	OCT '17	OCT '16	OCT '15	OCT '14
Price/Sales	4.53	6.06	4.90	5.07	5.39
Price/Earnings	7.47	60.72	-	23.59	82.14
Price/Book Value	3.35	5.11	3.57	7.22	6.76
Price/Tangible Book Value	-	-	-	-	-
Price/Cash Flow	10.63	16.31	19.03	14.93	19.60
Price/Free Cash Flow	11.45	19.49	24.15	20.06	30.06
Dividend Yield (%)	3.20	1.61	1.14	1.26	1.31
Enterprise Value/EBIT	21.69	42.55	107.19	22.81	41.56
Enterprise Value/EBITDA	12.37	15.42	21.97	15.01	22.34
Enterprise Value/Sales	5.61	6.48	6.34	6.18	6.90
Total Debt/Enterprise Value	0.15	0.15	0.16	0.09	0.19

Source: FactSet

Broadcom: Valuation

Company Name	Fiscal Period	Price	Market Value	Enterprise Value	Sales	EV/EBIT	EV/EBITDA
Broadcom	11/04/2018	265.51	105,170.0	118,371.0	20,848.0	21.97x	12.53x
Average		79.32	109,838.1	116,753.8	28,590.4	16.21x	12.25x
Median		79.49	81,943.4	85,396.4	18,645.0	15.65x	12.55x
QUALCOMM	12/30/2018	54.03	65,392.8	71,463.8	21,506.0	16.50x	12.15x
Texas Instruments	12/31/2018	104.95	98,494.0	99,329.0	15,784.0	14.79x	12.95x
Analog Devices	02/02/2019	105.68	38,923.4	44,552.1	6,223.4	22.68x	16.11x
Intel	12/29/2018	52.60	236,542.0	251,670.0	70,848.0	10.85x	7.80x

Source: FactSet

Broadcom: Valuation

Broadcom Free Cash Flow Yield - LTM

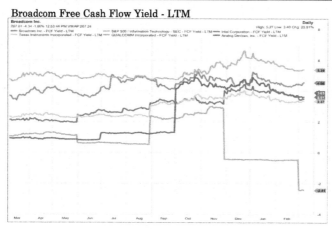

Source: FactSet

Broadcom: Valuation

Broadcom Free Cash Flow Yield - NTM

Source: FactSet

Broadcom: Valuation

Broadcom P/E- LTM

Source: FactSet

Broadcom: Valuation

Broadcom P/E- NTM

Source: FactSet

Broadcom: Valuation

Broadcom P/E- FY2

Source: FactSet

Broadcom: Stock Price (3 Year)

Source: FactSet

Broadcom: Comparison to Xilinx

Broadcom: Comparison to Xilinx

Broadcom:
- Movement towards "Everything-as-a-service" (XaaS)
- Movement towards being an Infrastructure Software Solutions company in addition to a Semiconductors Solutions company
- Acquisition of CA Technologies

Xilinx:
- Movement towards "FPGA-as-a-service"
- Acquisition of DeePhi Tech
- Strong management team

Broadcom: Opportunities and Weaknesses

Opportunities:
- Infrastructure Software Solutions
- PLAs
- Full reversal of negative sentiment

Weaknesses:
- Added debt to balance sheet
- Vulnerability of shifting business segments
- Size

Xilinx: Opportunities and Weaknesses

Opportunities:
- FPGA-as-a-service movement
- Involvement in AI and IoT innovation (DeePhi Tech)
- Momentum

Weaknesses:
- Dependence upon others for manufacturing and sales
- Potential premium reversal
- Cash Flow

Broadcom: Price Comparison to Xilinx

Source: FactSet

Broadcom: PE Comparison to Xilinx

Source: FactSet

Broadcom: FCFY Comparison to Xilinx

Source: FactSet

Broadcom: Purchase Rationale

- Broadcom has a similar story to Xilinx
  - Development into an XaaS company
  - Movement into high-growth industries
  - Extensive experience of management

- Broadcom has more long-term growth potential than Xilinx
  - Xilinx stock appreciation is slowing
  - Broadcom stock is primed for appreciation
  - Broadcom growth more diversified

- Broadcom has strong Free Cash Flow Yield to balance out increases in debt

Recommendation

BUY   SELL

Ansys, Inc.

Ansys: Company Profile

- Founded in 1994; added to the S&P 500 on June 19, 2017
- Headquartered in Pittsburg, Pennsylvania
- Ansys designs and sells engineering solutions software for Aerospace and Defense, Automotive, Semiconductor, Energy, Chemical processing, Healthcare, and Hardware industries.
  - Enables companies to simulate product performance from concept stages to final testing stages
  - Maintains and services software license packages periodically.
- Largely international revenue streams
- Customers include Dell, Intel, and Microsoft, Rolls Royce, and Samsung

Source: FactSet, 10-K

Ansys: Management

Dr. Ajei S. Gopal, President and CEO of Ansys	Maria T. Shields, SVP and CFO of Ansys	Prith Banerjee, CTO of Ansys

Source: Company website

Ansys: Investment Thesis

BUY
- Primed for organic and inorganic growth through R&D investment and Acquisition.
  - 18% of revenue went toward R&D in 2017
  - 2017 acquisitions included CLK Design Automation, Computational Engineering International, and 3DSIM.
  - 2018 acquisitions included OPTIS
- International presence
- Reasonably valued

Ansys: Revenue Streams

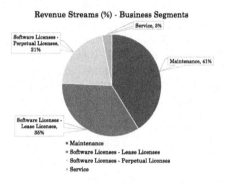

Revenue Streams (%) - Business Segments

Source: FactSet

Ansys: Revenue Streams

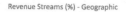

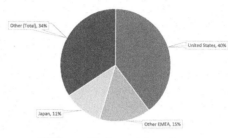

Source: FactSet

Ansys: Opportunity

- Highly productive partnerships:
  - Partnership with CAD expected to integrate Ansys Discovery Live real-time simulation software with PTC Creo 3D software in first half of 2019.
  - Partnership with SAP expected to produce first real-time cloud-based engineering solutions platform in 2019.
- Greatest expected growth is in the Americas
- Analysts expect double-digit sales growth through 2020
- Expansion beyond core industries (semiconductors, aerospace, and industrials):
  - Electrification of vehicles, autonomous driving, and IoT.

Source: 10-K, Bloomberg

Ansys: Risk

- Fast-paced industry
- Increased R&D and operating expenses could adversely affect earnings
- Continued use of perpetual license and lease-based sales model

Ansys: Balance Sheet Analysis

Balance Sheet Analysis	DEC '18	DEC '17	DEC '16	DEC '15	DEC '14
Current Ratio	2.50	2.09	2.17	2.22	2.39
Quick Ratio	2.50	2.09	2.17	2.22	2.39
Cash Ratio	1.48	1.45	1.53	1.62	1.70
Cash & ST Inv/Current Assets (%)	59.29	69.42	70.37	72.89	71.03
CFO/Current Liabilities (%)	92.70	70.73	66.19	75.91	82.84

Source: FactSet

Ansys: Earnings Analysis

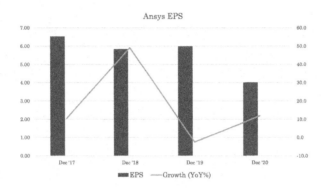

Source: FactSet

Ansys: Earnings Analysis

Source: FactSet

Ansys: Earnings Analysis

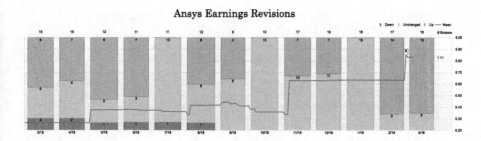

Source: FactSet

Ansys: Competition

Ansys: Valuation

Source: FactSet

Ansys: Valuation

Valuation	DEC '18	DEC '17	DEC '16	DEC '15	DEC '14
	365 Days	365 Days	366 Days	365 Days	365 Days
Price/Sales	9.49	11.70	8.32	8.98	8.25
Price/Earnings	29.29	49.53	30.93	33.51	30.37
Price/Book Value	4.51	5.53	3.59	3.72	3.36
Price/Tangible Book Value	13.81	17.51	11.34	12.71	11.52
Price/Cash Flow	25.25	29.78	23.06	23.03	20.05
Price/Free Cash Flow	26.43	31.17	23.89	24.09	21.50
Enterprise Value/EBIT	23.45	28.68	18.71	20.83	19.15
Enterprise Value/EBITDA	20.86	24.55	15.81	17.08	15.50
Enterprise Value/Sales	8.64	10.54	7.19	7.82	7.11
Total Debt/Enterprise Value	0.00	0.00	0.00	0.00	0.00

Source: FactSet

Ansys: Valuation

Cpmpany Name	Fiscal Period	Price	Market Value	Enterprise Value	Sales	EV/EBIT	EV/EBITDA
ANSYS	12/31/2018	178.79	14,977.6	14,200.2	1,293.6	29.80x	26.50x
Average		119.77	43,813.3	43,954.4	3,263.2	83.69x	55.58x
Median		67.75	3,939.1	3,467.8	411.8	83.69x	55.58x
Altair Engineering A	12/31/2018	36.10	2,551.5	2,550.2	396.4	122.30x	71.06x
Adobe	11/30/2018	255.46	124,949.0	125,845.0	8,981.4	45.08x	40.10x
2U	12/31/2018	67.75	3,939.1	3,467.9	411.8	—	—

Source: FactSet

Ansys: Valuation

Ansys P/E- LTM

Source: FactSet

Ansys: Valuation

Ansys P/E- NTM

Source: FactSet

Ansys: Valuation

Ansys Free Cash Flow Yield - LTM

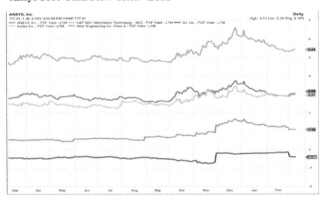

Source: FactSet

Ansys: Valuation

Ansys Free Cash Flow Yield - NTM

Source: FactSet

Ansys: Comparison to Applied Materials

Ansys: Comparison to Applied Materials

Ansys:
- Sells engineering solutions software
- Utilizes a license-based (perpetual and lease) sales model
- Thrives on successful R&D investments, partnerships, and acquisitions
- Large international presence with little exposure to China

Applied Materials:
- Sells manufacturing equipment, manufacturing solutions, and LCDs to semiconductor manufacturing companies
- Greatest source of growth from Display (LCDs) segment
- Large exposure to tariff wars
- Largest R&D expenditures in industry

Ansys: Opportunities and Weaknesses

Opportunities:
- Productive partnerships with SAP and CAD
- Increasing exposure to American markets
- Fairly priced

Weaknesses:
- Continued use of License-based sales model
- Acquisitions sometimes adversely affect operating expenses and earnings

Applied: Opportunities and Weaknesses

Opportunities:
- Exposure to semiconductor industry
- Potential upside of economic improvements in China
- Fairly priced

Weaknesses:
- Over-exposure to Asian markets (91% of sales)
- Over-exposure to semiconductor industry
- Concentrated customer base

Ansys: Price Comparison to Applied

Source: FactSet

Ansys: P/E comparison to Applied

Source: FactSet

Ansys: EV/EBITDA comparison to Applied

Source: FactSet

Ansys: Comparison to Applied Materials

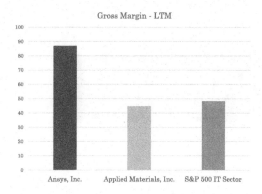

Gross Margin - LTM

Source: FactSet

Ansys: Purchase Rationale

- Healthy international exposure
- Healthy valuation relative to competitors and relative to Applied Materials
- Healthy blend of organic and inorganic growth
- Excellent Free Cash Flow Yield relative to competitors
  - Especially important considering the focus of Ansys upon acquisitions
  - Especially important considering the focus of Ansys upon R&D investment
- Healthy fundamentals:
  - Industry-leading Gross Margin
  - Industry-leading revenue growth

Recommendation

BUY   SELL

(Source: Baylor University Spring 2019 IT Sector Presentation.)

IT Sector Portfolio Summary

Exhibit 7.5 Examples of Baylor University's discussion summaries

Summary of discussion for potential stock purchase

Sector: Consumer Cyclicals.
Recommendation: Starwood Hotels & Resorts (HOT).

1. Summary of presentation
   - Discussed industries within Consumer Cyclicals sector
   - Discussed why I chose Starwood Hotels
   - Explained Starwood background, competitive strengths, and management
   - Covered the state and the risks associated with the lodging industry, and discussed competitors
   - Mentioned balance sheet and income statement highlights
   - Touched on 4Q00 highlights
   - Had the valuation discussion, thoroughly discussing value, hybrid, and growth criteria
   - Discussed key growth drivers, future projections, and analyst opinions for Starwood
2. Summary of discussion
   - Discussed many of the above topics thoroughly
   - Asked questions including:
     - What are the profit margins for others in the industry?
     - What are the occupancy rates for competitors?
     - What do you perceive as the two most relevant risks for Starwood? (Responded the state of the economy in general on the industry, and tax risks associated with possibly not qualifying as REIT)
     - Do you know how much revenue each country/region generates? (Top five included North America, Europe, Asia, Latin America, and Africa)
   - Explained concerns about ROE and ROA, including explanation about historical ROEs, purchase of ITT in 1998, price paid for ITT, impact on stock price and overall profitability, how the acquisition is currently impacting profitability, and projections about future ROE

3. Summary of voting

   - Seven students voted for the purchase of HOT
   - One students voted against the purchase of HOT
   - One student abstained from voting
   - Three remaining students were absent

Summary of Cendant "sell" discussion

Sector: Industrials.
Recommendation: Sell Cendant (CD).

1. Summary of presentation
   - Recommendation: sell Cendant (CD) and buy general dynamics (GD)
     - Voted to sell CD if we found a better stock on October 4, 2004
   - Cendant:
     - Foremost provider of travel and real estate services in the world

- Industry overview:
  - Companies in this sector are diverse
  - Performed better in 2004 after lagging margins
  - Ranks in top half of timeliness ranking
- Company overview:
  - World's largest real estate brokerage franchiser
  - Own and operate 920 Coldwell Banker locations
  - One of the largest vehicle rental operations in the world with Avis and budget
- Acquisitions
  - Recently purchased Orbitz on September 29, 2004
    - Purchased at a 35% premium for $1.25 billion in cash
    - Previously owned by top five US airlines
  - Planning to purchase Ramada Hotel and Resorts

- Risks:
  - Pending trials of 1998 Accounting fraud
  - Possibility of heightened terrorism may reduce travel
  - Higher than anticipated interest rates could affect real estate–related business
  - Increasing oil prices increase travel costs

2. Summary of discussion
   - Is this stock cheap for a reason?
     - Currently underperforming the market
     - Lower PE ratio yet lacking a promising outlook
   - Purchasing of Orbitz
     - Will this easily integrate in Galileo International?
     - Is it worth the premium price?
     - Growth potential

3. Summary of voting

   - 8:4 for selling the security

Summary of general dynamics "buy" discussion

Sector: Industrials.
Recommendation: Buy general dynamics (GD).

1. Summary of presentation
   - Recommendation: Sell Cendant (CD) and Buy General Dynamics (GD)
     - Voted to sell CD if we found a better stock on October 4, 2004
   - General dynamics:
     - Uniquely qualified to engineer, manufacture, and integrate complex land, air, and maritime platforms with leading-edge information technology
   - Industry overview:
     - Signs of pickup in jetliner demand
     - Military budget expected to rise 6% in 2005
     - Concentrate on stocks with timeliness of 2 or better

- Reasons for selection:
  - ValueLine timeliness ranking of 2, safety ranking of 1
  - FWD PE less than the industry
  - Market capitalization greater than $5 billion
  - Diversification of revenues
- Acquisitions
  - Recently agreed to purchase Alvis of Britain
    - Maker of Challenge II battle tank
    - Positions GD to win combat vehicle orders in US, Britain, and Sweden

- Veridian corporation:
  - Provider of network security and enterprise protection
- Creative technology:
  - Supports intelligence community and Department of Defense
- Risks:
  - Foreign currency exchange rate risk
    - Inter-company transactions in foreign currencies

- Environmental laws:
  - Indirectly/directly involved in the release of hazardous materials at former sites
  - In some cases, rely on 1 or 2 sources of supply for their product
  - Possibility of terminated projects

2. Summary of discussion
   - GD's business jet division on the rise
     - World's leading producer of mid-size and intercontinental business jet aircraft
   - Conservative stock for the future
   - Diversifies Dorr Portfolio
   - Good finances and strong free cash flows project future acquisitions

3. Summary of voting

   - 7–6 for purchasing security

---

learn from past members, understand the original rationale behind the purchase of portfolio securities, and evaluate the investment process.

External presentations

In addition to the internal reports and presentations that investment organizations produce to make organizational and portfolio decisions, reports and presentations must be made to communicate with external constituents and stakeholders. External presentations by investment managers are usually produced for two purposes: client service and business development. A client service presentation's primary objective is to retain a current client, while business development presentations aim to attract new clients or new money from existing clients. As such, the focus of external presentations differs somewhat from internal presentations. External presentations tend to focus more on the overall organization, portfolio, and performance and less on the details surrounding a specific buy or sell decision.

We consider presentations to oversight boards to fit into the client service category, though some presentations to oversight boards might have elements of internal presentations. For example, reports and presentations by mutual fund advisors (investment managers) to the mutual fund's board of directors would generally be considered client service presentations, since the board represents the interests of the mutual fund's shareholders, who are the ultimate client of the investment manager's services. However, boards also typically have authority for decisions regarding how the portfolio is managed. Therefore, such presentations might share some elements of the internal presentations discussed earlier. Furthermore, oversight boards for student-managed investment funds typically have shared interests with the investment managers beyond that of the portfolio's performance. Specifically, a student-managed investment fund's board typically would not choose to "fire" the managers by dissolving the fund in the same way a pension fund client might decide to fire an investment manager. Moreover, some SMIF oversight boards play an active role in investment decisions by participating in some of the internal presentations discussed above.

A key differentiating factor between internal and external presentations is that the audience of an external presentation is unlikely to be as familiar with or conversant in the content of the presentation. That is, members of an investment organization live and breathe the methods and data used in making portfolio decisions. The investment philosophy and process and their implications are dealt with in detail every day. External constituents, such as clients, typically have multiple investment managers who each have their own investment philosophy and process. The clients might be familiar with each of their manager's investment philosophies and processes, but they only focus on any specific investment process during those few times per year that they interact with that particular investment manager. Therefore, it is important that each external presentation seizes the opportunity to remind the audience of the framework in which the investment manager operates. Depending on the specific purpose of the presentation, it should almost always include a review of the organization, its purpose, and its investment philosophy and process in order to provide context for other content within the presentation.

Some content from internal presentations, especially those used to discuss security selection or portfolio construction, might be appropriate to include in external presentations. Indeed, such content can provide further clarification and detail regarding the investment process. However, such content should be presented in a way that recognizes the external audience's potential lack of familiarity with and context for the details and complexities of the investment process.

An investment manager's report or presentation to an existing client, also called a "client review," is typically provided on a quarterly basis. The primary purpose of a client review is to update the client on the performance of their assets that have been entrusted to the investment manager. It is the investment manager's responsibility to go beyond the performance numbers to provide insight into the performance of the assets so that the client understands why the performance is good or bad. As discussed above, an understanding of the performance is best achieved through an understanding of the investment process. An example of such a client review is show in Exhibit 7.6, in which Jill Foote discusses Rice University's Wright Fund report and presentation to its oversight board. Because of its top-down investment process, the Wright Fund's strategy is best understood in the context of the economic and market environment, which is reviewed at the beginning of the presentation. The economic discussion provides relevant context for further details about the fund's performance. While we performance reporting and analysis was discussed previously in Chapter 5, we note that a presentation of performance and analysis that reveals further insights into the sources of out- and under-performance is a critical element of reports and presentations to clients and oversight boards.

Exhibit 7.6 External presentation example from Rice University's Wright Fund

By: Jill Foote

The Wright Fund reports to an Oversight Board consisting of Rice University's Vice President for Investments and Treasurer; the Dean of the Jones Graduate School of Business; and prominent investment professionals. The Board typically meets three times per year: twice at the end of each school semester to hear a formal presentation by Fund Officers on performance and activities, and once otherwise to discuss strategic initiatives and curriculum changes.

Oversight board reporting

Each semester, the Fund Officers issue a short (2-page) mid-term Board Report and provide a formal end-of-semester presentation to the Oversight Board.

The end-of-semester Board presentation will typically cover the following agenda items:

- Semester strategy
  - Economic and market strategies
- Performance/Results
  - Performance vs. benchmark for fund and sectors
  - Best and worst stock performance
  - Attribution analysis
  - Risk metrics
- Events and initiatives
  - Conferences, speakers, and initiatives
- Awards and achievements

  - Scholarship winners
  - Best reports and Best Analyst Group

Agenda

- **Introduction**

- **Macroeconomic Review**

- **Fund Performance and Strategy**

- **Sector and Stock Spotlights**

- **Events & Initiatives, Awards & Achievements**

RICE UNIVERSITY 🦉 M.A. WRIGHT FUND   0

(Source: Fall 2019 WF Oversight Board Presentation.)

Strategy

The strategy segment of the Board presentation typically follows the WF's top-down approach. Both the Chief Investment Officer (CIO) and the Chief Economist (CE) will provide macro-level views on the economy and the market overall. Then the CIO will give an overview of the Fund strategy pursued for the semester, and typically changes to the strategy from the previous semester. Included in the strategy section will be asset allocation among Equities, Fixed Income, and Cash; and overweighting/underweighting of sectors.

U.S. Economy In 11 Year Bull Cycle

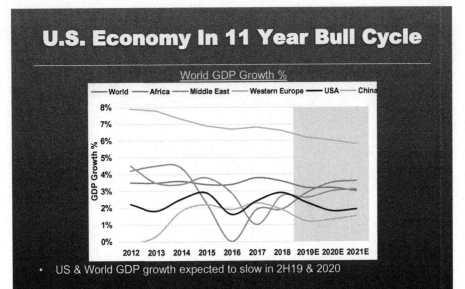

World GDP Growth %

- US & World GDP growth expected to slow in 2H19 & 2020

- Consumer demand is driving US GDP growth – Lagging

- US Business Investments & Exports are declining – Leading

RICE UNIVERSITY 🐾 M.A. WRIGHT FUND   0

Consumer Confidence Remains Strong

- Consumer confidence - All time highs in 2019
  - Driven by healthy employment, wage growth

- August lowest level in 2019....but starting to improve! – Positive

- Takeaway: Consumer confidence is strong. But considered lagging indicator!

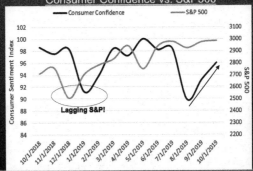

Consumer Confidence vs. S&P500

RICE UNIVERSITY 🐾 M.A. WRIGHT FUND   1

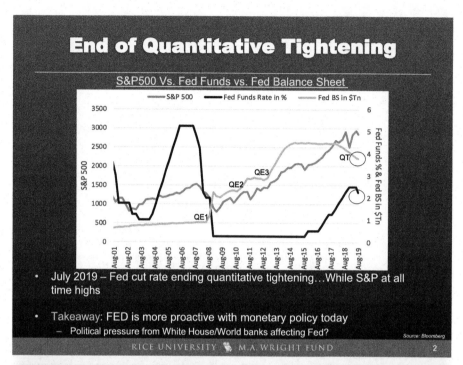

End of Quantitative Tightening

S&P500 Vs. Fed Funds vs. Fed Balance Sheet

- July 2019 – Fed cut rate ending quantitative tightening…While S&P at all time highs

- Takeaway: FED is more proactive with monetary policy today
  - Political pressure from White House/World banks affecting Fed?

Source: Bloomberg

RICE UNIVERSITY 🦉 M.A. WRIGHT FUND   2

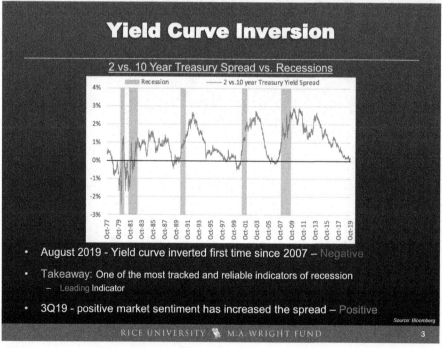

Yield Curve Inversion

2 vs. 10 Year Treasury Spread vs. Recessions

- August 2019 - Yield curve inverted first time since 2007 – Negative

- Takeaway: One of the most tracked and reliable indicators of recession
  - Leading Indicator

- 3Q19 - positive market sentiment has increased the spread – Positive

Source: Bloomberg

RICE UNIVERSITY 🦉 M.A. WRIGHT FUND   3

Interest Rate Cuts & Stimulus

- World Banks cut interest rates & increase stimulus to limit growth slowdown
  - Big driver of economy and sentiment

- Takeaway: Positive for markets in short term...but what about long term?

- October Prediction: FED leaves rate at 1.50-1.75%

S&P 500 vs. Fed Funds

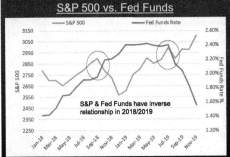

Historical Fed Funds

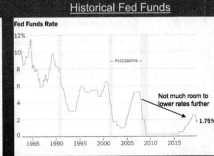

RICE UNIVERSITY 🦉 M.A. WRIGHT FUND

4

US – China Trade War Update

- December 2019 – US & China reach Phase 1 of trade deal:
  - Tariffs that start Dec 15th will be cancelled
  - China agrees to buy US agriculture/exports
  - Expected to sign early January

- Prediction: This is still far from being over

- Takeaway: Huge driver of growth for world economies

Trade War Timeline

Date	Description
Oct 10-11	Chinese Vice Premier Liu He meets Lighthizer and Mnuchin to continue trade talks Tariffs still active
Oct 15	Tariffs on $250bn Chinese imports rising to 30% from 25%
Oct 31	Brexit
Nov 13	Deadline for decision on auto tariffs
Nov 18	The "temporary general licenses" for US firms' sales to Huawei expire Tariffs below halted
Dec 15	15% tariffs for $156bn Chinese goods and China's retaliatory tariffs effective
Ongoing	Impeachment inquiry

Source: FactSet

RICE UNIVERSITY 🦉 M.A. WRIGHT FUND

5

Fall 2019 Outlook (Aug-Dec)

- August Thesis: US Economy is doing better than people think

Fall 2019 Outlook (as of August)		
Thesis	1. Strong unemployment & wage growth supports consumer confidence	Positive
	2. Expected interest rate cuts should benefit US economy	Positive
	3. World interest rate cuts & stimulus should reduce risk of recession	Positive
	4. Inverted yield curve signals caution	Negative
	5. Trade war not likely to be resolved until 2020	Negative
Outlook	**Aug-Dec 2019 Outlook:** S&P 500 = **Flat**(-5% to +5%) Bullish: US, Emerging economies Bearish: China, Europe, Commodities	Positive
	Long Term (2021+) Outlook Correction Awaits	Negative

RICE UNIVERSITY 🦉 M.A. WRIGHT FUND   6

Spring 2020 Outlook (Jan-Jun)

- December Thesis: Positive momentum going into 2020

Spring 2020 Outlook (as of December)		
Thesis	1. Stronger than expected economic data & earnings should provide upside going into 1H20	Positive
	2. Unlikely Fed cuts or raises interest rates in 1H20	Positive
	3. Trade war optimism should continue into 2020, but can change significantly with a tweet	Positive
	4. Election year brings more uncertainty	Negative
	5. Key issues need to be resolved: Trade War, Brexit, Impeachment, US budget, etc.	Nuetral
Outlook	**Jan-June 2020 Outlook:** S&P 500 = Up (0% to +10%) Bullish: US, Emerging economies Bearish: China, Europe, Commodities	Positive
	Long Term (2021+) Outlook Correction Awaits	Negative

RICE UNIVERSITY 🦉 M.A. WRIGHT FUND   7

Sources

- BBC
- Bloomberg
- Bureau of Economic Analysis (BEA)
- Bureau of Labor Statistics
- BIS
- China's National Bureau of Statistics
- FactSet
- Federal Reserve
- National Association of Realtors
- Peterson Institute for International Economics
- Standard and Poor's
- Statista

RICE UNIVERSITY · M.A. WRIGHT FUND · 8

(Source: Fall 2019 WF Oversight Board Presentation.)

Performance/results

Both risk and return are covered in the performance section. Continuing with a top-down approach, the usual flow of the presentation section first covers overall Fund performance (both for the semester and one or more longer terms of performance, such as YTD and 5-year performance), followed by sector performance, and then individual stock performance, usually best and worst performers. Attribution analysis, discussing the contribution to performance by allocation, selection, and interaction effects, is included. Risk measures such as portfolio Beta, Sharpe Ratio, and Value at Risk are reviewed. Depending on the goals of the presenting officers, sometimes other material, such as a styles analysis, will be included.

Investment Thesis For Fall 2019

1 Large-Cap Growth will Outperform

2 Avoid Energy, Materials and Industrials

3 Avoid Sectors exposed to Declining Interest Rates (Financials)

4 Overweight IT for Growth, Other Overweight Sectors Defensive

RICE UNIVERSITY M.A. WRIGHT FUND   0

Objectives and Fund Profile (Fall 2019)

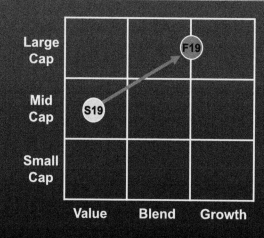

Portfolio Statistics

	WF	S&P 500
Beta	0.94	1.00
Div. Yield	1.48%	1.85%
P/E	25.5x	20.9x
P/CFO	17.5x	15.0x
P/B	4.1x	3.5x
D/E	99%	124%
ROA	4.90%	3.33%

Note: Statistics as of December 11, 2019

RICE UNIVERSITY M.A. WRIGHT FUND   1

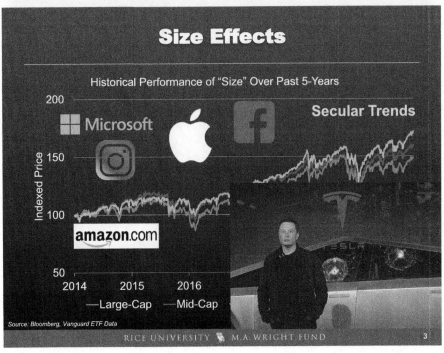

Target Areas of Focus (Over/Under Weight)

	Target Weight	S&P 500	Target vs. S&P 500
Real Estate	7.0%	2.9%	4.13%
Consumer Staples	10.0%	7.3%	2.74%
Information Technology	25.0%	23.0%	2.02%
Healthcare	16.0%	14.1%	1.88%
Utilities	5.0%	3.3%	1.73%
Consumer Discretionary	10.0%	9.7%	0.28%
Materials	2.0%	2.6%	-0.65%
Industrials	7.0%	9.2%	-2.23%
Energy	2.0%	4.3%	-2.26%
Communication Services	5.0%	10.4%	-5.35%
Financials	6.0%	13.3%	-7.27%
Cash	5.0%	0.0%	
Total	100.0%	100.0%	

Source: Wright Fund Weekly

RICE UNIVERSITY   M.A. WRIGHT FUND   4

Invested Position

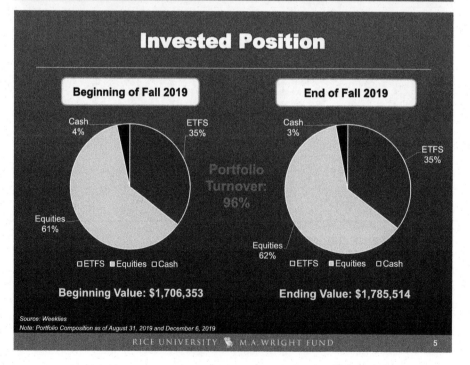

Beginning of Fall 2019 — Cash 4%, ETFS 35%, Equities 61%. ☐ETFS ■Equities ☐Cash

End of Fall 2019 — Cash 3%, ETFS 35%, Equities 62%. ☐ETFS ■Equities ☐Cash

Portfolio Turnover: 96%

Beginning Value: $1,706,353   Ending Value: $1,785,514

Source: Weeklies
Note: Portfolio Composition as of August 31, 2019 and December 6, 2019

RICE UNIVERSITY   M.A. WRIGHT FUND   5

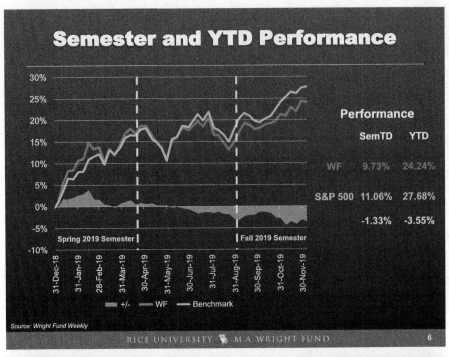

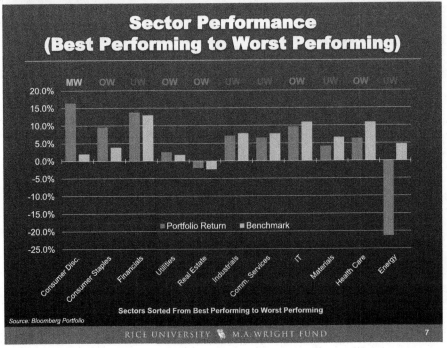

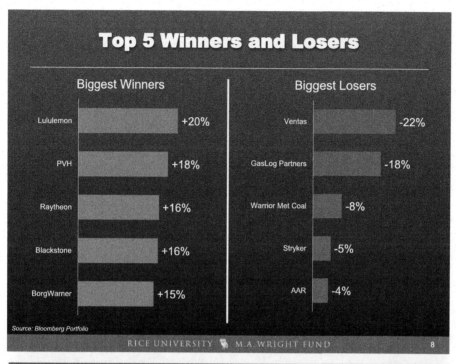

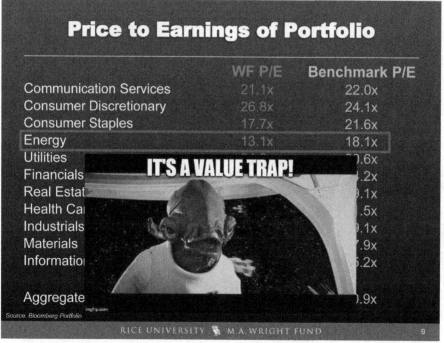

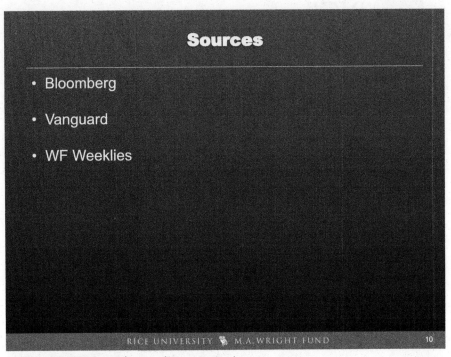

(Source: Fall 2019 WF Oversight Board Presentation.)

Forward view/looking ahead

In similar fashion to the strategy, often the CIO and CE will present their forward looking view after the Performance/Results Section. The Oversight Board members have expressed an interest in hearing the forward view of the officers at the point in time when they are most knowledgeable (at the end of their term).

Sector presentation—Best performer

The Board presentation includes a few slides by one or two sectors that performed particularly well on either an absolute or a relative basis. The presenting AGs are judgmentally chosen by the Officers and the Faculty Director.

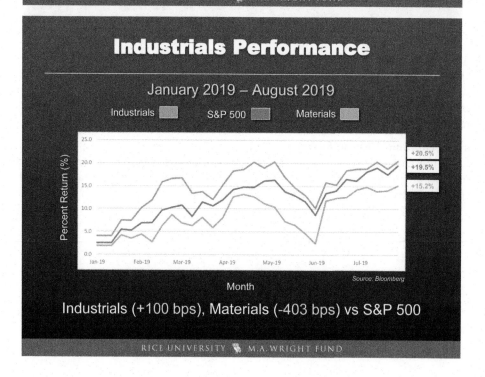

Thesis Drivers

US/China Trade War

Declining Economic Indicators

FOMC Rate Cuts

RICE UNIVERSITY M.A. WRIGHT FUND

Investment Thesis

1. Target industries with low betas

2. Eliminate exposure to commodity equities

3. Focus on industries that will sustain demand in late stages of business cycle

WF F19 Strategy: Large-cap, growth equities

Target Weighting: Underweight Industrials (2.0%)

Underweight Materials   (0.7%)

RICE UNIVERSITY M.A. WRIGHT FUND

Commercial Services and Supplies

- Industry Beta: 0.80 (2-Year, Weekly)
- Technological innovation increasing auto scrap rates
- "Green initiatives" have raised recycling rates from 10.0% in 1980 to over 35.0% today

Source: Bloomberg

RICE UNIVERSITY 🦉 M.A. WRIGHT FUND

Screener

Growth Metrics ☐   Quality Metrics ☐

Screener Item	Screener Value	Rationale
30-day Avg Volume	> 250,000	Liquidity check
Market Capitalization	≥70th Percentile	Target large-cap stocks
Earnings per Share	>0	Value indicator
Revenue 5Yr CAGR	> 5.71 [Industry Median]	Target growth
Momentum	[50 Day MA / 100 Day MA]>1	Target momentum
P/E	Display Field	Differentiate value
Total Debt/Total Equity	Display Field	Highlight leverage
ROA	Display Field	Highlight strong returns
ROE	Display Field	Highlight strong returns

RICE UNIVERSITY 🦉 M.A. WRIGHT FUND

Watchlist

STOCK NAME AND TICKER	RATIONALE	RANKING
Copart Inc (CPRT)	• Large cap company that specializes in auto salvage; industry is utilized regardless of economic cycle • Momentum present • High P/E / Low leverage / High ROE	1
Rollins Inc (ROL)	• Large cap company that specializes in pest and termite control; industry is an industrial staple • High P/E / High ROE	2
Cintas Corporation (CTAS)	• Large cap company that specializes in the production of industrial uniforms; uniforms are a requisite for employers • Momentum present • High P/E / High ROE	3
Waste Management (WM)	• Large cap company that specializes in waste management; industry is an industrial staple • Momentum present • High P/E / High ROE	4
Republic Services (RSG)	• Large cap company that specializes in waste management; industry is an industrial staple • Momentum present • High P/E value	5

WF Industrials Semester Performance

Industrials	WF	Benchmark	+/-
Capital Goods	11.1%	10.9%	0.2%
RAYTHEON COMPANY	17.0%	4.7%	12.3%
AAR CORP	-3.9%	0.0%	-3.9%
LOCKHEED MARTIN CORP	0.8%	-0.1%	0.9%
Commercial & Professional Services	5.9%	0.7%	5.2%
COPART INC	13.6%	5.8%	7.8%
WASTE MANAGEMENT INC	-2.6%	-2.6%	0.0%
Transportation	2.7%	7.2%	-4.5%
OLD DOMINION FREIGHT LINE	6.4%	0.0%	6.4%
NORFOLK SOUTHERN CORP	-0.6%	-1.4%	0.8%
Total Industrials Performance	7.7%	9.3%	-1.5%

Performance Drivers
• Strong performance by defense contractors
• Copart's inaugural entrance into Europe
• Mistiming in Transportation liquidations

Incyte Corporation (INCY)

Sell-Side Equity Research Analysis

Dec 17, 2019

RICE UNIVERSITY 🦉 M.A. WRIGHT FUND

Incyte Corporation Overview

- Discovers, develops, and commercializes proprietary therapeutics
- Strong revenue growth: 72% CAGR 2009-2019

How Effective is Jakafi?

It is effectively used to treat polycythemia vera or myelofibrosis that are otherwise known as bone marrow conditions that mainly affects the blood cell production in the body.

Source: ePainAssist

- Leadership in niche market
  - Jakafi and Iclusig

Trade Name	Generic Name	Target	Indications	Therapeutic Area
Olumiant	Baricitinib	JAK1/JAK2	Rheumatoid arthritis	Inflammation
Iclusig	Ponatinib	BCR-ABL	Chronic myeloid leukemia (CML) and Philadelphia-chromosome positive acute lymphoblastic leukemia (Ph+ ALL)	Oncology
Jakafi	Ruxolitinib	JAK 1/JAK2	Myelofibrosis (MF)	Oncology
			Polycythemia Vera (PV)	Oncology
			Steroid-refractory acute Graft-Versus-Host Disease (GVHD)	Oncology
Jakavi	Ruxolitinib	JAK 1/JAK2	Myelofibrosis (MF), Polycythemia Vera (PV), Steroid-refractory acute Graft-Versus-Host Disease (GVHD)	Oncology
In-registration	Capmatinib	MET	Non-small cell lung cancer (NSCLC) with MET exon 14 skipping mutations	Oncology
In-registration	Pemigatinib	FGFR1/2/3	Cholangiocarcinoma	Oncology

Source: Company Data

RICE UNIVERSITY 🦉 M.A. WRIGHT FUND   9

Investment Thesis 1: Long-term Growth

				Incyte Portfolio			
Disease	**Phase 1**	**Phase 2**	**Phase 3**	**Pre-Registration**	**Marketed**	**Total**	**% by Disease**
Oncology	1	13	0	2	3	19	52.8%
Immunology	0	2	5	0	1	8	22.2%
Dermatology	0	0	5	0	0	5	13.9%
Inflammation	0	2	1	0	1	4	11.1%
Total	**1**	**17**	**11**	**2**	**5**	**36**	100.0%
% by Phase	*2.8%*	*47.2%*	*30.6%*	*5.6%*	*13.9%*	*100.0%*	

Source: Company data

- Heavy investment in R&D
  - **54.3%** of revenue vs 33.03% peer median

- Attractive portfolio
  - **33% phase 3, 47% phase 2, 3% phase 1**
  - **53% oncology, 22% immunology, 14% dermatology, 11% inflammation**

- Efficient sales force
  - **$1.4 million sales / employee, 75% higher than peer median ($ 0.8 mm)**

Investment Thesis 1: Long-term Growth (Cont.)

Long-Term Focused CEO Compensation

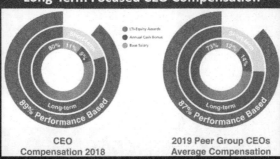

CEO Compensation 2018   2019 Peer Group CEOs Average Compensation

Source: Company data

- **INCY: 80%** Long-Term Incentive
- Peer Average: **73%**

Investment Thesis 2: Strong Outlook of Cancer Treatment Markets

- **INCY focuses on markets with strong outlook**
  - Therapeutics: Tyrosine Kinase Inhibitors (TKIs), **$23 bn** in 2018
  - **Market growth (CAGR):** leukemia **8%**, lung cancer **14%**

The Tyrosine Kinase Inhibitor Cancer Treatment Market

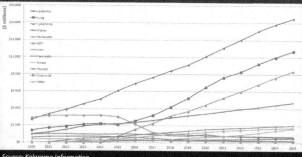

Source: Kalorama Information

Investment Thesis 3: High Probability of FDA Approval

- **New Drug Application (NDA)**
  - **Capmatinib:** only therapeutic for non-small cell lung cancer (NSCLC)

  - **Pemigatinib:** only targeted therapy for a type of cholangiocarcinoma

- **From NDA to Approval: 85.3% probability**

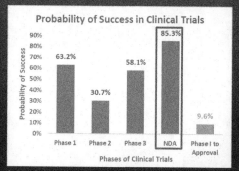

Sources: Biotechnology Innovation Organization, Biomedtracker, AMPLION

Valuation & Recommendation

- ## Valuation Methods
  - Discounted Cash Flow
  - Multiples

- ## Recommendation: BUY
  - **Target Price: $105.00**
  - Current Price: $92.66 (as of 12/16/2019)
  - % return to target: 13.3%

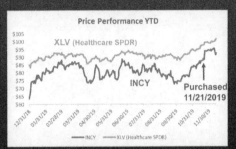

Source: FactSet

Sources

- AMPLION
- Biomedtracker
- Biotechnology Innovation Organization
- Cancer.org
- Cleveland Clinic
- Company data
- Current Oncology
- FactSet
- Journal of Hematology & Oncology
- Journal of Market Access & Health Policy
- Lungcancer.org
- Medscape
- MPN Research Foundation
- Nature
- WebMD

On my honor, I have neither given nor received any authorized aid on this assignment

Blackstone Group (BX)

12/17/2019

RICE UNIVERSITY 🦉 M.A. WRIGHT FUND

Macro-Economic Trends

Investors to Reward Lower Interest Rate Exposure

✗ Large Lending Practices   ✓ Fee-Based Companies

REITs have been seeing a renaissance

- Volatile low interest rate environment driving REIT growth

- Private REITs offer more stability vs Public REITs

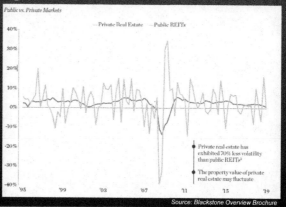

Public vs. Private Markets

— Private Real Estate   — Public REITs

- Private real estate has exhibited 70% less volatility than public REITs[2]

- The property value of private real estate may fluctuate

Source: Blackstone Overview Brochure

RICE UNIVERSITY 🦉 M.A. WRIGHT FUND   17

The Public Sees BX as just a PE Co.

As of 12/12/2019, BX news headlines included…

PE-Focused Stories

Reuters | 12/5/2019: PAI Partners, Lego owner to buy German insulation foam maker from Blackstone…

Reuters | 11/30/2019: UPDATE 2-Tallgrass Energy CEO leaves amid Blackstone takeover proposal…

New York Business Journal | 11/14/2019: Bumble, affiliated dating apps valued at $3B as Blackstone invests

Barron's | 12/12/2019: Apollo, Carlyle, and 3 Other Alternative-Asset Mangers That Have Sealed Their Dividend Payouts

VS

Real-Estate Stories

Bloomberg | 12/9/2019: Blackstone's Buyout of Coffee Day's Tech Park Stalls

Dallas Business Journal | 12/12/2019: Real Estate company buys 1M-SF Whirlpool distribution center from Blackstone

BX is *much more* than that…

BX has no true comparable companies, but is rather three separate companies…

% Rev	Comparable Companies
REITS — 43%	MACK-CALI Realty Corporation PROLOGIS' LPT
Alternative Investment — 33%	KKR OAKTREE THE CARLYLE GROUP GLOBAL ALTERNATIVE ASSET MANAGEMENT
Credit / Other — 24%	APOLLO

Investment Thesis

Investors are…

	Time of Investment	NOW

- Appreciating BX's limited interest rate exposure

- Valuing BX's REIT as a *private* REIT

- Valuing BX's C-Corp Conversion Correctly

RICE UNIVERSITY M.A. WRIGHT FUND

20

Combining all 3 BU's Shows...

Company Name	Ticker	Price	Market Cap ($B)	Ent. Value ($B)	Div Yield	EPS CY	EPS TTM	P/E TTM	P/E NTM	5 Yr Avg	EV/EBITDA TTM	EV/EBITDA NTM	EV/EBITDA 5 Yr Avg	PEG	P/TBV	P/FCF
BLACKSTONE GROUP	BX	50.22	33.2	77.1	4.1%	2.29	1.79	24.8	17.5	22.6	25.3	20.3	13.8	1.9	15.0	81.6
REITs (43%)																
MACK-CALI REALTY	CLI	21.77	2.0	5.3	3.7%	2.03	2.65	8.8	202.3	63.7	20.6	20.1	16.3	4.6	1.2	112.7
PROLOGIS	PLD	85.78	54.1	49.0	2.5%	2.12	2.72	29.5	46.6	67.0	18.1	19.1	29.8	7.4	2.4	31.7
LIBERTY PROPERTY TRUST	LPT	51.54	8.1	9.3	3.2%	1.81	3.19	15.7	31.9	22.7	21.5	19.9	20.4	4.8	2.3	22.9
Private Equity (33%)																
CARLYLE GRP	CG	25.69	2.8	11.1	5.7%	1.67	2.36	9.6	11.3	30.5	13.0	9.2	13.9	3.3	3.7	12.5
KKR & CO	KKR	27.32	14.9	56.9	1.8%	1.70	2.69	9.4	14.0	14.5	27.7	26.0	29.2	1.2	1.6	-
OAKTREE CAP GRP	OAK	51.52	3.9	11.0	4.9%	3.85	3.01	16.4	15.2	18.8	22.7	13.4	32.2	-	6.2	3.2
Credit / Other (24%)																
GOLDMAN SACHS GROUP	GS	208.97	75.1	451.3	7.4%	22.73	23.86	8.6	8.6	13.6	-	-	-	1.7	1.0	96.8
APOLLO GLOBAL MANAGEMENT	APO	35.88	8.6	11.1	5.1%	2.36	1.20	28.6	13.9	24.1	11.4	9.0	13.9	1.6	10.9	8.1
JPMORGAN CHASE	JPM	117.72	376.4	964.7	3.1%	10.19	9.80	11.4	11.3		-			2.1	2.0	15.9
Source: FactSet		Mean	48.4	132.0	3.5%	4.45	4.90	15.5	47.4	33.8	18.3	16.0	21.8	3.6	3.2	36.2
		Median	22.8	116.0	3.7%	3.88	4.41	12.6	27.4	38.1	19.1	15.1	21.7	3.2	2.7	20.0
		High	376.4	964.7	5.7%	22.73	23.86	29.5	202.3	67.0	27.7	26.0	32.2	7.4	15.0	112.7
		Low	2.0	5.3	1.8%	1.67	1.20	8.6	8.6	13.6	11.4	9.0	13.8	1.2	1.0	3.2

BX offers *higher* div yield
- BX: 4.1%
- Comp Set: 3.5%

 YET

BX trades at P/E *discount*
- BX: 22.6x
- Comp Set: 33.6x

RICE UNIVERSITY M.A. WRIGHT FUND

21

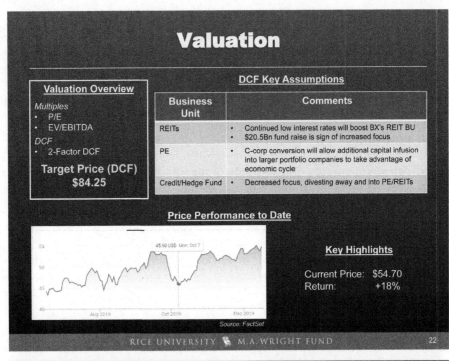

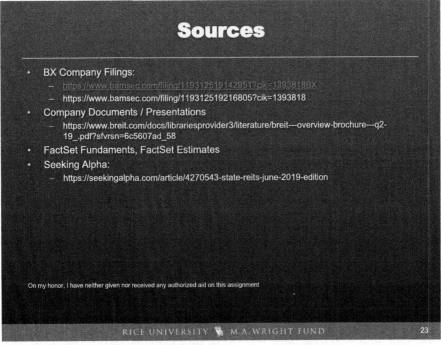

(Source: Fall 2019 WF Oversight Board Presentation.)

Events

In addition to performance reporting, the Fund Officers also present a few slides on events in which the WF was involved including training, speakers, conferences, and volunteerism in the Houston community. Initiatives, such as improvement in tools, new or updated assignments, and fund raising, are also covered in this section.

A Q&A session is held after Events, but before Awards are announced, so that the presentation can end after Awards.

Awards and achievements

For the past few years, the Wright Fund has recognized individual and analyst group (AG) achievement with several awards. These awards, along with WF scholarship recipients and any WF students receiving other recognition (such as winning competitions at conferences or receiving CFA Institute scholarships) are announced at the finale of the Oversight Board presentation.

Best report

For each of the major report assignments, the WF Officers and Faculty Director agree on the "best report." This individual or team is recognized both to the Fund at the time and to the Oversight Board. Copies of the winning reports are shared with Oversight Board members.

AG award

At the end of the semester, an AG award is voted on by the entire class. Votes are cast with the following in mind: sector strategy, sector performance, quality of presentations and class participation by AG members, and excellent on-going communication with the Fund. Analysts are not permitted to vote for their own AG. Each member of the winning AG receives a prize of "incalculable value."

Concluding with awards and achievements makes for a nice finale to the presentation.

Beyond discussing the investment process and its recent performance, the client review typically provides an update on the organization. Any significant changes to the organization, especially turnover in key personnel or changes in ownership and control, would be presented to the client to assist the client in their continued due diligence responsibility. The organizational update also provides an opportunity for notifying the client of enhanced product or service capabilities. In the case of student-managed investment funds, this section of the presentation can be appropriately used to provide a review of student and organizational achievements, such as awards, competitions, or job placements. As noted in the exhibit, the Wright Fund's presentation concludes with recognition of student awards.

CFA Research Challenge presentation material

The CFA Institute Research Challenge is a global financial analysis competition. Teams from universities around the world compete as CFA judges test the students on their research reports. Each team acts as a research analyst and conducts an in-depth evaluation of a stock leading to a buy/sell recommendation. The competition rules limit the report to 10 pages with an appendix limited to 20 pages (Exhibit 7.7).

CFA judges evaluate each report against a rubric, with the sections of the rubric matching the required sections of the report.

Section	Maximum points
Business description	5
Industry overview and competitive positioning	15
Investment summary	20
Valuation	20
Investment risks	15
Corporate governance	5
Total	*100*

In each local competition, the teams with the top research reports compete in the second round with a 10-min oral presentation followed by 10 min of questions and answers with the judges.

Sections of the research report

The research report's length is 10 pages. At the local level, all teams are analyzing the same company. The judges will know in advance which company is the topic. Thus, they will have more detailed knowledge of the company and will have probably conducted their own analyses. At levels beyond the local competition, each school will have a different stock. The judges may or may not know in advance the companies and thus, may not have as comprehensive knowledge as the local-level judges. Therefore, the research report needs enough details to satisfy local judges but also provides enough background information to inform judges in later competition rounds. The teams cannot revise the report between rounds of the competition.

Each section of the research report provides information used in another part of the analysis. A successful report will undergo several revisions. Business description, industry overview, and competitive positioning inform the valuation because these sections highlight the key value drivers.

Executive summary

While not explicitly required to have an executive summary, most reports use the first page of the research report to summarize the report. The appearance of the first page resembles a stock tear sheet.

Key items to include in the executive summary is the recommendation and the analysis that substantiates that recommendation. For a well-known company, the report only needs a cursory business description review. However, for lesser-known firms, the report must provide enough detail to inform the reader of the critical value drivers.

The first page also includes the investment recommendation. More than just the buy/sell recommendation, the summary must delineate the various financial models used to reach that recommendation.

Because firm valuation exists within an industry structure, the executive summary also presents key industry features that influence the valuation.

Notice how the executive summary provides substantiation to the recommendations on future price and trading.

The tone of the first page is analytical and not a sales pitch. Additionally, each point included on the first page supports the overall thesis of the report. If the stock recommendation is a buy, each point supports the buy and provides confidence to the buy. If the stock recommendation is a sell, each point presents why the stock is a sell and, while the company may be a fine, the valuation of the stock is not favorable.

A hold recommendation is permissible. However, in the Q&A phase of the competition judges tend to question why the team chose a hold and not a sell. Thus, the team must write a hold recommendation that includes why the recommendation is not a stronger recommendation of a sell.

Business description

Business description typically starts page 2 and carries a weight of 5% in the judging rubric. Depending on how well-known the company is, the initial description detail changes. Because of the page-limitation, the team should focus on the main divisions in order of profitability and revenue generation. As the team describes each division, the emphasis is on what that division does, how it operates in the marketplace, and on how the segment affects overall firm revenue and profitability.

For example, if a firm has three divisions, the center of the business description is on the main division with the two other divisions presented as to how they contribute to the success of the primary division. If the overall recommendation is a sell, the tone of the analysis is how the main division is not propelling the firm forward or how one of the divisions is a drag on overall firm performance.

If the company is a growth company, the team could choose to focus on the company strategy to describe the firm. For example, in a retail model, the firm may acquire existing stores and rebrand them, create new stores in new areas, and create new connections with existing retailers. In this thematic option, the report focuses on how the firm grows and which division or strategy generates the highest revenue and profit growth.

Teams typically write the business description early in the analysis process. A key to success is to revise this section after the valuation is complete to alter the tone to match the recommendation.

The sidebars of this section typically include charts visualizing the segments. Potential visuals include a graph of the number of stores, a map of the stores or production sites, critical highlights on the size of the firm, revenue and/or cash flow breakdown by segment.

The business description informs the next section by identifying the significant segments for firm revenue, cash flow, and profit. Industry overview and competitive positioning extend this analysis to include where the firm lies within the industry map.

Industry overview and competitive positioning

Industry overview presents the main macroeconomic variables that affect the industry and firm. The theme of this section is informative with conclusion statements with each variable that leads the reader to understand how a change in the variable affects the firm's financial performance. A chart, table, or another visual in the sidebar area should accompany each variable. These sections carry a weight of 15% of the rubric's total value.

It is essential to note word choice in this section. Sometimes students will use words like "correlate" or "significant" without showing the proof of these statistical words. The team can alleviate this concern by a chart demonstrating the correlation or further information in the appendix.

While the number of macroeconomic variables is limitless, the team should focus on the top three to five that have the largest effect. As the team attempts to distinguish themselves from the other teams, choosing interesting variables has a benefit. While the team would not want to ignore obvious variables such as oil prices for an energy company or disposable income for a retailer, the addition of a unique variable allows the analysis to stand apart. For example, greater fuel efficiency is a threat to oil and gas companies. However, an increase in vehicle miles traveled negates some of this threat. The report that includes both the obvious (price of oil) and the unique (vehicle miles traveled), especially when the unique counters the common concern and likely judges' question (fuel efficiency), demonstrates a more thorough analysis.

After identifying the macroeconomic environment, this section extends to include the position of the firm within the industry. Additional industry variables and unique industry characteristics complete the picture of the competitive landscape. Generally, the focus is on demand drivers. If the firm's revenues are quantity driven, the analysis identifies the variables that influence quantity such as how quickly downstream firms are growing, how demographics are changing, or how substitutes have slowed revenue growth. If the revenues are price driven, the focus is on elasticity or variables such as income and interest rates affect the price at which customers are willing or able to purchase.

If innovation drives the industry, this section examines research and development, time to market for new innovations, patents, and other traits that provide exclusivity to the firm.

If scale drives the industry, this section examines the role of the firm in acquiring new divisions, expanding geographically, controlling costs, or other traits that provide a cost or size advantage to the firm.

This section of the analysis may be from the viewpoint of a SWOT analysis or Porter's Five Forces. The benefit of Porter's Five Forces is that it gives structure to the SWOT analysis and allows the team to analyze the competitive environment in a well-known thematic process. Additionally, the spider diagram (also known as a radar chart) allows the team to present a visual on how significant each force is to the firm.

Relationship between business description and competitive positioning

While the two sections of business description and competitive positioning are separate, the two sections need to flow together. The business description introduces themes of the research, which competitive positioning expands.

If a firm a few main customers, the business description introduces those customers while competitive positioning presents which of the customers will be most important in the future, how their business outlook is, and any substitutes that could remove market share from your firm. If a firm has a wide variety of products, the business description familiarizes the reader with the major products, while competitive positioning presents the growth prospects of those products.

Typical value chain linkages between the two sections include geographic drivers, technology or innovation drivers, and consolidation drivers. If one considers demand as the intersection of willingness to buy and the ability to buy, these two sections scrutinize the main revenue drivers through this conceptual framework.

Somewhere in these sections, a team may want to consider providing a timeline of major events in the firm's history. If a theme of the report is mergers and acquisitions, the timeline is of the significant changes to scale. If the theme is growth, the timeline is of substantial expansions or growth milestones. If a theme is regulation, a timeline is of major laws and ruling along with any corresponding company-specific information.

Investment summary

Investment summary, which is 20% of the rubric score, starts with the buy/sell recommendation and the target price. The recommendation is immediately followed by essential information from the various valuation methods. The report will discuss all the critical points in greater detail in the next three sections, but investment summary starts with the conclusion.

After presenting the recommendation, the report typically presents the investment drivers. The drivers are the valuation inputs into the various models. For example, if the report has identified revenue growth as a critical part of the investment thesis, the investment summary presents revenue growth with the explanation of what is the team's consensus growth rate used in the discounted cash flow model. If relative valuation is a significant part of the overall valuation, the section presents the P/E or P/Sales multiple used in the calculations.

While the investment summary presents the justifications for the recommendation, it also presents caveats for each of the contributing factors. In the revenue growth example, the section would include the conditions that need to occur for the firm to achieve the growth rate.

The team would also address any additional concerns with the valuation in this section.

Valuation

While the investment summary presented the overall recommendations and main considerations, valuation presents the finer points of the analysis. Valuation is another 20% of the rubric's score. Thus, investment summary and valuation together are 40% of the overall score and the significant reason that a team moves forward into the next round. If two teams are very close, the judges typically view these sections as the deciding factor.

Almost all valuations include and start with a discounted cash flow analysis (DCF). A vital part of the DCF is a revenue forecast. This section of valuation presents the thought process and justification for the revenue forecast. The information refers to themes from the business description, industry overview, and competitive positioning as the team demonstrates how they took the concepts of those sections and translated them into values for the financial analysis.

The revenue growth forecast is the crucial first step. Errors in this forecast will throw off the entire valuation. Additionally, in the Q&A, the judges will ask detailed questions requiring the team to justify the number. It is important in this section to present the linkage from the prior sections of industry overview and competitive positioning as reasoning. For example, if a team identifies that revenue growth is dependent on market share expansion, the team is obligated to demonstrate how the market share expansion will occur and how it translates into the revenue forecast using numbers not just words.

Consider a health care firm. The team determines that total patient visits is the key revenue driver. The identification of this variable occurred in the industry section and is supported through a correlation value comparing total patient visits with revenue. Thus, the analysis established the importance of the variable in a prior section. In valuation, the variable is directly linked to the revenue forecast. The team forecasts total patient visits, which forecasts revenues, which forecasts the rest of the income statement and financial statements.

If a firm's revenue is more price driven, the analysis is parallel but focuses on changes in price. Consider an oil and gas firm with the price of oil as the key revenue driver. Forecasting future oil prices is trickier than total patient visits. Additionally, oil prices fluctuate based on macroeconomic and political factors, while total patient visits are more likely to follow a trend. In this case, the team may calculate a bull, bear, and middle forecasts based on the oil price. It is more work at this stage of the valuation. However, oil and gas firms do not have as many nuances in the later stages of the valuation.

Generally, the team forecasts the financial statements for 5 years. Then the team calculates a long-term growth rate in the calculation of the terminal value. A second subsection presents this methodology and numerical conclusion.

An integral part of this subsection is the calculations of the free cash flows (FCF) to the firm and to equity. Free cash flow is what remains after the firm has paid operating expenses and required capital expenditures. Free cash flow is what is available for growth. FCF is also available for dividends if the firm is an income stock.

The required rate of return calculation is the next essential step of this section. The methodology and justification for the calculation of the beta are central to this discussion. The weighted average cost of capital approach is the most common method. Teams must take care to use the correct equity and after-tax cost of debt values. For the cost of equity, the most common approach is the capital asset pricing model (CAPM). While the risk-free rate and market risk premium are assumptions, it is the calculation of the beta on which the judges focus.

The terminal value is a perpetuity using the discount rate and the long-term cash flow growth rate. Depending on the firm, the calculation could be the dividend discount model, but because most of the companies chosen are growth firms, the analysis is more likely to use the discount model using cash flows instead of dividends. The formula is just the dividend discount model (DDM) altered for cash flows.

$$\text{Terminal value} = [(\text{Final year forecasted cash flow})*(1 + \text{the long} - \text{term cash flow growth rate})] / (\text{Discount rate} - \text{the long} - \text{term cash flow growth rate})$$

Depending on the analysis, the sensitivity analysis of the future price to the long-term growth rate and the required rate of return is next or merely the results of the sensitivity analysis are next while the calculation is in the appendix. The team conducts the sensitivity analysis on the important assumptions of the DCF. While the team can do more sensitivity analyses, these two major assumptions are basic to the model.

If the firm pays dividends and it already has not been presented in the calculation of the terminal value, the report examines the dividend discount model (DDM). Even if the DDM is not the best way to value the firm, most reports include for completeness. If it is not relevant, the report presents the shortcomings of the model in regard to the firm. The justification typically revolves around the focus of the DDM on income stocks, which is inconsistent with the valuation of the team's growth stock.

A next common valuation method is a relative valuation. Reports typically demonstrate several relative valuation models and then present the justification for the better model. Sometimes teams will do a weighted average of the results of the various relative valuation models.

Typical relative valuation models include EV/EBITDA, price to operating cash flow, price to earnings, price to free cash flow, and price to earnings growth (PEG). Just as with the DDM, the relative models' justifications include a discussion on the companion variables in addition to the presentation of the conceptual analysis to values.

Because of the complexity of the calculations and the limits to the page length of the report, the appendix is an important companion to this section. In the appendix, the team can delineate the details of the calculation with further presentation of assumptions and sensitivity analysis.

For example, early in the appendix, the team presents the balance sheet with the 5–6 years of forecasted values and a common sized balance sheet. The next page is the same information but for the income statement. The statement of cash flows is next. The statements precede the financial ratios and the DuPont ratios, including forecasted ratios.

The pages that follow the basics of the financials are the assumption, calculation, and sensitivity analyses of the various valuation methods. Typically, the DCF is in greater detail, particularly in outlining team assumptions regarding growth rates and forecasted values.

The next model in the report is the Monte Carlo analysis. There are many ways to do a Monte Carlo, but the main idea is to test the sensitivity of the future price calculation against the key variables. While the variables tested differ for each firm, common variables are the required rate of return, revenue growth rate, interest rate, price of a significant input, tax rate, and industry growth rate. The simulations examine the frequency of the likely market price outcome.

It may seem odd to do a sensitivity analysis and then a Monte Carlo analysis on the same variables. A team could skip the sensitivity analysis. However, the Monte Carlo analysis is typically at the end of the valuation section, while the DCF is at the start of the section. A judge may not place the two valuation methods together. Thus, it is a safer action to include a sensitivity with the DCF to demonstrate to the judges that the team understands the importance of the key assumptions of the DCF. Additionally, the Monte Carlo analysis provides a further rationale for the future price recommendation. The sensitivity analysis is for the DCF while the Monte Carlo analysis is for the future price recommendation. Both results should reinforce each other and the report's overall recommendation.

A team can include additional valuation methods as it sees fit. If the firm is likely to be acquired, the team could include an acquisition or merger value or a leveraged buyout valuation, depending on the information available. These are more advanced methods and requires that the team has an opinion on who would do the purchasing. The negative of including these methods is that a judge may expect that the team has also completed a valuation impact on the buyer's financials of the acquisition.

Financial analysis

Either within the investment summary section or the valuation section, the team may present important financial ratios and other assumptions. The most likely position is after the investment summary and before valuation. The financial analysis, while not a specific line on the rubric, allows the team to present their rationale for other assumptions in their forecast.

A common piece of the financial analysis is a discussion on margins and whether the team expects operating margins to expand, contract, or remain constant.

In the DuPont Analysis, the team may have identified strengths or weaknesses of the firm, particularly with return on equity.

A team may discuss the interest burden on a firm with significant debt, including any drag on the earnings and cash flow.

Because of space limitations, the financial analysis typically presents the conclusions with greater detail in the appendix.

Investment risks

Before concluding the valuation topic, the report's next section is investment risk, comprising 15% of the rubric total. A thematic way to present the risks is to include a visual highlighting the probability of the risks with the impact of the risks. Risks plotted near the origin have a low probability and a low impact. Risks in the top-right part of the graph have a high probability and a high impact.

The investment risk section acts as a conclusion to the valuation section and allows the team to revisit various topics already presented in prior sections with a cohesive and unified comparison.

While the number of potential risks is limitless, common risks are regulation, revenue driver risk, technology risk, operational risk, liquidity risk, substitute product risk, and entry of new firm risk. As in much of the discussion, the type of firm informs the risks. An energy firm generally has fewer risks, but each risk has a substantial impact. In comparison, a retail firm has many risks of varying impact and probability.

Teams should view this section as a summary section that presents the caveats. It is also a section that allows the team's in-depth research to presents the nuances of the analysis. The team can stand out from other teams by delineating how their analysis is superior to other teams. At the local level, while all the teams will do valuation, the numbers will differ but, most likely, be in the same general area. For example, one team might find a future price of $53.87, while another team calculates $48.56. These are real differences, but if the thought process is solid, each teams' numbers can be justified. In contrast, investment risks have a greater tendency to differ among the teams, especially in presentation.

Corporate governance

The last section of corporate governance is 5% of the rubric point total. While the rubric lists it last, it does not have to be in last position. Depending on how long the various sections are, a team may decide to move corporate governance to a location where there is white space or to a place to help even out the appearance of the report. If one of the risks of the firm is management, especially succession, the position of corporate governance may be near the investment risks section.

Corporate governance tends to provide a quick overview of the management team. More detailed information on the insiders is in the appendix. If compensation is an issue, the report needs to address compensation. As mentioned above, if succession or age of management is a risk, the report presents it in the conceptual framework of firm valuation and growth. For firms with high or low institutional holdings compared to competitors, the report discusses these implications.

Environmental, social, and governance issues as they relate to stakeholder goals is a necessary section. For a firm such as oil and gas, the report must address the environmental considerations. While the team may be positive on the firm and industry, some judges will not share that viewpoint. The report must address environmental concerns evenly.

Other things to include

- Each section should have a concluding statement that reinforces the main themes of the analysis. The statement or phrase should be bolded or highlighted.
- Headings should be used frequently to help guide the reader and strengthen the investment themes.
- Each chart, table, and graphic must have a source.
- The stock price chart with major events highlighted can be in the main report or the appendix, wherever there is appropriate space.
- The appendix must have a reference section.
- The appendix might have a glossary page for industry terms that may not be familiar to the reader.
- The appendix might have a page on competitors and/or the supply chain as a visual companion with greater detail that what the section on competitive positioning provides.
- A more in-depth SWOT and a Porter's Five Forces analyses may be in the appendix.

A common theme of the list is that the appendix provides greater detail, and the report provides the summary and highlights. For example, a student who will write on industry overview and competitive positioning may first write the appendix SWOT and Five Forces. The team summarizes the information into the main body of the report.

Exhibit 7.7 Example CFA Institute Research Challenge presentation

CFA Institute Research Challenge
hosted by
CFA Societies Texas, Louisiana and Oklahoma
Local Challenge – Southwest U.S.
West Texas A&M University

February 5, 2017
Industry: Healthcare
Sector: Medical Services

U.S. Physical Therapy
New York Stock Exchange

Recommendation: **SELL**

Ticker: **USPH [NYSE]**
Current Price: **$71.45 (2/6/17)**

Price Target: **$65.64**
Discount: **8.13%**

USPH Stock Price
Source: Team Calculations and Nasdaq Data

Business Description: USPH is the third largest public company providing outpatient physical therapy. Their strategy is to acquire physical therapy clinics and provide back office administrative activities, marketing, and billing support. USPH's current stock price of $71.45 per share is at an all-time high. USPH has been able to successfully acquire quality clinics. Their strategy is to acquire clinic in areas with higher reimbursement rates. They have strong debt management and significant cash availability. We project USPH's revenue to increase by 7.5% annually through 2021.

Industry: The industry is highly fragmented. USPH owns approximately 1.4% of total rehabilitation centers in the U.S. No one in the market owns more than 10%. Revenue growth for the physical therapy rehabilitation industry is expected to grow at 1.8% in the next five years.

While USPH is financially sound, their current stock price is overvalued. We recommend a sell based on six models:

1. Running a Discounted Cash Flow analysis calculated an intrinsic value of $65.64 per share. The intrinsic value price is discounted 8.13% below their current market price of $71.45.
2. Price multiples between competitors show USPH to be overvalued. All ratios indicate that investors are paying more per dollar for income related to competitors. USPH has a current P/E ratio of 33.3, approximately 200% above their competitors.
3. A Monte Carlo simulation using a tax rate of 32%, shows that 57% of scenario prices are overvalued compared to the current market price. The assumption of using 32% tax rate is based on the historic USPH tax rate.
4. While revenues are increasing, the revenue growth rate is decelerating. Six revenue models identity total patient visits as the single most influential variable. Even at a projected 7.5% growth rate, we conclude that this growth does not justify the current stock price. Revenue per patient plateaus indicate USPH has reached a limit on their efficiency gains. As the market turns to consolidation, fewer clinics will be acquirable; this will decrease the amount that USPH will be acquiring, which will slow growth in total patient visits.
5. The Dividend Discount model predicts the net present value of returns over the next five years. This model indicates that the price per share is $20.16 under the current market price. Investors cannot expect to be properly compensated from the dividends received to justify current stock price.
6. A DuPont Ratio analysis indicates that Return on Equity (ROE) is decreasing. ROE in 2011 was 17%. In 2016, 11%, and is forecasted to be 10% by 2021.

The multiple models used to analyze USPH's stock provide consistent evidence that the current market price is overvalued. These models confirm our recommendation to sell.

Valuation Summary	
DCF	65.64

Other Valuation	
DDM	51.28
Multiples:	
P/EG	64.73
P/E	33.30
P/CF	16.46

EXPECTED EARNINGS GROWTH

Market Profile	
52 Week Price Range	$45.76 - $73.05
Average Daily Volume (3m)	81,104
Beta (3m)	0.85
Shares Outstanding	12.52M
Market Capitalization	894M
Institutional Holdings	12.47
Insider Holdings	0.33
Book Value per Share	$14.28
Debt to Equity	0.2

Source: Morningstar, Nasdaq

Comparison	USPH	SEM	HLS
Forward P/E	$33.33	$13.30	$15.30
Earnings Growth (1-3 yr.)	9	8.8	5.8
P/EG Ratio	3.7	1.51	2.64

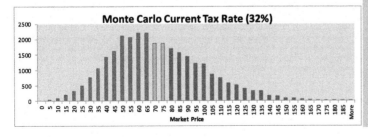

U.S. PHYSICAL THERAPY, INC.

Figure 2

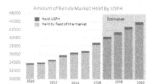

Amount of Rehab Market Held By USPH

Source: Team Calculations, IBIS World

Figure 3

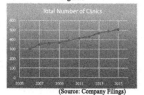

Total Number of Clinics

(Source: Company Filings)

Figure 4

UPSH Revenue Breakdown

(Source: Company Filings)

Figure 5

Name and Position	Year	Stock Awards
Christopher J. R.	2015	$1,140,253.00
-CEO	2014	$1,552,200.00
	2013	$974,400.00
Lawrence W. M.	2015	$570,126.00
-CFO	2014	$776,100.00
	2013	$487,200.00
Glenn D M.	2015	$570,126.00
-COO	2014	$776,100.00
	2013	$487,200.00

(Source: Company Filings)

Business Description

US Physical Therapy (USPH) was founded in Houston, TX in 1990. Outpatient physical therapy clinic acquisitions and start ups are their specialty. In addition, they manage twenty-one clinics for third parties. They are a general partner in their wholly owned clinics, while they can own interest from 49% to 99% in their limited partnerships depending on the developed agreement with the existing therapist. In the majority of clinic partnerships, USPH owns a limited partnership interest of 64%. Starting with just 55 clinics in 1994, USPH has grown into one of the largest groups of physical therapy clinics in America. USPH went public two years after starting, first being listed on the NASDAQ, changing to the NYSE in 2012. USPH provides physical therapy services through its subsidiaries for a variety of rehabilitation needs from injuries and pre/post operation. The majority of patient visits come from physician referrals. Patients are treated on a multi-weekly basis, usually for an hour a day. Depending on physician recommendation, patients therapy recovery time is around 6 weeks. They are paid on a fee for service basis from insurance reimbursement, workers compensation, and government plans. Due to their large market share, they attract new clinics by the management services they provide and the ability to negotiate insurance rates. These services include accounting, billing, marketing campaigns, and guidance with legal compliance. In return, subsidiaries are able to focus on the patient's needs and satisfaction with service.

By emphasizing growth through the starting of de novo clinics and the acquisition of established facilities, USPH has grown to 540 clinics (2016) in 42 states and currently employs approximately 3,400 employees. Currently being ranked the third largest in the industry, USPH only owns approximately 3.4% of the total physical therapy practices. This emphasizes the amount of fragmentation that exists in this industry. Unlike many competitors, USPH has a primary focus on physical therapists, which has perpetuated attraction by quality partnerships, growing company revenue, and increasing market share. Their revenue strategy is to own the majority interest of the clinic, while allowing the original physical therapist to own a specified minority. Successful physical therapists will be able to increase their minority interest up to 35%, which encourages growth in revenue and patient referrals.

The industry is highly regulated by government entities that also control reimbursement rates for a portion of the business making it subject to certain risks. With an average return of approximately 33.7% annually, USPH is categorized as an aggressive growth stock.

Company Strategy
Understanding the fragmentation in the industry, USPH focuses on five specific areas:

- **Acquiring Established Growth Oriented Clinics-** USPH profits from the acquisition of quality physical therapy facilities located in suburban areas that have high reimbursement trends and high relative populations. They attract therapists who are actively pursuing efficient growth with a large referral base. They market to those who are looking to narrow their focus to their medical practices without completely losing control of their business. This appeals to physical therapists who do not want to operate under a corporate name but want the efficiency of one.

- **De Novo/Satellite Clinics -** USPH focuses on underserved areas in the development of their own wholly owned clinics, while also focusing on expansion through the development of satellite clinics. Successful clinics gain management of satellite clinic, which further increase USPH market shares and overall company efficiency.

- **Diversified Revenue That Provides Higher Reimbursement Rates-** The physical care industry is threatened by constant change in reimbursement rates for Medicare/Medicaid. USPH has looked to diversify payment risk by minimizing exposure to government reimbursement. USPH has kept their Medicare/Medicaid reimbursement on average of 24% by pushing their business towards claims dealing with contractual agreements in company worker's compensation, middle class customers likely to have private insurance, and athletic injuries. Though it is more difficult to obtain this customer base, USPH has focused on the higher reimbursement rates these claims provide.

- **Relationship Oriented -** Before an acquisition, USPH executives examine each physical therapy group to better gain understanding on their future growth potential. On a personal level, they will get to know the therapist and their families to evaluate how they would fit within the ethical (and quality driven) structure of the company. This continues on a lower level, as each physical therapist is encouraged to engage with the community; USPH wants their subsidiaries to build relationships with their communities. Considering the personal nature of physical therapy, this methodology has allowed USPH to be successful on a micro level.

- **Referral Connections -** USPH has recognized the importance of physician referrals, considering most insurance companies require customers to be referred by a physician to be treated by a physical therapist. When evaluating areas of acquisition, USPH will observe the physical therapist with the most developed relationships with physician clinics. This area is a major focus within the company, as it is the best method of increasing total patient visits; a big driver for their net patient revenues.

Corporate Governance

Upper management - A large part of the success in the healthcare industry is dependent upon quality management. USPH has pushed for the success of their management in relation to their stock and company equally. Christopher Reading (CEO) and Lawrence McAfee (CFO) both have a seat on the board of directors. Reading and McAfee have held seats and those positions since 2004. USPH is unique from its competitors in that their upper management all have a therapist/hospital background which has given them a unique perspective on their business operations. (See appendix for information on specific corporate compensation structuring).

- **Insider Trading –** As explained in figure 5, USPH has given generous stock options to management for successful years. To ensure continual earning growth, USPH awards stock and cash bonuses to their senior management. Annual fiscal earnings incentives give Christopher Reading (CEO), Lawrence McAfee (CFO), and Glen McDowell (COO) the ability to earn up to 125% of their base salaries in cash bonuses for EPS goal attainment. There are also long term stock incentives for EPS goal attainments from the previous years: up to 16,000, 8,000, and 8,000 shares respectively. All upper-management persons are able to receive stock options based on senior management decisions. Management salaries are a large portion of stock options, and "insiders" have been selling since August 2015. Because of this, it is inconclusive to state the possible reasons for insider stock sales.

Figure 6

- ■ Neuberger Berman Group
  1,091,731 - 8.4%
- ■ Blackrock Fund Advisors
  927,868 - 7.14%
- ■ Royal Bank of Canada
  790,671 - 6.1%
- ■ Vanguard Group INC
  598,286 - 4.6%
- ■ Renaissance Technologies LLC
  573,654 - 4.4%

TOP 5 HOLDINGS

(Source: Nasdaq.com)

Figure 7

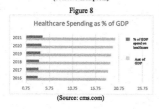

(Source: Nasdaq.com)

Figure 8

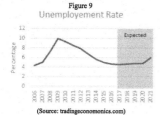

(Source: cms.com)

Figure 9

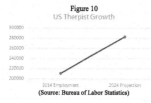

(Source: tradingeconomonics.com)

Figure 10

(Source: Bureau of Labor Statistics)

Figure 11

Average Price for Each Major Surgury

(Source: Harvard Medical Review, Spinehealth.com, and Team)

Board of Directors - The board of directors, in addition to the insider directors and the non-director officer, own 4.3% composite in stock shares. In accordance with the NYSE standards, there are 7 independent board of directors, who have no relationship with the company in question, defined by the Securities Exchange Commission (Securities Exchange Act of 1934).

- **Responsibilities** - USPH Board has adopted a Code of Ethics, created a compliance committee, meets four times a year, declares dividends and compensation, repurchase/issue shares of stock, and selects an auditing firm. Final decisions are voted on by shareholders, with one share equaling one vote.

Institutional Holdings - Currently USPH has 13 million shares outstanding with a total value at approximately $838 million. The top three institutional holders are Neuberger Berman Group (8.4%), Blackrock, Inc (7.14%), and RBC Global Asset Management (U.S.) Inc (7.1%), with total institutional holdings at 98.51% (1/17). Large shifts in institutional buying or selling of UPSH stock may negatively or positively affect USPH price.

- **New/Sold Out** - Investors have had the tendency to buy USPH with almost three times as many new positions as there was sold out positions. This is representative of our consensus in market over - buying.
- **Decrease/Increase** - USPH has had fewer investors decrease their position. We estimate this is due to institutions wanting to rebalance or capitalize on recent price appreciation.

Industry Overview & Competitive Positioning

USPH is a part of the healthcare sector within the outpatient physical therapy clinic industry accounting for $30 billion in annual revenue that is anticipated to grow at 1.6% in the next five years. The main sources of demand come from Medicare/Medicaid customers from government plans, private insurance held by young athletes and upper - middle class persons aged 35-65, and workers compensation claims through contractual agreements. See appendix J for "food supply chain" of outpatient physical therapy clinics.

Economic Drivers:

- **GDP** – The United States has been proven the wealthiest industrialized country globally with a GDP of 18.04 trillion dollars in production. The regulated United States growth is more favorable than the economy of countries like China because of the steady and constant nature it provides. This demonstrates long term future benefits as GDP is expected to grow at 2.2% in 2017, and 2.3% in 2018, far above most other developed countries. In addition, expected further growth is anticipated as the newly elected administration carries out its focus on economic growth.
- **Unemployment rate** - The low unemployment rate of 4.6% has created the ability for individuals to consume. As Americans enter the workforce their disposable income is increasing; further positively affecting GDP and ability to hold private insurance.
- **Healthcare Spending** - US healthcare spending increased 5.8% in 2015 to $3.2 trillion, composing 17.8% of annual GDP. This percentage of GDP significantly increases available cash flow circulation that will allow USPH to grow.
- **ACA-** The Affordable Care Act has increased demand in all aspects of the healthcare industry by requiring insurance for all with a fine for noncompliance. More people are covered than ever before, which has decreased money reserves available for insurance companies to pay for rising costs, causing premiums to increase. This decrease in money supply has also caused insurance companies to find cheaper alternatives. The inexpensive and long term successful nature of physical therapy has led many insurance companies to push easily recoverable customers to physical therapy care. The profits to be realized from an increased insured population have caused many rehabilitation institutions to enter the market to capture economic profits.

Industry Growth and Demand:

The healthcare industry as a whole has had strong and continuous growth patterns above most other industries in years past. The physical therapy industry specifically has been in a growth phase, considering its alternative cost to expensive procedures and successful treatment rate. Because of decreasing margins, insurance companies are continually looking for cost affective and less recurring alternatives to surgery.

- The physical therapy rehabilitation centers industry is expected to slow in growth at 1.6% for the next five years, while previously growing at 2.2%.
- Physical therapist jobs are forecasted to increase on average by 33% over the next 10 years. The demand for physical therapists have significantly increased because of this growth rate, as it was the 8th fastest growing jobs in 2015.

Demand for Low Cost Alternatives Has Increased Demand for Physical Therapy

To better govern costs, emerging electronic health records (EHR) has given Government entities the ability to track outcomes for medical services. The Center for Medicare & Medicaid Services (CMS) has pushed all forms of medical services to an E.H.R. requirement that tracks the type of patient, treatment plans, and success of treatment. This technology has become a requirement for any medical services institution that has reimbursement from Medicare/Medicaid. Quality is now being pushed more than ever, and is now more able to be quantified. The CMS has outlined their plan for medical services in the coming years:

1. Achieve better overall health care by making care more person-centered, reliable, accessible and safe;
2. Keep people and communities healthier by supporting proven interventions that address behavioral, social and environmental determinants of health; and
3. spur smarter spending of health care dollars that ultimately will reduce the cost of health care for everyone.

Insurance companies are piggy-backing off of the CMS's requirements by following the medical services that meet the technological standards of quality. Both government entities and private insurance are pushing for better quality and low cost methods. Harvard business medical review recently performed multiple studies relating spinal fusion surgery and physical therapy outcomes. For lower lumbar spinal stenosis (averaging $115,000 + 6 weeks of physical therapy), 169 persons were reviewed: half received back surgery with 6 weeks of physical therapy, the other half received just physical therapy. After two years, there was no difference in pain or function between the surgery and physical therapy groups. In addition, 25% reported recurring complications from surgery, while only 10% reported recurring complication from physical therapy. More than 650,000 spinal surgical procedures are being performed annually in the United States, with costs exceeding $20 billion. Of these 650,000 performed, it would only take 25% success rate of that number to save over $5.8 billion using physical therapy, though actual success rates would be close to surgery (tens of billions savings). The evidence is there for insurance and government to observe through technology. Companies will move into the market to capture the demand from insurance. It is estimated that over 15,000 new rehabilitations will enter the market by 2021. This could negatively affect USPH, as the flood of entrants is also accompanied with lowering ability to control pricing.

Figure 12

ACO Increases 2011-2016

(Source: healthpayorintelligence.com and Team)

Figure 13

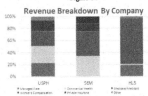

Uninsured Rate by Percent of Population

Where the Industry is Moving: ACO's - Accountable Care Organizations (ACO) were expedited through the ACA as a way to lower costs by working together as a cohesive group. Created by either large insurance companies or private sector organizations, an ACO is an organization that works together with all aspects of the medical delivery model to maintain a higher quality service while decreasing costs. This is achieved by keeping medical professionals accountable for their success rates by the use of technical information, which will help to reduce the amount Medicare, Medicaid and Insurance companies are paying. Since inception, ACOs have been growing in popularity: approximately 70% of the population can be served by an ACO. The amount of ACOs have grown since 2011 to over 800 groups today (Figure 12). Insurance companies are using ACO's to ensure that quality care is taken, which mitigates the risk that is accompanied with different treatment. Because of this large trend in quality, it is important to be on the receiving end of an ACO partnership. Due to their efficient care models, ACOs can profit from the utilization of a therapist; therapists benefit by the referral of a new stream of patients. However, it is difficult, if not impossible, for a single physical therapist to become a part of an ACO. If there is an ACO in the area, USPH brings the ability to negotiate on a individual providers behalf, in order to possibly gain entry into the organization. Because of this, group clinic and individual clinics will demand the services USPH provides in areas with ACO groups. USPH has proven their quality, and will be able to easily negotiate with their size and fiscal soundness. As more ACO groups are formed, however, USPH may be hindered from entering certain markets.

Increase in Prime Earning Year Customers Increasing Demand for Physical Therapy - The time that USPH has taken to acquire each clinic has allowed them to be strategically placed within each age demographic of the United States. Though they service people in all age groups, they have an increased portion of patients in the **45-54** age group. This age group is the largest demographic of private insurance holders, which benefits USPH's high insurance market share. This also lowers no show rates, as this age group is most likely to show up to appointments at the scheduled time. As the population is aging, lower unemployment rates allow more people in this age group to hold jobs that offer insurance. Longer life spans are causing people to remain working, keeping employment insurance in place for a longer period. This trend benefits USPH, as they have been able to fill the demand caused by this wave of the working class. In addition, population ages 65+ will be increasing exponentially in the next years, which will cause government spending on Medicare to increase. USPH capitalizes by marketing to each age group for its unique characteristics: see Appendix S for a more in-depth analysis of each age group.

Competitive Positioning

The industry is largely fragmented and only has a few large players each holding less than ten percent of market share. There are approximately 32,000 physical therapy rehabilitation centers in the U.S. and USPH has ownership rights of over 500. Because of fragmentation, USPH has been hesitant to expand in certain states with a high saturation of clinics. Though these clinics may not be owned by their main competitors, large groups of physical therapy clinics dot across the US, leaving less market share acquirable. There are few differentiated characteristics between these physical therapy institutions, so competition must be segmented through business operation differentials. USPH is one of the few companies who operates solely in the outpatient therapy rehab sector, however, while other competitors also have stake in specialty hospitals and inpatient at-home physical therapy. Because of this, there are no perfect competitors available for stock comparison. Based on the similarity in business operations, our team found the following to be USPH's main competition:

Figure 14

Revenue Breakdown By Company

(Source: Company 10K and Team)

Table 1

Company	Correlation
USPH	-0.042
SEM	0.21
HLS	0.08

(Source: Company 10K and Team Calculations)

Figure 15

Accepted PTCAS Aplicants By Age

■ 0-19 ■ 20-25 ■ 26-30 ■ 31-35 ■ 36-40 ■ 41-45 ■ 46+

(Source: ptcas.org and Team)

- Healthsouth Corporation (HLS) is an internationally operating provider of medical rehabilitation (109 outpatient clinics in the U.S.), specialty hospital, and home health. Their locations total more than 1,900 clinics with facilities in United Kingdom and Australia. Operating in 34 states, Healthsouth was organized in 1984. Net revenues for Healthsouth reached $3,162,900,000 in 2015 from their various focuses on professional sports and major corporate partnerships.

- Select Medical Corporation (SEM) expanded to outpatient physical therapy through the acquisition of Physiotherapy. Both outpatient and inpatient specialty hospitals clinics total approximately 1,500 clinics and are located in 46 states. With net revenues reaching $2,804,507,000 in 2015, clients served by Select Medical range from critically ill individuals to elite athletes.

- ATI Physical Therapy is a privately held company founded in 1996 that acquires various physical therapy specialties along with home health care services. Focusing on patient relationships, they emphasis meeting the goals of their clients and gaining satisfaction. ATI has grown to 600 clinics in 24 states.

Favorable Revenue Streams - For business operations, USPH has been able to produce a significantly less portion of their revenue from Medicare/Medicaid (24.5%). Because of the flux in government spending for Medicare and Medicaid, USPH has had more stable revenues throughout the years. Using percentage changes from government spending on Medicare/Medicare per year and percentage changes in revenue in each company, it can be seen that competitors with higher percentages of revenue from Medicare/Medicare have revenues that correlate more with fluctuating government spending on Medicare and Medicaid. The low correlation for USPH is positive for USPH in more stable revenue, and less uncertainty with pending government adjustment costs. USPH is able to better diversify their revenue streams, i.e. 50% of USPH's revenue comes from private insurance. USPH has taken advantage of their positioning by appealing to physicians for referrals that will also have a diversified mix of payers. This situation allows USPH to negotiate a larger portion of their revenue with insurance companies rather than take fixed amount from the federal government. However, this also subjugates USPH to certain risks related to a dependence upon private insurance. See Appendix L for USPH competitor revenue breakdown.

Progressive Business Model that Appeals to a Growing Generation - The upcoming millennial generation have unique characteristics that USPH will capture. Millennials are less likely to be entrepreneurial in nature, meaning they are less likely to develop business' of their own. According to a recent Harvard Business Review study, millennials are more relationship oriented, wanting to be able to focus solely on the quality of their work and relationships in their work. Consequently, they are more prone to focus on separation of specified work (physical therapy) and everything that is involved in running a business. USPH has recognized this need, and will continue to market acquisitions to therapists of this growing demographic by allowing focus to be placed on the actual physical therapy; creating value by supplementing accounting, legal, technical, and logistically based areas of the business operation. Considering the millennial (especially ages 20-25) generation is also the largest group of recent physical therapy licensures, the model USPH utilizes will continue to allow growth.

Table 2

Top 10 Urban States in US		
State	% of Urban State	% of USPH Total
CA	92.6%	0.19%
NJ	89.4%	2.96%
HI	89.0%	0.00%
NV	88.3%	0.56%
AZ	87.3%	2.22%
UT	87.0%	0.00%
RI	86.0%	0.00%
FL	84.8%	1.48%
IL	84.6%	0.93%
MA	84.3%	0.37%

(Source: Company filings and Bureau of Labor)

Table 3

Top 10 States for USPH		
State	% of USPH Total	% of Urban (AVG 67%
TX	13.2%	80.30%
TN	13.2%	60.90%
MI	9.3%	70.50%
VA	8.0%	69.40%
WA	6.9%	76.40%
MD	5.7%	81.30%
GA	5.0%	63.20%
OR	4.8%	70.50%
PA	3.9%	68.90%
WI	8.9%	65.70%

(Source: Company filings and Bureau of Labor)

Figure 18

Average Patient Per Day, Per Clinic

(Source: Company filings and Team)

Figure 19

Cost of the Most Disabling Injuries

(Source: Liberty Mutual Research and Team)

Figure 20

Porter's Five Forces

(Source: Team Projections)

Progressive Business Model that appeals to an exit-ing generation
Capitalizing on the other end of the demographic spectrum, USPH will appeal to the entrepreneurial generation getting close to retirement. Those looking for an exit strategy will benefit from USPH buying a portion of their business and slowly lifting the load, while guaranteeing the purchase of the business as a whole from the owner upon retirement.

Pinnacle ACO positioning for past/present/future acquisitions - Due to their previous employment as physical therapists, the personal experience of each USPH executive have given them unique insights. Understanding the importance of relationships between patient/therapist/management dynamics is valuable. More valuable is the management mindset for personal relationships, allowing them to focus on both present and future revenue potential based on the individual clinic's business model and values. In an industry where quality is becoming paramount, this atmosphere of management will continue to allow growth. The time taken to assure quality acquisitions have allowed USPH to acquire preferred clinics. The market movement to Accountable Care Organizations will continue to raise demand for USPH's model through their beneficiary capability, an increased focus on clinical outcomes will help ensure success in the ACO era.

Location, location, location... - USPH has developed their clinics in areas with less market supply. This has created an advantage to their insurance revenue mix, considering private insurance allowables are higher in markets with more demand (less supply of providers). USPH has consistently owned markets in which they are able to take a majority. While capturing a majority, the areas chosen are more suburban in nature, which also constitute higher fee schedules. Their large revenue mix of workers compensation has also led them to develop clinics in more manufacturing based areas. More manufacturing based areas give way to more demand from the need for hedging liabilities of high injury prone jobs. Physical therapy prevents workplace accidents and companies can decrease their insurance cost by putting in specific preventative measures. USPH creates contracts like Fit2Wrk to capture the market in their areas. USPH has also correlated their clinics with areas that have larger relative percentages of ages 45-55; these are the customers most likely to have private insurance. (see Appendix R for more detail on locations for specified demand qualities).

Employee Attraction - USPH's business model profits on the quality of their employees connections within their community. Considering the labor intense nature of physical therapy, it is important to capture the best talent. USPH out performed their competitor by attracting the best employees in the market with their benefit packages. Allowing profit sharing up to 35% encourages physicians to remain active in growing their business model. As discussed, taking on the back office activities USPH attracts physical therapists who want to focus on providing quality therapy to a larger volume of patients.

Increasing Net Revenue Per Visit – Adding extra visits per-day per-clinic has allowed USPH to be able to grow their revenues at a higher rate than their increases in acquisitions and developments. USPH's management supplementation has allowed their clinics to focus primarily on patients, which has increased the amount of patient visits per day. USPH has continually stated their intent to push clinic groups to better daily productivity. Because of the time taken for each clinic acquisition, USPH upper management ensures each clinic has that goal in mind, which has been demonstrated with the growth of each clinic's average visit per day. To continue in this trend, USPH must increase the number of visits per day at a greater extent. We believe USPH is close to peak efficiency in their operations.

Revenue from Workers compensation - At 18.5%, USPH has been able to secure revenue through workers compensation plans more than any of their competition. According to OSHA, there are 4.1 million work related injuries and illnesses per year. Injuries from workplace injuries can impose substantial costs to employers. USPH recognized this need and implemented the program Fit2Wrk to give preventative care for injury prone work environments. Negotiated contracts with companies allow less time and cost from injuries, while expediting job return time. These contracts guarantee patients, and the increasing costs for companies will continue the need for USPH's Fit2Wrk service. Recently, USPH has had a recent dip in revenue from workers comp. We estimate that it will be difficult to continue to keep high streams of revenue from workers compensation as the industry grows and mean population age increases, leaving more revenue from Medicare/Medicaid.

Porter's Five Forces:
- **Competitive Rivalry** - SIGNIFICANT
This industry remains highly fragmented with a large amount of physical therapist owning their own clinics, which increase competition for USPH. However, because USPH operates solely in the physical therapist area and is publically traded (unlike most of their competitors), they have been able to acquire more strategic locations and bypass low margin practices.
- **Bargaining Power of Suppliers** - AVERAGE
Over 70% of USPH's revenue comes from set insurance and government rates. However, USPH acquires locations within suburban areas where the fee schedule are set at a higher rate. Because reimbursement rates are set by location and demand, USPH has mitigated supplier power with their location strategy. USPH has been efficient in their operations, which appeals to insurance and government entities that are looking for better outcomes. The size of USPH has also given them power in rate setting, as they are more able to bargain for their clinics.
- **Bargaining Power of Customers** - LOW
The bargaining power of suppliers is directly related to the power of customers, considering over 93% of patients come in with alternative payments methods. Customers that try to bargain rates with their insurance companies are the only source of bargaining threat to USPH, though the likelihood of this occurring on a large scale basis in very minimal.
- **Threat of new Entrants** - AVERAGE
The cost to enter this industry as a physical therapist is fairly low. With high demand for this service, it would be fairly easy for therapists get started. USPH's business has pushed the market to therapists joining a group practice, rather than creating an individual clinic. Due to the new nature of acquiring and consolidation, however, it may be easier for some groups to become a larger part of the market through acquisitions. USPH remains highly competitive with the large number of clinics it owns and the methodology in its acquiring.
- **Threat of Substitute Products or Services** - LOW
All suitable substitutions to physical therapy are more costly and on-going pain management difficulties. These are the reasons why USPH has become the alternative to many of the available substitutes. Insurance companies have focused on USPH as the cheapest/most favorable option due to the expensive nature of surgery, other costly procedures, and medications.

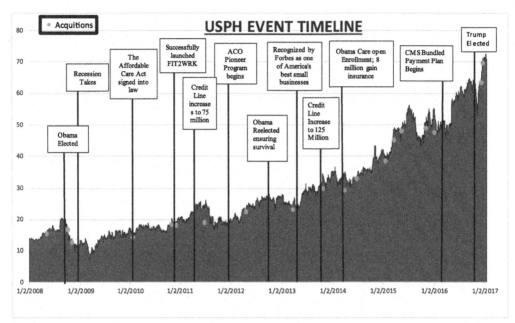

Figure 21

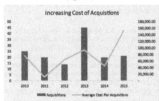

Source: Company Filings and Team Calculations

Figure 22

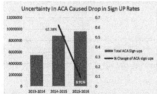

Source: Team Calculations and CMA

Figure 23

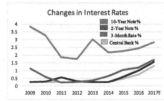

Source: Bloomberg

Investment Summary

We issue a sell recommendation for USPH with a target price of $65.64, primarily using a discounted cash flow to equity method. This is a 8.13% under the current price of 71.45 (2-3-17). USPH is currently experiencing a price of an all time high since its inception in 1992. Investors have showed support for the success of USPH through their expectations and price appreciation. USPH is a well-managed company with solid financials and cash availability for growth opportunities. The macro-environment favors the company with possible tax rate cuts. As we incorporate all the positive aspects and potential of the company in a forecast, the stock is still close to a hold. We do not deny their merit; USPH has proven their ability to be a successful company. The sell issue does not reside in problems with USPH: we attribute the overvaluation to recent market run-ups. This has caused price per share to increase beyond its intrinsic value. Investors would be better finding investments with more growth opportunities. We expect the market to adjust in the near future. We outline the causes for this consensus below:

- **High P/E Ratio Coupled with Unjustified Earnings**: USPH has a forward P/E ratio of 33.3 with a relative P/E of 1.40x. Our team estimates that earnings per share for 2016 are $1.92, creating a current P/E of 37. We expect earnings per share to grow at 7.82%. P/E will have to rise high above the current number to supplement an investor for price appreciation and return. As we except that as earnings grow at this rate, investors will be less willing to pay for the earnings growth at the current price and sell for capital gains. If USPH managed to keep their forward P/E at 33.3, we estimate that future price would be at $91.24 by 2021. This would only annualize to a 6.3%; less than our required rate of 8.4%. Any scare in expectations could cause a severe price dip: the recent price hike of $20 was from their earning announcement in November of 2016. Before this, stock price was falling quickly. If earnings do not meet the new market expectation increases, there could be a sharp decline in price. We anticipate earnings will not meet current price expectations.

- **Increasing Price of Future Acquisition Targets:** The price per acquisition has had an increasing trend; should this trend continue, USPH will be subject to a decrease in cash flow that will negativity effect their current debt structure. Funds being drawn away from cash flows could hinder growth potentials and cause investors to scare in response, lowering stock price. To increase earnings by the current prices expectations, USPH would have to acquire at a higher rate than expected. As the price of acquisitions continues to increase from less market supply, USPH will have to pay more for their clinics. We estimate that USPH will not acquire at the rate to justify current market price.

- **Uncertainty in the Environment Increases Risk:** USPH has been able to successfully diversify their payments between different sources. USPH primarily focuses on insurance, as insurance provides the highest reimbursement rates. This has given USPH competitive advantages in the past. Because of this large percentage in revenue, however, USPH is subject to certain risks that private insurance are also subject. The uncertainty regarding congressional rule may hinder profits through interstate insurance, lowering reimbursement rates from excess supply of insurance providers. Some of the largest health insurance companies have stated their intention of leaving the ACA, with estimates of only one health insurance company available through the ACA in 2017 . If USPH has a customer base from ACA, they will likely lose this customer visits. This could potentially severely effect their total patient visits; one of the main revenue drivers. For a detailed outline of possible congressional rulings effects, see appendix for details.

- **Interest rates:** USPH has a revolving line of credit for 125 million with interest of LIBOR + 1.5% -2.5%. As interest rates increase, cost of debt will increase. This could reduce cash flow and create an unattractive view towards investors. This also contributes to DCF. As interest rates rise, investors will expect more from their returns. Assuming higher interest rates, investors could find better opportunity for investments with higher returns.

ROE Composition Breakdown: For an In-depth Analysis , See Appendix

USPH	Historical							Forecast				
	2010	2011	2012	2013	2014	2015	2016E	2017E	2018E	2019E	2020E	2021E
ROE	13%	17%	13%	8%	12%	12%	11%	11%	11%	11%	10%	10%
ROA	11%	13%	10%	6%	9%	8%	8%	8%	8%	8%	9%	9%
Profit Margin	7%	9%	7%	5%	7%	7%	7%	7%	7%	7%	7%	7%
Tota Asset Turnover	150%	145%	147%	118%	125%	118%	113%	119%	118%	122%	124%	126%
Equity Multiplier	121%	134%	128%	148%	146%	145%	1.42	1.33	132%	126%	122%	1.19

Figure 25

RETURN ON EQUITY

Source: Team Calculations

Financial Analysis

Profitabilty Ratio	2013	2014	2015	2016E	2017E	2018E	2019E	2020E	2021E
Total Margin	4.82%	6.84%	6.72%	6.74%	6.76%	6.83%	6.87%	6.88%	6.95%
Operating Margin	59.92%	60.09%	60.35%	60.59%	60.51%	60.18%	59.67%	59.14%	58.76%
Cash Flow Margin	14.68%	15.00%	14.28%	14.28%	14.14%	14.11%	13.97%	13.82%	13.78%
Return on assets	11.60%	12.44%	11.32%	10.75%	11.23%	11.14%	11.44%	11.55%	11.78%
Return on equity	17.22%	18.19%	16.41%	15.24%	14.98%	14.68%	14.40%	14.12%	13.96%
Cash flow to equity	25.67%	27.37%	24.49%	22.89%	22.51%	22.00%	21.42%	20.92%	20.60%
Econimc value added	9,336x	12,843x	10,537x	10,451x	11,947x	12,562x	13,914x	14,832x	16,321x
Ecominc to capital	4.74%	6.07%	4.18%	3.72%	4.04%	3.93%	4.16%	4.18%	4.36%
Liquidity Ratio									
Current ratio	2.14x	2.15x	3.17x	2.64x	3.07x	3.21x	3.23x	3.54x	3.69x
Capital Structure Ratios									
Debt Ratio	30.79%	28.61%	27.85%	26.87%	22.91%	21.56%	17.79%	15.41%	12.91%
Coverage Ratios									
Cushion Ratio	9.46x	7.24x	8.74x	6.39x	6.52x	7.76x	9.23x	11.37x	15.73x

Figure 26

PROFIT MARGIN

Source: Team Calculations

As the Market Consolidates, Growth Will Slow
The physical therapy rehabilitation industry is expected to grow at 1.6% for the next five years. Slower than the previous five years of 2.2%. As economic profits decrease due to the fragmented nature of physical therapy rehabilitation centers, the market will continue to consolidate as larger, more efficient firms take the market. USPH has had a competitive advantage in their market strategy by their ability to purchase successful clinics, driven by quality and efficiency. The fragmented industry has also allowed larger groups like SEM, ATI, HLS, and KND to acquire in large quantities like USPH. As this market becomes more consolidated and fewer individual groups are available for purchase, USPH will be forced to acquire fewer clinics at a higher cost. In time, revenue growth will slow. Figure 27 shows the expected increase in total rehab clinic. USPH is not acquiring quickly enough to keep up with the market. As the market grows, there will be less availability as the market closes on its main additives.

Figure 27

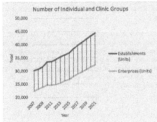

Number of Individual and Clinic Groups

Source: IBIS World and Team Calculation

As Wages Increase, Margins will Narrow - Operating margin increased from 54.61% in 2009 to 60.35% in 2015. Plateaus in efficiency and low cost acquisitions, operating margin have slowed in growth. As physical therapy job growth increases, wages are expected to grow in relation to revenue (See Figure 28). USPH has had high wages historically due to the efficiency they demand from each clinic. The increase in wages could further decrease USPH's operating margins. We estimate that margins will decrease by approximately .7% each year due to market consolidation and wage growth.

Return on Equity - Return on Equity shows the efficiency at which USPH has been able to generate profits with the amount of equity given. There was a large dip in ROE in 2013, primarily due to the closure costs of $5.5 million they incurred. They were able to successfully increase ROE the next year to 18.19% in 2014. There was drop to 16.41% in 2015, which was the lowest ROE has dropped since the large closure costs they incurred. We estimate this trend will continue. USPH will not be acquiring clinics and increasing visits fast enough to keep up with the amount of equity given by shareholders.

Strong Cash Flow from Past Successful Management Strategies Contribute to Future Growth
The ability for management to handle debt has increased their cash flow availability. Cash flows have been steadily increasing each year, showing management only acquires clinics based on present financial cash flow requirements. USPH has historically paid off the cash used for business purchases in the same year on a consistent basis. It is unlikely that they will make a large enough acquisitions to risk not paying off their debt to keep on good terms with their line of credit. The relationship built by management has guaranteed steady growth through future financing needs, holding unforeseen factors constant. Cash Flows Margin started to decrease in 2015, mostly due to decreases in EBITDA from salary cost increases. The prior year was higher at 15% from USPH's keeping clinical costs low. As these costs increase, we expect cash flow margin to decrease to 13.78% by 2021. This margin is still competitive; USPH will still have sufficient cash to use in operations, assuming they are able to keep their management of debt under control similar to prior years. USPH has had sufficient cash flows, but these cash flows are not being reinvested through growth at a quick enough rate.

Figure 28

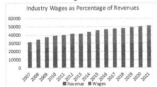

Industry Wages as Percentage of Revenues

Source: IBIS World and Team Calculation

By State Competitions: The overall United States physical therapy market is extremely fragmented. Looking at each state as a separate market, however, shows that USPH only has 1-5 clinics in each market. While it is strategically advantageous to have a footprint in as many states as possible for diversification and future expansion prospects, insurance companies offer differing contracts depending the state in which a clinic resides. Because of this, the bargaining power of USPH is reduced in these areas where they are not the primary physician supplier operating. In addition, USPH is cut off from some of the high population markets such as California and New York due to the barriers of entry from their competitors that have focused on those individual states. The barriers and cost of entering these markets put a lockdown on USPH venturing into these areas. The market is moving towards zones with high reimbursement and high populations. All aspects of the health care market have shifted focus to these areas in attempt to capitalize. This has caused competition in certain areas to increase, making it difficult for USPH to remain relevant and hold market share. This will continue to result in difficulty acquiring in certain market areas, putting a strain on the bottom line.

Table 4 DCF Valuation*

[RFR+β*(Rmarket-RFR)]	
Required Return	8.42%
NPV FCFE 2017	$27,999,644
NPV FCFE 2018	$26,548,236
NPV FCFE 2018	$40,529,011
NPV FCFE 2020	$34,055,068
NPV FCFE 2021	$37,818,929
NPV Terminal	$654,804,093
	$821,754,980.58
Shares Outstanding	12,520,000
Intrinsic Value FCFE	$65.64
Closing Price (2/3/17)	$71.45

Source: Team Calculations

*DCF based on FCFF and WACC yields an intrinsic value of
$56.56, consistent with our sell recommendation.

Figure 29

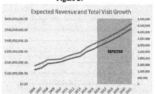

Expected Revenue and Total Visit Growth

Source: Company Filings, Team Calculations

Figure 30

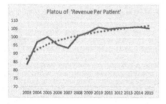

Platou of 'Revenue Per Patient'

Table 5

Sensitivity Analysis	
Intrinsic Value FCFF	56.56
57.89% are overvauled	
Recommendation	Sell

Source: Company Filings, Team Calculations

Valuation

Various valuation methodologies were utilized in obtaining a target price for USPH. These included DCF, Relative Multiples, Sensitivity Analysis, Dividend Discount Model, and two versions of the Monte Carlo Valuation based on different tax rate scenarios.

The **DCF** valuation led to an intrinsic value of $65.64, which represents an 8.13% discount from the current market price of $71.45. We calculated the required rate of return (RRR) of 8.42% using the CAPM model. The required rate of return was then used to discount free cash flow to equity (FCFE) estimates through 2021 and a terminal value using a 2.5% terminal growth rate. The Risk-Free Rate of 1.92% is based on a 5–year treasury constant maturity rate. As interest rates rise and expectations spur, five-year treasury bonds better capture the rising interest rates. We calculated beta by running regressions between the returns of USPH and multiple indices. We chose the beta from the 3-year S&P 500 index as the most appropriate, considering USPH tracks similar in each of the three indices. See Appendix L for team beta calculations. We obtained the terminal growth rate by using the expected GDP growth of 1.9% (world bank estimate), while considering that the healthcare industry has historically tracked slightly above GDP growth (.6%).

Revenues:

Our team estimates USPH's revenue will grow at approximately 7.5% per year, lower than the historic geometric mean of 8.02%. To find expected revenue, our team used the strongest predictor of patient revenues: 'Total Patient Visits'. Total Patient Visits has the highest correlation with patient revenues (R=.98, see Appendix M). Total Patient Visits was also identified as the most influential variable when modeling revenue using data mining techniques. A Simple Linear Regression predicts revenues using this formula: 115.9 * Total Patient Visits – Constant. To project total patient visits for the next five years, historic growth rates in total clinics were used to limit the variability in total patient visit increases due to efficiency differences. (See appendix H for specific process of revenue growth model predictions). The increase of patient visits allowed USPH's revenue to grow by 8.02% between the years of 2010-2015. Patient visits increased by a total of approximately 1.2 million during this period. Although we project patient visits will increase by approximately 1.6 million over the next five years, on a percentage basis, this is a smaller increase (35%) than the 1.2 million increase from 2010-2015 (40%). USPH has stated that they will continue their strategy of slow, meaningful acquisition and development. This slow acquisition growth does not justify the current stock price. They do not have the ability to increase total clinics or visits by a large enough percentage to stimulate increases in revenue growth rates above 8.02%.

USPH has been able to increase revenue per patient by being more efficient in their use of current clinics. This is a result of improvements in operational efficiency. Our analysis shows a limit to the revenue per patient fluctuating around $105 (See figure 30). This observation means that in order to grow patient revenues, USPH's strategy must be to increase Total Patient Visits by a larger percentage. We estimate this will not take place for three reasons:

• USPH has historically used their revolving line of credit to purchase interest in individual clinics and clinic groups. The interest rate on this line of credit is LIBOR+1.5%-2.5%. Thus, as interest rates increase, so will financing charges. This will cause USPH to keep their acquisition process relatively constant to continue their strong cash flow availability. In order to use the revolving line of credit in future acquisitions, USPH will need strong cash flows to comply with the consolidated fixed charge coverage ratio and consolidated leverage ratio in their amended credit agreement. USPH will be less likely to accelerate acquisitions, thus keeping total clinics increasing at a stable rate.

• We estimates that as the market turns to acquiring larger consolidated clinic groups, there will be less for USPH to acquire. The company has recently stated their intention of straying from larger clinic groups (i.e. they prefer to acquire clinics in the 1-to-3 million dollar revenue stream range). As clinic groups gets larger, the quality clinic groups USPH does acquire in this range will have to be bought at a higher price. The subsequent result will cause USPH to acquire clinics at a stable rate to keep cash flows higher.

• USPH is developing a new technology that will allow them to track where patients go from physician referrals. This will help identify potential acquisitions more quickly by taking away the first step in acquisitioning; theoretically making acquiring easier. Though there is no guarantee, it should add speed up the process. This technology will allow them to keep increasing clinics at a constant rate. If they did not have this technology, the growth rate in revenues could start to drop at larger rates. The net affect will be total patient visits and total clinic growth increasing at a stable rate, leading projected revenues to increase in a linear form, with the growth rate slowing at 0.1% per year. We conclude the stock price is overinflated for USPH's revenue growth rate.

Salaries and Related Costs:

Our predictions for Salaries and Related costs track with the common size statements as a percentage of net revenue at 55.28%. This is constant for projections through 2021. The Physician Extender Model ties into this percentage because salaries and related costs as a percentage of net revenue have increased steadily over the last 10 years. The percentage was 51.29% in 2006 and rose to 54.49% last year. We assumed another increase up to 55.28% for the coming years, though we estimate that the percentage remain steady to capture the Physician's healthcare extender model. As physical therapy moves more and more towards physician assistants being heavily involved in the treatment process, salaries will decrease from the ability to use the low priced assistants wages to compensate for the increasing wages from PT's. USPH is trending towards that strategy and thus related costs will slowly start to increase at a decreasing rate. For an in-depth explanation of the extender model and associated laws, see appendix V.

Sensitivity Analysis We conduct sensitivity analysis using RRR and terminal growth rate. We find that USPH is overvalued with approximately 57.89% of the scenarios below the current market price of $71.45. See Appendix G for an in-depth presentation of the analysis.

Monte Carlo Analysis:

The first Monte Carlo simulation is used with FCFE based on the past marginal corporate tax rate of 32%. We account for three different variables: growth rate in patent visits, RRR, and long-term growth rate. We use dour 7.07% forecasted growth rate in patient visits to calculate a standard deviation of .047. RRR was also tested with a manually calculated standard deviation of .0135. Lastly, we include the long term growth rate of 2.5% with a manually calculated deviation of .0075. The results of the original Monte Carlo show a frequency range of likely outcomes of $55.00-$66.00 for intrinsic values. The most likely value is $65.40, consistent with our intrinsic value of $65.64 from DCF. The current trading price of $71.45 is on the outside of the upper control limit on the analysis, further indicating overvaluation of the stock. Among the 30,000 iterations we run, 17,000(57%) falls bellow the current market price. This simulation is further explained in Appendix I.

Though we expect most of our forecasts to follow historical patterns in the next 5 years, the possible corporate tax reduction brings high uncertainty to our valuation. A change in income taxes could significantly affect USPH's net income, and subsequently FCFE. As the new administration comes in and lobbies for tax rate decreases, many stocks are responding positively for potential higher cash flows. We estimate the possible effects of the change using Monte Carlo simulations with a corporate tax rate of 20.11%, which is calculated based on the federal rate of 15% and the average sate rates of 5.11% in the states USPH operates in. The alternate Monte Carlo results show a frequency for the most likely outcomes to be in the range of approximately $57.00-$71.00. The single most likely outcome from the Monte Carlo was an intrinsic value of $60.00. Approximately 13,000 (33%) iterations fall below the current market price. The median of the new simulation is $75.79, approximately 5.7% above the current market price., valuing USPH at closer to a "hold." However, we recognize that 20.11% represents significant reduction in taxes, and the valuation of $75.79 is a result from the most optimistic scenario, while the actual tax cut might not be as low. In addition, if the tax rate decrease does occur, all companies with significant domestic revenue will benefit. Considering the high relative valuation as we discuss below, we expect investors to find better investment opportunities elsewhere. Our alternative tax simulation is explained further in Appendix I.

Figure 31

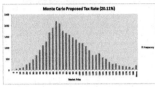

Source: Team Calculations

Dividend Discount Model
In DDM, future dividends were estimated, and discounted to find the present values. USPH started paying dividends in 2011 and has paid steady dividends of 0.17 each quarter from 2015 until present. Based on previous dividend issues, we estimate that they will continue to increase dividends $0.02 every quarter for the next five years. Based on the calculation, and using a discount rate of 8.42%, we value the stock at $51.27. It is important to note the limitations of DDM in this case as the model is traditionally used with companies that have had established dividend growth. Even with these limitations, the stock is still valued 20$ below current price. Investors should also note that increase in dividend growth are still not likely to supplement capital gains.

Table 6

Comparison	USPH	SEM	HLS
Forward P/E	$33.33	$13.30	$15.30
Earnings Growth (1-3 yr.)	9	8.8	5.8
P/EG Ratio	3.7	1.51	2.64

Source: Team Calculations

Table 7

Competitor Average P/Eg	1.78
Historic USPH Premium (5 Years)	90%
USPH NORMALIZED P/Eg	3.382
USPH Current P/Eg	**3.700**
Premium	9.40%
Current Trading Price (02-3-2017)	71.45
Insitrinsic Value	**64.73**

Source: Team Calculations

Relative Valuation
Relating financial ratios to competitors in the same industry gives the ability to discern possible misevaluation in the market between companies. The **P/EG ratio** shows the willingness of investors to pay for earnings, while also considering the growth in those earnings. If earnings are not high enough to compensate a high P/E, the P/EG ratio helps investors understand an overpriced stock. This is the case for USPH. USPH has a significantly higher P/EG ratio than their competition - exponentially above prior years. USPH has a current P/EG of 3.7, which represents an additional 9.4% premium to their normal relative ratios. We calculate the P/EG based valuation at $64.73, consistent with our DCF valuation (See Table 7). USPH's earnings growth is not rising at the same rate as the its increasing price. Future earnings are expected to increase in absolute value, but there is no indication that it will clime at a relatively higher rate to alleviate justification in current higher price. Our team estimates earnings to grow at a geometric growth rate of 8.494% over the next five years (see appendix H).

Figure 32

Source: Company Filings, Team Calculations

Price to Free Cash Flows shows the price that investors are willing to pay for cash flows. It is also beneficial to show cash after expenses have been subtracted to see freedom in growth opportunities. For a company that uses the majority of cash flow to acquire clinics, FCF is paramount in determining that firms ability to acquire and grow. USPH has historically had P/FCF at a premium of 28.95% above their competitors. In 2015, USPH had a premium 50% above that ordinary premium. This number is expected to have risen in 2016: our team estimates free cash flow and current price to produce a P/FCF of 16.46 at the current price of $71.45. Since there is no indication for reasons in future cash flow hikes to lower this ratio, we are confident in our consensus of "sell." To better understand the industry ratio, we added total patient visits to represent the relationship between cash flow per patient and market price (See table 8). It can be seen that cash flows per are not increasing by a large enough amount to justify the current stock price. Adding the companion variable of total patient visits indicates USPH is still over-valued.

Table 8

Year	P/(FCF/TPV) USPH	P/(FCF/TPV) SEM	P/(FCF/TPV) HLS
2015	3.59	0.34	0.056
2014	2.19	0.39	0.048
2013	1.55	0.21	0.042
2012	1.43	0.14	0.053
2011	1.39	0.15	0.068
2010	1.11	0.21	0.064

Source: Team Calculations

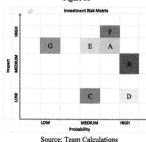

Figure 33

Source: Team Calculations

Figure 34

Source: Quarterly Calls

Table 10

Current Ratio	
2011	2.8
2012	2.78
2013	2.14
2014	2.15
2015	3.17
2016	2.64
2017	3.07
2018	3.21
2019	3.23
2020	3.54
2021	3.69

Source: Team Calculations

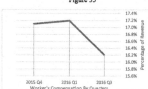

Figure 35

Source: Team Calculations

Investment Risks

Uncertainty in the Affordable Care Act – [A]

One of the most prominent issues that the new administration lobbied for was repealing and replacing the Affordable Care Act. Universal healthcare is a democrat ideology and the republican party will most likely try to alter a significant amount of the Act, and if allowed, repeal it entirely. There is much uncertainty on the subject of replacement. Considering 23.5% of USPH's revenue is tied to Medicare/Medicare, a repeal or alteration could hurt USPH's business operations. Altering the ACA slightly without replacing it could lead to complications for the consumers and the US economy. Similarly, if the Act is repealed and replaced with another system, there could be disaster in the healthcare insurance sector, which would affect USPH doubly. Though there is much uncertainty, USPH is in a better place than other healthcare industries. Because of the inexpensive nature of physical therapy, and the fact that republicans are pushing for lower costs, USPH may be at an advantage with a push of quality therapy. It also may be that, if the act is replaced by what republicans have proposed so far, fewer lower income individuals will be able to acquire Medicaid. In this case, when they come to age for Medicare, they will be in poorer health, and, will ultimately drive up costs from their poor health. In this regard, USPH may be able to make up some of the lost revenue from Medicaid reductions. Additionally, Medicare/Medicaid percentages of revenue is lower for USPH, which leaves them less susceptible to the possible detrimental effects of federal budget cuts to these government programs. Because of the uncertainty regarding the situation, there is no clear answer to mitigate this risk. See appendix for possible outcomes for ACA and the effects on USPH.

Certain government Medicare/Medicaid reductions may hinder profits [B]

Though USPH has diversified their revenue, 24% comes from Medicare/Medicaid. In 2015, the sustainable growth rate (SGR) formula for reducing Medicare expenditures was eliminated. The Medicare Access and CHIP Reauthorization Act of 2015 (MACRA) was signed into law, that decreased fee schedule payment rate by .3%. Through 2017 to 2019, however, fee schedule payments rates will increase by .5%. It is uncertain how MACRA could be affected by the new administration. While USPH is less affected by this than their competitors due their diversified payer mix, the reduction in payment from government causes increases risk to USPH future cash flows which directly flows into the EPS and then the stock price. This payment reduction is magnified as payment structures with the government are non-negotiable. USPH bases much of their strategy on clinic location, but the government is blind to this and sets the amount they will reimburse regardless of geographic location. The largest population base in the US is baby boomers (ages 53-71). Revenue diversity decreases as this large customer base approaches Medicare eligibility, this risk will increase the importance of Medicare for USPH as these people qualify for government services. This will decrease revenue opportunities because of the low profitability of government insurance. Investors viewing USPH as a long term growth stock will be concerned as distant future revenues are less lucrative. We feel this scenario could encourage the position of a sell.

Lengthy Acquisition Process hindering potential gain [C]

Historically, USPH has strategically chosen clinics for acquisitions. This lengthy process may have hindered their potential of entering new markets. As smaller companies consolidate together, USPH could miss out on potential growth opportunities due to the long selection process they implement. Considering stock prices tends to jump with each set of acquisitions, investors have demanded USPH to hasten their process. However, USPH has stated they will not change their methodology. To maintain quality selections, USPH has obtained extensive technology that shows that track which physical therapist physicians refer to. This will show USPH where physician referrals are coming from in each clinic, which will help them decide which clinics are worth acquiring. This helps them quicken their selection of clinics and decreases projected closure costs. If USPH does not accelerate their acquisition process, it could severely limit revenue growth and deter value investors that are interested in USPH stock.

Government Regulation [D]

The healthcare industry as a whole is highly regulated. Because of the extensive regulations, parameters implemented by government could hinder USPH from actively changing their policies in benefiting their stockholders. Recently, there has been a push for hospital care regulation to extend into the physical therapy sector. HIPAA put in place technologies for security purposes based on customer records. These required technologies are expensive to implement and costly to avoid.

Technology Risks [E]

From the attempts to comply with government electronic monitory records, UPSH has invested capital in new technology for their business. Shown by their integration attempts with the changing market they have found a new technology that has allowed for a better understanding of clientele characteristics (age, demographics, and specified type of ailment), as well as better monitoring of government and insurance policy. USPH has strived to maintain strong relationships with their therapists, working to continually monitor and ensure quality. This technology helps guarantee their quality standards are implemented. However, UPSH still remains behind some of their competitors who have moved their therapy sessions to an online bases allowing for an increase in patients visits and sequentially net patient revenues.

Operational Risks [F]

In the past USPH has been able to increase revenues by eliminating inefficiencies in their billing systems. They have been able to capitalize on more profitable codes when requesting reimbursement and streamlining of back office activities into the same system, which lowers the per-patient cost of business administration. This is represented by the per/patient/day/clinic revenue. The amount of growth USPH is experiencing here has began to slow. This means while USPH is a solid company, they have worked out most of their inefficiencies, and therefore the only way for them to increase revenues would be to increase the amount of patients they are seeing. It is beneficial to be operating at this level of efficiency, yet from an investor perspective, efficiency limits their ability for extra growth year on year. If this continues it could adversely affect the value of

USPH moving forward.

Liquidity Risks: [G]

In a market that is always changing it is important to remain liquid in order to pay off debts and avoid bankruptcy. This explains why cash flow is such an important part to USPH. Their current ratio while it fluctuates, it is projected to remain strong and slightly increasing finishing at 3.69 by 2021. This ability to pay off short term debt with on hand cash is important because liquidity problems indicate cash flow issues. This is where equity growth is and payout is derived from. Investors will be more likely to get a high dividend from a company with high cash flows.

Appendix A: Balance Sheet (Team Calculations)

	Historical										Forecast					
($ in Thousands)	2006	2007	2008	2009	2010	2011	2012	2013	2014	2015	2016E	2017E	2018E	2019E	2020E	2021E
Assets																
Current Assets																
Cash & cash equivalents	10,952	7,976	10,113	6,429	9,179	9,983	11,671	12,898	14,271	15,778	17,779	20,480	23,354	22,932	26,031	31,705
Patient accounts receivable, gross	23,070	27,758	28,128	24,130	27,004	30,487	27,568	32,250	34,560	37,675	41,530	43,979	46,572	49,318	52,225	55,305
Allowance for doubtful accounts	1,567	2,184	2,275	1,830	2,190	2,154	1,595	1,430	1,669	1,444	1,960	1,881	2,095	2,164	2,320	2,442
Patient accounts receivable, net	21,503	25,574	25,853	22,300	24,814	28,333	25,973	30,820	32,891	36,231	39,570	42,098	44,477	47,154	49,905	52,863
Accounts receivable - other	775	1,150	898	1,331	1,555	1,614	1,703	1,844	1,503	2,388	2,163	2,375	2,623	2,753	3,072	3,210
Other current assets	2,251	1,333	1,857	2,959	3,736	5,737	5,975	4,098	6,186	5,785	10,800	9,750	11,125	9,827	11,273	9,963
Total current assets	**35,981**	**36,033**	**38,721**	**33,019**	**39,284**	**45,667**	**45,322**	**49,660**	**54,851**	**60,182**	**70,312**	**74,703**	**81,579**	**82,666**	**90,282**	**97,741**
Furniture & equipment	23,718	28,782	30,947	31,973	33,563	35,103	36,316	38,965	42,003	44,749	47,607	50,601	53,784	57,167	60,763	64,585
Leasehold improvements	15,226	17,352	18,061	19,012	19,590	20,385	20,858	21,891	22,806	25,160	27,276	28,913	30,647	32,486	34,436	36,502
Fixed assets, gross	38,944	46,134	49,008	50,985	53,153	55,488	57,174	60,856	64,809	69,909	74,883	79,514	84,432	89,654	95,199	101,087
Less accumulated depreciation & amortization	25,573	29,342	33,167	36,646	39,230	42,299	44,158	45,896	49,045	53,255	57,654	60,669	64,263	68,362	72,700	77,235
Fixed assets, net	13,371	16,792	15,841	14,339	13,923	13,189	13,016	14,960	15,764	16,654	17,229	18,845	20,169	21,291	22,499	23,852
Goodwill	20,997	37,650	55,886	57,247	79,424	92,750	100,188	143,955	147,914	171,547	193,648	197,478	216,687	225,010	233,823	243,151
Other intangible assets, net	-	3,930	6,452	5,955	7,308	9,603	12,146	14,479	24,907	30,296	32,881	34,507	34,275	39,256	42,702	45,524
Other assets	1,108	1,847	1,347	869	922	2,043	1,042	1,081	1,115	1,234	1,392	1,523	1,617	1,716	1,859	2,008
Total assets	**71,457**	**96,252**	**118,247**	**111,429**	**140,861**	**163,252**	**171,714**	**224,135**	**244,551**	**279,913**	**315,462**	**327,056**	**354,327**	**369,940**	**391,164**	**412,277**
Liabilities and stockholders' equity																
Current Liabilities																
Accounts payable - trade	1,601	1,555	1,481	1,292	1,237	1,809	1,732	1,722	1,782	1,636	2,154	2,358	2,465	2,591	2,775	3,062
Accrued salaries & related costs	2,244	4,900	6,498	9,133	8,989	9,275	8,941	11,686	15,400	9,414	14,141	11,916	12,512	12,677	12,132	12,676
Accrued group health insurance claims	1,063	1,141	1,049	977	1,324	1,168	991	2,023	2,116	2,276	2,265	1,934	2,123	2,143	2,148	2,122
Credit balances & overpayments due to patients & payors	1,088	1,166	1,932	1,283	702	793	813	2,371	1,834	1,472	2,019	2,210	2,580	2,518	2,664	2,971
Other accrued expenses	1,925	1,864	2,273	1,066	1,729	2,846	3,371	4,545	3,489	3,434	4,555	4,006	3,871	3,966	4,100	3,986
Accrued expenses	7,007	9,071	11,752	12,459	12,744	14,082	14,116	20,625	22,839	16,596	22,979	20,066	21,086	21,304	21,044	21,755
Current portion of notes payable	-	812	1,380	1,013	250	433	459	825	883	775	1,511	1,930	1,846	1,696	1,696	1,696
Total current liabilities	**9,170**	**11,438**	**14,613**	**14,764**	**14,231**	**16,324**	**16,307**	**23,172**	**25,504**	**19,007**	**26,645**	**24,354**	**25,397**	**25,591**	**25,515**	**26,514**
Long-term liablities																
Notes payable	797	959	1,012	-	250	284	175	650	234	4,335	4,021	2,207	2,789	3,375	4,276	4,151
Revolving line of credit	-	7,000	11,400	400	5,500	23,500	17,400	40,000	34,500	44,000	41,000	38,000	35,901	22,745	15,380	6,428
Deferred rent	1,273	1,104	1,103	1,027	966	941	894	996	991	1,395	1,313	1,441	1,561	1,673	1,842	1,936
Other long-term liabilities/Deffered Taxes	829	696	2,297	3,013	3,531	623	2,279	4,196	8,732	9,223	11,775	8,929	10,760	12,442	13,269	14,206
Total liabilities	**12,069**	**21,197**	**30,425**	**19,204**	**24,478**	**41,672**	**37,055**	**69,014**	**69,961**	**77,960**	**84,754**	**74,931**	**76,407**	**65,826**	**60,281**	**53,234**
Stockholders' equity																
Common stock	137	141	142	138	139	139	141	143	145	146	148	149	149	149	149	149
Additional paid-in capital	36,304	41,452	43,648	43,210	45,570	36,133	37,489	40,569	43,577	45,251	49,506	50,735	51,995	53,286	54,609	55,965
Retained earnings (accumulated deficit)	50,704	59,442	69,446	75,632	89,876	102,405	111,321	119,206	134,186	149,016	164,547	181,340	199,265	218,376	238,624	260,495
Treasury stock at cost	31,628	31,628	31,628	31,628	31,628	31,628	31,628	31,628	31,628	31,628	31,628	31,628	31,628	31,628	31,628	31,628
Total U.S. Physical Therapy, Inc. shareholders' equity	**55,517**	**69,407**	**81,608**	**87,352**	**103,957**	**107,049**	**117,323**	**128,290**	**146,280**	**162,785**	**182,573**	**200,597**	**219,781**	**240,183**	**261,754**	**284,981**
Noncontrolling interests	-	-	-	4,873	12,426	14,531	17,336	22,727	20,934	30,325	39,967	44,557	49,147	53,738	58,328	62,918
Total equity	**55,517**	**69,407**	**81,608**	**92,225**	**116,383**	**121,580**	**134,659**	**151,017**	**167,214**	**193,110**	**222,540**	**245,154**	**268,928**	**293,920**	**320,082**	**347,899**
Redeemable non-controlling interests	-	-	-	-	-	-	-	4,104	7,376	8,843	8,169	6,971	8,992	10,194	10,801	11,144
Total Liabilities and Shareholders Equity	**71,457**	**96,252**	**118,247**	**111,429**	**140,861**	**163,252**	**171,714**	**224,135**	**244,551**	**279,913**	**315,462**	**327,056**	**354,327**	**369,940**	**391,164**	**412,277**

Common Sized Balance Sheet

	Historical										Forecast					
($ in Thousands)	2006	2007	2008	2009	2010	2011	2012	2013	2014	2015	2016E	2017E	2018E	2019E	2020E	2021E
Assets																
Cash & cash equivalents	15.33%	8.29%	8.55%	5.77%	6.52%	6.12%	6.80%	5.75%	5.84%	5.64%	5.64%	5.72%	5.71%	5.67%	5.68%	5.69%
Patient accounts receivable, gross	32.29%	28.84%	23.79%	21.66%	19.17%	18.67%	16.05%	14.39%	14.13%	13.46%	13.16%	13.79%	13.64%	13.51%	13.52%	13.61%
Allowance for doubtful accounts	2.19%	2.27%	1.92%	1.64%	1.55%	1.32%	0.93%	0.64%	0.68%	0.52%	0.62%	0.61%	0.61%	0.59%	0.61%	0.61%
Patient accounts receivable, net	30.09%	26.57%	21.86%	20.01%	17.62%	17.36%	15.13%	13.75%	13.45%	12.94%	12.54%	13.17%	13.03%	12.92%	12.92%	13.01%
Accounts receivable - other	1.08%	1.19%	0.76%	1.19%	1.10%	0.99%	0.99%	0.82%	0.61%	0.85%	0.69%	0.74%	0.72%	0.75%	0.73%	0.74%
Other current assets	3.15%	1.38%	1.57%	2.66%	2.65%	3.51%	3.48%	1.83%	2.53%	2.07%	3.42%	2.46%	2.62%	2.64%	2.79%	2.63%
Total current assets	**50.35%**	**37.44%**	**32.75%**	**29.63%**	**27.89%**	**27.97%**	**26.39%**	**22.16%**	**22.43%**	**21.50%**	**22.29%**	**22.09%**	**22.08%**	**21.99%**	**22.11%**	**22.07%**
Furniture & equipment	33.19%	29.90%	26.17%	28.69%	23.83%	21.50%	21.15%	17.38%	17.18%	15.99%	15.09%	16.41%	16.17%	15.91%	15.89%	16.10%
Leasehold improvements	21.31%	18.03%	15.27%	17.06%	13.91%	12.49%	12.15%	9.77%	9.33%	8.99%	8.65%	9.18%	9.04%	8.96%	8.96%	9.03%
Fixed assets, gross	54.50%	47.93%	41.45%	45.76%	37.73%	33.99%	33.30%	27.15%	26.50%	24.98%	23.74%	25.59%	25.20%	24.88%	24.85%	25.13%
Less accumulated depreciation & amortization	35.79%	30.48%	28.05%	32.89%	27.85%	25.91%	25.72%	20.48%	20.06%	19.03%	18.28%	19.46%	19.20%	18.99%	18.98%	19.16%
Fixed assets, net	18.71%	17.45%	13.40%	12.87%	9.88%	8.08%	7.58%	6.67%	6.45%	5.95%	5.46%	6.13%	6.00%	5.89%	5.87%	5.97%
Goodwill	29.38%	39.12%	47.26%	51.38%	56.38%	56.81%	58.35%	64.23%	60.48%	61.29%	61.39%	61.85%	61.25%	61.44%	61.48%	61.50%
Other intangible assets, net	0.00%	4.08%	5.46%	5.34%	5.19%	5.88%	7.07%	6.46%	10.18%	10.82%	10.42%	9.47%	10.23%	10.24%	10.09%	10.01%
Other assets	1.55%	1.92%	1.14%	0.78%	0.65%	1.25%	0.61%	0.48%	0.46%	0.44%	0.44%	0.46%	0.45%	0.45%	0.45%	0.45%
Total assets	**100.00%**	**100.00%**	**100.00%**	**100.00%**	**100.00%**	**100.00%**	**100.00%**	**100.00%**	**100.00%**	**100.00%**	**100.00%**	**100.00%**	**100.00%**	**100.00%**	**100.00%**	**100.00%**
Liabilities and stockholders' equity																
Current Liabilities																
Accounts payable - trade	2.24%	1.62%	1.25%	1.16%	0.88%	1.11%	1.01%	0.77%	0.73%	0.58%	0.68%	0.69%	0.67%	0.66%	0.68%	0.67%
Accrued salaries & related costs	3.14%	5.09%	5.50%	8.20%	6.38%	5.68%	5.21%	5.21%	6.30%	3.36%	4.48%	4.84%	4.75%	4.36%	4.61%	4.64%
Accrued group health insurance claims	1.49%	1.19%	0.89%	0.88%	0.94%	0.72%	0.58%	0.90%	0.87%	0.81%	0.72%	0.82%	0.81%	0.79%	0.78%	0.80%
Credit balances & overpayments due to patients & payors	1.52%	1.21%	1.63%	1.15%	0.50%	0.49%	0.47%	1.06%	0.75%	0.53%	0.64%	0.74%	0.66%	0.64%	0.67%	0.68%
Other accrued expenses	2.69%	1.94%	1.92%	0.96%	1.23%	1.74%	1.96%	2.03%	1.43%	1.23%	1.44%	1.53%	1.41%	1.40%	1.45%	1.45%
Accrued expenses	9.81%	9.42%	9.94%	11.18%	9.05%	8.63%	8.22%	9.20%	9.34%	5.93%	7.28%	7.94%	7.62%	7.19%	7.51%	7.57%
Current portion of notes payable	0.00%	0.84%	1.17%	0.91%	0.18%	0.27%	0.27%	0.37%	0.36%	0.28%	0.48%	0.37%	0.37%	0.37%	0.40%	0.38%
Total current liabilities	**12.83%**	**11.88%**	**12.36%**	**13.25%**	**10.10%**	**10.00%**	**9.50%**	**10.34%**	**10.43%**	**6.79%**	**8.45%**	**9.00%**	**8.67%**	**8.23%**	**8.58%**	**8.62%**
Long-term liabilities																
Notes payable	1.12%	1.00%	0.86%	0.00%	0.18%	0.17%	0.10%	0.29%	0.10%	1.55%	1.27%	0.80%	0.93%	1.14%	1.04%	0.98%
Revolving line of credit	0.00%	7.27%	9.64%	0.36%	3.90%	14.39%	10.13%	17.85%	14.11%	15.72%	13.00%	15.17%	14.50%	14.60%	14.31%	14.64%
Deferred rent	1.78%	1.15%	0.93%	0.92%	0.69%	0.58%	0.52%	0.44%	0.41%	0.50%	0.42%	0.44%	0.44%	0.45%	0.44%	0.44%
Other long-term liabilities/Deferred Taxes	1.16%	0.72%	1.94%	2.70%	2.51%	0.38%	1.33%	1.87%	3.57%	3.29%	3.73%	3.12%	3.43%	3.39%	3.42%	3.34%
Total liabilities	**16.89%**	**22.02%**	**25.73%**	**17.23%**	**17.38%**	**25.53%**	**21.58%**	**30.79%**	**28.61%**	**27.85%**	**26.87%**	**28.53%**	**27.96%**	**27.80%**	**27.79%**	**28.02%**
Stockholders' Equity																
Common stock	0.19%	0.15%	0.12%	0.12%	0.10%	0.09%	0.08%	0.06%	0.06%	0.05%	0.05%	0.06%	0.05%	0.05%	0.05%	0.05%
Additional paid-in capital	50.81%	43.07%	36.91%	38.78%	32.35%	22.13%	21.83%	18.10%	17.82%	16.17%	15.69%	16.94%	16.66%	16.36%	16.41%	16.60%
Retained earnings (accumulated deficit)	70.96%	61.76%	58.73%	67.87%	63.80%	62.73%	64.83%	53.18%	54.87%	53.24%	52.16%	53.36%	53.41%	53.04%	52.99%	53.20%
Treasury stock at cost	44.26%	32.86%	26.75%	28.38%	22.45%	19.37%	18.42%	14.11%	12.93%	11.30%	10.03%	12.09%	11.59%	11.25%	11.24%	11.54%
Total U.S. Physical Therapy, Inc. shareholders' equity	77.69%	72.11%	69.01%	78.39%	73.80%	65.57%	68.32%	57.24%	59.82%	58.16%	57.87%	58.27%	58.53%	58.21%	58.22%	58.31%
Noncontrolling interests	0.00%	0.00%	0.00%	4.37%	8.82%	8.90%	10.10%	10.14%	8.56%	10.83%	12.67%	10.55%	10.65%	11.18%	11.26%	10.91%
Total equity	**77.69%**	**72.11%**	**69.01%**	**82.77%**	**82.62%**	**74.47%**	**78.42%**	**67.38%**	**68.38%**	**68.99%**	**70.54%**	**68.82%**	**69.18%**	**69.38%**	**69.48%**	**69.22%**
Redeemable non-controlling interests	0.00%	0.00%	0.00%	0.00%	0.00%	0.00%	0.00%	1.83%	3.02%	3.16%	2.59%	2.65%	2.85%	2.81%	2.73%	2.76%
Total Liabilities and Shareholders Equity	**100.00%**	**100.00%**	**100.00%**	**100.00%**	**100.00%**	**100.00%**	**100.00%**	**100.00%**	**100.00%**	**100.00%**	**100.00%**	**100.00%**	**100.00%**	**100.00%**	**100.00%**	**100.00%**

Appendix B: Income Statement (Team Calculations)

	Historical										Forecast					
($ in Thousands)	2006	2007	2008	2009	2010	2011	2012	2013	2014	2015	2016E	2017E	2018E	2019E	2020E	2021E
Revenue																
Net patient revenues	$ 133,376	$ 149,437	$ 182,939	$ 195,322	$ 204,101	$ 226,579	$ 244,443	$ 258,283	$ 299,009	$ 324,293	$ 348,990	$ 382,262	$ 411,195	$ 442,174	$ 475,342	$ 510,856
Other revenues	34	304	4,747	6,087	7,132	10,427	7,645	5,775	6,065	7,009	7,658	7,964	8,283	8,614	8,959	9,317
	135,194	**151,686**	**187,686**	**201,409**	**211,233**	**237,006**	**252,088**	**264,058**	**305,074**	**331,302**	**356,648**	**390,226**	**419,478**	**450,788**	**484,301**	**520,173**
Expenses																
Salaries & related costs	69,340	79,191	100,269	105,737	110,872	125,117	132,824	141,840	163,417	180,514	197,144	215,717	231,887	249,196	267,722	287,552
Rent, clinic supplies, contract labor & other clinic operating costs	27,896	32,581	39,814	40,502	40,944	47,396	51,620	52,887	61,209	68,046	71,360	78,917	84,620	91,066	97,969	104,903
Provision for doubtful accounts	2,115	2,553	3,073	3,348	3,241	3,785	4,848	4,384	4,112	4,170	3,864	4,142	4,455	4,791	5,150	5,535
Closure costs	-	-	432	91	163	59	211	246	169	211	204	244	193	211	252	248
Total clinic operating costs	**99,351**	**114,325**	**143,588**	**149,678**	**155,220**	**176,357**	**189,503**	**199,357**	**228,907**	**252,941**	**272,572**	**299,019**	**321,155**	**345,263**	**371,093**	**398,237**
Gross margin (loss)	35,843	37,361	44,098	51,731	56,013	60,649	62,585	64,701	76,167	78,361	84,076	91,207	98,323	105,525	113,208	121,935
Corporate office costs	17,247	17,326	20,222	23,479	22,823	24,718	24,782	25,931	30,399	31,067	33,137	36,019	39,151	42,556	46,258	50,281
Operating income (loss) from continuing operations	**18,596**	**20,035**	**23,876**	**28,252**	**33,190**	**35,931**	**37,803**	**38,770**	**45,768**	**47,294**	**50,939**	**55,188**	**59,171**	**62,969**	**66,951**	**71,655**
Interest & other income, net	-	-	-	8	586	5,445	6	7	18	81	78	45	56	69	84	82
Interest expense	-	301	542	352	236	496	557	538	1,088	1,031	1,271	1,211	1,165	787	592	319
Income (loss) before income taxes from continuing operations	**13,250**	**14,280**	**16,509**	**27,908**	**33,540**	**40,880**	**37,252**	**38,239**	**44,698**	**46,344**	**49,746**	**54,022**	**58,062**	**62,251**	**66,442**	**71,419**
Provision for income taxes	5,057	5,465	6,505	7,934	8,840	11,097	11,034	12,236	14,274	14,653	15,832	17,287	18,580	19,920	21,262	22,854
Net income from continuing operations including non-controlling interests	**8,193**	**8,815**	**10,004**	**19,974**	**24,700**	**29,783**	**26,218**	**26,003**	**30,424**	**31,691**	**33,914**	**36,735**	**39,482**	**42,331**	**45,181**	**48,565**
Less: net income attributable to non-controlling interests	-	-	-	-8,207	-9,055	-8,809	-8,285	-8,273	-9,571	-9,412	-9,878	-10,343	-10,830	-11,340	-11,874	-12,433
Discontinued Operations	-1,897	-77	-	-	-	-	-	-5,007	-	-	-	-	-	-	-	-
Net income attributable to common shareholders	**6,296**	**8,738**	**10,004**	**11,767**	**15,645**	**20,974**	**17,933**	**12,723**	**20,853**	**22,279**	**24,036**	**26,392**	**28,652**	**30,991**	**33,307**	**36,132**
Weighted average shares outstanding - basic	11,690	11,643	11,907	11,703	11,638	11,814	11,804	12,063	12,217	12,392	12,489	12,629	12,770	12,913	13,058	13,204
Weighted average shares outstanding - diluted	11,731	11,718	12,055	11,807	11,870	11,977	11,904	12,082	12,221	12,392	12,489	12,629	12,770	12,913	13,058	13,204
Year end shares outstanding	11,467	11,838	12,037	11,614	1,168	11,705	11,915	12,101	12,273	12,421	12,520	12,660	12,802	12,946	13,091	13,237
Earnings (loss) per share from continuing operations - basic	**$ 0.54**	**$ 0.76**	**$ 0.84**	**$ 1.01**	**$ 1.34**	**$ 1.78**	**$ 1.52**	**$ 1.05**	**$ 1.62**	**$ 1.77**	**$ 1.92**	**$ 2.09**	**$ 2.24**	**$ 2.40**	**$ 2.55**	**$ 2.74**

Common Sized Income Statement

	Historical										Forecast					
($ in Thousands)	2006	2007	2008	2009	2010	2011	2012	2013	2014	2015	2016E	2017E	2018E	2019E	2020E	2021E
Revenue																
Net patient revenues	98.66%	98.52%	97.47%	96.98%	96.62%	95.60%	96.97%	97.81%	98.01%	97.88%	97.85%	97.71%	97.85%	97.86%	97.83%	97.82%
Other revenues	0.03%	0.20%	2.53%	3.02%	3.38%	4.40%	3.03%	2.19%	1.99%	2.12%	2.15%	2.29%	2.15%	2.14%	2.17%	2.18%
	100.00%	**100.00%**	**100.00%**	**100.00%**	**100.00%**	**100.00%**	**100.00%**	**100.00%**	**100.00%**	**100.00%**	**100.00%**	**100.00%**	**100.00%**	**100.00%**	**100.00%**	**100.00%**
Expenses																
Salaries & related costs	51.29%	52.21%	53.42%	52.50%	52.49%	52.79%	52.69%	53.72%	53.57%	54.49%	55.28%	55.28%	55.28%	55.28%	55.28%	55.28%
Rent, clinic supplies, contract labor & other clinic operating costs	20.63%	21.48%	21.21%	20.11%	19.38%	20.00%	20.48%	20.03%	20.06%	20.54%	20.01%	20.22%	20.17%	20.20%	20.23%	20.17%
Provision for doubtful accounts	1.56%	1.68%	1.64%	1.66%	1.53%	1.60%	1.92%	1.66%	1.35%	1.26%	1.08%	1.45%	1.36%	1.30%	1.29%	1.30%
Closure costs	0.00%	0.00%	0.23%	0.05%	0.08%	0.02%	0.08%	0.09%	0.06%	0.06%	0.06%	0.07%	0.07%	0.06%	0.06%	0.06%
Total clinic operating costs	**73.49%**	**75.37%**	**76.50%**	**74.32%**	**73.48%**	**74.41%**	**75.17%**	**75.50%**	**75.03%**	**76.35%**	**76.43%**	**75.70%**	**75.80%**	**75.86%**	**76.03%**	**75.96%**
Gross margin (loss)	26.51%	24.63%	23.50%	25.68%	26.52%	25.59%	24.83%	24.50%	24.97%	23.65%	23.57%	24.30%	24.20%	24.14%	23.97%	24.04%
Corporate office costs	12.76%	11.42%	10.77%	11.66%	10.80%	10.43%	9.83%	9.82%	9.96%	9.38%	9.29%	9.66%	9.62%	9.58%	9.51%	9.53%
Operating income (loss) from continuing operations	**13.76%**	**13.21%**	**12.72%**	**14.03%**	**15.71%**	**15.16%**	**15.00%**	**14.68%**	**15.00%**	**14.28%**	**14.28%**	**14.65%**	**14.58%**	**14.56%**	**14.47%**	**14.51%**
Interest & other income, net	0.00%	0.00%	0.00%	0.00%	0.28%	2.30%	0.00%	0.00%	0.01%	0.02%	0.02%	0.01%	0.01%	0.02%	0.02%	0.02%
Interest expense	0.00%	0.20%	0.29%	0.17%	0.11%	0.21%	0.22%	0.20%	0.36%	0.31%	0.36%	0.29%	0.30%	0.32%	0.32%	0.32%
Income (loss) before income taxes from continuing operations	**9.80%**	**9.41%**	**8.80%**	**13.86%**	**15.88%**	**17.25%**	**14.78%**	**14.48%**	**14.65%**	**13.99%**	**13.95%**	**14.37%**	**14.29%**	**14.25%**	**14.17%**	**14.20%**
Provision for income taxes	3.74%	3.60%	3.47%	3.94%	4.18%	4.68%	4.38%	4.63%	4.68%	4.42%	4.44%	4.51%	4.54%	4.52%	4.49%	4.50%
Net income from continuing operations including non-controlling interests	**6.06%**	**5.81%**	**5.33%**	**9.92%**	**11.69%**	**12.57%**	**10.40%**	**9.85%**	**9.97%**	**9.57%**	**9.51%**	**9.86%**	**9.75%**	**9.73%**	**9.68%**	**9.71%**
Less: net income attributable to non-controlling interests	0.00%	0.00%	0.00%	-4.07%	-4.29%	-3.72%	-3.29%	-3.13%	-3.14%	-2.84%	-2.77%	-3.03%	-2.98%	-2.95%	-2.92%	-2.93%
Discontinued Operations	-1.40%	-0.05%	0.00%	0.00%	0.00%	0.00%	0.00%	-1.90%	0.00%	0.00%	0.00%	0.00%	0.00%	0.00%	0.00%	0.00%
Net income attributable to common shareholders	**4.66%**	**5.76%**	**5.33%**	**5.84%**	**7.41%**	**8.85%**	**7.11%**	**4.82%**	**6.84%**	**6.72%**	**6.74%**	**6.45%**	**6.31%**	**6.61%**	**6.57%**	**6.54%**
Weighted average shares outstanding - basic	8.65%	7.68%	6.34%	5.81%	5.51%	4.98%	4.68%	4.57%	4.00%	3.74%	3.50%	4.10%	3.98%	3.87%	3.84%	3.86%
Weighted average shares outstanding - diluted	8.68%	7.73%	6.42%	5.86%	5.62%	5.05%	4.72%	4.58%	4.01%	3.74%	3.50%	4.11%	3.99%	3.87%	3.84%	3.86%
Year end shares outstanding	8.48%	7.80%	6.41%	5.77%	0.55%	4.94%	4.73%	4.58%	4.02%	3.75%	3.51%	4.12%	4.00%	3.88%	3.85%	3.87%

Appendix C: Statement of Cash Flows

	Historical										Forecast					
($ in Thousands)	2006	2007	2008	2009	2010	2011	2012	2013	2014	2015	2016E	2017E	2018E	2019E	2020E	2021E
Operating Activities																
Net income (loss) including noncontrolling interests	6,296	8,738	10,004	19,974	24,700	29,783	26,218	20,996	30,424	31,691	33,914	36,735	39,482	42,331	45,181	48,565
Depreciation & amortization	4,494	4,986	5,966	5,897	5,667	5,449	5,287	5,562	6,740	7,952	8,104	8,108	8,609	9,142	9,707	10,308
Provision for doubtful accounts	2,197	2,636	3,073	3,348	3,241	3,785	4,848	4,384	4,112	4,170	3,864	4,142	4,455	4,791	5,150	5,535
Equity-based awards compensation expense	1,038	1,277	1,574	1,573	1,292	2,032	2,102	2,743	3,363	4,491	4,784	4,427	5,011	5,525	6,055	6,394
Loss (gain) on sale of business & fixed assets	-	-	-	-	-333	182	175	7,335	35	84	-	-	-	-	-	-
Excess tax benefit from exercise of stock options	-	-184	-128	-44	-336	-217	1,351	-695	-948	-947	-863	-919	-910	-897	-909	-905
Deferred income tax	-373	313	1,922	714	452	3,833	3,738	2,369	6,275	7,001	7,100	7,200	7,302	7,405	7,510	7,616
Write-off of goodwill	-	-	49	-	-	-	-	-	135	180	90	-	142	187	-	182
Patient accounts receivable	-3,434	-3,543	-1,566	165	-4,169	-5,147	-1,663	-5,389	-5,388	-5,519	-5,653	-5,790	-5,931	-6,075	-6,223	-6,374
Accounts receivable - other	-73	-87	252	-468	-297	-990	-561	-5	341	-852	225	-212	-248	-130	-319	-138
Other assets	168	-160	-257	-855	206	-1,972	-585	1,803	-2,493	-1,477	-5,015	1,050	-1,375	1,298	-1,446	1,310
Accounts payable & accrued expenses	1,623	-655	1,873	595	-292	1,190	-340	4,833	1,868	-7,013	6,902	-2,148	-600	895	500	340
Other liabilities	571	338	470	415	804	-275	-1,321	859	730	1,482	783	376	376	469	725	706
Net cash flows from operating activities	**18,472**	**19,047**	**30,172**	**30,944**	**30,521**	**32,655**	**39,249**	**44,795**	**45,194**	**41,243**	**54,235**	**52,967**	**56,313**	**64,940**	**65,931**	**73,538**
Investing Activities																
Purchase of fixed assets	-4,655	-4,034	-4,299	-3,876	-3,673	-3,222	-4,234	-4,637	-5,167	-6,263	-7,100	-4,631	-4,918	-5,222	-5,545	-5,888
Purchase of businesses, net of cash acquired	-5,206	-19,504	-19,589	-1,178	-18,197	-9,451	-7,929	-46,628	-12,270	-18,965	-17,000	-16,078	-17,348	-16,809	-16,745	-16,967
Acquisitions of noncontrolling interests	-1,234	-519	-1,096	-2,329	-682	-20,439	-2,244	-1,876	-5,490	-7,083	-5,500	-6,024	-6,497	-6,007	-6,457	-6,572
Proceeds on sale of business & fixed assets, net	-	-	-	57	919	6	64	459	47	71	42	-	-	-	-	-
Net cash flows from investing activities	**-8,846**	**-23,536**	**-24,876**	**-7,326**	**-21,633**	**-31,606**	**-14,104**	**-52,449**	**-22,880**	**-32,240**	**-29,558**	**-26,734**	**-28,762**	**-28,038**	**-28,747**	**-29,427**
Financing Activities																
Distributions to noncontrolling interests	-5,489	-5,651	-7,295	-9,438	-9,580	-9,767	-9,332	-9,164	-9,913	-9,632	-11,271	-10,343	-10,830	-11,340	-11,874	-12,433
Cash dividends to shareholders	-	-	-	-	-	-3,789	-9,017	-4,838	-5,873	-7,449	-8,493	-9,598	-10,727	-11,880	-13,058	-14,261
Proceeds from revolving line of credit	0	12,000	20,900	24,450	46,300	118,900	79,900	150,800	134,300	103,000	117,000	126,275	120,144	105,742	114,635	112,548
Payments on revolving line of credit	0	-5,000	-16,500	-35,450	-41,200	-100,900	-86,000	-128,200	-139,800	-93,500	-120,000	-129,275	-122,243	-118,898	-123,000	-123,500
Payment of notes payable	-245	-588	-887	-1,379	-1,013	-250	-434	-459	-825	-884	-775	-1,511	-1,930	-1,846	-1,696	-1,696
Tax benefit from stock options exercised	-	-	-	-	-	217	1,351	695	948	947	863	919	910	897	909	905
Other financing activities	-	-	-	-	-	-	75	47	222	22	-	-	-	-	-	-
Net cash flows from financing activities	**-11,026**	**1,513**	**-3,159**	**-27,302**	**-6,138**	**-245**	**-23,457**	**8,881**	**-20,941**	**-7,496**	**-22,676**	**-23,533**	**-24,677**	**-37,325**	**-34,085**	**-38,437**
Net increase (decrease) in cash & cash equivalents	-1,400	-2,976	2,137	-3,684	2,750	804	1,688	1,227	1,373	1,507	2,001	2,701	2,874	-423	3,100	5,674
Cash & cash equivalents - beginning of period	12,352	10,952	7,976	10,113	6,429	9,179	9,983	11,671	12,898	14,271	15,778	17,779	20,480	23,354	22,932	26,031
Cash & cash equivalents - end of period	**10,952**	**7,976**	**10,113**	**6,429**	**9,179**	**9,983**	**11,671**	**12,898**	**14,271**	**15,778**	**17,779**	**20,480**	**23,354**	**22,932**	**26,031**	**31,705**
Cash paid during the period for income taxes	3,844	5,481	4,400	8,445	7,804	9,037	6,361	4,111	9,253	7,779	15,832	17,287	18,580	19,920	21,262	22,854
Cash paid during the period for interest	34	263	484	324	179	325	639	352	1,103	884	1,271	1,211	1,165	787	592	319

Appendix D: Financial Ratios (Team Calculations)

Profitability Ratio	2006	2007	2008	2009	2010	2011	2012	2013	2014	2015	2016E	2017E	2018E	2019E	2020E	2021E
Total Margin	4.66%	5.76%	5.33%	5.84%	7.41%	8.85%	7.11%	4.82%	6.84%	6.72%	6.74%	6.76%	6.83%	6.87%	6.88%	6.95%
Operating Margin	51.88%	53.63%	54.14%	54.61%	59.25%	59.24%	60.40%	59.92%	60.09%	60.35%	60.59%	60.51%	60.18%	59.67%	59.14%	58.76%
Cash Flow Margin	13.76%	13.21%	12.72%	14.03%	15.71%	15.16%	15.00%	14.68%	15.00%	14.28%	14.28%	14.14%	14.11%	13.97%	13.82%	13.78%
Free Cash Flow Margin	3.86%	2.14%	4.28%	6.91%	9.12%	9.60%	9.83%	9.02%	9.83%	9.25%	9.45%	9.31%	9.30%	9.25%	9.18%	9.19%
Operating Cash Flow Margin																
Free operating cash flow margin																
Return on assets	11.47%	9.16%	8.46%	17.93%	17.54%	18.24%	15.27%	11.60%	12.44%	11.32%	10.75%	11.23%	11.14%	11.44%	11.55%	11.78%
Cash flow to assets	26.02%	20.82%	20.19%	25.35%	23.56%	22.01%	22.02%	17.30%	18.72%	16.90%	16.15%	16.87%	16.70%	17.02%	17.12%	17.38%
Return on equity	14.76%	12.70%	12.26%	21.66%	21.22%	24.50%	19.47%	17.22%	18.19%	16.41%	15.24%	14.98%	14.68%	14.40%	14.12%	13.96%
Cash flow to equity	33.50%	28.87%	29.26%	30.63%	28.52%	29.55%	28.07%	25.67%	27.37%	24.49%	22.89%	22.51%	22.00%	21.42%	20.92%	20.60%
Basic Earning power	26.02%	20.82%	20.19%	25.35%	23.56%	22.01%	22.02%	17.30%	18.72%	16.90%	16.15%	16.87%	16.70%	17.02%	17.12%	17.38%
Growth rate in equity	3.82%	25.02%	17.58%	13.01%	26.19%	4.47%	10.76%	12.15%	10.73%	15.49%	15.24%	10.16%	9.70%	9.29%	8.50%	8.69%
Econimc value added	6,446x	5,520x	6,041x	11,859x	13,489x	13,468x	13,163x	9,336x	12,843x	10,537x	10,451x	11,947x	12,562x	13,914x	14,832x	16,321x
Econimc to capital	11.03%	6.97%	6.20%	12.27%	10.65%	9.17%	8.47%	4.74%	6.07%	4.18%	3.72%	4.04%	3.93%	4.16%	4.18%	4.36%
Liquidity Ratio																
Current ratio	3.92x	3.15x	2.65x	2.24x	2.76x	2.80x	2.78x	2.14x	2.15x	3.17x	2.64x	3.07x	3.21x	3.23x	3.54x	3.69x
Days in patiensd accoutn receivale	63.13x	67.80x	56.12x	45.09x	48.29x	49.11x	41.16x	45.58x	42.19x	42.40x	43.44x	41.99x	41.34x	40.71x	40.10x	39.51x
aVERAGE PAYMENT PERIOD	33.69x	36.52x	37.15x	36.00x	33.46x	33.79x	31.41x	42.43x	40.67x	27.43x	35.68x	29.73x	28.86x	27.05x	25.10x	24.30x
Capital Structure Ratios																
Debt Ratio	16.89%	22.02%	25.73%	17.23%	17.38%	25.53%	21.58%	30.79%	28.61%	27.85%	26.87%	22.91%	21.56%	17.79%	15.41%	12.91%
Equity ratio	77.69%	72.11%	69.01%	82.77%	82.62%	74.47%	78.42%	67.38%	68.38%	68.99%	70.54%	74.96%	75.90%	79.45%	81.83%	84.38%
Debt / Equity	0.22x	0.31x	0.37x	0.21x	0.21x	0.34x	0.28x	0.46x	0.42x	0.40x	0.38x	0.31x	0.28x	0.22x	0.19x	0.15x
Capitalization ratio	4.96%	12.93%	16.23%	4.59%	8.09%	17.25%	13.55%	23.29%	23.29%	21.00%	20.71%	17.10%	15.94%	12.04%	9.80%	7.13%
Coverage Ratio																
TIE Ratio	0.00x	66.56x	44.05x	80.26x	140.64x	72.44x	67.87x	72.06x	42.07x	45.87x	40.08x	45.57x	50.78x	80.04x	113.08x	224.89x
Cash flow to total debt	2.80x	180.01x	141.89x	294.83x	261.17x	172.97x	189.92x	104.18x	113.59x	108.96x	108.04x	129.99x	135.78x	168.16x	195.55x	236.32x
Debt service coverage ratio	0.00x	34.28x	22.46x	41.48x	131.54x	77.59x	69.27x	52.75x	40.32x	47.04x	32.91x	31.01x	34.45x	44.58x	51.51x	62.43x
Cash flow coverage	1.60x	1.50x	1.41x	1.80x	2.02x	1.89x	1.79x	1.72x	1.68x	1.65x	1.65x	1.61x	1.61x	1.62x	1.61x	1.61x
Cushion Ratio	#DIV/0!	7.17x	5.26x	4.71x	18.89x	10.75x	11.49x	9.46x	7.24x	8.74x	6.39x	6.52x	7.76x	9.23x	11.37x	15.73x
Capital expense ratio	18.92%	19.54%	17.96%	18.37%	18.68%	18.06%	17.74%	17.58%	16.43%	16.39%	16.52%	15.86%	15.60%	15.34%	15.13%	14.91%
Asset efficincy																
Total asset turnover	1.89x	1.58x	1.59x	1.81x	1.50x	1.45x	1.47x	1.18x	1.25x	1.18x	1.13x	1.19x	1.18x	1.22x	1.24x	1.26x
Fixed asset turnover	10.11x	9.03x	11.85x	14.05x	15.17x	17.97x	19.37x	17.65x	19.35x	19.89x	20.70x	20.71x	20.80x	21.17x	21.58x	21.81x
Current asset turnover	3.76x	4.21x	4.85x	6.10x	5.38x	5.19x	5.56x	5.32x	5.56x	5.51x	5.07x	5.22x	5.14x	5.49x	5.36x	5.32x
Other financial ratios																
Capital expenditure growth rate	39.10%	37.61%	36.85%	37.29%	36.86%	36.74%	36.48%	35.97%	35.19%	35.99%	36.42%	36.36%	36.30%	36.24%	36.17%	36.11%
Replacement viability ratio	152.29%	157.23%	147.76%	139.13%	135.49%	131.18%	129.48%	132.60%	132.14%	131.27%	129.88%	131.06%	131.38%	131.14%	130.95%	130.68%
Market to book ratio	4.28x	2.40x	1.97x	2.13x	0.20x	1.89x	2.44x	2.67x	3.08x	3.45x	3.95x					
Price to earnings ratio	38.33x	18.55x	15.87x	16.76x	14.79x	11.06x	18.12x	31.68x	25.90x	30.33x	36.48x					
Price cash flow ratio	7.03x	4.37x	3.72x	3.47x	0.36x	3.20x	4.66x	5.60x	6.48x	7.85x	9.60x					
Historical Prices	20.70	14.10	13.33	16.93	19.82	19.68	27.54	33.26	41.96	53.68	70.20					

Appendix E: DuPont (Team Calculations)

Using the DuPont analysis, we looked at the trends from ROE. ROE has leveled around 11% after being at a high of 17% in 2011. The equity multiplier has been high to maintain the ROE number because the Total Asset Turnover has fallen from 1.47 to a projected 1.13 at the end of 2016. The low Total Asset Turnover indicates that the company is not using its assets as efficient in producing sales. The equity is on a slightly downward trend and our projections continue the decrease the Equity multiplier. A service company such as USPH doesn't expect to have a great Total Asset Turnover because of the nature of the business. One aspect that further reduces this number is that USPH acquires clinics annually that do not produce high returns until they turn into mature clinics especially when they purchase clinics in December which usually occurs as acquisitions purchase prices are immediately incorporated into the balance sheet but do not yield increases in earnings if they are bought later in the year. Every year their assets produce revenue the year after purchase. This delay can cause low numbers for Total Asset Turnover if they acquire different number of clinics each year. The decreasing ROE and TAT still indicate that the company is becoming less efficient in return to investors. This shows that the stock price appears to be inflated higher than its true intrinsic value and is overvalued.

USPH	Historical						Forecast					
	2010	**2011**	**2012**	**2013**	**2014**	**2015**	**2016E**	**2017E**	**2018E**	**2019E**	**2020E**	**2021E**
ROE	13%	17%	13%	8%	12%	12%	11%	11%	11%	11%	10%	10%
ROA	11%	13%	10%	6%	9%	8%	8%	8%	8%	8%	9%	9%
Profit Margin	7%	9%	7%	5%	7%	7%	7%	7%	7%	7%	7%	7%
Tota Asset Turnover	150%	145%	147%	118%	125%	118%	113%	119%	118%	122%	124%	126%
Equity Multiplier	121%	134%	128%	148%	146%	145%	1.42	1.33	132%	126%	122%	1.19

Appendix F: Discounted Cash Flow and Assumptions (Team Calculations)

Forecast	2017E	2018E	2019E	2020E	2021E	Terminal
Net Operating Cash Flow	52,967	56,313	64,940	65,931	73,538	
Add: Interest Expense*(1-Taxrate)	824	792	535	403	217	
Exclude: Capital Expenditure	-26,734	-28,762	-28,038	-28,747	-29,427	
FCFF	27,057	28,343	37,438	37,587	44,327	
Add: Net Borrowing	4,511	4,029	15,002	10,061	12,648	
Exclude: Interest Expense	-1,211	-1,165	-787	-592	-319	
FCFE	30,357	31,207	51,653	47,056	56,657	$980,976,039.88
NPV FCFE	$27,999,643.86	$26,548,235.93	$40,529,011.35	$34,055,067.62	$37,818,929.06	$654,804,092.75

Current Risk-free Rate	1.92% 5-Year Treasury Constant Maturity Rate-FRED
Beta	0.85479 Team projections
Historican Market Return	9.53% Annual returns on S&P 500 stocks 1928-Current. Domaodaran. Geometric Mean
Long-Term Growth Rate	2.50% GDP is expected to grow at 2% based on the World Bank HC Stock track above GDP
Cost of Debt	4.23% LIBOR + 2.5%. LIBOR equals 1.73 on 2/3/2017
Tax Rate	32.00%
Weight of Equity	91.21% See calculations on the right
Weight of Debt	8.79% See calculations on the right
WACC	7.93% Weighted Average Cost of Capital

[RFR+β*(Rmarket-RFR)]	
Required Return	8.42%
NPV FCFE 2017	$27,999,644
NPV FCFE 2018	$26,548,236
NPV FCFE 2018	$40,529,011
NPV FCFE 2020	$34,055,068
NPV FCFE 2021	$37,818,929
NPV Terminal	$654,804,093
	$821,754,980.58

Shares Outstanding	12,520,000
Intrinsic Value FCFE	$65.64
Closing Price (2/3/17)	$71.45

Appendix G: Sensitivity Analysis (Team Calculations)

	Currently overvalued					Price (as of 2/3/2017):		$71.45			
	Currently undervalued										
						Long-Term Growth Rate					
	1.25%	1.50%	1.75%	2.00%	2.25%	2.50%	2.75%	3.00%	3.25%	3.50%	3.75%
5.72%	$92.07	$96.87	$102.27	$108.41	$115.42	$123.53	$133.00	$144.21	$157.69	$174.21	$194.91
6.02%	$86.03	$90.18	$94.82	$100.04	$105.95	$112.70	$120.48	$129.54	$140.25	$153.08	$168.73
6.32%	$80.71	$84.34	$88.36	$92.84	$97.88	$103.57	$110.06	$117.53	$126.22	$136.45	$148.66
6.62%	$75.99	$79.17	$82.69	$86.58	$90.91	$95.78	$101.27	$107.52	$114.69	$123.02	$132.79
6.92%	$71.77	$74.59	$77.68	$81.08	$84.85	$89.04	$93.74	$99.03	$105.05	$111.95	$119.93
7.22%	$67.98	$70.48	$73.22	$76.22	$79.52	$83.17	$87.22	$91.76	$96.87	$102.67	$109.30
7.52%	$64.55	$66.79	$69.23	$71.88	$74.79	$77.99	$81.53	$85.46	$89.84	$94.77	$100.36
7.82%	$61.43	$63.45	$65.63	$68.00	$70.58	$73.41	$76.51	$79.94	$83.74	$87.98	$92.74
8.12%	$58.59	$60.41	$62.38	$64.50	$66.80	$69.31	$72.06	$75.07	$78.39	$82.07	$86.17
8.42%	$55.99	$57.64	$59.41	$61.33	$63.39	$65.64	$68.07	$70.74	$73.66	$76.88	$80.44
8.72%	$53.60	$55.10	$56.71	$58.44	$60.30	$62.31	$64.49	$66.87	$69.45	$72.29	$75.41
9.02%	$51.40	$52.77	$54.23	$55.80	$57.49	$59.30	$61.26	$63.38	$65.69	$68.20	$70.95
9.32%	$49.36	$50.61	$51.95	$53.38	$54.91	$56.55	$58.32	$60.23	$62.29	$64.53	$66.98
9.62%	$47.46	$48.62	$49.84	$51.15	$52.54	$54.04	$55.64	$57.36	$59.22	$61.23	$63.41
9.92%	$45.70	$46.77	$47.89	$49.09	$50.37	$51.73	$53.18	$54.75	$56.42	$58.23	$60.19
10.22%	$44.06	$45.04	$46.08	$47.18	$48.35	$49.60	$50.93	$52.35	$53.87	$55.51	$57.27
10.52%	$42.53	$43.44	$44.39	$45.41	$46.49	$47.63	$48.85	$50.14	$51.53	$53.02	$54.61
10.82%	$41.09	$41.93	$42.82	$43.76	$44.75	$45.80	$46.92	$48.11	$49.38	$50.73	$52.18
11.12%	$39.74	$40.53	$41.35	$42.22	$43.14	$44.11	$45.13	$46.23	$47.39	$48.62	$49.95

(Row label at left: **Required Rate of Return**)

Our sensitivity analysis looked at the potential results with variations in the required rate of return and the long term growth rate. The required rate of 8.42% and our long term growth rate of 2.5% gave us an intrinsic value of the bolded number seen above. In order to identify potential outcomes from variations in required rate of return and long term growth rate we inputted discounted and premiums on both variables. Looking to see how changes in these variable would interact with each other giving different stock values scenarios, we ranged the required rate of return from 5.72% to 11.12% and ranged the long term growth rate from 1.25% to 3.75%. By looking at the analysis it is clear to see that more often than not, our stock is overvalued as indicated by the grey shaded boxes. This is proven when the larger number of scenarios give an intrinsic value that is below the current market value. This shows that the company needs more favorable than currently predictable conditions in order to become valuable. In situations such as this, the stock is given a sell decision.

Appendix H: Breaking down DCF and Assumptions (Team Calculations)

USPH Projected Revenues

2016	2017	2018	2019	2020	2021
$348,990,000.00	$382,262,038.52	$411,195,095.51	$442,173,623.75	$475,342,231.25	$510,855,749.36
$7,658,000.00	$7,964,000.00	$8,283,000.00	$8,614,000.00	$8,959,000.00	$9,317,000.00
$356,648,000.00	$390,226,038.52	$419,478,095.51	$450,787,623.75	$484,301,231.25	$520,172,749.36

As explained in Appendix M and page 9, the revenue driver for USPH is Total Patient Visits. Our estimates are that acquisitions will not grow by a large number, because of interest rate increases and fewer clinics to acquire, thus contributing less to revenue each year. Because of this, growth in total patients will also contribute less to revenue each year. Lastly, revenue per patient is at a probable plateau because of USPH peaking in efficiency. We represented attributes that will contribute to USPH's revenue growth of 7.5% as:

- Total Patient Visits Growth

- Total Clinics Growth

- Clinical Efficiency Growth

	2016	2017	2018	2019	2020	2021
Effincey contribution to Total Patient Visit Growth	**1.51%**	**1.85%**	**1.48%**	**1.47%**	**1.46%**	**1.46%**
Clinic Contribution to Total Patient Visits Growth	5.99%	7.37%	5.87%	5.85%	5.82%	5.80%
Total Patient Visits Contribution To Revenue Growth	7.50%	9.23%	7.35%	7.31%	7.29%	7.26%
Other Revenues	0.153%	0.188%	0.150%	0.149%	0.149%	0.148%
Total Revenue Growth	7.65%	9.41%	7.50%	7.46%	7.43%	7.41%

(Source: Team Calculations)

* Spikes in 2017 revenue are due to the January 2017 clinic acquisition of 17 clinics. Since these clinics were bought early in the year, they will bring more revenue for the year due to a full year of operations. We cannot assume this will happen in any other year, so our assumption of linear growth is used - linear growth accounts better for overall yearly acquiring than other methods.

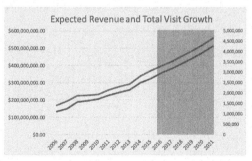

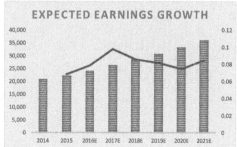

Salaries and Related Costs - Though salaries fluctuate with decisions by management for raises and other forms of compensation due to operational efficiencies and success in areas that USPH decide to work on, our team estimates that as revenues rise, salaries will grow from as a larger percent of revenue. This is due to the growing labor market in Physical therapy. We estimate that Salaries and Related Costs will account for an average of 55.28% of revenue in the next five years.

Revolving Line of Credit - As USPH continues to accumulate cash and growth in net income, they will be less inclined to use their line of credit. As interest rates start to increase, they will also be less likely to use their line of interest. Our estimates had the resolving line of credit decreasing approximately 8.09% a year.

Goodwill - USPH has historically recorded their purchases of business in Goodwill. Our estimate of goodwill is highly tide to revenues, considering as total clinics increases, revenues increase from new patient visits. We estimate that Goodwill will remain relatively constant at 61.5% of total assets.

Corporate Office Costs - These costs are associated to management pay and the internal technology costs associated with clinic acquisition research and health record information. This technology is at their headquarters in Houston and is related to Office Costs. USPH benefits from Economies of Scale, by adding each clinic acquisition to their network. Houston rental rates are not expected to increase in the future. Due to this, our team estimates Corporate Office costs to remain relatively constant, with some decreases. Corporate Office costs are projected at an average of 9.53% of total revenues.

Appendix I: Monte Carlo Simulation (Team Calculations, taxrates.org)

State	Lower limit	Upper limit
Alaska	0.00%	0.00%
Arizona	2.59%	4.54%
Connecticut	3.00%	6.70%
Delaware	2.20%	6.60%
District of Columbia	4.00%	8.95%
Florida	0.00%	0.00%
Georgia	1.00%	6.00%
Idaho	1.60%	7.40%
Illinois	3.75%	3.75%
Indiana	3.30%	3.30%
Iowa	0.36%	8.98%
Kansas	2.70%	4.60%
Louisiana	2.00%	6.00%
Maine	6.50%	7.95%
Maryland	2.00%	5.75%
Massachusetts	5.20%	5.20%
Michigan	4.25%	4.25%
Mississippi	3.00%	5.00%
Missouri	1.50%	6.00%
Nebraska	2.46%	6.84%
Nevada	0.00%	0.00%
New Jersey	1.40%	8.97%
Ohio	0.53%	5.33%
Oklahoma	0.50%	5.25%
Oregon	5.00%	9.90%
Pennsylvania	3.07%	3.07%
Tennessee	6.00%	6.00%
Texas	0.00%	0.00%
Vermont	3.55%	8.95%
Virginia	2.00%	5.75%
Washington	0.00%	0.00%
Wisconsin	4.00%	7.65%
Wyoming	0.00%	0.00%
Total rates	77.46%	168.68%
# of Clinics	33	33
Average Rates	2.35%	5.11%

Monte Carlo Original:
The Monte Carlo Valuation is a random sampling system that gives a wide range of different numerical possibilities. The system takes various inputs and assorts all the different possibilities based on how those inputs affect each other. The algorithm then delivers the individual results based on the data interaction. Each possibility is called an iteration. Millions of iterations can be run but for our Monte Carlo valuations we implemented 30,000 iterations as it is the max our excel add-in would allow. This number is still sufficient to demonstrate the most likely outcomes of our inputs and indicate where the stock price is most common.

Our Monte Carlo simulation accounted for three different variables. As discussed, the main driver of revenue growth is total patient visits (and acquisitions which is correlated with patient visits). We used our 7.07% growth rate of patient visits calculated from our historical changes in visits to calculate a standard deviation of .047. The Required Rate of Return was also tested with a manually calculated standard deviation of .0135. Lastly, we tested the long term growth rate of 2.5% with a manually calculated deviation of .0075. These variables were tested to return the potential intrinsic value of USPH's stock. The intrinsic value from the Discounted Cash flow model of $65.64 was the watch cell of which the outputs were based.

Monte Carlo Alternative:
Our second Monte Carlo simulation was run to help project the results potential tax reductions would have on our stock. The first simulation showed how the three most important variables relating to our intrinsic value would affect our stock. As stated, there is a potential new variable moving USPH to a lower tax rate that could breed beneficial results for our stock. Instead of the historical effective tax rate of 32%, we took the base tax rate of 15% (stated by the government administration) plus state taxes. The table shows the upper and lower corporate tax limits that USPH operates in (any states with only one clinic were omitted). The average rate was found; we went with the upper limit of 5.11% in order to be conservative. When added to our base figure of 15%, we project a potential future tax rate of 20.11%.

We applied this tax rate to our projections to see the effect of this lower tax rate.

By looking at the income from continuing operations before and after our tax provision changes, it is clear that there is a substantial difference to the financial statements from this tax reduction and income that will flow through to the Cash flow statement is sizably greater as can be seen.

Original statement:

Provision for income taxes	17,287	18,580	19,920	21,262	22,854
Net income from continuing operations including non-controlling interests	36,735	39,482	42,331	45,181	48,565

Statement with 20.11% tax rate:

Provision for income taxes	10,864	11,676	12,519	13,362	14,362
Net income from continuing operations including non-controlling interests	43,158	46,386	49,733	53,081	57,056
32% Tax Rate Net cash flows from operating activities	52,967	56,313	64,940	65,931	73,538
20.11% Tax Rate Net cash flows from operating activities	59,391	63,217	72,342	73,831	82,030

These numbers change the DCF noticeably and lead to a new intrinsic value of $75.79 from $65.64. This new intrinsic value is what we used to run another Monte Carlo with the same variables as used in the first analysis: patient visits, growth rate, and required rate of return.

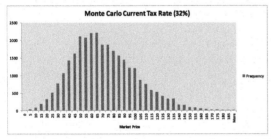

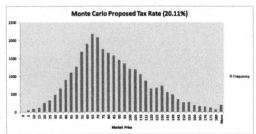

Appendix D: Retained Earnings

($ in Thousands)	Historical										Forecast					
	2006	2007	2008	2009	2010	2011	2012	2013	2014	2015	2016E	2017E	2018E	2019E	2020E	2021E
Previous retained earnings (accumulated deficit)	44,408	50,704	59,442	69,446	75,632	89,876	102,405	111,321	119,206	134,186	149,016	164,547	181,340	199,265	218,376	238,624
Purchase & retirement of treasury stock	-	-	-	5,581	1,401	4,656	-	-	-	-	-	-	-	-	-	-
Cash dividends to shareholders	-	-	-	-	-	3,789	9,017	4,838	5,873	7,449	8,493	9,598	10,727	11,880	13,058	14,261
Retained earnings (accumulated deficit)	50,704	59,442	69,446	75,632	89,876	102,405	111,321	119,206	134,186	149,016	164,559	181,340	199,265	218,376	238,624	260,495

Appendix J: Physical Therapy Rehab Center Food Supply Chain and Glossary (Team Calculations)

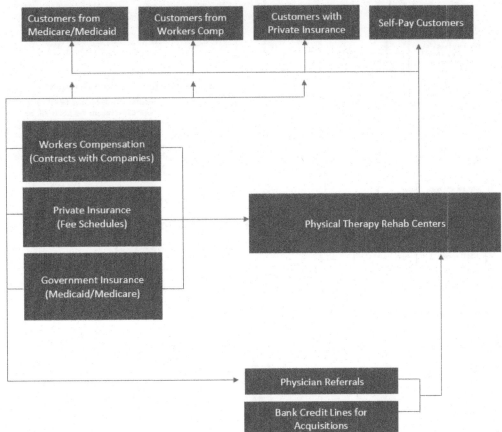

The Physical Therapy Industry is a complicated system between "suppliers" and the subsequent "consumer." It is important to understand the "food chain" for a company to better understand where their demand comes from and the factors that can influence it. The three main supplier-types for the USPH food chain are government insurances, private insurances, and workers compensation. These are the factors that most influence demand for USPH, which is why we focused our analysis on these factors. By identifying critical factors in revenue flows, USPH is more able to be strategic in their operations within their specific supply chain. Considering USPH is dependent on suppliers, they have difficulty controlling their risk factors. However, these risks can be strategically mitigated through business operations in a well managed firm. Unlike any other industry, healthcare providers are subject to supplier entities more than they are subject to the consumer. USPH tries to appeal to their customer base with quality and care but they are equally, if not more concerned, about the insurers who give them ability to have customers. This is why they encourage the development of relationships between their local therapists and physicians. It is important to have well rooted physician relationships because it produces a strong customer base. Physicians are also concerned with the type of payment these customer holds (private insurance or government plans). USPH has pushed for more private insurance customers, so they must develop good relationships with the physicians that also have a focus on this niche market of private insurance customers. As consumers gain insurance, physical therapists supply the ability to satisfy the growing demand. Private Insurance companies negotiate rates by cities which can determine USPH's ability to have customers. Though it seems as though private insurance has all the power, USPH has been able to leverage themselves favorably through their size in negotiating and low supply areas. USPH is subject to governments in regulation requirements and Medicare/Medicaid limits and requirements. Governments ask for quality outcomes at a cheaper price. USPH has strayed away from this supplier as much as possible; it has been one of their main goals. They have done this successfully with only 24.5% of their revenue coming from insurance. Lastly, the ability to acquire has been perpetuated by their revolving credit agreement. By being able to pay off their debt efficiently, they have been able to establish a well rooted relationship with Bank of America. Their Credit is used to acquire which is how they are able to increase patient visits and company revenue. Their ability to manage debt will allow them to continue to benefit from this relationship.

Appendix K: Possible Outcomes for Congressional Rulings (Team Calculations)

For every 1 new regulation 2 have to be removed: Purpose is to encourage small business growth and a decrease in price controls

Cuts tax rates to 15%

USPH profit margins increase

Increase in speed and ability of small business growth

Business are encouraged to expand domestically

Higher profit margins allow companies to hire more

More are able to go to the doctor cause of an increase in personal income

USPH revenue will be increased by these factors

More are covered by employer insurance (who are in favor of physical therapy)

Results of Administration Decisions

It is important to note the uncertainty in determining the affects the new administration will have on USPH. We estimate that USPH will fair well under most conditions. However, there are aspects that could make it easier – or more difficult- for USPH to continue to grow net income at a steady rate. Below is outlined a flow chart of possible congressional ruling and their affects on USPH. This information is taken at its most extreme levels and variations of occurrence.

Congressional Ruling

Redefine the term Hardship allowing increase amounts who opt out of insurance under ACA

Transitional Activity that could happen without actually repealing ACA

USPH revenue decreases because their payment mix is insurance heavy

Current payment subsidies insurers receive are ended allowing them to leave ACA

Insurance is allowed to freely cross state borders

Agencies are free to use their interpretations of the ACA

Contracts between insurance companies and ACA terminate due to this subsides ending

USPH can implement favorable contracts in more locations increasing revenue

Insurance is allowed to decide how long they will cover each illness, reducing the amount of days they will pay for

USPH revenue will increase because it will still be the low cost solution

Allows insurers to drop sick patients approved only through ACA

Less sick patients are referred to medical solutions rather than physical therapy because of shorter time frame

Physical therapy does not take on the extremely sick so revenues will not be as effected by them losing coverage. UPSH business model looks for younger and healthier

Repeal ACA

If done without a replacement

Up to 20 Million Lose insurance

USPH becomes more Medicare/ Medicaid focused to maintain profits

USPH patients decrease due to lower quantity of people insured

Under these condition it is unclear how significant of an impact it will have on profit margins of USPH

New administration are able to do it at a lower cost

Gives insurance to those who lost it when ACA was implemented

Coverage loss is kept to a minimal

Repeal and Replace ACA

Government Insurance is not expanded; looking for ways to save money

Government begins to seek out physical therapy

Quantity of USPH patients increase rises as a cheaper solution for government

Appendix L: Competition Positioning (Team Calculations, Company Filings)

Competition Positioning	USPH	KND	SEM	HLS
Number of Rehab Properties	508	604	1023	121
Revenue	$324.3M	1.58B	3.74B	2.65B
% of Revenue from Medicare/Medicaid	24.50%	83.00%	40.50%	73.20%
% of Revenue from Private Insurance	51.0%	8.0%	46.9%	19.0%
% of Revenue from Workers Compensation	18.5%	<1%	12.6%	1.1%

USPH has been able to mitigate their payment risks by diversifying their payment methods. Decreasing the amount of revenue you receive from the government, they have made themselves less susceptible to future regulations. Comparing USPH to their competitors, who have a substantial amount of revenues coming from the government, they have been are more appealing to investors. Combining this information with their beta based on the NYSE Healthcare index of .76 USPH has placed them in a favorable position for investors. When conservative investors are looking to diversify their portfolio they could benefit from adding USPH stock rather than some of their competitors.

Appendix L: Beta Analysis of USPH and Competitors (Team Calculations and Value Line)

Beta Analysis of USPH		
Year/Index	**Beta**	**R-Squared**
5Y S&P 500	1.074	0.253
3Y S&P 500	0.85	0.156
5Y RUT	0.928	0.351
3Y RUT	0.864	0.267
5Y NYP	1.043	0.208
3Y NYP	0.762	0.142

Beta Comparison		
USPH	SEM	HLS
0.85	1.15	1.1

When analyzing the level of risk USPH presents we found their beta compared to several indexes. We found that USPH beta almost always moved less than the market regardless of which index was used for comparison. This is beneficial to USPH because it shows they are less volatile then other companies. The first index we compared was the S&P 500 because it gives a base level for the market as a whole. This is the beta most companies will use when comparing different companies. Here we found that USPH 5 year beta moved more than the market but in recent years they have decreased their risk and have stabilized some of their validity. USPH is a smaller company who has potentials for growth. When listening to their CEO we found that they compared themselves to the Russell 2000 due to the broader outlook it gives. This larger view on the market let us compare USPH movement by looking at companies who were statically more likely to be equal in size and growth as USPH. These factors led us to compare USPH with the RUT. Her we found that we offer less risk. For an investor looking to invest in a growth company with less movement compared to the market, they may be interested in placing their money in USPH. The last index we used when comparing was the NYSE Healthcare index. The team felt it would be important to include this one in our analysis because it shows how USPH is moving as compared to their industry. For an investor looking to diversify their risk but still interested in the profits from the healthcare industry, they may look at this beta and feel confident in what USPH can offer On the right we have the betas of USPH and their competitors. Because beta shows how influenced a company is based on market swings we felt it important to compare these. USPH is the only one out of their competitors who is volatile than the market. In economic downturns this component interprets USPH being a safer investment choice in comparison with their competitors.

Appendix M: Dividend Discount Model (Team Calculations)

Using the Dividend Discount Model, we value the price of USPH by using dividends growth and then discounting the stock price to present value. This model has some limitations because it requires a constant growth rate of dividend. USPH had some dividend growth fluctuations over the years. USPH only started paying out dividends in 2011 so a historic trend cannot be established for a long period of time. For our model, we assumed USPH would continue their traditional increase in dividend payout. USPH paid stable dividend at $0.17 paid each quarter in 2015 until present. Using an estimate increase of $.02 every quarter for the next 5 years based on the past years increases which has had 3 of the last 4 years seeing a $.08 increase. We used the model to obtain an estimation of the value of the stock. Based on the calculation, and using a discount rate of 8.42%, we valued the stocks intrinsic value to be worth $51.58. It is important to note the limitations of the DDM model as the model is traditionally used larger companies that pay a more predictable amount of dividends. USPH dividends experienced an anomaly in 2012 with a sharp rise in payout, followed shortly with a huge decline. Since then USPH has trended dividend increases with 8 cent extra per year per share. Even with these limitations, the stock is still valued 20$ below current closing price. While the amount under may be argued, it is a substantial difference that show USPH is overvalued. This future amount shows how USPH stock price has been on the rise and is unlikely to get much higher even with the growth in their dividends.

Historical		
Year		**Dividend**
2011	$D_1 =$	0.32
2012	$D_2 =$	0.76
2013	$D_3 =$	0.4
2014	$D_4 =$	0.48
2015	$D_5 =$	0.6
2016	$D_6 =$	0.68
Year		**Dividend**
2017	$D_7 =$	0.76
2018	$D_8 =$	0.84
2019	$D_9 =$	0.92
2020	$D_{10} =$	1
2021	$D_{11} =$	1.08
	$P_5 =$	71.45
		Overvalued
	Value =	51.2751

Appendix M: Revenue Growth Model (Team Calculations)

Data Mining Results							(Source: Team Estimates)
Model Used:	Simple Variable Linear Regression	Gaussian Processes	Isotonic Regression	Linear Regression Model	Linear Node 0	SMO Regression	ZeroR model
Correlation Coefficent	0.9993	0.8796	0.903	0.9848	0.9989	0.9986	0.7951
(Closer to 1 the better)							
Relative Absolute error	13.34%	76.36%	5439.03%	33.61%	18.25%	26.83%	66.46%
(The lower the better)							

Growth rate is forecasted to increase at 7.5% through 2021 . For USPH, growth rate is based on net patient revenues . The best predictor of net patient revenues is total patient visits. Total patient visits was used in a simple linear regression model to predict revenues, which resulted in the "best model" fit over other more complicated models. Confirming this fact, we used the simple linear regression model to forecast USPH's revenues for 2017-2021. Many variables were analyzed to find which had a strong correlation with net patient revenues (See Above). Of the nine variables analyzed, total patient visits had the highest positive correlation with revenue; as total patient visits increase, revenue increases. Next, seven statistical and data mining models were investigated to create equations that could be used to forecast future revenues. Table 'Data Mining Results' shows the model correlation to the data and the best fitting model demonstrated by the lowest absolute error value. The SLR uses a feature selection algorithm to find the most influential variable and removes the less influential variables from the model, giving the formula 'Net Patient Revenue' = 115.9 * 'Total Patient Visits' – (2,699,416). The last term is a constant derived by the model. **Both the correlation analysis and the SLR modeling confirm that total patient visits is the most influential variable in predicting net patient revenue.** This equation is confirmed by the observation that USPH has focused in operations that increase total patient visits. Other improvements have increased the payments rates from patient visits. Next, we forecasted total patient visits using a combination of historic trends of total patient visits and total clinics. The formula used for this was 'Increase in Patient Visits' = .50 * Δ 'Total Patient Visits' (2010-2015) + .50 * Δ 'Total Clinics' (2010-2015). Total clinics was used to adjust for variability in efficiency of each clinic. Since total clinic changes has a high correlation with total patient visits at a coefficient of 98.4, total clinic increases were used to further justify the increase in total patient visits. This forecasted the growth rate of total patient visits is 7.07%. This growth rate is important to the Monte Carlo simulations described in Appendix I in this report to determine if the stock price is properly valued and thus influence the buy, hold, sell recommendation . Using this rate in the SLR formula equates to a growth rate of 7. 5%.

Appendix N: SWOT Analysis (Team Calculations)

SWOT Analysis:

The team felt that in addition to Porter's Five Forces, analyzing the SWOT gave a broader look at the industry USPH is operating in.

Strengths: 5

USPH has focused on acquisitions in states with high population and high reimbursement rates. Their target location is within rural suburban areas where they can be in personal relationship with the community yet strategic with a large number of patients. Preferring physicians who are already fairly efficient at operating with multiple clinics, USPH is interested in the future development rather clinics needing to be fixed Becoming excellent debt managers, USPH keeps modest financial leverage when acquiring physicians' clinics. With a revolving line of credit they have been able to buy into quality clinics with a mass of data. From the combination of clinics across the states USPH uses this data to better analyze where would be the most profitable location to acquire next. USPH has benefitted from economies of scale marginal technology costs lower with each increase in total clinics.

Weaknesses: 2

Their slow acquisition process may leave them at a loss in the growing consolidation market. Also, considering USPH's acquisitions are not forced to follow similar branding, marketing expenses are created for the hiring of multiple brand positions. Because the need for physical therapy is increasing and there is a decrease in the amount of available therapy graduates, USPH stands in a position with a decrease labor sector which increases labor costs. This combined with the limited reimbursements on Medicare/Medicaid, USPH faces opposition of future expansion at their current rate.

Opportunity: 3

Growing numbers in ages 65+ will likely increase Medicare rates in the future. Though USPH has strategically penetrated high insurance markets, they could easily tap into the Medicare market in a broader way, which could help them grow if they felt the need. Unlike their competitors, they have currently developed their revenue to a younger, active market, but are also in a favorable position to pursue another market. Similar to other industries, USPH has not created a solid online physical therapy presence yet. The technology advancement has made online physical therapy a profitable solution to those who are facing reimbursement limitations. Expanding their services online has create potential for future success of USPH.

Threats: 3

The limited ability for therapist to see a certain number of patients, coupled with growing technological ability have led companies like eWellness to create an online based physical therapy clinic. Though this cannot reach a majority of patients needs, the growing popularity of "not having to leave home mindset" could hurt USPH's business by taking over this customer base. This is also an opportunity for USPH if they pursue it correctly; a high threat if non handled correctly. Another area USPH has substantial threat in is they have worked out all inefficiencies for daily client billing. In addition, management has pushed for their physical therapists trying to see more patients per day the past which has been the large source of increased profit, however they have reached a plateauing area making it difficult for this amount of gain to continue at this rate in the future.

Strengths	Weaknesses
High Reimbursement	Slow Acquisitions
Personal Relationships	Marketing Expenses
Large Number of Patients	Growth rate Increases at Decresing rate
Efficient at Operating	Interest Paid to RLC
Multi Clinic Managements	Substitute Products
Debt Management	Increasing Labor Costs
Mass of Data	Medicare/Medicaid Reimbursement Limits
Profitable locations	
Opportunity	**Threats**
Aging Population	Daily Patients Restraint
Increase in Medicare Rates	No Online Base
Moving to Online Therapy	Daily Revenue/Patient Plateu
Growth in Total Patients	Market Condensing decreases amount USPH Acquires
Large Line of Credit for Acquistions	Barriers to Entry
Technology that Finds quality Acquistions	

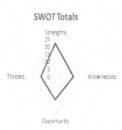

SWOT Totals

Appendix O: Market Share By State and Board of Director Holdings <small>(Team Calculations Company Filings)</small>

(Source: Team Estimates)

Because of the fragmentation of the industry, it is important for USPH to be separated from their competitors. ATI and SEM are the purest competitors of USPH so they are the ones placed for comparison in this graph. In areas with less competition, reimbursement rates are higher for both government and insurance entities. As seen in the map above, USPH has chosen clinic areas that are not heavily saturated by their competition. These high reimbursement rate areas, however, are appealing to their competitors. There are no barriers to entry for their larger competitors, so they are subject to market infiltration. Additionally, USPH 's high concentration in certain market may pose certain risks by lack of diversification. However, USPH has positioned themselves well bhy capturing the market before mas infiltration.

Appendix P: Board of Director Holdings <small>(Team Calculations and USPH Proxy)</small>

			(02/03/2017)	
	# of Shares	% of Total	Market Value	Non Exec Totals
Jerald L. Pullins	24596	0.2%	$ 1,757,384.20	$ 251,043.00
Christopher J. Reading	116877	0.9%	$ 8,350,861.65	-
Lawrance W. McAfee	45212	0.4%	$ 3,230,397.40	-
Daniel C. Arnold	128654	1.0%	$ 9,192,328.30	$ 177,043.00
Mark J. Brookner	53750	0.4%	$ 3,840,437.50	$ 188,543.00
Harry S. Chapman	33750	0.4%	$ 2,411,437.50	$ 204,543.00
Dr. Bernard A. Harris, Jr	34834	0.4%	$ 2,488,889.30	$ 189,543.00
Marlin W. Johnston	36849	0.3%	$ 2,632,861.05	$ 188,543.00
Edward L. Kuntz	5750	-	$ 410,837.50	$ 191,543.00
Reginald E. Swanson	6881	0.1%	$ 491,647.45	$ 115,295.00
Clayton K. Trier	11250	0.1%	$ 803,812.50	$ 214,043.00
Glenn D. McDowell	42771	0.3%	$ 3,055,987.95	-
Totals	541174	4.5%	$ 38,666,882.30	$ 1,720,139.00

Appendix Q: USPH Clinic Percentage by State Related to Market <small>(Team Calculations Bureau of Labor Statistics, Company Filings)</small>

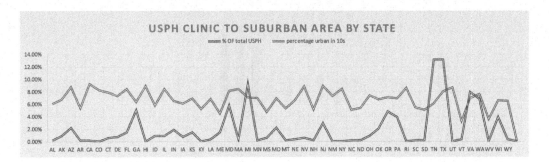

USPH has stated many times their strategy in developing clinics in suburban areas. The reason for this is that areas with less demand have higher reimbursement rates for both low supply, and less condense areas of population. Both insurance and government entities follow this trend, so it is important for USPH to capitalize. If the reimbursement rate is dollars more per patient, the higher rate can translate to millions of dollars in difference. This may be why USPH has been able to keep their margins so high with respect to how many clinics they have. This graph was found using census bureau information. The information was the percentage of urban areas by state. Dividing each states number of clinics owned by USPH by the total clinics found the higher areas of clinics by state. Comparing these number graphically depict higher suburban areas correlating with higher concentration of USPH clinics. This is true in most areas except Florida. USPH has stated they tend to stay away from Florida and the East Coast due to the low reimbursement rate, considering the market saturation of physical therapy clinics in Florida.

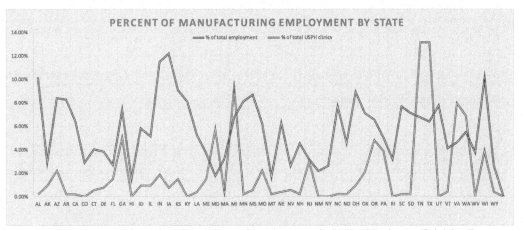

USPH lies alone among their competition with their high revenue from workers compensation (18.6%). USPH seeks out specific deals that will help benefit their revenue streams by giving companies preventative care. Preventive care has two benefits for manufacturing companies: it lowers workplace accidents and the insurance costs associated with a workplace accidents are also lowered. USPH has helped to lower the overall costs these manufacturing companies incur by keeping their employee on the job. USPH has been able to go into these companies to provide service to them before the accidents occur. The affect of entering into a deal to prevent harm helps OSHA look favorably onto the respective companies. USPH understands their market, and has been able to correlate many of their clinics to manufacturing states. Above is a graph with the percentage of USPH clinics by state, related to the percentage of employment in manufacturing by state. This was found using census bureau numbers to find total manufacturing employment by state, and dividing that by the total number of employment by state. In the future, USPH will further be able to capitalize with the manufacturing market considering the increased infrastructure plans that the new administration will be implementing: other manufacturing stocks have responded favorably to this news.

Appendix R: USPH's Market to In Each Age Group (Team Calculations and Census Bureau)

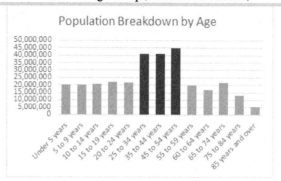

Demographics

0-18

USPH targets high school athletes as a client base. To help accomplish this, USPH encourages physical therapists to attend local events. Considering it is important to have parents trust, the relationship-oriented PT's help USPH By attending the sporting events of the high school athletes they have been able to build this referral source through high school sports events.

18-24

As millennials enter the workforce they have been categorized as being less entrepreneurial. This mindset that is spreading across the age category works in advantage for USPH because of the established business model they have set up. As the population ages and the older generation who established USPHs acquired clinics retire, USPH is able to hire these millennials to take over the therapist's position. USPH provides a way for this age group to do the job they want to do and not have to worry about added stress.

This age group also hold the statistic that 50% of Americans will develop some form of musculoskeletal injury and the recovery process will last on average three years. Physical therapy is one of the only sources of healing for these types of injuries, further increase demand of USPH services. Because USPH presents themselves as the most cost effective solution to an age group who haven't necessarily established themselves financially yet, they have been able to capture this market

26-34

As the population is aging, more people are becoming - and remaining - physically active. This increase the chance for injury or muscle straining and the demand for USPH. Extending this, more people have played some type of sport when they are younger and some of the delayed effects of this show up in this age demographic.

With the unemployment rate in the United States dropping, more people are able to hold jobs. Coming out of college and looking for work, this age is more likely to have a hire job rate that offered company offered insurance. Due to the favor of physical therapist's in the insurance industry, this increases the amount of individuals getting insurance.

35-54

This age group is the most likely group to have insurance. This is the prime target areas for USPH because they are the most likely to both complete treatment as well as fully pay their portion of the bill. Because they will have insurance and most of USPH payments come from some sort of insurance claims this is important to the revenue structure of USPH. This group accounts for 50,000,000 persons, which is higher than any other age group. Also, because they usually have families or some sort of responsibility they are more inclined to have stable jobs. With this stability, the chances of worker's compensation claim occurring increases. USPH has strategically placed themselves in the workers compensation subsection because an employer is mandated to have it. This decreases the possibility for uncollected bills because a company has set aside provisions for this event.

55-64

As the population ages, the median age limit is continuously increasing. These longer life spans are causing people to work longer at their jobs and they are wearing out their bodies more and more. The longer their bodies are working, ligaments and joints are more likely to wear down and cause pain. This is good for USPH because they have been able to help reduce some of this pain and provide a necessary service to these individuals.

Insurance companies and employers have found it better to remain proactive in the caring/curing of patients. One way they have found ot do this is by physical therapy. This age and older is at a higher risk of disabilities. When a short term disability occurs rather than ignoring the first sign of a pattern they have adopted the trend of taking care of it to reduce the chances of it becoming a more expensive chronic illness.

65+

As people age, they begin to recover slower and less efficiently but they are at a greater need/frequency for healthcare services. While everyone in this age group qualifies for government assistance, USPH tries to be careful at taking on large portions of these clients. This is due primarily to the fact that the government has a set reimbursement rate that are non negotiable with limits on how much can be used. In addition they also have provisions to take back payments if patients are not being served at their required quality standards or are having to come in for a repeat case. Because the older population is already at a higher risk for repeating illnesses and injuries, they pose the potential higher cost to USPH.

Appendix S: Breaking Down State Factors of USPH (Team Calculations and Census Bureau, Bureau of Labor Statistics, nfhs.org Company 10K)

			Physical Therpy Information By State					
State	Employed PTs	% of USPH Total	Manufacturing Employees	% of Rural	% of Uninsured	% of Urban	# of HS Athletes	Population
Alabama	2050	0.19%	252400	39.6%	13.0%	60.4%	123339	4779736
Alaska	510	0.93%	13500	32.5%	10.3%	67.5%	24374	710231
Arizona	2990	2.22%	156100	12.5%	13.7%	87.5%	122185	6392017
Arkansas	1940	0.19%	153500	46.5%	9.6%	53.5%	61263	2915918
California	19000	0.19%	1271000	7.4%	11.8%	92.6%	797101	37253956
Colorado	4560	0.00%	140100	17.6%	10.3%	82.4%	128600	5029196
Connecticut	3780	0.56%	160700	20.9%	6.4%	79.1%	111211	3574097
Delaware	660	0.74%	25700	27.0%	7.4%	73.0%	29665	897934
Florida	12020	1.48%	335700	15.2%	15.7%	84.8%	267954	18801310
Georgia	5230	5.00%	373700	15.2%	15.9%	63.2%	197537	9687653
Hawaii	710	0.00%	13500	36.8%	4.2%	89.0%	36871	1360301
Idaho	1010	0.93%	62200	11.0%	15.2%	57.4%	44524	1567582
Illinois	10590	0.93%	572500	42.6%	8.7%	84.6%	340972	12830632
Indiana	4580	1.85%	519300	15.4%	10.8%	64.9%	152552	6483802
Iowa	1830	0.74%	216100	35.1%	6.3%	60.6%	136138	3046355
Kansas	1570	1.48%	161000	39.4%	11.0%	69.1%	102593	2853118
Kentucky	2580	0.00%	240200	30.9%	7.5%	51.8%	96525	4339367
Louisiana	2670	0.37%	148800	48.2%	15.7%	68.1%	101311	4533372
Maine	1240	1.48%	50000	31.9%	8.8%	44.6%	51624	1328361
Maryland	4580	5.74%	102400	55.4%	7.5%	81.3%	118102	5773552
Massachusetts	8010	0.37%	249800	18.7%	3.5%	84.3%	226925	6547629
Michigan	8370	9.26%	598000	15.7%	7.6%	70.5%	295660	9883640
Minnesota	3960	0.19%	314900	29.5%	5.8%	69.9%	235243	5303925
Mississippi	1510	0.56%	141000	30.1%	14.7%	47.1%	113136	2967297
Missouri	3950	2.22%	260700	52.9%	11.6%	68.7%	171937	5988927
Montana	1010	0.19%	18700	31.3%	13.3%	52.5%	31355	989415
Nebraska	1540	0.37%	95300	47.5%	10.6%	66.1%	77137	1826341
Nevada	1530	0.56%	42000	33.9%	14.5%	88.3%	45033	2700551
New Hampshire	1430	0.19%	67500	11.7%	8.8%	51.0%	45028	1316470
New Jersey	7590	2.96%	245600	49.0%	9.7%	89.4%	279377	8791894
New Mexico	1120	0.00%	27900	10.6%	12.8%	73.0%	49713	2059179
New York	15970	0.00%	450500	27.0%	8.6%	84.3%	389475	19378102
North Carolina	5910	0.19%	460200	15.7%	14.4%	50.4%	194352	9535483
North Dakota	550	0.19%	26000	49.6%	6.9%	53.3%	25073	672591
Ohio	7310	0.93%	688200	46.7%	7.6%	74.1%	319929	11536504
Ohklahoma	1870	2.04%	133600	25.9%	16.5%	67.7%	114675	3751351
Oregon	2530	4.81%	186400	32.3%	7.3%	70.5%	100176	3831074
Pennsylvania	10760	3.89%	568000	29.5%	7.4%	68.9%	319562	12702379
Rhode Island	1010	0.00%	41900	31.1%	5.6%	86.0%	28486	1052567
South Carolina	2550	0.19%	231600	14.0%	12.3%	54.6%	95390	4625364
South Dakota	670	0.19%	44000	45.4%	10.6%	50.0%	29160	814180
Tennessee	4320	13.15%	331500	50.0%	13.0%	60.9%	109349	6346105
Texas	13060	13.15%	866700	39.1%	22.3%	80.3%	804598	25145561
Utah	1540	0.00%	125300	19.7%	12.4%	87.0%	59988	2763885
Vermont	740	0.37%	30700	13.0%	4.7%	32.2%	14889	625741
Virginia	5400	7.96%	234400	67.8%	12.6%	69.4%	173283	8001024
Washington	4720	6.85%	292200	30.6%	7.4%	76.4%	160245	6724540
West Virginia	1210	0.00%	48300	23.6%	7.7%	36.1%	35981	1852994
Wisconsin	4360	3.89%	472800	63.9%	5.9%	65.7%	186595	5686986
Wyoming	390	0.37%	9900	35.0%	14.0%	65.0%	19020	563626

The team did an analysis on variables that play into to the expansion of clinics in multiple states. USPH focuses on patient who are young and active, submitting worker compensation claims, and those in underserved areas with high populations. Looking at the percentage of USPH in each state we are able to see how they have tried to position their clinics in areas with a higher amount of manufacturing workers.

Appendix T: Stock Price and Point and Figure Chart (Team Calculations, Nasdaq.com, and stockcharts.com)

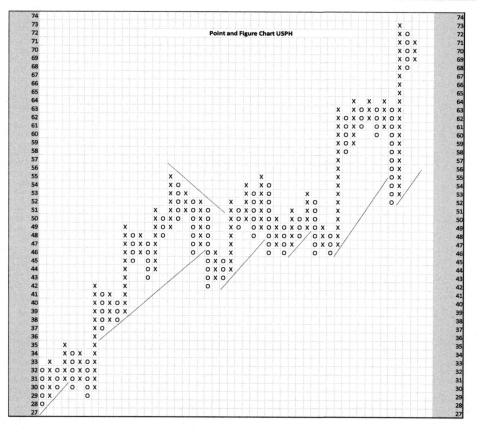

This point and figure graph our team created from information provided by stockcharts.com shows the historical frames of buying and selling for USPH. The benefit of using a point and figure chart is that it ignores the issue of time which will eliminate extensive noise of normalized daily activity for the investor. By only placing an X or O when it the price moves a specified amount, this helps to see what the trend is for USPH stock and what is likely to happen in the future. By looking at the upward, or downward trends, the team was able to verify prediction based on the resistance lines it naturally creates.

Shows Inflated Price

Appendix U: USPH Board of Directors Descriptions and Compensation (Team Calculations, Proxy, and USPH Website)

Name and Position	Year	Salary	Stock Awards	Non-equity Incentive Plan Compensation	All other Compensation	Total Compensation
Christopher J. Reading	2015	$616,500	$1,140,253	124,950	$1,289	$1,882,992
-Chief Executive Officer	2014	$575,692	$1,552,200	$721,250	$1,242	$2,850,384
	2013	$558,730	$974,400	$369,516	$1,242	$1,903,888
Lawrence W. McAfee	2015	$445,769	$570,126	$90,300	$3,701	$1,109,896
-Chief Financial Officer	2014	$419,231	$776,100	$525,000	$2,322	$1,722,653
	2013	$409,577	$487,200	$278,880	$2,322	$1,177,979
Glenn D McDowell	2015	$413,615	$570,126	$84,000	$2,411	$1,070,152
-Chief Operating Officer	2014	$376,077	$776,100	$471,250	$2,322	$1,625,749
	2013	$363,942	$487,200	$230,408	$2,322	$1,083,872

Upper management

USPH has showed their continual effort in the balance of retaining and appealing to talented management, the success of the company, and the success of the shareholders (both short and long term). Reading, McAfee, and Glenn D. McDowell (COO) are paid above their base pay according to the difference in actual performance and objective performance of their company. It can be clearly seen that UPSH sticks to this policy, according to decreases and increases in their pay in less successful years. All three officers can be paid based on company performance and EPS through cash . If EPS is above the objective, cash bonuses are given based on a percentage of base income, increasing as the EPS is further above projection. To keep future growth momentum prominent, the officers are paid a percentage stock options based on EPS goal attainment, which can be higher in value than the cash bonuses based on past performance. Most of the stock also have vesting options, which shows the longevity of this method. Earnings per share were 1.77, 1.62, 1.05, and 1.52 for 2015, 2014, 2013, and 2012 respectively. 2013 Non-equity Incentive Plan Compensation was due in part to company performance. USPH had a large loss of 4.5 Mil from discontinued operations, which contributed to their low EPS. USPH awarded their management for a "job well done" in dealing with the unfortunate circumstance from closure costs and regulation changes from ACA implementation.

USPH takes a great emphasis in having quality leadership. Their board members all have backgrounds in physical therapy and the healthcare industry. With the variety of people USPH has brought together for their board they have been able to gain expertise on multiple business decisions causing USPH to propel forward.

Jerald L. Pullins, Chairman of the Board has been with USPH since 2011 and has been a member beginning 2003. Mr. Pullins has interest in development and managing private companies in the healthcare field. Beginning in 2007, he has served as Chairman of the Board of Directors of Pet Partners, LLC, which is a private enterprise dealing with the acquisition and management of small animal veterinary hospitals.

Lawrance W. McAfee, EVP, CFO and Director became Executive Vice President and a member of USPH Board of Directors November 2004. Mr. McAfee also has served as our Chief Financial Officer of USPH since 2003. In the past, Mr. McAfee's has served as Chief Financial Officer of three publicly traded companies and was the President of two private companies.

Mark J. Brookner, Director has served on USPH Board since August 1998. Current-ly a private investor, he served as USPH Chief Financial Officer from 1992 to 1998 as well as Secretary and Treasurer for parts of that time frame.

Dr. Bernard A. Harris, Jr., Director joined USPH board 2005. Dr. Harris was Presi-dent and Chief Executive Officer of Vesalius Ventures, a venture capital firm that invests in early stage medical informatics and technology. He has served as a Class III director of Sterling Bancshares, Inc., a bank holding company. Also Dr Bernard was Chief Medical Officer and Vice President for Space Hub, an aerospace compa-ny. He finished his residency at the Mayo Clinic.

Edward L. Kuntz, Director USPH board member since 2014, is the former Chair-man and Chief Executive Officer of Kindred Healthcare. From 1999 through May 2014, he served as Chairman of the Board of Directors of Kindred and as Chief Executive Officer from 1999 to 2004. Mr. Kuntz serves as a director of Rotech Healthcare and American Electric Technologies, Inc.

Christopher J. Reading, President, CEO and Director was a physical therapist promoted to President and Chief Executive Officer in 2004. He was elected to USPH Board of Directors November 2004. Prior to 2004, Mr. Reading served as our Chief Operating Officer at USPH in 2003. From 1990 to 2003, Mr. Reading served in various executive/management positions with HealthSouth Corporation. One distinct position that plays into USPH Mr. Reading held was Senior Vice President of Operations covering 200 facilities located in 10 states.

Daniel C. Arnold, Director joined as Chairman of the Board in 2004. Mr. Arnold is a private investor who is currently engaged only USPH board activities and his personal investment activities. Previously Mr. Arnold was Chairman of the Board of Trustees for Baylor College of Medicine.

Harry S. Chapman, Director has been a board member since 2010. Mr. Chapman serves as the Chairman and the Chief Executive Officer of Chapman Schewe, Inc., which is a healthcare insurance and employee benefits consulting firm. Previously, he served as a Corporate Senior Vice-President and Managed Care Officer of CIGNA's South Central Region, and had involvement in HMO and PPO plans in several states. Mr. Chapman's also served as a head of EQUICOR's Health Plan and sales operation in Houston and as a Regional Vice-President for Lincoln National Insurance Compa-ny's Central Region.

Marlin W. Johnston, Director joined USPH Board in 1992. Mr. Johnston was a man-agement consultant at Tonn & Associates since 1993. Mr. Johnston also served as a consultant to the Texas Department of Health and the Texas Department of Protective and Regulatory Services.

Reginald E. Swanson, Director joined our Board 2007. Mr. Swanson is Managing Director of STAR Physical Therapy, LP, a subsidiary of USPH. Mr. Swanson started STAR Physical Therapy, LLC, in 1997. As a licensed athletic trainer he has been involved with sports medicine and physical therapy for over 25 years.

Clayton K. Trier, Director is a private investor who joined USPH board in 2005. He was a founder of U.S. Delivery Systems, Inc., which developed the first national network providing same-day delivery service.

Appendix V: Physical Therapist Industry (Team Calculations, Bureau of Labor Statistics)

The physical therapy industry as a whole has been in steady growth over the past years. This is due in part to the increase demand of physical therapy from insurance companies. This has caused an expected job outlook increase for physical therapy at 33% from 2014 to 2014. With the climbing prices of surgeries, physical therapy has grown in popularity due to being a good substitute. Study have shown physical therapy can offer the same result as an expensive surgery. They have identified it as a source of savings, which further increases the demand. Below is a graph of the growing need of physical therapy by state. This shows which states USPH may decide they want to expand further into by looking at who has the creates amount of need. Looking at these areas we can interpret them as underserved areas who may have increased reimbursement rates. The growing demand of therapists is coupled with the increased demand of physical therapist assistant jobs as well. Physical therapist assistants have a predicted growth of 40% from 2014-2024.

This could be attributed to the extender model many therapists have begun to implement. Varied by a case study from Louis C. Gapenski, the extender model has a business setup where physical therapy assistants are doing the majority of the patient treatments and then the physical therapist will come into each session and check on the patient to make sure it all went well. While the payment for a visit with just a physical therapist assistant is only reimbursable up to 85%, if the physical therapist is present for a portion of the time they can bill for the full reimbursement amount. This offers a way for therapists to extend the amount of patient they see each day and further increase the amount of revenue they bring in. There are limits on the amount of physical therapist assistants any one physical therapist may supervise. While this varies by state it averages to about 3:1 assistants to therapists. While it is unknown to what extend USPH is using this extender model, we do know that if they have not started, there are benefits from the implementation of physical therapist assistant extenders. If USPH has already implemented this it has potential to be magnified on a larger scale further reducing salaries paid and patients seen. There is a growing demand for physical therapist (assistants) and it verifies the opportunity for growth in patient visits by using this extender model. Because USPH total revenue is driven off of total patient visits, this offers another way for them to boost their now stagnating per patient revenues. Physical therapist assistant's annual wages are about half of what a normal therapist is making, so if implemented strategically, USPH would be able to not only raise the per patient revenue but also the costs they are incurring from salaries of each employees.

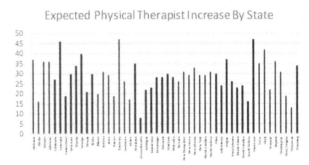

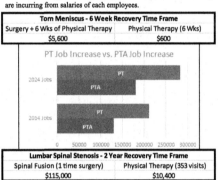

Torn Meniscus - 6 Week Recovery Time Frame	
Surgery + 6 Wks of Physical Therapy	Physical Therapy (6 Wks)
$5,600	$600

Lumbar Spinal Stenosis - 2 Year Recovery Time Frame	
Spinal Fusion (1 time surgery)	Physical Therapy (353 visits)
$115,000	$10,400

Appendix X: Macroeconomics Factors

Macroeconomic Factors Expanded

	2009	2010	2011	2012	2013	2014	2015	2016	2017	2018
Real GDP YoY%	-2.8	2.5	1.6	2.2	1.7	2.4	2.6	1.6	2.3	3.3
Consumer Spending YoY%	-1.6	1.9	2.3	1.5	1.5	2.9	3.2	2.7	2.6	2.5
Industrial Production YoY%	-11.4	5.5	2.9	2.8	1.9	2.9	0.3	-1	1.4	2.3
unemployment %	9.3	9.6	8.9	8.1	7.4	6.2	5.3	4.8	4.6	4.5
CPI YoY%	-0.3	1.6	3.2	2.1	1.5	1.6	0.1	1.3	2.4	2.4
CORE PCE YoY%	1.2	1.3	1.5	1.9	1.5	1.6	1.4	1.7	1.8	2
central bank rate %	0.25	0.25	0.25	0.25	0.25	0.25	0.5	0.75	1.3	-
3-month rate %	0.25	0.3	0.58	0.31	0.25	0.26	0.61	1	1.57	-
2-year note %	1.14	0.6	0.24	0.25	0.38	0.67	1.05	1.19	1.7	-
10-year note %	3.84	3.3	1.88	1.76	3.03	2.17	2.27	2.45	2.83	-

The economy has been improving with the lowering of unemployment rates inherently coupled with an increase in GDP. The numbers above are pulled from Bloomberg and show the year over year percentage change in key economic factors. The rising percentage each year of GDP is helping to put people back to work, helping them return to their jobs. This allows them to gain health insurance and start going to the doctor. One of the areas that is expected to increase is the industrial production. This increase is important to USPH because they work closely with manufacturing companies by implementing worker compensation programs helping to prevent workplace accidents. This increase amount of workers increases the statistical likelihood of workplace accidents occurring. USPH has a strategic positon in this area because they contract with companies to prevent the accidents helping to prevent large procedures with regular visits of industrial employees. Then when accidents do occur the companies are already in contact with USPH , causing USPH to have a double win from this one contract area.

A large concern for USPH is the rising interest rates shown above. A large portion of their revenues goes to paying for the acquiring of physical therapist clinics. This has the potential to make their business practices more expensive. This would then affect the amount of free cash flow they have available to either acquire other clinics or pay back to their shareholders. The rising rate will not only make it more expensive to purchase businesses but can also make the interest payments they have on their revolving line of credit more expensive.

Appendix W: Natural Events That Indirectly Effect USPH (Team Calculations, cdc.gov, usnews.com, moveforwardpt.com)

Car Wrecks: Increases in the number of car wrecks per year could be linked to the low unemployment rate. Over the past years, the unemployment rate has been steadily decreasing while the amount of car wrecks has been on the rise. Several researches feel these could be linked. With a larger amount of people on the road, traveling to and from work, coupled with the low gas rates in the US, these factors have inadvertently caused more individuals to be in car wrecks. These rising numbers are predicted to continue into the recent future. The most common injury from a car wreck is whiplash. This injury is curable, especially with the help of a physical therapist. While no one likes the idea of being in a car wreck, it is important to get quality help for your injuries it important to get quality help for injuries after the fact. USPH has a unique competitive advantage from this unpredictable economic event.

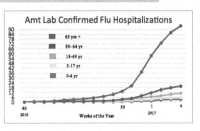

Flu: USPH CEO stated in transcript calls there was a significant decrease in patients visits due to an increase in the amount of flu infected patients. Illnesses, such as the flu, could pose a substantial threat to USPH revenues because it directly decreases the amount of visits they perform. According to the Center of Disease Control, 2016 had a hospitalization rate of 20.3 per 100,000 for flue infected patients. The national baseline for flu illnesses is 2.2%. January 2017 had a 3.9% infection rate which has started the year out above average. The amount of time someone is effected ranges from 1 to 20 weeks long with the average landing at 13 weeks. If a patient is suppose to be attending therapy visits– whose average visit length is 6 weeks– they could miss the entire session. In addition to this, statistics show those who miss their physical therapy visits are less likely to make up those visits at a later date. The probability of them making up these visits decreases with each week that passes. While it is not possible to predict who will get the flu, those who do could cause adverse effects for the revenue stream of USPH. One advantage USPH has over this is they market to a younger generation of patients who are less likely to have the flu. However, as the population ages and they begin switching into the older demographics this will have a larger effect of their business.

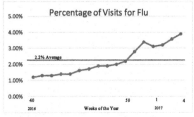

Vacations: USPH CEO stated the amount of patient visits for USPH could be adversely effected by the increasing rate of Americans on vacation. As the level of disposable income rises, the amount of trips people are taking are expand as well as the length they are on those trips. As individuals leave home for the summer, USPH patient visits in those specific months drop. USPH CEO stated patient visits have historically been down in July. This drop in patient visit trend could continue to rise as more people have the ability to go on vacations. As people miss their physical therapy visits, they are unlikely to reschedule those visits at a later date. This creates a deficit in USPH projected revenues. If America's spending trends continue to rise in this area, USPH revenues could be greatly penalized.

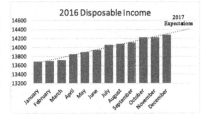

Obesity: According to a study found by Move Forward PT and confirmed by the Center for Disease Control, 68% of the American population is considered overweight and approximately 36% are considered to be obese. This growing amount growth in obese individuals can have negative effects on multiple areas of their lives leading towards chronic diseases and can escalate to early death. Physical therapy has been one solution in this area. By working with patients to increase their mobility and flexibility they are able to reduce the negative affects obesity takes on the human joints. Working to reduce the pain this causes they are able to improve the standard of living for these patients. By developing each patient an individualized physical activity plan they are able to work with these patients to fight obesity or at least the effects it causes on the body. Creating workout plans that their patients enjoy they are able to decrease the negative effects in a way that protects the muscles and tissues. When done without a physical therapist there is a greater risk of injury occurring. USPH is benefiting from this cliental because this is an effect that would take multiple visits to overcome, which increases the amount of billable. Also, those who are serious about losing weight are less likely to skip out of their appointments.

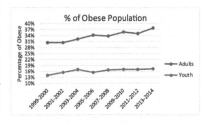

Weather: One of the most unpredictable factors, yet has one of the greatest effects is the weather patterns. In USPH's 10K they discuss how they anticipate different weather patterns limiting their ability to see patients. Because people view physical therapy as an elective procedure, many times it holds less importance to the individual. This means when heavy storms hit an area, patients will not risk the trip to the physical therapist. This holds a potential decrease in the amount of billable patient visits for USPH. A greater problem the climate has is the mass effect it has on patients. In other events it is only a few who are effected by the event; however, when a storm hits it has the potential to decrease all of the clinic visit. This could end up decreasing the bottom line revenues for USPH by $12,517.79. The graph on the right shows an example of the revenues that could be lost assuming one clinic is removed from operations for one week and they have been operating at max efficiency. If these patterns hit an area where there are multiple clinics, or if it is an event that could last for several weeks (such as Hurricane Katrina) the bottom line effects could be substantially escalated.

Effects of a Storm 2015			
Per Patient/Per Clinic Revenues	$ 105.28	$ 105.28	$ 105.28
Average Patients/Day/Clinic	23.78	23.78	23.78
Number of Days Lost	5	5	1
Number of Clinic Effected	1	5	10
Total Losts from Storm	$12,517.79	$62,588.96	$ 25,035.58

Appendix X: USPH Stock in Relation to Major Insurance Companies (Team Calculations, Nasdaq.com)

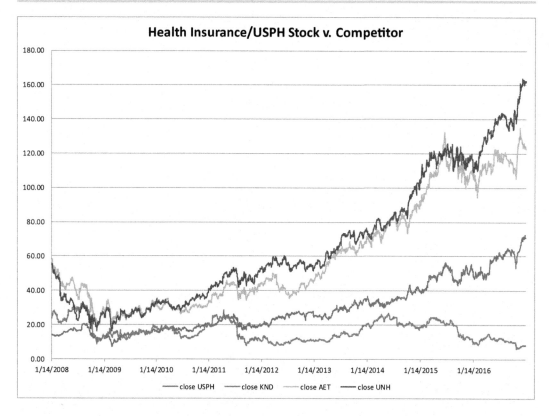

Company Stock	Stock Correlation
USPH/AET Correlation	0.96
KND/AET Correlation	-0.020
USPH/KND Correlation	-0.149
AET/UNH Correlation	0.98
USPH/UNH Correlation	0.98

This graph shows a comparison of four different stocks: USPH, Aetna (AET), United Health Corp (UNH), and Kindred (KND). USPH has a correlation of .96 and .98 with these major companies stocks. This shows that USPH 's stocks respond in a similar manor to insurance stocks news. As USPH's stock continues to track major insurance companies stock, potential investors should monitor factors that could significantly affect major insurance changes. This is also consistent with the large percent of revenue coming from private insurance. Unlike their competitors (KND), who have a low percent of revenue from private insurance.

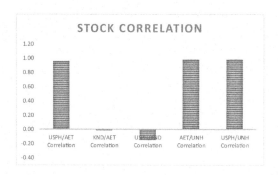

(Source: West Texas A&M University CFA Institute Research Challenge.)

Disclosures:

Ownership and material conflicts of interest:
The author(s), or a member of their household, of this report does not hold a financial interest in the securities of this company.
The author(s), or a member of their household, of this report does not know of the existence of any conflicts of interest that might bias the content or publication of this report.

Receipt of compensation:
Compensation of the author(s) of this report is not based on investment banking revenue.

Position as a officer or director:
The author(s), or a member of their household, does not serve as an officer, director or advisory board member of the subject company.

Market making:
The author(s) does not act as a market maker in the subject company's securities.

Disclaimer:
The information set forth herein has been obtained or derived from sources generally available to the public and believed by the author(s) to be reliable, but the author(s) does not make any representation or warranty, express or implied, as to its accuracy or completeness. The information is not intended to be used as the basis of any investment decisions by any person or entity. This information does not constitute investment advice, nor is it an offer or a solicitation of an offer to buy or sell any security. This report should not be considered to be a recommendation by any individual affiliated with CFA Society of Austin, CFA Society of Dallas Fort Worth, CFA Society of Houston, CFA Society of Louisiana, CFA Society of San Antonio, CFA Institute or the CFA Institute Research Challenge with regard to this company's stock.

CFA Institute Research Challenge

Summary of key points

- An internal report or presentation is an efficient and effective means for communicating important ideas and facilitating discussions within an organization.
- Internal reports and presentations are common within student-managed investment funds in support of security selection decisions.
- External presentations are used to communicate outside the organization and most often have a business development or client service objective.
- All presentations should be concise with clear points or takeaways summarized in the introduction and conclusion.

Exercises

1. Choose a current holding in your portfolio. Write an analyst report on the security. Be sure to clearly state a hold or sell recommendation.
2. Choose a security that is not currently held in your portfolio. Write an analyst report on the security. Be sure to clearly state a buy or pass recommendation.
3. Choose two competing companies in the same sector and industry from the S&P 500. Write an analyst report that makes the case to purchase (or sell) one stock over the other.
4. Develop and draft an outline for an internal stock selection presentation.
5. Develop and draft an outline for an internal portfolio construction presentation.
6. Develop and draft an outline for an external business development presentation under each of the following two scenarios. In each case, be sure to include sections that anticipate questions or concerns from the target audience.
   a. You are proposing the launch of a new student-managed investment fund.
   b. You are proposing an increase in the size of an existing student-managed investment fund.
7. Locate past internal and external presentations from your organization. Critique the presentations by noting the good aspects and those that are missing or need improvement. Be sure to articulate specifically how you would improve the presentation.

CHAPTER 8

Tools

Just as photographers need cameras and lenses, investment managers need tools that are appropriate to their trade. This chapter summarizes commonly used tools and resources in the investment management profession. Some of the most widely used tools in the profession are licensed, such as those from Bloomberg, S&P CapitalIQ, FactSet, Morningstar, and Refinitiv. Recognizing the resource constraints of colleges and universities, we also try to highlight tools that are currently freely available, even if they are not as commonly employed in the most prestigious investment firms. In some cases, we simply list a tool and describe some features that are relevant to a student-managed investment fund. In other cases, we provide examples of uses of the tool. Our purpose in providing more detail about some and not others is not intended to favor or endorse one tool over another. Furthermore, we do not suggest that this chapter provides a comprehensive list of available tools. Rather, we aim to provide examples of how tools might be employed in a student-managed investment fund and leave it to each organization to determine which tools meet their needs and offer the best value for their limited resources.

Throughout this text, we have already utilized the most ubiquitous business and investment management tool: Microsoft Excel. We hope that its exclusion from any list in this chapter emphasizes its importance. Without Excel, the other tools discussed below are of little or no value, as Excel is the primary means of analysis for investment professionals. Indeed, most of the tools listed in this chapter have explicit Excel links, either in the standard of exporting data in an Excel format or in the ability to interface directly with Excel. From building valuation models, to analyzing macroeconomic trends, to performing portfolio attribution and analysis, Excel's largest asset is its flexibility and adaptability to all of the various tasks. With this flexibility comes the ability and responsibility of the Excel user to create specialized or customized tools that fit the particular needs of an investment process. Every member of a student-managed investment fund must become not only familiar with Excel but also proficient in using it.

As with every other aspect of investing, the choice of tool is determined within the context of an organization's investment philosophy and process. A tool that might be essential to one investment manager might be superfluous to another if the investment processes are very different. For example, a bottom-up investment process might heavily rely on tools that provide detailed firm-specific information, while an investment process more focused on

Student-Managed Investment Funds. https://doi.org/10.1016/B978-0-12-817866-9.00008-X

asset allocation might find little use for such a resource. Finally, we caution that the quality and the quantity of tools are not the primary determinants of the quality of the investment decisions. There is a saying in the practice of photography that the most important piece of equipment is the person behind the lens. This sentiment is especially true in investing, since every tool mentioned in this chapter is available to anyone or anyone who pays to access that tool. What differentiates one investor from another is the investment ideas that result from their investment philosophy and process. It is our hope that the tools described in this chapter will help facilitate the discovery and expression of such ideas in student-managed investment funds.

Primary data sources

Vendor	Website
Companies	Various Company Websites
Federal Reserve Economic Data (FRED)	fred.stlouisfed.org
International Monetary Fund	www.imf.org
U.S. Securities and Exchange Commission	sec.gov/edgar/searchedgar/
EDGAR	companysearch.html
World Bank	data.worldbank.org

We begin our list of data sources with the ultimate sources from which nearly all hard data on companies begin: the companies themselves. Nearly all companies in the United States maintain an investor relations website on which the company's financial statements and other disclosures are available. For example, the investor relations site for Apple is investor.apple.com and Microsoft's investor relations site is www.microsoft.com/investor. Such sites often also have archived recordings or transcripts of quarterly earnings calls and links to the company's SEC filings. In addition, most company websites contain valuable background information about the history of the firm, identification about subsidiaries, divisions or offices, biographies of key executives, and details about its products and services.

The U.S. Securities and Exchange Commission's EDGAR Online provides access to filings made by companies whose securities are publicly traded in the United States. These filings are made available through a search interface as shown in Exhibit 8.1. As shown in the exhibit, when placing Apple's ticker symbol, "AAPL," on the search page, the site's user has access to the list of the company's SEC filings results. Exhibit 8.2 shows an 8-K filing by Apple, while Exhibit 8.3 shows an example of a 10-Q filing. Some filings can be viewed in interactive mode, allowing quick access to items in a menu on the left side of the page, as shown in Exhibit 8.4. Finally, Exhibit 8.5 shows an EDGAR page of Apple's insider holdings and recent changes to those holdings as reported on Form 4.

We discuss many different data vendors below, but stress that the filings that are freely available on the EDGAR are the primary source of financial statement information from nearly all vendors. Members of student-managed investment funds might find it useful to verify the accuracy of data from other vendors by consulting this primary source. Since all publicly traded companies in the United States must file these documents, students and investors who do not have access to other vendor's resources should be confident in knowing that they have the highest quality financial statement information available by accessing it on EDGAR.

The Federal Reserve Bank of St. Louis maintains the Federal Reserve Economic Data site, known as FRED. As shown in Exhibit 8.6, the site has a wealth of data on macroeconomic variables, such as interest rates, employment, and GDP. Note that most series on FRED can be downloaded individually to Excel spreadsheets, or even in bulk .zip files.

Exhibit 8.1 U.S. Securities and Exchange Commission EDGAR

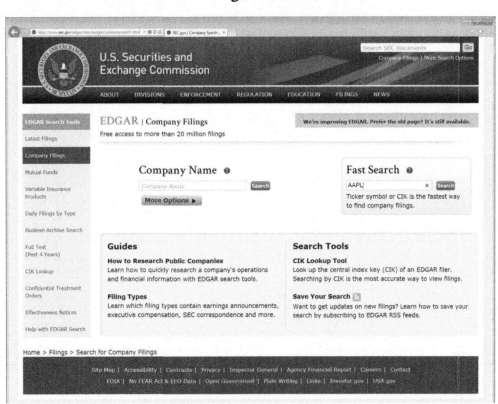

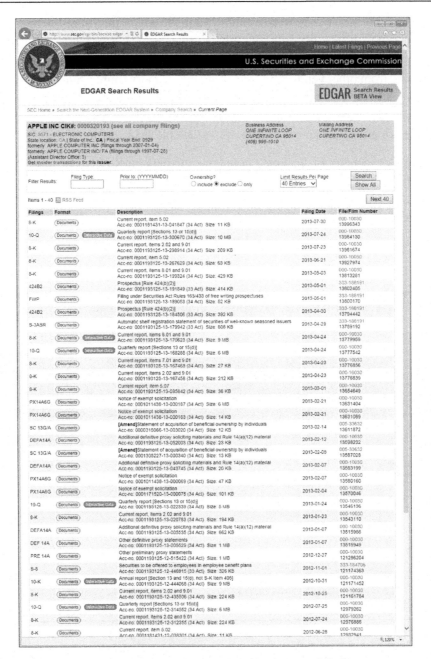

(Credit: SEC EDGAR Filings: https://www.sec.gov/edgar/searchedgar/companysearch.html.)

The International Monetary Fund (IMF) and World Bank compile global macroeconomic data. Unfortunately, the IMF and World Bank do not make all of their data freely available via their websites. However, some data are available for free and others by subscription. Some universities and colleges may already subscribe to these databases (e.g., through the library), so members of student-managed investment funds should determine if these sources are available at their institutions. Some IMF and World Bank data series are also available through other vendors, such as Bloomberg.

Exhibit 8.2 Apple's 8-K on EDGAR

8-K 1 d571814d8k.htm FORM 8-K

UNITED STATES
SECURITIES AND EXCHANGE COMMISSION
Washington, D.C. 20549

FORM 8-K

CURRENT REPORT
Pursuant to Section 13 or 15(d) of
The Securities Exchange Act of 1934

July 23, 2013
Date of Report (date of earliest event reported)

APPLE INC.
(Exact name of Registrant as specified in its charter)

California	000-10030	94-2404110
(State or other jurisdiction of incorporation)	(Commission File Number)	(I.R.S. Employer Identification Number)

**1 Infinite Loop
Cupertino, California 95014**
(Address of principal executive offices) (Zip Code)

(408) 996-1010
(Registrant's telephone number, including area code)

(Former name or former address, if changed since last report)

Check the appropriate box below if the Form 8-K filing is intended to simultaneously satisfy the filing obligation of the registrant under any of the following provisions:

☐   Written communications pursuant to Rule 425 under the Securities Act (17 CFR 230.425)

☐   Soliciting material pursuant to Rule 14a-12 under the Exchange Act (17 CFR 240.14a-12)

☐   Pre-commencement communications pursuant to Rule 14d-2(b) under the Exchange Act (17 CFR 240.14d-2(b))

☐   Pre-commencement communications pursuant to Rule 13e-4(c) under the Exchange Act (17 CFR 240.13e-4(c))

Item 2.02   Results of Operations and Financial Condition.

On July 23, 2013, Apple Inc. ("Apple") issued a press release regarding Apple's financial results for its third fiscal quarter ended June 29, 2013 and a related data sheet. A copy of Apple's press release is attached hereto as Exhibit 99.1 and a copy of the related data sheet is attached hereto as Exhibit 99.2.

The information contained in this Current Report shall not be deemed "filed" for purposes of Section 18 of the Securities Exchange Act of 1934, as amended (the "Exchange Act"), or incorporated by reference in any filing under the Securities Act of 1933, as amended, or the Exchange Act, except as shall be expressly set forth by specific reference in such a filing.

Item 9.01   Financial Statements and Exhibits.

(d)   Exhibits

The following exhibits are furnished herewith:

Exhibit Number	Description
99.1	Text of press release issued by Apple Inc. on July 23, 2013.
99.2	Data sheet issued by Apple Inc. on July 23, 2013.

SIGNATURE

Pursuant to the requirements of the Securities Exchange Act of 1934, the registrant has duly caused this report to be signed on its behalf by the undersigned hereunto duly authorized.

APPLE INC.

Date: July 23, 2013

By: /s/ Peter Oppenheimer
Peter Oppenheimer
Senior Vice President,
Chief Financial Officer

EXHIBIT INDEX

Exhibit Number	Description
99.1	Text of press release issued by Apple Inc. on July 23, 2013.
99.2	Data sheet issued by Apple Inc. on July 23, 2013.

🔍 130% ▼

EX-99.1 2 d571814dex991.htm EX-99.1

Exhibit 99.1

Apple Reports Third Quarter Results

Sales of 31 Million iPhones Set New June Quarter Record

CUPERTINO, California—July 23, 2013—Apple today announced financial results for its fiscal 2013 third quarter ended June 29, 2013. The Company posted quarterly revenue of $35.3 billion and quarterly net profit of $6.9 billion, or $7.47 per diluted share. These results compare to revenue of $35 billion and net profit of $8.8 billion, or $9.32 per diluted share, in the year-ago quarter. Gross margin was 36.9 percent compared to 42.8 percent in the year-ago quarter. International sales accounted for 57 percent of the quarter's revenue.

The Company sold 31.2 million iPhones, a record for the June quarter, compared to 26 million in the year-ago quarter. Apple also sold 14.6 million iPads during the quarter, compared to 17 million in the year-ago quarter. The Company sold 3.8 million Macs, compared to 4 million in the year-ago quarter.

Apple's Board of Directors has declared a cash dividend of $3.05 per share of the Company's common stock. The dividend is payable on August 15, 2013, to shareholders of record as of the close of business on August 12, 2013.

"We are especially proud of our record June quarter iPhone sales of over 31 million and the strong growth in revenue from iTunes, Software and Services," said Tim Cook, Apple's CEO. "We are really excited about the upcoming releases of iOS 7 and OS X Mavericks, and we are laser-focused and working hard on some amazing new products that we will introduce in the fall and across 2014."

"We generated $7.8 billion in cash flow from operations during the quarter and are pleased to have returned $18.8 billion in cash to shareholders through dividends and share repurchases," said Peter Oppenheimer, Apple's CFO.

Apple is providing the following guidance for its fiscal 2013 fourth quarter:

- revenue between $34 billion and $37 billion
- gross margin between 36 percent and 37 percent
- operating expenses between $3.9 billion and $3.95 billion
- other income/(expense) of $200 million
- tax rate of 26.5%

Apple will provide live streaming of its Q3 2013 financial results conference call beginning at 2:00 p.m. PDT on July 23, 2013 at www.apple.com/quicktime/qtv/earningsq313. This webcast will also be available for replay for approximately two weeks thereafter.

This press release contains forward-looking statements including without limitation those about the Company's estimated revenue, gross margin, operating expenses, other income/(expense), and tax rate. These statements involve risks and uncertainties, and actual results may differ. Risks and uncertainties include without limitation the effect of competitive and economic factors, and the Company's reaction to those factors, on consumer and business buying decisions with respect to the Company's products; continued competitive pressures in the marketplace; the ability of the Company to deliver to the marketplace and stimulate customer demand for new programs, products, and technological innovations on a timely basis; the effect that product introductions and transitions, changes in product pricing or mix, and/or increases in component costs could have on the Company's gross margin; the inventory risk associated with the Company's need to order or commit to order product components in advance of customer orders; the continued availability on acceptable terms, or at all, of certain components and services essential to the Company's business currently obtained by the Company from sole or limited sources; the effect that the Company's dependency on manufacturing and logistics services provided by third parties may have on the quality, quantity or cost of products manufactured or services rendered; risks associated with the Company's international operations; the Company's reliance on third-party intellectual property and digital content; the potential impact of a finding that the Company has infringed on the intellectual property rights of others; the Company's dependency on the performance of distributors, carriers and other resellers of the Company's products; the effect that product and service quality problems could have on the Company's sales and operating profits; the continued service and availability of key executives and employees; war, terrorism, public health issues, natural disasters, and other circumstances that could disrupt supply, delivery, or demand of products; and unfavorable results of other legal proceedings. More information on potential factors that could affect the Company's financial results is included from time to time in the "Risk Factors" and "Management's Discussion and Analysis of Financial Condition and Results of Operations" sections of the Company's public reports filed with the SEC, including the Company's Form 10-K for the fiscal year ended September 29, 2012, its Form 10-Q for the quarter ended December 29, 2012, its Form 10-Q for the quarter ended March 30, 2013, and its Form 10-Q for the quarter ended June 29, 2013 to be filed with the SEC. The Company assumes no obligation to update any forward-looking statements or information, which speak as of their respective dates.

Apple designs Macs, the best personal computers in the world, along with OS X, iLife, iWork and professional software. Apple leads the digital music revolution with its iPods and iTunes online store. Apple has reinvented the mobile phone with its revolutionary iPhone and App Store, and is defining the future of mobile media and computing devices with iPad.

Press Contact:
Steve Dowling
Apple
dowling@apple.com
(408) 974-1896

Investor Relations Contacts:
Nancy Paxton
Apple
paxton1@apple.com
(408) 974-5420

Joan Hoover
Apple
hoover1@apple.com
(408) 974-4570

NOTE TO EDITORS: For additional information visit Apple's PR website (www.apple.com/pr), or call Apple's Media Helpline at (408) 974-2042.

Apple Inc.
UNAUDITED CONDENSED CONSOLIDATED STATEMENTS OF OPERATIONS
(In millions, except number of shares which are reflected in thousands and per share amounts)

	Three Months Ended		Nine Months Ended	
	June 29, 2013	June 30, 2012	June 29, 2013	June 30, 2012
Net sales	$ 35,323	$ 35,023	$ 133,438	$ 120,542
Cost of sales (1)	22,299	20,029	83,005	66,281

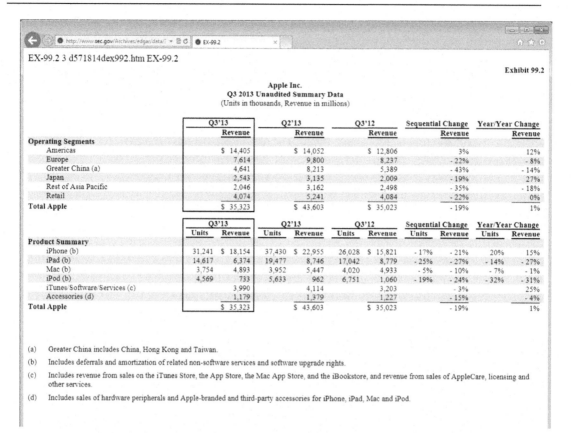

EX-99.2 3 d571814dex992.htm EX-99.2

Exhibit 99.2

Apple Inc.
Q3 2013 Unaudited Summary Data
(Units in thousands, Revenue in millions)

	Q3'13 Revenue	Q2'13 Revenue	Q3'12 Revenue	Sequential Change Revenue	Year/Year Change Revenue
Operating Segments					
Americas	$ 14,405	$ 14,052	$ 12,806	3%	12%
Europe	7,614	9,800	8,237	- 22%	- 8%
Greater China (a)	4,641	8,213	5,389	- 43%	- 14%
Japan	2,543	3,135	2,009	- 19%	27%
Rest of Asia Pacific	2,046	3,162	2,498	- 35%	- 18%
Retail	4,074	5,241	4,084	- 22%	0%
Total Apple	$ 35,323	$ 43,603	$ 35,023	- 19%	1%

	Q3'13 Units	Q3'13 Revenue	Q2'13 Units	Q2'13 Revenue	Q3'12 Units	Q3'12 Revenue	Sequential Change Units	Sequential Change Revenue	Year/Year Change Units	Year/Year Change Revenue
Product Summary										
iPhone (b)	31,241	$ 18,154	37,430	$ 22,955	26,028	$ 15,821	- 17%	- 21%	20%	15%
iPad (b)	14,617	6,374	19,477	8,746	17,042	8,779	- 25%	- 27%	- 14%	- 27%
Mac (b)	3,754	4,893	3,952	5,447	4,020	4,933	- 5%	- 10%	- 7%	- 1%
iPod (b)	4,569	733	5,633	962	6,751	1,060	- 19%	- 24%	- 32%	- 31%
iTunes/Software/Services (c)		3,990		4,114		3,203		- 3%		25%
Accessories (d)		1,179		1,379		1,227		- 15%		- 4%
Total Apple		$ 35,323		$ 43,603		$ 35,023		- 19%		1%

(a)   Greater China includes China, Hong Kong and Taiwan.

(b)   Includes deferrals and amortization of related non-software services and software upgrade rights.

(c)   Includes revenue from sales on the iTunes Store, the App Store, the Mac App Store, and the iBookstore, and revenue from sales of AppleCare, licensing and other services.

(d)   Includes sales of hardware peripherals and Apple-branded and third-party accessories for iPhone, iPad, Mac and iPod.

Exhibit 8.3 Apple's 10-Q on EDGAR

10-Q 1 d552802d10q.htm FORM 10-Q

UNITED STATES
SECURITIES AND EXCHANGE COMMISSION
Washington, D.C. 20549

Form 10-Q

(Mark One)
☒ QUARTERLY REPORT PURSUANT TO SECTION 13 OR 15(d) OF THE SECURITIES EXCHANGE ACT OF 1934

For the quarterly period ended June 29, 2013

or

☐ TRANSITION REPORT PURSUANT TO SECTION 13 OR 15(d) OF THE SECURITIES EXCHANGE ACT OF 1934

For the transition period from _____ to _____.

Commission File Number: 000-10030

APPLE INC.

(Exact name of registrant as specified in its charter)

California	94-2404110
(State or other jurisdiction of incorporation or organization)	(I.R.S. Employer Identification No.)

1 Infinite Loop	
Cupertino, California	95014
(Address of principal executive offices)	(Zip Code)

Registrant's telephone number, including area code: (408) 996-1010

Indicate by check mark whether the registrant (1) has filed all reports required to be filed by Section 13 or 15(d) of the Securities Exchange Act of 1934 during the preceding 12 months (or for such shorter period that the registrant was required to file such reports), and (2) has been subject to such filing requirements for the past 90 days.

Yes ☒ No ☐

Indicate by check mark whether the registrant has submitted electronically and posted on its corporate Web site, if any, every Interactive Data File required to be submitted and posted pursuant to Rule 405 of Regulation S-T (§232.405 of this chapter) during the preceding 12 months (or for such shorter period that the registrant was required to submit and post such files).

Yes ☒ No ☐

Indicate by check mark whether the registrant is a large accelerated filer, an accelerated filer, a non-accelerated filer, or a smaller reporting company. See the definitions of "large accelerated filer," "accelerated filer" and "smaller reporting company" in Rule 12b-2 of the Exchange Act.

| Large accelerated filer | ☒ | Accelerated filer | ☐ |
| Non-accelerated filer | ☐ (Do not check if a smaller reporting company) | Smaller reporting company | ☐ |

Indicate by check mark whether the registrant is a shell company (as defined in Rule 12b-2 of the Exchange Act)

Yes ☐ No ☒

908,497,000 shares of common stock issued and outstanding as of July 12, 2013

PART I. FINANCIAL INFORMATION

Item 1.   Financial Statements

APPLE INC.

CONDENSED CONSOLIDATED STATEMENTS OF OPERATIONS (Unaudited)
(In millions, except number of shares which are reflected in thousands and per share amounts)

	Three Months Ended		Nine Months Ended	
	June 29, 2013	June 30, 2012	June 29, 2013	June 30, 2012
Net sales	$ 35,323	$ 35,023	$ 133,438	$ 120,542
Cost of sales	22,299	20,029	83,005	66,281
Gross margin	13,024	14,994	50,433	54,261
Operating expenses:				
Research and development	1,178	876	3,307	2,475
Selling, general and administrative	2,645	2,545	8,157	7,489
Total operating expenses	3,823	3,421	11,464	9,964
Operating income	9,201	11,573	38,969	44,297
Other income (expense), net	234	288	1,043	573
Income before provision for income taxes	9,435	11,861	40,012	44,870
Provision for income taxes	2,535	3,037	10,487	11,360
Net income	$ 6,900	$ 8,824	$ 29,525	$ 33,510
Earnings per share:				
Basic	$ 7.51	$ 9.42	$ 31.67	$ 35.89
Diluted	$ 7.47	$ 9.32	$ 31.44	$ 35.48
Shares used in computing earnings per share:				
Basic	918,618	936,596	932,388	933,672
Diluted	924,265	947,059	939,172	944,440
Cash dividends declared per common share	$ 3.05	$ 0	$ 8.35	$ 0

See accompanying Notes to Condensed Consolidated Financial Statements.

2

APPLE INC.

CONDENSED CONSOLIDATED BALANCE SHEETS (Unaudited)

(In millions, except number of shares which are reflected in thousands)

	June 29, 2013	September 29, 2012
ASSETS:		
Current assets:		
Cash and cash equivalents	$ 11,248	$ 10,746
Short-term marketable securities	31,358	18,383
Accounts receivable, less allowances of $104 and $98, respectively	8,839	10,930
Inventories	1,697	791
Deferred tax assets	3,193	2,583
Vendor non-trade receivables	4,614	7,762
Other current assets	7,270	6,458
Total current assets	68,219	57,653
Long-term marketable securities	104,014	92,122
Property, plant and equipment, net	16,327	15,452
Goodwill	1,522	1,135
Acquired intangible assets, net	4,353	4,224
Other assets	5,421	5,478
Total assets	$ 199,856	$ 176,064
LIABILITIES AND SHAREHOLDERS' EQUITY:		
Current liabilities:		
Accounts payable	$ 15,516	$ 21,175
Accrued expenses	13,470	11,414
Deferred revenue	7,333	5,953
Total current liabilities	36,319	38,542
Deferred revenue – non-current	2,672	2,648
Long-term debt	16,958	0
Other non-current liabilities	20,553	16,664
Total liabilities	76,502	57,854
Commitments and contingencies		
Shareholders' equity:		
Common stock, no par value; 1,800,000 shares authorized; 908,442 and 939,208 shares issued and outstanding, respectively	19,024	16,422
Retained earnings	104,564	101,289
Accumulated other comprehensive (loss)/income	(234)	499
Total shareholders' equity	123,354	118,210
Total liabilities and shareholders' equity	$ 199,856	$ 176,064

See accompanying Notes to Condensed Consolidated Financial Statements.

4

APPLE INC.

CONDENSED CONSOLIDATED STATEMENTS OF CASH FLOWS (Unaudited)

(In millions)

	Nine Months Ended	
	June 29, 2013	June 30, 2012
Cash and cash equivalents, beginning of the period	$ 10,746	$ 9,815
Operating activities:		
Net income	29,525	33,510
Adjustments to reconcile net income to cash generated by operating activities:		
Depreciation and amortization	4,974	2,296
Share-based compensation expense	1,698	1,292
Deferred income tax expense	2,524	4,066
Changes in operating assets and liabilities:		
Accounts receivable, net	2,091	(2,278)
Inventories	(906)	(346)
Vendor non-trade receivables	3,148	(293)
Other current and non-current assets	484	(3,238)
Accounts payable	(4,740)	2,450
Deferred revenue	1,404	2,575
Other current and non-current liabilities	3,556	1,686
Cash generated by operating activities	43,758	41,720
Investing activities:		
Purchases of marketable securities	(122,681)	(121,091)
Proceeds from maturities of marketable securities	13,963	10,344
Proceeds from sales of marketable securities	81,734	73,140
Payments made in connection with business acquisitions, net	(443)	(350)
Payments for acquisition of property, plant and equipment	(6,210)	(4,834)
Payments for acquisition of intangible assets	(560)	(1,067)
Other	(188)	(56)
Cash used in investing activities	(34,385)	(43,914)
Financing activities:		
Proceeds from issuance of common stock	335	433
Excess tax benefits from equity awards	644	1,036
Taxes paid related to net share settlement of equity awards	(1,001)	(1,145)
Dividends and dividend equivalent rights paid	(7,795)	0
Repurchase of common stock	(17,950)	0
Proceeds from issuance of long-term debt, net	16,896	0
Cash (used in) generated by financing activities	(8,871)	324
Increase/(decrease) in cash and cash equivalents	502	(1,870)
Cash and cash equivalents, end of the period	$ 11,248	$ 7,945
Supplemental cash flow disclosure:		

Exhibit 8.4 EDGAR interactive mode

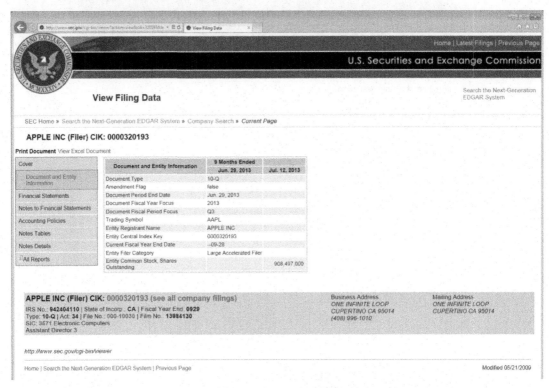

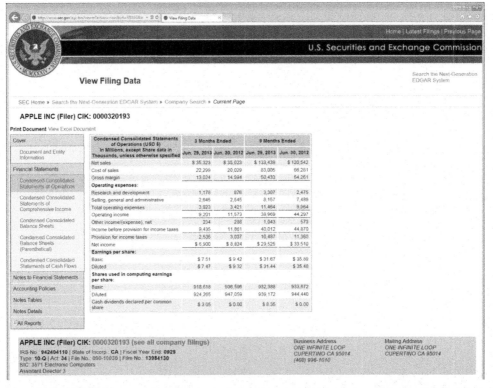

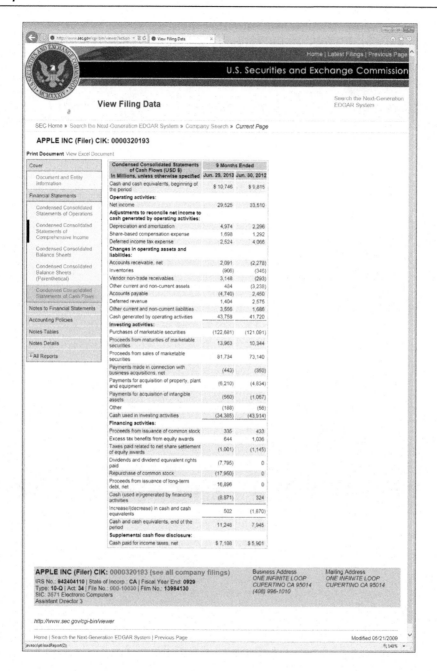

U.S. Securities and Exchange Commission

View Filing Data

Search the Next-Generation EDGAR System

SEC Home » Search the Next-Generation EDGAR System » Company Search » *Current Page*

APPLE INC (Filer) CIK: 0000320193

Print Document View Excel Document

| Cover |
| Document and Entity Information |
| Financial Statements |
| Condensed Consolidated Statements of Operations |
| Condensed Consolidated Statements of Comprehensive Income |
| Condensed Consolidated Balance Sheets |
| Condensed Consolidated Balance Sheets (Parenthetical) |
| Condensed Consolidated Statements of Cash Flows |
| Notes to Financial Statements |
| Accounting Policies |
| Notes Tables |
| Notes Details |
| All Reports |

Condensed Consolidated Statements of Cash Flows (USD $) In Millions, unless otherwise specified	9 Months Ended	
	Jun. 29, 2013	Jun. 30, 2012
Cash and cash equivalents, beginning of the period	$ 10,746	$ 9,815
Operating activities:		
Net income	29,525	33,510
Adjustments to reconcile net income to cash generated by operating activities:		
Depreciation and amortization	4,974	2,296
Share-based compensation expense	1,698	1,292
Deferred income tax expense	2,524	4,066
Changes in operating assets and liabilities:		
Accounts receivable, net	2,091	(2,278)
Inventories	(906)	(346)
Vendor non-trade receivables	3,148	(293)
Other current and non-current assets	484	(3,238)
Accounts payable	(4,740)	2,450
Deferred revenue	1,404	2,575
Other current and non-current liabilities	3,556	1,688
Cash generated by operating activities	43,758	41,720
Investing activities:		
Purchases of marketable securities	(122,681)	(121,091)
Proceeds from maturities of marketable securities	13,963	10,344
Proceeds from sales of marketable securities	81,734	73,140
Payments made in connection with business acquisitions, net	(443)	(350)
Payments for acquisition of property, plant and equipment	(6,210)	(4,834)
Payments for acquisition of intangible assets	(560)	(1,067)
Other	(188)	(56)
Cash used in investing activities	(34,385)	(43,914)
Financing activities:		
Proceeds from issuance of common stock	335	433
Excess tax benefits from equity awards	644	1,036
Taxes paid related to net share settlement of equity awards	(1,001)	(1,145)
Dividends and dividend equivalent rights paid	(7,795)	0
Repurchase of common stock	(17,950)	0
Proceeds from issuance of long-term debt, net	16,896	0
Cash (used in)/generated by financing activities	(8,871)	324
Increase/(decrease) in cash and cash equivalents	502	(1,870)
Cash and cash equivalents, end of the period	11,248	7,945
Supplemental cash flow disclosure:		
Cash paid for income taxes, net	$ 7,188	$ 5,901

APPLE INC (Filer) CIK: 0000320193 (see all company filings)

IRS No.: **942404110** | State of Incorp.: **CA** | Fiscal Year End: **0929**
Type: **10-Q** | Act: **34** | File No.: **000-10030** | Film No.: **13984130**
SIC: **3671** Electronic Computers
Assistant Director 3

Business Address
ONE INFINITE LOOP
CUPERTINO CA 95014
(408) 996-1010

Mailing Address
ONE INFINITE LOOP
CUPERTINO CA 95014

http://www.sec.gov/cgi-bin/viewer

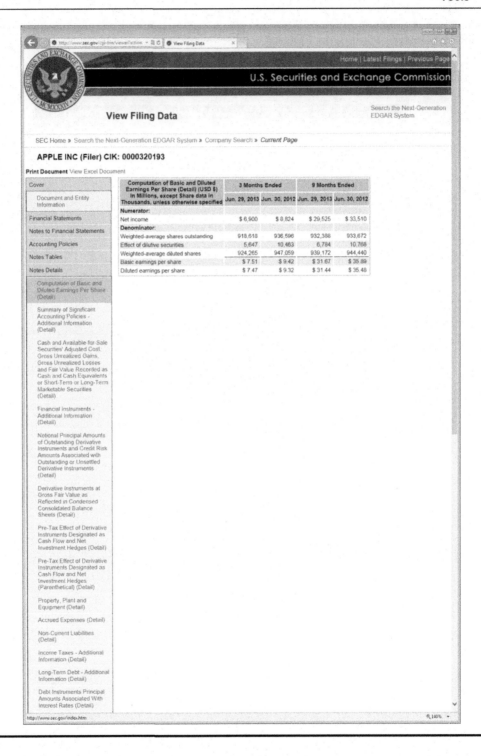

Exhibit 8.5 Insider trading on EDGAR

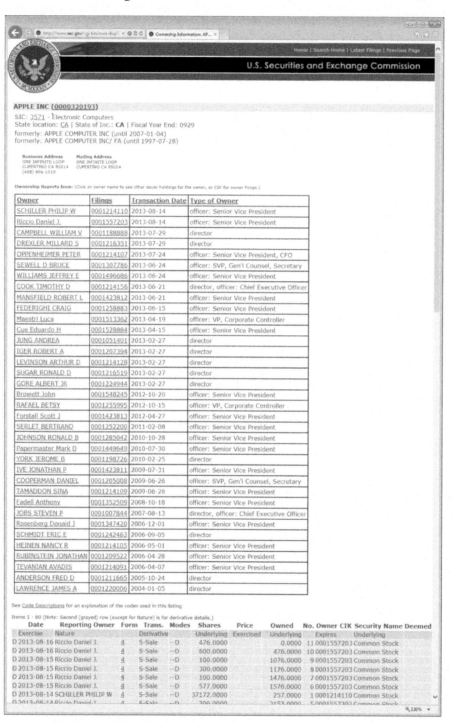

Exhibit 8.6 Federal Reserve Economic Data (FRED)

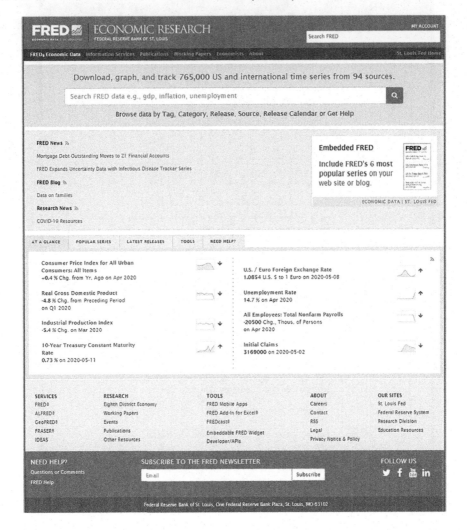

FRED | ECONOMIC RESEARCH
FEDERAL RESERVE BANK OF ST. LOUIS

MY ACCOUNT

Search FRED

FRED® Economic Data   Information Services   Publications   Working Papers   Economists   About

St. Louis Fed Home

Filter by:

Concepts   View All

Passenger   (30)
Flight   (24)
Miles   (24)
Travel   (22)
Air Travel   (16)
Domestic   (16)
Freight   (10)
Revenue   (10)
Indexes   (8)
Transportation   (8)

Sources

Bureau of Transportation
Statistics   (51)
Federal Highway Administration   (4)
Cass Information Systems, Inc.   (2)

Releases

Travel Volume Trends   (4)

Seasonal Adjustments

Seasonally Adjusted   (31)
Not Seasonally Adjusted   (26)

Citation & Copyright

Public Domain: Citation
Requested   (33)
Copyrighted: Citation Required   (2)

Need Help?

Learn about Tags
Tutorials
FAQs
Email Us

Transportation

Categories > Production & Business Activity

Motor Vehicles

☐ [Add to Data List] [Add to Graph] [Add To Dashboard]   [Sort by Popularity ▾]

Moving 12-Month Total Vehicle Miles Traveled

Millions of Miles, Monthly

☐ Not Seasonally Adjusted   Dec 1970 to Mar 2020 (1 day ago)
☐ Seasonally Adjusted   Dec 2000 to Mar 2020 (1 day ago)

Vehicle Miles Traveled

Monthly

☐ Millions of Miles, Not Seasonally Adjusted   Jan 1970 to Mar 2020 (1 day ago)
☐ Millions of Miles, Seasonally Adjusted   Jan 2000 to Mar 2020 (1 day ago)
☐ Millions, Seasonally Adjusted   Jan 2000 to Jan 2020 (Apr 20)
☐ Millions, Not Seasonally Adjusted   Jan 2000 to Jan 2020 (Apr 20)

Cass Freight Index: Shipments

☐ Index Jan 1990=1, Monthly, Not Seasonally   Jan 1990 to Apr 2020 (17 hours ago)
Adjusted

Freight Transportation Services Index

Monthly, Seasonally Adjusted

☐ Chain-type Index 2000=100   Jan 2000 to Mar 2020 (1 day ago)
☐ Percent Change from Preceding Period   Feb 2000 to Mar 2020 (1 day ago)

Truck Tonnage

☐ Truck Tonnage Index, Monthly, Seasonally   Jan 2000 to Feb 2020 (Apr 20)
Adjusted

Load Factor for U.S. Air Carrier Domestic and International, Scheduled Passenger Flights

Percent, Monthly

☐ Not Seasonally Adjusted   Jan 2000 to Jan 2020 (Apr 20)
☐ Seasonally Adjusted   Jan 2000 to Jan 2020 (Apr 20)

Rail Freight Carloads

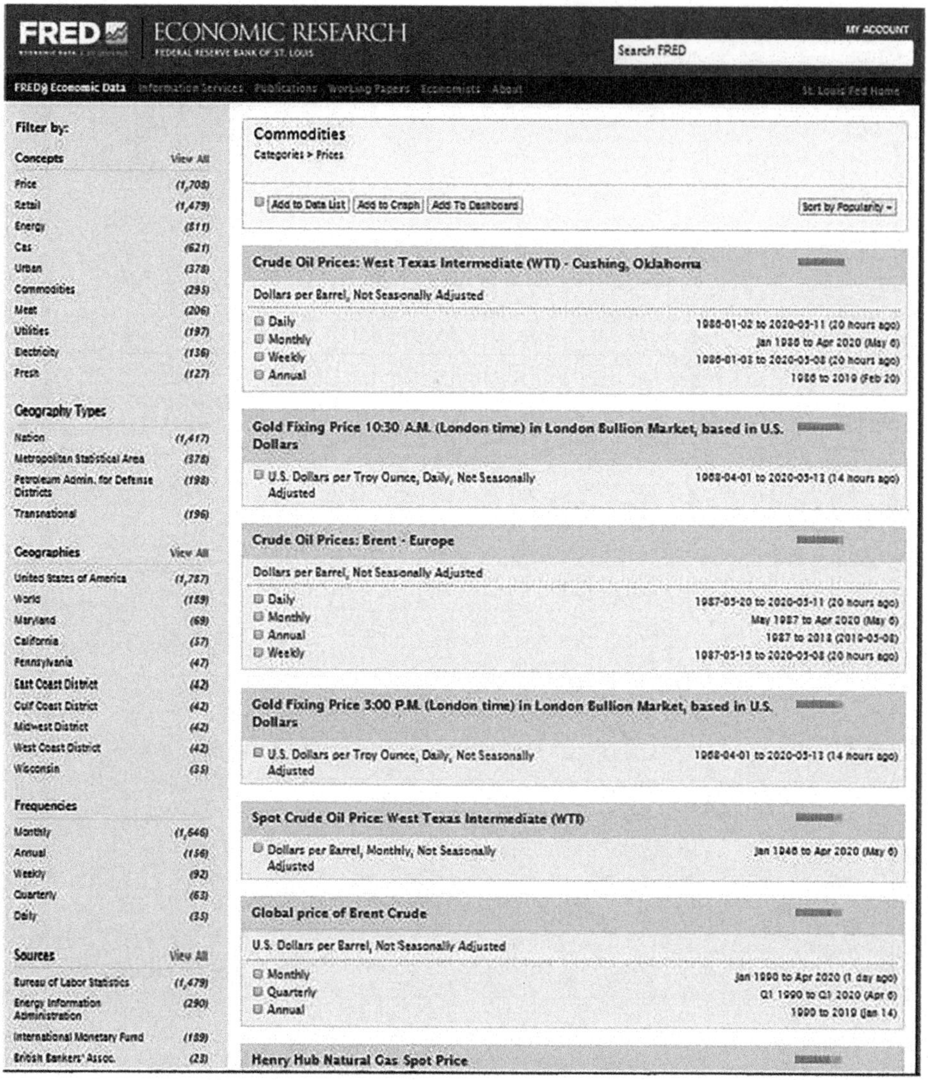
FRED
ECONOMIC RESEARCH
FEDERAL RESERVE BANK OF ST. LOUIS
MY ACCOUNT
Search FRED
FRED® Economic Data
Information Services
Publications
Working Papers
Economists
About
St. Louis Fed Home
Filter by:
Concepts
View All
Price (1,708)
Retail (1,479)
Energy (811)
Gas (621)
Urban (378)
Commodities (295)
Meat (206)
Utilities (197)
Electricity (136)
Fresh (127)
Geography Types
Nation (1,417)
Metropolitan Statistical Area (378)
Petroleum Admin. for Defense Districts (198)
Transnational (196)
Geographies
View All
United States of America (1,787)
World (189)
Maryland (69)
California (57)
Pennsylvania (47)
East Coast District (42)
Gulf Coast District (42)
Midwest District (42)
West Coast District (42)
Wisconsin (35)
Frequencies
Monthly (1,646)
Annual (156)
Weekly (92)
Quarterly (63)
Daily (35)
Sources
View All
Bureau of Labor Statistics (1,479)
Energy Information Administration (290)
International Monetary Fund (189)
British Bankers' Assoc. (23)
Commodities
Categories > Prices
Add to Data List
Add to Graph
Add To Dashboard
Sort by Popularity
Crude Oil Prices: West Texas Intermediate (WTI) - Cushing, Oklahoma
Dollars per Barrel, Not Seasonally Adjusted
Daily 1986-01-02 to 2020-05-11 (20 hours ago)
Monthly Jan 1986 to Apr 2020 (May 6)
Weekly 1986-01-03 to 2020-05-08 (20 hours ago)
Annual 1986 to 2019 (Feb 20)
Gold Fixing Price 10:30 A.M. (London time) in London Bullion Market, based in U.S. Dollars
U.S. Dollars per Troy Ounce, Daily, Not Seasonally Adjusted
1968-04-01 to 2020-05-12 (14 hours ago)
Crude Oil Prices: Brent - Europe
Dollars per Barrel, Not Seasonally Adjusted
Daily 1987-05-20 to 2020-05-11 (20 hours ago)
Monthly May 1987 to Apr 2020 (May 6)
Annual 1987 to 2018 (2019-05-08)
Weekly 1987-05-15 to 2020-05-08 (20 hours ago)
Gold Fixing Price 3:00 P.M. (London time) in London Bullion Market, based in U.S. Dollars
U.S. Dollars per Troy Ounce, Daily, Not Seasonally Adjusted
1968-04-01 to 2020-05-12 (14 hours ago)
Spot Crude Oil Price: West Texas Intermediate (WTI)
Dollars per Barrel, Monthly, Not Seasonally Adjusted
Jan 1946 to Apr 2020 (May 6)
Global price of Brent Crude
U.S. Dollars per Barrel, Not Seasonally Adjusted
Monthly Jan 1990 to Apr 2020 (1 day ago)
Quarterly Q1 1990 to Q1 2020 (Apr 6)
Annual 1990 to 2019 (Jan 14)
Henry Hub Natural Gas Spot Price

FRED | ECONOMIC RESEARCH
FEDERAL RESERVE BANK OF ST. LOUIS

MY ACCOUNT

Search FRED

FRED® Economic Data   Information Services   Publications   Working Papers   Economists   About   St. Louis Fed Home

Filter by:

Concepts	View All
House Price Index	(672)
Price	(672)
Price Index	(672)
Appraisers	(445)
High Tier	(32)
Low Tier	(32)
Middle Tier	(32)
Sales	(27)

Geography Types

Metropolitan Statistical Area	(508)
State	(61)
Census Division	(45)
Metropolitan Division	(33)
Nation	(17)

Geographies	View All
California	(33)
Texas	(29)
Florida	(27)
Ohio	(20)
Wisconsin	(20)
Indiana	(19)
Michigan	(19)
Georgia (U.S. state)	(18)
North Carolina	(18)

Frequencies

Quarterly	(473)
Monthly	(201)

Sources

Federal Housing Finance Agency	(491)
S&P Dow Jones Indices LLC	(181)
National Assoc. of Realtors	(2)

Releases

S&P/Case-Shiller Home Price Indices	(181)

Seasonal Adjustments

Not Seasonally Adjusted	(576)
Seasonally Adjusted	(96)

House Price Indexes
Categories > Prices

☐ [Add to Data List] [Add to Graph] [Add To Dashboard]   Sort by Popularity ▾

S&P/Case-Shiller U.S. National Home Price Index

Index Jan 2000=100, Monthly

☐ Not Seasonally Adjusted	Jan 1987 to Feb 2020 (Apr 28)
☐ Seasonally Adjusted	Jan 1987 to Feb 2020 (Apr 28)

S&P/Case-Shiller 20-City Composite Home Price Index

Index Jan 2000=100, Monthly

☐ Seasonally Adjusted	Jan 2000 to Feb 2020 (Apr 28)
☐ Not Seasonally Adjusted	Jan 2000 to Feb 2020 (Apr 28)

All-Transactions House Price Index for the United States

☐ Index 1980:Q1=100, Quarterly, Not Seasonally Adjusted	Q1 1975 to Q4 2019 (Feb 25)

S&P/Case-Shiller CA-San Francisco Home Price Index

Index Jan 2000=100, Monthly

☐ Seasonally Adjusted	Jan 1987 to Feb 2020 (Apr 28)
☐ Not Seasonally Adjusted	Jan 1987 to Feb 2020 (Apr 28)

S&P/Case-Shiller CA-Los Angeles Home Price Index

Index Jan 2000=100, Monthly

☐ Seasonally Adjusted	Jan 1987 to Feb 2020 (Apr 28)
☐ Not Seasonally Adjusted	Jan 1987 to Feb 2020 (Apr 28)

S&P/Case-Shiller NY-New York Home Price Index

Index Jan 2000=100, Monthly

☐ Seasonally Adjusted	Jan 1987 to Feb 2020 (Apr 28)
☐ Not Seasonally Adjusted	Jan 1987 to Feb 2020 (Apr 28)

S&P/Case-Shiller WA-Seattle Home Price Index

Index Jan 2000=100, Monthly

☐ Not Seasonally Adjusted	Jan 1990 to Feb 2020 (Apr 28)

FRED — ECONOMIC RESEARCH
FEDERAL RESERVE BANK OF ST. LOUIS

Search FRED

MY ACCOUNT

FRED Economic Data   Information Services   Publications   Working Papers   Economists   About   St. Louis Fed Home

Filter by:

Concepts   View All

16 Years +   (34)
Unemployment   (31)
Rate   (17)
Labor   (16)
Labor Underutilization   (10)
Civilian   (8)
Labor Force   (8)
Part-Time   (6)
Workers   (6)

Seasonal Adjustments

Seasonally Adjusted   (31)
Not Seasonally Adjusted   (10)

Need Help?

Learn about Tags
Tutorials
FAQs
Email Us

Current Population Survey (Household Survey)
Categories > Population, Employment, & Labor Markets

The Current Population Survey (Household Survey) is a monthly survey of households conducted by the Bureau of Labor Statistics. It provides a comprehensive body of data on the labor force, employment, unemployment, persons not in the labor force, hours of work, earnings, and other demographic and labor force characteristics. Read More

Civilian Labor Force (683)	Labor Force Participation Rate (15)
Civilian Labor Force Participation Rate (62)	Multiple Jobholders (20)
Employment (2,337)	Duration of Unemployment (18)
Employment Population Ratio (75)	Losers and Leavers (8)
Unemployment Level (748)	Earnings (3,507)
Unemployment Rate (319)	Entrants and Reentrants (4)
Not in Labor Force (59)	Labor Force Status Flows (90)

☐ Add to Data List   Add to Graph   Add To Dashboard   Sort by Popularity ▾

Total Unemployed, Plus All Persons Marginally Attached to the Labor Force, Plus Total Employed Part Time for Economic Reasons, as a Percent of the Civilian Labor Force Plus All Persons Marginally Attached to the Labor Force (U-6)

Percent, Monthly

☐ Seasonally Adjusted   Jan 1994 to Apr 2020 (5 days ago)
☐ Not Seasonally Adjusted   Jan 1994 to Apr 2020 (5 days ago)

Unemployment Rate - Black or African American

☐ Percent, Monthly, Seasonally Adjusted   Jan 1972 to Apr 2020 (5 days ago)

Population Level

☐ Thousands of Persons, Monthly, Not Seasonally   Jan 1948 to Apr 2020 (5 days ago)
   Adjusted

Number Unemployed for 27 Weeks & Over

☐ Thousands of Persons, Monthly, Seasonally   Jan 1948 to Apr 2020 (5 days ago)
   Adjusted

Not in Labor Force

☐ Thousands of Persons, Monthly, Seasonally   Jan 1975 to Apr 2020 (5 days ago)
   Adjusted

Employment Level - Part-Time for Economic Reasons, All Industries

FRED ECONOMIC RESEARCH
FEDERAL RESERVE BANK OF ST. LOUIS

Search FRED

MY ACCOUNT

FRED® Economic Data   Information Services   Publications   Working Papers   Economists   About   St. Louis Fed Home

Filter by:

Concepts	View All
Percent	(330)
Manufacturing	(191)
Indexes	(115)
Price	(112)
Diffusion	(110)
Employment	(64)
Paid	(56)
Expenditures	(40)
Business	(32)
Business Sentiment	(32)

Geography Types

State	(235)
Federal Reserve District	(88)
Nation	(16)

Geographies

United States of America	(264)
New York	(175)
Texas	(160)
Philadelphia Fed District	(88)

Sources

New York Fed	(192)
Dallas Fed	(160)
Philadelphia Fed	(88)
Census	(10)
Chicago Fed	(5)

Releases

Texas Manufacturing Outlook Survey	(160)
Manufacturing & Trade Inventories and Sales	(10)

Seasonal Adjustments

Not Seasonally Adjusted	(233)
Seasonally Adjusted	(222)

Citation & Copyright

Copyrighted: Citation Required	(445)
Public Domain: Citation Requested	(10)

Manufacturing
Categories > Production & Business Activity

Inventories (386)	Unfilled Orders (148)
New Orders (170)	Unfilled Orders to Shipments (15)
Inventory to Shipments (48)	Shipments (254)

☐ Add to Data List   Add to Graph   Add To Dashboard   Sort by Popularity ▾

Current General Business Conditions; Diffusion Index for New York
Index, Monthly

☐ Seasonally Adjusted   Jul 2001 to Apr 2020 (Apr 15)
☐ Not Seasonally Adjusted   Jul 2001 to Apr 2020 (Apr 15)

Manufacturers: Inventories to Sales Ratio
Ratio, Monthly

☐ Seasonally Adjusted   Jan 1992 to Feb 2020 (Apr 15)
☐ Not Seasonally Adjusted   Jan 1992 to Feb 2020 (Apr 15)

Future Capital Expenditures; Diffusion Index for FRB - Philadelphia District
Index, Monthly

☐ Seasonally Adjusted   May 1968 to Apr 2020 (Apr 16)
☐ Not Seasonally Adjusted   May 1968 to Apr 2020 (Apr 16)

Manufacturers Sales
Monthly

☐ Millions of Dollars, Seasonally Adjusted   Jan 1992 to Feb 2020 (Apr 15)
☐ Percent Change, Seasonally Adjusted   Feb 1992 to Feb 2020 (Apr 15)
☐ Millions of Dollars, Not Seasonally Adjusted   Jan 1992 to Feb 2020 (Apr 15)
☐ Percent Change, Not Seasonally Adjusted   Feb 1992 to Feb 2020 (Apr 15)

Current New Orders; Diffusion Index for New York
Index, Monthly

☐ Seasonally Adjusted   Jul 2001 to Apr 2020 (Apr 15)
☐ Not Seasonally Adjusted   Jul 2001 to Apr 2020 (Apr 15)

Current Employment; Diffusion Index for FRB - Philadelphia District
Index, Monthly

FRED | ECONOMIC RESEARCH
FEDERAL RESERVE BANK OF ST. LOUIS

MY ACCOUNT

Search FRED

FRED® Economic Data   Information Services   Publications   Working Papers   Economists   About   St. Louis Fed Home

Filter by:

Concepts	View All
Manufacturing	(338)
Industry	(314)
Goods	(310)
Durable Goods	(162)
Fabrication	(146)
Production	(146)
Nondurable Goods	(120)
Materials	(68)
Finished	(64)

Geography Types

Nation	(322)
State	(48)
Federal Reserve District	(16)

Geographies

United States of America	(370)
Texas	(32)
Philadelphia Fed District	(16)
New York	(16)

Frequencies

Monthly	(383)
Quarterly	(3)

Sources View All

Census	(316)
Dallas Fed	(22)
New York Fed	(16)
Philadelphia Fed	(16)
Bureau of Economic Analysis	(4)
St. Louis Fed	(2)

Releases

Manufacturer's Shipments, Inventories, & Orders Surv.	(316)
Texas Manufacturing Outlook Survey	(32)

Seasonal Adjustments

Seasonally Adjusted	(196)
Not Seasonally Adjusted	(190)

Citation & Copyright

Inventories

Categories > Production & Business Activity > Manufacturing

[ ] Add to Data List   Add to Graph   Add To Dashboard   Sort by Popularity ▾

Real Manufacturing and Trade Inventories

Chained 2012 Dollars, Seasonally Adjusted

▢ Monthly	Jan 1967 to Feb 2020 (Apr 30)
▢ Monthly	Jan 1997 to Feb 2020 (Apr 30)
▢ Monthly	Jan 1967 to Dec 1997 (2018-07-31)
▢ Quarterly	Q1 1967 to Q4 2019 (Mar 27)
▢ Quarterly	Q1 1997 to Q4 2019 (Mar 27)
▢ Quarterly	Q1 1967 to Q4 1997 (2018-07-31)

Value of Manufacturers' Total Inventories for Durable Goods Industries

Million of Dollars, Monthly

▢ Seasonally Adjusted	Jan 1992 to Mar 2020 (May 4)
▢ Not Seasonally Adjusted	Jan 1992 to Mar 2020 (May 4)

Value of Manufacturers' Total Inventories for All Manufacturing Industries

Million of Dollars, Monthly

▢ Seasonally Adjusted	Jan 1992 to Mar 2020 (May 4)
▢ Not Seasonally Adjusted	Jan 1992 to Mar 2020 (May 4)

Value of Manufacturers' Total Inventories for Nondurable Goods Industries

Million of Dollars, Monthly

▢ Seasonally Adjusted	Jan 1992 to Mar 2020 (May 4)
▢ Not Seasonally Adjusted	Jan 1992 to Mar 2020 (May 4)

Value of Manufacturers' Total Inventories for Capital Goods: Nondefense Capital Goods Industries

Million of Dollars, Monthly

▢ Seasonally Adjusted	Jan 1992 to Mar 2020 (May 4)
▢ Not Seasonally Adjusted	Jan 1992 to Mar 2020 (May 4)

Value of Manufacturers' Total Inventories for Information Technology Industries

Million of Dollars, Monthly

▢ Seasonally Adjusted	Jan 1992 to Mar 2020 (May 4)
▢ Not Seasonally Adjusted	Jan 1992 to Mar 2020 (May 4)

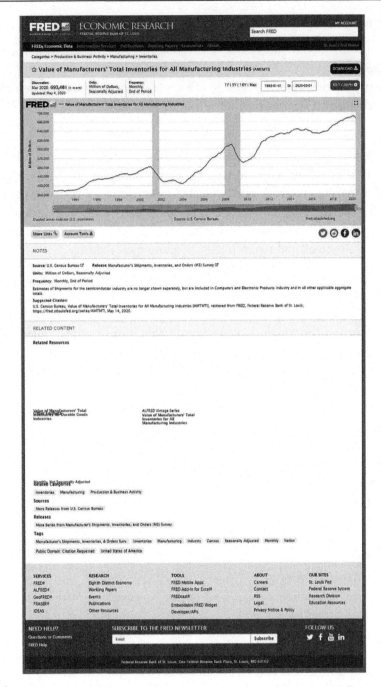

Source: FRED® graphs and images provided courtesy of the Federal Reserve Bank of St. Louis. © 2020 Federal Reserve Bank of St. Louis. All rights reserved. FRED® and the FRED® logo are the registered trademarks of the Federal Reserve Bank of St. Louis and are used with permission.

Other information and data sources

Vendor	Website
Industry Associations	Various association websites
World Health Organization	who.int

Many industry associations exist for the purpose of promoting or lobbying on behalf of the entire industry. As such, the information provided on these websites is as varied as the sites themselves. However, these organizations can provide valuable information for both company-specific and industry- or sector-specific research. For example, an industry trade association might produce white papers on new applications, markets, products, or services within its industry. Some associations might also track and report trends affecting their industry.

Finally, some organizations might provide both soft (e.g., commentary or viewpoints) and hard (e.g., objective data) information on issues of interest or related to their specific areas. Again, this information can help shape an investment analyst's understanding of issues affecting the companies for which they are responsible. For example, data from the World Health Organization (WHO) might be used by an analyst who is trying to forecast the revenues for a biotech or pharmaceutical firm's new drug to treat a specific disease. The WHO might have data on the global incidence of the disease, as well as information about what other therapies are available. The WHO might even have estimates of the cost of competing treatments.

Web portals, search engines, and business news

Vendor	Website
CBS Market Watch	marketwatch.com
CNBC	cnbc.com
CNNMoney	money.cnn.com
Financial Times	ft.com
Google Finance	google.com/finance
Wall Street Journal	wsj.com
Yahoo! Finance	finance.yahoo.com

Web portals, such as Google and Yahoo! Finance, can be convenient sources of investment data for individual investors and student-managed investment funds. In some sense, these sites offer free "one-stop shopping" for information that might be useful for company analysis and security selection. For example, a user of Yahoo! Finance can enter a stock name or ticker and have access to a profile of the company, recent company or industry news, financial statements, competitor information, and market statistics. Similar information can be found on Google. In addition, portfolios can be set up in each site and tracked, with performance updated throughout the day (though perhaps not in real time).

Other sites, such as those listed above, also have news or security-specific information and, in some cases, portfolio tracking features. A potentially nice feature of some of these sites, such as Yahoo! Finance, is that they can be set to provide alerts when there is news in tracked securities.

We caution that the quality control on some sites is unclear and suggest that any information obtained on such sites be confirmed with other trusted sources. For example, at this writing, Google appears to offer a "Stock Screener" feature—a tool that could be useful in narrowing the list of securities for more in-depth analysis as discussed in Chapter 2. However, when trying Google's Stock Screener, we found the results to be inconsistent with other professional-level tools. As with any tool, the user should understand the tool's purpose and limitations when trying to apply it. This is especially true of freely available tools from third parties. While the convenience of financial statement data from one of these sites might be useful in the initial analysis of a security, we recommend verifying the data against the company's EDGAR filings prior to final investment decisions that rely on such data.

Brokers and financial service providers

Vendor	Website
Fidelity	www.fidelity.com
Morningstar	www.morningstar.com

Brokerage firms often provide investment tools to their clients and, in some cases, the public. Members of a student-managed investment fund might have access to these tools via their fund's account or their own personal accounts. The tools available include stock screeners, sector information, index constituent information, analysts' ratings and reports, and risk analysis. We list Fidelity and Morningstar because these two vendors currently have a number of tools available freely, in addition to "premium" tools that are available to their clients or by subscription. Fidelity offers much of the same stock-level information as found on Yahoo! Finance, in addition to a number of other tools that might be useful to student-managed investment funds. Specifically, the publicly available stock screener in Fidelity appears to have a number of options that are typically found on other professional-level screeners, such as Bloomberg. The results of a stock screen can then be downloaded and opened in Excel. Though Morningstar's free screener might seem basic by comparison, it can be useful in quickly narrowing down a list of securities. In addition, Morningstar offers free portfolio tracking, allowing customized views of portfolio holdings.

Index providers

Vendor	Website
Barclays Index Products	indices.barcap.com
FTSE Russell Indices	ftserussell.com/index
Morningstar® Indexes	indexes.morningstar.com
MSCI Global Equity Indices	msci.com/index-solutions
S&P Dow Jones Indices	us.spindices.com/

Index providers can be an excellent source for information about the composition of benchmark portfolios for specific asset classes. Since the composition of an index is proprietary to the index provider, very few offer free access to real-time constituents and weights. Indeed, most index providers charge fees to investment managers for index data. In some cases, educational institutions might be able to negotiate an agreement with an index provider at a reduced fee (or perhaps even for free). In addition, most sites have index returns, descriptive statistics, and methodology information freely available. In some cases, sector or industry weightings are also available, which can be useful to a student-managed investment fund's portfolio construction and performance analysis.

Licensed Services

Vendor/platform	Website
Bloomberg Professional	bloomberg.com/professional/
Center for Research in Security Prices (CRSP)	crsp.com
Compustat	hspglobal.com/marketintelligence/en/? product=compustat-research-insight
FactSet	factset.com
Morningstar® Direct℠	morningstar.com/products/direct
Refinitiv (formerly Thomson Reuter)	refinitiv.com
S&P CapitalIQ	spglobal.com/marketintelligence/en/ solutions/sp-capital-iq-platform
Value Line	http://www.valueline.com/

Students who participate in student-managed investment funds are generally doing the same work and are faced with making the same decisions as analysts, strategists, and portfolio managers at real investment firms. This experience is what makes student-managed investment funds such valuable opportunities. The experience is further enhanced to the extent that members can utilize the same tools that professionals use in conducting the business of an investment firm.

Such experience is an added asset to SMIF members as they begin their careers. Some of the most widely used professional tools are listed above. Since the development of and maintenance of these tools represents a significant source of revenue for these vendors, these tools can be expensive to academic institutions that do not use such tools to generate investment management revenues. In many cases, colleges and universities may negotiate academic licenses at reduced fees compared to what professional investment firms pay. Since many of the vendors above offer comparable tools, student-managed investment fund programs that are resource-constrained might further economize by choosing only one or two. Indeed, many investment firms choose one vendor's platform over another rather than spending money on redundant resources.

At a basic level, most of these professional tools provide raw data that can be found in other tools described in this chapter, some of which are freely available. However, these tools generally provide true "one-stop shopping" for most of the raw data and organize it in readily accessible format. For example, we illustrate some of the capabilities of Bloomberg Professional below. In many cases, the data are derived primarily from company annual reports, SEC filings, and market data that are available from free sources. However, it would likely take an analyst days to collect the information for a single stock and additional time to organize the data prior to conducting analysis. On professional platforms, such as Bloomberg, Morningstar Direct, CapitalIQ, FactSet, and Refinitiv Eikon, these data are available to an analyst with only a few keystrokes or clicks of a mouse. Moreover, these vendors have an interest in maintaining the quality and consistency of the data that are provided on their platforms, reducing the likelihood of errors. In short, publicly and freely available tools do not begin to approach the quantity and quality of the functions that organize and analyze data that are found in these professional-level tools.

We have also included other vendors on this list that are more specialized in the product or service they offer. For example, ValueLine has a long-standing tradition of providing independent investment analysis and is available in many university libraries. On the other hand, FactSet specializes in quantitative analysis of portfolios and their underlying securities. Exhibit 8.7 provides an overview from FactSet about the ways in which it might be deployed in student-managed investment funds. Finally, CRSP (Center for Research in Security Prices) is a data vendor originating from the University of Chicago, providing one of the most comprehensive databases of U.S. securities returns. While CRSP might not have the fundamental data that would be useful in security analysis, the historical returns can be used for a student-managed investment fund to perform back-testing and simulations of quantitative investment processes. Many research universities already subscribe to CRSP as an academic research resource, so it may already be available to many student-managed investment funds. Since CRSP is primary a data vendor, analysis of the data must be done on another platform, such as FactSet or Excel.

Next we provide several examples of data and analysis tools that might be useful to a student-managed investment fund. Note that these examples only scratch the surface of the scale and scope of what is possible with these tools.

Exhibit 8.7 FactSet in a student-managed investment fund

Tasks a student within an SMIF might do
1. *Portfolio Trading Scenario?*

Find new companies
1. *Screen for new companies*
2. *Research ideas*

Analyze companies as potential investments
1. *Examine financials*
2. *Examine estimates*
3. *Compare to other competitors*

Managing portfolio
A. *Equity Portfolio Analysis*

1. *Track Performance in Real Time*

Analyze performance, risk, composition, style, and characteristics for multiple portfolios and portfolio managers in real time. With the most current analytics possible, you have a more accurate picture of your portfolio and increased clarity on the impact of changes you are considering.

2. *Customize Interactive Reports and Charts*

Interactively examine reports and charts with double-click sorting, drill down group- and security-level details, and formatting options. Spectrum functionality lets you view multiple reports and charts side-by-side, with intelligent linking that carries the portfolio, benchmark, and other details across all views. Set a standard display of reports and charts to open automatically when you launch FactSet.

3. *Access Streaming Global Data*

Combine your proprietary holdings with FactSet content or third-party data sources, including extensive benchmark data and global exchange indices. Integrate your holdings via a nightly upload or intraday connection to your firm's OMS. FactSet seamlessly integrates intraday prices with historical data to produce any report on an up-to-the-second basis.

B. *Composition and Characteristics*

Gain insight into portfolio and benchmark weights using custom groupings in reports and charts.

4. *Analyze Weights*

Customize Weights reports with multiple portfolios and benchmarks. Launch charts to see portfolio weights, benchmark weights, the difference between them, and weights over time.

5. *Examine Top-Level and Group Characteristics*

Use Characteristics reports to view weights on a portfolio-level basis, including market capitalization, valuation measures, growth rates, profitability ratios, and other financial ratios for your portfolios and selected benchmarks. For a security-level view, examine the current valuation for individual holdings, groups, and the total portfolio using P/E, forward P/E, price to book, and dividend yield. Customize Valuation reports by adding ratios that apply to your portfolio.

C. *Performance Analysis*

View performance versus a benchmark between any two selected dates, or for more in-depth analysis see portfolio performance from two perspectives: attribution and contribution.

6. *Analyze Relative and Absolute Performance*

Research the performance of a portfolio relative to a benchmark to see if your portfolio outperformed and how each group contributed to overall performance. Understand how management decisions such as group allocation, security selection, and currency tilts may have affected results. Within the Attribution report, view allocation, selection, and interaction effects at a glance. FactSet links to your proprietary holdings and benchmark index portfolios on a daily or intraday basis. Audit returns, attribution effects, weights, and characteristics data for greater transparency. You can also assess performance on an absolute basis. View how price changes and dividend payments contributed to total return and survey each company's weight, price change, market value, total return, and contribution to return.

7. *Customize Groups*

Examine how segments of your portfolio performed by grouping by sector, industry, market cap, or your own custom groupings. Choose groupings by sector, region, or country, or create groupings of the highest and lowest securities in your portfolio based on factors like market value, P/E, or growth rate. For more flexibility, choose grouping definitions from FactSet, vendors such as S&P, or your own proprietary definitions. You can also incorporate risk-based performance attribution or fixed income attribution into your reports. Add risk factors from Barra, Axioma, APT, Northfield, and R-Squared to a report and then group by factor. For fixed income performance attribution, integrate yield change, duration, or credit quality into attribution reports to view attribution for both equity and fixed income portfolios at once.

D. *Dynamic Chartings*

Study performance over time or throughout the day with flexible charts.

8. *Chart Performance from Multiple Perspectives*

Chart the performance of your portfolio management decisions over a series of months, quarters, years, or other periods, and plot this data against the overall effect. View intraday performance relative to a benchmark with Performance Heat Maps to uncover problem sectors, and then examine each sector to see which individual securities helped or hurt that sector during the day. See at-a-glance performance with reports like Top/Bottom Contributors, which shows only the best and worst performing securities in your portfolio during the report period.

9. *Customize Chart Options*

FactSet charts are dynamic, so you can quickly customize colors, labels, and other formatting aspects or look at raw data and charts simultaneously in a split view.

E. *Analysis That Fits Your Strategy*

FactSet gives you the flexibility to analyze according to your unique investment style, whether it includes fixed income, alternative assets, a long/short strategy, or currency hedging.

10. *Analyze Across All Asset Classes and Strategies*

Understand how counterparties and issuers relate to each other and what a firm's true exposure is by evaluating exposure to issuers across asset classes. To reveal the exposure of index futures, ETFs, or mutual funds to a particular security or risk factor, choose whether these composite assets should be analyzed as-is or as their underlying securities. Examine long/short and long-only portfolios by splitting the portfolio into long and short positions and creating a market neutral benchmark.

11. *Track the Impact of Ideas*

Understand how anticipated security changes in your portfolio or portfolio changes to your composite will impact composition and characteristics. Simulate trades before they are executed, and view the implications for predicted risk, style, or fundamental characteristics and weights.

12. *Present Portfolio Results*

Instantly create reports for client communications by combining key portfolio analytics with your proprietary portfolio information and commentary. Choose the reports and charts you want to include and publish presentation-ready documents using your firm's custom layout, colors, and design.

13. *Upload Holding Information*

FactSet integrates portfolio holdings and transactions through automated nightly synchronization with your accounting system or custodian. View portfolio holdings more current than the previous day's positions with an intraday connection to your firm's OMS. Link to your accounting system to leverage transaction-based returns for greater accuracy.

14. *Rely on Unsurpassed Support*

To provide the best client service in the industry, FactSet strives to be as accessible to our clients as possible. Round-the-clock client support reinforces FactSet's dedication to providing clients with superior service. Whether you have a quick question or need step-by-step guidance through a complex task, our highly trained Portfolio Analytics specialists will help you find answers and maximize the value of FactSet.

Style, performance, and risk analysis
FactSet's returns-based portfolio analysis solutions provide reports and charts that help you study a portfolio relative to a benchmark, competitor fund, or peer group.

A. *Style Analysis*

Two portfolios with a similar benchmark and stated style can exhibit significantly different style attributes.

1. Style Characteristics

When comparing your portfolios to competitors, it's important to understand style consistency or the purity of the current style. For institutional competitors, a returns-based analysis may be the only way to compare style characteristics. For competitor funds, a returns-based comparison can leverage much more frequent competitor data and complement other portfolio analysis performed in FactSet. Based on Nobel Laureate William Sharpe's concept of the "Effective Asset Mix," FactSet's style reports and charts determine how your selected portfolio and competitor returns correlate with asset class, size, and style indices.

1. *Manager Style Box*

Plot your selected portfolioss or competitor funds into a Manager Style quadrant to identify where they lie in terms of large cap, small cap, value, or growth characteristics.

2. *Rolling Manager Style Box*

Chart your portfolio over a rolling time period to identify style consistency.

3. *Rolling Asset Allocation*

Conceptually similar to the Rolling Manager Style Box, the Rolling Asset Allocation chart focuses on a single portfolio. This area chart emphasizes the indices that comprise your style section.

4. *Customized Style Analysis*

FactSet lets you create custom style sets using any combination of indices or portfolios. Specify any start date, end date, data frequency, and rolling period for analysis. Control every element of a chart from colors and markers to headers and footers.

B. *Risk Analysis*

With the extensive historical performance data in FactSet, you can research the historical risk and risk-adjusted performance of your portfolio and competitors. Choose from more than 120 risk/return statistics, including annualized return, standard deviation, beta, tracking error and upside/downside capture.

5. *Multi-Horizon*

Display any statistic for your selected portfolios, benchmarks, and competitors for various sub-periods within your selected time period.

6. *Multi-Statistic*

Compare risk and return statistics with the Multi-Statistic report. Customize your report by selecting from regression, semi-variance, and up-down statistics.

7. *Rolling Multi-Horizon*

The Rolling Multi-Horizon report is similar to Multi-Horizon but uses rolling periods instead of finite sub-periods for more of a trend analysis.

8. *Cumulative Return*

Chart the cumulative performance of portfolios, benchmarks, and competitors over any time period. You can also display the growth of your selected currency.

9. *X-Y Chart*

Create a scatterplot of two risk/return statistics, such as standard deviation and annualized return.

C. *Peer Universe Analysis*

Peer Universe analysis helps you understand how your portfolios compare to a broad range of competitors. This perspective is essential to effectively position your products in the competitive marketplace.

10. *Competitor Returns*

Choose Peer Universe reports and charts to examine portfolio returns relative to a selected peer group. Analyze portfolios against a variety of peer universes from Lipper, Morningstar, eVestment Alliance, RogersCasey, and PSN.

11. *Multi-Horizon*

Use the Multi-Horizon report and its corresponding chart to display peer rankings for a specific statistic over various time periods. Choose from over 120 Modern Portfolio Theory statistics and any time period.

12. *Multi-Statistic*

Compare risk and return statistics with the Multi-Statistic report. Add as many available risk/ returns statistics as you want.

13. *Customize Peer Universe Analysis*

Create your own customized peer group by combining universes, removing particular funds from a universe, or archiving a list of screened funds.

14. *Universe X-Y Chart*

Study risk and return for your entire universe with the Universe X-Y chart. This chart illustrates two risk/return statistics for your universe, with the axes' intersection representing the median fund manager.

D. *Returns-Based Research*

Beyond analyzing particular portfolios, use FactSet to research the optimal allocation of a set of indices or products. When you don't know the products, use fund screening to identify all portfolios that meet your exact criteria.

15. *Efficient Frontier Analysis*

Returns-based Efficient Frontier analysis focuses on creating optimal portfolios from an initial set of assets (indices and products) and asset constraints, such as asset returns (historical or expected), risk, and weight. Using these inputs, create and compare a variety of optimal
portfolios at different risk/return levels. Once a preferred allocation of products is decided, save that combination as a composite for additional analysis of its style, risk, or peer ranking.

16. *Fund Screening*

The fund screening utility lets you screen for all funds, separate accounts, or hedge funds passing any criteria you wish.

   i. Freely combine style, performance, and risk in your screening parameters
  ii. Include multiple data sets in the same screen
 iii. Mix time periods
 iv. Include other quantitative and qualitative characteristics in your screen, such as whether the separate account is open to new assets, the number of holdings in the fund, or the tenure of the manager
  v. Apply complex logical, statistical, and mathematical criteria
 vi. You can save the results of your screen to use as a custom peer group or as a list to be considered individually in FactSet reports

How to use Morningstar Direct^{SM}^a

In terms of using MorningStar Direct^{SM} to research stock fundamentals, the following cover page is a starting point to choose various modules in the column on the left side. MorningStar Direct^{SM} (Direct) is operated by each tab key which links to each module. Direct is a good analytics for at conducting portfolio management, performance measurement, and benchmarking. It is also very efficient to download a large amount of historical data for a large number of stocks. Users should be familiar themselves with each function by clicking on each tab in the left column of the Reuters page. For example, if you want to see how a particular portfolio performs, click on "portfolio performance" tab. It will return performance measurements for a specific portfolio. In the following section, a sample screen for each module is presented.

"Home" page

The easiest way to tour the service is to click on one box on the left side at a time. The boxes contain a wealth of information and analytics that perform every step of portfolio management (Exhibit 8.8).

Exhibit 8.8 Morningstar Direct^{SM} "Home" page

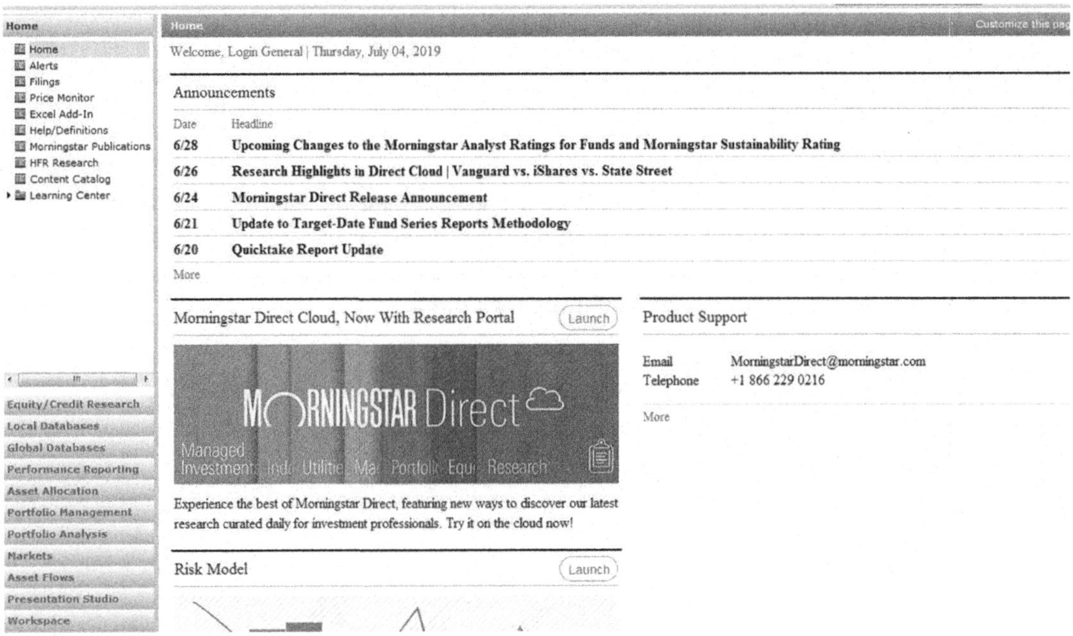

(Source: ©2020 Morningstar, Inc. All Rights Reserved. Reproduced with permission.)

a ©2020 Morningstar, Inc. All Rights Reserved. The information contained herein: (1) is proprietary to Morningstar and/or its content providers; (2) may not be copied or distributed; (3) does not constitute investment advice offered by Morningstar; and (4) is not warranted to be accurate, complete or timely. Neither Morningstar nor its content providers are responsible for any damages or losses arising from any use of this information. Past performance is no guarantee of future results. Use of information from Morningstar does not necessarily constitute agreement by Morningstar, Inc. of any investment philosophy or strategy presented in this publication.

"Research Portal" page

This page collects professional research work (Exhibit 8.9).

Exhibit 8.9 Morningstar Direct^{SM} "Research Portal" page

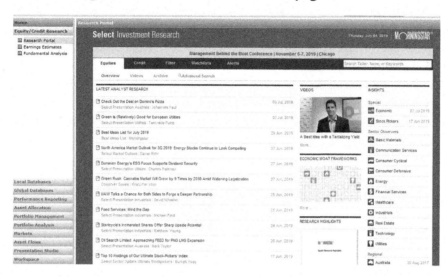

"Snapshot" page

This is a typical description page of a stock, a quick and easy way to start to know the stock. The detailed and specific information can be found in the boxes on the left side (Exhibit 8.10).

Exhibit 8.10 Morningstar Direct^{SM} "Snapshot" page

"Industry Peer" page

This is a self-explanatory peer stock comparison page (Exhibit 8.11).

Exhibit 8.11 Morningstar Direct^{SM} "Industry Peer" page

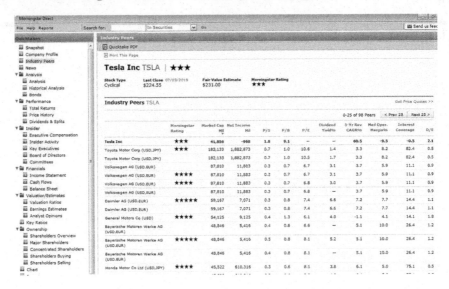

"Executive Compensation" page

See Exhibit 8.12.

Exhibit 8.12 Morningstar Direct^{SM} "Executive Compensation" page

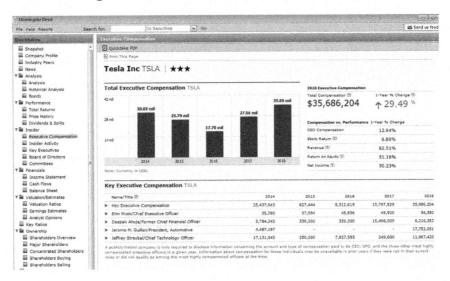

"Presentation Studio" module

This is a unique module that helps you to develop a professional presentation package (Exhibit 8.13).

Exhibit 8.13 Morningstar Direct^{SM} "Presentation Studio" module

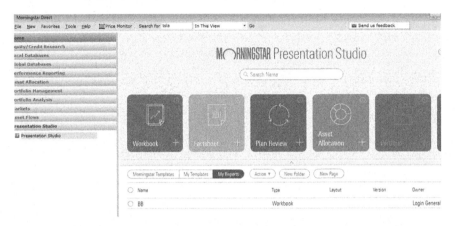

"Model Portfolio" module

See Exhibit 8.14.

Exhibit 8.14 Morningstar Direct^{SM} "Model Portfolio" page

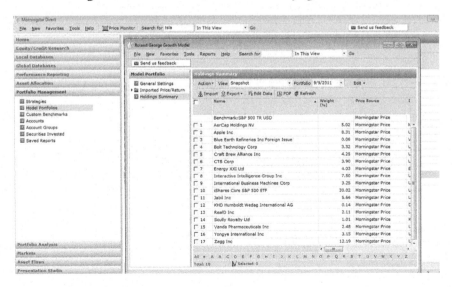

"Valuation Ratios" module

See Exhibit 8.15.

Exhibit 8.15 Morningstar Direct^{SM} "Valuation Ratios" module

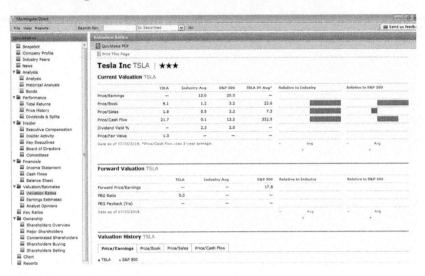

"Key Ratios" module

See Exhibit 8.16.

Exhibit 8.16 Morningstar Direct^{SM} "Key Ratios" page

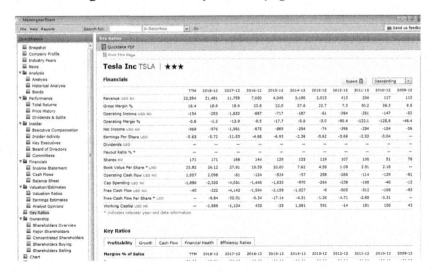

"Portfolio" reports

See Exhibit 8.17.

Exhibit 8.17 Morningstar Direct^{SM} "Portfolio" reports

	Name Report Currency: Base Currency	Morningstar Rating Overall	6/30/2019 - 7/2/2019 (Last Week End - Last Market Close (-1 day)) Return	Peer group rank	GIF Sector rank	# of investments ranked in GIF sector	7/1/2019 - 7/2/2019 (Last M Close (-1 day)) Return	Peer group rank
1	**Unclassified**							
2	Ambev SA ADR							
3	American International Group Inc	*****	0.96	9			0.96	9
4	Apple Inc	***	2.43	3			2.43	3
5	Bolt Technology Corp							
6	C&J Energy Services Inc							
7	Cameco Corp	*****	0.09	11			0.09	11
8	Cisco Systems Inc	***	1.97	5			1.97	5
9	Deere & Co	***	(0.35)	14			(0.35)	14
10	Flowserve Corp		0.28	10			0.28	10
11	Freeport-McMoRan Inc		(1.38)	16			(1.38)	16
12	Halliburton Co	****	(0.40)	15			(0.40)	15
13	International Business Machines Corp	***	1.68	6			1.68	6
14	Jack In The Box Inc		0.01	12			0.01	12
15	John Bean Technologies Corp		1.67	7			1.67	7
16	KHD Humboldt Wedag International AG		0.00	13			0.00	13
17	Movado Group Inc		(2.04)	18			(2.04)	18
18	Royal Caribbean Cruises Ltd	***	(1.79)	17			(1.79)	17
19	Scully Royalty Ltd		5.11	1			5.11	1
20	Stanley Black & Decker Inc		1.38	8			1.38	8
21	The Walt Disney Co	***	2.07	4			2.07	4
22	Zillow Group Inc A		3.65	2			3.65	2
23	*Benchmark 1: S&P 500 TR USD*		1.07				1.07	
24	*Benchmark 2: MSCI EAFE PR USD*		0.77				0.77	
25	*Peer Group: Display Group*							

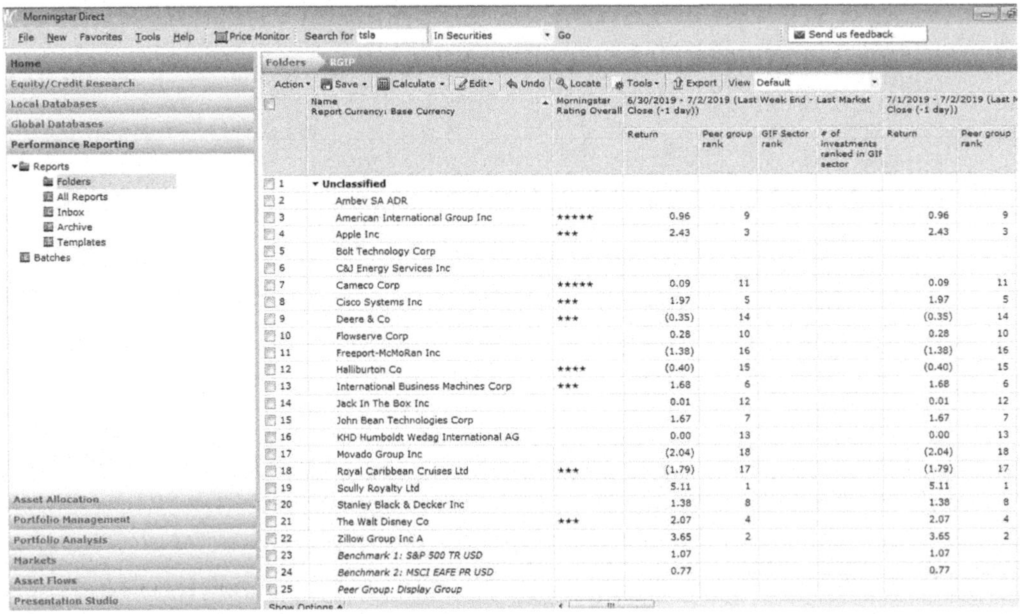

(Source: ©2020 Morningstar, Inc. All Rights Reserved. Reproduced with permission.)

How to use Refinitiv Eikon

In terms of using Refinitiv Eikon Equity Product to research stock fundamentals, the following equity page is a good starting point. Reuters is operated by each tab key at the top of the overview screen. Users should be familiar themselves with each function by clicking on each tab at the top of the Refinitiv Eikon page. For example, if you want to see company's recent earnings estimates, click on "Estimates" tab. It will return many sub-command for more specific information. In the following: A sample screen for the first command in each of the tab for the company Tesla (NASDAQ: TSLA.O) is presented.

"Overview" tab

See Exhibit 8.18.

Exhibit 8.18 Refinitiv Eikon "Overview" tab

(Source: Eikon from Refinitiv.)

"Description" tab

See Exhibit 8.19.

Exhibit 8.19 Refinitiv Eikon "Description" tab

(Source: Eikon from Refinitiv.)

"Price & Charts" tab

See Exhibit 8.20.

Exhibit 8.20 Refinitiv Eikon "Price & Charts" tab

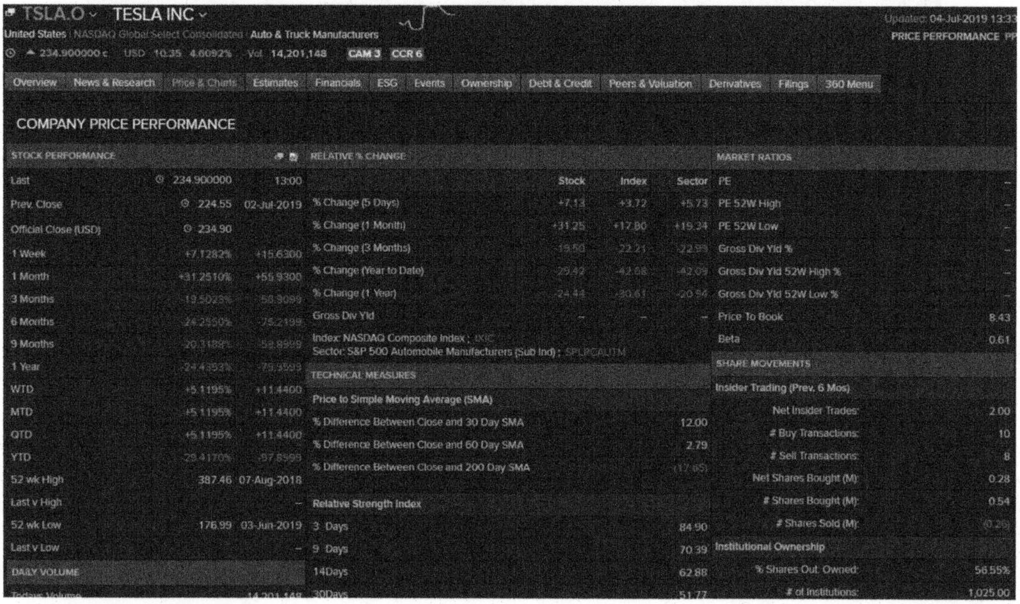

(Source: Eikon from Refinitiv.)

"Estimates" tab

This is where users can get most updated street consensus estimates of various metrics. Both the historical actual financials and future forecasts are laid out in a friendly format that can be downloaded into an excel file (upper right corner) for further analysis. Use the upper right button to change the default setting of the date range. Use the boxes on the right side to select items to be shown. This is a very useful and efficient way to see what the market is forecasting of company's future financials (Exhibit 8.21).

Exhibit 8.21 Refinitiv Eikon "Estimates" tab

(Source: Eikon from Refinitiv.)

"Financial" tab

This is where users can download a large amount of historical 10Qs or 10Ks in an useable format (Exhibit 8.22).

Exhibit 8.22 Refinitiv Eikon "Financial" tab

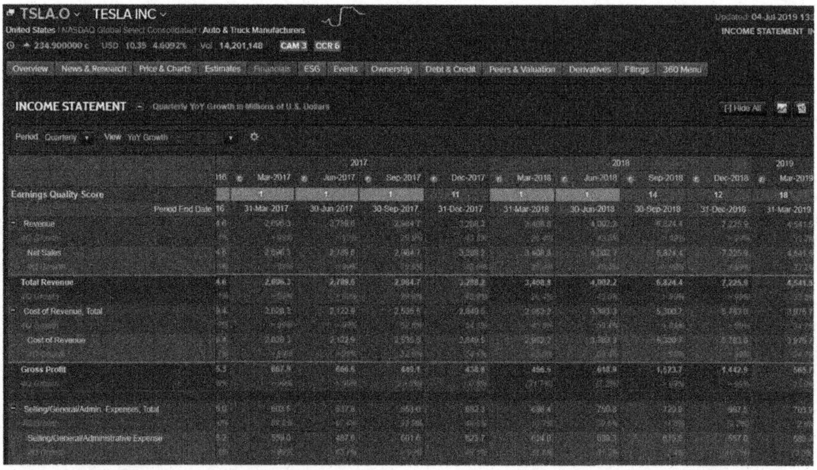

(Source: Eikon from Refinitiv.)

"Derivative" tab

See Exhibit 8.23.

Exhibit 8.23 Refinitiv Eikon "Derivative" tab

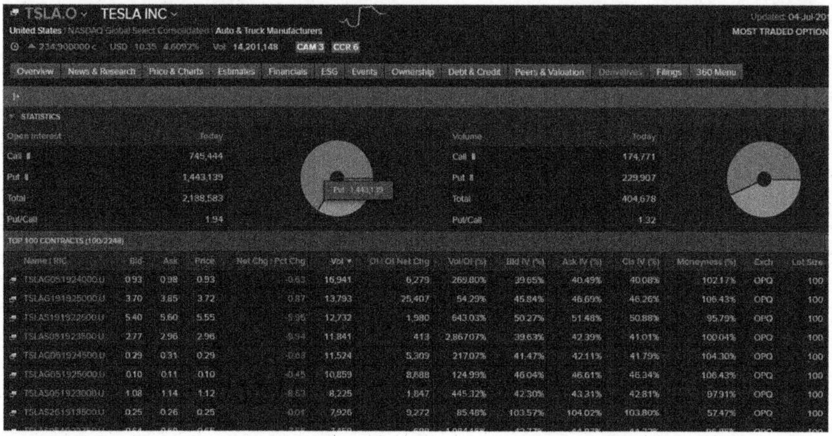

(Source: Eikon from Refinitiv.)

"Event" tab

See Exhibit 8.24.

Exhibit 8.24 Refinitiv Eikon "Event" tab

(Source: Eikon from Refinitiv.)

"Price & Chart" tab

The page allows users to put multiple market data items and tickers on the same page for comparison (Exhibit 8.25).

Exhibit 8.25 Refinitiv Eikon "Price & Chart" tab

(Source: Eikon from Refinitiv.)

"ESG" tab

This page displays company's ratings on "environmental," "sustainable," and "governance" (ESG) fronts (Exhibit 8.26).

Exhibit 8.26 Refinitiv Eikon "ESG" tab

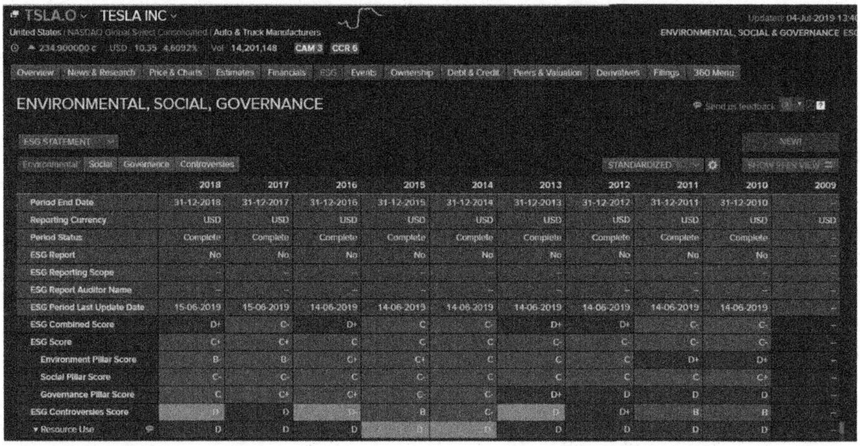

(Source: Eikon from Refinitiv.)

"Ownership Summary" tab

This page displays a snapshot of the owners of the company's stock (Exhibit 8.27).

Exhibit 8.27 Refinitiv Eikon "Ownership Summary" tab

(Source: Eikon from Refinitiv.)

"Social Media Valuation" tab

Only available on Reuter's Eikon's product, social media valuation shows the relationship between a social media score, measured mainly by the commentators' tweet contents, and the company stock prices (Exhibit 8.28).

Exhibit 8.28 Refinitiv Eikon "Social Media Valuation" tab

(Source: Eikon from Refinitiv.)

How to use Bloomberg

In terms of using Bloomberg to research stock fundamentals, the following equity function page is a good starting point. Users should familiarize themselves with each function by typing the white-letter command on the top of the Bloomberg page. For example, if you want to see company's recent news or research reports, type "CN" or simply clicking on the "CN" line. It will return with pages of requested information. In the following: the purpose of each functional key and a sample screen for the company Tesla (NASDAQ: TSLA) are described.

THE TITLE PAGE

The following table lists some of the most used commends (functions) in the title page. Users can either click on the first-level command (e.g., "Company Overview") or go directly on the second-level, sub-command (e.g., "DES") (Exhibit 8.29).

Exhibit 8.29 Examples of Bloomberg commands

Company Overview >		Charting and Reporting >	
DES	Security Description	GP	Line Chart
MFID	MiFID Descriptive Data	GF	Graph Fundamentals
CF	Company Filings	CMAP	Company Map
CN	Company News		
		Security Surveillance >	
Company Analysis >		EVT	Company Events
FA	Financial Analysis	BQ	Bloomberg Quote
OWN	Ownership Summary		
CRPR	Credit Rating Profile	**Trade Analytics >**	
		IOIA	IOI and Advert Overview
Research and Estimates >		MDM	Market Depth Monitor
EE	Earnings and Estimates	VWAP	Price and Vol Dashboard
BRC	Research Portal: Single Sec		
BICO	BI Company Primer	**Derivatives >**	
		OMON	Option Monitor
Comparative Analytics >			
EQRV	Equity Relative Valuation		
RV	Relative Valuation		

Key: If you don't know where to start specifically, always use the first-level command which has covered a complete list of the second-level commands. The second-level commends shown in the title page are only the most often used ones.

Bloomberg Function Examples (key words in quote, description in parentheses)

"DES" (Security Description)

Company Information/Profile, brief overview of a company's financials and industry, and includes links to other functions. This is the first place an investor wants to start to know the facts and descriptive information of the company and its stock. It also gives the most recent financials and stock data.

"MFID" (MiFID Descriptive Data)

Transparency Information on the security's liquidity and market data, classification, identifiers and Pre-Post-Trade data. (Regulatory disclosures for particular markets).

"CF" (Company Filings)

Provides access to publicly available filings for research purposes (10-K, 8-K, earnings call, etc.) This is where you find all the filings and relevant news of the company. This is where investors can find qualitative news, events, regulatory, legal, financial announcements, as well as earnings releases, conference call transcripts.

Key: Users are advised to download the actual files and search the files with key words for specific information.

"CN" (Company News)

Provides company specific news in the order of publishing time. This is where you can find recent news and comments and analysis from reputable sources. The articles can be searched using a specific time range.

Key: These functions can bring you a wealth of historical factual data and current real-time news and events relevant to the company.

"FA" (Financial Analysis)

Provides access to company's financial statements, financial ratios, company's segment breakdown, company specific metrics (# of cars sold for Tesla), and ESG (Environmental-Social-Governance) data. This page is probably most useful page for investors to get historical (10Q and 10K) financials.

Key: Remember to put them in an excel format to be easily used for analysis. Make sure to check on segment financials which are harder to get from typical financial databases. Also, users should be aware of some hidden gems of the proprietary data, such as Supply Chain Analysis ("SPLC") and Private Company database which are very difficult and expensive to obtain from other sources.

"OWN" (Ownership Summary)

Provides a breakdown of the company's ownership information over time by entities (institutions, public companies or private parties) and by geography.

Key: Bloomberg has the best layout of institutional holding. In fact, they are the only one which shows historical time series ownership data which is downloadable to an excel file. Note that Bloomberg is the only one that weekly ownership data can be downloaded over a historical period. Users should always know that it is more important to analyze the changes in ownership, rather than just the current data.

"CRPR" (Credit Rating Profile)

Allows for analysis of credit worthiness of the company's debt issuances. It displays both current and historical credit rating from different rating agencies.

Key: This is a good place to show you the ratings for different components of the debt at one page.

"EE" (Earnings and Estimates)

Provides a snapshot of aggregated analysts'/broker earnings projections, surprise earnings data and a summary of earnings history. This is the first place you look for street consensus of a company earnings report. It has a wealth of current and historical estimates on more than a dozen financial metrics. This page and its extension also cover analysts' recommendations, surprises, and also the market reaction to the announcements. Click on the words in white will lead to the extensions. Most (historical) data is downloadable into excel easily.

Key: The icing on the cake is that Bloomberg Intelligence gives you the current and historical analysis done by the Bloomberg analysts.

"BRC" (Research Portal)

Displays research reports for the company. You can find opinion and analyses from mainly professional sell-side analysts.

Key: This is the largest collection of analyst reports among all data services.

"BI" (Bloomberg Intelligence)

Provides in-depth analysis, commentary, and datasets on the companies, industries, government factors, credit issuances, and litigation from a team of independent experts.

Key: User should aware that these reports show Bloomberg analysts historical reports and their thought processes. As they utilize mainly Bloomberg data to support their conclusions, user can read their reports to learn how to use Bloomberg data to do a professional street research.

"EQRV" (Equity Relative Valuation)

Compares a company's present valuation to its historical averages over different periods of time and the company's peers.

Key: This is a good place to (1) find the competitors and (2) quick comparisons for the relative valuations.

"RV" (Relative Valuation)

Provides peer group relative valuation analysis

"GP" (Line Chart)

Graphs the company's historical price performance. This is the most powerful tool (GP) to graph pretty much everything Bloomberg has on the same graph. Investors can easily test their "prior" by putting them in a graph. All data from GP can be downloaded into an excel sheet.

"GF" (Graph Fundamental)

Allows for visual comparison between a company's financials with those of other companies, indices, commodities, and economic data

Key: GF is most useful graphing tool for beginners. You can pick multiple stocks' multiple financial metrics on the same graph. Visualization the relationship can help develop a good economic story.

"CMAP" (Company Map)

Shows a company's headquarters, factories and power plants on a world map

"EVT" (Company Event)

Event Calendar for company specific events

"BQ" (Bloomberg Quote)

Provide detailed quotes, valuation and earnings ratios, peer activity, consensus forecast, past performance trends, and related news.

"MDM" (Market Depth Monitor)

Monitor best bids and offers for the selected security

"VWAP" (Price and Volume Dashboard)

Provides a snapshot of VWAP (Volume Weighted Average Price) analysis

"Bank" (Broker Ranking)

Broker Dealer Rankings and shows advertised trade volume information

"OMON" (Option Monitor)

Displays options strikes available and other option pricing data. This function also provides real-time Greeks.

Summary of key points

- The quality of an investment decision is due more to the care, skill, knowledge, and insights of the analyst than the tools that the analyst uses.
- Data, information, and financial analysis functions are tools that are helpful in the practice of investment management.
- Many tools and data are freely available. Company and government websites provide access to high-quality economic and financial statement data.
- Access to one or more professional tools provides the opportunity for members of student-managed investment funds to gain practical experience with industry-standard data, functions, and platforms.
- Professional-level tools provide efficient access to a wealth of high-quality information and analysis methods.
- When students become actively engaged in utilizing these tools, the potential exists to more effectively manage the underlying student-managed portfolios.
- Professional level tools further facilitate students' active learning by immersing them in the professional environment they are studying.

Exercises

1. Suppose a biotech company is working on a drug that promises to be an effective treatment or therapy for hepatitis-C. This would be the primary source of revenues for the company. Assuming the drug is approved for use in the United States, estimate the firm's revenues from the drug over the next 5 years in the United States? What about worldwide revenues? In your answer, please address the following issues. What percentage of the U.S. (or world) population has hepatitis-C? Estimate how many people have hepatitis-C. How many new cases of hepatitis-C are reported each year? What current therapies exist for the treatment of hepatitis-C? How much do they cost per year for an individual with hepatitis-C? Assuming this new treatment is at least as effective as existing therapies and that it is priced similarly, how much market share do you estimate it can gain?

2. Choose two publicly traded companies in two different sectors. Locate their last two years' financial statements from as many sources as possible, including the company's own website, EDGAR, professional-level services, and freely available sites (e.g., Morningstar, Google, and/or Yahoo!). Are the financial statements identical regardless of the source? In cases where there are discrepancies, which sources are correct? Do some sources provide more/different details than others?

3. Using the tools in this chapter, try to separate the revenue in a company's latest income statement by geographic region (e.g., continent). Some companies that you might try are Microsoft, Caterpillar, and Tupperware.

4. Use a "stock screener" from at least two different vendors. For example, try Fidelity, Morningstar, and Google. If you have access to professional-level tools, also use their screener.

Compare the results of the various screeners. Which screeners appear to have the most options? Which screeners appear to have the best quality of results? Some suggestions for screens follow. When specific indexes are not available in a screening tool, you might try to "mimic" the index by using market capitalization criteria.

a. Build a list of S&P 500 Index stocks from the healthcare sector with a P/E ratio below 20.

b. Build a list of stocks between a market capitalization of $100 m and $1 b in the energy sector.

c. Build a list of the 50 stocks with the highest book-to-market ratios within the Russell 2000 Index.

d. Build a list of S&P 500 Index stocks with the best (or worst) 6-month (or 12-month) stock price performance.

e. Build a list of the 100 stocks with the highest dividend yield within the Russell 1000 Index.

f. Build a list of stocks with a beta between 0.50 and 0.80.

g. Build a list of corporate bonds rated lower than investment grade.

5. How would you estimate the before-tax and after-tax cost of debt for a firm? Specifically, what tools would you use and how would you use them?

6. Choose three companies: one large cap stock (e.g., from the S&P 500), one mid cap stock (e.g., from the S&P 400) and one small cap stock (e.g., from the Russell 2000). Estimate each stock's beta that you would use to estimate the firm's cost of equity capital according to the

CAPM. What data sources do you use? What methods do you use (e.g., frequency of data, horizon, index, etc.)? Compare the beta that you estimate with the beta available from sources such as Yahoo!, Google, Fidelity, and Morningstar. What method does each employ to estimate beta?

Advisors guide to organization of a SMIF

The focus in the text up to this point was on an individual's or organization's investment philosophy and process, stock selection, specific investment vehicles such as ETFs, bonds and derivatives, portfolio construction, performance evaluation, trading and operations, presentations and investment tools. Placing the investment philosophy and process along with the other essential applied investment topics first was intentional, as this is the proper focus for an individual or organization whose primary responsibility is to invest money. That is, the student-managed investment fund exists to both educate and invest. As such, its approach to investing is an important consideration. Now we turn attention to the practical matter of how a faculty advisor might go about the business of setting up, organizing and operating a SMIF which is part art and part science (Yerkes, 2018). The operational structure should follow from and be consistent with the investment approach. Most student-managed investment funds have two goals: (1) enhance finance and investment education by providing students hands-on experiential learning opportunities and (2) achieve investment growth (i.e., good performance or outperformance) in the fund's investments. By focusing on the latter, the former can be achieved. The experiential learning benefits offered by SMIFs prepare students for the workforce by requiring them to work in self-governed teams, give presentations, write research reports and solve real world problems. All of these activities encourage the development of leadership, analytical, problem solving and communication skills which are in high demand by employers (Demong, Pettit and Campsey, 1979; Neely and Cooley, 2004). This hands-on format also helps students understand and apply difficult finance concepts (Philpot and Peterson, 1998; Riley and Montgomery, 1980; Peng, Dukes and Bremer, 2009). The SMIF experience is essentially equivalent to an internship since students are effectively security analysts and portfolio managers responsible for managing real money (Markese, 1984). SMIFs are among the most cutting edge and innovative experiential learning opportunities due to the high stakes involved (Lawrence, 1994). In the remainder of this appendix, we consider a student managed investment fund's organizational structure, oversight, roles and responsibilities, academic structure, fund structure, operating guidelines, role of the security trading room and maximizing its use and application of the CFA Institute's Code of Ethics and Standards of Professional Conduct.

All of the organizational issues and many of the investment issues are typically discussed in the student-managed investment fund's operating guidelines. The last section of this appendix has an example of a complete set of operating guidelines from Baylor University's student-managed investment fund. Throughout this appendix, we will consider organizational issues that arise in both conceiving and operating a student-managed investment fund, offering both discussion and examples of various items along the way. Some of these issues are codified in operating guidelines, while others simply comprise the operating policies or practices of the organization.

Regardless of the organizational form within which the student-managed investment fund operates, the vehicle within which the portfolio is managed must be chosen, usually based on the source of the portfolio's assets under management. With respect to the organization, we place an emphasis on the student-managed investment fund as a type of investment organization. Specifically, we explore the organizational form in terms of its most common forms: a volunteer student club or organization versus a for-credit class. Within these two types of student-managed investment funds, the operational structure of the organization must be chosen.

Even in this discussion of organizational form and structure, we will emphasize the relevance of the investment approach. We take the approach of first discussing the ultimate goal of the organizational structure—answering the question, what structure facilitates the best implementation of the organization's investment philosophy and process? This provides a framework for understanding the key elements of an investment organization. We then discuss other organizational considerations, such as whether to have a student fund as a class or as a volunteer organization, and some of the organizational issues that present particular challenges to a student-managed investment fund. Finally, we discuss the fund structure—as opposed to the organizational structure—to explore the issue of the investment vehicle through which an organization offers its portfolio. As in the previous chapters, the diversity of investment approaches suggests diversity of organizational forms. Indeed, there are multiple ways to structure an organization to effectively deliver on any particular investment approach. Therefore, we will place an emphasis on the common elements of most organizations but also try to give examples of alternatives to or variations on a common theme.

First and foremost, a fund must put the interests of its beneficiaries ahead of all other considerations. By structuring the organization around the investment approach, the organization stays true to this primary focus on beneficiaries' interests. For ease of exposition (and to further the interest of thinking of student-managed investment funds as operating as real investment firms), we will call these beneficiaries "clients." We recognize that the "client" label will be perfectly appropriate for student-managed investment funds managing money for their universities' endowment funds but might not apply so strictly to other funds. However, even when the fund's beneficiaries are the students themselves or other investors, the "client" label is likely to be useful.

Organizational structure

The organization of a student managed investment fund must be structured with the proper roles in order to realize the previously mentioned fund objectives. Exhibit A1.1 provides examples of the mission or objectives of several student managed investment funds. Most roles and responsibilities are reflected at the first level in titles on an organizational chart. The titles should give hints to the responsibilities of the individual in that role. Most investment firms have a familiar hierarchical organizational structure and student investment firms might chose to mimic this structure or choose one that is "flatter." For example, student managed funds are frequently organized by asset classes and in industry research teams reporting to a director of research and chief investment officer and/or fund president (Moses and Singleton, 2005). Additional positions may be necessary to handle responsibilities such as compliance, economics, performance measurement and others. A faculty member or faculty advisor generally oversees fund operations subject to an investment policy statement and is responsible for educating students in portfolio management and security analysis best practices and theory (Nawrocki, 2017; Dolan and Stevens, 2010). While the faculty advisor may execute trades and may have veto power, they generally should not have access to transfer funds and should allow investment decision making authority to remain with the students (Tatar, 1987). Caution should also be exercised in the selection of a fund custodian to avoid any potential conflicts of interest while an anonymous voting system may be used to avoid undue influence by a single individual (Cooley and Hubbard, 2012; Johnson, Alexander and Allen, 1996). An additional performance benefit of an anonymous voting system is reported by Dorn (2018). Dorn notes the performance of Drexel University's Dragon Fund investment recommendations

---

Exhibit A1.1 Objective of student investment funds

Wright Fund (Rice University)
Educational objectives
The primary educational objectives of the Wright Fund are to provide Rice MBA students with:

- A challenging and stimulating opportunity to learn, develop, and practice professional stock analysis and portfolio management styles and techniques.
- Exposure to practices employed by professional fund managers including sound investment research, diverse investment philosophies, and ethical investment management.
- Insights into the structure, culture, and career choices in the investment industry.

Investment objectives
The Wright Fund's investment objectives are to:

- Achieve risk-adjusted returns superior to the Fund's benchmark.
- Award scholarships to Jones School students.
- Preserve capital and grow portfolio assets.

Cayuga Fund (Cornell University)

The Cayuga MBA Fund aims to: (1) provide a competitive rate of risk-adjusted return to its investors; and (2) enhance the educational and professional opportunities of Cornell Johnson. School MBA students through experiential learning. The fund invests in stocks traded in the United States.

Student Managed Investment Fund (University of Connecticut)

The primary objective of the Fund is to provide participating students an opportunity to gain valuable hands-on experience in security research, valuation of risky assets, asset allocation, and portfolio management. While performance will remain the primary focus, and will be reviewed at regular intervals, we do not presume that the students will be able to beat the market on a consistent basis. Rather, this is another SBA endeavor to deliver high quality practical education in an area of considerable interest to students and employers alike. The fund will increase the marketability of SBA students in industries such as equity research, investment banking, commercial banking, and corporate finance.

A long-term benefit of the fund will be the enhanced reputation of SBA as a school offering challenging, integrated, analytical projects using real time capital market data. This should enable us to attract more academically gifted and motivated students to the SBA.

Student Managed Investment Fund (Butler University)

Educational Objective

The SMIF should strengthen students' skills and abilities in security and market analysis, financial research, oral and written communication, and teamwork. Further, the fund should provide the opportunity for students to gain exposure to administrators (i.e., the Endowment & Investment Committee), investment advisors, alumni, professional money managers, and other industry practitioners. As such, in all facets the SMIF should provide experiential learning consistent with the mission of Butler University.

Investment Objective

The SMIF is designated by the Endowment & Investment Committee (hereafter, Committee) as a large-capitalization portfolio. Given the nature of the SMIF, the Committee authorizes the SMIF to further concentrate investments in the largest, most well-known stocks, which are represented by the S&P 500 index. The benchmark for the portfolio will thus be the S&P 500 index.

Although the goal of the SMIF is to meet or exceed the return of the S&P 500, the Committee recognizes the constraints (i.e., limited meeting time and research resources) associated with managing the SMIF in the context of an academic setting. Thus, the stated performance objective is to trail the S&P 500 by no more than 100 basis points per year.

Saluki Student Investment Fund (Southern Illinois University Carbondale)

Educational Objective

Provide students at Southern Illinois University Carbondale with hands-on experience in portfolio management and investment research.

Investment Objective

Manage a portion of the Southern Illinois University Foundation portfolio with a Midcap Core Strategy. Invest to maximize long-term capital appreciation relative to the benchmark as the primary objective.

anonymously approved outperformed their benchmark by 300 basis points in the 12 weeks following the recommendation while investment recommendations anonymously rejected underperformed by −290 basis points. In any case, the structure must start with the responsibilities for oversight and develop from there the roles and responsibilities for the student members.

Oversight

Oversight of a student-managed investment fund can take several forms. Most student-managed investment funds are overseen on a day-to-day basis by a faculty advisor who may have prior or current professional investment management responsibilities. In addition, many funds include an advisory board in their organizational structure. This board is typically made up of individuals who have professional experience and expertise in the investment management industry and/or university administrators and endowment investment committee members. In addition to oversight, advisory boards can provide important mentoring and networking opportunities for students. These professionals can draw on their experience to help shape the organization, investment approach and focus. As discussed below, the oversight might also depend on the structure of the actual fund in terms of the investment vehicle. For example, the oversight role of the advisory board might be replaced by university administrators and the endowment fund's investment committee if the student-managed investment fund is managed as part of the university's endowment fund.

Bryant College's Archway Investment Fund, shown in Exhibit A1.2, provides an example of many of these attributes. The fund spells out the role for the advisory board. Notice the emphasis on the Bryant University Board of Trustees as the ultimate client and the additional oversight offered by way of the board's Investments Committee.

Roles and responsibilities

The hierarchical structure is usually shaped like a pyramid, with reporting lines leading to the person or group with ultimate responsibility. With regard to the investment function only, the top of the pyramid is usually the role Chief Investment Officer, portfolio manager or perhaps an investment committee, in whom all responsibility and authority rests for the final buy and sell decisions in the portfolio. Below the portfolio manager, there could be industry sector or asset class team leaders or managers, who direct the work of industry or asset class specific research analysts. The hierarchical structure allows individuals to focus on specific tasks and to specialize on a specific set of skills. This can benefit an organization through efficient execution and even enhanced capabilities from specialization recognizing the labor-intensive nature of security analysis (Belt, 1975). The hierarchical structure also has the benefit of clear paths for growth or promotion and provides students with leadership and

Exhibit A1.2 Job Description for Archway Investment Fund Advisory Board Members (Bryant University)

Role of Advisory Board members

The primary role of Advisory Board members will be to:

- Validate and refine course design ideas to ensure that we create an experience for students that captures key aspects of working in the investments industry;
- Serve as a guest speaker from time to time if he/she has a specific area of expertise that is relevant to the operation of the fund;
- Serve on the panel that reviews the performance of student analysts and portfolio managers;
- Provide encouragement, advice, and access to ideas and opportunities that might otherwise be unavailable to students;
- Mentor individual students as the need or opportunity arises.

From time to time, Advisory Board members may also be asked to provide guidance to student managers by suggesting high level investment themes, commenting on proposed portfolio strategies, or proposed changes to the investment policy statement which specifies the guidelines under which student managers operate the Fund. Note, however, that in all cases this input is advisory in nature. Student managers are ultimately accountable to the Investments Committee of the Bryant University Board of Trustees, and in that sense they are the "client."

Key meetings

- February or March—Annual Financial Services Forum hosted by Archway Investment Fund student managers. The annual meeting of the Advisory Board is normally held on the same day as this event.
- Early May—Spring Semester Report: Student managers report on first quarter performance.
- Early December—Fall Semester Report: Student managers report on first 3 quarters performance.

While it is understood that most Advisory Board members will not be able to attend all three of the meetings listed above, it is hoped that each member will be able to attend at least one event per year and participate in at least one of the roles/activities outlined in the previous section.

---

self-governance opportunities. As such, it requires clear succession planning and methods to identify and develop future leaders.

Typical roles and responsibilities are outlined in Exhibit A1.3. These roles apply to a generic investment organization or firm. As such, each role might be somewhat different in any particular organization or even non-existent in some. As indicated above, these roles should be consistent with the investment philosophy and process of the firm. For example, a firm with a top-down investment process that begins with an overall economic view would have significant human resources in the economist roles. In contrast, a firm that employs a bottom-up approach might not even have a Chief Economist. Likewise, a "quant" firm would have significant resources dedicated to technology. The list in Exhibit A1.3 is intended to be indicative of the

Exhibit A1.3 Role and responsibilities in an investment organization

Role	Responsibility
Overall Firm	
Chief Executive Officer President	Overall strategy and operations
Investment Functions	
Chief Investment Officer	Overall investment strategy, decisions, and implementation
Portfolio Manager	Specific portfolio strategy and decisions
Chief Economist	Macroeconomic analysis
Economist	
Director of Research	Research on specific sectors, firms, or aspects of the economy
Research Analyst	
Sector Analyst	
Quantitative Analyst	
Research Support Analyst	
Client Portfolio Manager	Investment professional resource for clients
Chief Risk Officer	Analysis of portfolio performance and risks
Director of Portfolio Analytics	
Portfolio Analyst	
Head Trader Trade Clerk	Execution of trades
Operations	
Chief Operating Officer	Overall firm operations
Director of Human Resources	Hiring and staffing
Business Analyst	Firm operating planning and processes
Operations Analyst	
Client Operations Specialist	Client reporting and operations resource
Client Reporting Specialist	
Chief Technology Officer	Technology and information systems
Technology Analyst	
General Counsel	Overall legal
Chief Compliance Officer	Compliance with laws, regulations, and firm and client policies
Compliance Officers	
Finance and Accounting	
Chief Financial Officer	Budgeting, financial management, and reporting
Corporate Accountant	
Portfolio Accountant	Portfolio accounting and reporting
Marketing, Sales and Client Service	
Director of Marketing	External communications and public relations
Director of Product Development	Development of products and services
Director of Sales and Distribution	Sales to new and existing clients
Director of Client Service	Client service
Client Relations Manager	
Client Service Specialist	

industry, but might apply exactly to a student-managed investment fund. As such, we discuss below the relevance of each role to a student-managed investment fund. For example, many investment funds have significant resources in the organization dedicated to distribution (i.e., sales) and client service. Indeed, without clients, there is no portfolio to manage! Therefore, the client-facing roles are extremely important and many investment firms find it valuable to have very knowledgeable investment professionals in those roles. For a student-managed investment fund, it would be tempting to simply dismiss that functional area. However, as most student-managed investment funds do manage money for their colleges' or universities' endowment funds, it is often desirable to consider the fact that these funds do have clients and therefore should not neglect client service. Furthermore, the marketing role can help fulfill the objective of helping create opportunities for graduates of the fund by managing the organization's external image and public relations.

As illustrated in the Wright Fund's Overview of Structure in Exhibit A1.4, the fund at Rice University follows the hierarchical structure with clearly assigned responsibilities and expectations for each role. The officers represent the top of the pyramid, with the base of the pyramid composed of analyst groups. Consistent with the hierarchical structure, each analyst group has senior and junior analysts, conveying a clear sense of responsibility and succession. An important aspect of the organizational structure for the University of Tulsa Student.

Investment Fund, shown in Exhibit A1.5, is the inclusion of non-investment functions within the hierarchical structure. Indeed, critical elements of any effective investment organization are functions that support both the investment decisions and the administrative operation of the organization (Yerkes, 2018). These functions include accounting, human resources (i.e., personnel or membership), operations (e.g., technology and information systems), marketing and external communications (e.g., public relations), and macroeconomic analysis, among others.

These functions also provide an opportunity for students (e.g., from majors other than finance) who are not necessarily interested in investment decisions to earn valuable experience in a real business setting. These students can make significant contributions to the fund's success through their roles in managing other aspects of the organization.

A flatter organizational structure usually has decision-making authority shared or spread out across individuals or even teams. The decisions for purchases or sales in the portfolio might be allocated to a specific asset class or sector team, or be decided upon by a group vote. For example, the organizational structure of the Saluki Student Investment Fund (SSIF) at Southern Illinois University Carbondale is relatively flat, as shown in Exhibit A1.6. The SSIF's flat structure has sector teams sharing responsibility and authority for making buy and sell decisions. According to the SSIF investment process, each sector team has the authority to buy or sell any stock within its assigned sector, subject to the other provisions of the investment process. Because there are usually only a handful of students on each sector team, each

Exhibit A1.4 Overview of Structure of the Wright Fund (Rice University)

The Wright Fund curriculum is designed for students with a sincere interest in the markets who hope to pursue a career in securities research or investment management. The Fund is a two-semester commitment, with half of the approximately 25 enrolled students rolling off each semester to provide for continuity of the Fund. In the first semester, students perform intensive research and analysis of individual stocks, making transaction recommendations for the entire Fund's consideration. First semester students are called "junior analysts." Second semester Fund members serve as "senior analysts" and are effectively portfolio managers responsible for the allocation, strategy, and risk-return management of one or two equity sectors. Three of the second semester students serve as elected officers to manage the fund under the guidance of the Faculty Director.

Officers
The three elected officers of the Wright Fund and their primary responsibilities are listed below.

- Chief Investment Officer:
  - Manages and tracks the performance and risks of the Fund, including trade review and approval
  - Provides the Fund with weekly updates and two formal presentations
  - Prepares and delivers the mid-term board report and end-of-semester board presentation.
- Chief Operating Officer:
  - Designs and administers the course including syllabus preparation and agenda
  - Administers the application/interview and officer election processes
  - Oversees marketing needs and arranges guest speakers.
- Chief Economist:
  - Tracks economic trends and their impact on the Fund
  - Provides the Fund with weekly updates and two formal presentations
  - Makes allocation and trading decisions for the Fixed Income sector.

All officers are expected to keep up on the financial markets, to read all research reports written by other students, and to be involved in the application/interview process.

Analyst groups
Non-officer students are divided into Analyst Groups ("AGs"), consisting of one or two Senior Analysts and one or two Junior Analysts, each of which focuses on one or two of the S&P industry sectors:

- Consumer Discretionary
- Financials
- Consumer Staples
- Healthcare
- IT/Telecom
- Energy/Utilities
- Industrials/Materials

The AG is responsible for tracking their assigned sectors and managing Fund holdings within those sectors as a portfolio. The AGs choose sector strategies, goals, risk/return parameters, and performance monitoring techniques, as well as conduct in-depth stock analysis resulting in buy, sell, or hold recommendations.

Exhibit A1.5 Organizational Chart for the Student Investment Fund (University of Tulsa)

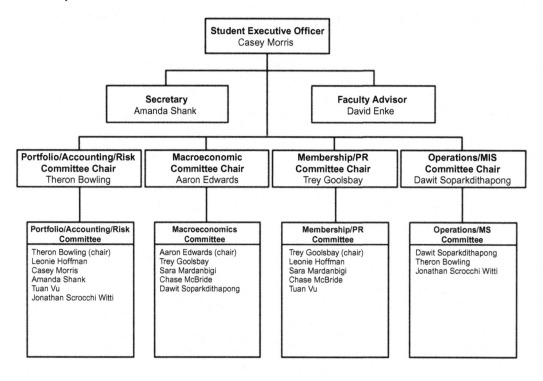

Exhibit A1.6 Organizational Chart for the Saluki Student Investment Fund (Southern Illinois University)

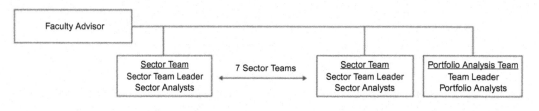

individual has a significant voice in choosing the portfolio investments without any single person having significantly more than another. In this way the resulting performance of the portfolio is truly shared across members. In addition, other functions of the organization, such as writing annual reports, are shared among the sector teams in this flat structure. As can be seen, even in this flatter organizational structure, some hierarchy exists in having team leaders. The role of the team leader exists to provide guidance and direction to each team from an experienced SSIF member, without implying seniority or increased authority. In this way, the structure facilitates continuity and succession without imposing a hierarchical structure.

The flat organizational structure is rarer in actual investment firms for various reasons including the benefits of having a single person with whom "the buck stops." However, given that the student-managed investment fund often has the luxury of focusing more exclusively on investment decisions this type of structure can work. A cost can arise in a flatter organizational structure in that efforts might be duplicated as the structure does not readily facilitate specialization. However, it also could have benefits in having members gain experience in accomplishing a broad spectrum of fund and organization activities.

The organizational structure must be rationalized to most effectively execute and implement the organization's investment process. Certain investment processes might give rise to a hierarchical structure, while others might suggest a flatter organization. An investment process that calls for very specialized skills might benefit more from a hierarchical structure than one that requires analysis across a large number of eligible securities. In this sense, it is convenient to think of the organizational structure as the shoe and the investment process as the foot. Putting the left shoe on the right foot might keep the foot dry but it will be an awkward fit at best. Over time, the wearing of the wrong shoe will adversely impact the foot and cause it to suffer. Therefore the design of an organization's structure should start with a list of responsibilities that result from the investment process. These responsibilities should motivate specific roles which help build a resulting organization chart. To conceive an organizational structure and then try to fit it on to an investment process risks orphaning or omitting some necessary functions and responsibilities. In summary, the investment philosophy and process should motivate the organizational structure, and not vice versa.

Academic structure

Student-managed investment fund as a for-credit course or a volunteer student organization

A key consideration at many universities is whether to offer the student-managed investment fund as a stand alone for credit course, as a component of another for credit course or as a volunteer student organization. Under any of these other considerations are include whether to allow participation by permission (or selection/application) or whether to have open (unrestrictive) participation. This section discusses the pros and cons of such considerations in the context of the benefits and challenges they create in an investment organization. As indicated elsewhere, this book takes the perspective of a student-managed investment fund having a goal to carry out its duties to the same standards of a professional investment management firm. Student-managed investment funds face specific organizational challenges that investment firms do not. These challenges are discussed below in the context of the both the organizational structure and the course credit/noncredit issue. Exhibit A1.7, "Challenges and Benefits of a Student-Managed Investment Fund at a Small Liberal Arts College" discusses how course credit issues were considered and dealt with at Austin College as they integrated a student-managed investment fund into the curriculum.

There are two key benefits of having the student-managed investment fund integrated into the curriculum, in general, and a portfolio management course, in particular. The most obvious benefit arises from the practical application of the course material to the management of the fund. This enhances the overall business education of the student by making the course material more tangible, more relevant and likely more interesting than it might otherwise be. As such, this first benefit accrues primarily to the students enrolled in the course in comparison to a similar course offering that does not have such a practical component.

Exhibit A1.7 The Challenges and Benefits of a Student-Managed Investment Fund at a Small Liberal Arts College

Steve Ramsey and Jerry Johnson
Austin College
Founded in 1849, Austin College, located about 60 miles north of Dallas, Texas, provides a fairly traditional undergraduate liberal arts education for about 1400 residential students. The college does not have a business school but does have a seven-member department of Economics and Business Administration, which consistently graduates one of the largest numbers of majors on campus.

While a student-managed investment fund (SMIF), using a substantial amount of "real money," is somewhat common in business schools, it is rare in a liberal arts college. We detail below our experiences incorporating such a fund into our curriculum. We try to identify the benefits to the students and to the school as well as some of the ongoing challenges we face. Teams of undergraduate students, in concert with faculty and alumni advisors, have been managing a fund that began with $1 million in fall 2007. The potential benefits from this gift included not only introducing a group of undergraduate students to portfolio management using real money, but also creating additional scholarships with our investment gains. The timing for starting a new fund probably could not have been much worse. However, in addition to learning a great deal about investing, our student portfolio managers have outperformed the market.

Curriculum considerations
Since this gift was not the result of a proposal that we had submitted, we had to start from scratch immediately upon being informed of the gift to design a program to incorporate a student-managed investment fund into our curriculum. Prior to receiving this funding, we had

only two finance courses in the curriculum — a junior-level managerial finance course and a senior-level international finance course. We decided that we needed to add a junior-level capital markets course to our spring 2007 course offerings so that by fall 2007 we would have a critical mass of sufficiently knowledgeable students available to manage the fund. One of our concerns was that with our small size we might have difficulty maintaining enough students in the pipeline to participate in the fund's management. The initial prerequisite courses for students who wanted to be fund managers included financial accounting, managerial finance, and the capital markets course. We launched an SMIF program that effectively limited involvement to seniors.

Setting up the fund

We decided to set up the fund as a course and give students ½ course credit per semester initially for successful participation in the fund's management with the expectation that students would be involved for a full year, both fall and spring semesters. The faculty member responsible for running the fund was given ½ FTE teaching credit per semester as well.

The SMIF course

With the guidelines, the bylaws, and the account set up, the focus shifted to the structure and operation of the course. We decided to make each student responsible for only one sector of the S&P 500. The intent was to simplify the process and make the students' experience resemble more closely the specialized responsibilities of true money managers.

The initial design of the course was to meet weekly at the beginning of the fall semester for 4 weeks to get the new students oriented to the structure of the class, the investment guidelines, and the expectations with regard to their research, presentations, and recommendations. Subsequent to that, we would meet every 2 weeks, sometimes more often, if needed.

Challenges

Many of our challenges are the result of our small size and liberal arts mission. Our biggest concern at the present time is having enough qualified students involved in the course and the management of the fund to make the individual student workload manageable, as well as having a course that serves a reasonable number of students. To address our desire to have more continuity and attract more students earlier, we recently restructured the prerequisites to make it easier for juniors to get involved in the fund. During their junior year, students can enroll in the SMIF course while they are completing the prerequisite courses. As juniors, they act primarily as researchers and receive ¼ credit per semester for their involvement as researchers for a maximum of two semesters, or a total of ½ credit. The following year they can become full-fledged managers. This adjustment appears to be getting more students involved in the fund for two full years, which gives the fund more continuity.

Given the workload and the time commitment involved, both the students and faculty thought that being a fund manager was worth more than the ½ credit per semester, we had originally decided to give. The problem was that if we gave students more credit, the SMIF could comprise an unacceptably high percentage of the total major credits required for graduation. As a liberal arts institution encouraging breadth of education, we have to be careful not to give too much credit for involvement in the SMIF. With our recent revision to the curriculum, increasing fund manager credit to ¾, and adding the ¼ credit researcher category, a student who serves two semesters as a researcher and two semesters as a fund manager can receive a total of 2.0 credits toward the major, which requires 8–9 total credits for graduation.

The second key benefit of having students participate in a student-managed investment fund through a formal course accrues primarily to the fund client vis-vis accountability and reward mechanisms. Specifically, the for-credit course structure usually requires students earn a grade in the course. The course grade can be used by the course instructor as a form of currency with which to compensate students who participate in the management of the portfolio. It might seem controversial to think of course grades as currency. However, the point is that a grade provides an incentive mechanism that allows the interest of the student to be aligned with that of the fund's client. In real investment firms, monetary compensation is used to provide incentives to employees to do a good job on behalf of the investment firm and its clients. If an employee is not meeting the requirements of the job, the employee might not be paid a substantial bonus, or might even be fired, causing the employee to forgo future compensation. Likewise, an employee can earn a nice bonus, raise, or promotion by performing well in a job. If the student is not meeting the requirements of a job or role in the operation and management of the student-managed investment fund, then the grade can reflect this performance, with the harshest penalty being a failure to get credit for the course. Likewise, a student making an outstanding effort and a significant contribution to the management of the fund can earn a high grade in recognition of such performance. It should be noted this notion of a course grade is consistent with the traditional notion of a course grade that reflects achievement in completing course requirements and mastery of course content, assuming that course content and requirements are relevant to the management of the portfolio. In summary, the for-credit course model of a student-managed investment fund recognizes the significant time commitment required by students and can serve to make up for the lack of compensation and provide an additional mechanism for aligning the incentives of the student fund managers with the interests of the fund beneficiaries. These aspects highlight the important issues with respect to a student-managed investment fund in putting the client's interest first. Other goals, such as the education of student-managed investment fund members, can be mutually compatible with the primary goal being that of serving the needs of the client.

The most common forms of for-credit student-managed investment funds are one-semester or two-semester courses. Examples of such structures are shown in Exhibit A1.8. Other forms include "labs" or practicum credit for participating in the fund outside of a traditional course structure, though still with integration into the curriculum and multiyear programs which can provide continuity otherwise lacking in the one- or two-semester form. Fund participation may be restricted to certain majors or require pre-requisite courses to ensure some baseline level of investment knowledge.

Student-managed investment funds organized outside a formal for-credit course structure face a challenge in overcoming the potential cost of incentive alignment, which arises as it does in almost any volunteer organization. Specifically, an individual is beholden to a volunteer organization only by the individual member's own will. If the individual loses the will to actively participate, there is no direct cost to the individual. For student-managed investment funds, this can be especially important around certain times of the semester, such as exam times

Exhibit A1.8 Course examples

Archway Investment Fund (Bryant College)

The Archway Investment Fund experience consists of a two course sequence with a securities analysis course in the first semester and a portfolio management course in the second semester. The progression of experiences that students are exposed to in these courses is intended to represent a mini "career path." Although the courses blend theoretical coverage of key topics with practical experience, heavy emphasis is placed on learning through experience. One objective of the course design is to replicate important elements of the look and feel of actually working in the industry.

Cayuga Fund (Cornell University)

Student Portfolio Managers are students officially enrolled in the Applied Portfolio Management class. Most student managers work in sector teams following an assigned economic sector. Others may be assigned to a quantitative research group or to investor relations/marketing or the student trader role. They are responsible for conducting thorough research of investment vehicles. They prepare and present proposed investment ideas to the class as a whole and positions are taken only after a 2/3 majority is achieved in a formal class vote. Student course grades are based on their formal reports, presentations, class participation, as well as portfolio performance relative to the sector benchmark.

Portfolio Practicum (Creighton University)

Portfolio Practicum is a two-semester "hands-on" undergraduate course in the College of Business at Creighton University. The class oversees a student-managed investment fund with approximately $2.7 million in equity investments for the Creighton University Endowment Fund. Eligible students apply for the class during the Spring semester of their Junior year. Applicants enter an interview process to gain acceptance to the class for the following academic year. The Fall semester of the class focuses on equity research and valuation techniques. Students also will revalue the existing stocks in the portfolio. In the Spring semester, students learn about the concepts central to portfolio construction and portfolio management. Students also present investments they believe would be good additions to the portfolio.

(e.g., final exams), social occasions (e.g., Homecoming or fraternity/sorority rush), or other extra-curricular activities (e.g., athletic tournaments). Student-managed investment fund members might find demands on their time from activities during these times that bring penalties (e.g., through lower grades or reduced social status) if they choose to divert attention away from those activities. This presents a challenge to the organization either to find means to mitigate these issues, to compensate members with other benefits that outweigh the costs associated with diverting time to the student-managed investment fund, and/or to attract and retain members for whom these issues are minor. The volunteer student investment club structure is best suited when there are no endowment sponsored funds available and often can be a precursor to having a more formal student managed fund. Ease of raising initial funds and avoiding stringent endowment investment guidelines and the fact students may be managing their own money are several advantages of the volunteer structure (Cox and Goff, 1996; Seiler and Seiler, 2000; Grinder, Cooper and Britt, 1999). Frequently for credit courses consist of juniors, seniors or graduate students while student investment clubs may be open to a broader audience including freshmen and sophomore and thus provide a significant recruiting opportunity for the finance program by exposing students to the finance discipline at an earlier point in their academic career (Vihtelic, 1996).

One of the primary forms of compensation in any student-managed investment fund is the wealth of knowledge and experience that the student gains from participating in the fund. This single factor helps mitigate much of the incentive alignment problem because a student who fails to devote the appropriate time and effort toward fund activities reaps little of the primary reward of such activities. Like anything else in life, the benefits that are realized from participating in a student-managed investment fund are proportional to the effort and energy put into it.

As discussed previously, consistency of approach can be maintained in either a for-credit or volunteer format by maintaining the fund's identity through its investment philosophy or policies and procedures manual. Block and French (1991) provide a comprehensive list of best practices for a policies and procedures manual including organizational structure. The volunteer structure can also have additional benefits compared to a for-credit course structure. In particular, because a volunteer structure is extracurricular, it does not count against (or toward) credit for other courses. In this way, it does not limit the participation of members to a specific time period, such as one or two semesters. Rather, the volunteer structure accommodates students who might participate in the fund for only one semester or even for the entirety of their college careers. Clearly, a first-year college student might have much more to learn about investing than the more seasoned student who has taken courses in finance and investing. However, as in any organization, there are myriad ways to contribute to both the investment function and the operation of the organization without having specific finance knowledge or training. For example, first year students can contribute by preparing reports, auditing statements and account positions, reviewing trades for compliance with policies, managing proxy voting procedures, maintaining records and preparing external communications. These functions simply require a bit of training of and diligence by the member. While duties such as these do not necessarily require in-depth finance knowledge, they are no less important to the operation of a fund. Moreover, these types of functions help initiate new members and provide them with training and education that can pay significant dividends for the fund as these members matriculate through the program and acquire more subject-matter knowledge. Thus, an open structure can help facilitate continuity in the fund over time and establish a depth and capacity in the organization.

Challenges to a student-managed investment fund

Regardless of a student-managed investment fund being organized as part of the curriculum in a for-credit course or as a volunteer organization, there are challenges student-managed investment funds face by virtue of having students as primary fund managers. Among others, one challenge is the fact students typically follow an academic calendar and successful students continuously graduate and leave the fund. Effectively a SMIF may experience 100% personnel turnover from semester-to-semester or year-to-year. It is tempting to suggest this challenge is unique to student-managed investment funds—implying investment firms do not face this challenge. However, this simply is not the case. All investment firms must make contingency plans for business disruptions and must deal with personnel turnover. While these challenging events might not be quite as numerous or regular in an investment firm compared to a student-managed investment fund, they are no less important. Indeed, these events can often have serious consequences for the investment firm, especially because, unlike in student-managed investment funds, these disruptions are often unscheduled and unexpected.

Personnel recruiting and turnover

A key determinant of the value of any organization is the people who comprise the organization. This is especially true of investment organizations. While the investment philosophy and process provide a basis for investment judgments, key decisions relating to the output of the organization are directly influenced by the organization's personnel. At an investment organization it is important to attract and retain motivated, knowledgeable and capable people. In a student-managed investment fund with equal emphasis on learning and investment performance, the key is to attract motivated individuals who will approach the responsibility with the diligence that money management deserves. Because (good) students cannot be "retained" indefinitely, the student-managed investment fund must also find ways to manage personnel turnover. We begin by discussing the selection of new members and then turn to considerations that arise due to turnover or matriculation and graduation of student members.

Whether a student-managed investment fund is offered in a for-credit course format or as a volunteer organization, the membership is either "open" to anyone who chooses to sign up or "selective" in restricting access only to those who meet certain criteria. As with the other organizational issues that are discussed throughout this chapter, there are costs and benefits to either approach. The selective organizational structure typically requires a specific course background (i.e., prerequisite courses), grade point average or status (e.g., seniors only) to be eligible. This is especially true in the for-credit course that is part of a specific curriculum. In addition, many student-managed investment funds carefully screen prospective members through an application process that often includes interviews, faculty recommendations and final selection by the faculty advisor (Cooley and Hubbard, 2012). Exhibit A1.9 shows examples of the selection process at several student-managed investment funds and Exhibit A1.10 shows example applications. This structure resembles a real investment firm that would typically try to choose the "best of the best" to hire. This structure can serve to ration the opportunity in a situation in which there is significantly more interest in participating than availability of "seats" in the organization. In turn, this helps to motivate both current members and prospective members. Current members might consider participation to be an honor,

Exhibit A1.9 Interview and selection process

Interview Process (Rice University)

Each semester, first-year students are invited to apply and interview for 12 to 14 positions. The application/interview process occurs in two stages. In the first stage, candidates must submit an application, resume, and stock analysis. Qualified applicants are then invited to interview with Fund Officers and the Faculty Director. Interviews consist of a presentation/pitch of the stock analysis completed in the first stage and a character/fit component. Strong preference is given to students pursuing careers in Investments fields.

Student Selection Process (Creighton University)

The selection of the students for the Portfolio Practicum begins in their junior academic year. Admission into the two-semester sequence is highly competitive. On average, 40 students apply for 16 positions. The application process includes a recommendation from a business professor, submission of a resume, a personal interview with the previous class participants and faculty members, and selection by a faculty committee. The Portfolio Practicum application requires that the prospective student get an application form (downloadable from the Portfolio Practicum section of Creighton University's website). The application form requires a signature from a College of Business professor. The student must submit a current resume. The student must also write a one-page letter of interest describing why s/he wants to be in the class. This size allows for individual consultation and has been very functional for forming groups of four members per team.

The Portfolio Practicum applicants must sign up and attend a personal interview during the selection process. Interview teams include a Finance professor and two or more members of the current portfolio class. Interviews are scheduled for 20 min each. Interviews are conducted on two consecutive evenings, Sunday and Monday, with two groups interviewing simultaneously for three to 4 h each. Students and professors rotate asking the questions and each interviewer makes an individual evaluation of the applicant.
The selection process then reviews the evaluations of each applicant in a Portfolio Practicum class. The process typically identifies eight applicants who are very good applicants. The remaining four slots are then determined from a vote of the finance faculty with the top vote getters being selected.

In the class selection process we look to see the proportion of males and females. For example, 1 year the Portfolio Practicum only had one female member. That year, only one female student applied for the class. The next year we advertised the fact that female applicants for the class had a 100% acceptance rate and the number of female applicants has increased ever since that year. International students offer diversity of opinion and perspective to the class, so it is also considered. Varsity athletes are another category of students who add diversity to the class. We consider the majors of the students as well. In the course of the life of the Portfolio Practicum it has evolved from a pure finance class into a financial accounting course, to a College offering for all majors, to a heavily focused CFA-type class primarily for accounting students, to an accounting and finance focused class for exceptional majors from all areas.

Once the students for the class have been selected notifications go to all the applicants regarding whether they were selected for the class or not. The selected students are invited to attend classes with the graduating class. They listen to the Portfolio Practicum students present their financial analysis reports and their buy, sell, or hold recommendations. The selected students choose the sectors they want to follow during the next academic year. They are assigned stocks from our current holdings to track during the summer. They are given a summer reading list. In their Fin 325 Investment Analysis class they do a stock valuation report that is designed to get them experience with the top-down approach to fundamental analysis. The students typically gravitate to the sector they studied in that class.

Selection Process (Bryant College)

Students apply to be admitted to the first course in very much the same way that they would apply for a job. To start the process students are required to send in a resume and a cover letter by sometime around the middle of the semester preceding the one in which they wish to begin the first course. Interviews are held during the following week, and are conducted by an interviewing panel consisting of one faculty member and two or three students from the current classes. During the interview an attempt is made to gauge the candidate's level of focus, discipline, and level of passion for investment management. As one might expect, these traits tend to be highly correlated with grade point average, but although a simple GPA cutoff would be more efficient in many respects, and experience has shown that it would result in almost the same admitted group, we have resisted moving in that direction. There are several reasons for this choice. First, the interviews are good practice for the candidates and they send a very clear signal that it is time for them to have a polished resume and to be able to clearly articulate their career aspirations and their strategy for achieving them. Since many candidates are juniors when they apply for the first course, a little bit of a push in this direction sometimes helps to bring priorities into focus. Second, doing the interview provides the candidate with information about the standard of professionalism expected of students involved in the Fund-related courses. Third, the interviews provide useful information on candidate personalities and interests, which is helpful when putting together teams. Fourth, and finally, interviewing has often proven to be a transformative experience for students serving on the interviewing panel. They regularly report that experiencing the monotony and mental exhaustion that goes with interviewing demystifies the process for them and makes them much less apprehensive about their own job interviews, which are often taking place at around the same time. They also gain a much better understanding of the importance of standing out in the interviewer's memory, and this seems to cause them to take a much more serious approach to the process of preparing for interviews.

Fund Membership (University of Tulsa)

1.2 New Members—Students who wish to become members of TUSIF are required to fill out an application, which shall be reviewed by the Membership Committee. Applicants who are approved by the Membership Committee shall then be interviewed by that committee during a Membership meeting which shall be held prior to the enrollment period for the following semester. Following each applicant's interview, the Members shall vote Yea, Nay, or Abstention. The Membership Committee shall then present every applicant before the class along with their recommendation. The class will then vote on the acceptance of the individuals. A vote of 2/3 of the class must be received for an applicant to become a new member of the TUSIF.

1.2A In the event that there are more applicants than Member positions available, the assignments will be made in the following manner: The Members of the Membership Committee will individually rank the Applicants in ascending numerical order with the number "1" being the most preferable choice. The rankings for each individual will then be tallied by the Student Executive Officer. The lowest total scores will receive first assignment. In the event that Applicants are still tied in rank, a vote between the Student Executive Officer, the Membership Chair, and the Faculty Advisor shall determine the final selection.

Exhibit A1.10 Membership Applications

Part A: MBA Portfolio Practicum Class Application—University of Toledo

Application for Student Managed Investment Fund

The University of Toledo
Student Managed Investment Fund
PLEASE TYPE OR PRINT CLEARLY *(All information is completely confidential.)*

Full Name:_____

Local Address:_____

_____

Local Phone:_____ E-Mail:_____

Major:_____ Minor:_____

Anticipated Graduation Date:_____

List your total credit hours in the following areas of study (including current semester):

Finance	
Accounting	
Economics	
Computer Information Systems	

List expected class schedule for next semester:

CLASS	CREDITS

Current GPA at UT:_____ Current GPA in Major:_____

Please answer the following questions on a separate piece of paper. Please limit your answer to no more than 100 words for each questions.

1. Why do you to be a member of the Fund?
2. What abilities and skills can you contribute to the succes of the Fund?
3. Attach a current resume.
4. Attach an unofficial copy of your undergraduate transcript. This can be obtained by logging onto the *myUT* web portal and clicking on the student self-service tab.
5. If you desire (not necessary), attach a faculty recommendation.

Your signature:_____ Date:_____

Part B: Student Investment Fund Membership Application—University of Tulsa

SIF Student Investment Fund
University of Tulsa

Student Investment Fund Membership Application

Name:_____ GPA:_____
E-mail:_____ Phone:_____
Majors(s)/Minor(s): _____
Expected Graduation Date: _____ Advisor: _____

Term for enrollment: □Spring   □Fall 2010

Classification: □Freshman   □Sophomore
                □Junior   □Senior
                □Graduate   □Other:_____

Finance Courses Completed:
(Undergrad): □Personal Investing   □FOB Finances/Finance 3003
              □Institution and Markets I   □Institututions and Markets II
              □Invest/Portfolio Mgt I   □Invest/Portfolio Mgt II
                (Required)
              □Portfolio Analysis   □Adv Portfolio Mgt.
              □Plan Cntrl/Capital Exp   □Fin Analysis/Working Cap Mgmt
              □Financial Statement Analysis □Int'l Business Finance
              □Other:_____
(Graduate):   □Finance Concepts   □Financial Admin 7003
                                             (Required for Non-Finance Majors
                                             in Undergraduate Students)
              □Portfolio Mgt   □Advanced Portfolio Mgt I
              □Investment Analysis & Mgt   □Behavior Fin Mkts
              □Long-Term Financial   □Other:_____
              □Decisions

On which committees would you be interested in serving (Check all that apply)?:
Portfolio   MIS   Accounting   Economics
Membership   Capitations   Public relations

Please list any offices you've held, awards you've received, or activities in which you
are involved: _____
_____
_____

Please describe any related work or internship experience you've had:_____
_____
_____
_____

Please explain what attributes you will bring to the Fund: _____
_____
_____

Thank you for taking the time to fill out this application. Please return to the Finance Dept.
Office Use only

Date Received: _____
SIF initials:_____

Part C: MBA Portfolio Practicum Class Application—University of Toledo
March 2009
Dear MBA students:

In This Job Market You Need an Edge
How about taking a professional quality analyst report on a company like Apple to your job interview? It's helped students over the years differentiate themselves from the pack. It can help you too. Whether you plan a career with an investment firm or hedge fund or just plan to take your MBA and get rich, hands-on experience in investments will be invaluable to your future success in managing someone else's or your own investments. In order to gain this knowledge, I encourage you to apply for the Portfolio Practicum class next year, FINA 6230/6231.

Get Experience Running a Live-Multi-million-Dollar Portfolio
I teach the MBA Practicum class and we manage a multi-million-dollar live portfolio that is part of the SMU endowment. We focus entirely on picking good stocks. The class functions like an institutional investment firm. You will be a stock analyst and you will come to the class with recommendations regarding the stocks you cover. You will learn techniques that I have used successfully at three of the largest money managers in the world: The Northern Trust, State Street Global Advisors, and Putnam Investments.

This Class Is Very Popular and Seats Are Limited
Please complete the attached information highlighting your grades, interests, and work history so you can make the best case for your participation. Please include information on your participation in the Buyside Club, if applicable.

I look forward to reviewing your application.

Director of the ENCAP & LCM Group Alternative Asset Management Center Cox School of Business.

MBA Portfolio Practicum Application
Fall 2009 FINA 6230/Spring 2010 FINA 6231
Name/SMU ID#:_____.
Mailing Address:_____.
E-Mail:_____ Tel:_____.

Please list courses taken in the areas of Economics, Finance, Investments, Valuation, and Financial Statement Analysis

Course #	Instructor	Grade	Hours/semester taken

Overall Cox GPA
EXPECTED DATE OF GRADUATION:
MBA PROGRAM (circle one): Full-time Professional.
Please return this completed form and attach:

- Required: A copy of your current resume
- Required: A one-page (maximum) typed statement explaining why you wish to participate in the course. Please include your career aspirations and any relevant experience in investments
- Optional: A copy of your transcript
- Optional: Up to three letters of recommendation

Please note that you must take this class BOTH semesters. Return this information IN HARD COPY to my mailbox in Fincher.
Deadline: Monday, March 30, 2009, at 5:00 PM

thereby increasing their dedication to and effort in the student-managed investment fund. Likewise, prospective members might work harder to achieve the proper credentials in preparing for application to the student-managed investment fund. Potential costs to a selective organizational structure include the accessibility to the opportunity and direct and indirect costs of maintaining the application and selection process.

Most student-managed investment funds have a significant goal of enhancing financial and investment education through the practical, hands-on experience that comes with managing an actual portfolio. As such, an open membership policy has the potential to maximize the realization of this goal with the widest reach in bringing this educational opportunity to students. The open organization also can accommodate students from virtually any major, especially in a volunteer organization not offered as part of a specific curriculum. Students outside a business school can bring fresh perspectives and unique capabilities contributing to both the management of the portfolio and the value of the organization. For example, engineering majors might make insightful contributions to research into materials or industrial companies, while pre-med, biology, or biochemistry majors might have a valuable perspective for understanding certain aspects of biotech, pharmaceutical, or other healthcare companies. In such a setting, students can specialize based on their backgrounds (e.g., major subject matter) and learn to collaborate with fellow team members from diverse backgrounds. Like the selective organizational structure, the open organizational structure has costs that might mitigate some of these benefits. Like any organization, it is likely that the bulk of the work will be concentrated on the most dedicated members. However, this may be more equitable than it might appear on the surface, as those who do the most work and achieve the most in such an organization also reap the largest rewards in terms of acquiring knowledge and experience. As discussed above, the lack of direct incentives (e.g., grades) in an open, volunteer organization makes it difficult to engage some members and rely on their consistent efforts. If others are free to join or resign at any time, coordination costs might be imposed on the most diligent members of the group as turnover can create uncertainty as to who has responsibility for what. The other issue with an open structure is the potential lack of investment knowledge of students outside the business school. A chemistry major can understand pharma better than any finance major but may have almost no idea of how to research or value a stock. Any fund that utilizes nonfinance students must be especially diligent in creating a structure that takes advantage of the diverse and specialized knowledge while compensating for the lack of basic investment knowledge.

All organizations must deal with turnover in personnel. While it might seem turnover in a student-managed investment fund is more severe than in a typical investment firm, the issue might not be as clear as it seems. On the one hand, a student-managed investment fund will experience turnover due to matriculation or graduation of its members. In a for-credit course structure, the entire "staff" of the fund might turn over every semester or every academic year. Given this seemingly extreme turnover and lack of consistency in staffing, few investors would be comfortable investing with a firm that had such extreme turnover. On the other hand, the predictability and regularity of the turnover in a student-managed investment fund makes its impact on the fund potentially far less disruptive than the turnover of personnel in a real investment firm. Consider that a real investment firm experiences turnover of the following forms: (1) firm-initiated termination of an employee; (2) employee-initiated separation due to employment at another firm; (3) employee death; and (4) employee-initiated separation due to retirement. The turnover of personnel at a student-managed investment fund looks most like the last form of turnover at a real investment firm. As such, this form of turnover can be planned for and managed. Succession planning is an important element in any business and especially important for an investment management organization. The other forms of separation between firm and employee are no less important and, because the timing of such events usually is unanticipated, they are potentially more disruptive. As such, an investment organization must assume that such turnover will occur and plan accordingly.

As discussed early on in a previous chapter, the most important inoculations against disruption from personnel turnover are a clear and well-documented investment philosophy and investment process statements (Block and French, 1991). Since the value of an investment organization is the service it provides in a consistent and ongoing manner, the philosophy and process are all that remain when the firm experiences a change in personnel. For firms lacking a specific investment approach as expressed in the investment philosophy and process, personnel turnover can leave the organization with nothing—or, at least, nothing familiar. Of course, the survival of the investment organization does not rest alone on the investment philosophy and process. Other aspects of how the organization functions also must be memorialized in policies and procedures to help the organization continue to operate in a consistent manner through time. These policies and procedures should cover all aspects of the organizational structure, including roles and responsibilities and methods of operation. Furthermore, care should be taken to maintain organization-related documents and work products in the possession of the organization and not of individuals who scatter far and wide after graduation. A shared file directory, central library or use of learning management system such as Blackboard can serve as a repository for documents including analyst reports from year-to-year and maintain a history that simulates the knowledge retained in a typical investment firm.

Academic calendar

At most U.S. colleges and universities, classes regularly meet during the academic year, consisting of fall and spring semesters or their academic quarter counterparts, starting around the end of August and lasting until around the beginning of May. While some institutions have summer classes, the number of students on campus, if any, is typically a fraction of the number attending during the academic year. Whether the student-managed investment fund is a voluntary organization or a for-credit course, this presents a challenge for the fund during semester breaks, such as the holiday between fall and spring semesters, and the lengthier summer break. Obviously, markets do not close and investment decisions are no less important during these times. The potential exists for significant information to come out about specific portfolio holdings, possibly posing a risk of a loss to the portfolio. Similarly, the risk of opportunity costs arises if information comes out that would have triggered a purchase of a security in the portfolio. These risks or losses could be in both absolute and relative (e.g., to a benchmark) terms. Generally, the more concentrated a portfolio, the larger the risk.

Plans must be made to manage the portfolio during these breaks in the academic calendar. As always, the way in which investment decisions are handled during these breaks should be consistent with the organization's investment philosophy and process. For a fund with a very long horizon and little turnover, the breaks are unlikely to require significant action. However, most funds would typically require at least some monitoring during the breaks to assure compliance with portfolio constraints and policies, and to respond to significant news that might trigger a decision to rebalance the portfolio. For example, a fund might have a policy constraining individual security weights to a specific amount, such as 5% or 10% of the portfolio. The fund's duty is to enforce these policies regardless of whether classes are in session. Similarly, if a significant event affects one of the portfolio's current holdings, other actions might be necessary. For example, suppose that a fund has a policy not to hold firms implicated in wrongdoing by the U.S. Securities and Exchange Commission or other authority. If news emerges of such wrongdoing by a company held in the portfolio then action would be necessary in the fund.

Fortunately, these scenarios have feasible solutions that take many forms. The most expedient solution might be to craft a fund policy that provides for action to be taken at the next earliest date when classes are in session. In essence, this creates two sets of rules: one set for when classes are in session and one set for when classes are not in session. While this type of policy would not likely be acceptable to a professional investment management firm, it addresses the issue in a transparent manner and sets the expectations of all parties as to how the assets of the fund are managed. This type of policy has the benefit of handling decisions in a deliberate manner. Another common approach is to liquidate individual stock holdings during extended breaks and move to a passive investment instrument such as index mutual funds or ETFs. As shown in Exhibit A1.11, Butler University specifies policies to cover its 4-week winter break period and the 20-week summer break period. In the shorter break case, the solution is to set limit order prices to transact based on the student-managed investment fund members' analysis of the individual securities. A passive approach is taken during the longer summer break.

An alternative approach is to establish explicit procedures for communication among student-managed investment fund members and perhaps the fund advisor during breaks. Modern technological conveniences, such as Skype, Face Time, Google Hangout, and teleconferencing can be used to facilitate meetings with participants who are not able to meet in the same

---

Exhibit A1.11 Academic Holiday Policies (Butler University)

Periods of inactivity and transition

Since the SMIF will operate in the context of a structured course that follows the academic calendar, there will be periods of time during which little oversight would exist. Specifically, Winter (~4 weeks) and Summer (~20 weeks) breaks represent the longest duration of inactivity. Further, when semesters end/begin, there will be a transition from one student team to another.

A. WINTER BREAK

At the end of the Fall semester, the SMIF team will designate target selling prices (above and below the current price) for each security held. With these prices, the Faculty Advisor will institute good 'til canceled stop orders that will automatically transact in the even the trigger price is reached. Further, the Faculty Advisor will monitor the account for unexpected market events. At the beginning of the Spring semester, the stop orders will be withdrawn and the new management team will assume control of the portfolio.

B. SUMMER BREAK

Given the extended nature of the Summer break, SMIF holdings in individual company securities (and related derivatives) will be liquidated and invested in index funds that track the S&P 500. Exceptions may be made on a case-by-case basis with approval of the Faculty Advisor.

It is possible, as enrollment numbers increase, that sufficient interest may exist to offer a summer section of the SMIF course. If this occurs, transition from one academic period to the next will follow the rules designated under the Winter Break section.

---

physical location. In most cases, a simple exchange of e-mails might suffice to conduct the necessary business of the fund. Regardless of plans for communication, procedures require forethought and planning to assure that all participants understand their individual responsibilities and the logistics of how and with whom to communicate. In some cases a "skeleton crew" might be appropriate with certain responsibilities normally resting with a team being delegated to an individual for a limited time period.

Finally, it is also important to consider access to information. Many tools such as Bloomberg Professional or proprietary databases might have availability limited to a physical location on the college or university campus. As such, plans must be made to access similar information from remote locations. For example, if portfolio weights are typically monitored through an Excel Spreadsheet linked to Bloomberg the same spreadsheet should be reworked to access up-to-date prices from another source with holdings being manually updated or entered. Publicly available sources such as Yahoo! Finance, Google Finance and Morningstar offer useful tools for this purpose. Similarly, these services offer an array of business and company news that can be monitored from anywhere. As indicated above, the important aspect of this issue is to plan appropriately and have contingency plans in place.

Fund structure

We conclude the discussion of organizational issues with a discussion of fund structure, or the actual investment vehicle through which the portfolio will exist. In addition to building a rational organizational structure in which the student-managed investment fund operates, decisions must be made as to the structure or form of the investment portfolio itself. In general, any investment strategy can be delivered in various forms known as "vehicles." The investment profession offers its services in two general vehicles to investors: separate accounts and pooled funds. Separate accounts (sometimes called "separately managed accounts," or SMAs) are often offered to institutional clients or very wealthy individuals. The key distinguishing feature of a separate account is it has a single entity (individual or institution) as its beneficiary. Separate accounts are therefore usually a large enough dollar amount to justify their individual attention. Because there is a single beneficiary for each separate account the oversight of the account is the sole responsibility of the beneficiary. An investment manager would be given discretion to trade a separately managed account according to the manager's investment process but usually would not be given custody of the assets of the account.

In this arrangement the investment manager would direct sales and purchases of securities within the account but would not be able to withdraw or otherwise divert the funds for its own use. Instead, the assets are usually held in an account at a brokerage firm or custodial bank in the name of the owner or beneficiary of the account. This structure of the account helps to provide some protection to the client since the investment manager cannot commit fraud or theft of the account's assets, yet still facilitates the specific investment strategy of the manager. Having an arrangement where the student-managed investment fund only directs trades in an account but cannot otherwise access the assets for withdrawal is prudent risk management for the fund.

The management fee paid to the investment manager for a specific separate account is negotiated between the account holder and the investment manager and is typically set as a percentage of assets under management (AUM) in the account. Therefore, the investment management fee from a single investment manager might vary across separate accounts, usually being a decreasing function of the account's AUM. Brokerage and custodial fees are typically charged directly to the account.

Smaller accounts from either individuals or institutions are usually more efficiently offered through a pooled fund because they lack the scale to justify the cost of handling the accounts individually. A pooled fund is managed as a single account or fund by the investment manager, but the fund has multiple beneficiaries (i.e., shareholders) having a proportional claim on the assets, returns and costs of the fund. In some cases, various share classes of the same underlying portfolio might exist to differentiate fees or costs, while in institutional pooled funds, like separate accounts, a client's fees are typically charged based on the AUM of the specific client. Because pooled funds have multiple, perhaps even numerous, shareholder or beneficiaries,

funds other than those organized as unit investment trusts may have a board of trustees or board of directors. Boards have oversight responsibility on behalf of the fund's shareholders.
For example, mutual funds subject to the Investment Company Act of 1940 are required to have a board of directors who oversee the fund and make decisions on the fees paid to the fund's investment manager or advisor. The investment manager makes regular reports to both the fund's board and the fund's shareholders. The general types of investment vehicles are summarized in Exhibit A1.12.

Student-managed investment funds can take either of the two main forms of fund structure. The source of the money for the fund usually dictates the fund structure. If the student-managed investment fund receives its assets under management from the university's endowment fund, then a separate account is typically the optimal structure. In this case, the student-managed investment fund is "hired" in the same manner as the endowment fund's other investment managers. The endowment fund's board of trustees, perhaps via an investment committee, provides oversight of the fund. In some cases, additional oversight might be established through a fund-specific board of advisors. Similarly, if a single sponsor or benefactor establishes a fund for students to manage, then a separate account is similarly appropriate. Again, oversight could be provided by the fund sponsor and/or through an additional board of advisors.

Some student-managed investment funds utilize a pooled structure to facilitate the addition of new investors and the "cashing out" of others. Some funds even create a pooled fund organized as a hedge fund or a mutual fund. In these cases specific accommodations must be made for accounting to facilitate the issuance of new shares and redemption of old shares. Additionally, organizing documents would spell out the oversight of such a fund, usually with a

---

Exhibit A1.12 Investment vehicles

Separate accounts

- Separately managed accounts.

Pooled accounts

- Pooled or Collective Trusts (available only to qualified retirement plans, such as 401(k) or defined benefit pension plans, regulated by the Office of the U.S. Department of Treasury/Comptroller of the Currency, no board of directors, trust account at a custodian or trust bank).
- Mutual Funds (Regulated by the SEC under the Investment Company Act of 1940, board of directors, restrictions on short-selling or use of leverage).
- Hedge Funds (SEC oversight but less regulation, may use leverage or short-sales, open to qualified investors only).

board of trustees or board of directors to whom the student fund managers report on a regular basis. If the fund is organized under the Investment Company Act of 1940, then shares must be valued daily and policies regarding the pricing of the fund's underlying shares must be maintained. For most student-managed investment funds a mutual fund structure is beyond what is feasible or practical.

The roll of security trading rooms in business schools

Security trading rooms provide specialized hardware and software and are particularly useful resources for student managed investment funds. Yet, the environment and tools promote information and financial literacy and support data analysis and research efforts for business students from any discipline. The trading room is also often home base for student managed investment funds providing a dedicated space for students to conduct research, faculty advisors to hold classes and for the fund to hold meetings and presentations. Most financial research databases such as Morningstar, Bloomberg, FactSet and CapitalIQ are on a subscription basis and while some of these tools can be delivered over the internet, via site license or through library services, others such as Bloomberg are terminal based. The security trading room can be outfitted with the same specialized hardware and software found on trading floors of investment firms around the world offering students exposure and training opportunities on these platforms prior to entering the workforce. Some platforms such as Morningstar and Bloomberg have training modules where students can receive a certificate of completion. For example, students may receive a certificate of completion for the Bloomberg Markets Concept (BMC) course or for the Morningstar Direct Certification program. These programs are typically complimentary training courses for software subscribers.

The finance lab can also serve to be a showcase aspect of a business school facility by leveraging stock tickers, financial information displays and a multitude of computer terminals. This helps convey a high-tech, business and financially savvy environment to the external community including prospective students, employers and donors. The University Finance Lab web site sponsored by Rise Vision, Inc. is an excellent resource for the design elements for a trading room. Rise Vision, Inc. is one of the leading providers of stock ticker and financial display hardware and software technology for trading rooms.

Maximizing the use of a trading room/finance lab

In order to maximize the return on investment (ROI) of a trading room/finance lab it will be important to drive student traffic and usage. This can be accomplished when faculty require the usage of resources found in these labs for assignments and provide students with the appropriate introduction and training. Some software providers such as Bloomberg will come on sight and conduct training orientation sessions with SMIFs and classes. For example, one assignment for a principles of finance course is a company research project where students research a company of interest and analyze the company's financial statements, financial ratios, stock price history, competitors, capital structure, credit ratings, etc. and make a short class presentation. For more advanced courses students may conduct a discounted cash flow or market comparable valuation, analyze derivative or fixed income instruments, conduct a top-down economic, industry and company analysis, or conduct performance attribution analysis on an actual or simulated portfolio. In any case, the key is providing the appropriate orientation, training and assignments to motivate the usage of the lab.

Application of the CFA Institute code of ethics and standards of professional conduct to a student managed investment fund

The CFA Institute Code of Ethics and Standards of Professional Conduct (2014) is a set of best ethical practices designed to promote integrity and trust in financial markets and within the investment profession. While the Code and Standards *must* be followed by CFA and CIPM Charterholders, CFA and CIPM Candidates, and members of CFA Institute, they may be voluntarily adopted and followed by other organizations or individuals. These best practices have been translated into 20 languages and these translations are available for download via CFA Institute's web page. Exhibit A1.13 contains a reprint of the Code of Ethics and Standards of Professional Conduct from CFA Institute's web page. The Code focuses on integrity and overall ethical conduct while the Standards are more specific to the practice of investment management. For example, broad categories covered within the Standards include: Professionalism, Integrity of Capital Markets, Duties to Clients, Duties to Employers, Investment Analysis, Recommendations and Actions, Conflicts of Interest and Responsibilities as a CFA Institute Member or CFA Candidate. Contained within each of these broad categories are more specific items with application to the investment management profession such as how to handle material nonpublic information (i.e. insider information). CFA Institute's Code and Standards is an excellent example for Student Managed Investment Funds to voluntarily adopt and follow and also provides the faculty advisor with content perfectly suited for a lesson on ethics for the investment management profession. By adopting the Code and Standards, a SMIF is conveying to the external community an adherence to the highest standards of integrity and professional conduct. Furthermore, it serves to reinforce a culture of ethical conduct and integrity for all SMIF activities and operations. Adopting the Code and Standards also prepares students for what will be expected of them if they obtain employment with a firm who has adopted the Code and Standards or if they become a CFA or CIPM Charterholder or Candidate.

Exhibit A1.13 CFA Institute Code of Ethics and Standards of Professional Conduct

 **CFA Institute**

CODE OF ETHICS
AND STANDARDS OF
PROFESSIONAL CONDUCT

PREAMBLE

The CFA Institute Code of Ethics and Standards of Professional Conduct are fundamental to the values of CFA Institute and essential to achieving its mission to lead the investment profession globally by promoting the highest standards of ethics, education, and professional excellence for the ultimate benefit of society. High ethical standards are critical to maintaining the public's trust in financial markets and in the investment profession. Since their creation in the 1960s, the Code and Standards have promoted the integrity of CFA Institute members and served as a model for measuring the ethics of investment professionals globally, regardless of job function, cultural differences, or local laws and regulations. All CFA Institute members (including holders of the Chartered Financial Analyst® [CFA®] designation) and CFA candidates must abide by the Code and Standards and are encouraged to notify their employer of this responsibility. Violations may result in disciplinary sanctions by CFA Institute. Sanctions can include revocation of membership, revocation of candidacy in the CFA Program, and revocation of the right to use the CFA designation.

THE CODE OF ETHICS

Members of CFA Institute (including CFA charterholders) and candidates for the CFA designation ("Members and Candidates") must:

- Act with integrity, competence, diligence, respect and in an ethical manner with the public, clients, prospective clients, employers, employees, colleagues in the investment profession, and other participants in the global capital markets.
- Place the integrity of the investment profession and the interests of clients above their own personal interests.
- Use reasonable care and exercise independent professional judgment when conducting investment analysis, making investment recommendations, taking investment actions, and engaging in other professional activities.

- Practice and encourage others to practice in a professional and ethical manner that will reflect credit on themselves and the profession.
- Promote the integrity and viability of the global capital markets for the ultimate benefit of society.
- Maintain and improve their professional competence and strive to maintain and improve the competence of other investment professionals.

STANDARDS OF PROFESSIONAL CONDUCT

I. PROFESSIONALISM

A. Knowledge of the Law. Members and Candidates must understand and comply with all applicable laws, rules, and regulations (including the CFA Institute Code of Ethics and Standards of Professional Conduct) of any government, regulatory organization, licensing agency, or professional association governing their professional activities. In the event of conflict, Members and Candidates must comply with the more strict law, rule, or regulation. Members and Candidates must not knowingly participate or assist in and must dissociate from any violation of such laws, rules, or regulations.

B. Independence and Objectivity. Members and Candidates must use reasonable care and judgment to achieve and maintain independence and objectivity in their professional activities. Members and Candidates must not offer, solicit, or accept any gift, benefit, compensation, or consideration that reasonably could be expected to compromise their own or another's independence and objectivity.

C. Misrepresentation. Members and Candidates must not knowingly make any misrepresentations relating to investment analysis, recommendations, actions, or other professional activities.

D. Misconduct. Members and Candidates must not engage in any professional conduct involving dishonesty, fraud, or deceit or commit any act that reflects adversely on their professional reputation, integrity, or competence.

II. INTEGRITY OF CAPITAL MARKETS

A. Material Nonpublic Information. Members and Candidates who possess material nonpublic information that could affect the value of an investment must not act or cause others to act on the information.

B. Market Manipulation. Members and Candidates must not engage in practices that distort prices or artificially inflate trading volume with the intent to mislead market participants.

III. DUTIES TO CLIENTS

A. Loyalty, Prudence, and Care. Members and Candidates have a duty of loyalty to their clients and must act with reasonable care and exercise prudent judgment. Members and Candidates must act for the benefit of their clients and place their clients' interests before their employer's or their own interests.

B. Fair Dealing. Members and Candidates must deal fairly and objectively with all clients when providing investment analysis, making investment recommendations, taking investment action, or engaging in other professional activities.

C. Suitability.
1. When Members and Candidates are in an advisory relationship with a client, they must:
   a. Make a reasonable inquiry into a client's or prospective client's investment experience, risk and return objectives, and financial constraints prior to making any investment recommendation or taking investment action and must reassess and update this information regularly.
   b. Determine that an investment is suitable to the client's financial situation and consistent with the client's written objectives, mandates, and constraints before making an investment recommendation or taking investment action.
   c. Judge the suitability of investments in the context of the client's total portfolio.
2. When Members and Candidates are responsible for managing a portfolio to a specific mandate, strategy, or style, they must make only investment recommendations or take only investment actions that are consistent with the stated objectives and constraints of the portfolio.

D. Performance Presentation. When communicating investment performance information, Members and Candidates must make reasonable efforts to ensure that it is fair, accurate, and complete.

E. Preservation of Confidentiality. Members and Candidates must keep information about current, former, and prospective clients confidential unless:
1. The information concerns illegal activities on the part of the client or prospective client,
2. Disclosure is required by law, or
3. The client or prospective client permits disclosure of the information.

IV. DUTIES TO EMPLOYERS

A. Loyalty. In matters related to their employment, Members and Candidates must act for the benefit of their employer and not deprive their employer of the advantage of their skills and abilities, divulge confidential information, or otherwise cause harm to their employer.

B. Additional Compensation Arrangements. Members and Candidates must not accept gifts, benefits, compensation, or consideration that competes with or might reasonably be expected to create a conflict of interest with their employer's interest unless they obtain written consent from all parties involved.

C. Responsibilities of Supervisors. Members and Candidates must make reasonable efforts to ensure that anyone subject to their supervision or authority complies with applicable laws, rules, regulations, and the Code and Standards.

V. INVESTMENT ANALYSIS, RECOMMENDATIONS, AND ACTIONS

A. Diligence and Reasonable Basis. Members and Candidates must:
1. Exercise diligence, independence, and thoroughness in analyzing investments, making investment recommendations, and taking investment actions.
2. Have a reasonable and adequate basis, supported by appropriate research and investigation, for any investment analysis, recommendation, or action.

B. Communication with Clients and Prospective Clients. Members and Candidates must:
1. Disclose to clients and prospective clients the basic format and general principles of the investment processes they use to analyze investments, select securities, and construct portfolios and must promptly disclose any changes that might materially affect those processes.
2. Disclose to clients and prospective clients significant limitations and risks associated with the investment process.
3. Use reasonable judgment in identifying which factors are important to their investment analyses, recommendations, or actions and include those factors in communications with clients and prospective clients.
4. Distinguish between fact and opinion in the presentation of investment analysis and recommendations.

C. Record Retention. Members and Candidates must develop and maintain appropriate records to support their investment analyses, recommendations, actions, and other investment-related communications with clients and prospective clients.

VI. CONFLICTS OF INTEREST

A. Disclosure of Conflicts. Members and Candidates must make full and fair disclosure of all matters that could reasonably be expected to impair their independence and objectivity or interfere with respective duties to their clients, prospective clients, and employer. Members and Candidates must ensure that such disclosures are prominent, are delivered in plain language, and communicate the relevant information effectively.

B. Priority of Transactions. Investment transactions for clients and employers must have priority over investment transactions in which a Member or Candidate is the beneficial owner.

C. Referral Fees. Members and Candidates must disclose to their employer, clients, and prospective clients, as appropriate, any compensation, consideration, or benefit received from or paid to others for the recommendation of products or services.

VII. RESPONSIBILITIES AS A CFA INSTITUTE MEMBER OR CFA CANDIDATE

A. Conduct as Participants in CFA Institute Programs. Members and Candidates must not engage in any conduct that compromises the reputation or integrity of CFA Institute or the CFA designation or the integrity, validity, or security of the CFA Institute programs.

B. Reference to CFA Institute, the CFA Designation, and the CFA Program. When referring to CFA Institute, CFA Institute membership, the CFA designation, or candidacy in the CFA Program, Members and Candidates must not misrepresent or exaggerate the meaning or implications of membership in CFA Institute, holding the CFA designation, or candidacy in the CFA program.

CFA Institute

www.cfainstitute.org

Summary of Key Points

- Student-managed investment funds often have both experiential learning and fund performance objectives. By focusing on the fund performance objective, the learning objectives can also be achieved.
- Because most student-managed investment funds perform the same primary function as an investment firm, it is useful to consider the structure of real investment firms.
- An investment organization's structure should be motivated by and consistent with the investment approach.
- The organization should have clearly defined roles and responsibilities.
- Regardless of whether a student-managed investment fund is a volunteer organization or part of a for-credit curriculum, incentives exist for students to diligently manage the fund on behalf of the fund's clients or beneficiaries.
- Student managed investment funds face several unique challenges. Continuity and consistency through time are critical and turnover in any organization is disruptive. Succession planning and processes should be in place to manage personnel turnover. Policies or procedures should exist for managing the fund during breaks in the academic calendar.
- The fund structure or vehicle should match the client's or beneficiary's needs.
- Trading Rooms, also known as finance labs or portfolio management rooms, can serve as a great compliment to and resource for student managed investment funds.
- In order to maximize the use of a trading room, faculty must encourage student participation through required course assignments.
- The CFA Institute Code of Ethics and Standards of Professional Conduct is a great example for SMIFs to follow and voluntarily adopt.

Exercises

1. If a student-managed investment fund has only six (6) students who participate at any given time, what roles are critical? Does the answer depend whether the investment approach is top-down or bottom-up? What if the fund is purely quantitative or purely fundamental?
2. If a student-managed investment fund has 30 students who participate at any given time, what organizational structure might be most efficient? Be sure to discuss what roles would be included in the structure.
3. Suppose that a large business school offers a student-managed investment fund as a volunteer organization. In the Fall semester of its first year, it attracts 70 students. By the end of the first semester, only 45 students remain. By the end of the Spring semester, only 25 students remain. Why is this undesirable for the fund? Discuss what policies or procedures the fund might.adopt in future years to protect the fund from having the same experience and discuss the potential cost/benefit tradeoffs of such policies.

4. Consider the following student-managed investment funds that have specific characteristics. For each fund, identify potential policies for managing the portfolio during short and extended semester breaks. What are the costs and benefits of the possible policies?
   a. Small-cap portfolio of 10 stocks, benchmarked to the S&P 400 index.
   b. Large-cap portfolio of 60 stocks, benchmarked to the S&P 500 index.
   c. Portfolio of 50 stocks, benchmarked to the Russell Midcap index.
   d. A balanced portfolio of mostly large-cap stocks and some government bonds.
   e. Tactical asset allocation strategy portfolio.
   f. Sector rotation strategy portfolio that holds sector ETFs.
   g. Hedged (long and short) portfolio with 40 open long and short positions.
   h. Large-cap portfolio with 25% turnover per year (or 4-year average holding period).
5. Identify and discuss the key advantages and disadvantages of offering a student-managed investment fund in a for-credit format.
6. Identify and discuss the key advantages and disadvantages of offering a student-managed investment fund in a volunteer (not for credit) format.
7. Identify and discuss the key advantages and disadvantages of being selective in restricting participation in a student-managed investment fund.
8. What roles might be appropriate for the following student with the given background?
   a. Freshman Accounting major.
   b. Sophomore Marketing major.
   c. Junior Finance major.
   d. Junior Marketing major.
   e. Junior Management major.
   f. Senior Finance major.
   g. Senior Economics major.
   h. Senior Education major.
   i. Psychology graduate student.
   j. Senior Chemistry major.

Operating Guidelines for Philip M. Dorr and Alumni Endowed Investment Fund

Baylor University—Hankamer School of Business

Objective The objectives of the Philip M. Dorr and Alumni Fund (henceforth, Fund) are: (1) to provide an investment fund by which business students can learn investment management principles and techniques by managing real money; (2) to provide scholarships out of the growth in market value of the Fund; and (3) to support the Southwest Securities Capital Markets Investments Center (henceforth, Center).

Education Students involved in managing the Fund will gain valuable hands-on experience in securities research, valuation of risky assets, and portfolio management. In so doing, students will develop skills in evaluating economic, industry, and firm data and integrating such data into securities analysis. In addition, students will gain practice in effectively communicating their research results to others.

The performance of the Fund will be reviewed twice per year (at the end of the Fall and Spring semesters) and compared with the performance of the S&P 500 (the benchmark portfolio). The investment goal of the Fund will be to maximize the long-term rate of return consistent with prudent risk limits. The Fund's main objective, however, is to deliver high-quality practical education in securities analysis and portfolio management.

The Fund should increase the employment opportunities of participating students in areas such as equity research, investment banking, commercial banking, and corporate finance. In addition, over time the Fund should enhance the reputation of Baylor as a university offering challenging, integrated, hands-on investment management experience using real-time capital market data. This, in turn, should enable Baylor to attract more academically gifted and motivated students.

Distributions and Scholarships: Beginning 2007, the Fund's *Endowment Value* will be defined as the average market value of the Fund at the end of the prior four calendar years. (Through year-end 2006, the Endowment Value will be the market value of the Fund as of the prior year end.) Each academic year, the Board of Trustees (henceforth, Board) of the Fund will review the University's *distribution rate* and set the Fund's distribution rate for that fiscal year. The *distribution amount* is the distribution rate times the Endowment Value. The distribution amount goes first to meet the operating budget for the Center for that fiscal year as approved by the Board. The estimated operating budget for 2004–2005 is $100,000 and reasonable increases in this budget should be expected. Unusual increases or new budget items must be approved by the Board. Each year, the Board will set a *scholarship amount*, which will be based on the distribution amount less the Center's operating budget. The Chairman of the Board, after consulting with other Board members, will select a *distribution date* for liquidating assets and distributing the scholarship amount, but it shall not be later than May 31, the end of the University's fiscal year. It is anticipated that at least one scholarship will be reserved to recruit an outstanding MBA candidate who is interested in a career in investment management. Other scholarship recipients will be athletes who are pursuing a business school degree based on the following priority structure: football first, men's and women's basketball second, and other sports as funds permit.

Fund amount The initial endowment of the Fund was $250,000 contributed by Mr. Dorr and an additional $250,000 of matching contributions from Baylor alumni and friends. The University endowment contributed approximately $500,000 to match this initial seed money. A donor and his alumnus wife donated approximately $2.3 million specifically to support the operations of the Center. The donor has approved that the funds should be managed as part of the Philip M. Dorr and Alumni Endowed Investment Funds. The University endowment matched this contribution with a gift of $2 million. The Fund will remain open for additional contributions. Endowed funds will be deposited in an investment account under student management with oversight by the Board of Trustees of the Fund and an Investment Advisory Committee.

Operating expenses Operating expenses are expenses incurred by the Center, Practicum, and Department for such Practicum-related items as technical support, teaching payments, administrative personnel, director compensation, computers, data sources, equipment, accounting and legal fees, books, journals, research materials, speaker honorariums, travel, annual report production, and newsletter production. No fees will be paid by the Fund to any students, either in cash or in kind.

Investment policy

Return goal

The return goal is to obtain a long-term return (calculated on a 5-year basis) as high as possible consistent with prudent risk limits, but at least as high as the return on the S&P 500 (with dividends reinvested). Since the Fund is exempt from federal and state taxation, the return goal is based on total return with no preference given to whether the return comes from dividends, interest, or capital gains. However, it is understood that the return on the Fund return will likely lag that of the benchmark portfolio in "up" markets due to the drag of lower returns on cash.

Risk tolerance

The normal or target asset allocation calls for a large allocation to equities. In addition, even though each class of students will manage the Fund for only one semester, the Fund has an infinite time horizon and should be managed as such. Consistent with this time horizon and the target asset allocation, the Fund has a high tolerance for risk.

Asset allocation

The Fund will be allowed to invest in any U.S. exchange traded securities of established firms. However, at no time will the Fund be allowed to use financial leverage. Consistent with the Fund's educational objective and goals, the target stock allocation should generally be 100%. The Fund's stock weight, however, may drop as low as 60%, permitting students to gain experience with other asset classes and to recognize that cash will exist after positions are liquidated. The purchase of derivative securities will not be allowed. Exchange traded funds, such as S&P Depository Receipts (SPDRs or "Spiders") and sector-specific exchange-traded funds such as sector Spiders, are acceptable investments. Mutual funds, too, will not be allowed for purchase except for investment of cash balances in a money market fund. Some liquidity must be maintained to provide cash for operating expenses. In addition, occasional liquidity will be needed to fund scholarship withdrawals.

Diversification

The Fund should be diversified across industry sectors and individual stocks. In general, each *sector's* weight in the Fund should be within either 50% of its weight in the S&P 500 or 5 percentage points of its absolute weight. Thus, a sector with a 20% weight in the S&P 500 could have a weight in the Fund of 10% to 30%, while a sector with a 3% weight in the S&P 500 could have a weight in the Fund of 0 to 8%. In addition, the maximum investment in any *one stock* should be no more than the larger of 7% or 5% in excess of its weight in the S&P 500. Thus, stocks with weights of 1% and 3% in the S&P 500 could have maximum weights in the Fund of 7% and 8%, respectively.

Exchange traded funds are not considered individual stocks for purposes of these calculations. However, the restrictions on industry weights and individual stock weights include the underlying exposure in ETFs. For example, suppose the Fund has $1 million and the technology sector's weight in the S&P 500 is 30%. The Fund could not invest $450,000 in technology stocks and the remaining $550,000 in S&P Depository Receipts (SPDRs). This would be an effective weight of 45% + 55% (0.30) = 61.5%, thus violating the restriction that the effective weight of the technology sector in the Fund must be between 15% and 45%.

Selection emphasis

The selection process will focus on stocks that have the potential for good returns. Although the S&P 500 is the benchmark portfolio, investments can come from U.S. securities outside that index. However, restrictions on industry weights and individual stock weights will still apply, meaning that no more than 7% of the Fund can be invested in a single stock outside the S&P 500. In addition, no more than 20% of the Fund can be invested in all stocks outside the benchmark portfolio.

Fund management

The Fund will be managed through a one-semester, three-hour Portfolio Management Practicum course (Practicum). The Practicum will be taught in the Fall and Spring semesters as a seminar open to graduate business students and senior undergraduate Finance majors. It is critical that at the close of the Fall and Spring semesters the Fund must satisfy the diversification requirements outlined above. The Fund will not be actively managed by the Practicum class between semesters. The Faculty Advisor and Chair of the Board of Trustees may liquidate investments during times that the Fund is not being managed by the Practicum class.

Class structure

The Practicum will be taught using a combination of lectures, homework, readings, and research reports (using a template developed by the Faculty Advisor) prepared by the students working in sector Teams. For example, in a 15-student class there could be 10 Teams, five with one student and five with two students. Each Team will be responsible for making presentations for stocks in its sector of the S&P 500. Although one Team will make the presentation for a given sector, all students are responsible for analyzing the stocks under consideration since all students vote for or against each stock recommendation.

The entire class will meet once a week to review the status of the Fund and discuss research reports and trade recommendations prepared by the various Teams on securities within their assigned sectors. Among these reports/recommendations will be an analysis every semester of each of the stocks in the Team's assigned sector(s) that are currently held in the Fund portfolio. Each recommended trade must be supported by a research report, which should be made available to non-team members of the class by Friday before the Monday night class. After discussion, the class will vote to execute the trade, not execute the trade, or postpone the decision.

At all times the class will make decisions consistent with maximizing the total return on the Fund through the avoidance of excessive transactions costs. In so doing, the class will be sensitive to the resulting costs associated with paying commissions and spreads from high turnover of the Fund's assets.

Student Fund managers may not hold themselves out, either privately or publicly, as *investment advisors* or *investment counsel* as defined by the Investment Advisors Act of 1970. Individual students, acting in their capacity as Fund managers, are specifically prohibited from using these descriptions in possible violation of state and federal regulations.

Execution of trades

Final authority to execute trades rests with the Faculty Advisor. Trades can only be executed by the Faculty Advisor or his designated representative. All trades must be supported by a research report and minutes of the class meetings in which the recommended trade was discussed. These documents must be made available to the Faculty Advisor with sufficient time for him or her to review them prior to the trade. The Faculty Advisor must approve all trades.

Brokerage account

All trades will be made through a brokerage account approved by the Board of Trustees of the Fund. The address of record of the brokerage account will be that of the Fund. The brokerage firm will provide to the Fund originals of all regular account statements and confirmations of all transactions made in the account on behalf of the Fund. In addition, the brokerage firm will be directed to provide duplicate statements to the Faculty Advisor and the University Investment Accounting Office.

End-of-semester report

At the end of Fall and Spring semesters the class will present a consolidated report to a meeting of the Board of Trustees of the Fund, outlining the results of the Fund to date. The report should discuss the performance of the Fund, especially relative to the return on the benchmark portfolio. Each Team will be responsible for reporting on its portion of the Fund portfolio.

Because of the important role of the Investment Advisory Committee (discussed below) in advising students about their stock selection process, members of this Committee will also be invited to attend these end-of-semester meetings. In addition, to provide continuity in managing the Fund from one semester to the next, students selected to take the Practicum during the succeeding semester will be asked to attend the last several class meetings, including the final class meeting, of the semester prior to their enrolling in the Practicum.

Oversight

Oversight of the Fund and the Practicum will be divided between the Board of Trustees of the Fund and an Investment Advisory Committee.

Board of trustees

The board of trustees of the Fund will include the Chief Investment Officer of Baylor University, the Dean of the Hankamer School of Business, the Chair of the Department of Finance, Insurance, and Real Estate, the holder of the Pat and Thomas R. Powers Chair of Investment Management, the original Fund donor or his representative, and the Faculty Advisor. The holder of the Powers Chair of Investment Management will serve as Chair of the Board and will call meetings of the Board as necessary but at least once near the end of each semester to review the end-of-semester report prepared by the class.

The Board will make policy level and administrative decisions to accomplish the objectives of the Fund. Policy decisions include all the guidelines articulated in this document, including, for example, guidelines relating to Investment Policy and Fund Management. Administrative decisions include nonpolicy matters such as selecting the brokerage firm to handle trades for the Fund and determining an annual scholarship distribution amount.

Investment advisory committee

The investment advisory committee will include the Faculty Advisor, who will serve as Chair of the Committee, select members of the Baylor faculty, and Baylor alumni and friends involved in professional money management. Committee members will serve strictly an advisory role, including advising Teams about their securities research and periodically attending class, either in person or via video- or tele conferencing, to discuss their securities-selection methods and other relevant investment topics.

Other matters

Amended and Restated Agreement: The Operating Guidelines document set forth herein supersedes the previously executed agreement dated September 28, 2000, entitled Philip M. Dorr and Alumni Endowed Investment Fund.

References

Belt, B., 1975. A securities portfolio managed by graduate students. J. Financ. Edu. 4, 77–81. Fall.

Block, S.B., French, D.W., 1991. The student-managed investment fund: a special opportunity in learning. Financ. Pract. Educ. 1 (1), 35–40. Spring.

CFA Institute, 2014. Code of Ethics and Standards of Professional Conduct. CFA Institute, Charlottesville, VA.

Cooley, P.L., Hubbard, C.M., 2012. FAQs about student managed funds. Adv. Financ. Edu. 10 (1 & 2), 72–84.

Cox, D.R., Goff, D.C., 1996. Starting and operating a student investment club. Financ. Pract. Educ. 6 (2), 78–86.

DeMong, R.F., Pettit, L.C., Campsey, B.J., 1979. Finance curriculum for the future: perceptions of practitioners versus academicians. J. Financ. Edu. 8, 45–48. October.

Dolan, R.C., Stevens, J.L., 2010. Experiential learning for undergraduates in economics and finance: a true top-down investment fund. J. Financ. Edu. 36 (1/2), 12–136. April 2010.

Dorn, D., 2018. Student managed portfolios: wisdom of independent crowds. J. Trad. 13 (1), 17–26. Winter.

Grinder, B., Cooper, D.W., Britt, M., 1999. An integrative approach to using student investment clubs and student investment funds in the finance curriculum. Financ. Serv. Rev. 8, 211–221.

Johnson, D.W., Alexander, J.F., Allen, G.H., 1996. Student-managed investment funds: a comparison of alternative decision-making environments. Financ. Pract. Educ. 6 (1), 97–101. Spring/Summer.

Lawrence, E.C., 1994. Financial innovation: the case of student investment funds in at United States universities. Financ. Pract. Educ. 4 (1), 47–53. Summer.

Markese, J.D., 1984. Applied security analysis and portfolio management. J. Financ. Edu. 13, 65–67. Fall.

Moses, E.A., Singleton, J.C., 2005. Teaching portfolio management with real dollar and imaginary portfolios: our experiences and class-tested exercises. Adv. Financ. Edu. 3, 36–71.

Nawrocki, D., 2017. An Organization Design for a Student Managed Investment Fund. Working paper Villanova University.

Neely, W.P., Cooley, P.L., 2004. A survey of student managed funds. Adv. Financ. Edu. 2, 1–9. Spring.

Peng, Z., Dukes, W.P., Bremer, R., 2009. Evidence on student-managed funds: a survey of U. S. universities. Bus. Edu. Accredit. 1 (1), 55–64.

Philpot, J., Peterson, C.A., 1998. Improving the investments or capital markets course with stock market specialist. Financ. Pract. Educ. 8 (2), 118–124. Fall/Winter.

Riley, W.B., Montgomery, W.H., 1980. The use of interactive computer programs in security analysis and portfolio management. J. Financ. Edu. 9, 89–92. October.

Seiler, M.J., Seiler, V.L., 2000. The ultimate in student investment clubs: putting your money where your mouth is. Rev. Bus. 21 (3/4), 53–57. Fall/Winter.

Tatar, D.D., 1987. Teaching securities analysis with real funds. J. Financ. Edu. 16, 40–45. Fall.

Vihtelic, J.L., 1996. Personal finance: an alternative approach to teaching undergraduate finance. Financ. Serv. Rev. 5 (2), 119–131.

Yerkes, R.T., 2018. The art and science of student managed investment portfolios. J. Trad. 13 (1), 39–51. Winter.

Forums, symposiums, and competitions

The investment and classroom activities of a student-managed investment fund allow students to experience and learn the portfolio management aspect of what professional investment managers must do. However, professional investment managers must, at some point in their careers, also present their investment philosophy and process to clients and prospective clients, such as pension plans, endowment funds, foundations, consultants, family offices, financial advisors, and high-net-worth individuals. In some cases, such presentations might be made to larger audiences at investment conferences. As discussed in Chapter 7: Presentations, these activities often support the business development (i.e., sales and marketing) efforts of the investment firm, which is also critical to the firm—after all, without clients, there are no assets to manage! Student-managed investment fund forums, symposiums, and competitions can provide meaningful practical experience in making such presentations. Furthermore, these activities facilitate the exchanging of ideas among student-managed investment funds from different colleges and universities, as well as among professional participants.

This chapter discusses student investment forums, symposiums, and competitions that have been offered in various regions around the United States. As with the Chapter 8—Tools, our purpose in using a particular example in this chapter is not intended to endorse that activity as the only or best example. Rather, we provide these examples to show the diversity in opportunities available. Features of the examples discussed in this chapter are available in other programs that currently exist and, undoubtedly, others that will come along. In areas where no such opportunities exist, we encourage student-managed investment funds to create such events. Indeed, we begin our chapter with an example of how universities in Texas did just that in creating the Texas Investment Portfolio Symposium. We also discuss other examples of regional symposiums and competitions, such as the Tennessee Valley Authority and Cornell-Fidelity MBA Stock Pitch Competition and national and international forums, such as the GAME forum hosted by Quinnipiac University.

Texas Investment Portfolio Symposium (TIPS)

Overview

The Texas Investment Portfolio Symposium (TIPS) conference, in its 17th year in 2020, is a forum for students, faculty, and investment professionals from Texas, Oklahoma, and Louisiana. TIPS provides participants with a wonderful opportunity to learn from and interact with industry professionals through keynote presentations and panel discussions with senior personnel from Texas investment management firms and several networking events.

TIPS is also home to two student competitions (described in further detail below): (1) the Portfolio Manager's Finalist Competition in which student teams "pitch" their investment process to a panel of judges; and (2) the CFA Institute Research Challenge – Southwest US in which finalist schools (10 schools as of 2019), based on a research report, present their stock research to a panel of judges. In addition to providing a terrific hands-on learning experience for the finalist schools, all TIPS attendees learn by watching these well-done presentations. TIPS is hosted by Texas universities and is generously sponsored by Texas investment firms and the CFA Societies Texas, Louisiana, and Oklahoma.

TIPS history

TIPS was inaugurated in 2004 by the combined efforts of Professor Brian Bruce of Baylor University and Southern Methodist University, who created the vision for TIPS, and Professor Jill Foote of Rice University, who endeavored to host the first two conferences as well as four more annual TIPS conferences since then. Initially, the large Texas universities, working collaboratively, thought the best hosting format would be an alternating 2-year cycle as there is a significant organizational start-up effort that must be expended in the first year. However, after 5 years, TIPS had grown to such a size and prestige level that it was deemed best to host the conference in a large Texas city, usually Houston or Dallas but also including Austin and San Antonio. In 2019, TIPS was held on February 23 at UT San Antonio. In 2020, TIPS was held on February 21–22 at Rice University. The list of host schools and participating colleges and universities is shown in Exhibit A2.1.

Portfolio managers finals competition

The Portfolio Managers Finals Competition (PMC or Finals Competition) is similar to a "finals presentation" that all investment firms make in order to compete to win an institutional client's business. Begun in 2006 and run annually by creator Professor Brian Bruce, the PMC allows student teams to truly get a real-world feel for the portfolio management pitch process through two stages of competition.

Preliminary application—First, universities that wish to be considered for the Finals Competition must submit a preliminary application (four pages maximum) providing:

- A description of the school's investment philosophy, decision-making process, investment style, and universe from which securities are selected.
- Presentation of long-term (minimum 3 years) investment results, including the results versus an appropriate benchmark.
- Other material may be included such as a discussion of risk controls or why the investment process adds value.

In order to compete in the PMC schools must have a real-money portfolio and must have a minimum of 3-years performance history.

Finals presentation—Then finalist teams (consisting of three to five students), selected based on excellence in the preliminaries, make a 10 minute presentation followed by a question-and-answer period at the TIPS conference. A typical presentation consists of an introduction of team members, a description of the team's investment philosophy, decision-making process, investment style, and a review of the long-term investment results. Basically, each team has 10 minutes to convince the judges that they should be hired to manage this hypothetical account.

These PMC Finals presentations are judged by a panel of practicing institutional investment professionals based on the same criteria used to judge a professional money manager: The judges select a winner based on their perceptions about which team's investment process will most likely produce the best results over time. Awards are presented to the winning teams at the Symposium, including a take home award for the top three teams and a Winner's Cup, which is passed each year to the new winning school. Recent winners of the Finals Competition are shown in Exhibit A2.1. Texas Lutheran University's winning presentation from 2019 is shown in Exhibit A2.2.

Exhibit A2.1 Texas Investment Portfolio Symposium (TIPS)

Universities represented
More than 40 universities have sent representatives to TIPS, with most years of the conference boasting 150–200 attendees.

Texas
Austin College
Baylor University
Houston Baptist University
Lamar University
Prairie View A&M University
Rice University
Southern Methodist University
Southwestern University
St. Mary's University
Stephen S. Austin State University
Texas A&M University
Texas A&M–Kingsville
Texas A&M–San Antonio
Texas Christian University
Texas Lutheran University
Texas Southern University
Texas State University
Texas Tech University
Texas Wesleyan University
Texas Woman's University

Trinity University
University of Houston
University of Incarnate Word
University of North Texas
University of St. Thomas
University of Texas
University of Texas at Arlington
University of Texas at Dallas
University of Texas at El Paso
University of Texas Rio Grande Valley
University of Texas at San Antonio
West Texas A&M University

Louisiana
Louisiana State University
Loyola University New Orleans
Nicholls State University
Northwestern State University of Louisiana
Southeast Louisiana University
Tulane University

Oklahoma
Cameron University
Oklahoma Christian University
Oklahoma State University
University of Central Oklahoma
University of Oklahoma
University of Tulsa

TIPS Host Universities.

2004	Rice
2005	Rice
2006	Baylor
2007	Baylor
2008	A&M
2009	Rice
2010	UT Dallas
2013	Rice
2014	SMU
2015	Rice
2016	TCU
2017	University of Houston
2018	SMU
2019	UT San Antonio
2020	Rice

Winner Universities in the CFA Institute Research Challenge—Southwest US.

2007	Rice
2008	U of H
2009	A&M
2010	U of H
2011	Rice
2012	UT San Antonio
2013	Texas State University
2014	Rice
2015	West Texas A&M
2016	SMU
2017	West Texas A&M
2018	Rice
2019	Baylor
2020	TCU

Note: Started as Texas region, but is now called Southwest US and includes TX, LA, and OK. In 2019, the Southwest US was the second largest region in the world after India.

Winning universities in the Portfolio Managers Finals Competition.

2006	SMU
2007	Baylor
2008	Baylor
2009	Rice
2010	U of H
2011	Baylor
2012	Rice
2013	University of Oklahoma
2014	University of North Texas
2015	Baylor
2016	TCU
2017	Tulane
2018	Texas Lutheran
2019	Texas Lutheran
2020	Texas Lutheran

Exhibit A2.2 Texas Lutheran University's winning presentation in the 2019 Portfolio Managers Finals Competition

Bulldog Investment Company

"Rule No. 1:
Never lose money.
Rule No. 2:
Don't forget Rule No. 1"
            - Warren Buffett

LOGIC · DISCIPLINE · VALUES

Texas Lutheran University

Introduction

Carlos Leal (Mentor)

Major: BBA Management
    MS Data Analytics
Tenure: 3 years

Esam Hijazi (Team Leader)

Major: BBA Finance
Tenure: 2 years

Caleb Bronnenberg (Team Leader)

Major: BBA Finance
    MS Data Analytics
Tenure: 2 years

*Average Member Tenure: 3.1 Years

Buffett's Rule #1

<u>Don't Lose Money</u>

- Volatility

- Permanent Impairment of Capital

Investment Strategies

Long-Term Compounders

Options Contracts

Cash-out Arbitrage

What Does Buffett Look For?

1. Can you **understand** the business?

2. Is the business **predictable**?

3. Is the business **consistent**?

What Does Buffett Look For?

4. Is there an "economic moat?"

- There are four types of moats:
  - Intangible Assets
  - Switching Costs
  - The Network Effect
  - Cost Advantages

✓ **Sustained Competitive Advantage**

What Does Buffett Look For?

5. Managerial Efficiency

- Return on Equity ≥ 15%

- Return on Capital ≥ 15%

What Does Buffett Look For?

6. Properly structured **long-term obligations?**

Long term debt
(+) Preferred stock
(+) Pension funding shortfall
(+) Leases multiplied by 7
(−) Cash
_____
Divided by Annual Net Income ≤ 5

• Analyze debt maturities

What Does Buffett Look For?

7. Is there a **valuation gap?**

Long-Term Compounders:
Dollar General

- Targeted Customer
  - Annual Household Income ≤ $40,000
- Affordable Products
  - 80% of items priced ≤ $5.00

Convenient Locations
  - 75% of Americans live within 5 miles

✓ **Understandable**

Long-Term Compounders:
Dollar General

- Sales have grown 265% since 2004
  - 10.7% per year

- Profits have grown 508% since 2004
  - 14.5% per year

✓ **Predictable & Consistent**

Long-Term Compounders:
Dollar General

Economic moat:
•Cost Advantages

✓ **Sustained Competitive Advantage**

Long-Term Compounders:
Dollar General

• Return on Equity/
  Return on Capital: ≥ 20% & improving

• Long-Term Obligation Ratio: ≤ 5

✓ Sustained Competitive Advantage

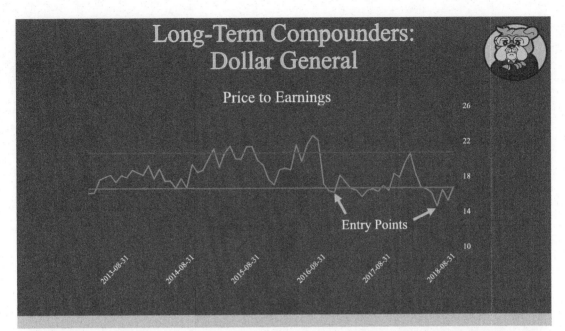

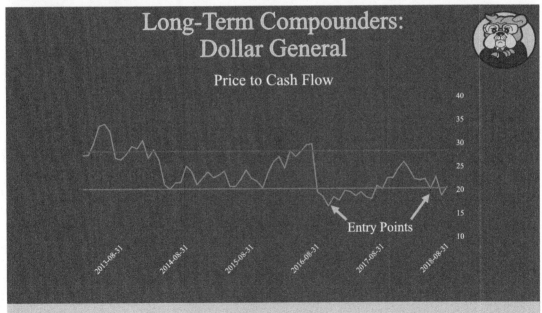

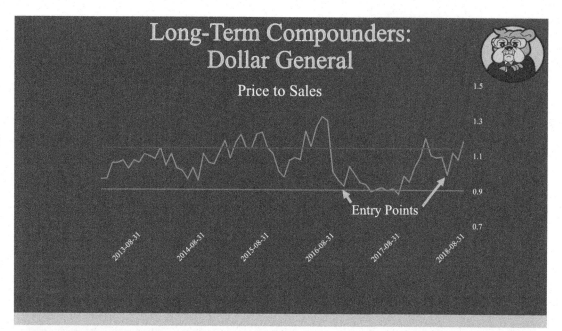

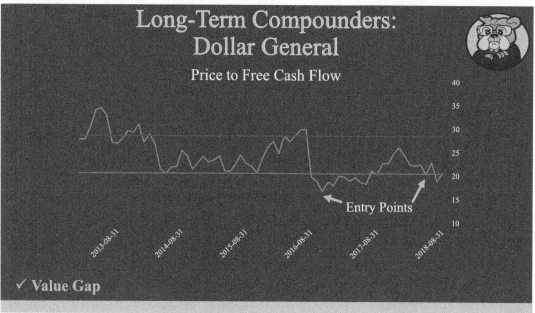

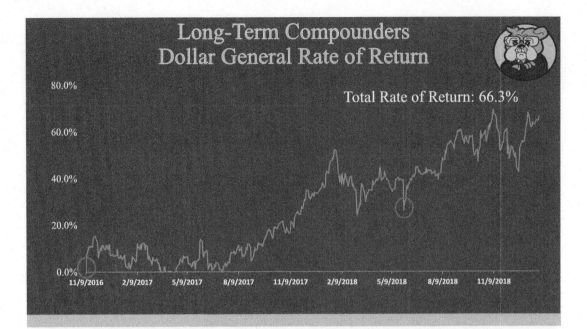

Option Contracts

Strategically target entry & exit points

Increases cash flow to the portfolio

Option premiums have added 1% to 2% of additional return per year

Put contracts are cash secured and call options are covered

Cash-out Arbitrage Requirements:

When one company announces a buyout of another

1. All cash deal

2. Friendly buyout

3. Few regulatory hurdles

4. Secured financing

5. Significant market price discount to cash out price

Cash-out Arbitrage: AveXis

• April 6, 2018 – Novartis announces acquisition of AveXis

• Cash out price: $218/share

• Entered on April 10, 2018 at a price of $207.11

• May 18, 2018 – Deal Completed

Cash-out Arbitrage:
AveXis

Number of days held: **28**

Gross Return: **5.3%**

Annualized Return: **68.6%**

Total Average Return of
Cash-out Arbitrage

Total Arbitrage Transactions: 17

Average Annualized Return: 36.5%

Our Sell Criteria:

Issues that merit further research:

- Historically high valuations

- Dramatic increases in debt

  - Breaking long-term obligation ratio

- Decreasing profit margins

- Eroding economic moat

- Opportunity cost

Our Sell Criteria:

Always Remember:

- Do **NOT** fall in love with any investment

Advanced Auto Parts (AAP) Performance

- Acquired CARQUEST on January 3, 2014

Advanced Auto Parts (AAP) Performance

Over the next 2 years:

- Long-term Debt nearly tripled

- Return on Equity fell from 38% to 17%

- Operating and Net Profit Margins were declining

- Inventory Turnover, Asset Turnover, Cash Conversion cycle were worsening

- Replaced Long-Time CEO

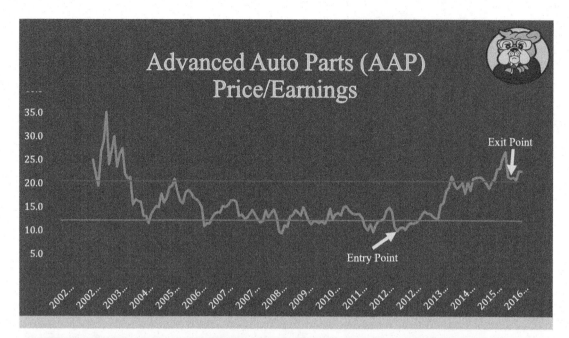

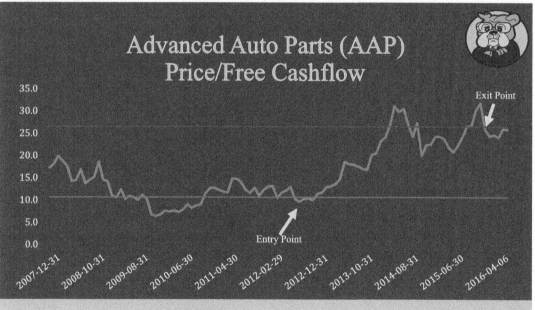

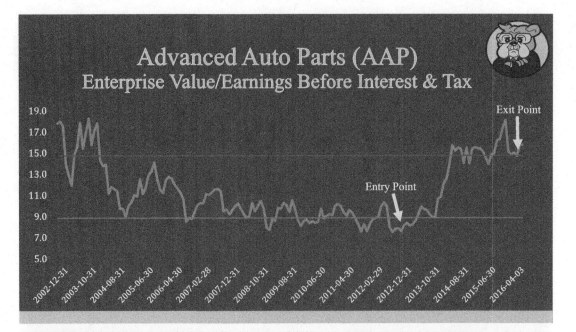

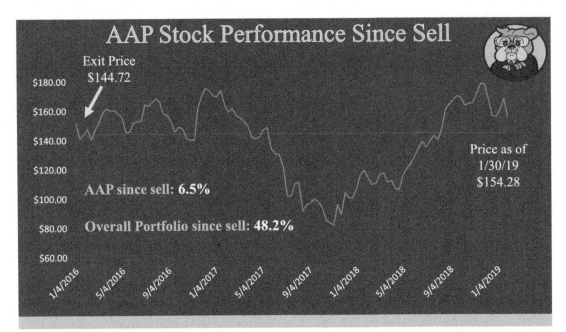

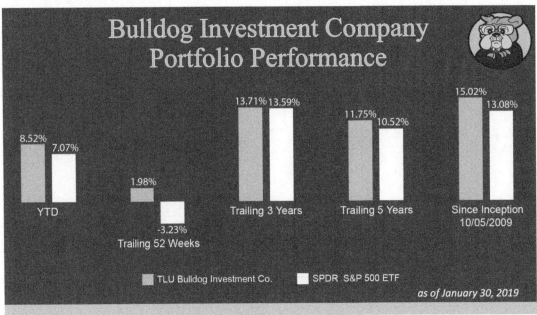

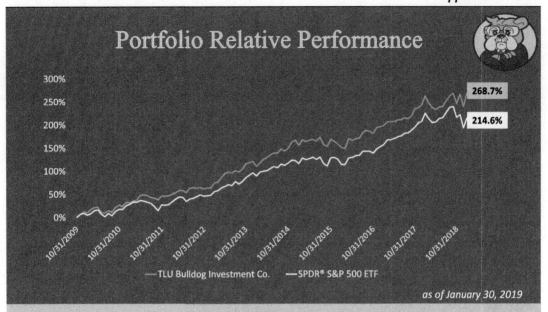

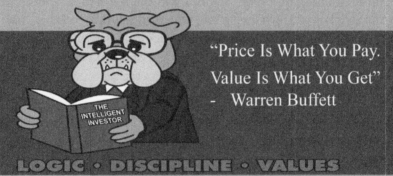

(Credit: Texas Lutheran University, Bulldog Investment Company, 2019.)

CFA Institute Research Challenge—Southwest US

History and the 2018–19 competition

In 2006, Sharon Criswell, then President of the CFA Society Dallas/Fort Worth, and Leah Bennett, then President of CFA Society Houston, teamed up to launch an exciting new initiative, the Investment Research Challenge—Texas (IRC-TX, Research Challenge or Challenge). In the initial year of the Research Challenge, student teams from four Texas Universities (Rice, A&M, TCU, and SMU) competed with each other on analyzing, writing, and presenting a report recommending a "Buy," "Sell," or "Hold" position on a publicly traded company. All four Texas societies provided mentors for the teams, judges, or graders. Finalist teams competed before an oral panel made up of leaders in our investment community at TIPS. The winning team went on to compete regionally against other winners hosted by the CFA Institute in New York City. Since then, the regional competition has expanded to include Oklahoma and Louisiana and is now called the CFA Institute Research Challenge—Southwest US. With more than 25 universities from Texas, Oklahoma and Louisiana involved in 2018–19, the Research Challenge—Southwest US is now the second largest region globally (after India). Since its inception in 2006, the Southwest US finals presentations for this prestigious competition have been held at the TIPS conference.

The Research Challenge—Southwest is managed and supported by all four CFA societies in Texas (Austin, Dallas-Fort Worth, Houston, and San Antonio) as well as the CFA Societies Louisiana and Oklahoma. The winning and second place team based on 50% score on written research/50% presentation then go on to compete in the "Americas Regional" which includes all local challenge winners across Canada, Latin America, and the United States. The top two teams in Americas then go on to compete against the winners from Europe, the Middle East and Africa, and Asia Pacific.

The 2018–19 competition was kicked-off in mid-November and 10 finalist teams competed at TIPS at UT San Antonio on February 23, 2019. The top two teams went on to compete in the Americas Regional on 23–25 April 2019 in New York City.

Exhibit A2.1 also shows the winners of the CFA Institute Research Challenge—Southwest US.

All regional Research Challenges, including the Southwest US Challenge, follow the same format. University teams made up of three to five MBA and/or undergraduate students compete with each other on analyzing and writing a research report recommending a "Buy," "Sell," or "Hold" position on a publicly traded company. Finalist teams, present their research before an oral panel made up of senior investment professionals.

The basic components of the Challenge include:

- Training: Students receive training by video seminars provided by the societies on Research Tools for Analysts, Research Report Analysis and Writing (both buy-side and sell-side), and Ethics.

- Analysis of a Public Company: Teams are assigned to research the same public company, selected by the CFA Societies Texas and located in the Southwest, including a presentation and question and answer session with senior company management. Teams are given a template to follow in completing their written analysis/report.
- Mentoring by a Professional Research Analyst: Each team is mentored by a professional research analyst, who reviews and critiques the team's report.
- Assessment of Written Research Reports: Written research reports are evaluated by a panel of senior investment professionals who choose finalist teams to present at TIPS.
- Finals Presentation: The finalist teams present their research to a high-profile panel of respected investment professionals. The Research Challenge Southwest winning team and second place are selected based on the combined scores for the written report and the presentation.

Each year the Texas and now Southwest region has grown. All four CFA Societies Texas—Austin, Dallas-Fort Worth, Houston, and San Antonio and the CFA Societies of Louisiana and Oklahoma—provide mentors for the teams, judges, or graders, and provide sponsorship of TIPS. Additionally, in the Southwest region, the sponsoring societies of the challenge pay 100% of enrollment for the winning team in the upcoming CFA exam at any level. Truly this Research Challenge Southwest has become a wonderful educational and collaborative effort between the CFA Societies, the involved universities, and TIPS.

The CFA Institute Research Challenge

History and growth of the CFA Institute Research Challenge

The CFA Institute Research Challenge as it is now called, was originated as the "Investment Research Challenge" by the New York Society of Security Analysts (now the CFA Society New York) in the 2002–03 academic year. The Challenge was started as a means to promote best practices in equity research among the next generation of analysts, through an annual 8-month initiative in which top industry professionals taught business and finance students how to conduct stock research and report on a publicly traded company. By the 2006–07 academic year, a number of other local CFA societies had started their own challenges, including those in Hong Kong, Boston, and the CFA Society Dallas-Fort Worth and CFA Society Houston (for Texas universities). CFA Institute (CFAI) was an initial sponsor for these early Challenges and as the Challenge has expanded over the years, has taken over as the global sponsor, providing a key role in global visibility and consistency of the Challenge as well as supporting local CFA societies that decide to roll out a Challenge. According the CFAI website: "This annual global equity research competition provides university students with hands-on mentoring and intensive training in financial analysis. Working in teams, students gain real-world experience as they assume the role of research analysts and are judged on their ability to value a stock, write a research report, and present their recommendations."

From starting with the four local regions (New York, Boston, Texas, and Hong Kong) and around 150 students from 30+ universities in 2006, the CFA Institute Research Challenge has expanded to 6,400 students at more than 1,100 universities in 98 countries participating and involving over 150 member societies hosting local competitions globally in 2020. Winners of the local competitions go on to compete regionally in three major competitions, the Americas region; the Europe, Middle East, and Africa region (EMEA); and the Asia Pacific region. The top two teams from the Americas regional and the winning teams from Asia Pacific and EMEA regions square off at the Global Finals, which is held in locations around the globe. The global winning team's university is then awarded US$10,000 for its students' achievement in the Global Research Challenge.

It is difficult to overemphasize the impact this Challenge has come to have. Administered by the CFAI and strongly supported by most of the local member societies across the globe, all student participants have the opportunity to get real-world experience in equity analysis, learn best practices and ethical decision making from investment professionals, interact with top management of public companies, and gain industry exposure for themselves and sometimes regional and/or global exposure for their universities. The CFA Institute Research Challenge teaches a discipline of effective research, sell-side research report writing, and strong presentation capabilities. From the initial educational sessions on report writing, research techniques, and ethics in the investment management industry, to interviewing public company management, to working on the actual analysis and research report, and then finally presenting the results to top industry professionals, this discipline encompasses many of the key skills and tools that students will later utilize as they complete their schooling and begin their careers.

Additionally through Research Challenge, investment professionals make a positive impact on the profession, public companies promote education and analyst independence, universities gain global exposure, and corporate sponsors reach universities, students, and finance professionals.

More information on the CFA Institute Research Challenge can be found on the CFA Institute's website at https://www.cfainstitute.org/societies/challenge.

The Quinnipiac University Global Asset Management Education (GAME) Forum

The Global Asset Management Education (GAME) Forum is held annually in the spring and is hosted by Quinnipiac University. GAME gathers together some of the most successful people in finance to share their knowledge, expertise and outlook for the future with graduate and undergraduate students. A roman numeral is affixed to the title of each subsequent year of the Forum to distinguish one year from another (e.g., GAME Forum I, GAME Forum II, GAME Forum III). GAME Forum X, is taking place March 26–28, 2020 in New York City at the New York Hilton Midtown Hotel.

The GAME Forum, Quinnipiac University, is acknowledged by many as the world's largest student-run financial conference in the world. At GAME IX held in 2019—there were more than 1500 attendees representing 158 colleges and universities from 50 countries and 46 states in the U.S. There were 148 speakers and 115 companies and organizations involved. Strategic partners that have lent their name in support of the program over the years have included such notable organizations as the Voya Investment Management, Americana Partners, Fidelity, J.P. Morgan Asset Management, TD Ameritrade, Bridgewater Associates and BlackRock. Additionally, Bloomberg Television and Bloomberg Radio broadcast live from the GAME Forum. Some students have the opportunity to be interviewed live on air.

The three-day conference (Thursday to Saturday), GAME features the following:

- Keynote panels and perspectives
- Concurrent breakout panels and workshops
- Career strategy panels
- Networking opportunities
- Optional portfolio competition
- Faculty-only discussion of best practices
- Nasdaq closing bell ceremony

On day one, keynote panels discuss the global economy, global markets, global portfolio and risk, and global investment strategy. Day two included a variety of breakout discussion panels, workshops and keynote perspectives covering portfolio management, equity analysis, asset allocation, risk and financial technology and innovation, among other topics. The forum concludes on day three with panels discussing best practices and advances in teaching student managed portfolio class and career opportunities within the financial services industry. Students and faculty may attend all three days of GAME, while professionals are welcome to register for the day one keynote panels.

The first day of the GAME Forum is modeled after the World Economic Forum and is generally composed of four 90-min keynote panels focusing on such topics as the economy, the markets, portfolio and risk management, and investment strategies. Often the Federal Reserve perspective and/or a leadership perspective are addressed in a keynote. Panelists number as many as eighteen each year, spread across the four keynote panels. They are leaders from the areas of business, government, labor, academics, and the media. In addition to interacting among themselves, keynote panelists interact with the audience as well through an interview-style discussion format. Following five-minute introductory remarks by each panelist regarding their thoughts on what they believe to be the issue of the day with regard to the topic at hand, the floor is opened to questions posed by students and directed to the panel. Spirited dialogue and debate ensue. The aim is to make the panel sessions dynamic and interactive as opposed to canned or scripted.

GAME Forum has been fortunate to attract such keynote luminaries as: David Kelly, Chief Global Strategist at JP Morgan; Richard Thomas, Managing Director of Research at Fidelity; Jeffrey Kleintop, Chief Global Investment Strategist at Charles Schwab; Rick Rieder, Managing Director and Chief Investment Officer of Global Fixed Income at BlackRock; Ethan Harris, Head of Global Economics Research at Bank of America Global Research; Peter Spiegel, U.S. Managing Editor at Financial Times, Catherine L. Mann, Managing Director and Global Chief Economist at Citibank; Eileen Murray, Co-Chief Executive Officer at Bridgewater Associates.

Needless to say, while the first day of the conference piques the interest of the academic audience, the high-profile lineup holds equal appeal for the professional men and women in attendance, many of whom qualify for continuing education credit toward a variety of professional designations.

Friday and Saturday programming, for attendance by students and faculty only, consist of a series of seven concurrent breakout sessions: two on Friday morning, three on Friday afternoon, and two on Saturday morning. Friday sessions focus on investment-related topics such as portfolio management, investment products, equity analysis, hedge funds, technical analysis, derivatives trading, socially responsible investing, asset allocation, financial technology and innovation, ethical dilemmas in investing, and so forth. Career networking events with industry-leading professionals in the greater New York area, designed with a special Q&A to prepare students for life in the workforces is also part of Friday sessions. Additionally, the CFP, CAIA, and FDP Institutes, traditionally offer a session on the requirements and benefits of their designations. Faculty are also invited to attend a session on investment education best practices. Friday breakout sessions take the form of panel discussions among industry professionals, presentations by investment strategists, and workshops offering more technical content. Panelists and presenters represent major firms from across the country. Friday programming terminates with a networking reception followed by an optional dinner.

Saturday morning panels include breakout sessions on financial technology, CDOs, market cycles, and exploration of career options within the financial services industry and corporate sector.

A number of the attending schools opt to participate in the GAME Forum's student-managed portfolio competition as well. Top three place performance is acknowledged in each of three categories in each of two divisions. The categories are based on portfolio style (growth, value, blend, and hybrid), and the division is defined by the program level of the preponderance of the fund's student managers (undergraduate vs. graduate). Winning portfolio teams are determined by comparison of the 12-month, risk-adjusted performances of the competing funds in each divisional category, and announced at the Friday evening dinner. Required materials are submitted by schools weeks before the conference so that competition involvement does not detract from Forum participation.

Competing schools are welcome to exhibit poster board displays describing their portfolios at the Friday afternoon networking reception, and a limited number of competing teams are invited to offer a 30-min presentation to a panel of national investment professionals for discussion and feedback.

For information regarding the GAME conference may be found on the Forum's website: game. qu.edu Questions may be emailed to game@qu.edu or call 203–582-5400.

TVA Investment Challenge

Overview

The Tennessee Valley Authority (TVA) Investment Challenge Program is a partnership between TVA and 24 universities in its service territory that provides a unique hands-on experience in financial asset management for the students and performance-based awards the university can use to enhance their business school resources. TVA's Investment Challenge program is one of the largest student-managed investment funds in the United States.

Student teams actively manage real stock portfolios for TVA, designing long-term investment strategies and selecting investments under the guidance of faculty members and within investment guidelines established by TVA.

TVA supports the program by utilizing some of its most experienced financial managers and analysts available to help students as they learn to apply financial management concepts to real-world situations. TVA representatives periodically visit campuses to discuss the students' portfolio management decisions and offer constructive feedback.

TVA is the largest public power provider in the United States, and is dedicated to partnering in education with colleges and universities to invest in communities and future leaders. TVA's Investment Challenge is a creative use of TVA's resources that offers opportunities for learning and training to the region's next generation of financial leaders.

The Investment Challenge is part of TVA's Asset Retirement Trust, which was created to offset the future cost of decommissioning TVA's power assets.

History

In 1998, TVA created the Investment Challenge by allocating $1.9 million to 19 universities to be managed, on behalf of TVA, in equity investment portfolios.

In 2003, TVA added 6 new universities to the program, bringing the total to 25. TVA also increased the total Investment Challenge portfolio allocation to $10 million after the success of the program demonstrated that student-managed portfolios performed competitively against performance benchmarks. A TVA trust fund provided the original $1.9 million for the program and the additional $8 million to expand it.

There are currently 24 universities participating in the program. Today, each of the participating universities manages funds of approximately $500,000, on average, which is invested in the stock market on behalf of TVA. Exhibit A2.3 shows a list of participating universities. More than 9,000 students have participated in the program since it began in 1998.

Structure

Consistent with what is required of professional investment managers, participating universities must sign an investment management agreement with TVA. The investment management agreement specifies the investment guidelines that must be followed.

Exhibit A2.3 Universities participating in the TVA investment challenge

Alabama A&M University
Austin Peay State University
Belmont University
Christian Brothers University
East Tennessee State University
Lipscomb University
Middle Tennessee State University
Mississippi State University
Mississippi University for Women
Murray State University
Tennessee State University
Tennessee Technological University
Trevecca Nazarene University
Union University
University of Alabama—Huntsville
University of Kentucky
University of Memphis
University of Mississippi
University of North Alabama
University of Tennessee—Chattanooga
University of Tennessee—Martin
Vanderbilt University
Western Carolina University
Western Kentucky University

(Credit: http://www.tvainvestmentchallenge.com/.)

Each university has a separate account with a trustee, where investment positions are held. Universities trade positions in the portfolio utilizing an online trading platform with a broker and have access to a trustee website application to monitor account positions.

The majority of participating universities have structured the learning experience in the form of a for-credit course focused on management of the portfolio. The universities generally use an application process for acceptance into the class. The portfolio management process typically involves a practical application of theory provided through academic instruction.

Investment guidelines

Each university agrees to abide by the investment guidelines described below. University portfolios are monitored for guideline compliance by TVA using a trustee software tool.

University investment manager guidelines

Goals

The investment goal of the portfolio is to provide TVA with a strategic allocation to the domestic equity market. Manager has been selected by TVA as the portfolio manager of this strategic allocation. Manager's assignment is to construct and actively manage the portfolio in a manner consistent with this investment goal and to add value relative to return opportunities that could be achieved from a passive exposure to this market segment.

Objective

The investment objective of the portfolio is to achieve long-term capital growth by investing in marketable U.S. common stocks with a risk profile that is similar to the risk profile of the market benchmark. Specific investment objectives are intended to define quantifiable measures by which the results of the portfolio will be measured and evaluated on an ongoing basis. The performance results and investment characteristics of the portfolio will be measured and evaluated relative to:

(1) An overall measure of the largecap segment of the domestic equity market,
(2) A universe of professionally managed large-cap core-oriented equity managers selected by TVA, and.
(3) A universe of other universities managing TVA decommissioning funds.

The relative domestic equity market benchmark is defined as the S&P 500 Index. In light of the above, the portfolio should strive to meet or exceed the following performance objectives:

• The portfolio is expected to match the return of the S&P 500 Index over one, three and 5 year horizons.

- The portfolio is expected to generate a total return that ranks in the top 50% of a large-cap core-oriented equity manager universe as may be selected by TVA from time to time.

Guidelines

The following points highlight the investment guidelines that have been established for the portfolio. Manager is expected to follow these guidelines carefully while implementing and executing its portfolio strategy. If Manager is in non-compliance with these guidelines, Manager will have 30 days to rebalance the portfolio to meet these guidelines. The 30-day period will begin after either TVA notifies Manager that it has determined Manager is not in compliance or Manager makes a self-determination of non-compliance.

Asset allocation

The portfolio is expected to be invested fully and exclusively in U.S.-listed equity securities. Any cash equivalent investment should represent "frictional" or operational amounts and not strategic allocations. Therefore, cash equivalents should not exceed 2.5% of the portfolio at any time. Should market conditions suggest an environment where this guideline may be detrimental to the financial well-being of TVA, Manager should communicate suggested tactical adjustments to this guideline with authorized representatives of TVA. Cash equivalent balances are expected to be invested in a short-term investment fund managed by the assigned custodian bank.

Diversification

Portfolio performance is expected to achieve value added results through active management decisions. However, the portfolio is expected to be diversified with respect to the exposures to economic sectors, industries, and individual stocks. The following diversification guidelines apply to the construction of the portfolio:

- The portfolio must consist of a minimum of 20 holdings excluding the portfolio's cash position.
- The portfolio will maintain minimum allocations to economic sector, as defined by S&P's Global Industry Classification Standards (GICS), not to be less than 3% (calculated on an absolute basis) below the economic sector weighting in the S&P 500 Index.
- The portfolio will not exceed maximum allocations to economic sectors, as defined by S&P's GICS, by more than 3% (calculated on an absolute basis) of the economic sector weighting in the S&P 500 Index.
- At the time of purchase, no single issue should exceed 5% (at market value) of the portfolio. Positions may be allowed to appreciate up to 8% (at market value) of the portfolio.

Market capitalization

The portfolio is expected to be primarily invested in well-established, large market capitalization companies. Therefore, the weighted average market cap of the portfolio is expected to be above $10 billion. The portfolio may also invest in less established, small capitalization companies. However, based on the strategic role of this portfolio in the context of the overall investment program, no more than 35% of the portfolio may be invested in small capitalization companies. For this purpose, small capitalization is defined as companies with a market capitalization of less than $1.5 billion. Companies with a market capitalization below $500 million at the time of purchase are prohibited. Positions that drift below $500 million in market capitalization after purchase shall be reported to TVA and monitored carefully. The portfolio shall not have more than 5% of the portfolio invested in securities whose market capitalizations have declined below $250 million.

Other transactions and policies

American Depositary Receipts (*ADRs*) may be used to construct the portfolio. However, because of the strategic role of the portfolio, positions in stocks traded as ADRs are limited to no more than 10% of the portfolio market value for calendar year 2017, and no more than 5% of the portfolio market value for calendar year 2018 and beyond. The limitations described above include foreign securities traded on U.S. exchanges that are not ADRs.

Exchange Traded Funds (*ETFs*) may comprise up to a maximum of 7.5% of the portfolio. The ETFs that can be purchased are limited to the S&P 500 Depository Receipts (SPY).

Prohibited Transactions—The portfolio is prohibited from investing in any of the following investment vehicles, or engaging in any of the following activities, unless approved in writing by an authorized representative of TVA:

- Fixed-income securities
- Non-marketable securities (including private debt securities and/or direct placements)
- Non-dollar-denominated securities
- Commingled funds (including mutual funds and ETFs except for the single ETF identified above)
- Convertible or preferred securities
- Warrants
- Commodities
- Real estate investments (excluding REITs)
- Short sales
- Margin purchases
- Swaps (including, but not limited to, index or rate of return swaps)
- Securities lending

Derivatives Policy—Manager is prohibited from using any derivative securities (including, but not limited to, options and futures).

Taxes—The assets of the portfolio are tax-exempt, and thus consideration does not have to be given to potential tax consequences to the portfolio from any transaction.

Performance

The combined portfolio of the Investment Challenge program has outperformed the S&P 500 benchmark by 0.52% since the inception of the program, through 2019, which represents an excess cumulative return of 48%. The composite university portfolio has exceeded the performance of the S&P 500 Index in 12 of the 22 of the years through 2019, as shown in Exhibit A2.4.

Exhibit A2.4 Composite annual performance of university portfolios in the TVA investment challenge

Year	Average university returns	S&P 500
2019	30.8%	31.5%
2018	−6.3%	−4.4%
2017	23.9%	21.8%
2016	8 0.3%	12.0%
2015	0.2%	1.4%
2014	10.5%	13.7%
2013	33.8%	32.4%
2012	12.6%	16.0%
2011	0.2%	2.1%
2010	17.8%	15.1%
2009	31.8%	26.5%
2008	−39.2%	−37.0%
2007	9.8%	5.5%
2006	12.9%	15.8%
2005	6.6%	4.9%
2004	16.0%	10.9%
2003	29.7%	28.7%
2002	−20.4%	−22.1%
2001	−7.5%	−11.9%
2000	−16.7%	−9.1%
1999	33.3%	21.0%
1998	15.6%	12.2%*

*Represents performance inception date of 11/1/1998.
Credit: http://www.tvainvestmentchallenge.com/

Performance awards

Each university that exceeds the performance of the S&P 500 Index over one full calendar year receives a performance-based award. The award amount is 20% of the alpha generated by the university, up to a cap of 2% of total assets managed. Alpha is defined as the excess return compared to the benchmark. The performance structure is similar to what is used with professional investment managers. Investment challenge teams have earned over $1.1 million in performance awards for their schools over the life of the program.

Future

The program has provided many benefits to TVA and the participating students and universities. Many of the faculty members and leaders of the participating universities value the program as a tool for integrating real-world learning opportunities into the curriculum. Student participants cite their experience in the Investment Challenge program as beneficial to their careers, and many believe the program improved their initial marketability for professional employment. TVA continues to benefit from the program as a way to invest in the communities it serves and enhance its relationship with those areas, and as a potential recruiting pipeline.

See tvainvestmentchallenge.com more information about the TVA Investment Challenge.

The Cornell-Fidelity MBA Stock Pitch Competition

The Cornell-Fidelity MBA Stock Pitch Competition (SPC) is organized and hosted by the Johnson School at Cornell University with lead sponsorship from Fidelity Investments. Initiated by the Johnson School, the annual MBA Stock Pitch Competition provides a forum for top MBA students to compete and showcase their stock-picking skills in front of a panel of distinguished judges. The event challenges teams of finance students from 12 top MBA programs to prepare and present buy/hold/sell recommendations and vigorously defend them. Judged by a panel of investment industry experts, the intense competition is designed to replicate the fast-paced, demanding experience of sell-side and buy-side analysts and asset managers.

In addition to gaining valuable experience and competing before judges, MBA students have a chance to shine before prospective employers. Recruiters from sponsoring firms come to shop for top talent. As one judge commented, "There's no one I wouldn't hire."

The names of the winning schools are inscribed on the Jack M. Ferraro Trophy, which honors the lead individual sponsor, a Johnson School alumnus. The SPC is generously supported by sponsors from the investment industry. Fidelity Investments is the lead corporate sponsor of the competition.

What happens at the MBA stock pitch competition?

Wednesday—Arrival: The event begins with an opportunity for student teams to meet each other at an informal dinner.

Thursday—Preparation: Students undergo a morning training session on software such as Capital IQ and FactSet at the Johnson School's Parker Center for Investment Research. After lunch, the judges assign two industries and a common stock, and give each team a list of the eligible universe of stocks. For the common stock, teams must decide whether to present it as a long (buy), neutral (hold), or a short (sell) recommendation. For each of the two assigned industries, they must select either a long or short candidate. Additional restrictions may be imposed on each selection (e.g., market capitalization, trading volume, investment style, etc.). Students have until midnight to prepare for the three presentations.

Friday—Competition/recruiting: In the morning preliminary round, each team pitches one common stock and one industry-specific stock. For each stock pitch, a single presenter from each team makes a 10-min presentation, followed by judges' questioning of all three team members for 5 min. For each stock pitch, teams feature a different team member as presenter. The event is held before a live audience, but other competing teams are not permitted to watch one another's presentations. The two highest scoring teams from each group in the preliminary round advance to the final afternoon round. After brief private practice sessions, the finalists make their final presentations and undergo the judges' rapid-fire questioning.

Late in the afternoon, awards are presented at a reception, and judges and recruiters have an opportunity to mingle with participants. The event has met with consistent praise over the years from judges, recruiters, and participants. Many sponsoring firms have stated that they often use the forum as an opportunity to identify strong potential hires.

Summary of key points

- Student-managed investment fund forums and symposiums are helpful in bringing students together to share their diverse approaches to portfolio management and to student members to hear from investment professionals on the diversity of approaches in the investments industry.
- Competitions among student-managed investment funds force fund members to articulate and defend their investment philosophies and processes, just as professional investment managers have to do in making finals presentations to prospective clients.
- Numerous competitions, forums, and symposiums take place around the world, providing student-managed investment fund members opportunities to learn and practice their aspects of portfolio management beyond what they do in their own funds or classrooms.

Index

Note: Page numbers followed by *f* indicate figures.

Printed in the United States
By Bookmasters